Le monde francophone
L'ASIE
L'EUROPE
L'AFRIQUE
L'OCÉAN INDIEN
L'AUSTRALIE
L'ANTARCTIQUE
la Pologne
la Belgique
le Luxembourg
la France
la Suisse
Monaco
la Moldavie
la Roumanie
la Bulgarie
l'Albanie
la Macédoine
la Syrie
le Liban
Israël
la Tunisie
le Maroc
l'Algérie
l'Égypte
le Sahara occidental
la Mauritanie
le Mali
le Niger
le Tchad
le Sénégal
la Guinée-Bissau
la Guinée
le Burkina-Faso
la Côte-d'Ivoire
le Togo
le Bénin
la République centrafricaine
Djibouti
le Cameroun
le Gabon
la République Démocratique du Congo
le Congo
le Ruanda
le Burundi
les Comores
les Seychelles
l'Angola
Mayotte (COM)
Madagascar
le Mozambique
l'île Maurice
la Réunion (DOM)
Pondichéry
le Laos
le Cambodge
le Vietnam
les îles St. Paul et Amsterdam
l'archipel Crozet
l'archipel Kerguelen
Terres australes et antarctiques françaises (COM)
Terre-Adélie
3,000 kilomètres
3,000 milles
MW01627448

La France : les régions /
les départements
La Mer
Du Nord
N
L'ANGLETERRE
L'ALLEMAGN
LA BELGIQUE
LE LUXEMBOURG
La Manche
NORD-PAS
DE CALAIS
Lille
Pas-de-Calais
Arras
Nord
Somme
Amiens
Seine-
Maritime
Rouen
Charleville-Mézières
Laon
Ardennes
Aisne
PICARDIE
Beauvais
Oise
HAUTE-
NORMANDIE
Manche
Caen
Saint-Lo
Calvados
Evreux
Pontoise
Val-d'Oise
Eure
Yvelines
Paris
Versailles
BASSE-
NORMANDIE
Orne
Evry
ÎLE-DE-FRANCE
Melun
Essonne
Seine-et-
Marne
Marne
Châlons-sur-Marne
LORRAINE
Meuse
Metz
Moselle
Bar-le-Duc
Nancy
Meurthe-et-Moselle
ALSACE
Strasb
Bas-
Rhin
Finistère
St-Brieuc
Côtes-du-Nord
Quimper
BRETAGNE
Morbihan
Vannes
Rennes
Ille-et-Vilaine
Alençon
Chartres
Mayenne
Laval
Le Mans
Sarthe
PAYS DE
LA LOIRE
Eure-et-Loir
Orléans
Loiret
CHAMPAGNE-ARDENNE
Troyes
Aube
Chaumont
Haute-
Marne
Epinal
Vosges
Colmar
Haut-Rhin
Territoire
de Belfort
Loire-
Atlantique
Nantes
Angers
Maine-
et-Loire
Tours
Blois
Loir-
et-Cher
Indre-
et-Loire
CENTRE
Auxerre
Yonne
Côte-d'Or
Dijon
Vesoul
Haute-Saône
Doubs
Besançon
L'OCÉAN
ATLANTIQUE
La Roche-sur-Yon
Vendée
Deux-
Sèvres
Poitiers
Vienne
Niort
Châteauroux
Indre
Bourges
Cher
Nièvre
Nevers
BOURGOGNE
FRANCHE-
COMTÉ
LA SUISS
Saône-et-Loire
Lons-le-Saunier
Jura
Moulins
Allier
Mâcon
Bourg-en-Bresse
Ain
Haute-Savoie
Annecy
Seine-Saint-Denis
Nanterre
Bobigny
Paris
Hauts-de-
Seine
Créteil
Val-de-Marne
La Rochelle
POITOU-
CHARENTES
Charente-
Maritime
Charente
Angoulême
Haute-
Vienne
Limoges
Guéret
Creuse
AUVERGNE
Clermont-Ferrand
Rhône
Loire
Lyon
RHÔNE-ALPES
Chambéry
Savoie
LIMOUSIN
Puy-
de-Dôme
Isère
St.-Étienne
Périgueux
Tulle
Corrèze
Cantal
Haute-Loire
Grenoble
L'ITALI
Bordeaux
AQUITAINE
Dordogne
Aurillac
Le Puy
Valence
Gironde
Lot
Privas
Ardèche
Drôme
Gap
Haute-
Alpes
Lot-et-
Garonne
Cahors
Aveyron
Mende
Lozère
Rodez
Landes
Agen
Tarn-et-
Garonne
MIDI-PYRÉNÉES
Gard
Vaucluse
Digne
Alpes de
Haute-Provence
Alpes-
Maritimes
Avignon
Mont-de-Marsan
Gers
Montauban
Albi
Tarn
Nîmes
Auch
Toulouse
Montpellier
Hérault
Bouches-du-
Rhône
PROVENCE-ALPES-
CÔTE-D'AZUR
Nice
MONA
Pyrénées-
Atlantiques
Pau
Tarbes
Haute-
Garonne
LANGUEDOC-
ROUSSILLON
Carcassonne
Marseille
Var
Toulon
Hautes-
Pyrénées
Foix
Ariège
Aude
Pyrénées-
Orientales
Perpignan
L'ANDORRE
Limite départementale
Limite régionale
Ardèche Nom du département
CENTRE Nom de la région
L'ESPAGNE
Bastia
Haute-
Corse
CORSE
Ajaccio
Corse-
du-Sud
La Mer
Méditerranée
200 kilomètres
200 milles

Chez nous

BRANCHÉ SUR LE MONDE FRANCOPHONE

Fourth Edition

Albert Valdman
Indiana University

Cathy Pons
University of North Carolina, Asheville

Mary Ellen Scullen
University of Maryland, College Park

Prentice Hall

Upper Saddle River London Singapore
Toronto Tokyo Sydney Hong Kong Mexico City

Senior Acquisitions Editor: *Rachel McCoy*
Senior Editorial Assistant: *Bethany Gilmour Williamson*
Senior Media Editor: *Samantha Alducin*
Media Editor: *Meriel Martinez*
Assistant Editor/Editorial Coordinator: *Jennifer Murphy*
Executive Marketing Manager: *Kris Ellis-Levy*
Senior Marketing Manager: *Denise Miller*
Marketing Coordinator: *William J. Bliss*
Senior Managing Editor: *Mary Rottino*
Associate Managing Editor: *Janice Stangel*
Project Manager: *Manuel Echevarria*
Senior Operations Supervisor: *Brian Mackey*
Operations Specialist: *Cathleen Petersen*
Senior Art Director: *Pat Smythe*
Art Director: *Miguel Ortiz*
Text and Cover Designer: *Lisa Delgado, Delgado and Company, Inc.*
Art Manager: *Gail Cocker*
Illustrator: *Steve Mannion*
Permissions: *Antonella Giglio/Veronica Oliva*
Manager, Visual Research: *Beth Brenzel*
Manager, Rights and Permissions: *Zina Arabia*
Image Permission Coordinator: *Ang'John Ferreri*
Manager, Cover Visual Research & Permissions: *Karen Sanatar*
Publisher: *Phil Miller*
Cover Image: *Tai Power Seeff, Getty/Image Bank*
Full-Service Project Management: *Francesca Monaco, Preparé Inc.*
Printer/Binder: *Quebecor World Book Services*
Cover Printer: *Lehigh-Phoenix Color*

Credits and acknowledgments borrowed from other sources and reproduced, with permission, in this textbook appear on appropriate page within text (or on page S1)

10 9 8 7 6 5 4 3 2 1

Prentice Hall
is an imprint of

www.pearsonhighered.com

ISBN 10: 0-13-503415-9
ISBN 13: 978-0-13-503415-6

Brief Contents

Scope & Sequence

Scope & Sequence

Scope & Sequence

Scope&Sequence

Preface

CHEZ NOUS, Fourth edition is a complete introductory French program designed for use at colleges and universities, over two or three terms/semesters, and is suitable for use in accelerated or intensive courses. Using a careful progression from skill-developing to skill-using activities and a sophisticated treatment of Francophone culture, the text and its full complement of supplementary materials help students develop listening, reading, speaking, and writing skills as well as insights into other cultures by exposing them to authentic, contemporary French and encouraging them to express themselves on a variety of topics.

Building on the success of earlier editions, CHEZ NOUS, Fourth edition offers a richly nuanced focus on the Francophone world through a highly integrative and process-oriented approach to the development of language skills. This approach is consistent with the **National Standards for Foreign Language Learning for the 21st Century**, widely recognized as a set of desired outcomes for foreign language instruction. Rather than functioning as discrete and occasional influences on the text, the National Standards constitute an essential underlying principle of the program as a whole. The "Five C's," as defined by the National Standards, are directly embodied in essential aspects of the CHEZ NOUS program. The National Standards also constitute a subtext throughout the program—for example, many practice activities introduce cultural realities from across the French-speaking world, and culture is explored through skill-using activities and discovery methods of language learning. CHEZ NOUS addresses the National Standards by:

- Emphasizing **communication** developed through authentic language samples and tasks (**Points de départ**, **Formes et fonctions**, and in all skill-development activities)
- Encouraging cultural **comparisons** (**Vie et culture** and **Venez chez nous !**)
- Presenting a broad cross section of French-speaking **communities** (**Points de départ**, **Vie et culture**, **Lisons**, **Écoutons**, **Observons**, and **Venez chez nous !**)
- Fostering **connections** by guiding students through a variety of disciplines, including history, geography, art, and literature (**Vie et culture**, **Lisons**, and **Venez chez nous !**)
- Promoting skill development within a distinctive **cultural** framework (**Vie et culture** and **Venez chez nous !**)

What's New in CHEZ NOUS, Fourth Edition?

1. **Substantive new content.** Language use and cultural realities are constantly changing, and this is reflected in CHEZ NOUS, Fourth edition.
   - Vocabulary presentations (**Points de départ**) have been significantly updated. For example, presentations related to the topics of education, health, media, technology, and ecology have been revised, along with their corresponding art. Some new themes have been added to allow students to discuss important topics such as civic responsibility and multiculturalism.
   - Correspondingly, nearly one-third of the cultural notes (**Vie et culture**) are new or revised to include additional topics (such as volunteerism) or updated information, offering a more contemporary and nuanced picture of France and the Francophone world.
   - More than a third of the skill-building activities (**Lisons, Écoutons, Observons, Parlons, Écrivons**) are new or revised for this edition, introducing new texts, video clips, and authentic tasks. In particular, half of the readings are significantly revised or new, including new literary selections and journalistic prose texts.
   - The themes of the **Venez chez nous !** cultural lessons have been broadened in **Chapitres 3** and **4**, to reflect the overall chapter focus.

Chapitre 3 now emphasizes study and work in Francophone countries, while **Chapitre 4** treats aspects of daily routines across the Francophone world.

2. **Further refinement of the cyclical scope and sequence.** Users' feedback has led to additional modification of the scope and sequence for enhanced linguistic effectiveness and flexibility in the classroom. Some highlights include the following:
   - The chapter treating food and its related grammatical content has been moved to the first half of the book (**Chapitre 5**); this allows for earlier treatment of useful vocabulary and structural features such as the partitive.
   - The treatment of direct- and indirect-object pronouns has been extended over two chapters (**Chapitres 6, 7**), for ease in acquisition; object pronouns are then reviewed in the final chapter (**Chapitre 12**), where their most frequent combinations are presented and practiced.
3. **Increased attention to the development of learner strategies.** The fourth edition focuses attention on learner strategies in new ways:
   - Revised **Écrivons** activities target explicit writing strategies, and a four-step process now encourages students to draft and revise their writing, focusing first on content and then on form.
   - A new feature, **Fiche pratique**, outlines practical strategies to help students learn specific lesson content (for example, showing them ways to organize the new material, how to interact with native speakers using new content or structures, or how to test themselves).
4. **Comprehension before production.** Within many of the practice sections for the **Formes et fonctions**, new comprehension-based activities allow students to make an initial form-meaning link as they learn new grammatical structures.
5. **Increased opportunity for individualized learning and practice.** With **MyFrenchLab**™, a new, nationally hosted online learning system, students and instructors have available a wide range of language-learning tools and resources. The learning experience is personalized through readiness checks and grammar tutorials, and students progress via individualized practice with recording capabilities. Incorporating the Student Activities Manual (SAM) and other types of practice, students can complete their assignments online, while instructors can tailor assignments and grade and monitor student progress in new ways, such as providing spoken comments and detailed markups of student writing.
6. **Music and film related activities.** New activities incorporating film and music videos found on video-sharing sites are now a feature of the Instructor's Resource Manual. Step-by-step classroom treatments offer many options for integrating music and film into the program.
7. **Incorporation of the Orthographic Reform.** Although championed in Canada, the Orthographic Reform of 1990 has met with limited success in France. CHEZ NOUS, Fourth edition incorporates a few of the most widely accepted elements of the Reform. Notably, changes related to the use of the **accent grave** have been implemented, affecting some verb conjugations in the future and conditional (for verbs like **préférer**) as well as the spelling of individual lexical items, such as **crèmerie** and **évènement**. Also, all numbers are now written with connecting hyphens, eliminating ambiguity and simplifying the learner's task: **cinq-mille-deux-cent-soixante-et-onze**.
8. **Focus on learner outcomes.** Chapter openers now provide an overview of expected learner outcomes. At the end of each chapter, a new self-assessment checklist encourages students to take stock of what they have learned to do.
9. **New design and art.** CHEZ NOUS, Fourth edition has an entirely new design intended to increase its user-friendliness. More abundant photos offer a richer depiction of the Francophone world and combine with updated line art to enhance the contemporary focus and visual appeal of the book.

HALLMARK FEATURES

While much is new in CHEZ NOUS, Fourth edition, we remain committed to the hallmark features that distinguish this program from all others:

- **Innovative treatment of grammar.** Structures are presented in the context of authentic communicative use of the language; for example, the periphrastic future (**aller** plus the infinitive) is not the notional equivalent of the inflected future (**le futur simple**), and this distinction is clearly made in the presentation and in practice activities. Grammar treatments, reflecting the spoken language, make important generalizations about the structure of French. For example, the presentation of adjectives is based on the concept that the masculine form of variable adjectives is derived from the longer feminine form by dropping the final pronounced consonant (**grande/grand**). Similarly, students learn that verbs with two stems have a longer stem in the plural, from which the singular can be derived by this general rule of final consonant deletion (**partent/part**).

  Use of a cyclical syllabus facilitates language acquisition by allowing the instructor to focus on frequent and simpler language features first. For example, instead of presenting the conditional in full paradigms and in complex sentences, we first present verbs used frequently in polite requests. A more complete presentation of the conditional follows the presentation of the future, which uses the same base form.
- **Process orientation to skills development.** The receptive skills (listening and reading) are developed using authentic materials that are just beyond students' productive skill level. Preview activities provide or activate background knowledge and introduce comprehension strategies; listening and reading activities guide and check comprehension as students encounter the material; and follow-up activities encourage them to reflect on what they have read or heard. The productive skills (speaking and writing) are likewise practiced via carefully sequenced activities that emphasize carrying out authentic tasks through a process approach. Pre-speaking and pre-writing preparation readies students to carry out the assigned tasks; frameworks for the actual speaking and writing assignments are provided; and thoughtful follow-up is encouraged. Through this process approach to development of the four skills, students gradually become confident and proficient at carrying out a wide variety of communicative tasks.
- **Pervasive and highly nuanced treatment of French and Francophone cultures.** Throughout each chapter, thematically interrelated lessons closely integrate the presentation of lexical and grammatical content within interesting and culturally authentic contexts. Nuanced cultural presentations also explicitly encompass the breadth and richness of the Francophone world, leading students to a deeper analysis and understanding of the diverse cultures of France and the French-speaking world. The cultural and thematic presentation of each chapter culminates in the final lesson, titled **Venez chez nous !**, which provides an in-depth and intellectually stimulating look at the chapter theme in the Francophone context. A rich pedagogical apparatus provides students with opportunities to further develop language skills while exploring the cultural topic and making cross-cultural comparisons.
- **Authentic texts and tasks.** Authentic texts and tasks form the basis for developing students' language skills in CHEZ NOUS. Listening activities and models for speaking reflect the everyday language of young people. Varied readings and writing tasks help students develop an awareness of appropriate style as they are exposed to a wide variety of Francophone writers and oral traditions. Throughout the textbook and supplements, practice of vocabulary and grammar is oriented toward real situations and authentic tasks.

ORGANIZATION OF THE TEXTBOOK

CHEZ NOUS, Fourth edition consists of a brief introductory chapter plus twelve full-length chapters. Each is built around a cultural theme introduced by informative photographs, line drawings, and realia. The user-friendly organization in the fourth edition divides each chapter into three lessons that pair lexical and grammar presentations, and the concluding fourth **Venez chez nous !** cultural lesson. The first three lessons in each chapter typically include the following components:

Points de départ. Reflecting the chapter theme, this opening section presents situationally oriented vocabulary through varied and appealing visuals and exchanges representing authentic everyday contexts. All language samples are recorded in the Text Audio component. The **Points de départ** section includes extensive and updated cultural notes (entitled **Vie et culture**) written initially in English, then in French (beginning in **Chapitre 5**). **Vie et culture** notes elaborate on the cultural references made in the vocabulary presentation. They incorporate photos and realia that students must analyze to discover features of French culture and make cross-cultural comparisons. Each **Points de départ** section offers a sequence of activities (**À vous la parole**) to be used in class to provide meaningful and personalized practice of the words and expressions through whole class, paired, and small group activities.

Sons et lettres. This section presents the main phonetic features and sound contrasts of French. It emphasizes the sound contrasts that determine differences in meaning, the major differences between French and English, and the relationship between sounds and spellings. Discrimination and oral practice exercises found in the text (**À vous la parole**) are also recorded in the Text Audio program.

Formes et fonctions. Clearly written grammar explanations in English focus on authentic usage and point out features of the spoken versus the written language. Numerous examples are provided and, where appropriate, color-coded charts summarize the forms. Similarly, verb conjugations are illustrated in charts whose color shadings indicate the number of spoken forms and show how forms are derived from the base. The **Formes et fonctions** section also includes class-friendly exercises that provide a full range of practice—from form-based to meaningful and personalized activities—incorporating the theme and the vocabulary of the lesson (**À vous la parole**). Where appropriate, grammar practice begins with a comprehension-based exercise to focus attention on the link between form and meaning before students are asked to produce the new grammatical feature. Icons clearly indicate pair and small group activities.

Lisons, Écoutons, Parlons, or Écrivons. Each of the first three chapter lessons concludes with one of these skill-oriented activities, allowing students to put into practice the vocabulary, grammar, and cultural knowledge acquired in the lesson. Through work with an authentic text or task in a reading, listening, speaking, or writing activity, students are guided in their development of receptive and productive skills.

Venez chez nous ! These newly revised cultural lessons allow students to explore the chapter theme in depth. Every **Venez chez nous !** lesson includes substantive process-oriented activities—**Lisons, Parlons, Écrivons**—that promote skill development while encouraging cultural analysis and cross-cultural comparisons. In addition, the **Observons** activities draw on clips from the video to incorporate authentic listening practice with rich visual and cultural elements.

Vocabulaire. This section is found at the end of the chapter, and it summarizes the key vocabulary targeted for students' productive use. Words and phrases are grouped semantically by lesson, and English equivalents are provided. These new words and expressions are recorded in the Text Audio program.

Appendices. Located at the end of the text, these include the **International Phonetic Alphabet** with key words; presentations of the **plus-que-parfait**, the **futur antérieur**, and the **passé du conditionnel**, along with a sequence of practice activities; **verb charts** for regular and irregular verbs; **French-English** and **English-French glossaries**; and an **Index** of grammar, vocabulary, and cultural topics found in the book. Targeted learner strategies are also listed in the **Index**.

Finally, a series of colorful updated **maps** are included in the front and back of the book.

OTHER PROGRAM COMPONENTS

Innovative supplements provide ample opportunities for practicing lexical and grammatical features while extending the breadth and depth of the cultural presentation and the introduction to the Francophone world. New and sophisticated electronic components build on the fourth edition's pedagogical and cultural presentations in interesting, creative ways.

Student Resources

Audio CDs to Accompany Text. Each chapter's **Points de départ, Sons et letters**, and **Écoutons** segments, as well as the end-of-chapter vocabulary lists, can be found on the Text Audio CDs. **Lisons** texts such as poems and play excerpts have also been included. Recorded material is indicated by an icon in the textbook, along with the track number, making it easy to find selections and incorporate them into class activities or assign as homework.

Student Activities Manual (SAM). The Student Activities Manual provides reading and writing practice along with listening activities related to the audio and video components. Written exercises provide meaningful and communicative practice, incorporating the vocabulary and structures introduced in each chapter and offering additional process-oriented activities. Exercises linked to audio recordings provide listening practice that progresses from comprehension to production, based on what students hear. The exercises stress authentic speech and real-life tasks, and recordings feature native speakers of French. Video-based activities complement the listening practice provided in the textbook, using additional video clips and expanded activities. Each chapter of the SAM concludes with a **Venez chez nous !** section that is closely tied to the chapter theme and allows students to delve deeper into the cultural focus of the **Venez chez nous !** lesson in the textbook through guided Web-based activities.

Answer Key to Accompany the SAM. A separately bound **Answer Key** is available for optional inclusion in course packages; it includes answers for all discrete and short-answer exercises in the SAM.

Audio to Accompany the SAM. Students and instructors have access to the audio recordings for the SAM in several formats: through Audio CDs, the Companion Website, and **MyFrenchLab™**.

Video Program. CHEZ NOUS, Fourth edition includes a beautifully produced video, shot on location, with several clips new to this edition. The video introduces native speakers from across the Francophone world who address the topics and themes of each chapter in varied settings and contexts. Carefully integrated with the **Vie et culture** sections and the **Venez chez nous !** lessons in the textbook, the video is easy to incorporate into daily lesson plans. The textbook's **Observons** exercises and the activities found in the SAM take a process-oriented approach to the development of viewing skills.

Instructor Resources

Annotated Instructor's Edition (AIE). Extensive, clearly labeled annotations make the AIE an indispensable handbook for the novice as well as the experienced instructor. Notes offer ideas for presenting material; for initial form-based practice; for implementation of activities; and for expansion, alternative practice, and review. Complete scripts for listening activities and keys to many exercises are provided. Other notes give in-depth linguistic and cultural information that the instructor may find useful.

Instructor's Resource Center. The IRC is located on *www.pearsonhighered.com* and provides password-protected instructor access to the Instructor's Resource Manual and Testing Program, in downloadable format.

Instructor's Resource Manual. An extensive introduction to the components of the CHEZ NOUS, Fourth edition program is included in the revised Instructor's Resource Manual (IRM). The IRM is available in traditional paper and in downloadable format via the Instructor's Resource Center. Sample syllabi for two- and three-term course sequences are outlined, along with numerous sample lesson plans. The extensive cultural annotations are a unique feature of this IRM, providing further information about topics introduced in the textbook. Information-gap activities, ready for classroom use, are provided for each chapter. New to this edition are suggested chapter-related activities that incorporate film and music videos. In addition, the IRM provides the scripts for the audio and video activities of the SAM.

Testing Program and Audio to Accompany the Testing Program. A revised and highly flexible testing program allows instructors to customize tests by selecting the modules they wish to use or by changing individual items. This complete testing program, available in paper and electronic formats, includes quizzes, chapter tests, and comprehensive examinations that test listening, reading, and writing skills as well as cultural knowledge. Special formats to test listening and speaking skills are also included. All oral sections are recorded for the instructor's use in a classroom or laboratory setting. For all elements in the testing program, detailed grading guidelines are provided.

Online Resources

MyFrenchLab™. This new, nationally hosted online learning system was created specifically for students in college-level language courses. It brings together—in one convenient, easily navigable site—a wide array of language-learning tools and resources, including an interactive version of the SAM and all materials from the audio and video programs. Readiness checks and grammar tutorials presented in English individualize instruction to meet the needs of each student. Instructors can use the system to make assignments, set grading parameters, listen to student-created audio recordings, and provide feedback on student work as well as to access the IRM, the testing program, and all the line-art images featured in the textbook. Instructor access is provided at no charge to adopting institutions. Students can purchase access codes online or at their local bookstore.

Companion Website. The clearly designed and regularly updated Companion Website (CW) makes a wealth of material available to the student and instructor. Organized by chapter, the site offers automatically graded vocabulary and grammar practice, Internet-based activities for language and cultural learning, resources such as dictionaries and study manuals, the complete audio program from the textbook, audio activities from the SAM, and game activities.

TO THE STUDENT

Why did you choose to study French? Most students of French wish to develop basic language skills that they can put to practical use and to learn about how the lives of French-speaking peoples compare to their own. The CHEZ NOUS, Fourth edition program is designed to help you meet those goals. Specifically, with the aid of this textbook and the accompanying materials, you can expect to accomplish the following:

- Become familiar with many features of everyday life and culture in France and in the three dozen countries where French is spoken. You will have the opportunity to reflect on how your life in North America and your values compare with those of French speakers across the globe.
- Speak French well enough to get around in a country where French is spoken. You should be able to greet people, ask for directions, cope with everyday needs, give basic information about yourself, and talk about things that are important to you. You should also be able to assist French-speaking visitors in this country.
- Understand French well enough to get the main ideas and some details from a news broadcast, lecture, or conversation that you hear. You should understand French speakers quite well when they speak slowly about topics with which you are familiar.
- Read French Web sites as well as newspaper and magazine articles dealing with current events or other familiar topics. With the help of a dictionary, you should be able to read more specialized material in fields of interest. You should also be able to enjoy short and simple pieces of literature in French.
- Write French well enough to take notes, write messages and letters for various purposes, and fill out forms.
- Gain an understanding of the structure of the French language: its pronunciation, grammar, and vocabulary. You will also gain insight into how languages function in societies. These insights may even help you to understand your native language better!

Assuring Your Success

Whether or not you have already studied French, you bring some knowledge of that language to your study. Many words of French origin are used in English (**soufflé**, **croissant**, and **diplomat**, for example). You also bring to the study of French your knowledge of the world in general and of specific events, which you can use to predict what you will read or hear. You can use your knowledge of a particular topic, as well as accompanying photos or titles, to predict what will come next. Finally, the reading and listening skills you have learned for your native language will also prove useful as you study a foreign language.

Many of the materials found in CHEZ NOUS, Fourth edition will seem challenging to you because you will not be able to understand every word you hear or read. That is to be expected—the readings in the textbook were written for native speakers, and listening exercises approximate native speech. The language used in CHEZ NOUS, Fourth edition is real and the topics current. You should use your background knowledge and prediction skills to make intelligent guesses about what you are hearing and reading. In this way, you can get the main ideas and some details, a good first step toward real communication in a foreign language.

Since access to native French speakers is limited in most parts of the United States, the classroom offers an important opportunity for you to practice your listening and speaking skills. Unless your instructor indicates otherwise, keep your book closed. Since what you are learning is explained in the textbook, you will not need to take notes during class. Instead, it is important that you *participate* as much as possible in classroom activities.

Adequate preparation is another key to success. Prepare each lesson as directed by your instructor before going to class. Be sure to complete assignments made by your instructor and review regularly, not just for an exam.

Using Your Textbook to Prepare

CHEZ NOUS, Fourth edition is made up of a brief introductory chapter plus twelve full-length chapters, each organized around a cultural situation that you are likely to encounter when you come into contact with native French speakers. Each chapter consists of three lessons that expand on this cultural situation. Each lesson includes the following sections:

The opening section called **Points de départ** provides a "point of departure" for the lesson by presenting vocabulary related to the chapter topic. The meaning of new words is conveyed through the use of art, photos, documents, dialogues, or brief descriptions in French. You can listen to recordings of these language samples. You should learn both the written and spoken forms of these words and expressions so that you can use them in your own speech and writing. Look over the exercises found under **À vous la parole** (*Your turn to speak*); many of these will be used in class. Your instructor may also assign additional practice from the Student Activities Manual (SAM), **MyFrenchLab™ (MFL)**, and the CHEZ NOUS Companion Website (CW) once you have dealt with the topic in class.

Vie et culture (*Life and culture*) sections challenge you to discover aspects of Francophone life and culture and to make comparisons with your own culture as you examine photos and various types of documents. Language cannot be separated from the culture of its speakers, and the activities in CHEZ NOUS, Fourth edition provide a cultural context for your study of French.

Sons et lettres (*Sounds and letters*) focuses on important pronunciation features of French and differences between French and English. This section also provides guidance in spelling French words. Exercises in the textbook can be practiced using the Text Audio program. These exercises, plus additional ones found in the SAM and in **MyFrenchLab™**, help you to first recognize, then produce, the French sounds.

Each lesson includes grammar presentations called **Formes et fonctions** (*Forms and functions*). The grammar forms taught can be combined with the lesson vocabulary to carry out specific tasks such as asking questions or ordering something to eat or drink. Read over the explanation in English and study the examples before the topic is presented in class; likewise, use the notes to review once the topic has been treated by your instructor. Often a color-coded chart will summarize forms. Look for similarities with other structures you have already learned. Some new vocabulary may be found in these sections, for example, a list of verbs or negative expressions. Once the material has been practiced in class, your instructor may assign additional exercises from the SAM/MFL and CW.

The last section in each lesson is designed to help you put into practice the vocabulary, grammar, and cultural knowledge you have acquired in this and earlier lessons. Through the exercises called **Lisons**, **Écoutons**, **Parlons**, and **Écrivons**, you will use your reading, listening, speaking, and writing skills to communicate in French with your instructor and with other class members.

At the end of each chapter you will find a colorful cultural lesson, **Venez chez nous !** (*Come to our place!*), that allows you to examine the chapter theme in depth as it relates to the Francophone world and to make cross-cultural comparisons. These cultural lessons also include an activity, **Observons**, based on video clips from the exciting video that accompanies CHEZ NOUS, Fourth edition. The **Venez chez nous !** activities found in your textbook are supplemented by exercises in the SAM/MFL and on the CW, which features links to interesting sites related to the topic of the cultural lesson.

You will also want to familiarize yourself with the sections of your textbook designed to give you special help. For example, each chapter ends with **Vocabulaire**, a list of the words and expressions that you should be able to use in your own speech and writing. For each lesson, the words are grouped by meaning, and English equivalents are provided. These words and expressions are recorded in the Text Audio program, so that you can practice recognizing and pronouncing them on your own. The appendices of CHEZ NOUS, Fourth edition include a guide to pronunciation that uses simple key words and phonetic symbols, charts with sample verb conjugations for both regular and irregular verbs, colorful maps of France and the Francophone world, and a **Lexique** that allows you to look up a word in French or in English and find its equivalent in the other language. For vocabulary that you should be able to use in your speech or writing, chapter and lesson numbers indicate where a particular word or expression was first introduced. You will also find vocabulary used in readings, in directions, or in the **Vie et culture** sections that you should be able to recognize or guess from context. Finally, the **Index** lists vocabulary, grammar, and cultural topics alphabetically so that you can easily find the section you wish to read or review.

CHEZ NOUS, Fourth edition and its accompanying materials will provide you with opportunities to develop your French language skills—listening, reading, speaking, and writing—by exposing you to authentic French and encouraging you to express yourself on a variety of topics. It will also introduce you to Francophone cultures around the world and invite you to reflect on your own culture. As you begin this endeavor, we wish you « **Bon courage !** »

Acknowledgments

The publication of the fourth edition of CHEZ NOUS represents the accumulated experience of many years of classroom instruction, as well as twelve years of planning, field testing, and fine-tuning, to which many instructors and students have contributed. We wish to thank our colleagues and students for their participation in this process, for their comments, and for their encouragement.

In particular, we would like to thank language coordinators who participated in an intensive two-day workshop in Montreal in October 2007; your willingness to be frank and to share your ideas encouraged our innovations. Your positive energy greatly inspired us.

Debra Bell – University of Georgia
Nathalie Dieu-Porter – Vanderbilt University, TN
Annie Duménil – University of South Carolina
Nezha Erradi – George Washington University, DC
Joyce Johnston – Stephen F. Austin State University, TX
Sharla Martin – University of Texas at Arlington
Kate Paesani – Wayne State University, MI
Pamela Paine – Auburn University, AL
Kelly Sax – Indiana University
Elizabeth D. Weber – University of Illinois-Chicago

We also extend our sincere thanks and appreciation to colleagues who reviewed the manuscript at various stages of development. We gratefully acknowledge their participation and candor:

Seda Chavdarian – University of California at Berkeley
Nathalie Dieu-Porter – Vanderbilt University, TN
Annie Duménil – University of South Carolina
Stacey Katz – University of Utah
Paul Chamness Miller – University of Cincinnati, OH
Christine E.B. Moritz – University of Northern Colorado
Caroline Nash – Louisiana State University
Daniel E. O'Sullivan – University of Mississippi
Kate Paesani – Wayne State University, MI
Kelly Sax – Indiana University
Jean Marie Schultz – University of California at Santa Barbara

We thank the following colleagues for their important contributions, without which the fourth edition would be incomplete: Virginie Cassidy of Georgetown College, for revisions to the Student Activities Manual and the Companion Website; Joyce Johnston of Stephen F. Austin State University, for revisions to the Test Package; Kate Paesani of Wayne State University, for the Instructor's Resource Manual; and the colleagues who contributed to **MyFrenchLab**™. Many thanks to Michèle Dussaucy for her careful proofing of the textbook manuscript.

At the University of North Carolina, Asheville, Cathy wishes to thank supportive colleagues and cooperative students who tried out new texts and activities and supplied helpful comments and enthusiastic encouragement. Special thanks go to my colleagues in French, Sandra Malicote and Ellen Bailey.

At the University of Maryland, College Park, Mel is particularly grateful to the amazing group of Graduate Teaching Assistants who have taught with CHEZ NOUS over the years and to the undergraduates who have studied with it; I have learned much from you about how the material in the book can really come alive in the classroom, and the fourth edition has benefited greatly from your suggestions, ideas, and critiques. A special thanks to all of you who go out of your way to provide material, answer questions, offer suggestions, and keep me up-to-date with the latest technology crazes. And to my group of language experts, *un énorme merci* for responding to an endless stream of random e-mail queries with patience, good humor, and insightful responses. Merci encore Eva, Caroline, Cybèle, Dorothée, Marilyn, Pierre et Virginie.

We would also like to acknowledge the many people on our Pearson team who contributed their ideas, talents, time, and publishing experience to this project. Thanks to Publisher for World Languages, Phil Miller, for his continuing support. Many thanks to Rachel McCoy, Senior Acquisitions Editor, for her energy, enthusiasm, miles logged, and continual encouragement and faith in us. Our special thanks go to our Development Editor, Barbara Lyons, who through four editions has become an indispensable colleague and dear friend, and whose careful reading, exacting standards, useful suggestions, and moral support have been invaluable in virtually every aspect of the project. Copy Editor Karen Hohner did her usual excellent job of readying the manuscript for production, and we greatly appreciate her eagle eye and our many e-mail discussions. Thanks also to Katherine Gilbert, who played a crucial role in working with Karen to code the manuscript for typesetting. We are indebted to the wonderful production crew both in Upper Saddle River and in Battipaglia. Mary Rottino, Senior Managing Editor, Janice Stangel, Associate Managing Editor, and Manuel Echivarria, Production Editor, proved to be unflappable and always ready to solve yet another crisis. Many thanks to Frank Weihening, Production Supervision, and Francesca Monaco, Editor, of Emilcomp/Preparé, who meticulously oversaw every detail to bring the fourth edition through production. *Grazie mille* especially to Francesca, whose endless supply of patience, good humor, and smiles were much appreciated at every stage of the production process.

We would also like to thank Samantha Alducin, Senior Media Editor, for being a tireless advocate for integrating new technologies into the fourth edition and for her implementation of **MyFrenchLab**™. We would be remiss to not thank Bob Hemmer, who has fearlessly led the My Language Lab charge and who has generously given of his time to bring us up to speed. Thanks also to Meriel Martínez, Supplements Editor, for carefully overseeing the preparation of the revised Student Activities Manual and Video, and to Jennifer Murphy, Assistant Development Editor, for helping to coordinate the revision of the Instructor's Resource Manual and supervising the permissions process. We would especially like to thank Antonella Giglio and Veronica Oliva for their invaluable assistance with securing the various text and electronic permissions. *Un grand merci* to Melissa Marolla Brown, Development Editor for Assessment, for her oversight of the Testing Program. Our thanks go to Kris Ellis-Levy, Executive Marketing Manager-World Languages, Denise Miller, Senior Marketing Manager, and Bill Bliss, Marketing Coordinator, for their energy and innovative ideas. We thank Bethany Gilmour, Editorial Assistant, for her attention to so many important details. Thanks also go to Francelle Carpeyan for her assistance with photo research and to Steve Mannion for his superb line art, which has greatly enriched the book.

And finally, we wish to thank our families, who have almost come to view the various CHEZ NOUS editions as siblings (or children) who are extremely demanding of our time and energy. We thank each of you for your patience and understanding and for all the sacrifices big and small that you have made, so that we could bring to life a new edition. *Merci* Andrew, Bertrand, Chikondi, Hilde, Kate, and Moyenda, we would like to dedicate the "new arrival" to you.

About the Authors

A native of Paris, Albert Valdman's interest in languages dates back to when, as a young teenager, he served as a shepherd in southwestern France. His contact with the local southern French Languedoc dialect stimulated a burning interest in the study of language as a cultural phenomenon. Valdman immigrated to the United States and eventually earned a Ph.D. in French linguistics from Cornell University. He started his career at the Foreign Service Institute of the U.S. Department of State and at the Pennsylvania State University before joining Indiana University, where he attained the distinguished rank of Rudy Professor of French, Italian, and Linguistics. He served as visiting professor at Harvard, the University of the West Indies (Jamaica), and several years at the University of Nice. He also taught at the University of Oregon summer institutes for high school French teachers at Tours and organized summer institutes for college teachers sponsored by the American Association of Teachers of French (AATF). At Indiana University, he created the program in French linguistics and the Creole Institute and directed the program of elementary and intermediate French, including the mentoring of graduate student instructors and coordinators. A constant in his career has been his interest in developing more effective approaches to the teaching of foreign languages, with a passionate focus on his native language, the training of teachers, and the preparation of pedagogical materials. Valdman held the posts of president of the AATF and, for two terms, of president of the International Association of Applied Linguistics. For his commitment to the teaching of French language and culture and his pioneering work in the description of French outside of France, he was named *Commandeur dans l'Ordre des Palmes Académiques* of France and named member of *l'Ordre des Francophones d'Amérique* of the government of Quebec province.

Cathy Pons grew up hearing French spoken by her grandparents but only began study of the language in high school. After completing a BA in French at the University of North Carolina at Greensboro, she spent a year in France as a Fulbright Teaching Assistant. Pons completed her doctorate in French linguistics at Indiana University where, as an Assistant Professor, she directed the elementary French program and the MA in French instruction. Pons served on the faculty of several AATF Summer Institutes and on the Executive Board of the Indiana chapter of AATF. Teaching at the University of North Carolina at Asheville since 1995, Pons is Associate Professor in the Department of Foreign Languages. She is past president of the Foreign Language Association of North Carolina and has received numerous grants in support of study abroad programs for students and faculty. With more than twenty-five years' experience in elementary French teaching and teacher preparation, Pons finds the classroom to be a stimulating environment.

Mary Ellen Scullen has been enamored of French from her first exposure in the seventh grade. After completing her BA in French at Kalamazoo College in Michigan, she went to Tours, France to be a French government sponsored teaching assistant for one year. Three years later, Scullen returned to the U.S. with a *Licence de Lettres modernes, mention Français Langue Étrangère* and a *Maîtrise de Français Langue Étrangère* from Université François Rabelais in Tours. After teaching at Kalamazoo College for a year, Scullen went to Indiana University, where she earned a joint Ph.D. in French Linguistics and Theoretical Linguistics in 1993. Scullen has taught French language, culture, and linguistics, coordinated the basic French language program, and supervised teaching assistants at the University of Louisville and, since 1998, at the University of Maryland, College Park. She also had the opportunity to teach French in southern Africa at the University of Malawi from 1995–1997 and to serve as the Resident Director for the Maryland-in-Nice program in Nice, France from 2002–2003. In 2005, she was named *Chevalier dans l'Ordre des Palmes académiques* of France. For the past several years, Scullen has been involved in training new teaching assistants not only in French, but also in Spanish, German, Russian, and Japanese. She finds working with new teaching assistants to be highly rewarding, if not occasionally frustrating, and she truly loves being in the classroom with first year students.

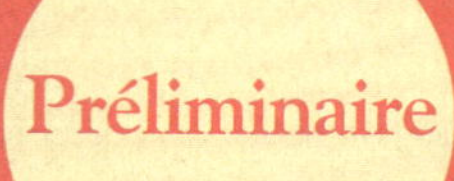

Préliminaire

Présentons-nous !

What does the photo tell you about where these French speakers are? What might their gestures tell you about their relationship?

Leçon 1 Je me présente

Leçon 2 Dans la salle de classe

Venez chez nous ! Le français dans le monde

After completing this chapter, you should be able to:

- Greet people, make introductions, and say good-bye
- Describe your classroom
- Follow and give instructions in class
- Spell words in French
- Identify places throughout the world where French is spoken
- Describe the public education system in France

Leçon  Je me présente

POINTS DE DÉPART

TEXT AUDIO
CD 1 TRACK 1

Moi, je parle français

CHLOÉ : Salut ! Je m'appelle Chloé. Et toi, comment tu t'appelles ?
ANTOINE : Je m'appelle Antoine.
CHLOÉ : Tu es de Paris ?
ANTOINE : Non, moi, je suis de Montréal.

LE PROF : Bonjour, mademoiselle, bonjour, monsieur.
CHLOÉ ET ANTOINE : Bonjour, madame.
LE PROF : Comment vous appelez-vous ?
CHLOÉ : Je m'appelle Chloé Lafont.
LE PROF : Et vous ?
ANTOINE : Paradis, Antoine Paradis.

Fiche pratique

As you begin the study of French, you will rely on a number of fixed expressions to help you navigate situations such as greeting people. Memorize these expressions in their entirety rather than trying to translate them literally.

Presentation: Present some of the material inductively by circulating around the room, shaking students' hands, greeting them, and introducing yourself using the expressions from the dialogues. You might consider preparing blank name tags for students to fill out. Include such phrases as *Bonjour, je m'appelle...* and *Je suis de...* on the name tags to help students respond to you.

Next, you may wish to show the dialogues and related drawings as you present them one by one (MFL, Ch. prélim.). Point out the learning strategy (**Fiche pratique**) for this lesson and provide some examples. Check comprehension and have students repeat key phrases. To conclude, show the illustrations without the dialogues and let students supply sample exchanges.

As you work through the exchanges, treat the cultural notes (**Vie et culture**) and have students 1) point out differences between the first two dialogues; 2) make a list of possible responses to the question *Comment ça va ?*; 3) make a list of ways to say "good-bye." Note that to say "good-bye," French Canadians often use *Bonjour* instead of *Au revoir*.

You might also use the opening montage of the *Chez nous* video to introduce students to the notion of the Francophone world as a focus of study; this is a colorful and exciting way to begin the course.

CHLOÉ : Salut, Loïc ! Comment ça va ?
LOÏC : Ça va. Et toi ?
CHLOÉ : Pas mal.
LOÏC : Bonjour, madame. Comment allez-vous ?
LE PROF : Très bien, merci. Et vous ?
LOÏC : Bien aussi, merci.

CHLOÉ : Madame, je vous présente Loïc Richard. Loïc, Madame Dupont.
LOÏC : Enchanté, madame.
LE PROF : Bonjour, Loïc.
CHLOÉ : Antoine, voici mon ami Loïc. Loïc, voici mon camarade de classe, Antoine.
ANTOINE : Salut, Loïc.
LOÏC : Salut.

LOÏC : Bon, au revoir, Chloé, au revoir, Antoine.
CHLOÉ : Salut, Loïc.
ANTOINE : À bientôt... Au revoir, madame.
LE PROF : Au revoir, Antoine. À demain.

Pour saluer et répondre

Comment ça va ?	*How are you?*
Très bien, merci.	*Very well, thanks.*
Ça va.	*Fine.*
Pas mal.	*Not bad.*
Comme ci, comme ça.	*So-so.*
Ça ne va pas très bien.	*Things aren't going well.*

Vie et culture

Bonjour !

Look at the photos here and watch the video segment *Bonjour*, in which people are greeting each other: what gestures and phrases do you notice?

When French people meet someone they know, or make contact with a stranger (for example, sales, office, or restaurant personnel), they always greet that person upon arriving and say good-bye when leaving. If the speakers are not on a first-name basis, the greeting includes an appropriate title, and the last name is not used. Usually a woman is addressed as **madame** unless she is very young:

Bonjour, monsieur.
Bonsoir, madame.
Au revoir, mademoiselle.

Se serrer la main, faire la bise

When they meet or say good-bye, French people who know each other almost always shake hands, using the right hand (**se serrer la main**). Good friends and family members kiss each other lightly on each cheek (**faire la bise**). When talking together, the French stand or sit closer to each other than Americans do. A French person would be offended if you kept moving away as he or she attempted to maintain normal conversational distance.

Tu et *vous*

When addressing another person in French, you must choose between **tu** and **vous**, which both mean *you*. Use **tu** to address a family member, a close friend, or another student. Use **vous** to address someone with whom you have a more formal relationship or to whom you wish to show respect. For example, use **vous** with people you do not know well, with older people, and with those in a position of authority, such as your teachers. Always use **vous** also to address more than one person. Do the people in the video clip use **tu** or **vous**?

ET VOUS ?

1. Think of how you typically greet people each day. Although we do not make a distinction in English like the **tu/vous** distinction in French, how do we vary our forms of address?
2. What do the practices of shaking hands and kissing on the cheek tell you about the importance of close physical contact in French culture? Would you feel comfortable with these practices? Why or why not? Compare your answers to these questions with those of your classmates. How would you explain any differences?
3. View the video segment again, paying close attention to the ways in which people greet each other; what can you conclude about their relationship in each case?

Implementation: Before going over **Vie et culture**, ask students to make inferences about the use of *tu* and *vous* based on the dialogues in the **Points de départ**. Test their understanding of the differences in usage by suggesting various people and letting students tell which form of address they would use. For example, with: a police officer; a pet; a grandparent; their best friend's mother, etc. Americans are generally considered very informal by the French, but French speakers are also becoming less formal, using the first name and *tu* more frequently among colleagues and acquaintances.

À vous la parole

P-1 Le mot juste. Give an appropriate response.

MODÈLE Comment vous appelez-vous ?
Morin, Nicolas Morin.

1. Bonjour, mademoiselle.
2. Comment tu t'appelles ?
3. Tu es de Montréal ?
4. Ça va ?
5. Comment allez-vous ?
6. Comment ça va ?
7. Voici mon ami David.
8. Je vous présente mon amie Claire.
9. Au revoir, monsieur.
10. Bon, à demain !

P-2 Présentez-vous. Get acquainted with some of your classmates and your instructor, following these suggestions.

MODÈLE Greet your instructor.
Bonjour, monsieur.
OU Bonjour, madame.

(Your instructor responds.)

Bonjour, mademoiselle.
OU Bonjour, monsieur.

1. Greet and introduce yourself to a person sitting near you.
2. Ask a classmate what his or her name is, then introduce yourself.
3. Ask a classmate whether he or she is from your city.
4. Greet a classmate and ask how he or she is today.
5. Introduce two people whom you have met in class.
6. Greet your instructor and ask how he or she is today.
7. Introduce a classmate to your instructor.
8. Say good-bye to several classmates.
9. Say good-bye to your instructor.

Implementation: P-3 Students can work in small groups to prepare exchanges, then act out their variations. You might also bring in photos/drawings of people greeting each other and have students create the dialogues. Use the photos in this lesson for the same purpose.

P-3 Le savoir-faire. What would you say and do in the situations described below? Act out each one with classmates.

MODÈLE You meet a very good friend.
É1 Salut, Anne ! Ça va ? (faire la bise)
É2 Ça va, et toi ?
É1 Pas mal.

1. You and a friend run into your instructor on campus.
2. You sit down in class next to someone you do not know.
3. You are with your roommate when a new friend joins you.
4. You run into your friend's mother while doing errands.
5. You are standing near a new teacher who does not yet know your name.
6. Class is over, and you are saying good-bye to a close friend.
7. Class is over, and you are saying good-bye to your teacher.

P-4 Faisons connaissance. Imagine that you are at a party with your classmates. Greet and introduce yourself to as many people as possible, and make introductions when others do not know each other. Tell what city you are from, then ask what city your classmates are from.

MODÈLE É1 Bonjour, je m'appelle Sean. Et toi ?
É2 Je m'appelle Natasha. Voici mon ami, Jérémie.
É1 Salut, Jérémie.
É3 Bonjour. Je suis de Chicago, et toi ?
É1 Moi, je suis de Lafayette, et toi, Natasha ?

Implementation: P-4 Use as a mixing activity at the end of class. Have students report back the names of people they met. You may wish to adapt this activity and use it a second time by passing out cards with French names written on them and having students introduce themselves to each other with their new identities.

FORMES ET FONCTIONS

1. *Les pronoms sujets et le verbe* être

Les pronoms sujets et le verbe être					
SINGULIER			**PLURIEL**		
je	**suis**	*I am*	nous	**sommes**	*we are*
tu	**es**	*you are*	vous	**êtes**	*you are*
il		*he is*	ils		
elle	**est**	*she is*	elles	**sont**	*they are*
on		*we are*			

- The verb **être** means *to be*. This form is called the *infinitive*; it is the form you find in the dictionary listing for the verb. Notice that a specific form of **être** corresponds to each subject. Because these forms do not follow a regular pattern, **être** is called an *irregular verb*.
- A subject pronoun can be used in place of a noun as the subject of a sentence:

—**Alex** est de Paris ? — *—Alex is from Paris?*
—Non, **il** est de Bruxelles. — *—No, he's from Brussels.*

As you have learned, use **tu** with a person you know very well; otherwise use **vous**. Use **vous** also when speaking to more than one person, even if they are your friends. Pronounce the final **-s** of **vous** as /z/ if the word following it begins with a vowel sound, and link it to that word:

Olivier, **tu** es de Paris ? — *Olivier, are you from Paris?*
Madame, **vous**‿êtes de Liège ? — *Madame, are you from Liege?*
Audrey et Fred, **vous**‿êtes de Genève ? — *Audrey and Fred, are you from Geneva?*

Presentation: Present inductively by questioning students about the city they are from: *Je suis de Chicago — et vous ? Vous êtes de... ? Elle est de ... — et toi aussi ?* Model the various verb forms in this way, then ask students to summarize meaning and forms. Display the chart. Point out that subject-verb agreement takes place in English as well: *I am, she is, we are.* Explain the organization of the verb chart, with singular forms on the left and plural forms on the right, and the division into first/second/third-person forms. Ask students to provide the meanings for each form. Use the textbook examples to illustrate the various points as students help you explain.

On is an indefinite pronoun that can mean *one, they,* or *people,* depending on the context. In conversational French, **on** is often used instead of **nous** to mean *we*. **On** always takes the singular form, **est**.

Nous, on est de Lille.	*We are from Lille.*

Elles refers to more than one female person or to a group of feminine nouns. **Ils** refers to more than one male person, to a group of masculine nouns, or to a group that includes both males and females or both masculine and feminine nouns.

Anne et Sophie, **elles** sont en forme.	*Anne and Sophie are fine.*
Jean-Luc et Rémi, **ils** sont stressés.	*Jean-Luc and Rémi are stressed out.*
Julie et Damien, **ils** sont occupés.	*Julie and Damien are busy.*

- Use a form of the verb **être** in descriptions or to indicate a state of being.

Elle **est** occupée.	*She's busy.*
Tu **es** malade ?	*Are you sick?*
Je **suis** stressé.	*I'm stressed out.*

- The final **-t** of **est** and **sont** is usually pronounced before a word beginning with a vowel sound.

Il est‿en forme.	*He's fine.*
Il est malade.	*He's sick.*
Elles sont‿en forme.	*They're fine.*
Elles sont stressées.	*They're stressed out.*

Comment ça va ?

Je suis en forme.	*I am fine.*
... fatigué/e.	. . . *tired.*
... stressé/e.	. . . *stressed.*
... très occupé/e.	. . . *very busy.*
... malade.	. . . *sick.*

- Use **c'est** and **ce sont** to identify people and things:

C'est Madame Dupont ?	*That's Madame Dupont?*
C'est un ami, Kevin.	*This is a friend, Kevin.*
Ce sont M. et Mme Lafarges.	*This is Mr. and Mrs. Lafarges.*

Presentation: Have students repeat the expressions in the shaded box; these provide vocabulary for use with *être*. This treatment does not create a problem for oral practice, since the adjectives have identical masculine and feminine spoken forms. Adjective agreement is treated in Ch. 1, L. 1.

Initial practice: Begin practice with a discrimination drill to ensure that students hear crucial distinctions: one or more than one? *Il est fatigué. Elles sont en forme. C'est un professeur. Ce sont des étudiants. Elle est stressée. Ils sont malades. Ce sont des profs. Elle est occupée.* Follow up with a simple substitution drill: *Je suis en forme ; vous → Vous êtes en forme*, etc. The spoken forms of these adjectives are identical, so students will never be wrong when they say these phrases. Exercises in the textbook with these adjectives should not be assigned as written work since students will not be able to produce the correct forms.

À vous la parole

P-5 Comment ça va ? Tell how everyone is feeling today.

MODÈLE Moi ? Fatigué/e.
→ Je suis fatigué/e.

1. Mme Hébert ? En forme.
2. Toi ? Fatigué/e.
3. Adrien ? Très occupé.
4. Cécile ? Malade.
5. Mathieu et toi ? En forme.
6. Julien ? Stressé.
7. Nous ? Fatigués.
8. Vous ?

Implementation: P-5 You may wish to point out that the verb *aller* is used in the questions *Ça va ?* and *Comment allez-vous ?* and that some answers to these questions would require using a form of *aller*, such as *Je vais bien* (that is, students cannot say, **Je suis bien*). The verb *aller* will be presented in Ch. 2, L. 3.
This can be cued with photos/drawings if you have some. This oral exercise does not require students to make written agreement of adjectives such as *occupé/e/s.*

P-6 Qui est-ce ? Identify the people from the opening dialogues pictured below.

MODÈLE ◆ C'est Chloé.

Implementation: P-6 You might allow students to look back at the **Points de départ** presentation as you display this exercise (MFL, Ch. prélim.).

P-7 Identité mystérieuse. Take on a new identity! Your instructor will give you a new name and city of origin, or you can invent one yourself. Circulate around the room and introduce yourself to at least three people. Be prepared to introduce someone you have met to the rest of the class!

MODÈLE É1 Bonjour, je m'appelle Mathilde.
É2 Tu es de Paris ?
É1 Non, je suis de Québec. Et toi ?
É2 Je m'appelle Louis-Jean, je suis de Port-au-Prince, à Haïti.

Implementation: P-7 Put names and cities on index cards to pass out (you can take these back and re-use them). You might also participate to provide students with practice using the *vous* form. Impose a time limit, and follow up by having students identify the people they met. Suggested names/cities: for women: Julie/Montréal, Marie-Claire/Marseille, Amira/Casablanca, Annick/Bruxelles, Honorée/Dakar, Kalida/Alger, Jennifer/Baton Rouge, Fatima/Paris, Jeanne-Marie/Port-au-Prince, Jamila/Tunis, Marine/Genève, Laura/Québec For men: Kevin/Lafayette, Abir/Tunis, Farid/Rabat, Benjamin/Nice, Badu/Tombouctou, Louis-Jean/Port-au-Prince, Habib/Beyrouth, Daniel/Louvain, Grégory/Dijon, Bakari/Kinshasa, Paul/Québec, Alex/Paris

2. *Les pronoms disjoints*

- You know that subject pronouns can be used in place of a noun (for example, a person or an object) as the subject of a sentence. *Subject pronouns* appear with a *verb*:

—Adrien est de Paris ?	—*Is Adrien from Paris?*
—Non, **il** est de Trois-Rivières.	—*No, he's from Trois-Rivières.*
—Pierre et Mélanie sont occupés ?	—*Are Pierre and Mélanie busy?*
—Oui, **ils** sont occupés.	—*Yes, they are busy.*

Preparation: Quickly review subject pronouns by having students pick the correct pronoun for the subject given: *Anne et Marie ? — Elles ; Geoffrey ? — Il ; Loïc et toi ? — Vous ; Jennifer et moi ? — Nous/On ; Moi ? — Je ; Max et Luc ? — Ils,* etc.

Presentation: To present the pronouns inductively, display a number of sentence examples on a transparency or slide that contrast the usage of subject pronouns and the corresponding stressd pronouns. Highlight forms using different colors. Read the examples, and ask students to help explain usage. Point out that *les pronoms disjoints* are called "stressed pronouns" precisely because they occur in places where they receive primary stress. Providing an exaggerated parody of Miss Piggy from the Muppets saying « *Qui, moi ?* » can help make this point in a humorous way. Remind students that they have seen examples of stressed pronoun usage from day one. You may point out that French usage is different from English in the case of complex subjets: *Damien et moi* vs. "Damien and I."

- A different type of pronoun, a *stressed pronoun*, is used:
  - in short questions that have no verb:

Je m'appelle Clémence, et **toi** ?	*My name is Clémence, how about you?*
Ça va bien, et **vous** ?	*I'm fine, and you?*

  - where there are two subjects in a sentence, one of which is a pronoun:

Damien et **elle**, ils sont fatigués.	*She and Damien are tired.*

  - to emphasize the subject of a sentence when providing a contrast:

Moi, je suis de Lausanne, mais **lui**, il est de Saumur.	*I'm from Lausanne,* *but **he**'s from Saumur.*

  - after **c'est** and **ce sont**:

—C'est Paul ? —Oui, c'est **lui**.	*—Is that Paul?* *—Yes, it is he.*
—Ce sont M. et Mme Dulac ? —Oui, ce sont **eux**.	*—Is that Mr. and Mrs. Dulac?* *—Yes, it is they.*

The stressed pronouns are shown below with the corresponding subject pronouns:

moi	je	**nous**	on/nous
toi	tu	**vous**	vous
lui	il	**eux**	ils
elle	elle	**elles**	elles

À vous la parole

Variation: P-8 Cue using the visuals from the introductions in the **Points de départ** (MFL, Ch. prélim.): *C'est Chloé ? —Oui, c'est elle ; C'est Loïc ? —Oui, c'est lui*, etc.

P-8 C'est ça. With your partner, confirm who these people are.

MODÈLE É1 C'est toi ?
É2 Oui, c'est moi.

É1 Ce sont Marie et Hélène ?
É2 Oui, ce sont elles.

1. C'est Christophe ?
2. C'est Jessica ?
3. C'est toi ?
4. C'est Arnaud ?
5. Ce sont Adeline et Nathalie ?
6. C'est vous ?
7. Ce sont Simon et Maxime ?
8. Ce sont Vanessa et Laurent ?

P-9 Et vous ? Interview each other in groups of three.

MODÈLE Je m'appelle... Et vous ?
É1 Je m'appelle Alex. Et vous ?
É2 Moi, je m'appelle...
É3 Et moi, je m'appelle...

1. Je m'appelle... Et vous ?
2. Moi, ça va. Et vous ?
3. Je suis de... Et vous ?

Implementation: P-9 Model with two students before putting students into small groups to work. Follow up by having them tell what they learned about their partners, providing additional practice with the various forms: *Lui, il est de..., elle, elle est de..., et eux, ils sont de....*

P-10 Présentez-vous ! Help out your forgetful instructor by identifying students in your classroom.

MODÈLE Lui, il s'appelle Matt ; elle, elle s'appelle Cindy.

Implementation: P-10 Cue student responses by asking for the names of students or by offering an incorrect name: *Lui, comment il s'appelle ? Et elle, elle s'appelle Nathalie ?*

Lisons

P-11 Des adresses en francophonie

A. Avant de lire. You will be looking at envelopes and postcards addressed to different people in the Francophone world. Before you read them, list the information you expect to find on an addressed envelope.

B. En lisant. How does the list you made compare with what you actually see on the envelopes and postcards? Do you see words or expressions with which you are not familiar or that you did not anticipate?

C. En regardant de plus près. Now examine the following aspects of the text more closely.

1. Given the context and its similarity to English, what do you think the phrase **Boîte Postale** means?
2. Given the context, what do you think the word **rue** means?
3. Provide the full forms in French for the following abbreviations:

   M. Mlle Mme B.P.

4. Although you do not see the phrase **code postal** in the addresses, most of them have one. What do you think the **code postal** is? What is the **code postal** for **Abidjan**, for **Tours**, for **Vieux-Québec**? What is different about the **code postal** for this last city?
5. One envelope includes the words **destinataire** and **expéditeur**. What do you think those terms mean?

Stratégie

Use your knowledge of the type of text you are reading to understand its content. When you are reading addresses, for example, you will expect to find certain kinds of information; you can use that knowledge to figure out the meaning of words and expressions that you do not know.

Implementation: Avant de lire We recommend that you treat this first reading in class to introduce students to the techniques used in this process approach. Be sure to explain to students the meaning of each subheading, because these will be used consistently throughout the textbook. Conduct this preliminary brainstorming activity with the class as a whole, putting the list up for all to see as it develops. Then ask students to match items in the list to actual information on the envelopes as you display them (MFL, Ch. prélim.).

Implementation: En lisant You might put students in pairs to complete this task, then have the class compare notes.

Implementation: En regardant de plus près This activity focuses on developing decoding techniques, so that students learn to rely on prior knowledge and contextual guessing rather than searching through a dictionary to discover the meaning of unfamiliar words and expressions. It is meant to build students' confidence. Work through the questions with them.
Point out interesting cultural information such as the frequent use of capital letters for last names, cities and countries; stamps and postmarks; the fact that the first two numbers in postal codes in France designate the *département*; CH as the abbreviation for *la Confédération Helvétique*, the official name for Switzerland (this last example is found in the **Après avoir lu**).

D. Après avoir lu. Now that you've studied the addresses, write envelopes for these two people.

1. Salut, je m'appelle Marie-Cécile Kabambé. Je suis de Kinshasa. Mon adresse, c'est Boîte Postale 357. Il n'y a pas de code postal. Kinshasa est au Congo bien sûr.
2. Bonjour, je m'appelle Marc Leblanc. Je suis de Genève. Mon adresse, c'est Case Postale 1602. Le code postal, c'est CH-1211 Genève 1. Vous savez que Genève est en Suisse, n'est-ce pas ?

Implementation: Après avoir lu This may be completed as a whole-class activity, displaying the addresses for all to see. As an additional follow-up, ask students to give their own address as they would explain it to a French speaker.

Leçon  Dans la salle de classe

POINTS DE DÉPART

TEXT AUDIO
CD 1 TRACK 2

La salle de classe

Presentation: You may wish to divide the material in this section into two groups. First, focus on classroom objects and the mini-dialogues. Continue with the **Vie et culture** notes and Ex. P-12 and P-13. In a subsequent class or later in the same period, present the classroom expressions and commands. Follow with Ex. P-14 and P-15. To present, describe the classroom, showing the labeled art (MFL, Ch. prélim.) or real objects in the classroom. You can also bring in a specially prepared backpack or bag filled with various items (i.e., *une règle, un stylo, une craie, un livre, un DVD*). Use items in the bag to present the vocabulary or as an identification drill. Students can take turns reaching into the bag, drawing out an item and saying what it is. Using the unlabeled art (MFL, Ch. prélim.) or objects in the classroom, check comprehension by having students point to objects you name. Drill using either/or questions to practice pronunciation: *C'est une porte ou une fenêtre ?* Other simple drills: 1) draw one of the items and let others guess what it is; 2) find the "odd word out" in a list of three or four items: *une craie, un stylo, une règle, un crayon... (une règle)*; 3) associations: What word do you associate with each of the following? *un professeur ? — un étudiant ; une craie ? — un tableau*, etc.

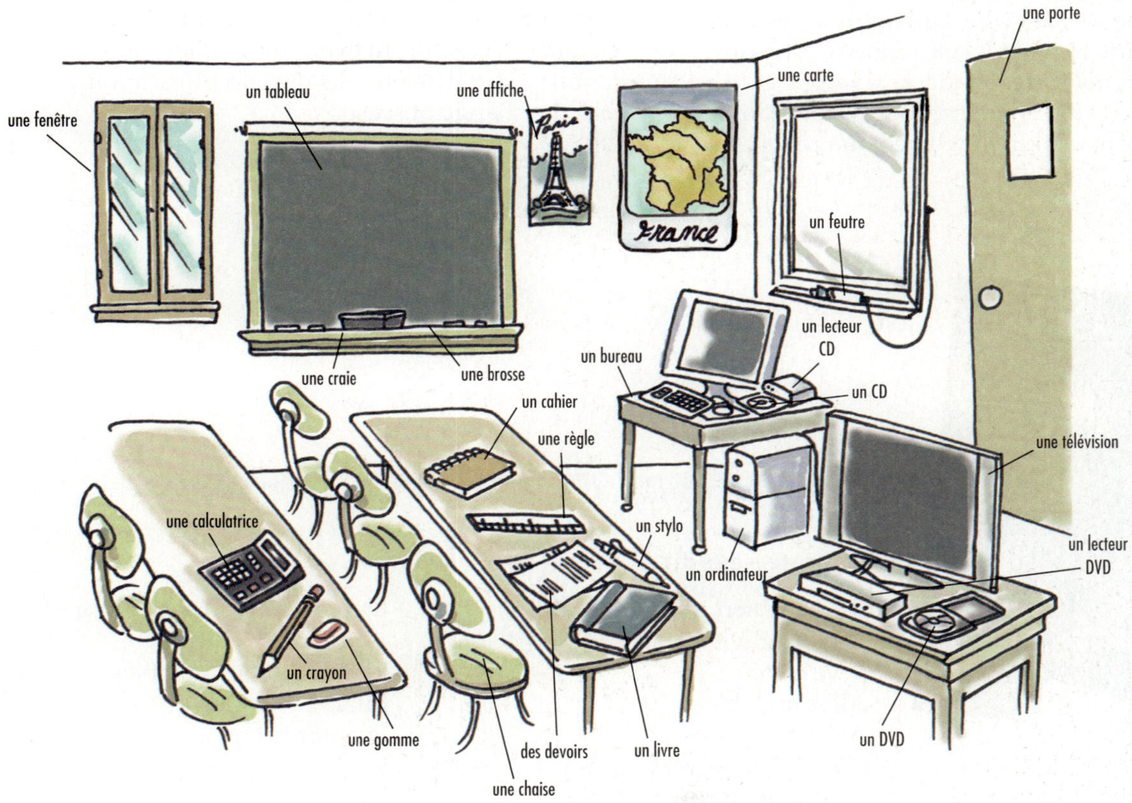

—Il y a un crayon sur le bureau ?
—Non, il n'y a pas de crayon, mais il y a un stylo. Voilà.

—Il y a des affiches dans la salle de classe ?
—Non, il n'y a pas d'affiches.

Presentation: Present the mini-dialogues, using examples of classroom objects; then move directly to the exercises. We avoid the traditional *voici/voilà* distinction because native speaker usage is highly variable. *Voilà* is the neutral term, acceptable in a wider variety of contexts. We present *voici* in Ch. prélim., L. 1, in the context of introductions: *Voici mon ami Loïc*, since native speakers are consistent in their use of *voici* in this context. *Il n'y a pas de* is taught here as a lexical item; negation is treated productively in Ch. 1, L. 3.

Vie et culture

La scolarité en France

This chart provides an overview of the French school system. As you examine the chart, answer the following questions.

1. What general information is provided about public schools in France?
2. Find the words **école, collège**, and **lycée** in the chart. To what levels of instruction do these terms correspond?
3. How does the French school system compare to the school system where you grew up?
4. Nearly all French children are enrolled in school by age three. Why do you think this might be the case?

La rentrée (*back to school*) for French schoolchildren generally takes place early in September and for university students, early in October. A significant event for retailers and families, **la rentrée** marks the end of vacation and the change of seasons.

Presentation: Use the standard TPR (Total Physical Response) sequence to introduce and practice classroom commands: 1) demonstrate; 2) hesitate as students respond; 3) students perform alone; 4) introduce novel combinations and series of commands; finally, if you wish, 5) reverse roles, letting students give commands. For more information on TPR techniques, see the IRM. The goal of this treatment of commands is for students to be able to function in an all-French classroom and to follow basic classroom instructions; the forms of the imperative will be treated in Ch. 2, L. 3. We assume that the instructor will use the polite form with students. You may wish to introduce the familiar forms as well.

Le professeur dit :

Écoutez bien, s'il vous plaît !
Regardez le tableau !
Levez-vous !
Allez au tableau !
Allez à la porte !
Ouvrez la fenêtre !
Fermez le livre !
Montrez-moi votre livre !
Montrez Paris sur la carte !
Ne parlez pas anglais !
Prenez un stylo !
Écrivez votre nom et votre prénom !
Lisez les mots au tableau !
Effacez le tableau !
Écoutez sans regarder le livre !
Répondez en français !
Donnez la craie à Marie-Laure !
Rendez-moi les devoirs !
Asseyez-vous !
Merci.
De rien.

Note: The Ch. 3 video segment, *Un peu d'histoire*, shows a Canadian speaker responding to *Merci !* with *Bienvenue !* Here we teach only *De rien*, but you might introduce other expressions: *Je vous/t'en prie, Il n'y a pas de quoi.*

Les étudiants répondent :

Pardon ? Je ne comprends pas.
Répétez, s'il vous plaît !
Parlez plus fort !
Comment dit-on « *board* » en français ?

LIRE EN PARTANT DU BAS DU TABLEAU

Enseignement	Établissement	Classe	Classe (voie professionnelle)	Âge
Enseignement supérieur	UNIVERSITÉS ou ÉCOLES SUPÉRIEURES			
Enseignement secondaire 2°	LYCÉE GÉNÉRAL, TECHNOLOGIQUE ou PROFESSIONNEL	Terminale pour Bac général ou Bac technologique	Bac professionnel (*en 2 ans*)	
		1ère	brevet d'études professionnelles ou certificat d'aptitude professionnelle	
		2ème	2ème professionnelle	
	COLLÈGE	3ème		14 – 15 ans
		4ème		13 –14 ans
		5ème		12 – 13 ans
		6ème		11 – 12 ans
Enseignement primaire 1°	ÉCOLE ÉLÉMENTAIRE	cours moyen 2	Cycle 3	10 – 11 ans
		cours moyen 1		9 – 10 ans
		cours élémentaire 2		8 – 9 ans
		cours élémentaire 1	Cycle 2	7 – 8 ans
		cours préparatoire		6 – 7 ans
	ÉCOLE MATERNELLE	Grande section		5 – 6 ans
		Moyenne section	Cycle 1	4 – 5 ans
		Petite section		3 – 4 ans 2 – 3 ans

En France, la scolarité est **obligatoire** de 6 à 16 ans. L' école est **publique**, **laïque** et **gratuite**.

Presentation: We use authentic documents to help students learn about culture through discovery techniques. Show students how to analyze the document: How is the information organized? What are the main headings? What vocabulary is used to identify the various levels of instruction? Highlight the terms *école*, *collège*, and *lycée* and discuss their equivalents in North American educational systems. Can students guess at meaning based on cognates, context, and their knowledge of the real world? Point out that *6ème* is roughly equivalent to sixth grade in the United States. Encourage cross-cultural comparisons: for what ages is school attendance mandatory? When do children generally begin school? At what age do they complete their secondary education? Note that almost 100% of French children are enrolled in school by age three. This may be in part explained by the high percentage of women who work: 80% of women aged 30–54 (Mermet, *Francoscopie 2007*, p. 268).

À vous la parole

P-12 Voilà ! As your instructor asks about various classroom objects, hand them over, point them out, or say there aren't any.

MODÈLES Donnez-moi un stylo, s'il vous plaît !
Voilà (*and you hand over a pen*).

Montrez-moi une carte de France, s'il vous plaît !
Voilà (*and you point to a map of France*).

Il y a des affiches ici ?
Oui, voilà des affiches (*and you point to some posters*).
OU Non, il n'y a pas d'affiches.

P-13 Dans la salle de classe. Write down as many different classroom objects as you can see. Now compare your list with that of a classmate. Cross off the items that are common to both lists, then give yourself a point for each item on your list that your partner did not name. Who has the most points?

MODÈLE É1 ~~un bureau~~, ~~une fenêtre~~, un livre, ~~une carte~~, une affiche, une télé
É2 ~~un bureau~~, un tableau, une craie, ~~une fenêtre~~, une porte, ~~une carte~~, un cahier
É1 = 3 pts, É2 = 4 pts

Implementation: P-12 This focuses on comprehension and repetition of the classroom vocabulary and allows students to use *voilà* in an authentic context. Suggestions: *Donnez-moi un stylo, un crayon, une craie, un livre, un cahier, une règle, une gomme. Montrez-moi une fenêtre, le tableau, la porte, un ordinateur, un bureau, une chaise, un étudiant. Il y a une carte ici ? un lecteur CD ? des règles ? un lecteur DVD ? des affiches ? des cahiers ?*
Modify by responding *Merci* each time a student gives you an object and suggesting that students reply appropriately.
To simplify, break down into two parts: 1) have students hand over or point out objects *(Donnez-moi ... / Montrez-moi ...)*; 2) have students respond with *il y a ... / il n'y a pas de.*

Variation: P-13 Make this a timed exercise so that students must write quickly; spelling is not critical as long as students have attempted the word. Follow up by finding out which students had the most points, then have the top two compare lists to declare a winner.

Additional activities: For further practice, put students in pairs or small groups and ask them to show each other what they have brought with them to class. For example, *Voilà un livre, un cahier, un stylo, un crayon et une gomme.* Alternatively, put several classroom objects into a bag and have students guess what is inside by asking questions: *Il y a un stylo ?—Non, il n'y a pas de stylo.* or *Oui, il y a un stylo. Voilà.* Turn this into a pair or small group activity by asking students to prepare bags with three items and having their classmates guess what's inside.

Exercice de mémoire: Have students look at a (complex) picture and then write down as many things as they can remember having seen; or display and then hide actual items.

P-14 C'est logique.

With a partner, complete each command in as many logical ways as possible.

Variation: P-14 Students are required to demonstrate comprehension of the verbs by adding an appropriate completion. To simplify, give students a list of possible completions from which they must choose.

MODÈLE Ouvrez…
→ Ouvrez la fenêtre.
OU → Ouvrez le livre.

1. Regardez…
2. Écoutez…
3. Rendez-moi…
4. Montrez-moi…
5. Fermez…
6. Effacez…
7. Répondez…
8. Allez…
9. Écrivez…
10. Prenez…

P-15 Qu'est-ce que vous dites ?

What could you say in each situation?

MODÈLE You want the teacher to speak up.
→ Parlez plus fort, s'il vous plaît !

1. You want to interrupt the teacher.
2. You want the teacher to repeat.
3. You don't understand.
4. You ask how to say *door* in French.
5. You want to thank someone.
6. You can't hear what's being said.
7. You don't know how to say *please* in French.
8. Someone says **Merci !** to you.

Note: This presentation focuses on orthography rather than pronunciation, so the International Phonetic Alphabet is not taught here. IPA symbols, along with key words in French, are provided in Appendix 1.

Presentation: You may want to present the alphabet to your students in phonetic groups:

[e] : b c d g p t v w
[ɛ] : f l m n r s z
[i] : i j x y
[a] : a k h
[y] : q u
Ce qui reste : e, o

First spell words and let students write them, then have students spell their name or another word that you provide. You may wish to teach students to say *deux èls*, etc., for double letters.

Sons et lettres

TEXT AUDIO CD 1 TRACK 3

L'alphabet et les accents

Here are the letters of the alphabet together with their pronunciation in French.

a	(a)	j	(ji)	s	(ès)
b	(bé)	k	(ka)	t	(té)
c	(sé)	l	(èl)	u	(u)
d	(dé)	m	(èm)	v	(vé)
e	(eu)	n	(èn)	w	(double vé)
f	(èf)	o	(o)	x	(iks)
g	(jé)	p	(pé)	y	(i grec)
h	(ach)	q	(ku)	z	(zèd)
i	(i)	r	(èr)		

Accents and other diacritical marks are an integral part of French spelling.

- **L'accent aigu** is used with **e** to represent the vowel /e/ of **stressé**:

  Andr**é**   Qu**é**bec   stress**é**   r**é**p**é**tez

- **L'accent grave** is used with **e** to represent the vowel /ɛ/ of **la règle**:

  la r**è**gle   le mod**è**le   tr**è**s   Gen**è**ve

It is also used with **a** and **u** to differentiate words:

la *the* vs. **là** *there* ou *or* vs. **où** *where*

- **L'accent circonflexe** can be used with all five vowel letters. It often marks the loss of the sound /s/ at an earlier stage of French. The **s** is still present in English words borrowed from French before that loss occurred.

être	s'il vous pla**î**t	bient**ô**t
la h**â**te *haste*	l'h**ô**pital *hospital*	co**û**ter *to cost*

- **Le tréma** indicates that vowel letters in a group are pronounced individually:

toi vs. Lo**ï**c /lo-ik/ Claire vs. Ha**ï**ti /a-i-ti/

- **La cédille** indicates that **c** is to be pronounced as /s/ rather than /k/ before the vowel letters **a**, **o**, or **u**:

ça fran**ç**ais Fran**ç**oise

À vous la parole

P-16 Les sigles. Practice saying each French acronym, then match it with its full form. Can you provide the English equivalent for each?

1. l'ONU	**a.** l'Union européenne
2. l'OEA	**b.** les États-Unis d'Amérique
3. l'OTAN	**c.** l'Organisation des Nations unies
4. l'UE	**d.** le syndrome d'immunodéficitaire acquise
5. le SIDA	**e.** l'Organisation des États américains
6. les USA	**f.** l'Organisation du traité de l'Atlantique Nord

P-17 Qu'est-ce que c'est ? Reorder the letters to identify things you find in the classroom, and spell the correct word aloud.

Key: P-17 1) livre 2) carte 3) tableau 4) chaise 5) porte 6) devoirs 7) étudiante 8) craie

MODÈLES LYSTO
S-T-Y-L-O, stylo.

NORACY
C-R-A-Y-O-N, crayon.

1. LERVI
2. TAREC
3. LATAUBE
4. ICASHE
5. TROPE
6. VISODER
7. DAUNITETÉ
8. CIERA

P-18 Les accents. Correct the following words or phrases by adding the missing accents and other diacritics, then spell each word aloud. (The asterisk indicates that these words are spelled incorrectly.)

1. le *francais
2. une *regle
3. une *fenetre
4. le verbe *etre
5. *repondez
6. *bientot
7. *repetez
8. *voila

Presentation: To present, begin with a series of either/or questions: *C'est un livre ou un cahier ? une affiche ou une carte ?*; then move to open-ended questions—*Qu'est-ce que c'est ?*—that require students to answer using familiar vocabulary and the indefinite article. Ask students how they decide whether to use *un* or *une* in their response. Their answers will help summarize the information provided in the textbook. Display the chart listing forms, and provide simple practice: *Un ou une ? livre, ordinateur, porte, bureau, fenêtre,* etc. Follow the same process in introducing the definite article.

FORMES ET FONCTIONS

1. *Le genre et les articles au singulier*

All French nouns are assigned to one of two noun classes—*feminine* or *masculine*—and are therefore said to have a *gender*. The gender of a noun determines the form of other words that accompany it—for example, articles and adjectives.

◆ **The indefinite article**

The indefinite articles **un** and **une** correspond to *a* or *an* in English. **Une** is used with feminine nouns and **un** with masculine nouns. **Un** or **une** can also mean *one*:

Voilà **un** bureau.	*Here's a desk.*
Donnez-moi **une** chaise.	*Give me a chair.*
Il y a **une** fenêtre dans la salle de classe.	*There's one window in the classroom.*

Before a vowel sound, **un** ends with an /n/ sound that is pronounced as if it were part of the next word: **un‿**ami, **un‿**ordinateur.

In negative sentences, the indefinite article is replaced by **de/d'**:

Il n'y a pas **de** lecteur DVD.	*There's no DVD player.*
Il n'y a pas **d'**ordinateur dans la salle de classe.	*There's no computer in the classroom.*

◆ **The definite article**

There are three forms of the singular definite article, corresponding to *the* in English: **la** is used with feminine nouns, **le** with masculine nouns, and **l'** with all nouns beginning with a vowel sound. As in English, the definite article is used to indicate a previously mentioned or specified noun.

Voilà **la** carte.	*Here's the map.*
C'est **le** professeur.	*That's the professor.*
Donnez-moi **l'**affiche.	*Give me the poster.*

In French the definite article also designates a noun used in a general or abstract sense. In such cases, no article is used in English.

J'aime **le** football.	*I like soccer.*
Ma sœur adore **la** musique.	*My sister loves music.*

Les articles

	MASCULIN	FÉMININ
indéfini	**un** cahier	**une** règle
	un‿ordinateur	**une** affiche
défini	**le** cahier	**la** règle
	l'ordinateur	**l'**affiche

- **Predicting the gender of nouns**

The following guidelines will help you identify the gender of many nouns.

- Nouns designating females are usually feminine and nouns designating males are usually masculine:

la dame	*the lady*	**le** monsieur	*the man*
une étudiante	*a (female) student*	**un** étudiant	*a (male) student*

- The names of languages are masculine:

le français	*French*	**le** créole	*Creole*

- Words recently borrowed from other languages are generally masculine:

le marketing	**le** yoga	**le** rap	**le** tennis

- Some endings are good predictors of the gender of nouns:

MASCULINE ENDINGS: **-isme, -age, -eau, -o**

le socialisme	**le** jardinage *(gardening)*	**le** tableau	**le** stylo

FEMININE ENDINGS: **-ion, -té**

la nation	**la** télévision	**la** liberté	**la** quantité

Fiche pratique

It is a good idea to learn a new noun with the indefinite article, so you can remember the gender. For example, learn **une affiche** rather than **affiche** or **l'affiche**.

Note: Although some students may have heard that nouns ending in **-e** are feminine, this is not necessarily the case. About half the nouns ending in **-e** are feminine, the other half are masculine.

À vous la parole

P-19 Qu'est-ce qu'il y a ? Look carefully at the list of classroom objects below. Note the form of the article in each case to determine if this object is found in the classroom or not.

	Il y a...	Il n'y a pas...	
MODÈLES	______	✓	... de carte.
	✓	______	... un tableau.
1.	______	______	... d'ordinateur.
2.	______	______	... un bureau.
3.	______	______	... une affiche.
4.	______	______	... de télévision.
5.	______	______	... un livre de français.
6.	______	______	... de lecteur CD.
7.	______	______	... une calculatrice.

In your opinion, what one object most needs to be added to make this a well-equipped classroom, and why?

Implementation: P-19 Begin practice with this comprehension-based exercise. To focus on form, use a discrimination drill: *masculin ou féminin ? Voici un ordinateur, une affiche, un stylo, une chaise, un crayon, une gomme, un crayon, une calculatrice.* Do the same for the definite article: *Voici la porte, le livre, le cahier, la brosse, le bureau, la télévision, le DVD, la règle.*
Follow with substitution drills, having students change first from the indefinite to the definite article (*Voilà un stylo* ⟶ *Voilà le stylo ; une gomme, un étudiant, une affiche, un crayon, un livre, une chaise*), then from the definite to the indefinite (*Voilà le professeur* ⟶ *Voilà un professeur ; le livre, le bureau, la brosse, le cahier, la calculatrice, la gomme, l'ordinateur*).

P-20 Dans la salle de classe. What can you name in this classroom?

MODÈLE Il y a un bureau,...

Implementation: P-21 Be sure to bring some of the items to class and have them prominently displayed. To incorporate the idea of possession, place items on students' desks throughout the room.

P-21 Voilà ! Can you find the following objects in your classroom? If so, take turns with a partner indicating to whom they belong.

MODÈLE un lecteur CD
Voilà un lecteur CD ; c'est le lecteur CD de Jacques.

1. un cahier
2. un crayon
3. une calculatrice
4. un livre
5. un stylo
6. un bureau
7. une règle
8. une gomme

Key: P-22 1) le 2) le 3) le 4) la 5) le 6) la 7) le 8) la

P-22 Quel genre ? Can you guess the gender of these unfamiliar words?

MODÈLE japonais
le japonais

1. rock
2. château
3. camouflage
4. solution
5. communisme
6. diva
7. métro
8. beauté

Presentation: For an inductive presentation, use written examples to elicit plural forms: *un livre, deux livre_ ? un bureau, deux bureau_ ? un cours, deux cours_ ?* Ask students to provide written plurals. Then contrast singular and plural forms to show that there is no difference in pronunciation of the noun, using first the noun alone, then the noun accompanied by a number or article: *bureau, bureaux ; un bureau, trois bureaux ; livre, livres ; le livre, les livres.*

2. *Le nombre et les articles au pluriel*

Plurals of nouns

Most French nouns are made plural by adding a written letter -s:

un livre	*a book*	deux livre**s**	*two books*
une fenêtre	*one window*	trois fenêtre**s**	*three windows*

Singular nouns that end in a written **-s** do not change in the plural; nouns ending in **-eau** add the letter **-x**:

un cours	*a course*	deux cours	*two courses*
un bureau	*one desk*	trois bureaux	*three desks*

Although a letter **-s** or **-x** is added to written words to indicate the plural, it is not pronounced. You must listen for a preceding word, usually a number or an article, to tell whether a noun is plural or singular.

◆ **Plurals of articles**

The plural form of the definite article is always **les**, which is pronounced /le/:

Note: Stress the pronunciation of the full vowel of the article in order to distinguish between singular and plural nouns.

le livre	*the book*	**les** livres	*the books*
la chaise	*the chair*	**les** chaises	*the chairs*

The plural form of the indefinite article is always **des**, which is pronounced /de/:

un cahier	*a notebook*	**des** cahiers	*notebooks, some notebooks*
une porte	*a door*	**des** portes	*doors, some doors*

In English, plural nouns often appear without any article; in French, an article almost always accompanies the noun:

Il y a **des** livres ici.	*There are books here.*
J'aime **les** affiches.	*I like posters.*

Before a vowel sound, the **-s** of **les** and **des** is pronounced as /z/:

les chaises vs. **les**‿images (/z/)   des bureaux vs. **des**‿ordinateurs (/z/)

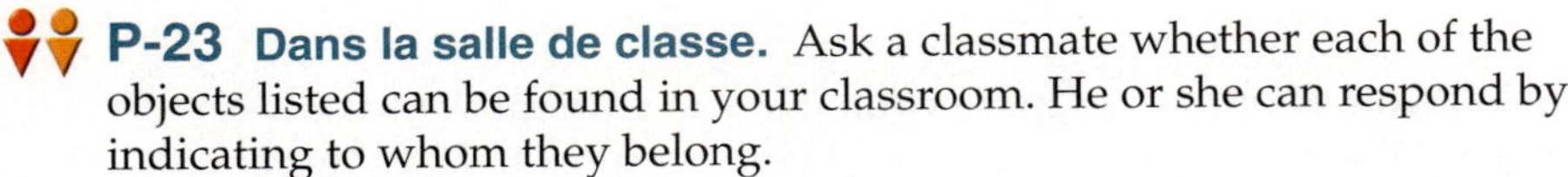

À vous la parole

Initial practice: Begin with a discrimination drill: one, or more than one? *Voici une chaise, des ordinateurs, un crayon, une brosse, des devoirs, des cahiers, une affiche, des stylos, un livre, une gomme.* Follow with a simple transformation drill, singular to plural: *Voici une chaise* ⟶ *Voici des chaises,* then plural to singular (which is more difficult, since students will need to produce the appropriate gender).

P-23 Dans la salle de classe. Ask a classmate whether each of the objects listed can be found in your classroom. He or she can respond by indicating to whom they belong.

MODÈLE CD

É1 Il y a des CD ?
É2 Oui, voilà les CD de Vincent.

1. cahiers
2. livres
3. stylos
4. cartes
5. règles
6. devoirs
7. DVD
8. gommes
9. affiches

P-24 Dans ta chambre. Ask a classmate questions to find out what objects are in his or her room.

MODÈLE É1 Il y a des affiches ?
É2 Oui, il y a des affiches.
OU Non, mais il y a des photos.

Script: Écoutons C'est Nicolas Sarkozy. Il est d'origine hongroise, mais il est né à Paris. C'est un homme politique. Il est élu président de la République française en 2007.
Elle, c'est Maryse Condé. Elle est de Pointe-à-Pitre à la Guadeloupe. Elle est professeur et écrivain, donc elle écrit des livres.
Voici Audrey Tautou. Elle est très élégante, non ? Elle est de Beaumont. C'est une petite ville en France qui s'écrit B-E-A-U-M-O-N-T. C'est une actrice de cinéma. Elle joue dans les films « Le fabuleux destin d'Amélie Poulain » et « le Code da Vinci ».
Lui ? C'est MC Solaar. Il est de la ville de Dakar, au Sénégal, mais il habite Paris. Il est chanteur. En fait, il chante du rap, donc il est rappeur.

Implementation: Après avoir écouté Review the answers with students and find out what they listened for to determine the correct responses. Discuss the follow-up questions as a class.

P-25 Sur mon bureau. In groups of three, compare what is on your desk at home by naming at least three items that are on it. What do you have on your desk that your partners don't have?

MODÈLE É1 Sur mon bureau, il y a un ordinateur, des livres et une photo.
É2 Et sur mon bureau, il y a...
É3 Sur mon bureau, il y a...

Presentation: Avant d'écouter Allow students to make guesses about the individuals pictured and listed in the chart, but do not confirm or deny. You might pronounce each name before students listen to the descriptions, to ensure they will recognize the names when they hear them.

Écoutons

P-26 Des francophones bien connus

A. Avant d'écouter. You will hear descriptions of four famous French-speaking people. Look at the chart below—do you recognize any of the names? Do you know anything about these individuals? Can you match their name to their photo?

B. En écoutant. The first time you listen, fill in the first column of the chart with the city where each person was born. Then, listen again and try to determine why these people are famous. Write their profession in the second column. See whether any of your initial ideas are confirmed.

Nom	Ville d'origine	Profession
Nicolas SARKOZY		
Maryse CONDÉ		
Audrey TAUTOU		
MC SOLAAR		

C. Après avoir écouté. Compare your answers with those of your classmates. Which of these people would you like most to learn more about? What would you like to learn about this person? Where would you go for more information?

Venez chez nous ! Le français dans le monde

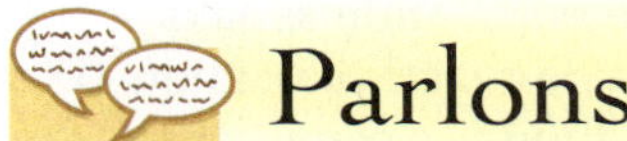

Parlons

P-27 Qui parle français ?

A. Avant de parler. What do you know about who speaks French, where, and for what purposes? Take the following quiz and see.

1. The French-speaking population of the world totals approximately . . .
   - **a.** 60 million
   - **b.** 175 million
   - **c.** 300 million
   - **d.** 450 million
2. In a Francophone country, everyone speaks French.
   - **a.** True
   - **b.** False
3. French is an official language in the United States.
   - **a.** True
   - **b.** False
4. In the eighteenth century, French was the Western world's major language of diplomacy and international affairs.
   - **a.** True
   - **b.** False
5. The world organization for countries where French is spoken is . . .
   - **a.** a political and economic federation, a kind of French commonwealth.
   - **b.** the only international organization based on a language.
   - **c.** a vehicle for recognizing the cultural diversity of French-speaking people.

Preparation: To preview the **Venez chez nous !** section, you might ask students to name places where French is spoken — create a list on the board for everyone to see, perhaps writing the place names in French. If you have not done so already, show the opening montage from the video to create interest; ask students to comment on what they see and to guess about the various locations for the segment.

Note: P-27 Unlike most **Parlons** sections, this activity is conducted in English.

Note: The continent with the largest percentage of French speakers is Africa — 11% of the total population. The regions with the highest percentages of French speakers (more than 15% of the total population) are the Maghreb, the Indian Ocean, and western Europe. The ten countries with the greatest number of French speakers are: France, Algeria, Canada, Morocco, Belgium, the Ivory Coast, Tunisia, Cameroon, the Republic of Congo, and Switzerland.

la Polynésie française

la Tunisie

la Guadeloupe

B. En parlant. Now compare your answers with those of a partner to see how you did.

Number 1

Did you answer . . . b. 175 million? You are correct. About 115 million people are native speakers of French: 60 million of these live in France; about 20 million live in countries where part of the population speaks French as an everyday language (Belgium, Canada, Switzerland); about 35 million live in areas where a majority of the population use some other language(s) for everyday communication. Another 60 million people speak French regularly as a second language. The number of French-speaking people in the world has tripled since 1945. Give yourself two points.

le Sénégal

Number 2

The answer is False; give yourself two points if you answered correctly. In a Francophone country, not necessarily everyone speaks French. In some countries, French is both an official language (used in government and education) and a vernacular language (used in everyday communication). Belgium is an example of a country in which French is both an official and a vernacular language. In Haiti, on the other hand, French serves as one of two official languages, but is spoken by only about 15 percent of the population. The vernacular language of all Haitians is Haitian Creole.

Number 3

The answer is True; give yourself two points if you answered correctly. Since 1968, French and English have been declared official languages in Louisiana. About a quarter million speakers of Cajun French live in southwest Louisiana.

le Québec

Number 4

Two points if you answered True. Philosophers such as Montesquieu, Voltaire, and Rousseau had a profound effect on the politics of the era. Both Benjamin Franklin and Thomas Jefferson spoke French and lived for a time in Paris, meeting many of the great French thinkers of the day. The influence of French philosophers is seen in our own United States Constitution: the notion of separation of executive, legislative, and judicial powers is an idea developed by Montesquieu in his work **L'Esprit des lois** (*The Spirit of Laws*).

le Mali

Number 5

The answer is both **b** and **c;** give yourself two points for either, four points if you answered both! In 1970, several African nations formed an entity to promote technological and cultural development across French-speaking countries. The current organization, **l'Organisation internationale de la Francophonie** (**l'OIF**), includes 53 member states, 2 associate members, and 13 observer nations. In 32 of these countries, French serves as an official language for some 175 million people, more than half of whom are fluent speakers of the language. A new charter, **La Charte de la Francophonie**, was adopted by the **OIF** in 2005, promoting human rights, cooperation, and development among member nations.

C. Après avoir parlé. How did you and your partner score? Did any of these answers surprise you? Why, or why not?

Implementation: Avant de lire As you focus on the reading strategy, looking for cognates, ask why there are so many similar words in French and English. You may explain that after the arrival of William the Conquerer (*Guillaume le Conquérant*) in England in 1066, many of the English nobles and middle class people began to use French as their everyday language. Gradually, many French words found their way into the English language.

Lisons

P-28 Titres de journaux

A. Avant de lire. Here is a series of headlines from the French-language press. As you read them, you will find that you are able to grasp their general meaning because they include a number of cognates. For example, you can guess that the article entitled **Dossier Beauté : Écolo Cosméto** probably has to do with cosmetics and ecology because of the words **Écolo** and **Cosméto**. What cognates can you find in the subtitle that help to confirm this guess?

Stratégie

Look for *cognates* (**des mots apparentés**) as you read a text. Cognates are words whose form and meaning are very similar in French and English. Focusing on cognates can help you to grasp the general meaning of a text.

B. En lisant. Watching for cognates, decide which headline/s deal/s with . . .

1. art
2. medical news
3. politics
4. a natural disaster
5. a scientific discovery
6. the economy
7. the environment

How did you make your decision in each case?

Key: En lisant 1) 6 2) 1 3) 5 4) 4 5) 2 6) 5 7) 3, 4
As you work with the headlines, point out to students that they can also use context to guess the meaning of unfamiliar words. For example, in the phrase **aérosols sans fréon**, they might guess that the word **sans** means *without*, since that would be an ecological improvement!

1. **Le vaccin antigrippal serait utile**
La nouvelle vaccination réduit de 48 % le risque de décès chez les personnes qui ont plus de 65 ans et de 27 % les risques d'hospitalisation pour pneumonie ou grippe pour tous, d'après une étude de l'Université du Minnesota à Minneapolis.

Le Soir en ligne (Bruxelles)

2. **Un dinosaure rare découvert à Lisbonne**
Un paléontologue français a découvert des morceaux de mâchoire d'un étrange dinosaure carnivore avec des dents « de crocodile ». C'est le baryonyx.

Le Soir en ligne (Bruxelles)

3. **DOSSIER BEAUTÉ : ÉCOLO COSMÉTO**
La cosmétologie se met à l'heure écolo. Shampooings biodégradables, crèmes aux plantes, aérosols sans fréon. . .

20 ans (Paris)

« Dossier beauté » 20 ANS no. 67, mars 1992

4. **CATASTROPHES NATURELLES**
Cayes - inondations : 3.000 familles sinistrées
Est-ce la manifestation du changement climatique ?
La ville des Cayes, troisième ville d'Haïti comptant 100.000 habitants, était en partie sous les eaux mardi. . .

Haïti en marche (Miami)

5. ***Politique québécoise***
L'Assemblée nationale reprend ses travaux sur fond d'économie
Plusieurs dossiers économiques majeurs attendent le gouvernement Charest cet automne.

Cyberpresse (Canada)

6. **Voirol ou le regard émerveillé d'un môme photographe**
. . . Portraitiste subtil, photoreporter nominé à l'European Kodak Award d'Arles, Xavier Voirol reste viscéralement attaché à son indépendance. Il travaille en freelance depuis 20 ans . . . .

L'Express (Neuchâtel)

Implementation: En regardant de plus près Show students how they use contextualized guessing in their native language, with examples such as the following: "Jancis, get the besom and sweep out my room a bit." "You did light a fire as will be hard to dout." In the first sentence, knowing what one does with a "besom" tells us what it must be: a broom. In the second, "dout" is something you do to a fire, clearly the opposite of "light." The examples are taken from *Precious Bane* by Mary Webb, which contains many examples of Welsh dialect that can be used to exemplify reading strategies for students. Help students practice additional decoding strategies related to each headline: 1) the many cognates along with contextualized guessing and background knowledge can help students decide that *la grippe* is "influenza/ flu"; have students also analyze the meaning of percentages used in the headline; 2) ask students to find the name of the dinosaur discovered and to identify the different nationalities involved in the story (French, Portuguese); 3) mention the tendency in French to abbreviate words (as in *métro, resto, McDo*); analyze the use of prepositions; 4) have students find what the proper name *Cayes* refers to; show how *-ième* is a productive suffix; point out that words that appear to be cognates can also be *faux amis*, such as *sinistrées* (which here means "threatened"); relate the French word *inondations* to the English expression "to be inundated"; 5) point out word order in noun phrases: noun + adjective; 6) have students find the artist's full name and the city where the Kodak Awards were presented (*Arles* is a significant location, as Vincent van Gogh painted there).

Script: Observons

EDOUARD : Bonjour, Je suis Edouard Fleuriau-Château. J'ai vingt-quatre ans, euh, je parle l'anglais, le français, l'espagnol... et bien sûr je suis français.

MARIE : Bonjour, je m'appelle Marie Éline Louis. Je suis de Port-au-Prince, Haïti, mais j'habite ici aux États-Unis. À la maison, on parle créole. Je parle aussi français et anglais.

FADOUA : Bonjour, je m'appelle Fadoua Bennani. J'ai vingt-cinq ans et j'habite à Nice. Mes parents vivent au Maroc. Euh, moi, je parle français et un peu arabe. Mon père il est marocain, donc lui il parle beaucoup plus arabe que moi, et ma mère est française.

BIENVENU : Je m'appelle Bienvenu Akpakla. Je suis du Bénin. Je parle le français, ma langue maternelle fongbé et l'anglais. Voici mon épouse, elle se présente.

HONORINE : Je m'appelle Honorine Akpakla, je viens du Congo. Je parle le français, ma langue maternelle et l'anglais.

MARIE-JULIE : Alors, je m'appelle Marie-Julie Keraro, je suis québécoise. Je suis originaire de Rimouski. J'habite les États-Unis depuis quelques années. Avant de venir ici, je parlais anglais, ce qui m'a aidé beaucoup.

C. En regardant de plus près. Now look more closely at these features of the headlines.

1. Point out at least one cognate in each headline.
2. Based on the context and use of cognates, indicate what the following words or expressions mean.
   a. Le vaccin antigrippal (#1)
   b. des dents « de crocodile » (#2)
   c. Écolo cosméto ; crèmes aux plantes, aérosols sans fréon (#3)
   d. le changement climatique (#4)
   e. Il travaille en freelance (#6)

Note: Après avoir lu These questions lead directly into the *Observons* exercise.

D. Après avoir lu. For each headline, the source has been indicated. What does this tell you about where French is used in the world today? Can you explain why French is used all over the world?

Preparation: P-29 To prepare this activity, pronounce for the class the name of each of the people shown, then pronounce the place names and languages listed in French. The entire **Observons** clip introduces nine speakers; only the first six are treated here. The remaining speakers are introduced in the SAM/MFL. You might complete this exercise in class and assign the remaining introductions as homework, with students completing the activities in the SAM/MFL. Point out to students that these speakers will appear in other video clips.

Observons

P-29 Je me présente

A. Avant de regarder. What information do people generally give when they introduce themselves? What expressions have you learned that people might use to provide this information in French?

B. En regardant. Watch and listen as the people shown introduce themselves, telling where they are from and what language(s) are spoken there. Match their photos with the places they come from and then find those places on the map inside the cover of your textbook. You can expect to listen more than once.

Bienvenu et Honorine AKPAKLA

1. Vous avez compris ?
   a. Who is from . . .

le Bénin ?	Haïti ?
le Congo ?	le Maroc ?
la France ?	le Québec ?

   b. How many people are from places where languages other than French are spoken?

Marie-Julie KERHARO

2. Which of the following languages are mentioned?

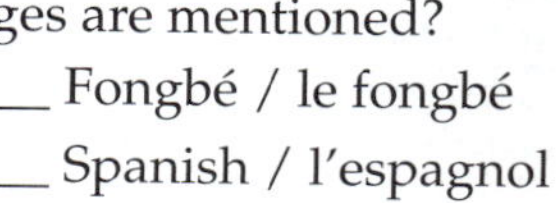

_____ Arabic / l'arabe	_____ Fongbé / le fongbé
_____ Creole / le créole	_____ Spanish / l'espagnol
_____ English / l'anglais	

Edouard FLEURIAU-CHÂTEAU

Marie Éline LOUIS

Fadoua BENNANI

C. Après avoir regardé. Discuss the following questions with your classmates.

1. What differences do you notice in the way these people look, dress, and speak?
2. What do these observations tell you about the Francophone world?

Expansion: You might also ask students to listen for expressions used to tell one's name: *je suis, je m'appelle* ; to tell where you're from: *je suis de, j'habite, je suis né/e* ; and to tell what language you speak: *je parle*. Regular *-er* verbs will be introduced in Ch. 1, L. 3.

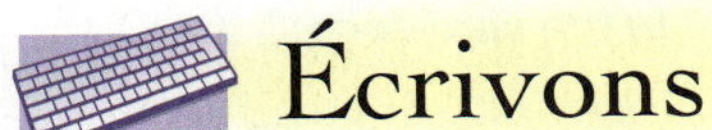

Écrivons

P-30 Voyages en francophonie

A. Avant d'écrire. On the inside cover of this textbook, a world map shows the Francophone countries and regions of the world. Take a look at this map.

B. En écrivant. On a separate sheet of paper, make two lists: (1) Francophone countries and regions that you have already visited (**J'ai déjà visité ...**); (2) Francophone countries and regions that you would like to visit in the future (**Je voudrais visiter ...**). Write out the name of each place in French.

MODÈLE

J'ai déjà visité :	Je voudrais visiter :
le Canada	la France
la Louisiane	le Maroc
etc.	etc.

C. En révisant. Now review the list you made: did you include an article with the name of each country (islands are exceptions)? Did you spell the name correctly in French, including accents?

D. Après avoir écrit. Compare your lists with those of other students in the class to see who has visited the most Francophone countries or regions. Talk about your experiences and why you'd like to visit the other places you named.

Stratégie

When writing in French, be attentive to spelling conventions such as capitalization and the use of accents. Do not hesitate to check a dictionary or another reference resource if you are not sure of spelling.

Implementation: P-30 We recommend conducting this writing activity in class, allowing students to work individually and in small groups, then following up with the class as a whole. Be sure to discuss the writing strategy and have students incorporate it into a revising stage.

Now that you have completed the *Chapitre préliminaire*, can you

- ☐ introduce yourself to a teacher? to a classmate? to a person at a party?
- ☐ greet and say good-bye to various people, using typical French gestures?
- ☐ identify objects in the classroom?
- ☐ follow classroom instructions in French?
- ☐ spell your name in French? write down a classmate's name when it is spelled?
- ☐ identify places where French is spoken throughout the world, and tell why?
- ☐ describe the public education system in France?

Leçon 1

pour vous présenter	to introduce yourself
Comment tu t'appelles ?	*What is your name?*
Comment vous appelez-vous ?	*What is your name?*
Je m'appelle Chloé.	*My name is Chloé.*
Je vous présente Loïc.	*I introduce/present Loïc to you.*
Voici...	*This/Here is/are . . .*
Enchanté/e.	*Delighted.*
Je suis de Montréal.	*I am from Montreal.*

pour saluer	to greet
Bonjour.	*Hello.*
Bonsoir.	*Good evening.*
Comment allez-vous ?	*How are you?*
Très bien, merci.	*Very well, thank you.*
Bien aussi.	*Fine, also.*
Salut.	*Hi.*
Comment ça va ?	*How's it going?*
Ça va, et toi ? / et vous ?	*Fine, and you?*
Pas mal.	*Not bad.*
Comme ci, comme ça.	*So-so.*
Ça ne va pas très bien.	*Things aren't going well.*

pour prendre congé	to take leave
Au revoir.	*Good-bye.*
À bientôt.	*See you soon.*
À demain.	*See you tomorrow.*
Salut.	*'Bye.*

des personnes	people
Madame (Mme)	*Mrs./Ma'am/Ms.*
Mademoiselle (Mlle)	*Miss*
Monsieur (M.)	*Mr./Sir*
un/e ami/e	*friend*
un/e camarade de classe	*classmate*
moi	*me*

quelques expressions avec le verbe *être*	a few expressions with the verb to be
être en forme	*to be fine*
être fatigué/e	*to be tired*
être malade	*to be sick*
être occupé/e	*to be busy*
être stressé/e	*to be stressed out*
c'est/ce sont...	*this is/these are . . .*

autres mots utiles	other useful words
oui	*yes*
non	*no*
ou	*or*

Leçon 2

dans la salle de classe	in the classroom
une affiche	*poster*
une brosse	*eraser (for chalk- or whiteboard)*
un bureau	*desk*
un cahier	*notebook*
une carte	*map*
une calculatrice	*calculator*
un CD	*CD, compact disk*
une chaise	*chair*
une craie	*piece of chalk*
un crayon	*pencil*
des devoirs (m.)	*homework*
un DVD	*DVD*
une fenêtre	*window*
un feutre	*felt-tipped marker*
une gomme	*eraser (for pencil)*
un lecteur CD	*CD player*
un lecteur DVD	*DVD player*
un livre	*book*
un ordinateur	*computer*
une porte	*door*
une règle	*ruler*
un stylo	*pen*
un tableau	*board*
une télé(vision)	*television*

des expressions pour la salle de classe	classroom expressions
Allez à la porte !	*Go to the door!*
Allez au tableau !	*Go to the board!*
Asseyez-vous !	*Sit down!*
Donnez la craie à Marie-Laure !	*Give the piece of chalk to Marie-Laure!*
Écoutez bien, s'il vous plaît !	*Listen carefully, please!*
Écoutez sans regarder le livre !	*Listen without looking at the book!*
Écrivez votre nom et votre prénom !	*Write down your last name and your first name!*

Effacez le tableau !	*Erase the board!*
Fermez le livre !	*Close the book!*
Levez-vous !	*Get up/stand up!*
Lisez les mots au tableau !	*Read the words on the board!*
Montrez-moi votre livre !	*Show me your book!*
Montrez Paris sur la carte !	*Point to Paris on the map!*
Ne parlez pas anglais !	*Don't speak English!*
Ouvrez la fenêtre !	*Open the window!*
Prenez un stylo !	*Take a pen!*
Regardez le tableau !	*Look at the board!*
Rendez-moi les devoirs !	*Hand in your homework!*
Répondez en français !	*Answer in French!*
Pardon ?	*Excuse me?*
Je ne comprends pas.	*I don't understand.*
Répétez, s'il vous plaît.	*Repeat, please.*
Parlez plus fort !	*Speak louder!*
Comment dit-on « *board* » en français ?	*How do you say "board" in French?*
Voilà ...	*Here/There is/are . . .*
Il y a ...	*There is/are . . .*
... (mais) il n'y a pas de ...	*. . . (but) there isn't/aren't any . . .*

pour remercier quelqu'un	***to thank someone***
Merci.	*Thank you.*
De rien.	*Not at all./You're welcome.*

des personnes	***people***
un/e étudiant/e	*student*
un professeur	*teacher*
une dame	*lady*
un monsieur	*man*

1 Ma famille et moi

What kind of occasion is shown here? Who are the people involved? Does this remind you of similar events in your own experience?

Leçon 1 Voici ma famille

Leçon 2 Les dates importantes

Leçon 3 Nos activités

Venez chez nous ! La famille dans le monde francophone

After completing this chapter, you should be able to:

- Talk about and describe family members
- Count from 0 to 100 and tell how old someone is
- Describe everyday activities
- Ask simple questions
- Talk about changing family structures across the French-speaking world

Leçon  Voici ma famille

POINTS DE DÉPART

Ma famille

Salut, je m'appelle Éric Brunet. Voici ma famille :

D'abord il y a mes grands-parents Brunet — ce sont les parents de mon père. Mon père a une sœur ; elle s'appelle Annick Roy. Paul Roy est son mari. Ma tante est divorcée et remariée. Loïc est le fils de son premier mari mais Marie-Hélène est la fille de son deuxième mari, Paul Roy.

Ma mère est d'une famille nombreuse. Elle a deux frères et trois sœurs. Alors, j'ai beaucoup d'oncles, de tantes, de cousins et de cousines. Ma grand-mère Kerboul habite chez mon oncle ; mon grand-père Kerboul est décédé.

Ma grande sœur Fabienne est fiancée. J'ai aussi un petit frère, Stéphane. Chez nous il y a des animaux familiers. On a un chien, César, deux chats, Minou et Cédille, et trois oiseaux.

Jean-Pierre Brunet
Madeleine Brunet (née Guilbaud)
Yves Brunet
Micheline Brunet (née Kerboul)
Annick Roy (née Brunet)
Paul Roy
Fabienne
Éric
Stéphane
Loïc
Marie-Hélène
César
Minou
Cédille
les oiseaux

Preparation: Preview Ch. 1 by showing the video montage *La famille dans le monde francophone.* Ask students to guess what the various family relationships depicted might be. What do they notice about the interactions they observe?

Presentation: Begin by having students listen to Éric's description of his family, thereby presenting some of the vocabulary inductively. Next present kinship terms more systematically, using the Brunet family tree (MFL, Ch. 1). Test comprehension as you go along. First have students pronounce all the names. Then begin: *Voici Éric. La mère d'Éric s'appelle Micheline. Comment s'appelle la mère de Marie-Hélène ? la mère d'Annick ?,* etc. Not all terms need to be presented on the first day of the lesson.

Presentation: As you introduce the family's names, point out the frequent use of hyphenated names in French; most are composed with *Jean* or *Marie.* Explain that, as in English, some names can be either masculine or feminine: *Claude, Dominique, Pascal/e.* Other names have both a masculine and a feminine spoken form: *Simon, Simone ; Jean, Jeanne ; François, Françoise.* If you or your students are interested in learning more about popular names in France and Québec, see the *Chez nous* Companion Website for links to interesting sites.

Note: The word *les parents* means both "parents" and "relatives." For example: *Mes parents habitent aux États-Unis* refers to the speaker's mother and father; *J'ai des parents au Canada* refers to other relatives.

Expansion: Present *beau-/belle-* as a productive form for step- and in-law relationships (note the exception, *le gendre,* son-in-law). Additional useful vocabulary for students may include: *fils/fille unique, des jumeaux/des jumelles, des triplés.*

Fiche pratique

As you learn new vocabulary, it can be helpful to organize words and expressions into pairs of logical opposites or counterparts, for example: **mère et père ; sœur et frère**.

La famille

le mari	la femme		
les parents		**les grands-parents**	
le père	la mère	le grand-père	la grand-mère
le beau-père	la belle-mère		
les enfants		**les petits-enfants**	
le fils	la fille	le petit-fils	la petite-fille
le frère	la sœur		
le demi-frère	la demi-sœur		
le cousin	la cousine		
l'oncle	la tante		
le neveu	la nièce		

célibataire fiancé/e marié/e divorcé/e décédé/e

Initial practice: Show the Brunet family tree (MFL, Ch. 1) as you practice the vocabulary. Begin with a comprehension drill: *Nommez la mère d'Éric, la fille d'Yves et de Micheline Brunet, le grand-père d'Éric,* etc. Follow with true/false statements that students must correct: *Annick Roy est la sœur d'Éric. — Non, c'est la tante d'Éric,* etc. Finally, have students describe each person in as many ways as possible: *Micheline Brunet ? C'est la femme d'Yves Brunet, la mère de Fabienne, d'Éric et de Stéphane,* etc. Point out the learning strategy and practice opposite relationships: *C'est le père de Marie. — C'est la mère de Marie,* etc. The chart above organizes the vocabulary into opposites.

À vous la parole

1-1 Relations multiples. Describe the relationships among the various members of Éric's family.

MODÈLE Paul Roy : Annick Roy, Éric
Paul Roy ? C'est le mari d'Annick Roy ; c'est l'oncle d'Éric.

1. Loïc : Marie-Hélène, Éric
2. Annick Roy : Yves Brunet, Paul Roy
3. Annick Roy : Madeleine Brunet, Fabienne
4. Loïc : Yves Brunet, Jean-Pierre Brunet
5. Fabienne : Annick Roy, Marie-Hélène
6. Éric : Jean-Pierre et Madeleine Brunet, Yves Brunet
7. Madeleine Brunet : Yves Brunet, Marie-Hélène
8. Jean-Pierre Brunet : Annick Roy, Fabienne

Variation: 1-2 This exercise includes *mon/ma* for receptive control; it can serve as an inductive presentation for the possessive adjectives. To simplify, complete the sentence and have students decide whether it is true or false. For a more challenging exercise, once possessives have been introduced have students provide the definition: *ma nièce ? — C'est la fille de mon frère ou de ma sœur.*

1-2 Le mot juste. Complete the definitions of these family relationships.

MODÈLE La mère de ma cousine est ma...
La mère de ma cousine est ma tante.

1. Le père de ma mère est mon...
2. La sœur de mon père est ma...
3. La fille de mon oncle est ma...
4. Le frère de ma cousine est mon...
5. Le mari de ma tante est mon...
6. La mère de mon père est ma...
7. Le fils de mon frère est mon...
8. La fille de ma sœur est ma...

Note: The **Lisons** activity in this lesson illustrates some of the trends described here, including an example of a couple announcing their *PACS*; generally couples refer to their relationship by saying, *Nous sommes pacsé/es.* If you have not done so already, show the video montage *La famille dans le monde Francophone* to provide an overview of francophone families. You might pause and have students describe each family pictured.

Vie et culture

La famille en France

The family is changing in France. Today's couples tend to marry later and have fewer children. Typically, French men marry at age 31 and French women, at age 29.

The divorce rate in France is rising; almost half of all marriages now end in divorce. In addition, nearly five million unmarried French men and women—more than one in six couples—live together. It is common for unmarried couples to have children together. Today, 59% of all first-time births are to unmarried women. It is also not unusual for couples to marry after the birth of one or more children. Since the creation of the **Pacte Civil de Solidarité (le PACS)** in 1999, unmarried couples living together, whether of the same or opposite sex, can legalize their union. Each year, increasing numbers choose to do so.

Although the family is changing, relations among family members still tend to be close and to have a strong influence in a French person's life. Young people have frequent contact with their extended family. They also tend to live in their parents' home for longer periods of time. Typically French men leave home after age 24 and French women, after age 22.

How does the typical French family compare to the typical American family, and to your own? Is the role of the family similar in France and in the United States, in your opinion?

Les animaux familiers

Pets are often an important part of the French family. Look at the video segment *Les animaux familiers*, and identify the types of animals you see and where you see them—are there any places that surprise you? How would you feel about dining in a restaurant where pets are allowed under the tables? What does this custom suggest about differences in French and American attitudes toward public spaces?

Implementation: The French own approximately 9.4 million cats, 8.5 million dogs, 36 million fish, 6.5 million birds, and 3.3 million hamsters, rabbits, mice, etc. (statistics from Mermet, *Francoscopie 2007*, p. 187). Ask students why they think cats outnumber dogs in France—it may be a function of urban living and smaller spaces.

Expansion: 1-3 Expand on this exercise using other works of art that show families. Some examples include: Henri Rousseau, « La carriole du père Junier » and « La Noce », Musée de l'Orangerie des Tuileries, Paris ; Pablo Picasso, « Famille de saltimbanques », National Gallery of Art, Washington, D.C. Personalized practice for presenting and describing one's family follows in the **Formes et fonctions** section on possessive adjectives.

1-3 Portrait d'une famille. Look at the family portrait by Impressionist painter Frédéric Bazille. The title of the painting is ***La réunion de famille***; the artist brought together ten of his close family members for this group portrait. You can see the artist's self portrait on the far left. With a partner, try to identify the members of his family.

MODÈLE Voilà l'artiste, et ici, c'est..., etc.

Frédéric Bazille, « La réunion de famille », Musée d'Orsay, Paris

Presentation: To present this information, have students discriminate between equivalent names spoken in English and French (Phillip/*Philippe*, Alice/*Alice*, *Paul*/Paul, Thomas/*Thomas*, Guy/*Guy*, *Jacques*/Jack, *Simone*/Simone, Juliette/*Juliette*, etc.). Ask students how they could tell which language was used. Usually students will mention stress/rhythm and vowel tenseness.

Presentation: Have students compare the pronunciation of English "say" and French *c'est* with a hand under their chin: in the first case, the chin will drop; in the second, it should not, and the lips should be spread. Use the hand under the chin as a way of monitoring production of a tense, unglided vowel. To help students produce /i/ and /u/ correctly, use rising intonation with /i/, falling intonation with /u/.

Sons et lettres

Les modes articulatoires du français : la tension et le rythme

Vowel tension and rhythm are distinctive qualities of spoken French.

- **Pronouncing French vowels**

  At the end of a syllable, French vowels are pronounced with lips and jaws tense. French vowels are usually shorter than corresponding English vowels, and the lips and jaws do not move as they are produced. In contrast, when you pronounce English vowels, your chin often drops or your lips move, and a glided vowel results.

  - French /i/, as in **Mimi**, is pronounced with the lips smiling and tense. The sound produced is high-pitched.
  - French /u/, as in **Doudou**, is pronounced with the lips rounded, tense, and projected forward. The sound produced is low-pitched and very different from the vowel of English *do*, because for the French /u/ the tongue is further back in the mouth.

- **Rhythm**

  French speech is organized in rhythmic groups, short phrases usually two to six syllables long. Each syllable within a rhythmic group has the same strength; each receives the same degree of stress. The last syllable tends to be longer than the others.

In English, some syllables within words are stronger than others. Consider the pronunciation of the following words:

re*peat*   *lis*ten   Chi*ca*go   Minne*a*polis

The syllables that are not stressed are usually short, and their vowel is a short, indistinct vowel. In French, each syllable and therefore each vowel is pronounced evenly and distinctly.

Listen to the pronunciation of the following English and French words. Then, as you pronounce each French word yourself, count out the rhythm or tap it out with your finger.

1-2		1-2-3		1-2-3-4	
English	**French**	**English**	**French**	**English**	**French**
Phillip	Philippe	*Canada*	Canada	*Alabama*	Alabama
machine	machine	*alphabet*	alphabet	*Francophony*	francophonie
madam	madame	*Isabel*	Isabelle	*introduction*	introduction

 À vous la parole 

1-4 Les animaux familiers. At a pet show, owners are calling their cats. Repeat what they say, paying particular attention to the /u/ and /i/ sounds.

1. Ici (*here*), Mistigri !
2. Ici, Minouche !
3. Ici, Mimi !
4. Ici, Foufou !
5. Ici, Loulou !
6. Ici, Fifine !
7. Ici, Cachou !
8. Ici, Minette !

Note: 1-4 The names provided are typical names for felines and, like many pet names and nicknames in French, often involve reduplication (*Mimi, Foufou*).

1-5 Slogan. In a French school zone you will find a sign urging motorists to drive slowly. Practice reading the warning aloud.

Pensez à nous ! Roulez tout doux !   *Think of us! Drive very slowly!*

1-6 Répétez. Practice pronouncing the following sentences with even rhythm. Count out the rhythm of each rhythmic group. The last syllable of each rhythmic group is printed in boldface characters.

1. 1-2   1-2   Bon**jour**/ma**dame**.
2. 1-2   1-2-3   Voi**ci**/Fati**ma**.
3. 1-2-3   1-2   Il s'ap**pelle**/Pa**trick**.
4. 1-2-3-4   1-2-3-4   C'est mon am**ie**/Sylvie Da**vy**.

FORMES ET FONCTIONS

1. *Les adjectifs possessifs au singulier*

Presentation: Present possessive forms inductively in class, using the Brunet family tree (MFL, Ch. 1) and your own family: *Voici Éric. Son père s'appelle Yves Brunet. Comment s'appelle son grand-père ? Sa sœur s'appelle Fabienne. Comment s'appelle sa mère ? Ma mère s'appelle Pauline. Et ta mère ?* Ask students to summarize the rules, then display the chart.

- Possessive adjectives indicate ownership or other types of relationships.

Voilà **ma** mère.	*There's my mother.*
C'est **ton** frère ?	*Is that your brother?*
Ce sont **tes** crayons ?	*Are these your pencils?*

Les adjectifs possessifs au singulier

SINGULIER			PLURIEL
masculin *+ consonne*	*masc/fém* *+ voyelle*	*féminin* *+ consonne*	
mon frère	**mon**‿oncle	**ma** tante	**mes** cousins
ton père	**ton**‿ami/e	**ta** mère	**tes** parents
son cousin	**son**‿ami/e	**sa** sœur	**ses**‿amis

Initial practice: Begin with discrimination drills to ensure that students hear meaningful distinctions before having to produce them: is the form students hear masculine or feminine? *C'est mon oncle. C'est ma sœur. C'est son prof. C'est ton bureau. C'est mon chien. C'est son cahier. C'est ta cousine. C'est mon livre. C'est sa règle. Voilà tes amis.* singular or plural? *Voilà mes cousins. Voilà son frère. Voilà ma sœur. Voilà mes tantes. Voilà ses devoirs. Voilà mon cahier. Voilà tes oncles.* Follow up with substitution (*Voilà ma cousine ; père. — Voilà mon père,* etc.) and transformation drills (*Voilà ma tante. — Voilà mes tantes,* and vice versa).

- The form of the possessive adjective depends on the gender and number of the noun that it modifies.

—C'est **le frère** de Sarah ?	—Oui, c'est **son** frère.	*Yes, it's her brother.*
—C'est **la tante** de Simon ?	—Oui, c'est **sa** tante.	*Yes, it's his aunt.*
—Voilà **les cousins** de Cédric.	—Voilà **ses** cousins.	*There are his cousins.*

- Use **mon**, **ton**, and **son** before any singular noun beginning with a vowel sound, and link the sound /n/ to the word that follows.

C'est **mon**‿amie Sandrine.	*This is my friend Sandrine.*
C'est **ton**‿oncle ?	*Is that your uncle?*

- For plural nouns beginning with a vowel sound, the **-s** of **mes, tes,** and **ses** is pronounced as /z/.

Voilà **ses**‿amies.	*There are his/her friends.*
Ce sont **mes**‿oncles.	*These are my uncles.*

 À vous la parole 

Implementation: 1-7 Go over the models carefully, demonstrating in particular how the second model elicits the third-person forms *sa/son/ses*. Point out that the masculine plural form, *mes neveux*, is used to indicate one's nieces and nephews, contrary to English usage. So, the response to #8, *Oui, ce sont mes neveux*, is ambiguous and could mean either "my nephews" or "my nieces and nephews."

1-7 C'est qui ? Imagine you are at a family gathering with a friend. Answer your friend's questions about various members of your family.

MODÈLES É1 Ce sont tes cousins ?
É2 Oui, ce sont mes cousins.

É1 C'est le frère de ton père ?
É2 Oui, c'est son frère.

1. C'est ta mère ?
2. Ce sont tes grands-parents ?
3. C'est ton frère ?
4. C'est ton oncle ?
5. Ce sont ton cousin et ta cousine ?
6. C'est la sœur de ta mère ?
7. C'est le mari de ta sœur ?
8. Ce sont ta nièce et ton neveu ?

1-8 Un arbre généalogique. Ask your partner questions so that you can draw his/her family tree.

MODÈLE É1 Paul, comment s'appellent tes grands-parents ?
É2 Mes grands-parents s'appellent Smith, ce sont les parents de ma mère.
É1 Et comment s'appelle ta mère ?
É2 Ma mère s'appelle Anne.
É1 Comment s'appelle ton père ?
É2 Mon père s'appelle David.
É1 Est-ce que tu as des frères ou des sœurs ? ...

Implementation: 1-8 Model for students by having them ask you questions as one student draws your family tree on the board. Students can work at their seats or at the board; as a follow-up, have some describe their partner's family while a third person draws the tree on the board. Encourage students to follow the model and use the question *Comment s'appelle/nt ...* to elicit the information they need.

1-9 Qu'est-ce que vous prenez ? Imagine that your dorm/house/apartment is on fire, and you have time to take only three things. What would you take? Make a list and share it with your partner.

MODÈLE
1. les photos de ma famille et de mes amis
2. mes deux chats, Mickey et Minnie
3. mon ordinateur

Implementation: 1-9 Complete in pairs, then compare responses for the class as a whole.

2. *Les adjectifs invariables*

Presentation: Use the labeled illustrations of opposite traits (MFL, Ch. 1). Remind students of the learning strategy for learning vocabulary using logical opposites; the presentation and the practice activities in this **Formes et fonctions** use this strategy. Once several sets of opposites have been introduced, switch to the images without labels (MFL, Ch. 1) to check students' comprehension: *Il est optimiste ? —Non, pessimiste.* or, *Nommez une personne qui est calme.* Follow comprehension checks with either/or questions to elicit repetitions of the vocabulary (*Il est réservé ou sociable ?*), then go on to the exercises in **À vous la parole**.

sympa(thique) ≠ désagréable **optimiste ≠ pessimiste**

sociable ≠ réservé/e

dynamique ≠ timide

idéaliste ≠ réaliste

discipliné/e ≠ indiscipliné/e

conformiste ≠ individualiste

raisonnable ≠ têtu/e

calme ≠ stressé/e

- Adjectives are used to describe a person, place, or thing. French adjectives agree in gender and number with the noun they modify. Look at the adjective endings in the examples below. Note the addition of **-e** for the feminine forms (unless the adjective already ends in **-e**) and **-s** for the plural.

SINGULIER	*f.*	Anaïs est	calme	et	réservé**e**.
	m.	Jordan est	calme	et	réservé.
PLURIEL	*f.*	Mes amies sont	calme**s**	et	réservé**es**.
	m.	Mes cousins sont	calme**s**	et	réservé**s**.

- All forms of adjectives like **calme** and **réservé**, whose masculine singular form ends in a written vowel, are pronounced alike. Because they have only one spoken form, they are called *invariable*. The feminine ending **-e** and the plural ending **-s** are only apparent in the written forms.

- Most French adjectives follow the noun they modify.

Sarah est une étudiante **sociable**.	*Sarah is a friendly student.*
Damien est un homme **raisonnable**.	*Damien is a reasonable man.*

Adjectives are also used in sentences with the verb **être**, where they modify the subject.

Laurent est **optimiste**.	*Laurent is optimistic.*
Marie-Louise est **calme**.	*Marie-Louise is calm.*

- With a mixed group of feminine and masculine nouns, the masculine plural form of the adjective is used.

Lucie et Madeleine sont **têtues**. — *Lucie and Marie are stubborn.*
Romain et Grégorie sont **réservés**. — *Romain and Gregory are reserved.*
Alexandre et Marie sont **disciplinés**. — *Alexander and Marine are disciplined.*

> The French often express a negative trait or thought by using its opposite in a negative sentence:
>
> Elle n'est pas très sympa ! — *She's not very nice!*
>
> *instead of*
>
> Elle est désagréable ! — *She's disagreeable!*

À vous la parole

1-10 Des jumeaux. Look at the adjectives below and decide whether they refer to Justine, to Jonathon, or to both twins.

	Justine	Jonathon
MODÈLES sympathiques	✓	✓
réservée	✓	
1. indiscipliné		
2. individualistes		
3. stressée		
4. têtu		
5. disciplinée		
6. réalistes		

Are the twins similar or different? Why?

Implementation: 1-10 This comprehension-based activity focuses students' attention on the written cues to number and gender. Emphasize, by modeling pronunciation, that there is no difference in the spoken form for masculine/feminine, singular/plural. Have students discuss the follow-up question to bring the focus back to how form informs meaning.

1-11 Le contraire. Answer each question using the opposite adjective.

MODÈLE Ces étudiantes sont disciplinées ?
Non, elles sont indisciplinées.

1. Ces femmes sont calmes ?
2. Ces professeurs sont idéalistes ?
3. Ces enfants sont sociables ?
4. Ces filles sont têtues ?
5. Ces hommes sont conformistes ?
6. Ces étudiants sont pessimistes ?
7. Ces étudiantes sont timides ?

Implementation: 1-11 Point out that this exercise allows students to practice the learning strategy presented earlier in the lesson.

1-12 Contrastes. Compare your ideas with those of a classmate.

MODÈLE le frère/la sœur idéal/e
É1 Pour moi, le frère idéal est calme et réservé.
É2 Pour moi, le frère idéal est calme aussi, mais il est sociable.

1. le frère/la sœur typique
2. le père idéal
3. le professeur idéal
4. l'étudiant/e typique
5. l'homme / la femme idéal/e

Implementation: 1-12, 1-13 Have students work in pairs and report back to the group. For **1-13**, have students suggest other people to be described, perhaps members of the class or celebrities.

Pour une description plus précise

un peu (*a little*) **assez** (*rather*) **très** (*very*) **vraiment** (*really*) **trop** (*too*)

 **1-13 Descriptions.** Describe each of the following people to a classmate.

MODÈLE ton/ta camarade de classe
Mon camarade de classe est un peu indiscipliné, mais il est très sympathique.

1. ton/ta camarade de classe
2. ton professeur préféré
3. ton/ta meilleur/e *(best)* ami/e
4. ton frère ou ta sœur
5. ton père ou ta mère

Stratégie

Certain types of documents—for example, announcements and invitations—are formulaic in nature. Your familiarity with such texts in English can help you anticipate and understand the content of similar texts in French.

Lisons

1-14 Des faire-part

A. Avant de lire. Here are three very similar documents to look over.

1. For what purposes have they been designed?
2. What kinds of information do you expect to find as you read them? Choose from the list:

__ addresses	__ names	__ professions	__ times
__ ages	__ places	__ relationships	__ weather
__ dates	__ prices	__ religion	__ web sites

3. In documents such as these, the type of information provided as well as the phrasing is often highly predictable. Think of some common examples in English. Where would you expect to find such phrases as *request the pleasure of your company* or *are pleased to announce*?

Key: Avant de lire In #3, *request the pleasure of your company* might be found in a dinner or wedding invitation; *are pleased to announce* would be commonly found in a birth or wedding announcement.

Key: En lisant 1) First announcement: wedding announcement; Guillaume, Nathalie Duguai, Bernard Gaillard; May 23, 2009; 4:30 P.M., 5:30 P.M.; Second: birth announcement; Nicolas, Jean-François, Robert et Annie Dupuis; February 10, 2009; 8:15 P.M. Third: PACS announcement; Christian Leblanc, Benoît Perrin; June 12, 2009, July 25; 5:30 P.M. Point out the use of the 24-hour clock. This will be addressed more thoroughly in Ch. 4, L. 2. 2) Students may be surprised to see that a child announces the marriage of his parents—this reflects the large number of couples who co-habit, have children, then marry.

B. En lisant. As you read, look for key information and answer the related questions.

1. Fill in the following chart as completely as possible.

	1er faire-part	2e faire-part	3e faire-part
Purpose:			
Names:			
Date:			
Time(s):			

2. What information do you find in these documents that you expected to find? Is there any information that you did not expect?

1.

Guillaume
a le plaisir de vous faire part du Mariage de ses parents
Nathalie et Bernard
La cérémonie se déroulera le Samedi 23 Mai 2009, à 16 heures 30 à la Mairie d'Albi.
Un Vin d'Honneur sera servi à 17 heures 30, à la salle des fêtes de Poulan-Pouzols.
Nathalie Duguai et Bernard Gaillard
19, rue Baptiste Marcet
81000 Albi
Tél : 05 63 64 30 52

2.

Le grand frère Nicolas
est heureux de vous annoncer
l'arrivée de son petit frère
Jean-François
qui est né le 10 février 2009 à 20 h 15
Il fait 3,5 kg pour 50 cm
Nos parents sont
Robert et Annie Dupuis

Nicolas
Jean-François

3.

Christian et Benoît
sont heureux de vous annoncer
qu'ils ont pacsé
le 12 juin 2009
Un vin d'honneur suivi d'un buffet froid
sera offert le samedi 25 juillet
au restaurant les Pyrénées
17 h 30
Christian Leblanc et Benoît Perrin
7 rue du Vieux Marché
21000 Dijon

C. En regardant de plus près. Now look more closely at some features of these documents.

1. They all begin in a very similar way:
   ...est/sont heureux de vous annoncer... *...a le plaisir de vous faire part...*
   Based on your familiarity with similar texts in English and on your knowledge of cognates, what do you think these first lines mean?
2. In France, marriage is first of all an official act. Look at the text for Nathalie and Bernard. Their wedding will take place in **la Mairie d'Albi**. Looking at their address, you'll see that Albi is where they live. Given this information, what do you think is the meaning of the word **la mairie**?
3. **Le vin d'honneur** is a ceremony during which guests drink wine, often champagne, to celebrate a happy event. In which of these **faire-part** are guests invited to a **vin d'honneur**? When and where will this take place?
4. In the second announcement, what do **3,5 kg** and **50 cm** refer to? Can you find the equivalent measures in another system?

D. Après avoir lu. Compare your responses to the questions below with those of your classmates.

1. What do you generally do when you receive an announcement of this type?
2. Having seen these three examples, design a similar announcement for yourself, a family member, or a friend.

Implementation: En regardant de plus près Point out that the couple getting married are having a civil service; many couples choose to have both a civil and a religious ceremony. Describe how, typically, the bride and groom go with their guests to the town hall for a civil ceremony. Afterward, there may also be a religious ceremony in a church, synagogue, or elsewhere. The video clip *Visitons Seillans* in Ch. 7 takes viewers to the *salle de mariage* in a small town hall; the **Venez chez nous !** of Ch. 7 provides more information about wedding customs in the Francophone world.

Key: 1) are happy/pleased/proud to annonce... 2) the town hall 3) Nathalie and Bernard : in the town of Poulan-Pouzols (Midi-Pyrénées), in the reception room, immediately following the ceremony at 5:30 P.M.; Christian and Benoît : in Dijon, at the restaurant Les Pyrénées, on July 25 at 5:30 P.M. 4) 3,5 kilograms = 7 pounds, 11 ounces; 50 centimeters = 19.7 inches.

Implementation: Après avoir lu Designing an announcement can be an in-class group writing activity, or it can be assigned as homework.

Leçon 2 Les dates importantes

Presentation: Show the illustrations of holidays and point out the significance of each date: *la fête nationale ; Noël ; la fête du Travail ; l'Armistice* (MFL, Ch. 1). Use the calendar to continue practice with months (MFL, Ch. 1).

POINTS DE DÉPART

Les fêtes et les anniversaires

Note: Days of the week are taught in L. 3 of this chapter; seasons in Ch. 8, L. 1. Liaison with numbers is treated in this lesson.

C'est le quatorze juillet.

C'est le vingt-cinq décembre.

C'est le premier mai.

C'est le onze novembre.

Presentation: Point out that months are not capitalized, and that the order day-month (*7/9, le sept septembre*) is used in writing and saying dates. Note the exception *le premier septembre* and that no elision is made before a date: *le onze novembre.*

Les mois de l'année

janvier	avril	juillet	octobre
février	mai	août	novembre
mars	juin	septembre	décembre

septembre

L	Ma	Me	J	V	S	D
		1	2	3	4	5
6	7	8	9	10	11	12
13	14	15	16	17	18	19
20	21	22	23	24	25	26
27	28	29	30			

C'est le 7 septembre. *It's September 7th.*

Les nombres cardinaux de 0 à 31

0 zéro	1 un	11 onze	21 vingt-et-un	31 trente-et-un
	2 deux	12 douze	22 vingt-deux	
	3 trois	13 treize	23 vingt-trois	
	4 quatre	14 quatorze	24 vingt-quatre	
	5 cinq	15 quinze	25 vingt-cinq	
	6 six	16 seize	26 vingt-six	
	7 sept	17 dix-sept	27 vingt-sept	
	8 huit	18 dix-huit	28 vingt-huit	
	9 neuf	19 dix-neuf	29 vingt-neuf	
	10 dix	20 vingt	30 trente	

Presentation: French speakers begin with their thumb when counting on their fingers. Show how the numbers 1–9 are typically written. Model pronunciation, then test comprehension: students write the number or date you say; they identify a) the higher or b) the lower of two numbers. Simple production drills: students say the number or date you write; count in even numbers (*les nombres pairs*), odd numbers (*impairs*), and backwards (*à rebours*).

Note: Based on the orthographic reform of 1990, all numbers are linked by hyphens. This reform makes the writing of numbers more uniform and eliminates ambiguity. Students may see numbers such as *vingt et un* written without hyphens, since the reform is not uniformally followed.

À vous la parole

1-15 Complétez la série. With a partner, take turns reading aloud each series of numbers and adding a number to complete it.

MODÈLE 2, 4, 6,...

É1 deux, quatre, six,...
É2 deux, quatre, six, huit

1. 1, 3, 5,...
2. 7, 14, 21,...
3. 6, 12, 18,...
4. 2, 4, 8,...
5. 5, 10, 15,...
6. 25, 27, 29,...
7. 31, 30, 29,...
8. 28, 26, 24,...

Expansion: 1-15 Have students provide additional groupings of numbers that form a series.

1-16 Cours de mathématiques. Create math problems to test your classmates!

MODÈLES É1 10 + 2 = ? (Dix et deux/Dix plus deux, ça fait combien ?)
É2 Ça fait douze.
É3 20 − 5 = ? (Vingt moins cinq, ça fait combien ?)
É4 Ça fait quinze.

Implementation: 1-16 Begin with addition and give several models. Have one student state the problem and designate another student to answer. You may have the second student write the problem on the board. The first student then judges the correctness of the response. When the student responds correctly, he/she then asks the next question. You might focus only on addition at first, then review and add problems using subtraction, multiplication, and division.

1-17 Associations. What number do you associate with the following?

MODÈLE la superstition
→ treize

1. le vote
2. une paire
3. l'alphabet
4. le premier
5. un imbécile
6. la chance
7. l'indépendance
8. Noël

Key: 1-17 1) 18 2) 2 3) 26 4) 1 5) 0 6) 2, 7 ou 11 7) 4, 14, 18 ou 21 8) 24 ou 25

Vie et culture

Bon anniversaire et bonne fête !

Take a look at the French calendar shown below. How is it similar to the calendar you use? How is it different? Notice that some dates are highlighted in color. With a partner, make a list of these dates and try to determine the significance of each. Do some dates coincide with important dates on your own calendar?

Also, note that a name is listed alongside most dates. Many French people celebrate two special days a year, their *birthday* (**Bon anniversaire !**) and their *saint's day* (**Bonne fête !**), the day associated in the Catholic tradition with the saint for whom they are named.

Implementation: Use the calendar to illustrate the discussion (MFL, Ch. 1). Point out that the French week runs from Monday to Sunday. Although France is *un état laïque*, the calendar is heavily influenced by the traditional religion, Catholicism. Most French are not devout, however. Religious holidays include: *Pâques* (Easter), *l'Ascension* (the ascent of Christ to heaven), *la Pentecôte* (the descent of the Holy Spirit among the apostles), *l'Assomption* (the ascent of the Virgin Mary to heaven), and *la Toussaint* (All Saints' Day, November 1). Legal holidays include: *la fête du Travail* (Labor Day, May 1), *le jour de la Victoire 1945* ou *la fin de la Seconde Guerre mondiale en Europe* (commemorating the Allies' victory over Nazi Germany in World War II, May 8), and *l'Armistice* (celebrating the signing of the armistice to end World War I, November 11). Although church and state are separate in France, the religious holidays listed above are also legal holidays, as are the Mondays following *Pâques* and *la Pentecôte*. When a legal holiday occurs on a Tuesday or a Thursday, many schools, businesses, and government offices opt to *faire le pont* ("make a bridge"), taking the extra day off to make a long weekend. Ask students which holidays on the calendar pictured here offer that possibility.

2009

JANVIER		
1	J	J. de l'An, Marie
2	V	Basile
3	S	Geneviève
4	D	Épiphanie, Odilon
5	L	Edouard
6	M	Melaine
7	M	Raimond
8	J	Lucien
9	V	Alix
10	S	Guillaume
11	D	Paulin
12	L	Tatiana
13	M	Yvette
14	M	Nina
15	J	Rémi
16	V	Marcel
17	S	Roseline
18	D	Prisca
19	L	Marius
20	M	Sébastien
21	M	Agnès
22	J	Vincent
23	V	Barnard
24	S	François de Sales
25	D	Conv. S. Paul
26	L	Paule
27	M	Angèle
28	M	Th. d'Aquin
29	J	Gildas
30	V	Martine
31	S	Marcelle

FÉVRIER		
1	D	Ella
2	L	Présentation
3	M	Blaise
4	M	Véronique
5	J	Agathe
6	V	Gaston
7	S	Eugénie
8	D	Jacqueline
9	L	Apolline
10	M	Arnaud
11	M	N. D. Lourdes
12	J	Félix
13	V	Carême, Béatrice
14	S	Valentin
15	D	Claude
16	L	Julienne
17	M	Alexis
18	M	Bernadette
19	J	Gabin
20	V	Aimée
21	S	P. Damien
22	D	Isabelle
23	L	Lazare
24	M	Mardi gras, Modeste
25	M	Cendres, Roméo
26	J	Nestor
27	V	Honorine
28	S	Romain

MARS		
1	D	Aubin
2	L	Charles
3	M	Guénolé
4	M	Casimir
5	J	Olive
6	V	Colette
7	S	Félicité
8	D	Jean de Dieu
9	L	Françoise
10	M	Vivien
11	M	Rosine
12	J	Justine
13	V	Rodrigue
14	S	Mathilde
15	D	Louise de M.
16	L	Bénédicte
17	M	Patrice
18	M	Cyrille
19	J	Joseph
20	V	Herbert
21	S	Clémence
22	D	Léa
23	L	Victorien
24	M	Cath. de Su.
25	M	Annonciation, Humbert
26	J	Larissa
27	V	Habib
28	S	Gontran
29	D	Gwladys
30	L	Amédée
31	M	Benjamin

AVRIL		
1	M	Hugues
2	J	Sandrine
3	V	Richard
4	S	Isidore
5	D	Irène
6	L	Marcellin
7	M	Jean Bap. de la S.
8	M	Julie
9	J	Gautier
10	V	Fulbert
11	S	Stanislas
12	D	PÂQUES, Jules
13	L	DE PÂQUES, Ida
14	M	Maxime
15	M	Paterne
16	J	Benoît-Joseph
17	V	Anicet
18	S	Parfait
19	D	Emma
20	L	Odette
21	M	Anselme
22	M	Alexandre
23	J	Georges
24	V	Fidèle
25	S	Marc
26	D	Alida
27	L	Zita
28	M	Valérie
29	M	Catherine
30	J	Robert

MAI		
1	V	F. du Travail, Andéol
2	S	Boris
3	D	Philippe, Jacques
4	L	Sylvain
5	M	Judith
6	M	Prudence
7	J	Gisèle
8	V	Vict. 1945, Désirée
9	S	Pacôme
10	D	Solange
11	L	Estelle
12	M	Achille
13	M	Rolande
14	J	Matthias
15	V	Denise
16	S	Honoré
17	D	Pascal
18	L	Eric
19	M	Yves
20	M	Bernardin
21	J	Ascension, Constantin
22	V	Emile
23	S	Didier
24	D	Donatien
25	L	Sophie
26	M	Bérenger
27	M	Augustin
28	J	Germain
29	V	Aymar
30	S	Ferdinand
31	D	Pentecôte, Ferdinand

JUIN		
1	L	Justin
2	M	Blandine
3	M	Kevin
4	J	Clotilde
5	V	Igor
6	S	Norbert
7	D	F. des Mères, Gilbert
8	L	Médard
9	M	Diane
10	M	Landry
11	J	Barnabé
12	V	Guy
13	S	Antoine de P.
14	D	Elisée
15	L	Germaine
16	M	J. F. Régis
17	M	Hervé
18	J	Léonce
19	V	Romuald
20	S	Silvère
21	D	F. des Pères, Rodolphe
22	L	Alban
23	M	Audrey
24	M	Jean Bapt.
25	J	Prosper
26	V	Anthelme
27	S	Fernand
28	D	Irénée
29	L	Pierre, Paul
30	M	Martial

JUILLET		
1	M	Thierry
2	J	Martinien
3	V	Thomas
4	S	Florent
5	D	Antoine
6	L	Mariette
7	M	Raoul
8	M	Thibaut
9	J	Armandine
10	V	Ulrich
11	S	Benoît
12	D	Olivier
13	L	Henri, Joël
14	M	F. Nationale, Camille
15	M	Donald
16	J	N.D. Mt-Carmel
17	V	Charlotte
18	S	Frédéric
19	D	Arsène
20	L	Marina
21	M	Victor
22	M	Marie Mad.
23	J	Brigitte
24	V	Christine
25	S	Jacques
26	D	Anne, Joachim
27	L	Nathalie
28	M	Samson
29	M	Marthe
30	J	Juliette
31	V	Ignace de L.

AOÛT		
1	S	Alphonse
2	D	Julien Eymard
3	L	Lydie
4	M	J.M. Vianney
5	M	Abel
6	J	Transfiguration, Hormisdas
7	V	Gaétan
8	S	Dominique
9	D	Amour
10	L	Laurent
11	M	Claire
12	M	Clarisse
13	J	Hippolyte
14	V	Evrard
15	S	Assomption Marie la Vierge
16	D	Armel
17	L	Hyacinthe
18	M	Hélène
19	M	Jean Eudes
20	J	Bernard
21	V	Christophe
22	S	Fabrice
23	D	Rose de L.
24	L	Barthélemy
25	M	Louis
26	M	Natacha
27	J	Monique
28	V	Augustin
29	S	Sabine
30	D	Fiacre
31	L	Aristide

SEPTEMBRE		
1	M	Gilles
2	M	Ingrid
3	J	Grégoire
4	V	Rosalie
5	S	Raïssa
6	D	Bertrand
7	L	Reine
8	M	Nativité N. D.
9	M	Alain
10	J	Inès
11	V	Adelphe
12	S	Apollinaire
13	D	Aimé
14	L	La Ste Croix
15	M	Roland
16	M	Edith
17	J	Renaud
18	V	Nadège
19	S	Emilie
20	D	Davy
21	L	Matthieu
22	M	Maurice
23	M	Constant
24	J	Thècle
25	V	Hermann
26	S	Côme, Damien
27	D	Vinc. de Paul
28	L	Venceslas
29	M	Michel
30	M	Jérôme

OCTOBRE		
1	J	Thérèse de l'E.J.
2	V	Léger
3	S	Gérard
4	D	François d'Assise
5	L	Fleur
6	M	Bruno
7	M	Serge
8	J	Pélagie
9	V	Denis
10	S	Ghislain
11	D	Firmin
12	L	Wilfried
13	M	Géraud
14	M	Juste
15	J	Thérèse d'Avila
16	V	Edwige
17	S	Baudouin
18	D	Luc
19	L	René
20	M	Adeline
21	M	Céline
22	J	Elodie
23	V	Jean de C.
24	S	Florentin
25	D	Crépin
26	L	Dimitri
27	M	Emeline
28	M	Simon, Jude
29	J	Narcisse
30	V	Bienvenue
31	S	Quentin

NOVEMBRE		
1	D	Toussaint
2	L	Défunts
3	M	Hubert
4	M	Charles
5	J	Sylvie
6	V	Bertille
7	S	Carine
8	D	Geoffroy
9	L	Théodore
10	M	Léon
11	M	Armistice 1918, Martin
12	J	Christian
13	V	Brice
14	S	Sidoine
15	D	Albert
16	L	Marguerite
17	M	Elisabeth
18	M	Aude
19	J	Tanguy
20	V	Edmond
21	S	Prés. de Marie
22	D	Christ Roi, Cécile
23	L	Clément
24	M	Flora
25	M	Catherine L.
26	J	Delphine
27	V	Séverin
28	S	Jacq. de la M.
29	D	Avent, Saturnin
30	L	André

DÉCEMBRE		
1	M	Florence
2	M	Viviane
3	J	Xavier
4	V	Barbara
5	S	Gérald
6	D	Nicolas
7	L	Ambroise
8	M	I. Concept.
9	M	P. Fourier
10	J	Romaric
11	V	Daniel
12	S	Jeanne F.C.
13	D	Lucie
14	L	Odile
15	M	Ninon
16	M	Alice
17	J	Gaël
18	V	Gatien
19	S	Urbain
20	D	Abraham
21	L	Pierre C.
22	M	Françoise-X. C.
23	M	Armand
24	J	Adèle
25	V	NOËL, Emmanuel
26	S	Etienne
27	D	Jean
28	L	Innocents
29	M	David
30	M	Roger
31	J	Sylvestre 1

1-18 C'est quelle date? What date corresponds to each holiday?

MODÈLE Noël
➤ C'est le 25 décembre.

1. le jour de l'An
2. la Saint-Valentin
3. la fête du Travail
4. la fête nationale américaine
5. la fête nationale française
6. l'Armistice 1918
7. la Toussaint

Expansion: 1-18 Have students work with a calendar to find other holidays and saints' days.

1-19 Votre anniversaire et votre fête. Find a partner and ask each other when your birthday is and when your saint's day is. Share what you have learned about your partner with the class.

MODÈLE
É1 Ton anniversaire, c'est quel jour ?
É2 C'est le 30 août. Et toi ?
É1 C'est le 9 mai.
É2 Et ta fête, Tom ?
É1 C'est le 3 juillet. Et toi, Jenna ?
É2 Il n'y a pas de « Sainte Jenna ».

Implementation: 1-19 In a class of 20 students, the probability is high that two will share the same birthday. Many students will not have a saint's day. Follow up by having students report back and listing dates of birthdays and saints' days on the board. Also list names without a corresponding saint's day. Remind students that French first names have traditionally been influenced by Catholic tradition.

Sons et lettres

La prononciation des chiffres

numeral alone	before a consonant	before a vowel
un	un jour	un‿an
une	une fille	une affiche
deux	deux cousins	deux‿amis
trois	trois frères	/z/ trois‿oncles
quatre	quatre profs	/z/ quatre étudiants
cinq	cinq filles	cinq‿enfants
six /sis/	six femmes	six‿hommes
sept	sept livres	/z/ sept‿images
huit	huit cahiers	huit‿affiches
neuf	neuf cousines	neuf‿amies
dix /dis/	dix mois	dix‿ans
vingt	vingt crayons	/z/ vingt‿affiches

In general, final consonant letters are not pronounced in French, for example: **le chat**, **mes parents**.

The numbers 1–10 are exceptions. Their pronunciation depends on whether they occur by themselves, as in counting (**un**, **deux**, **trois** ...), or whether they are followed by another word (**un‿ami**, **deux‿enfants**, **six chiens**).

Note: In normal conversational style, *quatre* is pronounced /kat/ before a consonant and in final position. Although there is some generational variation, *cinq* has a pronounced final consonant in most contexts; an exception is the expression *cinq cent(s)...*, where the /k/ is never pronounced. There is also a tendency among native speakers to pronounce the final consonant of *six*, *huit*, and *dix* before a consonant in dates: *le huit /t/ mars*. In contrast, the final *-t* of *quatre-vingt-un*, etc., is never pronounced.

Initial practice: Begin with a discrimination drill. Give students a list of nouns and have them write in the number you call out (as if you were taking inventory). Begin student production with substitution drills, changing either the number or the noun: *Il a dix ans ; six. — Il a six ans*, etc.; *Elle a cinq frères ; oncles. — Elle a cinq oncles*, etc. To practice the isolation form, use the following exercise:

É1 Il a six euros.
É2 Combien ?
É1 Six.

Except for **quatre** and **sept**, all numbers have two or three spoken forms.

Neuf has a special form before the words **ans** and **heures**; **f** is pronounced /v/:

Il a neuf ans.	*He is nine years old.*
Il est neuf heures.	*It's nine o'clock.*

À vous la parole

1-20 À la réunion de la famille Brunet. Repeat each expression.

Il y a...

un grand-père	un arrière-grand-père (*great-grandfather*)
trois tantes	trois oncles
dix filles	dix enfants
huit garçons	huit étudiants
cinq cousins	cinq animaux familiers

Implementation: 1-21 Point out that *nous irons au bois* means "we'll go to the woods"; *cueillir des cerises*, "to gather cherries"; *dans mon panier neuf*, "in my new basket"; *elles seront toutes rouges*, "they'll all be red." Explain to students that *neuf* is a homonym which means "nine" and "new." Refer students to the SAM/MFL for a French Canadian version of this counting rhyme.

Additional activity: For further practice with numbers, have students tell each other the number of people or animals there are in their families in the following categories: *grands-parents ; petits-enfants ; étudiants ; arrière-grands-parents ; garçons ; enfants ; cousins ; oncles ; chats ; chiens*. For example, *— Il y a deux grands-parents*. If there is no one in a given category, students should use the structure *Il n'y a pas de...* For example, *— Il n'y a pas de grands-parents*.

1-21 Une comptine. Repeat the following counting rhyme.

Un, deux, trois, nous irons au bois,
Quatre, cinq, six, cueillir des cerises.
Sept, huit, neuf, dans mon panier neuf.
Dix, onze, douze, elles seront toutes rouges.

FORMES ET FONCTIONS

1. *Le verbe* avoir *et l'âge*

Presentation: Remind students that subject-verb agreement takes place in English as well: "I have," "she has." Remind them of the use of *avoir* in the idiomatic expression *il y a*, "there is/are." Point out that *je* becomes *j'* before a vowel.

- The irregular verb **avoir** (*to have*) is used to indicate possession and other relationships.

J'**ai** une sœur.	*I have a sister.*
Tu **as** un crayon ?	*Do you have a pencil?*

- **Avoir** is also used to indicate age.

Vous **avez** vingt ans ?	*Are you 20 years old?*
Mon grand-père **a** cent ans.	*My grandfather is a hundred.*

In addition to the numbers you already know, the following numbers will be useful for talking about ages.

40 quarante	80 quatre-vingts
50 cinquante	81 quatre-vingt-un
60 soixante	90 quatre-vingt-dix
70 soixante-dix	91 quatre-vingt-onze
71 soixante-et-onze	100 cent
72 soixante-douze	

- Here are the forms of **avoir**, shown with the subject pronouns. Notice that the subject pronoun **je** becomes **j'** before a vowel. Pronounce the final **-s** of **nous, vous**, and **ils/elles** as /z/, and link it to the plural form of **avoir** that follows.

AVOIR *to have*

SINGULIER			PLURIEL		
j'	**ai**	*I have*	nous‿	**avons**	*we have*
tu	**as**	*you have*	vous‿	**avez**	*you have*
il	**a**	*he/it has*	ils	**ont**	*they have*
elle	**a**	*she/it has*	elles	**ont**	*they have*
on	**a**	*we have*			

- Use **ne... pas de** to express the idea of *not having any*. Notice that both **ne** and **de** drop their final **-e** before a vowel sound.

Je **n'**ai **pas de** sœurs.	*I don't have any sisters.*
Elle **n'**a **pas d'**oncle.	*She doesn't have an uncle.*

À vous la parole

1-22 Qu'est-ce que vous avez ? Compare with a partner what you brought to class today, and report back to your classmates. See how many different items you can name.

MODÈLE Ben et moi, nous avons des cahiers. J'ai aussi un stylo et un livre. Ben a un crayon et un CD.

Presentation: Review numbers 0–30 with a quick round of math problems on the day you plan to treat this topic. Display the numbers and ask students to look for patterns. The pattern of counting in 20s is a relic of the Gaulish language spoken in France before the arrival of Julius Caesar and Latin; the same pattern is found today in Celtic languages. In some dialects of eastern France, in Belgium, French-speaking Switzerland, Zaire, and Rwanda, 70 is *septante* and 90 is *nonante*, 80 is *huitante* in some parts of Switzerland. Model pronunciation and test comprehension by having students write the number you say. Note that the *-t* of *quatre-vingts* is never pronounced. When no other number follows, *quatre-vingts* ends in the letter *-s*, this *-s* can be heard in liaison when it is followed by a vowel: *quatre-vingts‿ans*.

Note: Based on the orthographic reform of 1990, all numbers are linked by hyphens. This reform makes the writing of numbers more uniform and eliminates ambiguity.

Presentation: Point out the following about pronunciation:
The first-person singular form is pronounced /e/: *j'ai*
The other singular forms are pronounced /a/: *tu as, il a*
Be sure students pronounce liaison /z/ for all the plural forms: *nous‿avons, vous‿avez, elles‿ont*

Note: A more detailed treatment of negation with *ne... pas* is presented in L. 3 of this chapter.

Initial practice: Begin with a discrimination exercise to ensure that students hear meaningful distinctions: one person, or more than one? *Ils ont un chien. Elle a un chat. Elles ont deux frères. Ils ont trois sœurs. Il a quinze ans. Elle a deux oiseaux. Ils ont dix-neuf ans. Elle n'a pas de chat. Ils n'ont pas de sœurs*, etc. Follow with a substitution drill: *J'ai un chat ; nous. —Nous avons un chat*, etc.

Implementation: 1-23 You might also use the diagram of the Brunet family tree to cue this exercise (MFL, Ch. 1). Add ages to the image before showing it.

1-23 La famille Brunet. Tell how old each of the Brunet family members is.

Additional activity: The following exercise may be cued using visuals:
Qu'est-ce qu'ils ont ? Tell what each person has.

MODÈLE je / 1 chat
J'ai un chat
nous / 2 chiens
Nous avons deux chiens.

1. les Marchand / 5 filles
2. vous / 6 amis
3. Stéphane et Pierre / 3 sœurs
4. je / 8 cahiers
5. tu / 4 CD
6. nous / 12 DVD
7. vous / 1 ordinateur
8. Fanny / 10 affiches

MODÈLE Quel âge ont les enfants de Jean-Pierre Brunet ?
Yves Brunet a cinquante-cinq ans et Annick Roy a quarante-neuf ans.

1. Quel âge a la mère de Loïc ?
2. Quel âge a le père de Marie-Hélène ?
3. Quel âge a la sœur d'Éric ?
4. Quel âge ont les parents d'Yves Brunet ?
5. Quel âge ont les enfants d'Annick Roy ?
6. Quel âge a la femme d'Yves Brunet ?
7. Quel âge ont les neveux de Paul Roy ?

1-24 Et ta famille ? Ask a classmate how old various members of his or her family are.

MODÈLES ta mère ?
É1 Quel âge a ta mère ?
É2 Ma mère a quarante-huit ans.

tes frères ?
É1 Quel âge ont tes frères ?
É2 Mon frère Robert a douze ans. Mon frère Kevin a quinze ans.

1. ta mère ?
2. ton père ?
3. tes frères ?
4. tes sœurs ?
5. tes grands-parents ?
6. tes nièces ?
7. tes neveux ?
8. tes cousins ?
9. tes animaux ?

Presentation: Review the singular-reference possessives, taught in Ch. 1, L. 1, before presenting the new forms. Use the Brunet family tree (MFL, Ch.1) to present these forms inductively: *Voici Fabienne, Éric et Stéphane. Leur père s'appelle Yves Brunet. Comment s'appelle leur mère ?* Similarly, model the three children describing their family: *Notre mère s'appelle Micheline.* You may prefer to present these forms in the same manner using personal family portraits or magazine photos of well-known families. Summarize forms, using the chart that is part of this grammar presentation.

2. *Les adjectifs possessifs au pluriel*

- Corresponding to the subjects **nous**, **vous**, and **ils/elles** are the following possessive adjectives:

Voici **notre** père.	*Here's our father.*
C'est **votre** mère ?	*Is that your mother?*
C'est **leur** tante.	*That's their aunt.*

  Remember that **vous/votre** can refer to one person (*formal*) or more than one.

- There is no distinction between masculine and feminine for **notre**, **votre**, and **leur**.

◆ For the plural forms, pronounce the final **-s** as /z/ before a vowel.

Ce sont **nos**‿oncles.	*These are our uncles.*
Voici **vos**‿affiches.	*Here are your posters.*
Ce sont **leurs**‿amis.	*These are their friends.*

Les adjectifs possessifs

SINGULIER			PLURIEL
masculin + consonne	*masc/fém + voyelle*	*féminin + consonne*	
mon frère	**mon**‿oncle	**ma** tante	**mes** cousins
ton père	**ton**‿ami/e	**ta** mère	**tes** parents
son cousin	**son**‿ami/e	**sa** sœur	**ses**‿amis
	notre mère		**nos** cousines
	votre oncle		**vos**‿amis
	leur père		**leurs**‿oncles

À vous la parole

1-25 C'est logique. Use the possessive to point out the person(s) indicated.

MODÈLE Nous avons une fille.
Voici notre fille.

1. Nous avons deux fils.
2. Vous avez un neveu.
3. Vous avez trois cousins.
4. Ils ont une nièce.
5. Ils ont trois enfants.
6. Nous avons une tante.
7. Elles ont deux oncles.

1-26 Décrivons la famille Brunet. With a partner, describe the family from the point of view indicated.

MODÈLES pour Jean-Pierre et Madeleine Brunet
É1 Leur fille s'appelle Annick Roy.
É2 Leurs petites-filles s'appellent Fabienne et Marie-Hélène.

pour Annick Roy
É1 Ses parents s'appellent Jean-Pierre et Madeleine.
É2 Sa nièce s'appelle Fabienne.

1. pour Fabienne Brunet
2. pour Jean-Pierre et Madeleine Brunet
3. pour Annick et Paul Roy
4. pour Loïc Leclerc et Marie-Hélène Roy
5. pour Yves Brunet
6. pour Fabienne, Éric et Stéphane Brunet

Initial practice: Begin with a transformation drill, singular to plural: *Voici notre tante* → *Voici nos tantes*, etc.

Implementation: 1-26 If this proves difficult for students, display the Brunet family tree (MFL, Ch. 1).

Alternative activity: At this point in the lesson, students generally know the Brunet family tree well. For a lively exercise using possessive adjectives, have class members take on the roles of various members of the Brunet family and test their memory of the family tree. Provide students with name tags and have them circulate in class asking each other questions such as [*à Fabienne, Éric et Stéphane Brunet*] : *Comment s'appelle votre mère ?* or *Comment s'appellent vos grands-parents ?* Students playing the role of these family members would respond: —*Notre mère s'appelle Micheline.* or —*Nos grands-parents s'appellent Jean-Pierre et Madeleine Brunet.* As an alternative, give students a card with their name on it, and have them circulate and ask questions to find their nuclear family: *Vous avez des enfants ? Combien ?* or *Je m'appelle Fabienne. Vous êtes ma mère ?*

 **1-27 Encore la famille.** Take turns asking and answering questions with a partner to describe your family.

MODÈLE des frères et des sœurs
É1 Tu as des frères et des sœurs ?
É2 Oui, j'ai deux frères.
É1 Comment s'appellent tes frères ?...
É2 Mes frères s'appellent Chris et Alex.

1. des frères et des sœurs
2. des parents
3. des nièces et des neveux
4. des cousins
5. des grands-parents
6. des neveux
7. des animaux

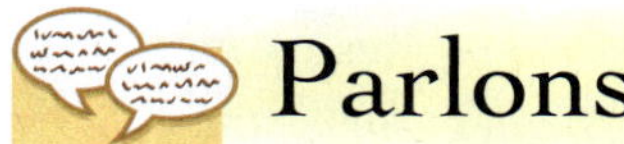

Parlons

Implementation: Avant de parler You may wish to complete this activity with the whole class. Students have only been exposed to asking questions with intonation and lexical phrases at this point. Questions with *est-ce que* are presented in L. 3 of this chapter. Possible questions include: *Ton anniversaire, c'est quel mois ? Ton anniversaire, c'est quelle date ? Ton anniversaire, c'est quand ? Tu as quel âge ? Tu as des frères et des sœurs ? Combien ? Tu as ton livre de français ?*

1-28 Trouvez quelqu'un qui...

A. Avant de parler. Try to find people in your class who correspond to the descriptions below. To prepare, brainstorm with a partner to come up with a list of the questions you can ask in order to get the required information. For example, to find out if someone has a birthday in May, you could ask the general question: **Ton anniversaire, c'est en quel mois ?** (or, **Votre anniversaire, c'est en quel mois ?** if you are asking your instructor).

B. En parlant. Now circulate among your classmates and ask the questions you have prepared. You may have to speak to several people before finding someone who fits a particular description—keep moving! Your instructor will call time in just a few minutes.

MODÈLE ... a son anniversaire au mois de mai
É1 Ton anniversaire, c'est en quel mois ?
É2 C'est en décembre.
(*You ask someone else the same question.*)
É1 Ton anniversaire, c'est en quel mois ?
É3 C'est en septembre.
(*You write this person's name down for #2.*)

1. ... a son anniversaire au mois de mai
2. ... a son anniversaire au mois de septembre
3. ... a son anniversaire le même (*same*) jour que vous
4. ... a son anniversaire le même mois que vous
5. ... a le même âge que vous
6. ... a le même nombre de frères et de sœurs que vous
7. ... n'a pas de frères ou de sœurs
8. ... a son livre de français et un cahier
9. ... a un ordinateur
10. ... a des affiches de France

C. Après avoir parlé. Did you find someone who matched every description before time was called? If not, ask one of your questions to the class as a whole; perhaps someone else found a match!

MODÈLE Qui a son anniversaire au mois de mai ?

Leçon  Nos activités

POINTS DE DÉPART

TEXT AUDIO
CD 1 TRACK 23

Presentation: Present the vocabulary inductively, using the visual of the Dupont family's activities (MFL, Ch. 1). First describe the activities, then test students' comprehension: *Qui travaille dans le jardin ?*, etc. Use either/or questions to elicit repetitions: *M. Dupont joue au tennis ou il joue au golf ?*, etc. Follow up with open-ended questions: *Qu'est-ce que Simon fait le mercredi après-midi ?* At this point, other visuals could be introduced, such as magazine photos, to elicit the new vocabulary. Contracted forms of *à* and *de* plus definite articles are presented here as lexical items for students to memorize. These forms will be treated in Ch. 2, L. 2.

Une semaine typique

Implementation: For the **Points de départ**, do not present forms of *-er* verbs, rather use the base form (*regarde/nt, joue/nt, écoute/nt*) with an appropriate subject to teach the lexical items. Point out that *rester* is a *faux ami.* The conjugation of *-er* verbs will be presented later in this lesson, in **Formes et fonctions.**

C'est une semaine typique chez les Dupont. Le lundi matin, M. Dupont travaille normalement au bureau et Mme Dupont travaille dans le jardin. Leur fils Simon a 12 ans ; il est au collège. Et leur fille Émilie a 16 ans ; elle est au lycée.

Aujourd'hui, c'est mardi. Mme Dupont parle au téléphone maintenant ; elle invite ses parents à déjeuner dimanche.

Le mercredi, après-midi, Simon n'a pas d'école. Il joue au foot avec ses copains.

Le jeudi après-midi, M. Dupont joue souvent au golf ; il aime le sport.

Le vendredi soir, Simon ne travaille pas, il écoute de la musique ou regarde la télé.

Le samedi, il n'y a pas d'école. Les enfants restent à la maison. Émilie joue du piano et elle prépare sa leçon de chant.

Dimanche, les grands-parents arrivent, et la famille déjeune ensemble.

Vie et culture

Implementation: Remind students that *le collège* is the equivalent to a "middle school." Let students examine the schedule and draw conclusions about the length of the school day in France and the length of the midday break; point out the use of the 24-hour clock. Make sure students notice the absence of afternoon classes on Wednesday. Point out that parents may have a similar break at noon and may work until six o'clock. Subsidized child care is available in France, and the mandated 35-hour work week makes parents' schedules more flexible.

La semaine

Look at the weekly schedule of a French middle school student. What do you notice about the times at which school begins and ends? the lunch break? the days on which there are classes? Many students devote part of the day on Wednesday to sports and cultural activities such as music or art lessons. Discuss the following questions with your classmates:

1. How might this schedule impact the family? What questions would you have about how French families handle child care or leisure time issues?
2. How does a typical week for young French students compare to that of North American students? What are the advantages and disadvantages of these varying schedules?

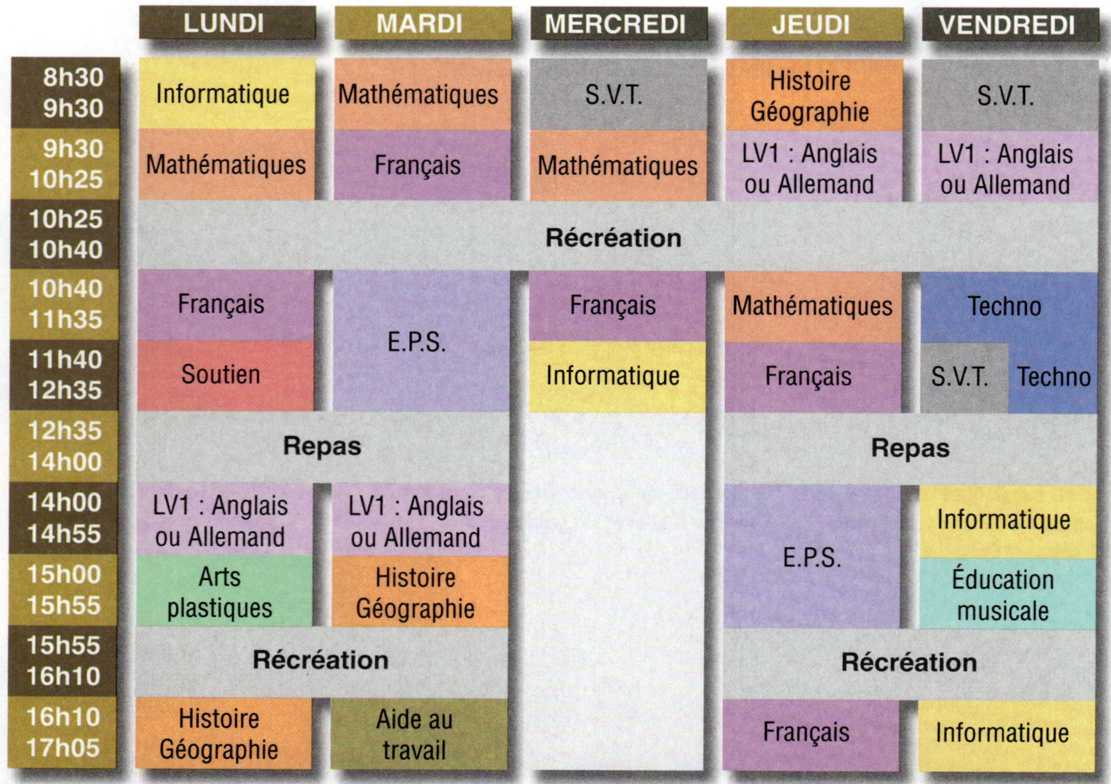

<table>
<tr><th></th><th>LUNDI</th><th>MARDI</th><th>MERCREDI</th><th>JEUDI</th><th colspan="2">VENDREDI</th></tr>
<tr><td>8h30
9h30</td><td>Informatique</td><td>Mathématiques</td><td>S.V.T.</td><td>Histoire
Géographie</td><td colspan="2">S.V.T.</td></tr>
<tr><td>9h30
10h25</td><td>Mathématiques</td><td>Français</td><td>Mathématiques</td><td>LV1 : Anglais
ou Allemand</td><td colspan="2">LV1 : Anglais
ou Allemand</td></tr>
<tr><td>10h25
10h40</td><td colspan="6">Récréation</td></tr>
<tr><td>10h40
11h35</td><td>Français</td><td rowspan="2">E.P.S.</td><td>Français</td><td>Mathématiques</td><td colspan="2">Techno</td></tr>
<tr><td>11h40
12h35</td><td>Soutien</td><td>Informatique</td><td>Français</td><td>S.V.T.</td><td>Techno</td></tr>
<tr><td>12h35
14h00</td><td colspan="2">Repas</td><td rowspan="5"></td><td colspan="3">Repas</td></tr>
<tr><td>14h00
14h55</td><td>LV1 : Anglais
ou Allemand</td><td>LV1 : Anglais
ou Allemand</td><td rowspan="2">E.P.S.</td><td colspan="2">Informatique</td></tr>
<tr><td>15h00
15h55</td><td>Arts
plastiques</td><td>Histoire
Géographie</td><td colspan="2">Éducation
musicale</td></tr>
<tr><td>15h55
16h10</td><td colspan="2">Récréation</td><td colspan="3">Récréation</td></tr>
<tr><td>16h10
17h05</td><td>Histoire
Géographie</td><td>Aide au
travail</td><td>Français</td><td colspan="2">Informatique</td></tr>
</table>

E.P.S. : Éducation Physique et Sportive ; S.V.T. : Sciences de la Vie et de la Terre ; Techno : Technologie ; Soutien : Français et Mathématiques

Les parties de la journée

le matin   l'après-midi   le soir

Les jours de la semaine

lundi   mardi   mercredi   jeudi   vendredi   samedi   dimanche

Des activités

arriver   déjeuner   dîner   écouter   inviter   jouer à/de   parler
préparer   regarder   rester   réviser   téléphoner   travailler

Presentation: Using the text in the **Points de départ** (MFL, Ch. 1), have students pick out which activities take place on a regular basis and which activities are one-time events. Make sure students notice that activities on a regular basis use *le*. Point out that in contrast to English, a preposition is never used with the days of the week or times: *le lundi* or *le soir*, in contrast to "*on* Monday(s), *in* the evening." Point out the use of *maintenant* to express an action occurring now.

The definite article **le** is used with days of the week or times of day to refer to an activity that always happens on that particular day of the week or at that particular time:

Le lundi, je travaille à la maison.	*Mondays, I work at home.*
Le samedi, on dîne au restaurant.	*On Saturdays, we eat out.*
Le soir, je regarde la télé.	*In the evening, I watch TV.*

Compare these examples with the sentences below, which do not use an article with the days of the week because they refer to specific, non-repeated activities.

Je joue au tennis avec des amis **mardi.**	*I'm playing tennis with friends on Tuesday.*
Dimanche, je dîne avec ma mère.	*Sunday, I'm having dinner with my mother.*

À vous la parole

1-29 Associations de mots. What words do you associate with each of the verbs listed? Work with a partner to find as many answers as possible.

MODÈLE regarder
→ la télé, un film, le tableau

1. écouter
2. jouer
3. rester
4. préparer
5. parler
6. travailler
7. aimer
8. inviter

Implementation: 1-30 To prepare, have students repeat the names of the days of the week. Drill by having them name the day after (*mardi ? —mercredi*) or the day before (*vendredi ? —jeudi*). This allows for practice of the vocabulary out of sequence. Then complete the exercise using Sophie's agenda (MFL, Ch. 1). Students produce only the third-person form of *-er* verbs, which is the base form. Note use of the 24-hour clock. Time is presented only for receptive control here; students should merely recognize whether an activity takes place in the morning, afternoon, or evening. Telling time is treated in Ch. 4, L. 2.

1-30 L'agenda de Sophie. Tell what Sophie has written in her pocket calendar for Thursday through Saturday.

MODÈLE Jeudi matin, elle a rendez-vous avec un professeur.

Jeudi 16 (09) SEPTEMBRE S. Édith	Vendredi 17 (09) SEPTEMBRE S. Renaud	Samedi 18 (09) SEPTEMBRE S. Nadège
9 h rendez-vous avec prof d'anglais	10 h examen de maths	9 h travailler dans le jardin avec maman
13 h déjeuner avec Alex	16 h jouer au tennis avec Julie	
19 h préparer examen de maths		20 h regarder un film avec Alex

Expansion: 1-31 Ask what students are doing tonight.

1-31 Qu'est-ce que vous faites le samedi ? Use the elements from each column to tell a classmate what you typically do on Saturday.

MODÈLE le matin / je révise / mes leçons
Le matin je révise mes leçons.

le matin	je travaille	le dîner
l'après-midi	j'écoute	mes copains à dîner
le soir	je joue	au tennis
	je révise	la télé, un film
	je regarde	à la maison
	j'invite	de la musique
	je prépare	mes leçons

Presentation: Present the verb paradigm inductively using a personalized story: *Le week-end, je ne travaille pas à la fac. Avec ma fille, on joue au tennis et on travaille dans le jardin. Et vous, vous travaillez ou vous regardez la télé habituellement le week-end ?*, etc. Ask students to provide the infinitive forms of verbs you have used, and to identify the various spoken forms. Remind students that English verbs also vary according to the subject: "I watch, he/she watches." Stress the fact that regular *-er* verbs in French have three spoken forms (and five written forms). As pointed out in the **Fiche pratique,** these verbs show a boot pattern: the third-person plural form is pronounced the same as the three singular forms.

FORMES ET FONCTIONS

1. *Le présent des verbes en -er et la négation*

Regular French verbs are classified according to the ending of their infinitive. Most have an infinitive form that ends in **-er**. To form the present tense of an **-er** verb, drop the **-er** from the infinitive and add the appropriate endings according to the pattern shown.

REGARDER *to look at, to watch*			
SINGULIER		**PLURIEL**	
je	regard**e**	nous	regard**ons**
tu	regard**es**	vous	regard**ez**
il / elle / on	regard**e**	ils / elles	regard**ent**

- Verbs ending in **-er** have three spoken forms. All singular forms and the **ils/elles** plural forms are pronounced alike. Their endings are important written signals, but they are not pronounced. The only endings that represent sounds are **-ons** and **-ez**, which correspond to the subject pronouns **nous** and **vous**.
- When a verb begins with a consonant, there is no difference in the pronunciation of singular and plural for **il/s** and **elle/s**. Use the context to decide whether the speaker means one person, or more than one.

Mon cousin, **il** joue du piano.	*My cousin, he plays piano.*
Mes frères, **ils** jouent au foot.	*My brothers, they play soccer.*

- When the verb begins with a vowel sound, the final **-s** of a subject pronoun is pronounced as /z/. This allows you to distinguish the singular **il/elle** form from the plural **ils/elles**.

il aime vs. ils‿aiment	*he likes, they like*
elle habite vs. elles‿habitent	*she lives, they live*
nous‿écoutons, vous‿arrivez	*we listen, you arrive*

- Remember that **on** is an indefinite pronoun that can mean *one, they,* or *people,* depending on the context. In conversational French, **on** is often used instead of **nous** to mean *we.*

On parle français ici.	*They speak French here.*
On joue au foot ?	*Shall we play soccer?*

- In French the present tense is used to talk about a state or an habitual action.

Je **parle** français.	*I speak French.*
Il **travaille** le week-end.	*He works on weekends.*

- It is also used to talk about an action taking place while one is speaking.

On **regarde** la télé.	*We're watching TV.*

Fiche pratique

Sometimes grammatical forms have a distinct visual pattern. For example, if you draw a box around the forms in the **-er** verb chart that are pronounced alike, you will see the shape of a boot. Think of the boot to remind yourself which forms have the same spoken form.

Can you provide the missing form of *jouer*?

Note: Although *ne*- deletion is extremely common in spoken French, we advocate teaching students to consistently use the two-part negative, to avoid being perceived negatively by native speakers.

Initial practice: Begin with a discrimination drill highlighting the presence or absence of liaison as a cue for number: one person, or more than one? *Ils habitent un appartement. Elle aime le rock. Ils écoutent de la musique. Elles arrivent. Il invite son ami. Elles aiment le sport*, etc. Follow with substitution drills: *Je joue au tennis ; nous. —Nous jouons au tennis*, etc. *J'aime la musique ; vous. —Vous aimez la musique*, etc.. *Je ne travaille pas ; nous. —Nous ne travaillons pas*, etc.

Implementation: 1-32 Display the images illustrating the Dupont family's weekly activities, used to present *-er* verb vocabulary (MFL, Ch. 1).

- To make a sentence negative, put **ne** (or **n'**) before the verb and **pas** after it.

Je **ne** travaille **pas**.	*I'm not working.*
Vous **n'**aimez **pas** le golf ?	*You don't like golf?*

In casual spoken French, native speakers will often drop the **ne**, so you may hear French speakers say sentences such as:

J'écoute **pas**.	*I'm not listening.*
Ils téléphonent **pas** ?	*They're not calling?*

À vous la parole

1-32 Une semaine chez les Dupont. Imagine that you're Mme Dupont, and describe your family's activities throughout the week.

MODÈLE lundi matin : Mme Dupont
Je travaille dans le jardin.

1. lundi matin : M. Dupont, les enfants
2. mardi : Mme Dupont
3. mercredi après-midi : Simon
4. jeudi après-midi : M. Dupont
5. vendredi soir : Simon
6. samedi matin : les enfants
7. dimanche : les grands-parents, la famille

Additional activity: Put students in pairs and have them tell each other one thing they are and are not doing this evening. Begin by modeling with a student: *Ce soir, je travaille à la maison. Je ne regarde pas la télé.* Student: *—Moi non plus, je ne regarde pas la télé. Je joue au tennis.* (*Moi non plus* is provided here as a lexical item.) Follow up by having students report back to the class: *On ne regarde pas la télé. Chris joue au tennis, et moi, je travaille.*

1-33 Vos habitudes. With a partner, take turns explaining when you or the people you know typically do the things listed.

MODÈLES vous / regarder la télé
Je regarde la télé le vendredi soir.
OU Je ne regarde pas la télé.

vos parents / téléphoner aux enfants
Ils téléphonent aux enfants le week-end.

1. vos amis / préparer leurs leçons
2. vous / regarder un film
3. vous et vos amis / jouer au tennis
4. votre père / préparer le dîner
5. vous / écouter la radio
6. votre frère ou sœur / téléphoner aux parents
7. vos parents / travailler
8. vous / rester à la maison

 **1-34 Cette semaine.** With a classmate, take turns telling some of the things you'll be doing later this week.

MODÈLE Jeudi soir, je révise mes leçons ; vendredi soir, je regarde un film avec mes copains ; samedi, je parle au téléphone avec mes parents...

Then report back to the class what you learned about your partner.

2. *Les questions*

There are two types of questions in English and French: *yes-no questions*, which require confirmation or denial, and *information questions*, which contain words such as **qui** (*who*) or **comment** (*how*) and ask for specific information.

Presentation: Introduce this topic by having students identify, by raising their hand, which of your utterances are questions: *Je m'appelle Sylvie. Elle s'appelle Nicole ? Comment ça va ? Ça va. Est-ce que tu habites Montréal ?*, etc. After many examples, ask students to explain how they identified these as questions. Students should then be able to provide additional examples. Information questions are presented in Ch. 2, L. 1 and in Ch. 8, L. 2.

- The simplest way to form yes-no questions in French is to raise the pitch level of your voice at the end of the sentence. These questions are said to have a rising intonation:

Émilie est ta cousine ?	*Emily is your cousin?*
Tu t'appelles Anne ?	*Your name is Anne?*

Another way of asking a yes-no question is by putting **est-ce que/qu'** at the beginning of the sentence. These questions are usually pronounced with a falling voice pitch:

Presentation: Show students that *est-ce que* functions like "do/does" in English: signaling a question, but not carrying meaning in itself.

Est-ce que vous parlez français ?	*Do you speak French?*
Est-ce qu'il joue au foot ?	*Does he play soccer?*

- If a question is phrased in the negative, and you want to contradict it, use **si** in your response:

Presentation: To drill the use of *si*, ask a series of questions and have students contradict you in every case, using *non* or *si* : *Vous jouez au foot ? — Non. Vous ne parlez pas français ? — Si*, etc. Follow up using the family tree and asking questions that require the answers *oui/non/si.*

—Tu n'es pas mariée ? —**Si,** voilà mon mari.	*—You're not married?* *—Yes (I am), there's my husband.*
—Tu n'aimes pas le français ? —**Si,** j'aime le français.	*—You don't like French?* *—Yes, I do like French.*

- When French speakers think they already know the answer to a question, they sometimes add **n'est-ce pas** to the end of the sentence for confirmation.

Vous êtes de Paris, **n'est-ce pas** ?	*You're from Paris, aren't you?*
Ton père parle français, **n'est-ce pas** ?	*Your father speaks French, doesn't he?*

However, be careful. French speakers do not use **n'est-ce pas** as frequently as American speakers use tag questions such as *aren't you? doesn't he? didn't you?*

À vous la parole

Implementation: 1-35 You may use the Brunet family tree (MFL, Ch. 1) to provide visual support; encourage students to invent other questions.

Expansion: Other visuals—the classroom (MFL, Ch. prélim.), the Dupont family's activities (MFL, Ch. 1)—can be used as a point of departure for students' questions.

Additional activity: Use the following as a mixing activity. Have students get up and circulate around the room, asking each person no more than two questions. When a person answers yes, his/her name is written down beside that activity. Give students about five minutes; they will probably not complete the list. As a follow-up, have them ask questions to complete their list: *Qui joue de la guitare ?* A student who found the response can then answer: *Jean joue de la guitare.* Other information can then be elicited: what type of music?, for example. At this point, treat the expressions *jouer de la guitare, jouer du piano, jouer au golf/tennis/foot* as lexical chunks for students to memorize. The distinction between *jouer à* and *jouer de* as well as contractions with these prepositions and the definite articles is treated in Ch. 2, L. 2.

Un remue-ménage ! Circulate around the classroom, asking your classmates questions to find out who does what. Limit your questions to two per person, write down your classmate's name when you get a positive response, and be ready to compare notes with the class as a whole.

MODÈLE *jouer de la guitare*

É1 Tu joues de la guitare ?

É2 Non, je joue du piano, mais pas de la guitare.

1. jouer de la guitare
2. travailler le week-end
3. rester à la maison le week-end
4. préparer le dîner
5. danser la valse (*waltz*)
6. travailler dans le jardin
7. écouter de la musique classique
8. ne pas regarder la télé
9. ne pas écouter de rap
10. jouer au golf

1-35 Encore la famille Brunet !

Ask for confirmation from your classmates concerning the members of the Brunet family.

MODÈLE La mère d'Éric s'appelle Micheline.

É1 Est-ce que la mère d'Éric s'appelle Micheline ?

OU La mère d'Éric s'appelle Micheline ?

É2 Oui, sa mère s'appelle Micheline.

1. Éric a une sœur.
2. Sa sœur s'appelle Fabienne.
3. Il a deux cousins.
4. Ses grands-parents sont Jean-Pierre et Madeleine Brunet.
5. Il n'a pas de frère.
6. Sa tante est divorcée et remariée.
7. Elle a deux enfants.
8. La demi-sœur de Loïc s'appelle Marie-Hélène.
9. Annick Roy a un frère.
10. Le mari de Micheline s'appelle Yves.

1-36 C'est bien ça ?

Draw a picture on the board. Your classmates will try to guess what it is.

MODÈLE (Vous dessinez un crayon.)

É1 Est-ce que c'est un stylo ?

É2 C'est une craie ?

É3 Ah, c'est un crayon !

Variation: 1-36 Common objects can also be hidden in a bag (Kim's game).

1-37 Une interview.

Interview a member of your class that you do not know very well to find out more about him/her. Use the suggested topics, and report to the class something you have learned about your partner.

MODÈLE avoir des frères ou des sœurs

É1 Est-ce que tu as des frères ou des sœurs ?

É2 J'ai une sœur, mais je n'ai pas de frères.

1. avoir des enfants
2. avoir des animaux familiers
3. travailler beaucoup
4. jouer du piano ou de la guitare
5. jouer au football ou au tennis
6. regarder la télé
7. préparer le dîner
8. regarder des films
9. inviter des copains à dîner

Expansion: 1-37 You might arrange for another teacher, a Francophone, or an advanced student to visit your class and be interviewed.

Écoutons

1-38 Le répondeur

A. Avant d'écouter. Fabienne has a lot of friends. Listen to the messages on her answering machine from people who are suggesting that she join them this week for various activities. Before you listen, think about the kinds of information you would expect to hear in a phone message.

Here is Fabienne pictured with one of the people who leaves a message on her answering machine. Can you guess who this might be? Where are they, and what are they probably doing?

B. En écoutant. As you listen, complete the first three columns of the chart below for each message.

	Who called?	Event suggested?	When?	Accept or refuse?
1.				
2.				
3.				
4.				

C. Après avoir écouté. Now, look over the chart again and decide which invitations you would accept and which invitations you would refuse if you were Fabienne. Fill in column four with this information, and discuss your responses with a classmate.

Script: Écoutons

1. Salut. C'est Jennifer. Mercredi soir, il y a un bon film à la télé que je veux regarder. Je t'invite. On peut préparer du pop-corn. Téléphone-moi si tu veux le regarder avec moi. Allez, ciao !
2. Bonjour, c'est Jean-Pierre à l'appareil. Samedi matin, je joue au golf avec des copains. Tu veux jouer avec nous ? On a rendez-vous à 11 heures au parc. Appelle-moi si ça t'intéresse. Bon, au revoir !
3. C'est maman. Je t'invite à manger à la maison dimanche après-midi. Tes grands-parents, ton oncle Paul et tes cousins déjeunent avec nous. Téléphone-moi si tu es libre. On a envie de te voir. Allez, je t'embrasse !
4. Salut, c'est Annie. Vendredi soir, il y a un concert de piano au conservatoire. Je sais que tu aimes la musique classique. Appelle-moi si tu veux te joindre à nous. O.K., salut !

Venez chez nous ! La famille dans le monde francophone

Preparation: If you have not done so already, show the video montage *La famille dans le monde francophone* to provide an overview of Francophone families. You might pause and have students describe each family pictured. You might review the information on the French family treated by the **Vie et culture** in L.1: How does the typical French family seem to compare to the typical North American family, and to your own? How would you characterize the role of family life in France? Is the role of family life in North America similar, in your opinion?

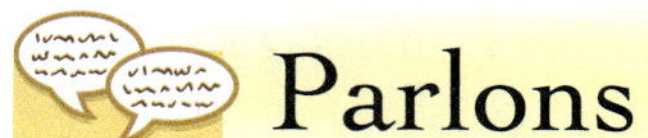

Parlons

1-39 Des familles bien diverses

A. Avant de parler. Choose one of the photos shown here or in another part of this **Venez chez nous** lesson. You will describe this family to a partner, who will then have to decide which family you have chosen. Before you begin, make a list of the people you see in the picture, using words you have learned in this chapter (**la mère, la sœur**...). Next, decide how old each person might be and jot down a few adjectives to describe each person. You may also be able to say where they are or what they are doing (**Ils déjeunent** ; **Ils sont dans le jardin**).

Expansion: 1-39 Bring in other photos of families to give students a wider choice. You might also use paintings of families by well-known artists as the basis for descriptions; some examples are provided with exercise **1-3**. Follow up on the **Parlons** by having students reflect on the families they have described. Could they find families like these where they live? Why or why not? The **Parlons** activity can also be used as preparation for the writing activity, where students are asked to write a portrait of their own family.

Voilà des familles francophones. Quelle famille habite en France? en Algérie? au Sénégal?

B. En parlant. Take turns describing the family in your photo and letting your partner guess which one you are talking about. Can either of you follow up by making suggestions to amplify your partner's description or otherwise to modify it?

C. Après avoir parlé. Now present your description to the class as a whole, while your partner points to each person you mention.

Stratégie

Use accompanying graphic elements to help understand a text. Often a graph or table, for example, will summarize at a glance the main points made in the text, serving as a useful point of reference both before and as you read.

Implementation: Avant de lire The table does not duplicate the text information exactly. Display the table and work through it with students, using the questions provided; point out how large numbers and percentages are expressed, using spacing and commas. When students have developed their lists of preliminary conclusions, have them share these with the class as a whole. Note that the Canadian census is taken every five years, whereas in the U.S. it is every ten years. To learn more about the latest census figures for Quebec families, see the **Chez nous** Companion Website for links to the Statistics Canada Web site.

Lisons

1-40 La famille au Québec

A. Avant de lire. This reading about families in Quebec is accompanied by a table that presents census statistics about married and unmarried couples in the province. Examining the table beforehand can help you better understand the related text. Consider the following questions:

1. What types of family structure are referred to in the table? The key expressions here are: **avec enfants**, **sans enfants**, and **en union libre**. Can you explain the meaning of each? Notice that the footnotes provide additional information.
2. The far right column provides comparative data; what information is being compared?
3. What general conclusions might the statistics in the table lead you to make about the family in Quebec? Work with a partner to make a list.

Familles comptant un couple selon la présence d'enfants, chiffres de 2006, pour le Québec

Structure de la famille :		Variation 2001–2006 :
Nombre total de couples	1 768 785	5,0 %
Couples mariés avec enfants[1]	522 100	–12,3 %
Couples mariés sans enfants[2]	634 825	9,4 %
Couples en union libre avec enfants[1]	308 170	19,2 %
Couples en union libre sans enfants[2]	303 685	21,4 %

[1]un couple avec au moins un enfant âgé de moins de 25 ans
[2]un couple et enfants âgés de 25 ans et plus

Source : http://www12.statcan.ca/english/census06/data/highlights/households/pages/Page.cfm?Lang=F&Geo=CMA&Code=24&Table=1&Data=Count&Age=2&StartRec=1&Sort=2&Display=Page

Implementation: En lisant You may wish to read the text aloud, asking students to circle the statistics. Do not ask students to read the text aloud, as it contains many unfamiliar words and large numbers. Afterward, review the statistics and have students explain their significance. Then address question #3, following up on the initial task and seeing whether students were able to draw correct conclusions. For #4, students should notice that information about same-sex couples is included in the 2006 census.

B. En lisant. The essential information in the text below, as in the preceding table, is statistical.

1. As you read, circle each statistic and focus on discovering its significance.
2. Which statistics are related to those in the preceding table?
3. Which of your preliminary conclusions based on analysis of the table can you now confirm?
4. What additional information does the text provide about how couples are defined by the census?

Québec : le nombre d'unions libres continue de monter

Au Québec, un grand nombre de couples vivent[1] ensemble sans être mariés, selon le Recensement de 2006. De 2001 à 2006, le nombre d'unions libres a augmenté de 20,3 % au Québec pour atteindre[2] 611 900.

Les couples mariés représentent seulement[3] 54,5 % des familles comptées en 2006. C'est une baisse par rapport à[4] la proportion de 58 % enregistrée[5] en 2001. Parallèlement, la proportion de couples vivant en union libre a augmenté considérablement, passant de 25 % à 34,6 %.

En 2006, seulement 3 familles sur 10 (29,5 %) au Québec sont des couples mariés avec des enfants de 24 ans et moins à la maison.

Le Recensement de 2006 fournit[6] aussi des données[7] sur les couples de même[8] sexe. Un total de 13 700 couples se sont identifiés comme étant[9] des couples de même sexe. En mars 2004, le Québec est la troisième province à légaliser les mariages entre conjoints de même sexe. Au Recensement de 2006, on constate que 9,2 % des couples du même sexe au Canada sont mariés.

Adapté de Statistique Canada « Portrait de famille : continuité et changement dans les familles et les ménages du Canada en 2006, Recensement de 2006 », catalogue 97-553-XWF2006001, paru le 12 septembre 2007. Accès : http://www12.statcan.ca/francais/census06/analysis/famhouse/index.cfm.

[1]habitent [2]*reach* [3]*only* [4]*in comparison with* [5]*recorded* [6]donne [7]*facts* [8]*same* [9]*as being*

Key: En regardant de plus près 1) selon le Recensement 2) monter, augmenter 3) une baisse 4) vivant en union libre

C. En regardant de plus près. Find the French words in the text corresponding to the following words and expressions in English:

1. according to the Census
2. to increase
3. a decline
4. living together without being married

D. Après avoir lu. Think about and then discuss the following questions with classmates.

1. What seems to be the primary trend in Quebec family life, as indicated by the statistics given in the text and illustrated by the related table? Based on what you have learned about current family life in France, is this trend similar to or different from what is happening in France? In what ways? Are the trends similar in your own community? Explain your answer.
2. What options are available to same-sex couples in Quebec? How are they similar to, or different from the options in France? How do they compare to the options where you live?

La famille en Afrique francophone

Families in Francophone Africa tend to be larger than European and North American families and to place more emphasis on the extended family and the obligation to help out family members. It is not uncommon for Africans studying and working in France to send money home to their families or to bring back books, school supplies, clothing, and household gifts when they return home for a visit. In many African societies, elderly people are greatly respected and they often live with their children and their families. Pensions and social security payments may be quite small or nonexistent, and older people rely on their children to provide for them.

Implementation: To encourage cross-cultural comparison, ask students what advantages or disadvantages they see in a system where family obligations and respect for elders receive more emphasis than in North America.

Observons

Note: 1-41 This exercise treats the first three interviews in the clip. Additional interviews are treated in the SAM/MFL. You might ask students to complete those activities on their own.

1-41 C'est ma famille

A. Avant de regarder. You will see three short interviews in which people describe their family. Watch the video clip a first time without sound. Try to determine which members of the family are being described by each speaker, and write down the relationships in French.

Marie-Julie et sa famille

	without sound	with sound
Speaker(s)	relatives inferred	relatives described
Pauline :		
Bruno, Diane et Claire :		
Marie-Julie :	*son mari, sa fille*	

Script: Observons

PAULINE : Toute ma famille habite à Paris. Euh, c'est-à-dire, euh, mes parents, mes frères, mes grands-parents, mes oncles, mes tantes, absolument tout le monde. Euh, j'ai donc, euh, j'ai deux frères qui s'appellent Maxime et Clément. Ils sont plus jeunes que moi. Euh, moi, je suis née en 1976. J'ai vingt-sept ans donc, et mes frères, euh, ont vingt-et-un ans et vingt-trois ans.

BRUNO : Bonjour, je m'appelle Bruno. J'ai sept ans. Voici mes deux sœurs, Claire et Diane.

DIANE : Bonjour, je m'appelle Diane. J'ai onze ans et demi. Voici ma grande sœur et mon petit frère.

CLAIRE : Tandis que moi, je m'appelle Claire. J'ai treize ans et j'ai un petit frère et une petite sœur qui s'appellent Diane et Bruno. Donc je suis la plus grande de toute la famille. Voilà.

MARIE-JULIE : Je vous présente ma fille, Laura. Laura est québécoise, française et elle est née américaine. Et voici mon mari, Patrick. Il est français d'origine, à moitié breton, à moitié du Midi.

B. En regardant. Now watch the video clip with sound and see if your list is correct and complete. Can you add to the list of family relationships based on what you hear?

C. Après avoir regardé. Discuss the following questions with a partner.

1. How are these Francophone families similar to, or different from, American families?
2. Can you draw at least a partial family tree for each speaker? What information is still missing? What additional questions might you ask each speaker?

Implementation: Après avoir regardé Allow students to work in pairs, then follow up to compare opinions, find out what questions students would ask, and compare partial family trees and descriptions of the photos.

Écrivons

1-42 Une famille louisianaise

A. Avant d'écrire. Read Amélie Ledet's description of her family's origins. Her family is typical of many in southwest Louisiana: some of her ancestors are of Acadian origin, others came directly from western France, and still others were earlier German settlers who were assimilated into the French-speaking population. Based on her description, and focusing on the key terms to name family members, sketch the part of Amélie's family tree that she describes.

Stratégie

Before you write a description, you may find it is helpful to organize your thoughts using a chart or a diagram. You can then refer to it as you write to be sure you are following your plan.

Implementation: Avant d'écrire Use a map to show where Amélie lives and where her ancestors came from. You might explain that the Cajun "myth" traces the ancestors of the Cajuns to Acadia, today New Brunswick. The Acadians were expelled after the British took control, in a movement known as **le Grand Dérangement**. Longfellow's epic poem, *Evangeline*, recounts this story. The reality is much more complex, however, with settlers of many ethnic origins mixing over the years. Some of the early settlers to Louisiana came from Germany, hence the place name *Lac des Allemands*, where they settled. Their German names were given a French equivalent, *La Branche* in the case of *Zweig*. If your own family has an interesting multiethnic origin, provide a brief description as another model for students.

A Louisiana family checks their fishing nets in the waters of the Atchafalaya swamp.

Mon nom, c'est Amélie Ledet. J'ai 22 ans et j'habite à Montagut dans la paroisse Lafourche. Mon arrière-arrière-arrière-grand-père du côté de mon père s'appelle Jules Desormeaux. Il est né[1] à Grand Pré, en Acadie, en 1745 et il est décédé en 1806. Sa femme s'appelle Marie Landry. Mon arrière-arrière-arrière-grand-mère est née à Port-Royal, Acadie, en 1751 et elle est décédée en 1810. Du côté de ma mère, mon arrière-arrière-arrière-grand-père s'appelle Pierre Arceneaux. Il est né à La Rochelle, en France, en 1772. Il est décédé en Louisiane en 1840. Sa femme, Louise La Branche (Zweig), est née au Lac des Allemands, en Louisiane, en 1780. Elle est décédée en 1845.

[1] *was born*

B. En écrivant.

1. Sketch your own family tree.
2. Now write a paragraph describing your family origins. Use Amélie's description as a model, incorporating vocabulary and expressions that she uses into your own writing.

C. En révisant. As you re-read your paragraph, think about the following questions and make any necessary changes.

1. Analyze the content: does your description match the family tree you drew?
2. Look at the style and form of your paragraph: did you use the appropriate kinship terms and possessives (**mon, ma, mes**)? Did you incorporate expressions from the model to tell where your relatives come from, when they were born, and when they died?

D. Après avoir écrit. Share your paragraph with your classmates to get a sense of the diversity within your own class.

Now that you have completed *Chapitre 1*, can you do the following in French?

- ☐ Talk about and describe your own family, or another family?
- ☐ Count from 0 to 100 and tell how old someone is?
- ☐ Use a variety of verbs to describe your everyday activities?
- ☐ Ask simple questions?
- ☐ Describe general trends among families across the French-speaking world?

Leçon 1

les relations familiales	family relations
un beau-père	stepfather, father-in-law
une belle-mère	stepmother, mother-in-law
un/e cousin/e	cousin
un/e enfant	child
une famille nombreuse	big family
une femme	wife, woman
une fille	daughter, girl
un fils	son
un frère	brother
un garçon	boy
une grand-mère	grandmother
un grand-père	grandfather
des grands-parents (m.)	grandparents
un mari	husband
une mère	mother
un neveu, des neveux	nephew, (nieces &) nephews
une nièce	niece
un oncle	uncle
des parents (m.)	parents; relatives
un père	father
une petite-fille, des petites-filles	granddaughter, granddaughters
un petit-fils, des petits-fils	grandson, grandsons
des petits-enfants (m.)	grandchildren
une sœur	sister
une tante	aunt

l'état civil	marital status
célibataire	single
décédé/e	deceased
divorcé/e	divorced
fiancé/e	engaged
marié/e	married
remarié/e	remarried

des animaux familiers	pets
un animal familier	pet
un chat	cat
un chien	dog
un oiseau	bird

le caractère	disposition, nature, character
calme	calm
conformiste	conformist
désagréable	disagreeable, grumpy
discipliné/e	disciplined
dynamique	dynamic
idéaliste	idealistic
indiscipliné/e	undisciplined
individualiste	individualistic
optimiste	optimistic
pessimiste	pessimistic
raisonnable	reasonable
réaliste	realistic
réservé/e	reserved
sociable	outgoing
stressé/e	stressed out
sympa(thique)	nice
têtu/e	stubborn
timide	shy

pour exprimer l'intensité	to express intensity
assez	rather
beaucoup	a lot
un peu	a little
très	very
trop	too much
vraiment	really

autres mots utiles	other useful words
chez	at the home of
chez nous	at our place
deuxième	second
habiter	to live
un homme	man
premier	first

Leçon 2

les mois (m.) de l'année (f.)	the months of the year
janvier	January
février	February
mars	March
avril	April
mai	May
juin	June
juillet	July
août	August
septembre	September
octobre	October

Vocabulaire

novembre	*November*
décembre	*December*
Quelle est la date	*What is the date*
... de ton anniversaire (m.) ?	*. . . of your birthday?*
C'est le premier mai.	*It's May 1.*
C'est le 4 septembre.	*It's September 4.*

l'âge (m.)	***age***
un an	*one year*
avoir	*to have*
Quel est ton/votre âge ?	*What is your age?*
Quel âge as-tu ?/Quel âge avez-vous ?	*How old are you?*
J'ai 19 ans.	*I am 19 years old.*

les nombres de 0 à 100

(see p. 43 for 0 to 31 and p. 47 for 40 to 100)

Leçon 3

pour dire quand	***to say when***
lundi	*Monday*
mardi	*Tuesday*
mercredi	*Wednesday*
jeudi	*Thursday*
vendredi	*Friday*
samedi	*Saturday*
dimanche	*Sunday*
aujourd'hui	*today*
la semaine	*week*
le week-end	*weekend*
le jour	*day*
le matin	*morning*
l'après-midi (m.)	*afternoon*
le soir	*evening*
maintenant	*now*

les activités	***activities***
aimer	*to like, to love*
arriver	*to arrive*
déjeuner	*to have breakfast/lunch*
dîner	*to have dinner*
écouter la radio/de la musique	*to listen to the radio/to music*
inviter	*to invite*
jouer au foot/du piano	*to play soccer/the piano*
ne... pas (Je ne joue pas.)	*not (I'm not playing/ I don't play.)*
parler au téléphone	*to talk on the phone*
préparer le dîner	*to fix dinner*
regarder un film/la télé/des photos	*to watch a movie/TV/look at photos*
rester à la maison	*to stay home*
réviser la leçon	*to review the lesson*
téléphoner à quelqu'un	*to call somebody*
travailler dans le jardin	*to work in the garden/ yard*

quelques lieux	***some places***
au bureau	*at the office*
à l'école	*at school*
au collège	*in middle school*
au lycée	*in high school*
à la maison	*at home*
au restaurant	*at the restaurant*

la musique	***music***
la musique classique	*classical music*
une guitare	*a guitar*

quelques sports	***some sports***
le foot(ball)	*soccer*
le golf	*golf*
le tennis	*tennis*

autres mots utiles	***other useful words***
avec	*with*
un copain/une copine	*friend*
ensemble	*together*
une leçon de chant	*singing lesson*
normalement	*usually*
si	*yes (after a negative question)*
typique	*typical*

2 Voici mes amis

Who are the people shown here and what are they doing? Does this remind you of experiences you've had with people you know?

After completing this chapter, you should be able to:

- Describe people's appearance and personality
- Talk about sports and leisure activities
- Ask for information
- Give commands and make suggestions
- Talk about French and American notions of friendship
- Talk about major sporting events across the Francophone world

Leçon  Mes amis et moi

POINTS DE DÉPART

Elles sont comment ?

Denise et Marie regardent un album de photos.

DENISE : C'est toi sur la photo là, avec le chapeau ?
MARIE : Bien sûr.
DENISE : Tu es jolie. Qui sont les autres filles ?
MARIE : Ce sont mes amies du collège.
DENISE : Comment s'appelle l'autre fille avec un chapeau ?
MARIE : Ça c'est Diane ; elle est maintenant à la fac avec moi. C'est ma colocataire. Elle est très intelligente et ambitieuse. Mais elle est amusante aussi ; elle adore les histoires drôles.
DENISE : Et la grande fille mince et rousse ?
MARIE : C'est Clara. Elle est très élégante. Elle travaille avec les personnes âgées ; c'est une fille gentille et généreuse.
DENISE : Et la blonde ?
MARIE : C'est Anne-Laure. Elle est super sportive et sociable ; pas du tout paresseuse, elle.
DENISE : Pas comme toi, donc !
MARIE : Arrête !

Preparation: Provide an overview of the lesson by showing the Ch. 2 video segment *Les amis.* Have students listen and watch, then describe the activities friends are sharing. This video clip may also be shown in conjunction with the **Vie et culture** section.

Presentation: Only feminine forms of variable adjectives are presented here, since in most cases the masculine spoken form can be easily derived from the feminine. This derivation rule will be taught in the **Formes et fonctions** section of this lesson. To present the vocabulary, use the girls' photo and the dialogue, as well as the boxed list of adjectives. Read or play the recorded dialogue, pointing out each person as she is described. Test comprehension by asking *Qui est blonde ?*, etc., or by creating statements that students must identify as true or false. Next, use either/or questions to elicit repetitions: *Clara est blonde ou rousse ?* Finally, have students provide opposites for adjectives: *Elle est grande ? —Non, elle est petite.* As follow-up, have students describe magazine photos of interesting-looking women.

Pour décrire les femmes			
jeune	d'un certain âge	âgée	
belle	jolie	moche	
grande	de taille moyenne	petite	
maigre	mince	forte	grosse
blonde	rousse	châtain	brune
élégante			
gentille		méchante	
généreuse		égoïste	
intelligente		bête	
ambitieuse	énergique	paresseuse	
sportive		pantouflarde	
sérieuse	drôle	amusante	

Note: Adjectives like *châtain*, derived from nouns, are invariable and never add an *e* or an *s*.

À vous la parole

Implementation: 2-1 This allows students to practice nuancing descriptions by using the negative and the qualifying adverbs taught in Ch. 1, L. 1.

Additional Activity: Ask students to describe one of the women in your class so that classmates can guess who it is. For example, *É1 Elle est d'un certain âge. Elle est blonde, grande et assez mince. É2 C'est le professeur ? É1 Oui.* Be aware that some students are sensitive about physical descriptions. As an alternative, you might bring in magazine photos and have students work in pairs to create a description; post all the photos, then have the class guess which one is being described.

2-1 En d'autres termes. Describe each young woman, using other words.

MODÈLE Clara n'est pas égoïste.
Clara est généreuse.

1. Clara n'est ni (*neither*) brune, ni blonde, ni châtain.
2. Clara n'est pas petite.
3. Clara n'est pas méchante.
4. Diane n'est pas très mince.
5. Diane n'est pas petite.
6. Diane n'est ni blonde, ni rousse, ni châtain.
7. Diane n'est pas bête.
8. Anne-Laure n'est pas paresseuse.
9. Anne-Laure n'est pas grande, mais elle n'est pas petite non plus.
10. Anne-Laure n'est pas pantouflarde.

Implementation: 2-2 Offer a few examples, then have students work in pairs or small groups to prepare a description. Each group gives out its information bit by bit; they receive one point for each statement they make before class members guess correctly.

2-2 Une personne connue. Describe a well-known girl or woman, real or imaginary, and have your classmates guess who it is.

MODÈLE É1 Elle est très jeune ; elle a environ (*about*) douze ans. Elle est petite, mince et rousse. Elle n'a pas de parents, mais elle a un chien, Sandy.
É2 C'est Annie, la petite orpheline.

Expansion: 2-3 To follow up, display all pictures in the classroom. As individual students share their description with the class, their classmates will listen to determine which person is being described.

2-3 Voici une amie / mes amies. Bring in a photo of a female friend or friends to describe to a partner.

MODÈLE Voici la photo d'une de mes amies. Elle s'appelle Julie. Elle est grande et blonde. Elle est intelligente et très énergique. Elle aime le tennis.

Presentation: If you have not yet shown it, use the Ch. 2 video segment *Les amis* to lead into this section or to follow up on discussion.

Vie et culture

Note: For more information, see Raymonde Carroll's chapter on friendship in her book *Évidences invisibles : Américains et Français au quotidien* (Éditions du Seuil, 1987); translated by Carol Volk as *Cultural Misunderstandings: The French-American Experience* (The University of Chicago Press, 1990). The quote featured here can be found on page 77.

Les amis

Concepts of friendship vary from culture to culture. In France, friendships are usually formed slowly, over many years. Once established, they tend to last a lifetime. American visitors and exchange students in France sometimes find it difficult to form friendships with French peers because of the brevity of their stays. French exchange students and visitors to the United States, on the other hand, often report that Americans make friends very quickly and seem to refer to many people as "my friend." This contrasts sharply with French usage where the word **ami** is reserved for those people with whom a strong bond of friendship has been established. In *Cultural Misunderstandings: The French-American Experience*, Raymonde Carroll, a French anthropologist living in the United States, explains the use of the word "friend" in American English:

> For an American, . . . this is merely a verbal shortcut which saves the trouble of explaining the differences between "friend" and all the other terms available (acquaintance, vague acquaintance, buddy, pal, chum, roommate, housemate, classmate, schoolmate, teammate, playmate, companion, co-worker, colleague, childhood friend, new friend, old friend, very old friend, family friend, close friend, very close friend, best friend, girlfriend, boyfriend, etc.).

However, Americans' casual use of the word "friend" leads French observers to conclude that their own concept of friendship is more durable and considerably more nuanced.

ET VOUS ?

1. What behaviors or features of American society might promote the perception among the French that friendships are formed quickly?
2. Think about the contexts in which you would refer to someone as "my friend." Do you agree with Carroll's observation that Americans tend to use the word *friend* rather loosely? What advantages and disadvantages are there to using *friend* to refer to a wide range of relationships?
3. Do you agree with the judgment that American friendships are less durable and less nuanced than French friendships? Explain your response.

Voici quelques amis qui discutent au café.

Key: Et vous ? Point out the tendency for Americans to use first names immediately on meeting someone, to invite people into their homes very soon after they have met, and even to hug or kiss business associates. Suggest to students that because Americans tend to change jobs and move frequently, often far from family and childhood friends, there is perhaps more of a necessity to form new friendships quickly.

Sons et lettres

Presentation: Present this topic in conjunction with *Les adjectifs variables.*

La détente des consonnes finales

As a general rule, final consonant letters are not pronounced in French:

l'enfa**nt** elle e**st** nou**s** somme**s** trè**s** jeune**s** beaucou**p**

However, there are four final consonant letters that are generally pronounced: **-c**, **-r**, **-f**, and **-l**. To remember them, think of the English word *careful*.

la fa**c** pou**r** neu**f** Danie**l**

An exception is the letter **-r** in the infinitive ending **-er** and in words ending in **-er** and **-ier**:

écout**er** dans**er** le dîn**er** le prem**ier** janv**ier**

The letter **n** is seldom pronounced at the end of a word. Together with the preceding vowel letters it represents a nasal vowel sound:

m**on** cop**ain** le chi**en** l'**en**fa**nt**

Initial practice: Reinforce with a discrimination drill to ensure that students hear pronounced final consonants: *un homme ou une femme ? Michel est amusant. Michèle est intelligente. Dominique est sérieuse. Dominique est généreux. Daniel est élégant. Danielle est petite. Renée est ambitieuse. René est paresseux. Andrée est sportive*, etc. Additional names that work well in this type of exercise include *Pascal/e* and *Claude*.

At the end of a word, one or more consonant letters followed by **-e** always stand for a pronounced consonant. These consonants must be clearly articulated, for they mark important grammatical distinctions such as feminine versus masculine forms of adjectives. The final **-e** doesn't represent any sound.

	Danielle es**t**	sérieu**se**	intelligen**te**	amusan**te**
vs.	Daniel es**t**	sérieu**x**	intelligen**t**	amusan**t**

À vous la parole

Implementation: 2-4 First have students go through and underline pronounced final consonants, and draw a line through silent final consonants.

2-4 Prononcer ou ne pas prononcer ? In which words should you pronounce the final consonant?

avec Robert	il aime danser	s'il vous plaît	pour ma sœur
neuf cahiers	le jour de Noël	le Québec	le singulier

2-5 Contrastes. Read each pair of sentences aloud and note the contrasts.

C'est Denise. / C'est Denis.
Voilà Françoise. / Voilà François.
Pascale est amusante. / Pascal est amusant.
Michèle est blonde. / Michel est blond.

FORMES ET FONCTIONS

1. *Les adjectifs variables*

- You have learned that adjectives agree in gender and number with the noun they modify. *Invariable* adjectives have only one spoken form. The feminine ending **-e** and the plural ending **-s** show up only in the written forms.

Ma sœur est stressé**e**.	Mes amies sont stressé**es**.
Mon frère est discipliné.	Mes amis sont discipliné**s**.
Mon père est calme.	Mes parents sont calme**s**.

- *Variable* adjectives have masculine and feminine forms that differ in pronunciation. Their feminine form ends in a pronounced consonant. To pronounce the masculine, drop the final consonant sound. The written letter **-s** or **-x** at the end of plural adjectives is not generally pronounced.

SINGULIER	*f.*	Anne est	amusan**te**	et	généreu**se**.
	m.	Cédric est	amusan**t**	et	généreu**x**.
PLURIEL	*f.*	Mes amies sont	amusan**tes**	et	généreu**ses**.
	m.	Mes copains sont	amusan**ts**	et	généreu**x**.

The feminine form of variable adjectives always ends in **-e**. The final **-e** is dropped in the masculine form; therefore, the final consonant sound, heard in the feminine form, is also dropped. Although some variable adjectives have spelling irregularities, this pronunciation rule still applies. For example, in the feminine form **généreuse** [ʒenerøz], the final consonant is pronounced, but it is dropped in the masculine form **généreux** [ʒenerø]. In the written form, the final **-e** is dropped in the masculine and the final **-s** is changed to **-x**. Other regular variable adjectives that show spelling changes include:

rou**sse** → rou**x**   gro**sse** → gro**s**   genti**lle** → genti**l**

Note: Point out that the irregularities involve changes in the final written consonant: *-ss→x; -ll→l*, etc.

- Adjectives whose masculine singular form ends in **-x** do not change in the masculine plural form.

Laurent est rou**x**.	Laurent et Matthieu sont rou**x**.

- As you have learned, with a mixed group of feminine and masculine nouns, the plural form of the adjective is always the masculine form.

Jessica et Laure sont **brunes**.	*Jessica and Laure are brunettes.*
Kevin et Marc sont **blonds**.	*Kevin and Marc are blonds.*
Max et Sylvie sont **roux**.	*Max and Sylvie are redheads.*

Note: You may wish to point out that some frequently used adjectives precede the noun. These include *belle, grande, jeune, jolie,* and *petite,* all of which were presented in the **Points de départ**. Prenominal adjectives will be treated in Ch. 3, L. 1 and L. 2.

Fiche pratique

Noun phrases in French typically include multiple written indications of number and gender: compare, for example, **une amie intelligente** with **un copain amusant** and **des profs sympathiques**. Because the written indications are not always heard in the spoken forms, it is a good idea to get into the habit of double-checking the number and gender of any nouns and adjectives that you write.

Presentation: What we call *invariable* adjectives have a single spoken form, but some have distinct written masculine and feminine forms as well as distinct plural written forms. This presentation focuses on spoken forms and is reinforced by the **Sons et lettres** treatment. Exercises in the SAM/MFL focus on the written forms of invariable and variable adjectives. To present variable adjectives, prepare a series of parallel examples describing *le couple idéal,* where the two members of the couple have identical personality and physical traits. Arrange the examples in two columns with *Elle est...* on the top of the first column and *Il est...* on the top of the second column. Then fill in the columns with examples such as: *élégante, élégant ; grande, grand ; ambitieuse, ambitieux ; brune, brun ; intelligente, intelligent ; amusante, amusant ; gentille, gentil ; généreuse, généreux.* As you read and display the forms, have students explain the written forms, then see whether they can give the rule for deriving the masculine spoken form from the feminine. Finish by asking students, *Est-ce que ce couple est vraiment un couple idéal ? Pourquoi ?*

Note: Point out that *belle* and *brune* involve vowel changes (i.e., from [ɛ] to [o] for *belle-beau* and from [y] to [ɛ̃] for *brune-brun*) as well as the loss of the final consonant; *sportive* shows a final consonant change from [v] to [f].

Initial practice: Begin with a discrimination drill, as in the **Sons et lettres**, so that students hear masculine and feminine forms of adjectives: *Michel est amusant. Michèle est intelligente. Pascal est sportif. Pascale est ambitieuse. Claude est blonde. Claude est petit. René est gros. Renée est élégante*, etc. Continue with a simple substitution exercise, such as the following: ***Des jumeaux***. Julien and Juliette are twins. Tell how they are alike: *Juliette est grande. — Et son frère, Julien, est grand aussi. Elle est rousse ; elle est un peu forte ; elle est assez amusante ; elle est très intelligente ; elle est vraiment gentille ; elle est généreuse.* Next reverse the direction of derivation by providing the masculine form and having students respond with the feminine. Stress the importance of over-articulating the final consonant, since it contains the signal for the gender: *Julien est très élégant. — Sa sœur, Juliette, est très élégante aussi. Il est sportif ; il est assez ambitieux ; il est très sérieux ; il est beau.*

Expansion: 2-7 You may also bring large photos, such as those found in fine art reproductions, catalogs, or magazines into class. Put students into pairs to work out their description, then bring all the photos to the front of the class. As each pair describes their person, the other students try to guess to which photo the description corresponds. You may wish to introduce expressions such as *avoir les cheveux courts/longs/bouclés/blonds*, as appropriate.

- Note the following irregular forms:

FÉMININ	MASCULIN
belle	beau
brune	brun
sportive	sportif

À vous la parole

2-6 Pas mes amis ! Your friends are quite different from what your mother thinks; tell how.

MODÈLE Tes amies sont paresseuses !
Ah non, elles sont énergiques.

1. Tes amis sont méchants !
2. Tes amis sont trop idéalistes !
3. Tes amies sont têtues !
4. Tes amis sont trop conformistes !
5. Tes amis sont trop bêtes !
6. Tes amis sont égoïstes !
7. Tes amies sont trop sérieuses !
8. Tes amis sont tous (*all*) pessimistes !

2-7 Les amis. Describe the appearance and personality of this group of friends to your partner.

MODÈLE Il y a trois femmes qui sont assez jeunes, une femme d'un certain âge et un homme...

 **2-8 Le monde idéal.** Ideally, what are the following people and pets like? Describe them to your partner.

MODÈLE le chien idéal

É1 Pour moi, le chien idéal est petit, gentil et intelligent.
É2 Pour moi aussi, le chien idéal est gentil et intelligent, mais il est grand.

1. le père idéal
2. la mère idéale
3. l'enfant idéal
4. le/la colocataire idéal/e
5. le professeur idéal
6. l'étudiant idéal
7. l'ami/e idéal/e
8. le chat idéal

Expansion: 2-8 To follow up, have each pair report back to the class and see how many people in the class have similar descriptions.

2. *Les adverbes interrogatifs*

◆ To ask a question requesting specific information, it is necessary to use an interrogative word or expression. Usually, the interrogative word or expression appears at the beginning of the question and is followed by **est-ce que/qu':**

Où est-ce que tes amis travaillent ?	*Where do your friends work?*
Quand est-ce qu' elle arrive ?	*When does she arrive?*

Some of the words or expressions frequently used to ask questions are:

comment	*how*	**Comment est-ce que** tu t'appelles ?
où	*where*	**Où est-ce qu'**il travaille ?
quand	*when*	**Quand est-ce que** tu arrives ?
pourquoi	*why*	**Pourquoi est-ce que** tu ne travailles pas ?
combien de	*how many*	**Combien d'**étudiants **est-ce qu'**il y a ?

The question **pourquoi ?** can be answered in two ways:

—**Pourquoi est-ce que** tu aimes tes amis ?	—*Why do you like your friends?*
—**Parce qu'**ils sont très amusants.	—*Because they're lots of fun.*
—**Pourquoi est-ce que** tu téléphones ?	—*Why are you calling?*
—**Pour** inviter mes amis à dîner.	—*To invite my friends to dinner.*

When used to ask *how many*, **combien** is linked to the noun by **de/d':**

Combien de frères est-ce que tu as ?	*How many brothers do you have?*
Combien d'enfants est-ce qu'ils ont ?	*How many children do they have?*

Presentation: Review formation of yes/no questions and the use of *si*, taught in Ch. 1, L. 3, before teaching this material; use exercises from those earlier sections. Present the new expressions using multiple-choice questions: *Quand est-ce que nous avons notre cours de français ? le matin ? l'après-midi ? le soir ? Où est-ce que nous avons notre cours de français ? au café ? à la maison ? à la fac ? Combien d'étudiants est-ce qu'il y a dans notre classe ? quinze ? vingt ? vingt-deux ? Comment est-ce que le prof de français s'appelle ? M. X ? Mme Y ? Mlle Z ?*

Note: Remind students that they have learned to form some information questions using simply a question word without rising intonation: *Comment tu t'appelles ? Il a quel âge ?*, but that these are very informal ways of asking a question.

Presentation: To show the two possible answers for *pourquoi*, display a humorous exchange such as: *Pourquoi est-ce que vous parlez anglais ? —Parce que nous sommes américains ; —Pour frustrer le prof.*

Note: Questions using *quel* will be treated in Ch. 8, L. 1; *qui, que,* and *quoi* will be treated in Ch. 8, L. 2.

Note: At this level, questions with inversion are presented largely for receptive control. Students should be able to recognize these questions and to be able to produce them in limited fixed expressions such as *Quel âge avez-vous ? Comment allez-vous ?* Students should be encouraged to form their questions with intonation or *est-ce que* and instructors should also make an effort to produce these types of questions in their spoken and written interactions with students.

Note: The verb *aller* is presented in L. 3 of this chapter.

- Another question construction, called *inversion*, is used in writing, in formal conversation, and in a few fixed expressions. In questions with a pronoun subject using *inversion*, the subject follows the verb and is connected to it with a hyphen. Notice that when the verb form ends in a vowel, the letter **-t-** is inserted before the pronoun and linked to it with a hyphen.

Comment **vas-tu** ?	*How are you?*
Comment **allez-vous** ?	*How are you?*
Quel âge **a-t-il** ?	*How old is he?*

Inversion is also more generally used with the verbs **aller** and **être** when the subject is a noun:

Comment **vont tes parents** ?	*How are your parents?*
Où **est ta sœur** ?	*Where's your sister?*

À vous la parole

Implementation: 2-9 To make the exercise more realistic, read each of the instructor's statements out loud, replacing the underlined material with static-like noise. For further practice, repeat this exercise and have students provide the complete questions.

2-9 Pardon ? You can't quite hear all that your instructor says, so use a question word or expression to ask for the missing information.

MODÈLE J'ai cinq cahiers.
Combien ?

1. Nous travaillons dans la salle de classe.
2. Il y a un examen mardi.
3. Il y a trois étudiants français.
4. Yannick est absent parce qu'il est malade.
5. Elle s'appelle Chloé.
6. Elle a deux sœurs.
7. Nous ouvrons le livre pour réviser un exercice.

Implementation: 2-10 Demonstrate an exaggerated pronunciation of *Ah bon ?*, and make sure students understand what it means. Challenge them to be expressive as they complete the exercise. You might put students in pairs to complete the activity.

2-10 À propos de Thomas. Your friend is telling you about her new boyfriend Thomas, and you want more details.

MODÈLE Thomas a deux colocataires.

Ah bon ? Comment est-ce qu'ils s'appellent ?
OU Ah bon ? Est-ce qu'ils sont aussi étudiants ?

1. Il est assez jeune.
2. Il n'habite pas dans la résidence (*dorm*).
3. Il est d'une famille nombreuse.
4. Il travaille le week-end.
5. Il arrive bientôt.
6. Il n'est pas en forme.
7. Il n'aime pas le sport.
8. Il a des chiens.

2-11 Au service des rencontres. Ariane has called a dating service. As you listen in on her end of the phone conversation, imagine the questions she is being asked.

Expansion: 2-11 This is good preparation for playing *Jeopardy!*, where students earn points by providing the question that elicits the information given.

Key: 2-11 1) Où est-ce que vous habitez ? 2) Combien de colocataires est-ce que vous avez ? Est-ce que vous avez des colocataires ? 3) Est-ce que vous avez des animaux familiers ? 4) Est-ce que vous travaillez ? 5) Où est-ce que vous travaillez ? 6) Quand est-ce que vous travaillez ? 7) Pourquoi est-ce que vous travaillez le week-end ? 8) Quand est-ce que vous avez des cours ?

MODÈLE Je m'appelle Ariane Patoine.
Comment vous appelez-vous, mademoiselle ?

1. J'habite à Ottawa.
2. Non, je n'ai pas de colocataire.
3. Oui, j'ai un chien et deux chats.
4. Oui, je travaille.
5. Je travaille dans un bureau.
6. Je travaille le week-end.
7. Parce que je suis étudiante.
8. J'ai des cours (*classes*) le lundi, le mardi, le mercredi et le vendredi.

2-12 Questions indiscrètes ? Interview one of your classmates, asking him/her questions about the following subjects. Report back to the class what you learned about your partner.

Expansion: 2-12 You might offer to let students ask you any questions they wish, or bring in a visitor to be interviewed.

MODÈLE la famille
Est-ce que tu as des frères ou des sœurs ?
Où est-ce qu'ils habitent ?...

la musique
Est-ce que tu aimes la musique ?
Quand est-ce que tu aimes écouter de la musique ?...

(*you report back*) Voici Ian. Il a un frère. Il habite à Baltimore. Ian n'aime pas la musique, mais...

1. la famille
2. les animaux
3. les amis
4. la musique
5. le sport

Work with a partner to see how many questions you can ask this family. For example: Est-ce que vous êtes français ? Où est-ce que vous habitez ? Comment s'appellent ..., etc.

Lisons

Stratégie

Use illustrations to predict content. To anticipate and better understand an author's descriptions in a text, make preliminary assumptions by studying the illustrations.

Preparation: 2-13 If your students are not familiar with *Les Misérables*, there are many online resources for both the show and the novel. To prepare for the reading (and the **Après avoir lu**), you could have students look for the synopsis and some details about the main characters on the Web. See the *Chez nous* Companion Website for links. You may also wish to show a short excerpt from one of the many films made of *Les Misérables*. In particular, before completing **Avant de lire**, you might show the scene where Valjean arrives at the Bishop's house; ask students to describe the characters they see.

Implementation: Avant de lire Students can work alone or in pairs. When everyone has come up with adjectives, lists could be compared in groups or though a whole-class discussion. Check to see whether some students are familiar with the story and know how these characters fit into the plot.

2-13 Les Misérables

A. Avant de lire. You are about to read an excerpt from the opening paragraphs of the novel ***Les Misérables*** by Victor Hugo, a well-known nineteenth-century French novelist, playwright, and poet. ***Les Misérables*** has been translated into many languages and has been a major musical for many years.

Three characters are introduced in the beginning of the novel, the Bishop of Digne and the two women in his household. Look at the illustrations of these three characters made by Georges Jeanniot for the first edition of ***Les Misérables***. Then make lists of adjectives you know in French that could be used to describe each person. Using the illustrations to make preliminary assumptions about these characters can help you follow the author's descriptions, even if you cannot understand every word.

L'évêque

Mme Magloire, Mlle Baptistine, Jean Valjean et l'évèque

B. En lisant. As you read the descriptions of the Bishop, Mlle Baptistine, and Mme Magloire, focus on getting a general sense of the passage. You will note that the author incorporates a number of adjectives into his description of the two women and gives an indication of each person's age. Then look for the answers to the following specific questions:

1. How old is the Bishop, M. Myriel?
2. Knowing that **moins** means *less,* indicate how old his sister is.
3. What is the name of the Bishop's sister?
4. What is the name of their household servant?
5. Give two adjectives in English to describe each woman.

En 1815, M. Charles-Francois-Bienvenu Myriel était[1] évêque de Digne. C'était un vieillard[2] d'environ soixante-quinze ans…

M. Myriel était arrivé[3] à Digne accompagné d'une vieille fille[4], Mlle Baptistine, qui était sa sœur et qui avait[5] dix ans de moins que lui.

Ils avaient[6] pour tout domestique une servante appelée Mme Magloire.

Mlle Baptistine était une personne longue, pâle, mince, douce[7]. Elle n'avait jamais[8] été jolie…

Mme Magloire était une petite vieille, blanche, grasse, replète[9], affairée, toujours haletante, à cause de son activité d'abord, ensuite à cause d'un asthme.

[1]*past tense of the verb* être [2]une personne âgée [3]*had arrived* [4]une femme d'un certain âge qui est célibataire [5]*past tense of the verb* avoir, sg. [6]*past tense of the verb* avoir, pl. [7]*gentle* [8]*never* [9]grosse

C. En regardant de plus près. Take a closer look at the following features of the text.

1. There are two words in the text that are synonyms and mean "household worker." What are they?
2. Mlle Baptistine is described with the adjective **longue**. Can you provide a synonym in French for this word? What point do you think the author is trying to make with the choice of this particular adjective?
3. Look at the adjective **affairée**. This is an adjective used to describe a very busy person. Do you know any other adjectives in French that could be used to indicate the same idea?
4. Mme Magloire is described as **haletante**. The rest of the sentence explains why she is described in this way. Given this context, and the illustration of Mme Magloire, what do you think the adjective **haletante** means?

D. Après avoir lu. How successful are the author's brief descriptions in painting a portrait of each of the three characters? Look back at the lists of adjectives you drew up in preparation for reading. How closely do your predictions coincide with what you read? Is there anything you would change in the drawings, based on the descriptions in the text?

Key: En lisant 1) 75 2) 65 3) Mlle Baptistine 4) Mme Magloire 5) Mlle Baptistine: tall, thin, pale, gentle; Mme Magloire: large, fat, busy, old, white-haired.

Key: En regardant de plus près 1) *domestique, servante* 2) *grande,* the author is probably stressing how tall and thin she is 3) *occupé/e,* maybe *stressé/e* 4) *à cause de son activité d'abord* — heavy people who are busy get out of breath easily; *ensuite à cause d'un asthme* — people with asthma sometimes have difficulty breathing.

Expansion: Help students to see how the two female characters differ in looks and manner. You could have them make a list of adjectives for each in French and identify the opposites.

Expansion: The central characters in *Les Misérables,* who are not introduced in these opening lines, include *Jean Valjean, l'Inspecteur Javert, Fantine, Marius,* and *Cosette.* You might ask whether any students have read the novel or seen a movie version or the musical and have them tell about it. Alternatively, students can look for information on the Web. As a follow-up assignment, ask students to work with a partner to prepare a two- or three-sentence description of one of the main characters mentioned above. Have them start by making a list of adjectives in French that fit the character. They should also indicate the person's age. Students may also describe the relationships between their character and other characters listed. After writing, groups may take turns sharing their description with the class; see if others can guess whom they have described.

Leçon  Nos loisirs

POINTS DE DÉPART

TEXT AUDIO CD 1 TRACK 44

Presentation: Students have already seen the verb *faire* in expressions such as *Qu'est-ce qu'il fait ?* and *Deux et deux, ça fait quatre.* Limit use here to the singular forms, *fais/fait.* The complete paradigm for *faire* is treated in the **Formes et fonctions** for this lesson.

Nos activités

Moi, je fais du sport ; je joue au foot avec des amis. On a un match tous les samedis.

Mes copains font de la musique. Ils jouent dans un groupe. Ils donnent un concert samedi soir. Mamadou joue de la guitare et Valentin joue du piano.

François et Léa organisent une fête. François fait les courses et Léa fait la cuisine.

Ma copine Amélie ne fait pas grand-chose ; elle reste à la résidence et elle regarde un film. Ses amies Vanessa et Anne-Laure jouent aux échecs.

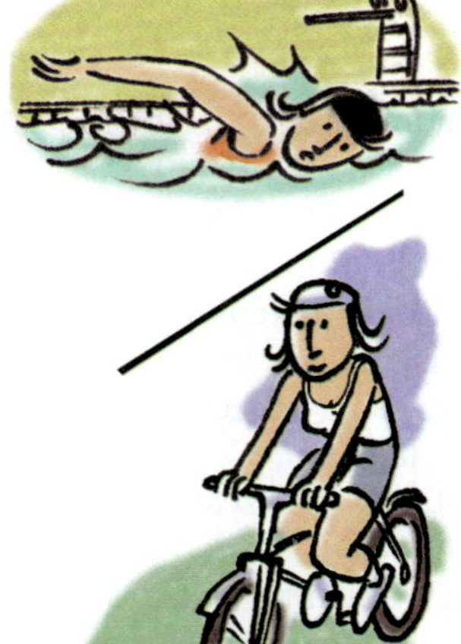

Nathalie est super sportive ; elle fait de la natation. Elle fait du vélo aussi.

Benjamin fait du bricolage et son amie Élodie fait du jardinage.

Presentation: Present this vocabulary by showing and describing the leisure activities (MFL, Ch. 2). Test comprehension by showing the unlabeled images (MFL, Ch. 2) and having students point to or mime the activity named. Use either/or questions to elicit repetitions of key vocabulary: *Il fait des courses ou il fait la cuisine ?* Have students repeat the new vocabulary, including the expressions in the boxed list. Then use visuals or miming (by the teacher or students) to get the class to recall the new vocabulary and identify activities. Use a quick substitution drill to review the forms of *-er* verbs like *jouer : Je joue au foot ; nous. —Nous jouons au foot,* etc.

Des loisirs

On fait...	On joue...
du sport de la natation, du vélo, du jogging	au football, au basket-ball, au tennis, au golf, au football américain, au rugby, au volley-ball, au hockey
On fait...	On joue...
de la musique	du piano, de la guitare, de l'harmonica, du saxophone, de la batterie, de la musique classique, du jazz, du rock
On fait...	On joue...
des courses, la cuisine, du bricolage, du jardinage	aux cartes, aux échecs, au Scrabble, au loto, aux jeux de société

Fiche pratique

Some French verbs require a preposition. For example, the verb **jouer** is followed by the preposition **à** or the preposition **de**, plus the definite article. To remember that **jouer** is followed by **à** for sports and games, and by **de** for musical instruments, memorize a couple of sentences that are personally meaningful. For example, you might come up with: **Je joue au foot** and **Mon frère joue de la guitare.**

À vous la parole

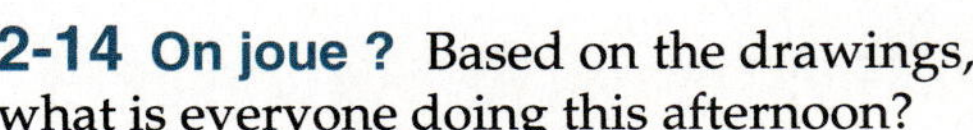

Note: The forms *le football, le basket-ball,* and *le volley-ball* are often abbreviated to *le foot, le basket,* and *le volley*. This is frequent in spoken French, particularly among students. Note that in Canada, *le football* is referred to as *le soccer, le football américain* as *le football*, and *le basket-ball* as *le ballon-panier.*

2-14 On joue ? Based on the drawings, what is everyone doing this afternoon?

MODÈLE On joue au tennis.

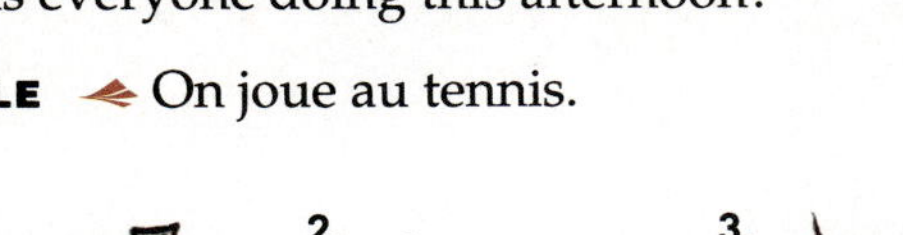

Implementation: 2-14 Show the visual cues for this exercise (MFL, Ch. 2).

1.
2.
3.
4.

5.
6.
7.
8.

2-15 Chacun à son goût. Based on the descriptions, figure out with a partner what these friends probably do in their spare time.

MODÈLE É1 Margaux est très réservée.
É2 Elle ne fait pas grand-chose ; elle reste à la maison et regarde un film.

1. Charlotte est très sociable.
2. Loïc est super sportif.
3. Delphine est une bonne musicienne.
4. Florian adore le cinéma.
5. Laurent est fanatique de jazz.
6. Céline aime préparer le dîner.
7. Alex préfère les jeux de société.
8. Rachid est très actif.
9. Anaïs est bricoleuse.

Implementation: All information is adapted from the 2007 edition of *Francoscopie* by Gérard Mermet and the most recent statistical data provided by INSEE on its Web site. Point out that *musculation* is related to the English word "muscles" and refers to strength training, and note that *gym = gymnastique* in French may refer to gymnastics but also refers to any type of physical exercise or stretching.

Vie et culture

Les loisirs des Français

The French devote more than one-third of their waking hours to leisure activities, about seven hours per day on average. They now enjoy the shortest workweek of any European country, 35 hours, and have five weeks of paid vacation each year. Typically, a little less than 20 percent of the total household budget is used for leisure activities.

The chart below indicates the percentage of French people who participated in various leisure-time activities at least once in the course of a year. Examine it with a partner: How many activities can you identify? How do these activities compare with your own leisure activities and those of people you know? How do you think a chart drawn up for North Americans would differ from this one?

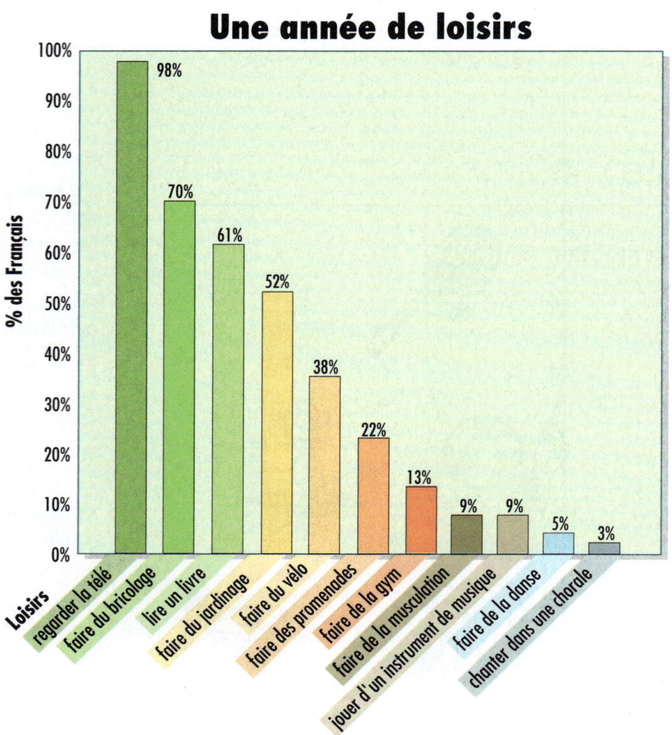

2-16 Et toi ? With the person sitting beside you, take turns telling three things you typically do on the weekend. Use only words and expressions that you know. Then share with your classmates what you have learned about your partner.

MODÈLE É1 Le week-end, je travaille un peu, je joue au basket et je fais la cuisine. Et toi ?

É2 Je ne fais pas grand-chose ; je reste à la maison et je prépare mes cours.

2-17 Un sondage. Poll your classmates to find out what percentage participate in each of the activities included in the chart in the **Vie et culture**. Designate one student in your group to ask the questions, and another to keep track of responses on the board. Compare your percentages with those presented for the French. What are your conclusions?

1. Posez des questions.

MODÈLE Qui fait du bricolage ? (*raise your hand if you do*)
Qui joue d'un instrument de musique ? (*raise your hand if you do*)

2. Comptez les réponses.
3. Annoncez les résultats.

MODÈLE Trois étudiants font du bricolage ; c'est 30 pour cent. (*if your group has 10 members*).
Un étudiant joue du piano ; c'est 10 pour cent.

Implementation: 2-17 Divide students into groups to make the data collection easier and allow more students the opportunity to participate. You may wish to postpone this activity until you have presented the conjugated forms of the verb *faire* in **Formes et fonctions 2** of this lesson to allow students to report back sentences such as *Cinq étudiants font du vélo.*

Expansion: 2-17 Discuss whether class results resemble those of the French poll. Why might they differ? Are there any activities not included in the French poll that would probably figure prominently in a poll of American leisure activities?

Sons et lettres

L'enchaînement et la liaison

Presentation: As you present this topic, review the notion of rhythmic groups.

In French, consonants that occur within a rhythmic group tend to be linked to the following syllable. This is called **enchaînement**. Because of this feature of French pronunciation, most syllables end in a vowel sound:

il a /i la/ sept amis /sɛ ta mi/ Élise arrive /e li za riv/

As you have learned, some final consonants are almost always pronounced; these include final **-c**, **-r**, **-f**, **-l**, and all consonants followed by the written letter **-e**:

Loïc ma sœur sportif Cyril arrête seize il aime

Other final consonants are pronounced only when the following word begins with a vowel. These are called *liaison consonants*, and the process that links the liaison consonant to the beginning of the next syllable is called *liaison*. Liaison consonants are usually found in grammatical endings and words such as pronouns, articles, possessive adjectives, prepositions, and numbers. You have seen the following liaison consonants:

- **-s**, **-x**, **-z** (pronounced /z/): vou**s**‿avez, le**s**‿enfants, no**s**‿amis, au**x**‿échecs, trè**s**‿aimable, si**x**‿ans, che**z**‿eux
- **-t**: c'es**t**‿un chapeau, elles son**t**‿énergiques
- **-n**: o**n**‿a, u**n**‿oncle, mo**n**‿ami

Note: Point out that liaison is never made with the final *-t* of the word *et*.

When you pronounce a liaison consonant, articulate it as part of the next word:

deux‿oncles /dø zɔ̃kl/ *not* */døz ɔ̃kl/
on a /ɔ̃ na/ *not* */ɔ̃n a/
il est‿ici /i le ti si/ *not* */il et i si/

Note: The asterisk in the examples is a linguistic convention used to show that this form is not part of a native speaker's repertoire.

À vous la parole

2-18 Contrastes : sans et avec enchaînement. Pronounce each pair of phrases. Be sure to link the final consonant of the first word to the following word when it begins with a vowel.

une copine	une amie
pour Bertrand	pour Albert
Luc parle	Luc écoute
neuf livres	neuf ordinateurs
quel cousin	quel oncle
elle fait ça	elle aime ça

2-19 Liaisons. Pronounce the liaison consonants in the following phrases. Be sure to link the consonant with the following word.

nous‿allons	vous‿écoutez
on‿a	un‿an
ils‿arrivent	elles‿habitent en ville
elles sont‿au bureau	elles vont‿à la maison
son petit‿ami	il a vingt‿ans
ton‿amie	son‿enfant

Presentation: To present this topic inductively, use examples with *jouer à, jouer de,* and *faire*. For example: *J'aime le tennis. Je joue au tennis. Ma mère adore la natation. Elle fait de la natation le lundi et le mercredi. Mon père aime bien le golf. Il joue au golf le week-end. Ma sœur adore la musique, surtout la guitare. Elle joue de la guitare dans un groupe.* Using sentences with the definite article in the presentation allows students to discover that *à* and *de* form contractions with the definite articles *le, la,* and *les*. After providing numerous examples, both orally and in written form, ask students whether they can explain the rules, and display a simple graphic with the contractions as illustrated here.

Presentation: Point out that French and English differ with regard to the types of objects used with verbs: *téléphoner à* (+ indirect object) vs. *écouter* (+ direct object). You might also want to contrast *parler à* and *parler de*.

FORMES ET FONCTIONS

1. *Les prépositions* à *et* de

- The preposition **à** generally indicates location or destination and has several English equivalents.

Elle habite **à** Paris.	*She lives* **in** *Paris.*
Il est **à** la maison.	*He's* **at** *the house.*
Elle va **à** une fête.	*She's going* **to** *a party.*

As you've seen, the preposition **à** is also used in the expression **jouer à**, *to play (sports or games).*

Nous jouons **au** tennis le lundi.	*We play tennis on Mondays.*
Ils jouent **aux** cartes le samedi soir.	*They play cards on Saturday evenings.*

With other verbs, **à** introduces the indirect object, usually a person who receives the action.

parler	Cédric **parle à** la petite fille.	*Cédric's speaking to the little girl.*
téléphoner	Nous **téléphonons à** nos amis.	*We're phoning our friends.*
donner	Elle **donne** la photo **à** son ami.	*She gives her boyfriend the photo.*

- **À** combines with the definite articles **le** and **les** to form contractions. There is no contraction with **la** or **l'**.

à + le → au	Il joue **au** golf.	*He plays golf.*
à + les → aux	Ils jouent **aux** échecs avec des amis.	*They play chess with friends.*
à + la → à la	Je reste **à la** maison vendredi soir.	*I'm staying home on Friday evening.*
à + l' → à l'	Je parle **à l'**oncle de Simon.	*I'm talking to Simon's uncle.*

- The preposition **de/d'** indicates where someone or something comes from.

Mon copain Justin est **de** Montréal.	*My boyfriend Justin is from Montreal.*
Elle arrive **de** France demain.	*She arrives from France tomorrow.*

As you've seen, **de** is also used in the expression **jouer de**, *to play* (*music or a musical instrument*).

Son ami joue **du** piano dans un groupe.	*Her friend plays piano in a group.*
Lui, il joue **de l'**harmonica.	*He plays the harmonica.*

De/d' also is used to indicate possession or other close relationships.

C'est le frère **du** professeur.	*It's the teacher's brother.*
Voilà le livre **de** Kelly.	*There's Kelly's book.*

- **De** combines with the definite articles **le** and **les** to form contractions. There is no contraction with **la** or **l'**.

de + le → du	Mon amie fait **du** jogging.	*My girlfriend goes jogging.*
de + les → des	On parle **des** projets pour le week-end.	*We're talking about plans for the weekend.*
de + la → de la	Moi, je joue **de la** guitare.	*I play the guitar.*
de + l' → de l'	Il joue **de l'**accordéon.	*He plays the accordion.*

À vous la parole

2-20 Ça cause. Tell what today's subjects of conversation are for Camille and her friends.

MODÈLE la copine de Bruno
→ Elles parlent de la copine de Bruno.

1. le professeur de français
2. le match de basket le week-end dernier (*last*)
3. les problèmes du campus
4. la nouvelle (*new*) colocataire de Camille
5. l'oncle d'Antoine
6. les devoirs d'anglais
7. le dernier film des frères Coen

Initial practice: Begin practice with simple substitution drills: *Il joue au foot ; loto. —Il joue au loto ; échecs ; basket ; cartes ; tennis ; jeux de société*, etc.; *Je joue du piano ; guitare. —Je joue de la guitare ; batterie ; harmonica ; saxophone ; musique classique ; jazz*, etc.

Variation: 2-21 Have students suggest other famous athletes, chefs, and musicians. **Key:** 1) Il joue de la guitare/Il chante. 2) Il fait du vélo. 3) Elle joue au foot. 4) Elle fait la cuisine. 5) Elle joue au tennis. 6) Elle joue du piano/Elle chante. 7) Il joue du saxophone. 8) Il joue au golf.

2-21 Des célébrités. What do these famous people do?

MODÈLE Kobe Bryant
➤ Il joue au basket-ball.

1. John Mayer
2. Lance Armstrong
3. Mia Hamm
4. Rachael Ray
5. Serena Williams
6. Alicia Keys
7. Kenny G.
8. Tiger Woods

Implementation: 2-22 Use as a mixing activity; impose a time limit, then have students ask questions to get missing information: *Qui joue de l'harmonica ?* Ask follow-up questions: *Tu joues dans un groupe ?*, etc.

2-22 Trouvez une personne qui... Circulate in the classroom to find someone who does each of the things listed. When your instructor calls time, compare notes to see who came closest to completing the list.

MODÈLE joue de l'harmonica

É1 Tu joues de l'harmonica ?
É2 Non. (*You ask another person.*)
OU Oui. (*You write down this person's name.*)

1. fait du vélo
2. fait de la natation
3. reste à la maison le dimanche soir
4. joue au golf le week-end
5. joue du piano
6. téléphone à ses parents le week-end
7. parle au professeur en français
8. joue du saxophone
9. joue souvent (*often*) aux cartes
10. fait du jardinage

Presentation: Present the verb inductively through a short narrative: *Le week-end, je fais des courses et je fais du jardinage. Mon mari fait du bricolage ; les enfants font du sport, etc. Et vous, vous faites du sport ?* Ask students to summarize the forms, and display the verb chart, re-modeling pronunciation. Remind students of where they have seen this verb before: in arithmetic problems and the question *Qu'est-ce qu'il fait ?*, as well as in the lexical items taught in the **Points de départ**.

2. *Le verbe* faire

- The verb **faire** (*to make, to do*) is used in a wide variety of expressions. Here are the forms of this irregular verb.

FAIRE *to make, to do*			
SINGULIER		**PLURIEL**	
je	fais	nous	**faisons**
tu	fais	vous	**faites**
il / elle / on	fai**t**	ils / elles	**font**

- A question using **faire** does not necessarily require using **faire** in the answer:

—Qu'est-ce que tu **fais** samedi ?	—*What are you doing on Saturday?*
—Je joue au golf.	—*I'm playing golf.*

- A form of the preposition **de** is used with the verb **faire** in some expressions.

—Elle fait **du** sport.	—*She plays sports.*
—Moi aussi, je fais **de la** natation.	—*Me too, I swim.*

- **Faire** is used in many idiomatic expressions related to everyday activities; it is one of the most common and useful French verbs.

Tu fais du sport ?	*Do you play sports?*
Nous faisons une promenade.	*We're taking a walk.*
On fait de la marche.	*We walk (for exercise).*
Elle aime faire la cuisine.	*She likes to cook.*
Il fait des courses.	*He's running errands.*
Ils font du jogging le matin.	*They jog in the morning.*
Vous faites de la danse ?	*Do you study dance?*
Je fais du français.	*I study French.*

Note: The expressions *faire une promenade* and *faire de la marche* can both be translated into English as "to take a walk," however, the nuances are quite different; *une promenade* is a leisurely walk or stroll, while *la marche* refers to vigorous walking, such as for exercise.

Ils font une promenade le dimanche après-midi. Est-ce que vous faites une promenade le week-end ?

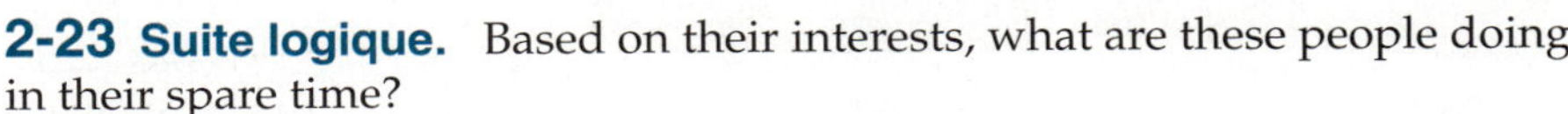

À vous la parole

Initial practice: Begin practice with a discrimination drill: one person, or more than one? *Elle fait des courses. Ils font une promenade. Il fait de l'anglais. Elles font du français. Elles font la cuisine. Elle fait du vélo. Ils font du jogging. Il fait du sport. Elles font de la musique*, etc. Follow with a simple substitution drill: *Je fais du foot ; vous. —Vous faites du foot ; toi ; eux*, etc.

2-23 Suite logique. Based on their interests, what are these people doing in their spare time?

MODÈLE Sylvie aime le ballet.
Elle fait de la danse.

1. Nous arrivons au supermarché.
2. Florent et Hamid aiment la nature.
3. Tu adores préparer le dîner.
4. Vous êtes fanatique de jazz.
5. Ludovic aime travailler dans le jardin.
6. Hélène et Béa sont vraiment sportives.
7. J'aime travailler à la maison.
8. David et moi sommes très paresseux.

2-24 Et vous ? Discuss with a partner your usual activities for each of the categories proposed.

MODÈLE la musique

É1 Je ne fais pas de musique, mais j'ai un lecteur CD et beaucoup de CD ; j'aime le jazz.

É2 Je fais de la musique ; je joue du piano et de la guitare.

1. la musique
2. le sport
3. les jeux
4. la cuisine
5. des travaux à la maison

Implementation: 2-24 Point out the use of *pas de* in negative expressions, as shown in the model. Have students report back what they found out from their partner. Compare answers for all class members. As an additional exercise, put up a frequency scale and let students indicate how often they do the things you ask about.

Preparation: Preview the activity by finding out which Francophone athletes students are already familiar with — have they heard of Zinédine Zidane, do they know that Tony Parker of the San Antonio Spurs is French? The theme of sports is further developed in the **Venez chez nous !** section of this chapter.

Script: Écoutons Tony Parker est un Français qui joue au basket dans le NBA. Il est né en 1982 en Belgique. Il est brun et assez grand. Tony est très sportif. Il aime regarder le football, le hockey et le base-ball, et il joue au tennis. Il aime bien la musique américaine et les fêtes entre amis, et il adore les jeux électroniques. Il a deux frères qui jouent aussi au basket-ball.

Hoda Lattaf joue au football pour l'équipe féminine de France et l'Olympique de Lyon. Elle est née au Maroc en 1978. Elle est brune, de taille moyenne, mince et très musclée. Elle n'aime pas beaucoup regarder le football à la télé ; elle préfère voir des amis et aller à la piscine. Elle a cinq frères.

Guillaume Latendresse joue au hockey pour l'équipe des Canadiens. C'est un très jeune joueur ; il est né le 24 mai 1987 à Sainte-Catherine au Québec. Il est blond, grand, musclé et très fort. Il est motivé et sérieux. Il aime beaucoup jouer au hockey et passer du temps avec sa famille. Son frère aîné, qui s'appelle Oliver, joue au hockey aussi.

Écoutons

2-25 Des portraits d'athlètes

A. Avant d'écouter. Look at the photos of three Francophone athletes. Which sport does each play? Can you think of two or three adjectives to describe each athlete? Have you ever seen any of these athletes in person or on television?

Tony PARKER

Hoda LATTAF

Guillaume LATENDRESSE

B. En écoutant. Listen to the descriptions of the three athletes and fill in the missing information in the chart below.

Name	Sport	Age	Appearance	Favorite Activities and Family Information
Tony PARKER				
Hoda LATTAF				
Guillaume LATENDRESSE				

C. Après avoir écouté. Now use the completed chart to summarize in a couple of sentences the information about the athlete who most appeals to you. Then add a sentence telling why this person is interesting to you.

MODÈLE Mon athlète préféré est... Je trouve cette personne intéressante parce qu'il/elle...

Leçon 3 Où est-ce qu'on va ce week-end ?

POINTS DE DÉPART

Destinations diverses

Presentation: Present the vocabulary showing the labeled drawing of the small town (MFL, Ch. 2); paraphrase or have students listen to the **Points de départ** text. Have students help describe in simple terms activities at each location, using *-er* verbs they know. Check comprehension by having students point to the places you name or describe. Have students repeat key words (as you point to the drawing): *C'est la librairie ou la bibliothèque ? — C'est la librairie.* The Ch. 6 **Observons** video segment (*Visitons Seillans*) is a visit to the small town of *Seillans*; play this sequence without sound to allow students to see what a small town in France looks like. Point out that the verbs *manger* and *nager* have a spelling peculiarity in the first-person plural, reflecting the pronunciation: *nous mang**eons***, *nous nag**eons***.

Le week-end, qu'est-ce que tu fais ? Tu aimes nager ? Alors tu vas probablement à la piscine. Tu pratiques un autre sport ? Alors tu vas probablement au stade, au gymnase ou au parc. Tu aimes les activités culturelles ? Tu vas peut-être voir un film au cinéma ou une exposition au musée ; ou bien tu assistes à une pièce, un ballet ou un concert au théâtre. Tu cherches un livre ? Voilà la bibliothèque ou bien la librairie. Tu ne fais pas la cuisine ? Alors va au restaurant, au café ou chez un ami pour manger.

Note: Point out that the word *église* in French usually refers to a Catholic church; a Protestant church is *un temple*. Jewish people worship in *une synagogue* and Muslims in *une mosquée*.

le stade
la piscine municipale
l'église
la mairie
le gymnase
LA PISCINE MUNICIPALE
MAIRIE
le parc
le monument aux morts
la place
le cinéma
Le Cinéma
Le Théâtre
Le Musée d'art
Exposition de Photos
BIBLIOTHÈQUE MUNICIPALE
le théâtre
le marché
le musée
la bibliothèque municipale
LA GARE SNCF
le café
Chez Pierrette
la librairie
l'hôtel
la gare
le café
le restaurant

Note: The presentation and the exercises that follow use only the singular forms of *aller : je vais, tu vas.* The complete paradigm is taught in the **Formes et fonctions** section of this lesson.

Vie et culture

Les petites villes

Small towns in France have a traditional structure. At the center is the Catholic church; a square, often with a veterans' memorial, is nearby. This is usually the location for the open-air market. The town hall is also in a central location. Older towns and villages often still have small merchants clustered around this central area. In many cases, a train station and a modest hotel are also close to the town center. Most communities also provide municipal sports centers for their residents. Young people and adults can swim at **la piscine municipale**, play basketball or take an exercise class at a local **gymnase**, or watch soccer games at **le stade municipal**.

Look at these maps of the town of Richelieu, population 2,194. Locate the following places: **la gare, le stade, la piscine, le gymnase, l'église, la mairie, la bibliothèque, la Place du Marché**.

Presentation: Help students use cognates and their world knowledge to figure out other locations on the map such as *le Trésor Public*, *l'Office de Tourisme*, and *La Poste*. To encourage cross-cultural comparisons, ask students how this layout corresponds to the layout of a small town that they may know or have visited. The town of Richelieu, located in the *département d'Indre et Loire*, was built under the direction of the Cardinal Richelieu between 1631 and 1642 by the same architect, Jacques Lemercier, who designed *la Sorbonne* and *le Palais-Royal* in Paris. Cardinal Richelieu was the powerful prime minister to Louis XIII. Point out the symmetry and other unique features of this town. Visit the *Chez nous* Companion Website for interesting links to sites about the history of Richelieu and the Cardinal.

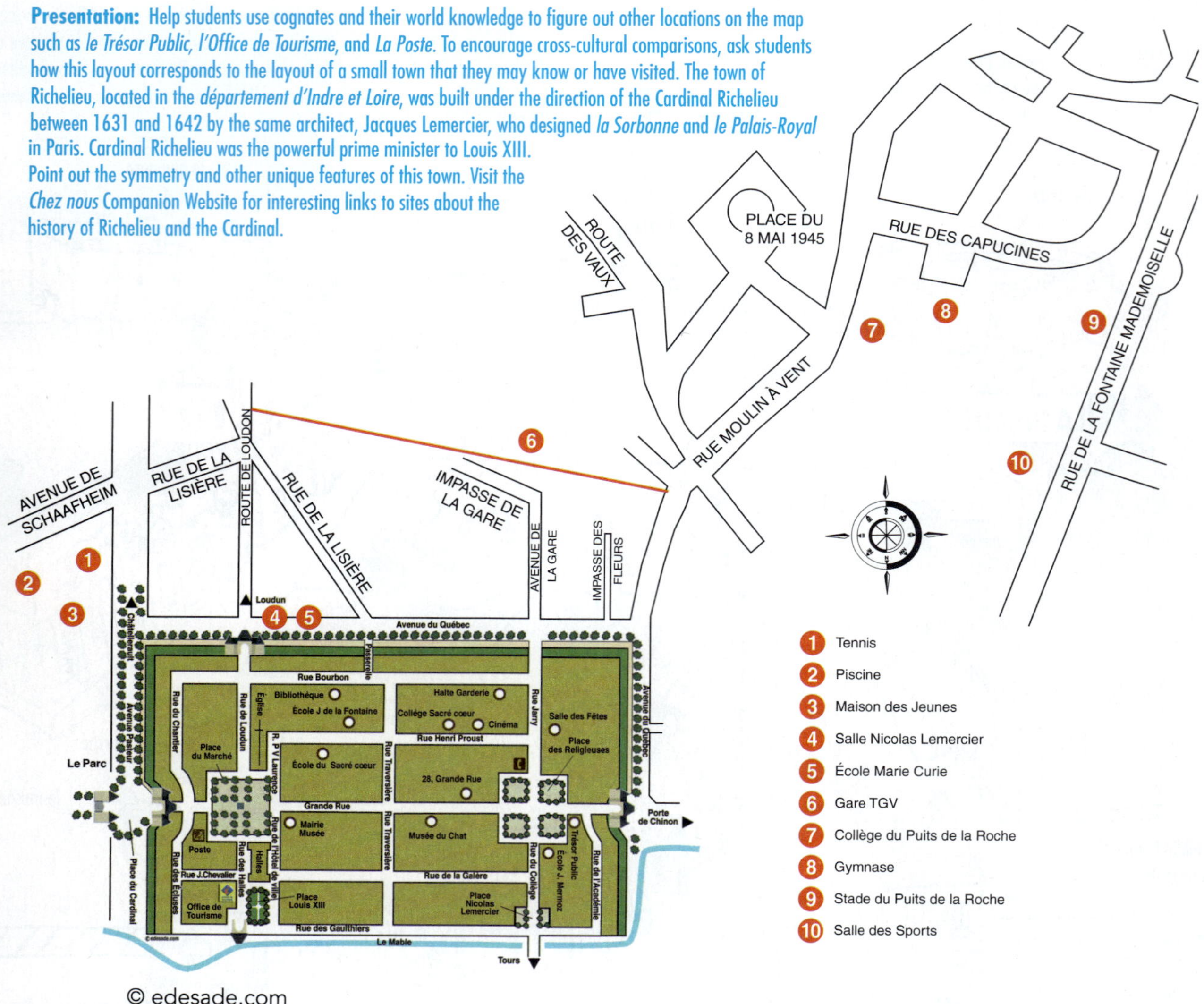

Which of these places are located in the **centre-ville** and which are located further out? Why do you think that might be? What other places indicated on the map can you identify?

ET VOUS ?

1. Is there a traditional structure for small towns in North America? Does this vary from region to region? Why do you think North American towns tended to evolve as they did? Compare your ideas with those of a partner.
2. What basic similarities and differences can you identify in the layout of traditional town centers in North America and France? How would you explain them?

Key: Et vous ? In many small towns in the U.S., the county courthouse is located in the center of town and the downtown is arranged around this square. In the Midwest, small towns are laid out in a grid. In the east, small towns often include a central green space, referred to as the mall or the commons. The layout of many towns probably followed the principles of organization that the settlers brought with them from their home countries. For example, towns in the original thirteen colonies tend to resemble towns in England.

Ville de Richelieu, vue aérienne. Est-ce que vous pouvez idéntifier la Place du Marché ? la bibliothèque ? le cinéma ? la Place Louis XIII ?

Preparation: Before beginning the exercises, review the preposition *à* using a quick substitution drill: *Il est au café ; piscine. —Il est à la piscine,* etc.

À vous la parole

2-26 Dans quel endroit ? Where would you hear people saying this?

MODÈLE « Du rosbif, s'il vous plaît. »
au restaurant

1. « Tu nages bien, toi ! »
2. « Le match commence dans dix minutes. »
3. « Regarde, c'est un mariage ! La mariée et le marié arrivent. »
4. « C'est mon ballet préféré. »
5. « Où sont les biographies, s'il vous plaît ? »
6. « On regarde la télé ce soir ? »
7. « La musique est excellente ce soir. »
8. « Encore un café ? »
9. « J'aime beaucoup cette statue. »
10. « C'est combien pour ces deux livres et un cahier ? »

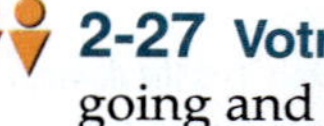

2-27 Votre itinéraire. With your partner, take turns telling where you're going and what you're doing this weekend. Then summarize your plans for your classmates.

MODÈLE É1 Ce week-end, je vais au restaurant. Mon copain et moi, nous dînons ensemble. Et toi ?
É2 Moi, je vais au musée. Il y a une exposition de photos.

2-28 Vos endroits préférés. Discuss with a partner your favorite place for each activity listed. How similar—or dissimilar—are your preferences?

MODÈLE pour dîner ?
É1 Moi, j'aime dîner chez ma mère. Et toi ?
É2 Moi, j'aime dîner au restaurant.

1. pour dîner ?
2. pour travailler ?
3. pour voir un film ?
4. pour discuter avec des amis ?
5. pour pratiquer un sport ?
6. pour écouter de la musique ?

Presentation: To present this verb inductively, provide a personal narrative and ask students questions about where they go: *Le week-end, je fais beaucoup de choses. Le matin, je vais au marché et après au café. L'après-midi, je vais au stade pour regarder un match de foot et quelquefois à la piscine pour nager. Et samedi soir, je vais souvent au ciné ; et vous ? Vous allez au marché ? au café ? au stade ? à la bibliothèque ? Et le soir ?,* etc. Have students summarize forms and display forms and sample sentences on a slide or transparency. You may wish to present the verb *aller* in its simple construction first and then present its use in the *futur proche* later in the lesson or in a subsequent lesson.

FORMES ET FONCTIONS

1. *Le verbe* aller *et le futur proche*

- The irregular verb **aller** means *to go.*

Je **vais** à la librairie.	*I'm going to the bookstore.*
Tu **vas** au ciné avec nous ?	*You're going to the movies with us?*

- You have already used **aller** in greetings and commands.

Comment ça **va** ?	*How are things?*
Comment **allez**-vous ?	*How are you?*
Allez au tableau !	*Go to the board!*

ALLER *to go*	
SINGULIER	**PLURIEL**
je **vais**	nous‿**allons**
tu **vas**	vous‿**allez**
il / elle / on **va**	ils / elles **vont**

- To express future actions that are intended or certain to take place, use the present tense of **aller** and an infinitive. This construction is called **le futur proche** (*the immediate future*). In negative sentences, place **ne ... pas** around the form of **aller**; the infinitive does not change.

Je **vais travailler** ce soir.	*I'm going to work this evening.*
Il **va téléphoner** à son père.	*He's going to call his father.*
Tu **ne vas pas danser** ?	*You're not going to dance?*

Presentation: To introduce the *futur proche,* tell students what you will be doing this afternoon, this evening, or this weekend. Ask them if you are speaking about the past, the present, or the future; then have them identify the forms that are used to express the notion of future, and ask them to explain how it is formed in French.

- To express a future action you may also simply use the present tense of a verb and an adverb referring to the future.

Mon copain arrive **demain**.	*My boyfriend arrives tomorrow.*
Tu joues **ce soir** ?	*Are you playing tonight?*

Here are some useful expressions referring to the immediate future:

ce soir	*tonight*
demain	*tomorrow*
ce week-end	*this weekend*
bientôt	*soon*
la semaine prochaine	*next week*
le mois prochain	*next month*
l'été prochain	*next summer*
l'année prochaine	*next year*

Presentation: Present these expressions by asking students to provide relevant examples for each, based on the actual date. For example, if you present this on Tuesday, October 3, for *ce soir* you could write *mardi 3 octobre à 6 heures ; demain* would be *mercredi 4 octobre,* and so forth.

À vous la parole

2-29 Maintenant ou plus tard ? Look at these statements about the activities of Sévérine, Yann, and their friends and decide if each activity is occurring now (**maintenant**) or will occur later (**plus tard**).

	Maintenant, ils	Plus tard, ils
MODÈLE … vont à la bibliothèque.	✓	____
1. … vont nager un peu.	____	____
2. … vont manger.	____	____
3. … vont au gymnase.	____	____
4. … vont au cinéma.	____	____
5. … vont travailler toute la journée.	____	____
6. … vont faire du jogging.	____	____
7. … vont au parc.	____	____
8. … vont voir un film.	____	____

Based on your answers above, are the friends busier now, or will they be busier later?

2-30 Où aller ? Based on their interests, where are these people probably going?

MODÈLE Anne adore nager.
→ Elle va à la piscine.

1. Rémi aime le basket.
2. Nous aimons les films.
3. Tu désires manger des spaghettis.
4. M. et Mme Dupont aiment l'art moderne.
5. Vous adorez jouer au foot.
6. Sandrine aime les livres historiques.
7. J'aime beaucoup parler avec mes amis.
8. Sophie et Angélique adorent faire de la marche le matin.

2-31 Les habitudes. Tell a partner where you usually go at the times indicated, and why.

MODÈLE le samedi soir

É1 Je vais au ciné avec mes amis pour voir un film.
É2 Moi, je vais à une fête chez des amis pour manger et pour écouter de la musique.

1. le lundi matin
2. le vendredi soir
3. le jeudi après-midi
4. le mercredi soir
5. le dimanche matin
6. le samedi matin
7. le samedi après-midi

Note: 2-29 is a comprehension-based activity focusing on the difference in the use of *aller* to express the present and the *futur proche*; 2-30 and 2-31 practice the present tense of *aller*, and 2-32 targets the *futur proche*. The additional activity, **Quoi faire ?** suggested in the marginal notes may be used after 2-29 to prepare students for 2-32.

Initial practice: Begin practice with a discrimination drill: one person, or more than one? *Il va au ciné. Elles vont chez elles. Elles vont à la bibliothèque. Ils vont à l'hôtel. Il va au parc. Elle va au gymnase. Ils vont au théâtre. Elles vont au restaurant*, etc. Follow with a substitution drill: *Je vais bien ; vous. — Vous allez bien*, etc., and then complete exercises 2-30 and 2-31 to practice *aller* in the present tense.

Implementation: 2-29 This activity focuses on the form distinction between the verb *aller* when it simply means 'to go' and when it is used in the *futur proche* construction to refer to a future event. It should be used as the initial exercise after presenting the use of *aller* in the *futur proche* construction, whether this is day 2 of your lesson or during the same day *aller* is presented.

Additional activity: Use this simple exercise after the comprehension-based activity in 2-29 and/or before 2-32. Here students repeat the subject and the verb and add an infinitive to practice the *futur proche*.

Quoi faire ? Based on where they're going, tell what these people are going to do.

MODÈLE → Je vais à la bibliothèque.
→ Je vais travailler.

1. Nous allons à la piscine.
2. Tu vas au stade ?
3. Elles vont au restaurant.
4. Vous allez à la résidence.
5. Christine va au ciné.
6. Je vais au bureau du professeur.
7. Marc va au gymnase.
8. Jean et Louise vont à la librairie.

Implementation: 2-31 Have students work in pairs or small groups to come up with imaginative responses, then compare notes.

 **2-32 Vos projets.** Interview a partner about his/her plans, and report back to the class what you have found out.

MODÈLE cet après-midi

É1 Qu'est-ce que tu vas faire cet après-midi ?
É2 Cet après-midi je vais travailler. Et toi ?
É1 Mon camarade et moi, nous allons jouer au tennis.

1. cet après-midi
2. ce soir
3. demain
4. ce week-end
5. le semestre/trimestre prochain
6. l'été prochain
7. l'année prochaine

Implementation: 2-32 As time permits, this activity can either be used as an extended interview, or you may limit it to one or two items for students to discuss, then report back to the class as a whole.

2. *L'impératif*

- To make a suggestion or a request, or to tell someone to do something, the *imperative* forms of a verb—without subject pronouns—may be used.
  - To address someone with whom you are on informal terms, the imperative is the same as the **tu** form of the verb in the present tense. Note, however, that for **-er** verbs (including **aller**), the final **-s** is dropped in the written forms.

Ferme la porte !	*Shut the door!*
Va au tableau !	*Go to the blackboard!*
Écris ton nom !	*Write your name!*
Fais tes devoirs !	*Do your homework!*

  - To address more than one person or someone with whom you are on formal terms, the imperative is the same as the **vous** form of the verb in the present tense.

Parlez plus fort !	*Speak louder!*
Écoutez-moi !	*Listen to me!*
Lisez à haute voix !	*Read aloud!*
Dites-moi votre nom !	*Tell me your name!*

  - To make a suggestion to a group of which you are part, the imperative is the same as the **nous** form of the verb in the present tense.

Jouons aux cartes.	*Let's play cards.*
Allons au cinéma.	*Let's go to the movies.*
Faisons une promenade.	*Let's go for a walk.*

- To be more polite, add **s'il te plaît** or **s'il vous plaît** as appropriate:

Ouvrez la fenêtre, **s'il vous plaît**.	*Open the window, please.*
Parle plus fort, **s'il te plaît**.	*Please speak louder.*

- To tell someone not to do something, put **ne** (**n'**) before the verb and **pas** after it:

Ne regarde **pas** la télé !	*Don't watch TV!*
N'écris **pas** en anglais !	*Don't write in English!*
N'oubliez **pas** vos devoirs !	*Don't forget your homework!*

Presentation: To present, review classroom commands, using first the *vous* form; next, call on students individually and use the *tu* form. Have students explain the difference in the two forms. Display examples of the imperative forms, and point out the written forms.

Note: The imperative forms for *être* and *avoir* are irregular and relatively infrequent. We suggest not presenting these forms here; you may wish to mention them when the subjunctive of irregular verbs is presented in Ch. 10, L. 1.

À vous la parole

Initial practice: Begin practice with a discrimination drill: have students decide whether they hear a command to one person or to a group: *Ferme la porte ! Parlons français ! Écoutez le professeur ! Travaille plus ! Va à la bibliothèque ! Mangeons à la cafétéria ! Ne parlez pas anglais ! Allons au cinéma ! Écrivez le devoir en français !*, etc. Follow with substitution drills; singular to plural: *Va au bureau ! —Allez au bureau !*; plural command to suggestion: *Allez au bureau ! —Allons au bureau !* In another simple exercise, have students associate verbs in the command form with nouns: *la fenêtre ? —Fermez la fenêtre ! Ouvrez la fenêtre !*

2-33 Impératifs. Use appropriate forms of the imperative to make requests to your friends and your instructor.

MODÈLE Dites à un/e ami/e de ne pas regarder la télé.
Ne regarde pas la télé !

Dites à un/e ami/e...

1. d'écouter le professeur
2. de fermer la porte
3. de ne pas parler anglais
4. de ne pas manger en classe

Demandez à votre professeur (n'oubliez pas d'être poli/e !)...

5. de répéter
6. de parler plus fort
7. de ne pas fermer la porte
8. de ne pas lire en anglais

Proposez à vos amis...

9. de jouer au basket
10. de faire du jogging
11. d'aller au cinéma
12. de ne pas travailler

Implementation: 2-34 Students can first work in pairs to come up with ideas. Variations: give advice to a fellow student who wants to improve his/her grade; give advice to someone who wants to relax over the weekend.

2-34 Pourquoi pas ? You'd like to do something different in French class today. What can you suggest to your instructor? Choose from this list of possibilities and include some of your own ideas as well: **aller**, **écouter**, **écrire**, **faire**, **jouer**, **oublier**, **parler**, **regarder**.

MODÈLE écrire
Écrivons un poème.

Variation: 2-35 As a fun variation, sit down in a chair facing your class. Tell students that they should give you commands. Students enjoy turning the tables and having the teacher do the things that they are frequently asked to do.

2-35 Situations. With a partner, give examples of a request or suggestion you'd be likely to hear in each situation. How many examples can you come up with?

MODÈLE une mère à son enfant
Écoute, mon chéri (*dear*).
ET Fais tes devoirs.

1. un professeur aux étudiants
2. une étudiante à un/e ami/e
3. un étudiant au professeur
4. un étudiant à son copain
5. un entraîneur (*coach*) de basket à ses joueurs
6. votre professeur, à vous
7. vos parents, à vous

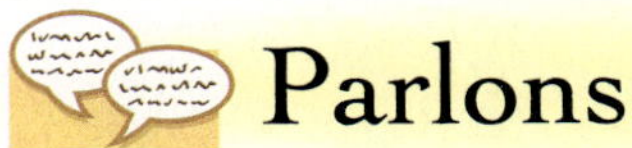

Parlons

2-36 Jouons ensemble

A. Avant de parler. To prepare for this game, a form of bingo, think about the questions that you will need to ask in order to find people who do the activities shown in the squares.

B. Parlons. Now, circulate among your classmates, asking them questions with the aim of completing a row (up, down, across, or diagonally). The first person to fill in a classmate's name in each square of a row is the winner.

MODÈLES É1 Est-ce que tu travailles à la bibliothèque le soir ?
É2 Non, je travaille chez moi. (*ask another student*)
É1 Est-ce que tu travailles à la bibliothèque le soir ?
É3 Oui, j'étudie à la Bibliothèque McKeldin le soir. (*write his or her name in the square*)

C. Après avoir parlé. Who first called "bingo"? Have that person check his or her responses by telling the class whose name was filled in for each activity. Play another round!

Implementation: Avant de parler You may provide students with a copy of the game board. Have students examine the game board and generate a few of the questions before beginning, so that you are sure they can complete the activity successfully.

l	o	t	o
aller au gymnase deux fois (*times*) par semaine	travailler à la bibliothèque le soir	aller à l'église le dimanche matin	pratiquer un sport trois fois par semaine
jouer du saxophone	chercher des livres à la librairie quelquefois	aller au musée quelquefois	aller au cinéma le week-end
aller souvent chez des amis	aller au supermarché le samedi	nager à la piscine municipale	aller au stade le samedi après-midi
aller au théâtre une fois par semestre	jouer au tennis le week-end	ne pas faire grand-chose le week-end	dîner au restaurant deux fois par semaine

Venez chez nous ! Vive le sport !

Preparation: Preview the lesson by discussing sporting preferences, both as fans and active participants, among the students in your class. Then find out what sports events in the Francophone world students are already familiar with—have any of them attended or watched the World Cup, the French Open, or the *Tour de France*? Show the video montage (*Vive le sport !*); have students identify the various sports being practiced in this fast-paced segment.

Les Bleus fêtent leur victoire après la Coupe des Confédérations en 2003.

Les sports dans le monde francophone

From Marseille to Madagascar, from Martinique to Morocco, sports are a unifying element in Francophone life. For example, in July, Europeans are glued to the TV watching the international bike race **Le Tour de France**. Throughout the year, you can find people all around the Francophone world listening to an exciting soccer match on the radio. French victories in the 1998 World Soccer Cup, the 2000 European Soccer Cup, the 2001 and 2003 Confederations Cups, and in the semi-finals of the 2006 World Soccer Cup fueled feelings of national honor and pride and great celebrations on the Champs-Élysées and throughout France. Traditionally, the players on the French national team have been ethnically diverse, and the team has been held up as a model of multi-cultural France. Several members of the current national team were born in Africa or the French Antilles, and eleven more were born in France to parents of North African, African, or Caribbean origin. This diversity has been a source of team strength as well as a buffer against intolerance.

Key: Et vous ? 1) In many small towns in the U.S., the fortunes of the local high school teams are closely monitored with extensive print and broadcast coverage that helps unify the community. In college towns, and in cities where there is a pro team, the same also holds true. The Olympic teams function in the same way for the country as a whole.
2) Some students may answer "yes" while others might argue that diverse teams may play into stereotypes about the perceived strength of one race over another or that the benefits might only accrue to the actual teammates and not to the spectators. 3) the Super Bowl, NCAA sports tournaments, the U.S. Open, the Indianapolis 500, the World Series.

Et vous ?

1. Are sports a unifying element in North America, as they are in Francophone countries? Are victories a source of national pride and celebration?
2. In your opinion, do ethnically diverse teams function as a buffer against intolerance? Why or why not?
3. Are there sports and sporting events in North America whose popularity rivals that of soccer in the Francophone world? If so, which ones?

Lisons

2-37 Le football : phénomène social.

Soccer is one of the most popular sports in France, and there are many professional soccer teams scattered throughout France. Many of France's top players also play for teams in other countries, such as Arsenal and Chelsea in England or Barcelona in Spain, but return to France to play on the national team during international competitions.

A. Avant de lire. Look closely at the title of this text about soccer fans in France and then at the accompanying photo in order to answer the following questions.

1. What is the title of the text? What does it suggest about the content of the reading?
2. How do you think the accompanying photo relates to the title of the text?
3. Does the accompanying photo remind you of any sporting events or behaviors that you have witnessed? Share your experience(s) with a partner.

B. En lisant. As you read the text, look for answers to the following questions.

1. How many fans go to soccer games each week?
2. Are soccer matches in France attended primarily by men or women? What percent of the fans are men?
3. Besides watching their favorite team win, what else are fans interested in, according to the author?
4. What are some of the signs of "belonging" cited by the author?
5. According to the author, victories by national teams are even more special than those of local teams. Why is this so?

Le spectacle sportif est un moyen[1] d'appartenance[2]...

Plus de 200.000 supporteurs vont chaque semaine dans les stades de football... ; la très grande majorité (90 %) sont des hommes, mais les femmes sont de plus en plus nombreuses...

La motivation de ces *aficionados* n'est pas seulement[3] de voir gagner « leur » équipe[4] mais aussi d'être membre d'un groupe... Il y a des signes concrets et évidents : vêtements[5], accessoires et objets aux couleurs de l'équipe ; emplacements réservés aux différents clubs de supporteurs dans le stade ; pratiques et rituels... ; réunions d'avant et d'après-match...

Ainsi, les supporteurs ne sont pas seulement spectateurs... mais aussi acteurs. Les grandes compétitions représentent... des moments intenses de la vie collective. Si la réussite[6] d'un champion est un évènement[7], l'exploit d'une équipe nationale a un caractère unique. Ainsi les titres obtenus par les Bleus à la Coupe du monde de football en 1998 et à l'Euro en 2000, puis leur qualification en finale de la Coupe du monde de 2006... sont des moments exceptionnels pour l'ensemble des Français, même pour les gens qui n'aiment pas le sport.

Adapté de G. Mermet *Francoscopie 2007*, p. 454. © Larousse 2006.

[1]*means* [2]*belonging* [3]*only* [4]*to see their team win* [5]*clothes* [6]*success* [7]*event*

Stratégie

Focusing on the title of a text can help you to anticipate and understand the content. Use the title to define the likely focus before you begin to read.

Preparation: 2-37 To preview this reading, find out if any of the students in your class are fans of a particular professional or collegiate sports team; ask them if they attend the games and if there are any rituals associated with them. If your school has a strong football tradition, you may want to mention the pre-game tailgates, any special cheers, special attire fans wear, and so forth. Compare what students are familiar with to the French soccer fan in the photo. This reading discusses fan behavior in connection with soccer in France. Help students to understand that although the sports are different, many of the rituals associated with fan behavior are similar and that big victories (such as the World Series or the Super Bowl in the U.S.) are celebrated as a unifying element, even by people who do not normally follow sports. Refer students to the *Chez nous* Companion Website for links to information about the French national team and the game of soccer in general.

Note: The spelling *évènement* reflects the orthographic reform of 1990; point out to students that they may see *événement* as well.

Key: En lisant 1) more than 200,000 2) mostly by men, 90% 3) They are not primarily interested in winning; they are more interested in being a member of a group. 4) Signs include: special clothing, accessories and other objects in team colors, special places to sit for various groups, special rituals and practices, pre- and post-game meetings. 5) Victories by the national team are unique and constitute exceptional moments for all French, even those who do not much like sports.

Key: **En regardant de plus près** 1) the word "place"; seating section or spot 2) reunions or get-togethers before and after the match 3) 1998 World Cup (Soccer), 2000 European Football Championship, the finals of the 2006 World Cup (Soccer)

C. En regardant de plus près. Now look more closely at the text to provide the following information.

1. Look at the phrase **emplacements réservés aux différents clubs de supporteurs dans le stade**. Most of these words are cognates or can be figured out using your knowledge of English. For example, what English word do you see in **emplacements**? Knowing this, along with the context, (i.e., something reserved for a particular group in the stadium), what do you think the word means?
2. The text also mentions des **réunions d'avant et d'après-match**. You know what **après** means (hint: think of **après-midi**); **avant** is the opposite. Knowing this, what do you think this phrase means?
3. Victories in several specific sporting events are mentioned in the text. Can you provide the English equivalent for each:
   - la Coupe du monde de football en 1998
   - l'Euro en 2000
   - en finale de la Coupe du monde en 2006

Implementation: Après avoir lu Ask students what types of events they have witnessed in person, on television, or in the newspapers surrounding the winning of a college bowl game, an NCAA championship, the World Series, the Super Bowl, or the NBA Finals. Refer students back to the introduction of the **Venez chez nous**, which points to large celebrations in Paris on the Champs-Élysées and in other major French cities when French national teams have won.

D. Après avoir lu. Think about and then discuss the following questions with your classmates.

1. Do you agree that attending sporting events is a way of belonging to a larger group? How has this been true in your own experience?
2. What customs surround sporting events on your campus or where you live? Are they similar to any of the customs observed by French soccer fans?
3. Can you remember a time when a favorite team won a championship? How did the team's victory make you and your friends and family members feel? Was there widespread elation like that after the major victories of the French teams?

Écrivons

2-38 Un/e athlète célèbre

Stratégie

When writing a description, try to paint a vivid picture by incorporating well-chosen adjectives and adverbs.

A. Avant d'écrire. Write a description of a Francophone or North American athlete whom you admire. You may choose Tony Parker, Hoda Lattaf, Guillaume Latendresse, or another athlete. Before you begin to write, complete the following steps:

1. List basic biographical information, including the person's name, sport, age, nationality, and marital status.
2. List several adjectives that describe the athlete's appearance.
3. List several adjectives that describe the athlete's personality.
4. Indicate, in a couple of sentences, why you admire this person.

Implementation: Refer students to the *Chez nous* Companion Website for helpful links to sites where they can find biographical information about Francophone athletes. Encourage students to use French language sites to discover more information about athletes.

B. En écrivant. Now, using your notes, write your description. Begin by providing factual information; next, describe the athlete's appearance and personality; and then conclude with your own thoughts.

MODÈLE Thierry Henry joue au football. Il est français, mais ses parents sont antillais. Sa mère est de Martinique et son père est de Guadeloupe. Thierry Henry est assez jeune ; il a 30 ans. Il est divorcé et il a une fille. Il est assez grand et mince ; il est beau. Il est intelligent, motivé, ambitieux, sportif et très rapide. Il aime regarder les matchs de basket-ball, et Tony Parker est un de ses amis. J'admire Thierry Henry parce qu'il joue très bien au football et il lutte (*fights*) contre le racisme dans le sport.

C. En révisant. As you revise your description, think about the following questions and make any necessary changes.

1. Reread your description. Did you include well-chosen adjectives and adverbs to make your description as evocative as possible? Are there any places where you might want to use a more specific adjective or maybe add one or two more?
2. Look closely at your paragraph to be sure that all the adjectives you have used agree in number and gender with the nouns they modify.
3. Find a photo of your athlete to include with your written description.

D. Après avoir écrit. Share your description with your classmates. Are certain individuals mentioned frequently? Based on how these athletes are described, is it possible to make any generalizations about what we admire in famous athletes?

Implementation: En regardant de plus près Refer students back to the **Fiche pratique** in Leçon 1, which focuses on adjective agreement in written French.

Expansion: Après avoir écrit You could ask students to post their descriptions and photos on a class Web site or blog and create an album of Francophone athletes.

Note: Students may not be familiar with *pétanque*. This game is very popular in the south of France, although it is played all over France and increasingly, around the world. The game is similar to the Italian game of *bocce*, which students of Italian-American descent may know. A Web-based exercise in the SAM/MFL explores this sport, and the *Chez nous* video features several images of people playing *pétanque*.

Parlons

2-39 Les évènements sportifs

Laurent Renucci joue dans le Tournoi de Pentecôte à Lyon en mai 2007. Ce tournoi de pétanque date de l'an 1894 !

Alize Cornet de France fête sa victoire dans la finale du tournoi juniors à Roland-Garros en juin 2007.

Implementation: Encourage students to do research on the Web to discover other Francophone sporting events. Students may work in pairs or small groups to prepare and give their oral reports. Use the model to teach students how to take notes in French to prepare for an oral presentation or a written report. Draw their attention to the short phrases used and show them how these phrases can be expanded to full sentences either orally or in written form.

A. Avant de parler. Look at the photos on the previous page. Many international sporting events are hosted each year in the Francophone world, ranging from the world-famous **Tour de France** to lesser-known events such as the annual **pétanque** competition, **le Tournoi de Pentecôte**, held each year in Lyon. Some of these events are pictured on the previous page. Look at the photos and identify the sport in each one. Which would you most like to attend? Why?

B. En parlant. Prepare a brief oral report to share with the class on one of the following sporting events: **le Roland-Garros, le Tour de France, la Coupe du monde de football**, or a similar Francophone event of your choosing.

1. Begin by doing research online to complete the chart below. As an example, information has been provided for **les Jeux de la Francophonie**.

Quoi ?	Quand ?	Où ?	Description
les Jeux de la Francophonie	*2009*	*à Beyrouth au Liban*	*une manifestation culturelle et sportive internationale*

2. Now, using the information that you have found, prepare written notes to summarize essential points for your oral presentation.

MODÈLE Les Jeux de la Francophonie

- en 2009, à Beyrouth au Liban
- une manifestation culturelle et sportive internationale
- beaucoup d'artistes et d'athlètes du monde francophone participent
- une occasion formidable pour fêter la francophonie, l'art et le sport
- tous les quatre ans après les Jeux Olympiques

3. Find a photo or the logo of the sporting event you are describing to share with the class.

C. Après avoir parlé. Share your report with your classmates and listen to their presentations to learn more about the wide variety of sporting events held in the Francophone world. Which ones especially caught your interest? Why?

Observons

2-40 Nos passe-temps

Implementation: Avant de regarder Do not provide answers for the previewing activity; instead, let students make guesses and see whether they are confirmed by the clip. This activity is based on the first three interviews in the clip; two additional interviews are treated in the SAM/MFL.

A. Avant de regarder. In this clip, several speakers describe their sports and cultural activities. Look at the following list of activities that they mention; can you guess—in cases where you don't already know—what each of these activities might involve?

l'athlétisme la danse classique la danse orientale le piano le tennis

As you watch this video segment, look for any clues that might support your guesses about unfamiliar activities.

B. En regardant. Who does which activities? Each speaker is listed in order; fill in the activities each person mentions.

Personne	Activité/s	Jour/s
Hervé-Thomas	*tennis*	
Caroline	*1.*	
	2.	
	3.	
Catherine (sa sœur)	*1.*	
	2.	
	3.	
	4.	
Fadoua		

Several of the speakers specify the days on which they do various activities; listen again and note those days on the chart.

C. Après avoir regardé. What is your impression of the types and number of activities in which these speakers are involved? How do their habits compare with your own habits and those of your family and friends?

Now that you have completed *Chapitre 2*, can you do the following in French?

- ☐ Describe people you know, talking about their appearance and personality?
- ☐ Talk about your favorite sports and leisure activities?
- ☐ Ask someone for information about his or her friends, family, and everyday activities?
- ☐ Give commands and make suggestions?
- ☐ Talk about differences in the American and French notions of friendship?
- ☐ Talk about important sporting events that occur in the French-speaking world?

Script: Observons Note that the elements in brackets reflect standard usage and have been added to the written transcripts. They were not pronounced by the speaker(s) in question.

HERVÉ-THOMAS : Je suis professeur de littérature et d'histoire de France, mais j'aime aussi le sport. Je fais beaucoup de sport : je joue beaucoup au tennis. Euh, en général, je joue au tennis le lundi, le mercredi et le samedi.

CAROLINE : En dehors de l'école on a un emploi de [du] temps très chargé, exemple : le mercredi,... j'ai une heure et demie de piano...

CATHERINE : Et moi, c'est le lundi.

CAROLINE : Le vendredi, on a deux heures d'athlétisme... et voici nos maillots. On en est fières.

CATHERINE : Très fières.

CAROLINE : Le samedi, on fait une heure et demie de danse. Voici les... chaussons de danse... les pointes.

CATHERINE : Et le dimanche, moi, je fais du tennis avec mon grand-père quand je peux. Parce que des fois il pleut, mais la plupart du temps je fais avec lui.

FADOUA : Donc je fais [de] la danse orientale à la faculté de Nice. Donc on... nous avons un gymnase où on peut faire [de] la danse ; nous avons un professeur qui est d'origine algérienne. Elle s'appelle Yamina. En fait j'aime bien faire [de] la danse orientale parce que ça me permet d'avoir un [une] attache... à mon pays.

Leçon 

le caractère	disposition, nature, character
ambitieux/-euse	*ambitious*
amusant/e	*funny*
bête	*stupid*
drôle	*amusing, funny*
égoïste	*selfish*
énergique	*energetic*
généreux/-euse	*generous, warm-hearted*
gentil/le	*kind, nice*
intelligent/e	*intelligent, smart*
méchant/e	*mean, naughty*
pantouflard/e	*homebody, stay-at-home*
paresseux/-euse	*lazy*
sérieux/-euse	*serious*
sportif/-ive	*athletic*

le physique	physical traits
âgé/e	*aged, old*
beau/belle	*handsome, beautiful*
blond/e	*blond/e*
brun/e	*brunette*
châtain	*chestnut colored, auburn*
de taille moyenne	*of average height*
d'un certain âge	*middle-aged*
élégant/e	*elegant*
fort/e	*strong, stout*
grand/e	*tall*
gros/se	*fat*
jeune	*young*
joli/e	*pretty*
maigre	*skinny*
mince	*thin, slender*
moche	*ugly*
petit/e	*short, little*
roux/-sse	*redhead, redhaired*

pour poser des questions	to ask questions
combien de	*how many*
comment	*how*
où	*where*
parce que	*because*
pourquoi	*why*
quand	*when*
qui	*who*

autres mots utiles	other useful words
adorer	*to adore, love*
arrête !	*stop it!*
autre	*other, another*
bien sûr	*of course*
un chapeau	*hat*
un/e coloc(ataire)	*roommate*
comme	*like, as*
donc	*then, therefore, so*
une fac(ulté)	*college*
une histoire drôle	*joke*
peut-être	*maybe*
une photo	*photo*
pour	*for, in order to*

Leçon 2

Note: Point out to students that h-initial words marked with an asterisk begin with an *h-aspiré*. These words behave as if they began with a consonant.

quelques sports (m.)	some sports
le basket(-ball)	*basketball*
le football américain	*football*
le *hockey	*hockey*
un match	*game (sports)*
le rugby	*rugby*
le volley(-ball)	*volleyball*

quelques jeux (m.)	some games
les cartes (f.)	*cards*
les échecs (m.)	*chess*
un jeu	*game, deck (of cards)*
un jeu de société	*board game*
le loto	*lottery*

la musique	music
le jazz	*jazz*
le rock	*rock*
une batterie	*percussion, drum set*
un concert	*concert*
un harmonica	*harmonica*
un saxophone	*saxophone*

d'autres activités	other activities
bricoler	*to do odd jobs, to tinker*
les loisirs (m.)	*leisure-time activities*
organiser une fête	*to plan a party*
rester à la résidence	*to stay in the dorm*

Vocabulaire

quelques expressions avec *faire*	*expressions using* faire
faire du bricolage	*to do do-it-yourself projects*
faire des courses	*to run errands*
faire la cuisine	*to cook*
faire de la danse	*to dance, to study dance*
faire du français	*to study French*
faire du jardinage	*to garden*
faire du jogging	*to go jogging*
faire de la marche	*to walk (for exercise)*
faire de la musique	*to play music*
faire de la natation	*to swim*
faire une promenade	*to take a walk*
faire du sport	*to play sports*
faire du vélo	*to go biking*
ne pas faire grand-chose	*to not do much*

Leçon 

en ville	*in town*
une bibliothèque (municipale)	*(municipal) library*
un café	*café*
un cinéma	*movie theater*
une église	*(Catholic) church*
une gare	*train station*
un gymnase	*gym*
un hôtel	*hotel*
une librairie	*bookstore*
la mairie	*town hall*
un marché	*market*
un monument aux morts	*veterans' memorial*
un musée	*museum*
un parc	*park*
une piscine (municipale)	*(municipal) swimming pool*
une place	*square (in a town)*
un restaurant	*restaurant*
un stade	*stadium*
un théâtre	*theatre*

activités culturelles	*cultural activities*
assister à...	*to attend . . .*
un ballet	*a ballet*
un concert	*a concert*
voir...	*to see . . .*
une exposition	*exhibition*
un film	*film (at a movie theatre)*
une pièce	*a play (theater)*

pour parler de l'avenir	*to talk about the future*
aller (Je vais manger.)	*to go (I'm going to eat./I will eat.)*
l'année (f.) prochaine	*next year*
bientôt	*soon*
ce soir	*tonight*
ce week-end	*this weekend*
demain	*tomorrow*
l'été (m.) prochain	*next summer*
le mois prochain	*next month*
la semaine prochaine	*next week*

autres mots utiles	*other useful words*
alors	*so*
chercher	*to look for*
dites-moi !	*tell me!*
manger	*to eat*
nager	*to swim*
oublier	*to forget*

3 Études et professions

Does this scene look familiar? Where do you imagine it is taking place?

Leçon 1 Nous allons à la fac

Leçon 2 Une formation professionnelle

Leçon 3 Choix de carrière

Venez chez nous ! Étudier et travailler en pays francophone

After completing this chapter, you should be able to:

- Talk about a university and courses of study
- Talk about jobs and the workplace
- Express preferences
- Compare education and the workplace in the United States, France, and Canada

Leçon 1 Nous allons à la fac

POINTS DE DÉPART

Presentation: You may present this vocabulary over two days. Present campus vocabulary on day 1 with Ex. 3-1 and 3-2; review the campus and present prepositions on day 2, completing Ex. 3-3. Present campus vocabulary using the labeled map (MFL, Ch. 3). Identify each location pictured, then have students help describe related activities, using verbs they know: *Dans le centre étudiant ? — On regarde la télé, on mange, on parle avec des copains.* Check comprehension by having students point to the places you name or describe. Ask questions as you point to the visual to elicit repetitions: *C'est le centre informatique ou le labo de chimie ? — C'est le centre informatique.* Reinforce the distinction between *la librairie* and *la bibliothèque.* You might supply the abbreviated expressions *la bibli* and *la B.U.*, which are frequently used in France, as is *le resto U.* Note that in France, students would say *Je vais à la fac,* and they would practice sports in a *centre des sports.* Demonstrate each preposition using the campus map. Have students name the places you describe: *Qu'est-ce qui est derrière le centre sportif ? — Ce sont les terrains de sport.* For additional practice, use the town map from Ch. 2, L. 3 (MFL, Ch. 2) and have students correct statements you make: *Est-ce que la mairie est loin de la place ? — Non, elle est près de la place.*

Presentation: Lead into one aspect of the cultural content of Ch. 3 by discussing reasons for the presence of French in Quebec. You might discuss how the universities of Quebec reflect its special situation as a French-speaking province in Canada. Ask students to provide examples of American universities that reflect divergent cultural identities; they may mention historically black colleges or schools in Louisiana.

À l'université

Je m'appelle Julie et je suis en deuxième année d'études à l'Université de Montréal. Je vais à l'université du lundi au vendredi. Après les cours, je retrouve mes amis au café dans le centre étudiant. J'habite en ville, mais j'ai des amis qui habitent en résidence. On mange ensemble quelquefois à la cafétéria et on fait du sport au centre sportif.

Voici un plan du campus. Si vous arrivez à UdeM en voiture, le garage se trouve à droite du pavillon principal. Il faut avoir un permis pour stationner sur le campus. Si vous arrivez en métro, il y a une station juste en face du pavillon principal. Pour circuler sur le campus, il y a la navette. Dans le pavillon principal, il y a une librairie et des bureaux administratifs. Les résidences se trouvent à gauche et le centre étudiant est juste à côté. Là-bas il y a un cinéma, un café, le bureau des inscriptions et des bureaux d'associations étudiantes. Le centre sportif est tout près des résidences, et les terrains de sport sont juste derrière.

Prépositions de lieu

à droite de	à gauche de
en face de	à côté de
dans	
près de	loin de
devant	derrière

Note: In Ch. 3 we begin to draw students' attention to regional differences in the French language. We focus on Quebec in the chapter on university studies, since the North American educational systems are more similar to each other than they are to the French system. The **Venez chez nous !** section presents issues related to **la loi 101** and the use of French as the only official language of Quebec.

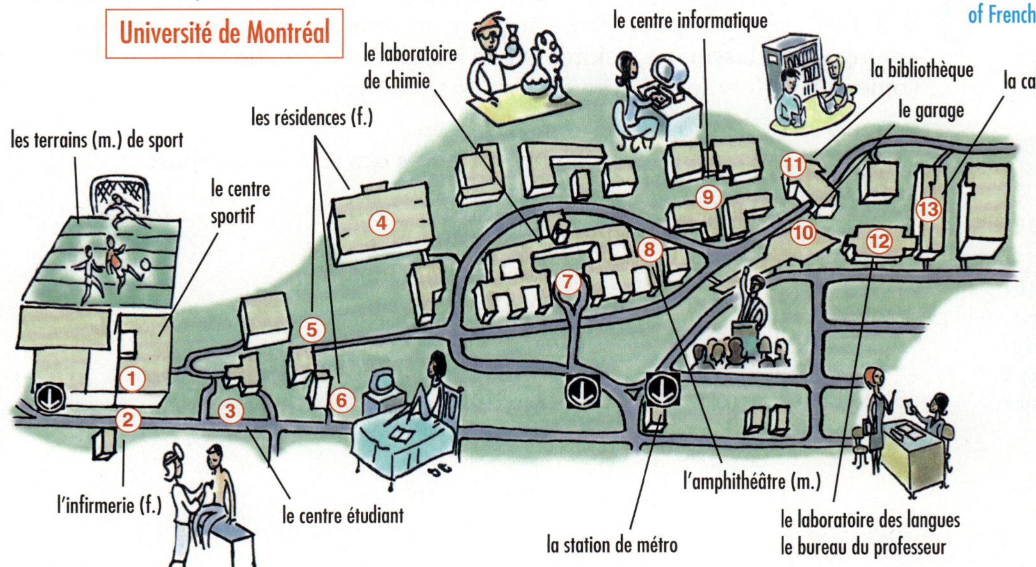

1. Centre d'éducation physique et des sports (CEPSUM)
2. Pavillon 2101, boul. Édouard-Montpetit
3. Pavillon J.-A.-DeSève (centre étudiant)
4. Résidence C (étudiants et étudiantes)
5. Résidence A (étudiants)
6. Résidence Thérèse-Casgrain (étudiantes)
7. Pavillon principal
8. Pavillon Claire-McNicoll
9. Pavillon André-Aisenstadt
10. Garage Louis-Colin
11. Pavillon Samuel-Bronfman
12. Pavillon Lionel-Groulx
13. Pavillon 3200, rue Jean-Brillant

Station de métro

À vous la parole

Preparation: 3-1 This exercise practices the key vocabulary used with the preposition *à*. Review forms, using a quick substitution drill: *Il est au café ; piscine — Il est à la piscine*, etc. You might also wish to review forms of *aller*; this can be practiced using a substitution drill and/or the campus visual (MFL, Ch. 3).

3-1 Dans quel endroit ? Where would you be likely to hear people asking these questions or making these comments?

MODÈLE Vous avez un permis pour votre voiture ?
au garage

1. Voilà le bureau de l'association.
2. Le match commence dans dix minutes.
3. Listen and repeat: number one.
4. Écoute ! C'est une explosion !
5. Où sont les biographies, s'il vous plaît ?
6. On regarde la télé ce soir ?
7. Où est le docteur Martin ?
8. Désolé, monsieur, je n'ai pas mes devoirs.
9. Tu as un autre CD ?
10. C'est combien pour ces deux livres et un cahier ?

Additional activity: As a brief personalized activity between Ex. 3-1 and 3-2, have students tell a partner where they are going after French class, then compare notes with the class as a whole.

3-2 Vos endroits préférés. Discuss with a partner your favorite place on campus for each activity listed. Then share your preferences with other classmates.

MODÈLE pour dîner ?

É1 Moi, je préfère la cafétéria ; c'est très pratique. Et toi ?
É2 Moi, je préfère le café au centre étudiant ; c'est plus calme.
É1 (*reporting back*) Pour dîner, je préfère la cafétéria, mais Anne préfère le café au centre étudiant…

1. pour dîner ?
2. pour travailler ?
3. pour voir un film ?
4. pour parler avec des amis ?
5. pour pratiquer un sport ?
6. pour préparer un examen ?

Implementation: 3-3 Follow-up by having students compare answers and choosing which is the best response.

Additional activities: 3-3 For further practice, show the image of the UdeM campus map (MFL, Ch. 3) and ask students to imagine that they are in the courtyard of the *pavillon principal*. Have them take turns asking and indicating where the following places are located: *la station de métro ; le terrain de foot ; le garage ; la Résidence A ; un café ; la piscine ; une librairie ; le centre étudiant*. For example,

É1 la station de métro, s'il vous plaît ?
É2 Ce n'est pas loin ; c'est juste en face d'ici.

Remind students of other ways to ask for directions: *Où se trouve… ? C'est loin / près d'ici… ? Je cherche… . C'est où… ?* As a follow-up, provide students with a map of your campus and have them work in pairs to label the map in French.

3-3 Sur votre campus. Pick one place on your campus, then circulate among your classmates, asking where it is located. See the list below for some ideas. How many different responses do you get?

MODÈLE É1 C'est où, la résidence Denton ?
É2 La résidence Denton, c'est près des terrains de sport.

OU É1 La résidence Denton, s'il vous plaît ?
É3 C'est en face du centre étudiant.

1. la bibliothèque
2. les bureaux de l'administration
3. le centre étudiant
4. la piscine
5. le bureau des inscriptions
6. le théâtre
7. la librairie
8. la cafétéria
9. la résidence…
10. les terrains de sport

Vie et culture

Note: In Montreal there are four universities: two are French-speaking, *l'Université de Montréal (l'UdeM)* and *l'Université du Québec à Montréal (l'UQÀM);* and two are English-speaking, *McGill* and *Concordia University.*

Le système éducatif au Québec

The educational system in the Canadian province of Quebec is organized somewhat differently than the educational system in the United States. Secondary school usually lasts five years; students normally graduate at 17 and then spend two years in a **CÉGEP** (**Collège d'enseignement général et professionnel**). Afterwards, many continue at a university where they may complete **un baccalauréat** (**un bacc**), **une maîtrise**, and **un doctorat**. These are equivalent to the American Bachelor's, Master's, and Ph.D. degrees respectively. Students in Canadian universities may pursue an honors degree in one discipline (**une spécialisation**) or they may choose to have a major (**une majeure** or **une concentration**) in one discipline and a minor (**une mineure**) in another.

L'Université de Montréal, the largest university in Canada, has an expansive campus located on the outskirts of town. It offers a wide range of majors and professional degrees.

La Sorbonne, l'Université de Paris IV, is at the heart of the busy Latin Quarter. Founded in 1253, it is surrounded today by cafés and bookstores that cater to the university clientele.

Le campus dans l'université française

Most French universities do not have a centralized campus. The different **facultés**, or schools, are often housed in buildings with historical significance that are scattered around town, usually in urban settings.

French students refer to their university as **la fac**; they say, for example, **Je vais à la fac**. To socialize and to study, students often go to a nearby café. Some French universities have residence halls located near classroom buildings, but most French students, in Paris and elsewhere, live at home or rent a room in town.

ET VOUS ?

1. Does your region have any institutions comparable to the **CÉGEP** in Quebec?
2. How is your campus similar to a French campus, and how is it different? You might compare location, size, type of buildings, and general campus layout.
3. Are students' living arrangements at your university similar to or different from those of typical French students?

Implementation: Point out that, whereas the *Québécois bacc* is equivalent to the American B.A. or B.S., the French *bac* is an examination that must be passed for graduation from the *lycée* and is a condition for admission to a university. The French *bac* is discussed further in the **Vie et culture** section of L. 2. Help students understand that the *CÉGEP* prepares Canadian students for university work and may account for a shorter time spent at university; recently, however, many Québécois universities have moved to a four-year *baccalauréat.*

Note: In early stages of acquisition, it is important to focus on the avoidance of glided vowels. For that reason, it is unwise to insist that student contrast /e/ and /ɛ/. Although that contrast is typical of Standard (Parisian) French (SF) and Canadian French speakers who differentiate between, for example, *le pré* (meadow) and *le prêt* (loan), it is not made by the majority of people in France. They follow what is called *la loi de position*: /e/ at the end of a word or syllable (open syllable); /ɛ/ before a consonant (closed syllable). This pronunciation is fully acceptable to SF speakers, who, in any case, exhibit a great deal of variation. You might want to follow this rule and use /e/ in *anglais, français, des, est*, and inside words in open syllables, for example, *intelligente*.

Sons et lettres

Les voyelles /e/ et /ɛ/

The vowels of **et** and **mère** differ by the degree of tension with which they are pronounced and where they occur in words. The vowel of **et**, /e/, must be pronounced with a lot of tension and without any glide; otherwise the vowel of the English word *day* is produced. To pronounce the French vowel, hold your hand under your chin to make sure it does not drop as you say **et**; your lips should stay in a smiling position and tense. The vowel /e/ occurs generally only at the end of words or syllables, and it is often written with **é**, or **e** followed by a silent consonant letter. It also occurs in the endings **-er**, **-ez**, and **-ier**.

la t**é**l**é**   **e**t   ass**ez**   janv**ier**   r**é**p**é**t**er**   **é**cout**ez**

The vowel of **mère**, /ɛ/, is pronounced with less tension than /e/, but still without any glide. It usually occurs before a pronounced consonant and is spelled with **è**, **ê**, or **e** followed by a pronounced consonant. It is also spelled **ei** or **ai** in **seize** or **j'aime**, for example.

la m**è**re   b**ê**te   je préf**è**re   **e**lle   il dét**e**ste

À vous la parole

Initial practice: Begin with a discrimination drill; have students indicate whether they hear the vowel /e/ or /ɛ/: *belle, les, mère, frère, janvier, et, elle, jouer*, etc.

3-4 Contrastes. Compare the pronunciation of each pair of words: the first word contains /e/ and the second /ɛ/.

anglais / anglaise	français / française	assez / seize
André / Daniel	préférer / je préfère	marié / célibataire

3-5 Des phrases. Read each of the sentences aloud. To avoid glides, hold the rounded, tense position of /e/ and do not move your lips or chin during its production.

1. Écoutez Hélène.
2. Hervé n'est pas bête.
3. Danielle est réservée.
4. Son père s'appelle André.
5. Sa grand-mère est âgée.

Note: Consistent with the presentation of variable adjectives in Ch. 2, L. 1, this presentation focuses on the spoken forms of adjectives and assumes the feminine as the base form, with a regular rule of final consonant deletion to derive the masculine. Plural forms are treated in L. 2 of this chapter.

FORMES ET FONCTIONS

1. *Les adjectifs prénominaux au singulier*

- Most adjectives follow the noun in French. A few, however, are placed before the noun.

Presentation: To present, first show students contrasting examples illustrating the position of adjectives: *C'est un professeur raisonnable ; C'est un jeune professeur.* Call attention to the learning strategy, and point out that the boxed list of adjectives is arranged according to the mnemonic. Go over the list and group the adjectives accordingly. Some mnemonic devices used in English include: "Thirty days hath September, . . . (the French count knuckles and the spaces between them); "A rat in Tom's house might eat Tom's ice cream" (to spell "arithmetic"). Then display and read aloud the sentence examples for prenominal adjectives, asking students how many different spoken forms these adjectives have. Ask specifically what they notice about the pronunciation of the masculine form before a vowel sound, versus before a consonant sound. Point out differences in written forms as well.

LES ADJECTIFS PRÉNOMINAUX

jolie/joli	
belle/bel/beau	
première/premier	dernière/dernier
jeune	vieille/vieil/vieux
nouvelle/nouvel/nouveau	
bonne/bon	mauvaise/mauvais
petite/petit	grande/grand
	grosse/gros

Fiche pratique

Use a mnemonic device to help you remember facts that you must learn by rote memory. For example, the list of adjectives that precede the noun is easy to remember if you use the acronym BRAGS as a reminder of their meaning—**b**eauty, **r**ank, **a**ge, **g**oodness, **s**ize. Can you think of mnemonic devices that you have used in English?

- In the singular, **jeune** and **joli/e** each have a single spoken form. For **joli**, add **-e** for the feminine written form: **jolie**.

une jeune étudiante	un jeune professeur
une jolie bibliothèque	un joli campus

- Most of the other adjectives that are placed before the noun have two spoken forms in the singular. Like other adjectives you know, the masculine form ends in a vowel sound and the feminine form ends in a pronounced consonant. However, because of liaison, the masculine form sounds just like the feminine form when followed by a word beginning in a vowel sound.

C'est une petite piscine.	C'est un petit‿amphithéâtre. C'est un petit laboratoire.
C'est une mauvaise bibli.	C'est un mauvais‿hôtel. C'est un mauvais prof.
C'est la première librairie.	C'est le premier‿ordinateur. C'est le premier jour.

Presentation: These examples allow you to demonstrate that the cue to knowing whether a word is masculine or feminine is found consistently in the indefinite article, *un/une*, and sometimes at the end of the noun (compare *étudiant–étudiante* with *ami–amie*). In presenting feminine and masculine forms followed by a word beginning with a vowel sound, stress that the pronounced final consonant forms a syllable with the next word (*enchaînement*): *un mauvais amphithéâtre* /mɔ vɛ zɑ̃ fi te atr/.

- **Belle**, **nouvelle**, and **vieille** also have two spoken forms in the singular. The feminine form and the masculine form used before a word beginning with a vowel sound end in the same pronounced consonant. (Note that the masculine form has a special written form.) However, when followed by a consonant, the masculine form is irregular.

C'est une belle étudiante.	C'est un **bel**‿étudiant. C'est un **beau** garçon.
C'est une nouvelle étudiante.	C'est un **nouvel**‿étudiant. C'est un **nouveau** prof.
C'est une vieille amie.	C'est un **vieil**‿ami. C'est un **vieux** copain.

- The adjectives **grande** and **grosse** have three spoken forms in the singular. When followed by a word beginning with a vowel sound, the masculine form has a final consonant sound different from the feminine form.

C'est une grande piscine. /d/	C'est un grand‿amphithéâtre. /t/ C'est un grand stade.
Regarde la grosse calculatrice ! /s/	Regarde le gros‿ordinateur ! /z/ Regarde le gros stylo !

Presentation: Demonstrate the pronunciation difference between *grand* [grɑ̃], *grand* [grɑ̃t] and *grande* [grɑ̃d], and *gros* [gRo], *gros* [gRoz], and *grosse* [gRos], when these words are followed respectively by masculine nouns beginning with a consonant, masculine nouns beginning with a vowel sound, and feminine nouns beginning with either a vowel or a consonant.

Initial practice: Begin practice with a discrimination drill, having students write or select the appropriate form of the adjective they hear: *Voilà un nouvel ordinateur ; une nouvelle étudiante ; un nouveau prof.* Point out the importance of the article in providing gender cues when the form of the adjective is ambiguous. Follow with simple substitution drills: *C'est un grand hôtel ; piscine ; amphithéâtre ; café ; bibliothèque ; stade ; mairie,* etc. *C'est un bon ordinateur ; nouveau ; vieux ; gros ; bel ; mauvais ; grand,* etc.

Variation: 3-7 Suggest additional emphatic statements: *Ah non !/Au contraire, c'est un jeune prof.* Encourage students to be expressive as they complete the exercise.

Implementation: 3-8 Use as a mixing activity and have students report back what they learned. Expand on each item, for example, asking all students: *Qui a un bon prof ? C'est un prof de quoi ?,* etc.

Presentation: Before presenting this topic, review *-er* verbs to highlight the differences in the number of stems and spoken forms. Stress the importance of a clear articulation of the final consonant in the third-person plural for *-re* verbs; it is this final consonant that distinguishes the singular from the plural in speech.

À vous la parole

3-6 Tout à fait d'accord ! Indicate that you agree.

Variation: 3-6 Suggest additional emphatic statements: *Ah oui/Mais oui/C'est vrai, c'est un bon cours.*

MODÈLE Le cours est bon ?
Oui, c'est un bon cours.

1. Le prof est mauvais ?
2. La fac est nouvelle ?
3. L'infirmerie est bonne ?
4. Le campus est grand ?
5. L'amphithéâtre est nouveau ?
6. Le stade est nouveau ?
7. L'ordinateur est beau ?
8. L'étudiante est jeune ?

3-7 Ce n'est pas vrai ! Contradict your partner!

MODÈLE É1 C'est un vieux professeur.
É2 Mais non, c'est un jeune professeur !

1. C'est un mauvais livre.
2. C'est un vieil ordinateur.
3. C'est le premier pavillon.
4. C'est une grande piscine.
5. C'est la dernière résidence.
6. C'est un petit ordinateur.
7. C'est un mauvais professeur.
8. C'est un nouvel amphithéâtre.

3-8 Trouvez une personne qui... Find someone in your class who . . .

MODÈLE a un bon prof de maths
É1 Est-ce que tu as un bon prof de maths ?
É2 Non, je n'ai pas de cours de maths. (*you ask another person*)
É1 Est-ce que tu as un bon prof de maths ?
É3 Oui, j'ai un bon prof ; il s'appelle M. McDonald. (*you write down the name of this student*)

1. a un bon prof de maths
2. a une bonne note en français
3. a un nouvel ordinateur
4. a son premier cours à huit heures du matin
5. a un gros dictionnaire
6. prépare un grand examen
7. est en première année de fac
8. est en dernière année de fac
9. a un bon cours d'histoire
10. a un vieil ami sur le campus

2. *Les verbes en -re comme* attendre

- Verbs ending in **-re** differ from the **-er** verbs you have already learned in two ways:
  - The singular forms have different written endings. Note that the final consonants in these singular forms are never pronounced.

    j'attends (*I wait*) tu entends (*you hear*) il répond (*he answers*)
  - With these verbs, you can always tell whether someone is talking about one person, or more than one, because the **-d** is pronounced in the plural forms.

    elles répondent vs. elle répond

ATTENDRE *to wait for*			
SINGULIER		**PLURIEL**	
j'	attend**s**	nous	attend**ons**
tu	attend**s**	vous	attend**ez**
il / elle / on	attend	ils / elles	attend**ent**

IMPÉRATIF : Attend**s** ! Attend**ons** ici.
Attend**ez** un moment !

◆ Here are the most common verbs ending in **-re**.

attendre	*to wait for*	Ils **attendent** la navette.
descendre	*to go down*	Je **descends.**
de	*to get off*	Elle **descend du** bus.
en ville	*to go downtown*	Vous **descendez en ville** ?
entendre	*to hear*	Tu **entends** cette musique ?
perdre	*to lose*	Il **perd** toujours ses cahiers.
rendre à	*to give back*	Le prof **rend** les essais **aux** étudiants.
rendre visite à	*to visit someone*	Nous **rendons visite à** nos parents.
répondre à	*to answer*	Vous **répondez à** sa lettre ?
en		Elle **répond en** anglais.
vendre	*to sell*	Ils **vendent** des magazines.

◆ Remember that English and French often differ in the use of prepositions with verbs:

J'attends le métro.	*I'm waiting* ***for*** *the subway.*
Il répond **au** professeur.	*He's answering the professor.*
Elle rend visite **à** sa mère.	*She's visiting her mother.*

 À vous la parole 

3-9 C'est logique. Complete each sentence logically, using an **-re** verb.

MODÈLE nous / le métro
→ Nous attendons le métro.

1. le professeur / en français en classe
2. l'étudiante / ses devoirs au professeur
3. nous / des livres à la bibliothèque
4. moi / mes parents à Québec
5. vous / le train ?
6. toi / au téléphone ?
7. elle / ses livres
8. Marc / le week-end pour dîner avec des amis

Presentation: Be sure to stress that *rendre visite à* is the equivalent of the English verb "to visit," when a person is involved. Make sure students understand that the cognate *visiter* can only be used with places (e.g., *Je rends visite à mes grands-parents. On visite le musée du Louvre*).

Initial practice: Begin practice with a discrimination drill: one person, or more than one? *Ils attendent le prof. Elle entend le téléphone. Elles vendent la maison. Elle attend la navette. Ils répondent au prof. Elle descend du bus. Elles perdent leurs cahiers. Ils entendent la musique. Il rend visite aux grands-parents*, etc. Follow up with a simple substitution drill. Start first with the contrast between the third-person plural and the third-person singular by visual cuing: *Elles descendent en ville.* (Show one finger) — *Elle descend en ville.* Then proceed with the other forms: *Nous descendons en ville ; je.* — *Je descends en ville.*

Key: 3-9 1) répond 2) rend 3) rendons 4) rends visite à 5) attendez 6) réponds 7) perd/vend 8) attend

Implementation: 3-10 Go over the exercise before students begin working, to ensure that they understand each item. As a follow-up, have students compare their responses.

3-10 Réponses personnelles. Ask your partner the following questions, and then share what you have learned with the rest of the class.

MODÈLE À qui est-ce que tu rends visite le week-end ?
É1 Je rends visite à mes parents.
OU É2 Et moi, je rends visite à mes amis.
É1 (aux autres) Nous, on rend visite à nos parents et à nos amis.

1. À qui est-ce que tu rends visite le week-end ?
2. Est-ce que tu perds souvent tes livres ? si oui, comment ?
3. Est-ce que tu vends tes livres à la fin du semestre ? pourquoi ?
4. Est-ce que tu réponds rapidement à tes messages ?
5. Quand est-ce que tu descends en ville, et pourquoi ?

Preparation: Parlons To prepare for this activity, bring copies of a campus map to class. Remind students that they are to indicate where places are located, as modeled, rather than providing directions for finding places. Use multiple models similar to the one included in the **En parlant** section to demonstrate the learning strategy.

Alternate activity: Tell students they are to prepare a walking tour of your campus, visiting five (or more) different sites. Assign as homework, and have students develop a script. You might have students record their tour, or present it live in class and have classmates offer suggestions for improving the tour.

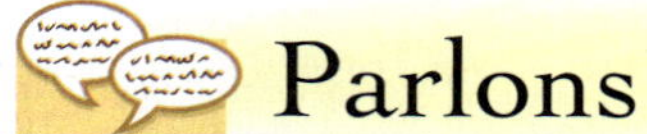

Parlons

3-11 Visitons le campus

A group of Francophone journalists is in town for a seminar and will be attending workshops on your campus. They may need help locating the things and places they need. Half of the class will play the role of journalists, the other half will be students working at the information desk in your student center.

A. Avant de parler. If you are a journalist, work with a partner to make a list of things and places to ask about, and practice formulating polite questions. If you are a student, brainstorm with a partner how you will indicate the location of various key places that your guests may ask about.

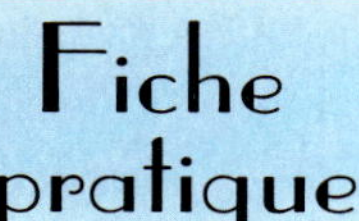

Fiche pratique

Ask for confirmation if you are not sure you have understood what someone has said to you. Get the person to repeat by saying *Pardon ?* or *Répétez, s'il vous plait.* If necessary, to make sure you have understood, repeat or rephrase what you have heard.

B. En parlant. Now take your places in front of or behind the information desk, asking questions or giving directions, as the case may be.

MODÈLE
É1, journaliste Bonjour, nous cherchons un café.
É2 Bonjour, monsieur. Ici dans le centre étudiant, il y a un petit restaurant et le café est très bon.
É1 C'est où exactement ?
É2 C'est à gauche, juste à côté de la librairie.
É1 À gauche ? Près de la librairie ? Merci bien !
É2 De rien, monsieur.

C. Après avoir parlé. Were you able to answer all of your classmates' questions, and were they able to understand your directions? Did they accept your advice? Which questions and answers did you like best?

Leçon  Une formation professionnelle

POINTS DE DÉPART

TEXT AUDIO
CD 2 TRACKS 5–7

Des programmes d'études et des cours

Claire Paradis

Gilles Robillard

Claire et Gilles sont étudiants à l'Université Laval. Claire prépare un bacc en chimie avec une concentration en chimie de l'environnement ; Gilles prépare un diplôme en économique. Ils parlent de leurs cours :

GILLES : Qu'est-ce que tu as comme cours ce semestre ?
CLAIRE : Un cours de chimie en labo, un cours de maths, un cours d'écologie et un cours de français.
GILLES : C'est intéressant, ton cours d'écologie ?
CLAIRE : En fait, c'est assez ennuyeux, mais c'est un cours obligatoire. Et ton cours de sciences po, ça va ?
GILLES : Ben, il est intéressant, ce cours, mais difficile.
CLAIRE : Il y a beaucoup d'examens ?
GILLES : Non, il y a seulement un examen final, mais il y a deux devoirs à faire. J'ai eu une note assez médiocre au premier devoir.

Presentation: Have students examine the boxed course listings and use cognates to determine what courses each student is taking and what each is likely to be majoring in. Have students pay attention to the course prefixes as well as the titles. These are actual courses found in the University of Laval catalog. Listen to the dialogue, then check comprehension: pose questions that can be answered with the appropriate student's name: *Qui suit un cours de chimie ? Qui a un cours de sciences politiques ?* Continue with more specific questions, such as the following: *Claire prépare un diplôme en sciences économiques ou en chimie ? Elle a une concentration en chimie physique ou en écologie ? Et Gilles, quel diplôme est-ce qu'il prépare ? Combien de cours est-ce qu'il suit ? Ce trimestre, Claire suit un cours d'écologie ? Pour quel cours est-ce qu'elle travaille au laboratoire ? Elle suit un cours de maths ?*

Presentation: Show the course listings as you model pronunciation for the disciplines and courses, and provide explanation where necessary. Ask: *Qui suit un cours de littérature ? C'est un cours de littérature américaine ou anglaise ?*, etc., to provide additional contextualization of the new words. As an early productive exercise, have students classify specific courses according to area of study: *la sociologie ? — C'est un cours de sciences humaines.*

Qu'est-ce que vous étudiez ?

les lettres :	l'histoire, une langue étrangère, la littérature, la philosophie
les sciences humaines :	l'anthropologie, la psychologie, les sciences politiques, la sociologie
les sciences naturelles :	la biologie, la botanique, la physiologie, la zoologie
les sciences physiques :	l'astronomie, la chimie, la physique
les sciences économiques :	la comptabilité, l'économie, la gestion
les arts du spectacle :	le théâtre, la danse, le cinéma
les beaux-arts :	le dessin, la musique, la peinture, la sculpture, la photographie

l'informatique	le droit	la médecine
les mathématiques	le journalisme	les sciences de l'éducation

Note: This vocabulary is provided to help students talk about their experiences as students and should be presented conversationally as you discuss courses and activities. Forms of the verbs *suivre* and *lire* are treated here as lexical items; their full conjugations should not be presented. Students already know the forms *écrivez* and *lisez*; complete paradigms for *écrire* and *lire* are presented in Ch. 7, L. 1. *Suivre* is used idiomatically in this context; English speakers "take" a course, but French students "follow" one.

Pour parler des cours :

Je suis un cours d'histoire.	*I'm taking a history course.*
J'ai des bonnes notes en maths.	*I have good grades in math.*
Je fais un devoir pour mon cours de sciences po.	*I'm writing an assignment for my poly sci class.*
Je lis un roman pour mon cours d'allemand.	*I'm reading a novel for my German class.*
Je passe un examen en cours de chimie lundi.	*I'm taking a chem exam Monday.*
Je vais réussir mon examen, je travaille beaucoup.	*I'm going to pass my exam, I'm studying hard.*
Je prépare un exposé pour le cours d'histoire.	*I'm preparing an oral presentation for history class.*
Je prépare un diplôme en biologie.	*I'm majoring in biology.*

À vous la parole

Implementation: 3-12 The terms *une majeure, une mineure* are used in Canada. Point out to students that the concept of a minor does not exist in France, and that the term *une spécialisation* is used there to indicate one's major.

Note: 3-12 The courses listed are actual course titles from the UdeM catalog.

3-12 La majeure. Based on the courses they're taking, what are these Canadian students probably majoring in?

MODÈLE Guillaume : Principes de chimie analytique ; Chimie physique moléculaire ; Mathématiques pour chimistes
Il prépare sans doute (*no doubt*) un diplôme en chimie.

1. Cécile : L'Europe moderne ; Introduction à l'étude des États-Unis ; Histoire générale des sciences
2. Arnaud : Civilisation allemande ; Allemand écrit 1 ; Cours pratique d'allemand parlé
3. Romain : Introduction aux concepts sociologiques ; Communication et organisation ; Psychologie sociale
4. Jennifer : Théorie macroéconomique ; Éléments de microéconomique ; Statistique pour économistes

5. Ben : Histoire politique du Québec ; Éléments de politique ; Géographie du développement
6. Anne-Marie : Biologie expérimentale ; Principes d'écologie ; Introduction à la génétique
7. Aurélie : Systèmes éducatifs du Québec ; Philosophie de l'éducation ; Sociologie de l'école

The French government has set as an educational goal to have 80% of all high school students obtain the *bac*. In 2005, the national statistic reached 62.5% (compared to 30% in the early seventies), with 82.2% of those who actually took the test passing. Compare this to 1982, when only 64.8% of candidates who took the test passed (*Francoscopie* 2007, p. 76). Ask students to compare requirements for entrance into American universities with those for French universities. What are the advantages and disadvantages of each? Unlike admission to the universities, admission to the *Grandes Écoles* is highly competitive and selective. Help students understand that the recent reforms are designed to allow students from one European country to move easily to another country to study, to complete an internship, or to work. Compare the North American system: Is it standardized? Is it easy to move from one place to another? What are the advantages of a standardized and a non-standardized system?

Vie et culture

L'université française et la réforme européenne

The educational system in France is organized quite differently from the American and Canadian systems. At the end of their high school curriculum, French students take a rigorous national exam called **le baccalauréat** (**le bac**). Students who pass are guaranteed entrance into the public university system, which is generally free, except for a low enrollment fee. Students may also opt to continue their studies in other, specialized institutions such as schools of business or engineering. The most prestigious and competitive of these are the **Grandes Écoles**, which are comparable to certain high-ranking graduate schools in North America. Students who plan to apply to the **Grandes Écoles** enroll in special **lycée** classes, called **classes préparatoires** or **prépas** for two years, after the **bac**. Many future politicians, business leaders, and professors are educated at the **Grandes Écoles**.

Un professeur à l'Université de Nice donne son cours dans un amphithéâtre.

Recently France has been reforming its university system in concert with 32 other European countries. This reform involves reorganizing the university year into two semesters (instead of the traditional October to June academic year); establishing a common system of credits; and awarding diplomas based on a common progression from **une licence**, after three years of study, to **un master** after five years, and **un doctorat** after eight years.

Look at the video clip *Je suis étudiant*, filmed at **l'Université de Nice**. Identify the places on campus you see and the subjects that each speaker studies (or teaches!).

ET VOUS ?

1. Comment on the **bac**. How would you feel about taking a rigorous national exam like this at the end of secondary school?
2. Think about the reforms of the French university system. What are likely to be some advantages and disadvantages of greater uniformity and transferability within Europe of university credits and diplomas?

Implementation: 3-13 We are using B.A. to reflect the experience of American students. Canadian students would prepare *un bacc* and French students *une licence* ou *un master*. You may wish to have students make a chart with their partner's schedule. Create a sample schedule using the list of courses for Claire or Gilles. Be sure to indicate only the days of the week when he or she has classes. Do not indicate or ask for specific times, as telling time is not introduced until Ch. 4, L. 2. Provide blank schedule forms and have students report back to the class.

3-13 Votre diplôme et vos cours. Compare your major and minor with a partner and discuss the courses you are taking this semester.

MODÈLE É1 Je prépare un B.A. en sciences politiques. J'ai une mineure en espagnol. Et toi ?
É2 Moi, je prépare un B.A. en mathématiques, mais je n'ai pas de mineure.
É1 Ce semestre, je suis deux cours d'histoire, un cours de sociologie et un cours de français.
É2 Bien sûr, je suis un cours de français et j'ai aussi trois cours de maths !

3-14 Le travail à faire. What are you working on in your courses this week? Compare your responsibilities with a partner.

MODÈLE É1 J'ai beaucoup de travail en ce moment : je prépare un exposé pour mon cours de sociologie et j'ai deux examens vendredi.
É2 Moi aussi, j'ai beaucoup de travail : je prépare un essai pour mon cours d'histoire et j'ai un gros projet pour mon cours de gestion.

Sons et lettres

Les voyelles /o/ et /ɔ/

Note: As was the case for the mid-vowel pair /e/ and /ɛ/, the most important goal for American speakers is to avoid the pronunciation of a glide. The pronunciation we present here reflects Standard French and does not strictly follow the *loi de position* mentioned in the annotation for the treatment of the other pair of mid-vowels. Speakers in the south of France routinely produce the vowel /ɔ/ in closed syllables, in words such as [gɔʃ] and [rɔz] for SF [goʃ] and [roz].

The vowel of **beau**, /o/, is short and tense, in contrast to the longer, glided vowel of English *bow*. Hold your hand under your chin to make sure it does not drop as you say **beau**; your lips should stay rounded and tense. The vowel /o/ generally occurs at the end of words or of syllables, and it is written with **o**, **au/x**, **eau/x**, or combinations of **o** and silent consonants:

au resto U | **au**x bure**aux** | le m**o**t | il est gr**os**

The vowel of **sport**, /ɔ/, is pronounced with less tension than /o/, but still without any glide. It usually occurs before a pronounced consonant and is spelled **o:**

le pr**o**f | il est f**o**rt | Yv**o**nne | il ad**o**re

In a few words, /o/ occurs before a pronounced consonant. In these cases, it may also be spelled **ô** or **au:**

le dipl**ô**me | les **au**tres | à g**au**che | elle est gr**o**sse

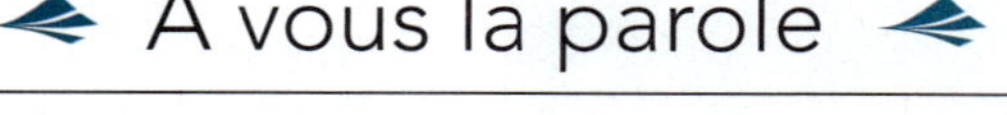

Initial practice: Begin with a discrimination drill, asking students to tell whether they hear the vowel of *beau* or that of *fort : gros, bureau, bonne, prof, mot, diplôme, fort, trop, golf.*

3-15 Contrastes. Compare the pronunciation of each pair of words or phrases. The first has the /o/ sound; the second the /ɔ/ sound.

le stylo / la gomme	Bruno / Yvonne	la radio / la porte
le piano / la note	Mme Lebeau / M. Lefort	il est beau / elle est bonne

3-16 Les abréviations. French students use many abbreviations to talk about their courses and other aspects of university life. Many of these abbreviations end in /o/ as in the list below. With a partner, practice saying each abbreviation and match it to its full form.

1. le labo	**a.** le dictionnaire
2. le resto U	**b.** le laboratoire
3. les sciences éco	**c.** la philosophie
4. les sciences po	**d.** les sciences politiques
5. la psycho	**e.** la sociologie
6. la philo	**f.** le restaurant universitaire
7. la socio	**g.** les sciences économiques
8. le dico	**h.** la psychologie

FORMES ET FONCTIONS

1. *Les verbes comme* préférer *et l'emploi de l'infinitif*

- For verbs conjugated like **préférer**, the singular forms and the third-person plural form of the present tense show a change from **é** /e/ to **è** /ɛ/. In all of these forms the endings are silent.

—Quel sport est-ce que vous préf**é**rez ?
—Nous préf**é**rons le tennis.
—Vous préf**é**rez le rugby ?
—Nous, on préf**è**re le football.
—Eux, ils préf**è**rent le hockey.
—Non, moi, je préf**è**re le golf.

PRÉFÉRER *to prefer*			
SINGULIER		**PLURIEL**	
je	préf**è**re	nous	préfér**ons**
tu	préf**è**re**s**	vous	préfér**ez**
il / elle / on	préf**è**re	ils / elles	préf**è**r**ent**

- Other verbs that show the same type of change are **répéter** (*to repeat*) and **suggérer** (*to suggest*):

Rép**é**tons après le professeur.
Qu'est-ce que vous sugg**é**rez ?
Rép**è**te après moi !
Qu'est-ce que tu sugg**è**res ?

- **Préférer** may be followed by a noun or by an infinitive:

Je préfère **le golf**.	*I prefer golf.*
Il préfère **jouer** au tennis.	*He prefers to play tennis.*

Presentation: To present inductively, discuss students' course preferences based on their majors, e.g., *Jessica prépare un diplôme en arts et spectacles ; elle préfère les cours de théâtre et de danse. La majeure de Steve, c'est l'histoire ; il préfère les cours d'histoire américaine.* Then display the verb chart and ask how this verb is similar to other *-er* verbs students have learned; you might draw a "boot" to illustrate the fact that all the singular forms and the third-person plural are pronounced alike. Be sure that students notice accent changes, and point out that these reflect the pronunciation discussed in the **Sons et lettres** of L. 1, /e/ in open syllables: *préférons* /pre fe rɔ̃/; /ɛ/ in closed syllables: *préfère* /pre fɛr/.

Expansion: In addition to *répéter* (introduced in Ch. Prélim., L. 2) and *suggérer*, you might provide other verbs conjugated like *préférer : espérer, compléter ;* only *préférer* will be practiced in this lesson. To practice *suggérer*, you might use:

SUGGESTION : Qu'est-ce que tu suggères ?
—Jouons aux cartes !
—Non, moi, je préfère jouer au golf.
OU Marie et moi, on préfère jouer au golf.

Presentation: Remind students of the placement of the negative in infinitive constructions.

◆ Use the following verbs to talk about likes and dislikes; all, like **préférer**, can be followed by a noun or an infinitive:

détester	*to detest*
aimer bien	*to like fairly well*
aimer	*to like or to love*
aimer beaucoup	*to like or love a lot*
préférer	*to prefer*
adorer	*to adore*

À vous la parole

Initial practice: Begin practice with a discrimination drill: have students write the letter *è* or *é* based on the form they hear: *je préfère, nous préférons,* etc. Follow with a substitution drill: *Je préfère le jazz ; vous. — Vous préférez le jazz,* etc.

Expansion: 3-17 Items may have more than one logical response; encourage students to think of several.

3-17 Les vacances. Based on the descriptions, figure out with a partner what these people probably prefer to do during their vacation.

MODÈLE Marie-Laure est très sociable.

É1 Elle préfère organiser des fêtes.

OU É2 Elle préfère dîner avec ses amies.

1. Fred et ses amis adorent le sport.
2. Mathilde est très réservée.
3. Nous aimons la musique.
4. Le copain de Sabrina est très énergique.
5. Vous n'êtes pas très énergiques.
6. La mère de mon amie aime bien travailler dans la nature.
7. Je suis assez paresseuse.
8. Tu n'aimes pas beaucoup le sport.

Expansion: 3-18 This is a good opportunity to recycle *faire* expressions and the difference between *jouer à* and *jouer de.* Expand on the exercise by asking students what they like to do.

3-18 Activités préférées. Everyone is supposed to be studying, but is instead thinking about his/her favorite activity! Tell what each person prefers to do.

MODÈLE Pauline préfère jouer au tennis.

 **3-19 Vos préférences.** Discuss your preferences with a classmate, then summarize them for the class.

MODÈLE les jeux : le Scrabble ou les échecs ?

É1 Est-ce que tu préfères jouer au Scrabble ou aux échecs ?
É2 Moi, je préfère jouer aux échecs, et toi ?
É1 Moi, j'adore jouer au Scrabble.

(*plus tard*) :
É2 Moi, j'aime les échecs, mais lui, il préfère le Scrabble.

1. les jeux : le Scrabble ou les échecs ?
2. la musique : le rock ou le jazz ?
3. les sports : le football ou le basket ?
4. les cours : le français ou les mathématiques ?
5. les animaux : les chats ou les chiens ?

Les Français préfèrent les chats. Ils ont 9,4 millions de chats et 8,5 millions de chiens.

2. *Les adjectifs prénominaux au pluriel*

- You have learned that a few adjectives precede the noun in French. These include:

MASCULIN SG.		MASCULIN PL.	FÉMININ SG.	FÉMININ PL.
jeune		jeunes	jeune	jeunes
joli		jolis	jolie	jolies
petit		petits	petite	petites
bon		bons	bonne	bonnes
mauvais		mauvais	mauvaise	mauvaises
premier		premiers	première	premières
dernier		derniers	dernière	dernières
grand		grands	grande	grandes
gros		gros	grosse	grosses
+ CONSONNE	+ VOYELLE			
beau	bel	beaux	belle	belles
nouveau	nouvel	nouveaux	nouvelle	nouvelles
vieux	vieil	vieux	vieille	vieilles

Additional activity: Have students discuss in pairs and then share with the class what they love to do, and what they absolutely hate doing. Be sure to provide clear models: *adorer :*

É1 Moi, j'adore travailler dans le jardin.
É2 Moi non, j'adore surtout écouter de la musique.

détester :

É1 Je déteste faire des courses le week-end.
É2 Moi aussi, je déteste ça.

To share with the class: *Moi, j'adore écouter de la musique, mais elle, elle adore travailler dans le jardin. On déteste faire des courses le week-end.*

Presentation: To introduce the new material, review adjective placement and singular prenominal adjective forms, taught in L. 1. Whereas the chart in L. 1 was meaning-based (using the *BRAGS* mnemonic), focus is on form in the chart provided here. Adjectives are grouped and shaded by the number of spoken forms (2, 4, and 5) and number of written forms. Note that *grand* and *gros* have four written forms, but five spoken forms; *beau, nouveau,* and *vieux* have five written forms, but four spoken forms (like *petit, bon,* etc.). To present, read a number of examples aloud and have students choose the appropriate form from a list, analyzing why they made the choice they did: *Voici des petits oiseaux : petit, petits, petites.* Summarize rules using the examples provided.
Remind students that although a letter *-s* or *-x* is generally added to written words to form the plural in French, this final letter is usually not pronounced. One must listen for a preceding word, usually a number or an article, to tell whether a noun is singular or plural. If the noun begins with a vowel, liaison can provide an additional clue: *cinq étudiants, des bureaux, mes‿affiches.*
Stress the importance of articles and liaison in signaling gender and number, since, for example, /ptit/ is both masculine (before a vowel) and feminine, singular and plural (feminine before a consonant).
Point out that *mauvais* and *gros* do not change spelling in the masculine plural. We are using the more frequent plural variant for the indefinite determiner: *des nouveaux étudiants* instead of *de nouveaux étudiants,* even though some conservative speakers might consider the latter form more "correct."

- The final letter of the plural form of these adjectives is usually not pronounced.

des jolies filles	des jeunes filles

However, when these adjectives precede a noun beginning with a vowel sound, you hear the liaison /z/.

des beau**x**‿enfants	des jeune**s**‿amis

For **jeune** and **joli**, there are two spoken forms in the plural. For all the other prenominal adjectives you have learned, there are four spoken forms in the plural, for example:

des grands labos	des grand**s**‿amphithéâtres
des grandes piscines	des grande**s**‿universités
des petits stades	des petit**s**‿amphithéâtres
des petites librairies	des petite**s**‿affiches

For the plural forms before a word beginning with a vowel, add the liaison /z/ to the form used before a consonant.

 À vous la parole 

Initial practice: Begin practice with a discrimination drill similar to that used for the presentation: *Voici des vieilles affiches : vieil, vieille, vieilles.* Follow up with substitution drills: *Voici des vieux musées ; résidences ; universités ; hôtels,* etc.

3-20 Décrivons l'université. Respond affirmatively to the following questions.

MODÈLE Les résidences sont nouvelles ?
→ Oui, ce sont des nouvelles résidences.

1. Les amphithéâtres sont vieux ?
2. Les laboratoires sont bons ?
3. Les ordinateurs sont mauvais ?
4. Les étudiants sont jeunes ?
5. Les terrains de sport sont beaux ?
6. Les bureaux sont grands ?
7. Les affiches sont belles ?
8. Les navettes sont nouvelles ?

Variation: 3-21 Vary this activity by having students adapt the passage to their own personal situation.

3-21 C'est le contraire ! Change the following narrative by substituting adjectives that have the opposite meaning.

MODÈLE Je suis étudiant dans une *petite* université.
→ Je suis étudiant dans une *grande* université.

Je suis étudiant dans une *petite* université. Nous avons des *vieilles* résidences ; moi, j'ai une *grande* chambre au *premier* étage. Il y a des *nouveaux* terrains de sport juste derrière notre *petit* centre étudiant. J'ai des *bons* cours et des *mauvais* cours. Dans mes cours, j'ai des *vieux* amis, et on travaille bien ensemble.

Implementation: 3-22 Point out that the adjectives are listed according to the *BRAGS* mnemonic, to reinforce the use of this learning strategy presented in L. 1. As a model, you might have the class as a whole describe the town where your university is located. Then put students into pairs to describe their hometown. Have them report back and briefly describe some aspect of their partner's hometown.

3-22 Votre ville natale. Describe your hometown to a classmate, commenting on the features outlined below. Use the correct form of adjectives from this list: **jolie**, **belle**, **première**, **dernière**, **jeune**, **nouvelle**, **vieille**, **bonne**, **mauvaise**, **petite**, **grande**, **grosse**.

MODÈLE des parcs
→ Dans ma ville natale, il y a des jolis parcs...

1. une mairie
2. des parcs
3. des hôtels
4. des piscines municipales
5. des universités
6. des cinémas
7. des maisons
8. des appartements

Écrivons

3-23 Une description de notre campus

A. Avant d'écrire. Write an e-mail to Jérémie, a student in France who is planning to visit your school. To help him visualize the campus, describe some of the important buildings and landmarks.

1. Make a list in French of four or five places on your campus that you will include in your description (for example, *la bibliothèque universitaire, la cafétéria,...*).
2. Look at a map of your campus, and decide how you can organize your description in a coherent manner. Note down by each place any prepositions or other indications you may use to tell where it is located.
3. Write a few adjectives in French that describe your campus in general or the specific places you will mention (for example, *le campus : assez petit, joli ; la bibliothèque : nouvelle et moderne*).
4. Write an introductory sentence or two to describe your campus.

B. En écrivant. As you write your description, begin with a general introduction, and then develop your ideas in a logical way. Keep in mind that for your French reader, the very idea of a campus might be somewhat foreign.

MODÈLE

Salut Jérémie,
Tu vas bientôt visiter notre université. Le campus de notre université est situé à proximité d'une grande ville. Le campus est assez petit mais joli. Au centre du campus, il y a la nouvelle bibliothèque. C'est un grand pavillon moderne, très pratique pour travailler et préparer les cours. Juste à côté, il y a...
À bientôt,
(your name)

C. En révisant. As you revise your e-mail, think about the following questions and make any necessary changes.

1. Check the content: did you provide an introductory overview of your campus? Did you describe several buildings and help your reader visualize them and where they are located?
2. Analyze the style and form of your description: did you include a variety of adjectives to make your description more vivid? Did you use appropriate prepositions to explain the location of buildings in relation to each other? Check also adjective agreement and the formation of prepositional phrases.

D. Après avoir écrit. Compare your description with those written by your classmates by reading them in small groups: what features are common to all the descriptions? What interesting differences do you notice?

Stratégie

When writing a description of a place, look for a logical way to organize the information. One effective approach is to help your reader visualize the setting by describing landmarks or points of interest in a logical sequence and in relation to each other.

Implementation: Another way to prepare students for this writing activity is to have them analyze the description of the UdeM campus provided in the **Points de départ** of L. 1. You might even revise this description as a whole-class writing activity, so that it better meets the requirements of this assignment. The revised description can then serve as a model for students' description of their campus.

Leçon 3 Choix de carrière

Presentation: Use the opening questions and other similar ones to introduce the topic; *vouloir* is treated here as a lexical item. Present the names of places, job types, and occupations using the labeled groupings (MFL, Ch. 3). Describe, in simple terms and using gestures, what each person does. Test comprehension by changing to the images without labels (MFL, Ch. 3) and having students point out the person you name; then elicit repetitions with either/or questions: *C'est une pharmacienne ou une infirmière ?*

Presentation: Point out that *la clinique* is a false cognate, referring to a private hospital. *Un/e fonctionnaire* is any government employee, including postal workers, *SNCF* employees, and teachers. Depending on the interests of your class, you may want to introduce additional professional vocabulary such as *un chef d'entreprise, un banquier, un cadre, un/e gérant/e, un directeur/une directrice, un/e psychologue, travailler dans la publicité,* etc.

Initial practice: For each place named, tell which person would not work there: *un bureau : un avocat, un secrétaire, un serveur.* Recycle vocabulary dealing with college coursework: *Pour être médecin ? — On étudie la biologie, la chimie, la médecine,* etc. Ask students what profession they associate with famous names: Pablo Picasso, Marie Curie, Whoopi Goldberg, Albert Schweitzer, Carl Bernstein, etc. Once they have been given a few examples, have students suggest others.

POINTS DE DÉPART

Qu'est-ce que vous voulez faire comme travail ?

Dans quel domaine est-ce que vous voulez travailler ? Est-ce que vous voulez aider les gens, comme les médecins, par exemple ? Est-ce que vous voulez voyager, comme certains journalistes ? Est-ce que vous êtes doué/e pour les mathématiques, comme les comptables ?

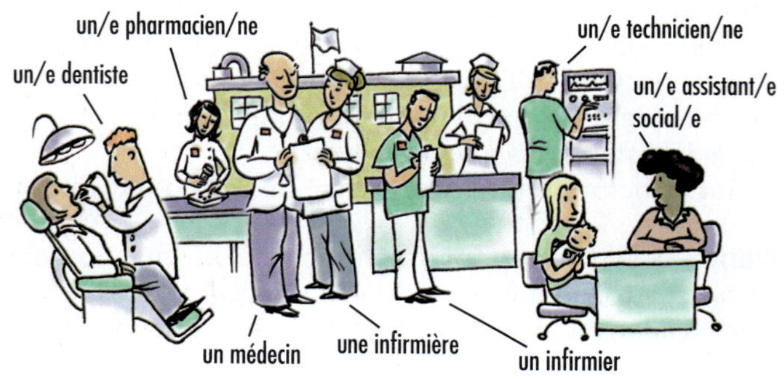

À l'hôpital ou à la clinique

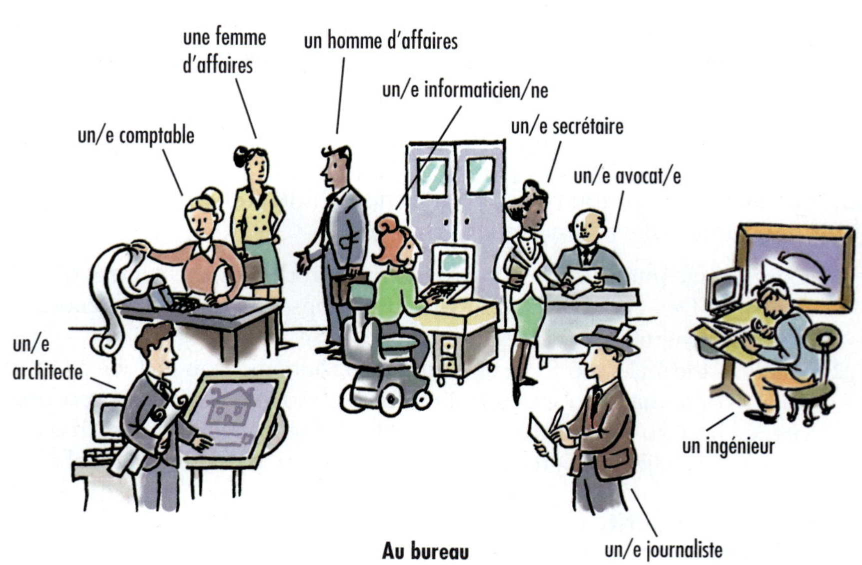

Au bureau

Les artistes

Les services

Les fonctionnaires

Presentation: Once students are familiar with the names of professions, introduce the chart of job characteristics. Have students provide an example for each job characteristic: *Dans quelle profession est-ce qu'on a beaucoup de prestige ? — Un médecin a beaucoup de prestige*, etc. For now, treat the relative pronoun *où* as a fixed expression; it will be presented in Ch. 9, L. 3.

Qu'est-ce qui vous intéresse ?

Je veux avoir...	Je cherche un travail où...
un bon salaire.	on peut voyager.
beaucoup de prestige.	on peut aider les gens.
beaucoup de responsabilités.	on n'est pas trop stressé/e.
un contact avec le public.	on est très autonome.
un travail en plein air.	on gagne beaucoup d'argent.

Initial practice: You might include drills that focus on form as a clue to gender. Begin with a discrimination drill: *un homme, une femme ou impossible à dire ? Michèle est informaticienne. Pascal/e est dentiste. René est avocat. Pascale est serveuse. Claude est infirmière. Pascal est infirmier. Michèle est vendeuse. André est représentant de commerce. Dominique est fonctionnaire*, etc. Remind students of the rule that derives masculine variable adjectives from the feminine by loss of the final pronounced consonant. The same rule applies to some professions: *Elle est avocate → Il est avocat*, etc. Review the importance of a strong release of the final consonant for the feminine. Be sure to treat the **Vie et culture** related to the feminization of names of professions.

À vous la parole

3-24 Classez les métiers. Name some jobs or professions that have the features listed.

MODÈLE On gagne beaucoup d'argent.
Un avocat gagne beaucoup d'argent.
OU Un acteur célèbre (*famous*) gagne beaucoup d'argent.

1. On est très autonome.
2. On travaille en plein air.
3. Un diplôme universitaire n'est pas nécessaire.
4. On n'est pas très stressé/e.
5. On a un contact avec le public.
6. On a beaucoup de prestige.
7. On peut travailler avec les enfants.
8. On peut voyager.

Expansion: 3-24 Expand on or vary this exercise by including the opposites, for example, *on ne gagne pas beaucoup d'argent* or *un diplôme universitaire est nécessaire.*

Vie et culture

Implementation: You might ask students to generate additional examples of this trend in English, such as police officer, mail carrier, and sales associate.

La féminisation des noms de professions

Throughout the world, women are making careers in professions that were once male-dominated. Language reflects this. The trend in English is toward more gender-neutral terms: instead of *waiter/waitress*, we say *server*; instead of *fireman*, *firefighter*. The French language tends toward specifying gender with regard to profession. For some professions that lack a feminine form, such as **un professeur**, a female professor has traditionally been addressed as **Madame le Professeur**, and students talking about their professors would say, **Mon professeur de chimie est Madame Durand**. Canadian and Swiss students, however, routinely use the form **une professeure** and might say, for example, **Ma professeure de psychologie est Madame Laurent**.

ET VOUS ?

1. Based on what you have learned in the **Points de départ**, provide some examples to illustrate how names of professions in French may have:
   a. one form
   b. a masculine or feminine article
   c. separate masculine and feminine forms
2. Why do you think that English speakers have opted for gender-neutral terms while in French-speaking countries the trend is toward gender-specific terms?

Un chef de bureau parle avec ses employés.

Key: Et vous ? Examples might include:
a. one form: *un professeur, un écrivain, un médecin, un ingénieur*
b. a variable article: *un/e dentiste, un/e architecte, un/e journaliste, un/e fonctionnaire , un/e agent/e de police*
c. separate masculine and feminine forms: *une avocate, un avocat ; un facteur, une factrice ; une infirmière, un infirmier ; une musicienne, un musicien ; une vendeuse, un vendeur.*

Note: Canadians and the Swiss have used the form *la professeure* for some time, while in France this form is frowned on. The French have no difficulty, however, using *la prof* in casual conversation. Additional feminine forms for professions include *une écrivaine, une ingénieure.* In countries like Switzerland and Canada, these terms have been officially accepted and are in use to some extent, especially among feminists and academics.

3-25 Aptitudes et goûts. Based on the descriptions, tell what each of these people will probably do for a living.

MODÈLE Rémy est sociable. Il aime aider les gens avec leurs problèmes.
→ Il va être assistant social.

1. Lucie s'intéresse au théâtre. Elle danse et elle chante très bien.
2. Kevin aime le travail précis. Il est très bon en maths.
3. Stéphanie est énergique et sociable. Elle aime voyager, et elle aime le contact avec le public.
4. Camille s'intéresse à l'informatique et elle aime créer des programmes.
5. Nicolas est très doué pour les sciences ; il aime travailler au laboratoire.
6. Nathalie adore la mode ; elle voudrait ouvrir une boutique un jour.
7. Charline s'intéresse à l'architecture; elle aime dessiner (*to design*) des maisons et des appartements.
8. Grégorie aime travailler avec les enfants ; il est calme et patient.

3-26 Vos projets de carrière. In a group of three or four students, find out what career each person wants—and does not want—to pursue.

MODÈLE
É1 Toi, Mike, qu'est-ce que tu veux faire comme travail ?
É2 Je veux être assistant social. J'aime travailler avec les gens.
É1 Et toi, Margot, qu'est-ce que tu ne veux pas faire ?
É3 Moi, je ne veux pas être avocate. On travaille trop et on est trop stressé.

Implementation: 3-26 You may need to introduce additional vocabulary, based on students' interests and career plans. Before completing in small groups, conduct a chain drill:

É1 Qu'est-ce que tu veux faire ?
É2 Je veux être dentiste. Et toi, qu'est-ce que tu veux faire ?
É3 Je veux être architecte. Et toi ?, etc.

Vouloir (*veux*) is treated here as a lexical item. This exercise can serve as an inductive presentation to the verb, which is presented later in this lesson.

FORMES ET FONCTIONS

1. C'est *et* il est

- There are two ways to indicate someone's profession:
  - Use a form of **être** + the name of the profession, without an article:

Julie **est** musicienne.	*Julie is a musician.*
Son frère **est** acteur.	*Her brother is an actor.*
Vous **êtes** professeur ?	*Are you a teacher?*

  - Use **c'est/ce sont** + the indefinite article + the name of the profession:

Julie, **c'est une** musicienne.	*Julie is a musician.*
Stéphane ? **C'est un** dentiste.	*Stéphane? He's a dentist.*
Leurs parents ? **Ce sont des** fonctionnaires.	*Their parents? They're government employees.*

- When you include an adjective along with the name of a profession, you must use **c'est/ce sont** + the indefinite article. Compare:

Anne **est** architecte.	*Anne is an architect.*
C'est une excellente architecte.	*She's an excellent architect.*
Ils **sont** artistes.	*They're artists.*
Ce sont des artistes très doués.	*They're very talented artists.*

Presentation: The functional difference between the two patterns is related to the notion of topic vs. comment. For example, if Julie has already been mentioned in the conversation, one is more likely to use the first pattern, *elle est musicienne*. If however Julie is being introduced into the conversation, one would be more likely to use *Julie, c'est une musicienne*. Display examples of the two patterns and explain usage.

À vous la parole

Initial practice: Using the unlabeled images of professions from the **Points de départ** (MFL, Ch. 3), have students identify the profession of each person shown: *C'est une infirmière*, etc.

Preparation: 3-27 Review adjectives, brainstorming about what kind of people usually have what professions: *infirmière = gentille, généreuse ; avocat = sérieux, ambitieux ; écrivain = individualiste*, etc.

3-27 Professions et traits de caractère. For each profession, specify a fitting character trait.

MODÈLE Anne est infirmière.
C'est une infirmière calme.

1. Delphine est avocate.
2. Rémi est assistant social.
3. Virginie est médecin.
4. Max est représentant de commerce.
5. Coralie est musicienne.
6. Florian et Sylvie sont informaticiens.
7. Hugo et Jessica sont serveurs.
8. Sandra et Alex sont professeurs.

Key: 3-28 1) C'est un ingénieur français. 2) C'est une chanteuse/une actrice américaine. 3) C'est un acteur français. 4) C'est un médecin français. 5) C'est une avocate américaine. 6) C'est un journaliste américain. 7) C'est un architecte américain. 8) C'est un écrivain américain.

Variations: Have students suggest additional possibilities; this could be structured as a game. Or simplify by having students give the profession only: *Jules Verne ? C'est un écrivain.*

3-28 Identification. Identify the nationality and profession of each of the following famous people. Choose from: **américain/e** or **français/e**.

MODÈLE Jules Verne
C'est un écrivain français.

1. Gustave Eiffel
2. Barbra Streisand
3. Gérard Depardieu
4. Louis Pasteur
5. Ruth Bader Ginsburg
6. Carl Bernstein
7. Frank Lloyd Wright
8. Toni Morrison

3-29 Quelle est leur profession ? With a partner, tell what some of the people you know well do for a living.

MODÈLE votre mère

É1 Ma mère est technicienne de laboratoire.
É2 Ma mère travaille à la maison ; c'est une femme au foyer (*homemaker*).

1. votre mère
2. votre père
3. votre frère ou sœur
4. les amis de vos parents
5. votre oncle
6. votre tante

Presentation: Present these verbs inductively by telling things you want to do, cannot do, and must do. For example, *Ce soir, je veux aller au ciné pour voir un film. Mais, je ne peux pas. Je dois préparer mon cours pour demain, et je dois corriger les essais. Et vous, qu'est-ce que vous voulez faire ce soir ? Vous voulez regarder la télé ? aller au match de basket ? Est-ce que vous pouvez ? Oui, c'est possible. ou Non, ce n'est pas possible. Qu'est-ce que vous devez faire : travailler ? préparer un examen ? faire les devoirs ?* Then show similar examples on a transparency or slide and have students provide quasi-synonyms for each: *vouloir = désirer, pouvoir = c'est possible, devoir = c'est nécessaire.* Finish by showing forms and asking students to find similarities among the verbs and others they know (i.e., all first-person forms are pronounced alike, although the spelling is different; similar to *-re* verbs, there is a pronounced final consonant in the third-person plural form, etc.)

2. *Les verbes* devoir, pouvoir *et* vouloir

- The verbs **devoir**, **pouvoir**, and **vouloir** are irregular.

DEVOIR *must, to have to, to be supposed to*			
SINGULIER		**PLURIEL**	
je	dois	nous	dev**ons**
tu	dois	vous	dev**ez**
il / elle / on	doit	ils / elles	doiv**ent**

POUVOIR *can, to be able*			
SINGULIER		**PLURIEL**	
je	peux	nous	pouv**ons**
tu	peux	vous	pouv**ez**
il / elle / on	peu**t**	ils / elles	peuv**ent**

VOULOIR *to want*			
SINGULIER		**PLURIEL**	
je	veux	nous	voul**ons**
tu	veux	vous	voul**ez**
il / elle / on	veu**t**	ils / elles	veul**ent**

- These verbs are often used:
  - With an infinitive:

Tu **dois** travailler ?	*Do you have to work?*
Je **veux** arriver demain matin.	*I want to arrive tomorrow morning.*
Tu ne **peux** pas arriver ce soir ?	*Can't you arrive this evening?*

  - To soften commands and make suggestions. Compare:

Travaillez plus !	*Work more!*
Vous **devez** travailler plus.	*You must work more.*
Fermez la porte !	*Shut the door!*
Vous **voulez** bien fermer la porte ?	*Will you shut the door?*
Vous **pouvez** fermer la porte ?	*Can you shut the door?*

- The verb **devoir** also has the meaning *to owe*:

Il **doit** 50 € à mon frère.	*He owes my brother 50 euros.*
Combien est-ce que je vous **dois** ?	*How much do I owe you?*

- **Vouloir** is used in a number of useful expressions:

Tu **veux** aller avec nous au ciné ?	*You want to go to the movies with us?*
Je **veux** bien.	*OK.*
Qu'est-ce que vous **voulez** (tu **veux**) dire ?	*What do you mean?*
Qu'est-ce que ça **veut** dire ?	*What does that mean?*

Presentation: Remind students of similar constructions they have learned: *aller* plus the infinitive in the *futur proche,* and verbs of preference plus the infinitive; remind them too of the placement of the negative in infinitive constructions.

À vous la parole

Initial practice: 3-30 Begin with this comprehension-based exercise. To practice forms, first use a discrimination drill: one person, or more than one? *Ils peuvent écouter. Elle veut dîner. Ils doivent travailler. Il peut chanter. Elles peuvent parler français. Ils veulent aller à une fête. Il veut danser. Elles peuvent jouer de la flûte. Il doit aider sa mère. Ils veulent faire du bricolage ce week-end. Elle veut faire de la natation,* etc. Follow up with substitution drills for *vouloir* and *pouvoir : Je veux travailler ; nous. — Nous voulons travailler,* etc. Next complete Ex. 3-31 and 3-32, which integrate practice of *vouloir* and *pouvoir*. To practice *devoir* as well, use Ex. 3-33.

3-30 Poli ou impoli ? Jean-Marc is a department manager. See his instructions to employees below, and decide in each case whether he is being polite or impolite.

	poli	impoli
MODÈLE Vous pouvez aider ces messieurs ?	✓	______
1. Apportez-moi les rapports !	______	______
2. Vous voulez bien préparer un mémorandum ?	______	______
3. Vous pouvez attendre un instant ?	______	______
4. Vous voulez bien lire ce message ?	______	______
5. Téléphonez à ces clients !	______	______
6. Vous pouvez répondre à ces questions ?	______	______
7. Vous voulez téléphoner au directeur ?	______	______
8. Fermez la porte du bureau !	______	______

Politeness is one indicator that a person is dealing well with stress; how is Jean-Marc doing today? Explain your response.

Expansion: 3-31 Have students describe their own interests, and let classmates suggest a suitable profession.

3-31 Une future profession. What can these people do for a living? With a partner, suggest possibilities.

MODÈLE Sarah veut gagner beaucoup d'argent, mais elle ne veut pas faire des études supérieures.

É1 Elle peut devenir (*become*) actrice de cinéma, par exemple.
É2 Elle peut aussi devenir chanteuse.

1. Adrien ne veut pas travailler dans un bureau ; il aime travailler en plein air.
2. Gaëlle et Alexandra veulent travailler avec les enfants.
3. Je veux voyager et je suis assez sociable.
4. Nous voulons un contact avec le public et nous préférons travailler le soir.
5. Jean-Baptiste veut aider les gens et il n'est pas doué pour les sciences.
6. Audrey est très douée pour la musique et très disciplinée.
7. Simon et David ne veulent pas un travail avec beaucoup de stress.

Implementation: 3-32 First brainstorm with the whole class some appropriate questions for each item. Examples:
1. Qu'est-ce que tu veux faire comme travail ?
2. Où est-ce que tu veux habiter ?
3. Où est-ce que tu veux voyager ?

4. Est-ce que tu veux avoir des enfants ? Combien ?
5. Est-ce que tu veux gagner beaucoup d'argent ?

Then put students in pairs to compare answers.

3-32 Vouloir, c'est pouvoir. What are your plans for the future? Compare your ideas with those of your partner.

MODÈLE faire comme travail

É1 Qu'est-ce que tu veux faire comme travail ?
É2 Moi, je veux être médecin ou dentiste. Et toi ?
É1 Moi, je ne veux pas être médecin ni (*nor*) dentiste ; je veux être architecte.

1. faire comme travail
2. habiter
3. voyager
4. avoir des enfants
5. gagner de l'argent

3-33 Trouvez une excuse. You don't want to go out (*sortir*) with your classmate's friend, so you must come up with a good excuse!

MODÈLE Je ne peux pas sortir ce soir avec ton ami/e ; je dois préparer un examen et aller chez mes parents.

Expansion: 3-33 As a follow-up, have each student share his/her excuse, then vote on who has the most original/the most plausible/the most far-fetched excuse.

Lisons

3-34 Petites annonces

A. Avant de lire. The text below consists of several job ads from a newspaper. When you read ads like these, you typically will be looking for specific pieces of information. You can scan the text—assisted by the design and layout—to find relevant ads, then focus more intensively on information of interest. Scan to find an ad:

1. for a teaching job
2. for a full-time permanent position
3. for a temporary position
4. for an office job
5. for which you need to speak two languages

Stratégie

Scan a text by searching quickly to locate specific information that you need. Then, when you find the desired information, read it carefully.

Key: Avant de lire 1) *CÉGEP* 2) *Fruits & Parfums, Rédacteur technique* 3) *Hygiéniste dentaire* 4) *Rédacteur technique* 5) *Fruits & Parfums, Rédacteur technique*

B. En lisant. Now find the answers to the following questions.

1. Find a sentence that indicates that all jobs are offered to both men and women. In spite of this, one ad is clearly written with women in mind. Which ad is it? Which ad(s) make(s) it clear that both men and women are encouraged to apply?
2. Which job requires knowledge of computers? You can find it by looking for names of computer programs.
3. Which job specifies that working some weekends is required? The expression used to express "weekend" is different from the word used in France, **le week-end**. How is this expressed in Canadian French?

Key: En lisant 1) *Tous les emplois annoncés s'adressent aux hommes et aux femmes ;* for women: *Hygiéniste Dentaire demandée ;* for both men and women: *enseignant(e), conseiller(ère), pharmacien(ne)* 2) *Rédacteur technique* 3) *Pharmacien(ne) ; une fin de semaine*

C. En regardant de plus près. Now that you have located particular pieces of information in the ads, focus on the following features.

1. Look more closely at the ad for a teaching job: Is this a full-time position? What qualifications are required, and what experience is desirable?
2. Based on their ad, what type of business is **Fruits & Parfums**?
3. If you wanted to apply for the job at **Fruits & Parfums**, what options do you have?
4. What particular personality traits does the technical writer need to exhibit?

Key: En regardant de plus près 1) the teaching job is a part-time position, requiring a *bacc* in the area taught, with pedagogical training and teaching experience desirable 2) a retail store offering luxury skin care, and home and gourmet products 3) one can apply by fax, by e-mail, or in person at the boutique 4) must be disciplined, able to take initiative and work independently.

carrières

Pour faire paraître vos annonces dans cette section composez 418-868-0237 ou envoyez un courriel à annoncescarrieres@presse.ca

Tous les emplois annoncés s'adressent aux hommes et aux femmes.

CÉGEP de St-Philippe

Le Cégep de Saint-Philippe requiert les services d'enseignant(e) afin de dispenser les charges de cours suivant :

CH-2006-04 Charge temps partiel en mathématiques

Exigence : baccalauréat en mathématiques

L'expérience en psychopédagogie et en enseignement est souhaitable.

Les personnes intéressées doivent faire parvenir leur curriculum vitae ***au plus tard le 7 mai à 17 h*** à l'adresse suivante :

Cégep de Saint-Philippe
Service des ressources humaines
Saint-Philippe (Québec) G2R 8K2
Télécopieur : (418) 261-9796

Fruits & Parfums

Fruits & Parfums, un réseau de boutiques offrant des produits de soins corporels, d'ambiance et de gourmet est à la recherche d'un(e)

CONSEILLER(ÈRE) AUX VENTES (temps plein)

– Vous avez un sens de la vente.
– Vous détenez un diplôme d'études secondaires.
– Vous êtes bilingue.

Si vous êtes un(e) passionné(e) de fragrances enivrantes, veuillez faire parvenir votre curriculum vitae au plus tard le 30 avril prochain, par télécopieur au (418) 296-2080, par courriel au *emploi@fruits-parfums.com* ou en vous présentant directement à la boutique située dans le Vieux-Québec.

Solutions Québec Tech recherche

Rédacteur technique pour travailler en collaboration avec des ingénieurs de télécommunications.

- Le candidat doit faire preuve d'initiative, être discipliné et apprécier le travail autonome
- Expérience avec Adobe FrameMaker, Illustrator, Photoshop, InDesign et Quark nécessaire
- Baccalauréat, soit en techniques de communication, en journalisme, en anglais, en informatique ou en communication avec science (ou l'équivalent)
- Forte habileté de rédaction en anglais
- La maîtrise du français pour communiquer avec les ingénieurs

S.V.P. faire parvenir c.v. à l'attention de Gilles Lamontagne

SOLUTIONS QUÉBEC TECH
4500, boul. de la Couronne
Québec (QC) G2F 2B9

HYGIÉNISTE DENTAIRE

demandée à Lac-Saint-Martin

Temps plein en remplacement d'un congé de maternité, 18 à 24 mois

Tél : **489-4271**

Pharmacien(ne)

Ville de Québec
(quartier Petit Champlain)
33 heures/semaine
Une (1) fin de semaine sur quatre (4)
Horaire flexible

Appeler Alain Paradis
459-3025

Key: Après avoir lu 2) One difference between similar ads in French and English is the need in French to make clear that jobs are for men and women by changing the ending of words.

D. Après avoir lu. Now discuss the following questions with your classmates.

1. Would you be qualified for any of the jobs listed? Explain why or why not. Do you find any of the jobs particularly interesting? Why?
2. Are these ads in any way different from ads for the same types of jobs in your own local newspaper?

Une vendeuse dans une parfumerie.

Venez chez nous ! Étudier et travailler en pays francophone

With the advent of globalization, many Americans now study and work overseas. Technology allows for rapid communication; universities encourage exchanges; and many businesses have international operations. Knowing even the basics of the French language increases opportunities for study and work across the globe. In this lesson we will explore what it is like to live, study, and work in a Francophone region.

NATO headquarters in Brussels, Belgium—what countries' flags do you recognize? Brussels serves, along with Strasbourg and Luxembourg, as one of the capitals of the European Union. Many internationals live and work there.

Implementation: An additional clip, in which a student and teacher discuss the history of Canada, is treated SAM/MFL. Discuss the questions in **Avant de regarder** with the class as a whole, or let students work in pairs or small groups. Show the location of Seillans on a map, and later, of Marseille, where Barbara completed her studies.

Observons

3-35 Études et travail

A. Avant de regarder. What profession are you considering? How will you prepare for this profession? List in French some of the positive and negative aspects of that field of work. In this video clip, you will hear Barbara describe her studies and her job. Barbara lives and works in Seillans, a small town in the south of France. Look at the picture here and guess what type of work she does.

Barbara au travail

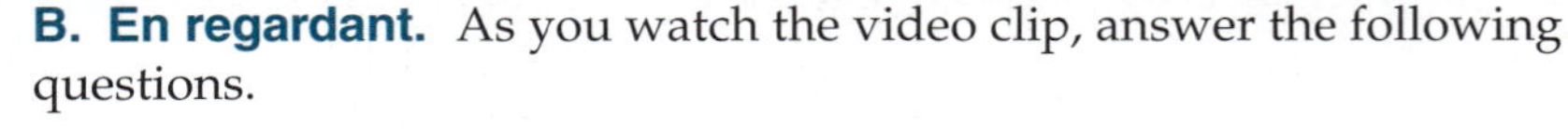

Note: The *École Normale Supérieure d'Architecture Marseille Luminy*, where Barbara studied, is a *Grande École*. Within the School of Architecture, the *Département de préparation à l'administration générale* prepares candidates for national examinations that are part of the professional credentialing process.

Script: Observons

BARBARA : Voilà, mais je suis architecte, je suis diplômée par le gouvernement, DPAG [Département de préparation à l'administration générale]. J'ai fait mon diplôme à Marseille, dans les Bouches-du-Rhône, à l'École d'Architecture et les Beaux-Arts. Et donc, euh je suis diplômée depuis 1986. J'ai fait sept ans d'études et puis trois ans après de spécialisation pour le, bah le bâtiment parasismique. J'aime beaucoup mon travail, parce que je suis ici principalement sur les maisons de Seillans, avec des projets de rénovation et un peu de création aussi. Et j'aime beaucoup ce métier parce que, on est disponible pour les horaires, on peut travailler à la maison, pour mes enfants, je peux travailler aussi euh, des rendez-vous de chantier, dehors et donc j'ai des horaires euh, c'est assez souple, voilà, au niveau des horaires. Donc j'aime beaucoup ce travail, et j'aime surtout euh, Seillans, parce que c'est, c'est vraiment typique, les maisons que l'on fait ici en Provence et c'est aussi très intéressant, mais il y a beaucoup aussi de clientèle anglaise, donc étrangère, qui vient de s'installer. Voilà. Mais c'est très intéressant.

Key: En regardant 1) b 2) d 3) b 4) d 5) a 6) a, d, e

B. En regardant. As you watch the video clip, answer the following questions.

1. Barbara works as a/an . . .
   a. journalist b. architect c. attorney d. teacher
2. She completed her studies in the city of . . .
   a. Strasbourg b. Toulon c. Paris d. Marseille
3. She studied at . . .
   a. la Faculté de Droit b. l'École d'Architecture et des Beaux-Arts
   c. une Grande École d. l'École d'Ingénieurs
4. With her studies and her specialization, Barbara has . . . years of professional training.
   a. three b. five c. seven d. ten
5. Does Barbara enjoy her work?
   a. yes b. no
6. Indicate her reasons for feeling the way she does about her job.
   a. She is available for her children.
   b. She has lots of responsabilities.
   c. She earns a good living.
   d. Her hours are flexible.
   e. Her work is interesting.

C. Après avoir regardé. Now discuss the following questions with classmates.

1. Would Barbara's job interest you? Why or why not?
2. Would you consider completing your own professional preparation in a foreign country? What might be some of the advantages or disadvantages of doing so?

Les francophones au Canada

Canada is officially bilingual, and almost seven million of the country's 31 million citizens speak French as their native language. Most French Canadians live in the province of Quebec, where approximately 80 percent of the inhabitants are native speakers of French. Montreal is the second largest Francophone city in the world, after Paris.

Dans le vieux Montréal, la place Jacques Cartier et l'Hôtel de Ville

In 1977, the provincial legislature made French the sole official language of Quebec with Bill 101 (**la Loi 101**). All official documents, however, are published in English and French, and the rights of

Anglophone minorities who are Canadian citizens are protected. The preamble to **la Loi 101** outlines its rationale and lists the five areas, in addition to the legal system, in which French will be used.

Note: This legislative text is easy to understand because of the large number of cognates. See whether students can find: 1) the name of the legislative body (*l'Assemblée nationale*); 2) the rationale for the creation of the bill, found in the opening sentence; 3) the five domains in which French will be used: the workplace, education, the media, commerce, and business affairs. The Preamble continues with a statement about the importance of respecting ethnic minorities and specifically grants the right to develop and maintain their native language and culture to the Inuit and the Amerindian peoples of Quebec. It also places this legislation in the wider global context of a revalorization of ethnic heritage. You may wish to have students read the full text of the Preamble to *la Loi 101*, found on the *Chez nous* Companion Website.
You might also discuss with students the movement for independence in Quebec. At the most recent referendum on this topic, in October 1996, the electorate was deeply divided: 49.5% for independence, 50.5% against.

Charte de la langue française

[Sanctionnée le 26 août 1977]

Préambule

Langue distinctive d'un peuple majoritairement francophone, la langue française permet au peuple québécois d'exprimer son identité.

L'Assemblée nationale reconnaît la volonté des Québécois d'assurer la qualité et le rayonnement de la langue française. Elle est donc résolue à faire du français la langue de l'État et de la Loi aussi bien que la langue normale et habituelle du travail, de l'enseignement, des communications, du commerce et des affaires.

Lisons

3-36 Emménager à Montréal

A. Avant de lire. This excerpt is from an informational magazine called **Emménager à Montréal** (*Moving to Montreal*), which is a guide for people who are relocating to Montreal. Skim the three paragraphs of the text and answer the following questions:

1. What is the general topic of the excerpt?
2. Each paragraph addresses a specific aspect of the general topic; explain what that is in each case.

B. En lisant. As you read more carefully, look for the following information.

1. In the first paragraph, why is Bill 101 mentioned? What exception to the law is described?
2. The second paragraph describes two "parallel branches," or systems; what does this refer to?
3. How could you get more information about learning French if you were moving to Quebec?

Stratégie

It is often useful to skim a text quickly to get the gist. This will orient you to the topic and help you to understand the content more readily as you read again.

Key: Avant de lire Answers will vary, but may include: 1) education, the school system (point out the words *éducation* and *école*, but also *enseignement*) 2) laws or government regulations related to education; the existence of French- and English-speaking schools; resources for learning French.

Key: En lisant Answers will vary, but may include 1) the law specifies that all children must be educated in French; an exception is made for temporary residents 2) there are parallel Anglophone and Francophone school systems 3) call the number listed, or visit the Web site

L'enseignement[1] au Québec

Au Québec, le ministère de l'Éducation est l'organisme gouvernemental responsable de la supervision de tous les niveaux[2] d'enseignement de la province. En 1977, la loi 101 – ou la Charte de la langue française — a été adoptée par le gouvernement du Québec. Selon la loi 101, tous les enfants doivent obtenir[3] leur éducation en français jusqu'au niveau post-secondaire. Il existe cependant des exceptions à cette règle[4]. Par exemple, les résidents temporaires du Québec peuvent fréquenter une école anglophone.

Le système scolaire, de la prématernelle et jusqu'à la cinquième année du secondaire, a deux branches parallèles, l'une anglophone et l'autre francophone. Les étudiants qui vont dans une école post-secondaire peuvent décider de la langue qu'ils désirent apprendre, et il n'est pas rare que des étudiants francophones choisissent de fréquenter une université de langue anglaise et vice-versa.

Bien s'exprimer en français

La vie de tous les jours peut s'avérer[5] compliquée si on ne possède pas au moins une connaissance[6] de base du français. Des cours sont offerts gratuitement aux nouveaux venus[7] en provenance d'un pays non francophone par le ministère des Relations avec les Citoyens et de l'Immigration. Pour de plus amples renseignements téléphonez au 514-864-9191 ou visitez www.immq.gouv.qc.ca.

[1]*teaching* [2]*all levels* [3]*obtain* [4]*rule* [5]être [6]*knowledge* [7]*newcomers*

Source: *Emménager à Montréal*, 2006–2007, www.movingto.com

Key: En regardant de plus près
1) there are five years of secondary school, rather than four, as in the United States
2) to choose; *peuvent décider de* 3) free of charge

C. En regardant de plus près. Now look more closely at the following features of the text.

1. In the second paragraph, Quebec's public education is described as « ... **de la prématernelle et jusqu'à la cinquième année du secondaire** ». What does this tell you about the length of public education in Canada?
2. Also in this paragraph, you see the verb **choisir : ils choisissent**. Based on the context, what do you think this verb means? There is another verb phrase in the same sentence with a similar meaning.
3. In the last paragraph, what is the meaning of **gratuitement** in the phrase « ... **des cours sont offerts gratuitement** » ?

D. Après avoir lu. Discuss the following questions with your classmates.

1. What is your opinion of the provision of **la Loi 101** mentioned in this excerpt? How do you think you would feel about this law and its provisions if you were going to be living in Quebec?
2. At this time, there is no national law specifying that English is the official language of the United States, although some groups have expressed support for such a law. Do you think an English-only law is necessary or would be beneficial? Why or why not?

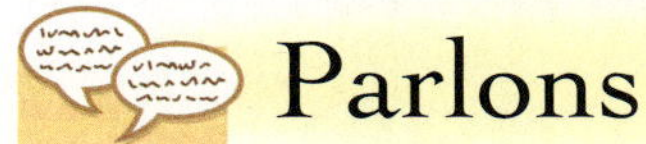

Parlons

3-37 Une langue bien de chez nous

A. Avant de parler. When you travel in the French-speaking world, you can expect to encounter regional differences in the language, much as you would note variations in English as spoken in different places. Consider how the following brief French-Canadian conversation differs from a conversation in Standard French, the French you are learning. Are there words and turns of phrase that you are not familiar with?

ALEX : Allô Julie. Ça va ?
JULIE : Pas pire.
ALEX : Je te présente ma blonde, Sabrina.
JULIE : Salut, Sabrina.
SABRINA : Salut, Julie.
ALEX : Excuse-nous, Julie, on ne peut pas jaser, on doit travailler à la bibli.
JULIE : O.K., c'est beau. Moi, je vais dîner à la cafétéria. Bonjour Alex, bonjour Sabrina.
SABRINA : Salut. À prochaine.

Here are some common expressions in Québécois French:

au Québec	en France
allô	bonjour
pas pire	pas mal
c'est le fun	c'est amusant
ma blonde	ma petite amie
mon chum	mon petit ami
la fin de semaine	le week-end
jaser	discuter
dîner	déjeuner
O.K. c'est beau	d'accord, c'est bon
bienvenue	de rien
à prochaine	à la prochaine
bonjour	au revoir

B. En parlant. Use some of the Québécois words and expressions listed above to create a dialogue with one or two classmates. Choose from the scenarios suggested below, or create your own. Act out your dialogue for the class.

1. You run into a friend on campus and introduce him/her to your boyfriend/girlfriend.
2. You call a friend and invite him/her to do something fun. Your friend wants to come, but there is a problem.
3. You run into a former boyfriend/girlfriend and try to impress him/her.

C. Après avoir parlé. Can you think of some examples of regional differences in your native language? Why might regional language differences exist?

Implementation: 3-37 This activity helps students grasp the idea that living languages evolve over time and vary from region to region. Our view is that no particular variety of French is superior to others, but rather that each regional variety functions in its own context. Students should be able to recognize regional linguistic differences, even if they don't produce them in their own speech and writing. For links to sites with lists of *québécois* vocabulary, visit the *Chez nous* Companion Website. Explain to students that the Standard French they are learning (sometimes called International French) is based on the French spoken in Paris. You might suggest that the differences found between the regional French spoken in Canada and that of France are similar to differences in American and British English: primarily differences of pronunciation, vocabulary, and fixed expressions. Display and read the sample dialogue and have students "translate" it into Standard French.

Implementation: En parlant Encourage students to develop their conversations orally, without writing down a script. Then have each group perform their dialogue—and let the class decide who did the best job!

Note: Après avoir parlé Some typical regional differences in English include: 1) pronunciation of merry/marry/Mary 2) usage of the words soda/pop/soft drink; students can probably add many more examples.

Stratégie

To write persuasively, use factual information to support your opinions. For example, in building a case for study abroad, research a specific program that is of interest and incorporate relevant facts into your presentation.

Implementation: See the *Chez nous* Companion Website for links to these universities. Show the Web sites for these universities and model how students might locate the information needed to complete the chart. If your university sponsors a study abroad program in a Francophone region, you might also use that program as a model for this activity.

Écrivons

3-38 Les universités francophones

A. Avant d'écrire. Enlist your French professor's support for including study abroad in your undergraduate program. Research a university that interests you online, then present persuasively to your professor your reasons for choosing to study there. He or she can become your strongest advocate!

1. Choose a university that you would like to know more about. Here are some possibilities:

   Université de Montréal (UdeM)
   Université de Québec à Montréal (UQÀM)
   Université de Nice
   Université de Paris
   Université de Liège (Belgique)
   Université de Neuchâtel (Suisse)
   Université Cheikh Anta Diop de Dakar (Sénégal)
   Université Mohammed V de Rabat (Maroc)

Une chambre d'étudiant en France.

2. Next, find the information needed to complete the chart below in French.

Nom de l'université : ______________________________
La langue des cours : ______________________________
Nombre d'étudiants : ______________________________
Nombre d'étudiants étrangers : ______________________________
Quelques majeures/spécialisations (une liste de 2 ou 3) : ______________________________
Quelques associations d'étudiants (une liste de 2 ou 3) : ______________________________
Équipes (*teams*) sportives : ______________________________
Ville et environs (*surrounding area*) : ______________________________

B. En écrivant

1. Begin your paragraph by stating why you have decided you would like to study at the institution you chose:

MODÈLE Je veux étudier à l'UdeM parce que…

2. Continue your paragraph by mentioning the features you like about the university and its location.

MODÈLE L'UdeM est située à Montréal, et c'est une grande ville. J'aime beaucoup les grandes villes... .

3. Explain why it would be beneficial to you to study at this university, and conclude your paragraph with a summary statement.

MODÈLE Je veux travailler comme avocate internationale, donc je pense (*think*) que c'est important de passer un semestre à l'UdeM. Après un semestre au Québec, je vais parler assez bien le français !

C. En révisant. As you revise your paragraph, think about the following questions and make any necessary changes.

1. Analyze the content: did you incorporate information from your research to explain your choice? Did you include an effective summary statement?
2. Analyze the style and form: does your paragraph read logically and persuasively? Did you use appropriate vocabulary related to university studies?

D. Après avoir écrit. Share your paragraph with a small group of your classmates.

1. What are the most frequently mentioned reasons for study abroad? Which do you think your French professor and others would find most persuasive?
2. Which universities are most often mentioned, and why?

Now that you have completed *Chapitre 3*, can you do the following in French?

☐ Talk about and describe your university's campus?

☐ Talk about and describe your courses and studies?

☐ Talk about and describe a variety of professions?

☐ Express your preferences?

☐ Talk about higher education in France and in Quebec?

☐ Describe language policy in Canada and Quebec?

Leçon 1

à l'université, à la fac(ulté)	***at the university, at the school***
un amphithéâtre	*lecture hall*
des associations (f.) étudiantes	*student organizations*
la bibliothèque universitaire (la B.U.)	*university library*
des bureaux (m.) administratifs	*administrative offices*
le bureau des inscriptions	*registrar's office*
le bureau du professeur	*professor's office*
la cafétéria	*cafeteria*
le centre sportif	*sports complex*
le centre étudiant	*student center*
un centre informatique	*computer center*
un garage	*garage*
une infirmerie	*health center*
un labo(ratoire) de chimie, de langues	*chemistry, language lab*
une navette	*shuttle, bus*
un pavillon (principal)	*(main) building*
un permis	*permit*
un plan du campus	*campus map*
la résidence	*residence hall*
le restaurant universitaire (le resto U)	*dining hall*
une station de métro	*subway, metro stop*
un terrain de sport	*playing field, court*

prépositions de lieu	***prepositions***
à côté de	*next to, beside*
à droite de	*to the right of*
à gauche de	*to the left of*
dans	*in, inside*
derrière	*behind*
devant	*in front of*
en face de	*across from*
loin de	*far from*
près de	*close to, near*

adjectifs prénominaux	***adjectives that precede the noun***
beau/bel/belle	*beautiful, handsome*
bon/bonne	*good*
dernier/dernière	*last*
grand/e	*tall*
gros/se	*big, fat*
jeune	*young*
joli/e	*pretty*
mauvais/e	*bad*
nouveau/nouvel/nouvelle	*new*
petit/e	*small, short*
premier/première	*first*
vieux/vieil/vieille	*old*

autres mots utiles	***other useful words***
après	*after*
un cours	*course*
ici	*here*
retrouver quelqu'un	*to meet someone*
se trouver	*to be located*
une voiture	*car*

Leçon 2

des cours (m.)	***courses***
l'allemand (m.)	*German*
le calcul	*calculus*
l'espagnol (m.)	*Spanish*

(See p. 116 for more courses)

les facultés (f.)	***colleges, schools, divisions***
les arts (m.) du spectacle	*performing arts*
les beaux-arts (m.)	*fine arts*
le droit	*law*
la gestion	*management*
le journalisme	*journalism*
les lettres (f.)	*humanities*
la médecine	*medicine*
les sciences (f. pl.) de l'éducation (f.)	*education*
les sciences (f. pl.) économiques	*economics*
les sciences (f. pl.) humaines	*social sciences*
les sciences (f. pl.) naturelles	*natural sciences*
les sciences (f. pl.) physiques	*physical sciences*

pour parler des études (f.)	***to talk about studies***
un bacc(alauréat) (en sciences économiques)	*B.A or B.S. degree (Can.) (in economics)*

verbes en -re	***-re verbes***
Voir à la page 113	*See page 113*

un dictionnaire	*dictionary*
un diplôme (en beaux-arts)	*degree (in fine arts)*
lire (je lis un roman)	*to read (I'm reading a novel)*
une majeure (en sociologie)	*major (Can.) (in sociology)*
une mineure (en français)	*minor (Can.) (in French)*
une note (avoir une note)	*grade (to have/receive a grade)*
préparer un diplôme (en chimie)	*to do a degree (in chemistry)*
un semestre	*semester*
une spécialisation (en français)	*major (in French)*
suivre un cours	*to take a course*
un trimestre	*trimester, quarter*

des devoirs (m.) — ***assignments, homework***

un devoir	*essay, assignment*
un essai	*essay*
un examen	*exam*
passer un examen	*to take an exam*
réussir un examen	*to pass an exam*
un exposé	*oral presentation*
un projet	*project*

pour décrire les cours, les examens, les notes — ***to describe courses, tests, grades***

difficile	*difficult*
ennuyeux/ennuyeuse	*boring, tedious*
facile	*easy*
final/e	*final*
intéressant/e	*interesting*
médiocre	*mediocre*
obligatoire	*required*

pour exprimer les préférences — ***to express preferences***

adorer	*to adore*
aimer	*to like or to love*
aimer beaucoup	*to like or love a lot*
aimer bien	*to like fairly well*
détester	*to detest*
préférer	*to prefer*

verbes conjugués comme *préférer* — ***verbs conjugated like* préférer**

répéter	*to repeat*
suggérer	*to suggest*

Leçon 3

où on travaille — ***where people work***

un bureau	*office*
une clinique	*private hospital*
un hôpital	*public hospital*

des métiers (m.) et des professions (f.) — ***jobs and professions***

un acteur/une actrice	*actor/actress*
un/e agent/e de police	*police officer*
un/e architecte	*architect*
un/e artiste	*artist*
un/e assistant/e social/e	*social worker*
un/e avocat/e	*lawyer*
un chanteur/une chanteuse	*singer*
un/e comptable	*accountant*
un/e dentiste	*dentist*
un écrivain	*writer*
un facteur/une factrice	*mail carrier*
une femme/un homme d'affaires	*businesswoman/businessman*
un/e fonctionnaire	*government worker*
un infirmier/une infirmière	*nurse*
un/e informaticien/ne	*programmer*
un ingénieur	*engineer*
un/e journaliste	*journalist*
un médecin	*physician*
un/e musicien/ne	*musician*
un/e pharmacien/ne	*pharmacist*
un professeur	*teacher, professor*
un/e représentant/e de commerce	*sales representative*
un/e secrétaire	*secretary*
un serveur/une serveuse	*server*
un/e technicien/ne	*lab technician*
un vendeur/une vendeuse	*sales clerk*

quelques mots utiles — ***some useful words***

l'argent (m.)	*money*
autonome	*independent*
une carrière	*career*
être doué/e	*to be talented*
les gens (m.)	*people*
en plein air	*outdoors*
le prestige	*prestige*
le public (un contact avec le public)	*the public (contact with the public)*
la responsabilité	*responsibility*
un salaire	*salary*
les services (m.)	*the service sector*
le travail	*work*

quelques verbes — ***some verbs***

aider les gens	*to help people*
devoir	*must, to have to, should*
gagner (de l'argent)	*to earn (money), to win*
s'intéresser à	*to be interested in*
pouvoir	*to be able to, can*
vouloir	*to want, to wish*
voyager	*to travel*

4

Métro, boulot, dodo

Where are these people and where are they going, in your opinion? How do they seem to be feeling?

Leçon 1 La routine de la journée

Leçon 2 À quelle heure ?

Leçon 3 Qu'est-ce qu'on met ?

Venez chez nous ! La vie de tous les jours à travers le monde francophone

After completing this chapter, you should be able to:

- Talk about your daily routine
- Tell time
- Make comparisons
- Describe clothing
- Compare daily routines and fashion in places where French is spoken

Leçon 1 La routine de la journée

POINTS DE DÉPART

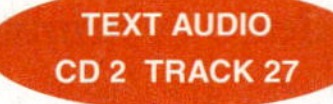

TEXT AUDIO CD 2 TRACK 27

La routine du matin

Il est huit heures du matin. La journée commence !

Chez les Bouchard, Thomas se réveille ; il va bientôt se lever.

Sa petite sœur Vanessa est déjà debout dans sa chambre ; elle se coiffe. Monsieur Bouchard est en train de se raser. Il va bientôt prendre une douche.

Madame Bouchard se maquille et elle s'habille pour aller au travail. Le bébé s'endort de nouveau.

Dans son appartement, Caroline se dépêche ; elle va bientôt à la fac. Elle se lave les mains et la figure, et elle se brosse les dents.

Chez les Morin, Madame Morin se douche et se lave les cheveux ; après, elle s'essuie. Son mari rentre à la maison. Lui, il travaille tard la nuit, donc il rentre tôt le matin pour se coucher. Il se déshabille, et il se couche.

Presentation: Use the cross section of the apartment building (MFL, Ch. 4) to present the new vocabulary. Describe the activities pictured, using the textbook description as a model. Test comprehension by having students tell who is doing what: *Qui se lave la figure ?*, etc. Have students repeat key phrases *(Il se douche ; elle se coiffe)*, then mime, or have students mime, activities while others guess what's being done. The verb *prendre* appears in this chapter in the expressions *prendre une douche, prendre le métro, prendre un café.* Treat these as lexical items and do not ask students to conjugate the verb, although you may wish to introduce the form *je prends une douche.* The full conjugation of *prendre* is presented in Ch. 5, L.1.

Note: Native speakers use the expressions *se doucher/prendre une douche* and *se laver les dents/se brosser les dents* interchangeably. The only forms practiced here are the third-person singular and the infinitive; the focus is on learning the meaning of the vocabulary. The forms of reflexive verbs are treated in the **Formes et fonctions** for this lesson.

Presentation: Use the video clip *La routine du matin* to help introduce or reinforce some of the new vocabulary; note that it is incorporated in the **Vie et culture** on the following page. Alternatively, the video can serve as an inductive presentation for **Formes et fonctions 1**. Note that in this segment, the two sisters use the form *nous nous levons*, etc., to describe their morning routine.

Vie et culture

Presentation: The SAM/MFL includes further activities to treat this video clip. You may wish to make a slide or a handout of the activities to use in class or assign as homework.

Métro, boulot, dodo

The expression **métro, boulot, dodo** epitomizes the daily routine of most Parisians. In the morning, many people take the **métro** (the highly efficient Paris subway), go to their **boulot** (a slang word for **un job/un travail**), then return home at night and crawl into bed to **faire dodo** (a child's expression for **se coucher/dormir**). In English, we often call this routine *the daily grind*. What does the expression **métro, boulot, dodo** lead you to believe about life in Paris? Describe a person whose daily routine could be summarized by this expression. Would this expression apply also to the daily routine of North Americans who live in big cities? Would it apply to life in your hometown?

Now watch the video clip *La routine du matin* as two girls describe their morning routine. Make a list of their activities, for example: **Elles se réveillent.** Is there anything that surprises you about their routine, or does it seem very familiar and logical?

Expansion: As a follow-up, ask students to come up with three words in French to evoke their own daily routine, perhaps words that describe their mornings, days, and evenings, respectively. Provide the following models: *Ma routine, c'est manger, étudier, dormir.* Or: *Ma routine, c'est pizza, télé, bibliothèque !*

Les articles de toilette

Presentation: Bring in items to illustrate toiletries; for example, show toothpaste and shampoo containers with labels in French, and an actual *gant de toilette*. Use the visual of toiletry items (MFL, Ch. 4) to present additional items and test comprehension. Have students point to items you name, then repeat by identifying items: *C'est un peigne ou une brosse à dents ?* Associate each item with an activity: *avec un rasoir ? —On se rase ;* or, *Qu'est-ce qu'il faut : pour se raser ? —un rasoir*, etc.

À vous la parole

4-1 Ordre logique. In what order do most people complete the following activities?

MODÈLE on se coiffe, on se douche
On se douche, et après on se coiffe.

1. on se lave, on s'habille
2. on se lave les cheveux, on se coiffe
3. on se lève, on se réveille
4. on se déshabille, on se couche
5. on mange, on se brosse les dents
6. on se couche, on se brosse les dents
7. on se couche, on s'endort
8. on s'essuie, on se lave

Note: Ex. 4-1 to 4-3 can serve as an inductive presentation of pronominal verbs, treated in this lesson. Verbs in *-ir* like *dormir*, *partir*, and *sortir* are treated in Ch. 4, L. 2.

4-2 Suite logique. Tell what these people are going to do next, choosing a verb from the list.

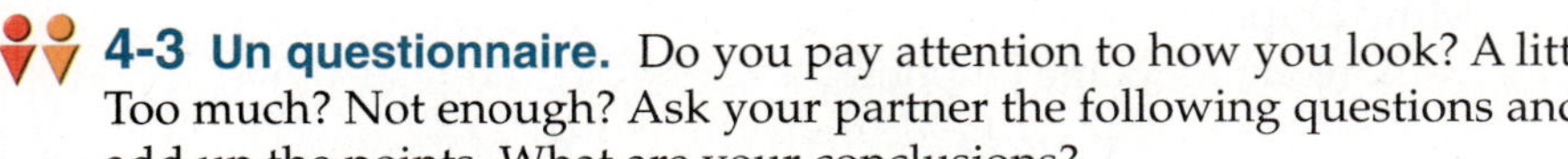

se coiffer	s'essuyer	se laver les cheveux
se coucher	s'habiller	se lever
s'endormir	se laver	se raser

MODÈLE Margaux a un teeshirt et un jean.
Elle va s'habiller.

1. Adrien a un rasoir.
2. Olivier va dans sa chambre.
3. Julie cherche le shampooing.
4. Fanny est très fatiguée.
5. Damien entend sa mère qui dit, « Allez, debout ! »
6. Grégory va prendre une douche.
7. Delphine termine sa douche.
8. Sandrine a un peigne.

4-3 Un questionnaire. Do you pay attention to how you look? A little? Too much? Not enough? Ask your partner the following questions and then add up the points. What are your conclusions?

Expansion: Follow up by asking how many students are in each of the point ranges.

1.	Vous prenez une douche ou un bain tous les jours ?	**oui**	**non**
2.	Vous vous lavez les cheveux tous les jours ?	**oui**	**non**
3.	Vous vous brossez les dents après chaque repas *(meal)* ?	**oui**	**non**
4.	Vous vous coiffez trois ou quatre fois pendant la journée ?	**oui**	**non**
5.	Vous vous habillez différemment chaque jour ?	**oui**	**non**
6.	Vous vous maquillez/vous vous rasez tous les jours ?	**oui**	**non**
7.	Vous vous mettez du parfum/de l'eau de Cologne ?	**oui**	**non**
8.	Vous faites très attention de ne jamais grossir *(gain weight)* ?	**oui**	**non**

Maintenant, marquez un point pour les réponses « oui », zéro pour les réponses « non » et ensuite additionnez vos points :

- Si vous avez 7 ou 8 points, vous vous intéressez peut-être un peu trop à votre apparence physique. Pensez un peu aux choses plus sérieuses.
- Si vous avez de 3 à 6 points, c'est bien. Vous faites attention à votre présentation, mais vous n'exagérez pas.
- Si vous avez moins de 3 points, attention ! Vous risquez de vous négliger.

Note: In American English, /uw/ (as in *do, two*) is intermediate phonetically between French /y/ and /u/. It is important to give students a clear acoustic model. Note that /y/ is acute and is most easily produced with the acute consonants /t/, /d/, /s/, /z /, as in *tu, du, su,* and *zut*. Have students think of /i/, the most acute vowel of French, as they produce /y/. Before practicing /y/, review /u/ and have students produce a tense and back /u/. That vowel is grave and most easily produced with the grave consonants /p/, /b/, /m/, as in *poux, boue,* and *moue*.

Initial practice: Begin with a discrimination drill; students raise their hand when they hear /y/: *tout, du, rue, qui, vous, Gilles, Camus, Lalou, boulot, Dumont, Manou, debout, douche, Bruno, couche, habille, Julie*.

Implementation: 4-5 Treat the contrastive pairs as nonsense syllables to focus on the pronunciation.

Implementation: 4-6 Before completing, remind students about the difference in formality when greeting a friend or someone with whom you have a more formal relationship. Point out that *Salut, Mme Dumont* would not be acceptable, although *Bonjour Suzanne* would be fine.

Sons et lettres

La voyelle /y/

The vowel /y/, as in **tu**, is generally spelled with the letter **u**. To pronounce /y/, your tongue must be forward and your lips rounded, protruding, and tense. As you pronounce /y/, think of the vowel /i/ of **ici**. It is important to make a distinction between /y/ and the /u/ of **tout**, as many words in French are distinguished by these two vowels.

À vous la parole

4-4 Imitation. Be careful to round your lips when pronouncing /y/!

tu du zut Luc Jules Bruno Lucie Suzanne

4-5 Contrastes. Be careful to distinguish between /y/ (spelled *u*) and /u/ (spelled *ou*).

tu	tout	bout	bu
du	doux	poux	pu
zut	tous	debout	début

4-6 Salutations. Practice greetings, using the following names.

MODÈLES Bruno
Salut, Bruno.

Mme Dupont
Bonjour, Madame Dupont.

1. Bruno
2. Lucie
3. Suzanne
4. Mme Dumont
5. M. Dumas
6. Mme Camus

FORMES ET FONCTIONS

1. *Les verbes pronominaux et les pronoms réfléchis*

- Verbs like **s'essuyer** (*to dry oneself off*) and **se laver** (*to wash up*) include a reflexive pronoun as part of the verb. In English, the word *-self* is sometimes used to express this idea.

Je **m'essuie**.	*I'm drying myself off.*
On **se lave**.	*We're washing up.*
Tu **te lèves** ?	*Are you getting up?*

Fiche pratique

The reflexive construction is used much more frequently in French than in English. In French, a reflexive verb is always accompanied by a reflexive pronoun. To remember that a verb is used reflexively, memorize its infinitive form along with the reflexive pronoun **se**. For example, learn **se laver** (*to wash up*) and **se raser** (*to shave*).

Here are the reflexive pronouns, shown with the verb **se laver**.

SE LAVER *to wash*

SINGULIER			PLURIEL		
je	**me**	lave	nous	**nous**	lav**ons**
tu	**te**	lave**s**	vous	**vous**	lav**ez**
il / elle / on	**se**	lave	ils / elles	**se**	lav**ent**

- Some verbs may be used both with and without a reflexive pronoun. Compare:

  Elle **lave** la figure de sa fille Clara. — *She is washing the face of her daughter Clara.*
  Elle **se lave** la figure. — *She is washing her (own) face.*

  The use of the reflexive pronoun means that the subject is acting upon himself or herself.

- Before a vowel sound, **me**, **te**, and **se** become **m'**, **t'**, **s'**.

  Je **m'**essuie les mains. — *I'm drying my hands.*
  Tu **t'**habilles ? — *Are you getting dressed?*
  Il **s'**essuie la figure. — *He wipes his face.*

- Note that reflexive pronouns always maintain their position near the verb, even in the negative and the immediate future.

  Il ne **se** lave pas. — *He's not washing up.*
  Je ne vais pas **m'**habiller. — *I'm not going to get dressed.*

- When a part of the body is specified, the definite article is used, since the reflexive pronoun already indicates whose body part is affected.

  Elle se lave **les** cheveux. — *She's washing her hair.*
  Ils se brossent **les** dents. — *They're brushing their teeth.*

- In an affirmative command, the reflexive pronoun follows the verb and is connected to it by a hyphen. Note the use of the stressed form **toi**. In negative commands, the reflexive pronoun precedes the verb.

  Lave-**toi** les mains ! — Ne **te** lave pas les mains !
  Dépêchez-**vous** ! — Ne **vous** dépêchez pas !

À vous la parole

4-7 C'est qui ? Read the sentences on the next page and indicate if the action Mathilde is performing in each case refers to herself (**elle-même**) or to someone else (**une autre personne**).

Presentation: Remind students that they have seen reflexive pronouns used with the verb *s'appeler*. Although this presentation does not treat forms of the verbs used reciprocally, you might wish to introduce here the notion of reciprocal pronominal verbs, corresponding to English "each other": *Ils s'embrassent, Ils se téléphonent, Ils se parlent souvent*, etc. Idiomatic pronominal verbs, such as *se fâcher* and *s'entendre*, will be presented in Ch. 7, L. 3. You may also wish to use the video segment *La routine du matin* as you present this topic.

Presentation: Point out the following irregularities: *lever/lève, essuyer/essuie* (the latter with loss of stem-final /j/). Full conjugations can be found in Appendix 5.

Presentation: To help students remember to use the definite article, you may want to recount the anecdote of a French speaker who has a hard time remembering to use the possessive in English because after all, "Whose face would I wash? Mine of course!"

Presentation: You may wish to delay presentation of the imperative forms and the accompanying Ex. 4-9 until day 2 of the lesson, so students can assimilate and practice verbs with reflexive pronouns before being confronted with the syntactic changes in the imperative.

Implementaion: 4-7 This comprehension-based activity focuses students' attention on the presence or absence of a reflexive pronoun. Have students discuss the follow-up question to bring the focus back to how form informs meaning and then continue with a substitution drill to practice forms: *Je me lave ; nous. —Nous nous lavons*, etc. Provide additional drills for the negative: *Elle ne se dépêche pas ; moi. —Je ne me dépêche pas*, etc., and *futur proche* : *Tu vas te coucher ; lui. —Il va se coucher*, etc.

Mathilde est très occupée ce matin. Elle…

	elle-même	une autre personne
MODÈLE … s'habille	✓	______
1. … se lave	______	______
2. … se coiffe	______	______
3. … réveille son petit frère	______	______
4. … coiffe sa sœur	______	______
5. … se dépêche	______	______
6. … brosse le chat	______	______

Based on your responses, did Mathilde spend more time today on herself or helping others?

4-8 Qu'est-ce qu'on fait ? Explain how people use the objects mentioned.

MODÈLE Moi, le shampooing ?
Je me lave les cheveux.

1. Les enfants, le savon et un gant de toilette ?
2. Jules, son rasoir ?
3. Vous, la serviette de toilette ?
4. Toi, le pull-over ?
5. Moi, le dentifrice ?
6. Nous, un peigne ?
7. Julie, du maquillage ?

Initial practice: Begin practice of command forms with simple transformation drills: (1) singular to plural, and vice versa: *Réveille-toi ! — Réveillez-vous !* (2) affirmative to negative, and vice versa: *Réveille-toi ! — Ne te réveille pas !*

Implementation: 4-9 Use objects if possible to make the exercise more realistic.

4-9 Fais ta toilette ! Your partner always has an excuse! Take turns asking and answering questions and making comments about grooming.

MODÈLE se raser

É1 Tu te rases ?
É2 Non, je n'ai pas de rasoir.
É1 Tiens, voilà un rasoir ; rase-toi donc !

1. se laver les mains
2. se laver la figure
3. s'essuyer les mains
4. se laver les cheveux
5. se brosser les dents
6. se coiffer

Implementation: 4-10 First go over the questions in the exercise to verify comprehension of key expressions such as *en premier, tous les jours, facilement.*

Additional activity: Ask students to describe three types of days to a partner: *une journée typique, une journée idéale, une journée horrible.* Provide a model such as this one for *une journée typique : je me lève pour aller à mes cours. Je me lave et je m'habille, et je vais en classe. Après, je vais au resto U pour manger. … Et toi ?*

4-10 La routine chez vous. At your house or in your family, who does the following things? Compare your answers with those of a partner.

MODÈLE se lève en premier ?

É1 Qui se lève en premier chez toi ?
É2 Ma mère se lève en premier. Et chez toi ?
É1 Moi, je me lève en premier.

1. se lève en premier ?
2. se douche en premier ?
3. se maquille tous les jours ?
4. s'habille avec beaucoup d'attention ?
5. se lave les cheveux tous les jours ?
6. se couche tard le soir ?
7. se réveille facilement le matin ?

2. *Les adverbes : intensité, fréquence, quantité*

- The adverbs listed below indicate to what degree something occurs.

trop	Elle travaille **trop**.	*She works too much.*
beaucoup	Elle se douche **beaucoup**.	*She showers a lot.*
assez	Nous mangeons **assez**.	*We eat enough.*
un peu	Je me dépêche **un peu**.	*I hurry a little.*
ne... pas	Il **ne** se rase **pas**.	*He doesn't shave.*

- These same adverbs, followed by **de/d'** plus a noun, indicate quantities.

trop de	Il prend **trop de** douches.	*He takes too many showers.*
beaucoup de	Elle a **beaucoup d'**amis.	*She has lots of friends.*
assez de	Vous avez **assez d'**argent ?	*Do you have enough money?*
peu de	J'ai **peu de** maquillage chez moi.	*I don't have much makeup at my house.*
ne... pas de	Tu **n'**as **pas de** rasoir ?	*Don't you have a razor?*

- Other adverbs indicate frequency, how often something is done. Notice that these adverbs follow the verb, like those you learned in the first section above.

Note: Longer adverbs such as *quelquefois* and those ending in *-ment* can also be placed at the beginning or end of a sentence: *Tu travailles ici quelquefois ? Normalement il travaille chez lui.*

tous les...	Je me lave les cheveux **tous les** jours.	*I wash my hair every day.*
toutes les...	Nous avons un match **toutes les** semaines.	*We have a game every week.*
toujours	Je me lève **toujours** en premier.	*I always get up first.*
souvent	Il prend **souvent** le métro.	*He often takes the metro.*
quelquefois	Tu travailles **quelquefois** ici ?	*Do you work here sometimes?*
rarement	Elle se maquille **rarement**.	*She rarely wears makeup.*
ne... jamais	Il **ne** se coiffe **jamais**.	*He never combs his hair.*

- Another useful expression to indicate frequency is formed with the noun **fois** followed optionally by **par** and a time expression.

Il se rase **une fois par semaine**.	*He shaves once a week.*
Je me brosse les dents **deux fois par jour**.	*I brush my teeth twice a day.*
Ma petite sœur prend une douche **trois fois par semaine**.	*My little sister takes a shower three times a week.*

À vous la parole

4-11 Vos habitudes. Be precise! Compare your habits with those of your partner.

Implementation: 4-11, 4-12 To assist students, show the scales from the first and third points on the previous page as they complete Ex. 4-11; show the scale from the second point for Ex. 4-12.

MODÈLE travailler le week-end

É1 Moi, je travaille beaucoup le week-end.
É2 Par contre, moi, je travaille rarement le week-end.

1. travailler le week-end
2. se réveiller tôt le matin
3. se brosser les dents
4. parler français
5. jouer au tennis
6. regarder la télé
7. aider les gens
8. se coucher de bonne heure (= tôt)

4-12 Combien ? How much or how many do you have? Compare your responses with those of your partner.

MODÈLE des livres

É1 J'ai beaucoup de livres.
É2 Moi, j'ai peu de livres.

1. des livres
2. des CD
3. des rasoirs
4. des serviettes
5. des peignes
6. du maquillage
7. des amis
8. de l'argent
9. des problèmes

Implementation: 4-13 You might also ask students to generate additional examples.

4-13 Stéréotypes et réalité. What is the stereotype, and what is the reality? Compare ideas with your partner.

MODÈLE É1 les Américains : manger au McDo ?
É2 Les Américains mangent très souvent au McDo.
É1 Mais moi, je ne mange jamais au McDo.

1. les Américains : manger dans des fast-foods ?
2. les Américains : se dépêcher ?
3. les Africains : être décontractés (*relaxed*) ?
4. les Suisses : avoir beaucoup d'argent ?
5. les Français : jouer au football ?
6. les Français : manger de la quiche ?
7. les étudiants : se coucher tard ?
8. les étudiants : travailler ?
9. les professeurs : se lever tôt ?
10. les professeurs : donner des devoirs ?

Lisons

TEXT AUDIO
CD 2 TRACK 31

4-14 Familiale

A. Avant de lire. Jacques Prévert (1900–1977) has probably been the most popular and widely read French poet since Victor Hugo. Prévert's first book of poetry, ***Paroles*** (*Lyrics*), appeared in late 1945, just as World War II was ending. The poem you are about to read is taken from that collection.

In ***Familiale***, Prévert uses the simple language of everyday life to make a profound statement about war and loss. He indicates in a matter-of-fact way what the three members of a family do:

La mère fait du tricot. / Elle tricote.	*The mother knits.*
Le père fait des affaires.	*The father does business.*
Le fils fait la guerre.	*The son wages war.*

As the poem reaches its climax, the poet's simple statements about the family members' lives are interrupted. The rhythm changes and verbs ultimately disappear from the narrative. Consider, as you read the poem, how these structural changes help evoke and reinforce the poet's troubling message.

B. En lisant. As you read silently or listen to the poem, which appears on the following page, answer these questions.

1. What is the nature of the characters' everyday life as conveyed in the first nine lines of the poem?
2. Like a play or a film, the poem builds to a climax. What is that climax? What happens afterward?

C. En regardant de plus près. Now look more closely at the structure of the poem.

1. The poem uses repetition to produce an effect and to convey meaning. For example, with what repeated phrase does Prévert suggest the characters' attitude toward their daily life? When this phrase recurs the third time, it has taken on new meaning and become associated with a terrible irony. Why? Can you point out some other instances of repetition that are significant in the poem?
2. What verb is used most frequently in the poem? What effect does this produce, and what is the effect when another verb is used instead? At what point do verbs disappear altogether?
3. Poetry is often characterized by a rhyme scheme. How would you describe the rhyme scheme in this poem? What might this type of rhyme scheme symbolize?
4. Look at the final line of the poem. How would you explain the seeming contradiction of the poet's reference to « La vie avec le cimetière » ?

Stratégie

Pay attention to both the meaning and form of the text when you read a poem. In an effective poem, form and meaning work together, so that variations in form—the poem's rhythm or structure, for example—contribute to the impact of its message.

Note: This change in structure might reflect the banalization of war, the routinized, rapid descent toward the destruction of a moral society which gives no thought to the consequences of its actions. War is "business as usual."

Key: En lisant 1) The characters all live routinized, monotonous lives. 2) The climax comes with the line, *Le fils est tué il ne continue plus*— the parents continue their routine, but incorporate the cemetery into it; meanwhile, everything around them disintegrates.

Key: En regardant de plus près 1) *elle/il trouve ça tout naturel*; it is somewhat shocking that the parents consider their trips to the cemetery *tout naturel*; repetition intensifies at the end of the poem to emphasize the machine-like life the family lives, unthinkingly 2) The verb *faire*, a very non-specific verb that can be used in many contexts, is repeated throughout the poem—again, this produces a routinized, machine-like effect. When a new verb appears, *le fils est tué*, it brings the routine to a halt; but then verbs disappear altogether, speeding up the tempo and suggesting little thought behind the actions. 3) Chart the rhyme scheme with students and show how it is simple and repetitive, reinforcing the notion of machine-like adherence to convention that Prévert wants to convey. 4) The line is ironic and reinforces the writer's view that the society's reaction to war is not normal.

Note: Students may notice that very traditional roles have been assigned to the parents; they may be surprised that the son's role is to go to war, but remind them of the date of publication of this collection — the poem was written during World War II, and it is a social commentary that places some blame for the war on the bourgeoisie. Students who have read Dickens may pick up on the literary allusion of the mother knitting (as in *A Tale of Two Cities*).

FAMILIALE°

La mère fait du tricot
Le fils fait la guerre
Elle trouve° ça tout naturel la mère
Et le père qu'est-ce qu'il fait le père ?
Il fait des affaires
Sa femme fait du tricot
Son fils la guerre
Lui des affaires
Il trouve ça tout naturel le père
Et le fils et le fils
Qu'est-ce qu'il trouve le fils ?
Il ne trouve rien° absolument rien le fils
Le fils sa mère fait du tricot son père des affaires lui la guerre
Quand il aura fini° la guerre
Il fera° des affaires avec son père
La guerre continue la mère continue elle tricote
Le père continue il fait des affaires
Le fils est tué° il ne continue plus°
Le père et la mère vont au cimetière
Ils trouvent ça tout naturel le père et la mère
La vie continue la vie avec le tricot la guerre les affaires
Les affaires la guerre le tricot la guerre
Les affaires les affaires et les affaires
La vie avec le cimetière.

Jacques Prévert, *Paroles.*

Familiale: *Family Life*; *trouve*: *thinks*; *rien*: *nothing*; *aura fini*: *finishes*; *fera*: *will do*; *tué*: *killed*; *ne … plus*: *no longer*

D. Après avoir lu. Now discuss the following questions with your classmates.

1. Poetry is meant to be read aloud. With a partner, or with your class as a whole, practice reading aloud ***Familiale***. Does this help you appreciate Prévert's efforts to convey meaning through the form and rhythm of his poem as well as through the words themselves?
2. Good literature has a timeless quality; readers in many different contexts can relate it to their circumstances. Do you believe Prévert's poem has this quality?

Presentation: Point out the expressions *Super !*, *Zut (alors) !*, *Mince !*, *Ouf !* and have students repeat them after you with the correct intonation. As suggested in the **Fiche pratique**, encourage students to build up their own collection of such expressions and to use them while speaking, in appropriate contexts.

Leçon 2 À quelle heure ?

POINTS DE DÉPART

TEXT AUDIO CD 2 TRACK 32

Je n'arrête pas de courir !

Presentation: Present the vocabulary by describing Delphine's day, using the illustrations (MFL, Ch. 4). Drill the main divisions of the hour using a clock face with moveable hands, or the multiple images (MFL, Ch. 4). Describe your own daily activities, incorporating each of the time expressions. At the end of the narrative, summarize expressions. Then test student comprehension by having them draw (for an analog) or write (for a digital clock) the times you give.

Presentation: Point out that *commencer*, like *manger* and *nager*, has a spelling change in the first-person plural: *nous commençons*. Explain that this change reflects the pronunciation. Full conjugations can be found in Appendix 5.

Delphine parle de sa journée :

Mon radio-réveil sonne à sept heures du matin. Mon premier cours commence à neuf heures, alors je quitte ma chambre à huit heures et demie pour aller à la fac.

Fiche pratique

As you develop your ability to speak in French, learn some phrases that you would like to use to express emotion; this will make your speech more natural and varied. Notice the phrases Delphine uses throughout her day, and select several to make part of your own vocabulary.

J'arrive en classe à neuf heures moins le quart. Super ! Je suis en avance ; je vais trouver une bonne place.

Le professeur arrive toujours à l'heure ; il entre dans la classe vers neuf heures moins cinq et il commence à parler.

À dix heures et quart, je regarde ma montre. Zut alors ! encore un quart d'heure ! Le cours continue jusqu'à dix heures et demie.

À onze heures moins vingt je prends un café. Je parle avec des camarades de classe pendant vingt minutes. Je regarde l'horloge. Mince, je suis en retard ! J'arrive au deuxième cours à onze heures dix. J'ai dix minutes de retard.

Entre midi et une heure de l'après-midi, je déjeune au resto U avec un ami, Jean-Baptiste.

L'après-midi, nous allons voir le nouveau film de Gérard Depardieu. On va à la séance de 14 h 55. C'est moins cher, et ça fait une petite pause dans une journée mouvementée. Ouf !

Vous avez l'heure ?

Note: *Demie* is written with a final *e* in all time expressions except *midi et demi, minuit et demi.* In the other forms, *demie* is an adjective modifying the feminine *heure.*

Il est deux heures et quart de l'après-midi. (Il est quatorze heures quinze.)

Il est neuf heures et demie du soir. (Il est vingt-et-une heures trente.)

Il est minuit moins le quart. (Il est vingt-trois heures quarante-cinq.)

Il est minuit. (Il est zéro heure.)

01:45

Il est deux heures moins le quart du matin. (Il est une heure quarante-cinq.)

À vous la parole

Implementation: 4-15 Ask students to convert to the informal system of telling time.

4-15 Une journée bien mouvementée. Look at Sophie's agenda and tell what she is doing today.

jeudi 15

(10) OCTOBRE — Th. d'Avila

8
9 *cours de littérature*
10 *h 45 rendez-vous avec prof d'anglais*
11 *h 30 manger au resto U avec Lucie*
12
13
14 *travailler à la B.U.*
15
16 *h 30 tennis avec Jean-Claude*
17
18
19
20 *dîner avec Maman*
21 *travailler chez Christine*

MODÈLE À neuf heures du matin, elle a son cours de littérature.

4-16 Dans le monde francophone. Look at the map below showing world time zones and tell what time it is in each of the Francophone cities shown. Then, based on the time, indicate what people are most likely to be doing.

MODÈLE À Paris. On déjeune ou on se couche ?
À Paris il est midi. On déjeune.

1. À La Nouvelle-Orléans. On se lève ou on travaille ?
2. À Cayenne. Les étudiants vont en classe ou ils rentrent chez eux ?
3. À Dakar. On va bientôt déjeuner ou on va bientôt dîner ?
4. À Marseille. On déjeune ou on fait la sieste ?
5. À Djibouti. On joue au foot ou on se douche ?
6. À Mahé. On nage ou on se couche ?
7. À Nouméa. On se couche ou on se réveille ?

Vie et culture

Le système des 24 heures

In this lesson you have already seen examples of the 24-hour clock (sometimes called *military time* in English). What might be the advantage of using a 24-hour clock? The expressions **et quart**, **et demie**, and **moins le quart** are not used when reporting times using the 24-hour clock. Instead, give the exact number of minutes after the hour: for example, **15 h 15** is read as **quinze heures quinze**.

Find examples of the 24-hour clock in the photos. Can you restate the equivalents in conventional time? What can you learn about typical business hours in France from these photos? In what ways are these hours similar to and different from business hours in North America? Which system do you prefer and why?

Presentation: In many countries, the 24-hour clock is used to avoid ambiguity in published schedules for classes, transportation, television programming, and public events. Compare the use of the 24-hour clock with the use of A.M. and P.M. in Anglophone countries. Students should be able to explain conversion from one system to the other. They should be able to deduce regular store hours from the photos. You may wish to point out that the A.M./P.M. system is also operative in France in ordinary conversations where people use the expressions *du matin* and *de l'après-midi* or *du soir* to situate the time. Using the photos, help students discover that most shops and businesses are closed on Sunday in France (with the exception of small food shops and shops where newspapers are sold, which are often open on Sunday mornings), and that many shops, banks, and businesses close for lunch, typically between the hours of noon and two P.M.

Implementation: **4-17** You could use this as a means of finding out how "compatible" partners are: could they function as roommates? If not, have them circulate to try to find a more compatible partner.

 **4-17 Votre journée typique.** What do you typically do at the times specified below? Share your responses with a partner, using some of the boxed suggestions. How similar—or dissimilar—are your responses?

aller en cours de/au labo de...	regarder la télé
faire...	se coucher
jouer à...	se lever
manger...	téléphoner à...
parler à...	travailler

MODÈLE à huit heures du matin

É1 Normalement, à huit heures du matin, je me lève. Et toi ?
É2 Moi, à huit heures, je suis en classe.

1. à huit heures du matin
2. à dix heures du matin
3. à midi et demi
4. à quatre heures de l'après-midi
5. à six heures du soir
6. à huit heures du soir
7. à minuit
8. à deux heures du matin

FORMES ET FONCTIONS

1. *Les verbes en* -ir *comme* dormir

Presentation: Before presenting this topic, review *-er* verbs to highlight the differences in the two verb classes. Stress the importance of a clear articulation of the final consonant in the third-person plural for *-ir* verbs; it is this final consonant that distinguishes the singular from the plural in speech.

- You have learned that regular **-er** verbs have one stem and three spoken forms in the present indicative. Unless the verb begins with a vowel sound, you must use the context to tell the difference between the third-person singular and plural:

Mon frère ? **Il regarde** la télé.	*My brother? He's watching TV.*
Mes amis ? **Ils regardent** le match de foot.	*My friends? They are watching the soccer game.*
Ma sœur ? **Elle écoute** la radio.	*My sister? She's listening to the radio.*
Ses amies ? **Elles‿écoutent** un CD. /z/	*Her friends? They are listening to a CD.*

- Verbs like **dormir** (*to sleep*) have two stems and four spoken forms. Their singular endings are **-s**, **-s**, **-t**; these letters are usually silent. The stem for the plural forms contains the consonant heard in the infinitive.

dormir (*to sleep*)	Ils dor**m**ent tard.	Il dort debout.
sortir (*to go out*)	Elles sor**t**ent souvent.	Elle sort le week-end.

DORMIR *to sleep*			
SINGULIER		**PLURIEL**	
je	dor**s**	nous	dorm**ons**
tu	dor**s**	vous	dorm**ez**
il / elle / on	dor**t**	ils / elles	dorm**ent**

IMPÉRATIF : Dor**s** bien ! Dorm**ez** tard ! Dorm**ons** ici !

◆ Here is a list of verbs conjugated like **dormir**, along with the prepositions often used with some of these verbs.

dormir jusqu'à	Je **dors jusqu'à** huit heures.	*I sleep until eight o'clock.*
s'endormir	Ils **s'endorment** tout de suite.	*They go to sleep right away.*
partir avec	Je **pars avec** mes parents.	*I'm leaving with my parents.*
de	Nous **partons de** Montréal.	*We're leaving from Montreal.*
pour	Vous **partez pour** la France ?	*Are you going to France?*
sortir avec	Elle **sort avec** ses amies.	*She goes out with her girlfriends.*
	Elle **sort avec** David.	*She's dating David.*
de	Les étudiants **sortent du** labo.	*The students are leaving the lab.*
servir	Qu'est-ce qu'on **sert** ce soir ?	*What are they serving tonight?*
mentir	Ce n'est pas vrai ; elle **ment** !	*It's not true; she's lying!*
à	Il **ment** souvent **à** ses copains.	*He often lies to his friends.*

◆ Note that the **-ir** verb **courir** (*to run*) is irregular and does not have the same pattern as **dormir; courir** has only three spoken forms in the present tense, as illustrated below.

COURIR *to run*			
SINGULIER		**PLURIEL**	
je	cour**s**	nous	cour**ons**
tu	cour**s**	vous	cour**ez**
il / elle / on	cour**t**	ils / elles	cour**ent**

IMPÉRATIF : Vas-y, cour**s** ! Cour**ez** plus vite ! Cour**ons** !

À vous la parole

Initial practice: Begin practice with a discrimination drill: one person, or more than one? *Ils dorment très tard. Elle sert du café. Elles partent demain. Il sort ce soir. Elles s'endorment rapidement. Elle sort souvent. Ils mentent. Il part en France. Ils servent du rosbif.* Follow up with a substitution drill. Start first with the contrast third-person plural vs. third-person singular by visual cuing: *Ils partent ce soir* ; (show one finger) *— Il part ce soir.* Then proceed with the other forms. *Nous partons demain ; je. — Je pars demain.*

4-18 C'est fini le boulot ! These people are leaving their place of work; identify their workplace.

Note: 4-18 This recycles professions and places of work from Ch. 3, L. 3.

MODÈLE Mlle Morin est vendeuse.
→ Elle sort de la boutique.

1. Nous sommes pharmaciens.
2. Florian est comptable.
3. Vous êtes infirmière.
4. Je suis actrice.
5. Jérémy et Audrey sont professeurs.
6. Tu es ingénieur.
7. Claire et Marine sont serveuses.

Implementation: 4-19 Since students need to use inference to choose among the *-ir* verbs, it is best to complete this as a group activity. To begin, either list the possible *-ir* verbs on the board or on a transparency or ask students to brainstorm to come up with this list before beginning. After an item is answered correctly, provide a variant to practice other forms of the verb; for example for #1: *Anne et Marie n'ont pas de problèmes d'insomnie ; elles s'endorment facilement.*

Key: 1) s'endort facilement 2) servez du café 3) sort 4) partent tôt 5) court 6) sors avec eux ; pars à 8 heures 7) part 8) mentent

4-19 Notre routine. Gaëlle is describing her family and friends. Use a logical verb in **-ir** to complete each description.

MODÈLE Mon frère, il n'est pas énergique. Le samedi matin, il...
→ Le samedi matin, il dort très tard.

1. Laure n'a pas de problèmes d'insomnie ; elle...
2. Gilles et toi, vous travaillez dans un café ; vous...
3. Mes amis et moi travaillons pendant la semaine. Mais le samedi soir, on . . .
4. Mes parents travaillent dans un bureau loin de la maison. Le matin, ils...
5. Karine se dépêche toujours ; pour aller à la fac, elle...
6. Tu vas au cinéma ce soir avec des amis ? Oui, je...
7. Mireille arrive ? Non, elle...
8. Les enfants disent toujours la vérité (*truth*) ? Non, quelquefois ils...

Additional activity: For further practice, use the following mixing activity. Compare notes at the end, and ask follow-up questions, many of which can be related to time expressions.

Nos habitudes. Try to find someone who does each of the things listed.

MODÈLE dormir l'après-midi
É1 Est-ce que tu dors l'après-midi ?
É2 Oui, je dors quelquefois l'après-midi.

1. s'endormir pendant les cours
2. sortir pendant la semaine
3. partir pour le week-end
4. servir le dîner dans un restaurant
5. dormir très tard le matin
6. mentir quelquefois à ses parents
7. partir de chez lui/elle très tôt le matin
8. dormir l'après-midi
9. partir en vacances
10. courir au parc le week-end

4-20 Je n'arrête pas de courir. Compare your weekly routine with your partner's. Then tell the class what you've learned.

Implementation: 4-20 Have students interview each other and report back what they learned about their partner.

MODÈLE Pendant la semaine, je dors jusqu'à...
É1 Moi, pendant la semaine, je dors jusqu'à 7 h.
É2 Moi, je dors jusqu'à 8 h 30 ; mon premier cours commence à 9 h.

1. Pendant la semaine, je dors jusqu'à...
2. Le week-end, je dors jusqu'à...
3. Le matin, je pars pour mon premier cours...
4. Souvent, je cours pour...
5. Je sors avec mes amis...
6. Je ne sors pas quand...
7. Le soir, je m'endors vers...

2. *Le comparatif et le superlatif des adverbes*

◆ You have learned to use adverbs to make your descriptions more precise.

Elle s'endort.	*She's falling asleep.*
Elle s'endort **tôt** le soir.	*She falls asleep early in the evening.*
Elle s'endort **facilement**.	*She falls asleep easily.*
Elle s'endort **souvent** en classe.	*She often falls asleep in class.*

Note: The comparison and superlative of adjectives are treated in Ch. 4, L. 3.

- The expressions **plus... que** (*more than*), **moins... que** (*less than*) and **aussi... que** (*as much as*) can be used with adverbs to make comparisons.

plus... que	Je dors **plus** tard **que** mon frère.	*I sleep later than my brother.*
aussi... que	Tu joues **aussi** bien **que** Stéphane.	*You play as well as Stéphane.*
moins... que	Il sort **moins** souvent **que** moi.	*He goes out less often than I do.*

When a pronoun follows **que** in a comparison, it must be a stressed pronoun.

- The adverb **bien** has an irregular comparative form **mieux**, as shown below:

Je chante bien.	*I sing well.*
Je chante **aussi** bien **que** toi.	*I sing as well as you do.*
Je chante **moins** bien **que** lui.	*I don't sing as well as he does.*
Tu chantes **mieux que** nous.	*You sing* ***better*** *than we do.*

- When comparing amounts, **plus**, **moins**, and **autant** are followed by **de** and a noun:

plus de... que	Elle a **plus de** travail **que** nous.	*She has more work than we do.*
moins de... que	Il a **moins de** devoirs **que** vous.	*He has less homework than you.*
autant de... que	J'ai **autant d'**amis **que** vous.	*I have as many friends as you.*

- To express a superlative, use the definite article **le** and **plus**, **moins**, or **mieux**:

Elle sort **le moins souvent**.	*She goes out the least often.*
Il a **le plus d'**amis.	*He has the most friends.*
Tu chantes **le mieux**.	*You sing the best.*

À vous la parole

4-21 Comparaisons. Who does it better? Compare your answers with those of your partner.

Note: 4-21 This exercise focuses on *mieux*, the most frequent comparative adverb.

MODÈLE Qui chante mieux, vous ou votre mère ?

É1 Ma mère chante mieux que moi.

É2 Moi aussi, je chante moins bien que ma mère.

1. Qui chante mieux, vous ou votre mère ?
2. Qui travaille mieux, vous ou votre meilleur/e (*best*) ami/e ?
3. Qui danse mieux, vous ou votre ami/e ?
4. Qui parle mieux le français, vous ou votre professeur ?
5. Qui mange mieux, vous ou votre père ?
6. Qui joue mieux au basket, vous ou votre frère/votre sœur ?
7. Qui s'habille mieux, vous ou votre meilleur/e ami/e ?

Implementation: 4-22 Have students work in pairs and report back to the class.

Additional activity: For additional practice, use the following exercise. If students do not have a roommate, encourage them to compare their routine with that of a brother, a sister, a spouse, or a parent.
Votre routine. Are these comparisons true or false? Explain your answer to a partner.

MODÈLE Je me lève plus tôt que mon/ma colocataire.
É1 C'est vrai : moi, je me lève à 7 h, et mon colocataire se lève à 8 h.
É2 Pour moi, c'est faux : mon colocataire se lève plus tôt que moi.

1. Je me lève plus tôt que mon/ma colocataire.
2. Mon/Ma colocataire travaille mieux que moi.
3. Je sors plus souvent que mon/ma colocataire.
4. Je vais moins souvent à la bibliothèque que mon/ma colocataire.
5. Mon/Ma colocataire part plus souvent que moi le week-end.
6. Mon/Ma colocataire dort moins profondément que moi.
7. Je travaille plus tard la nuit que mon/ma colocataire.
8. Mon/Ma colocataire s'endort plus facilement que moi.

4-22 Plus ou moins ? Look in your backpack or book bag, and compare what you have with what your partner has.

MODÈLE Qui a le plus de stylos ?
Moi, j'ai le plus de stylos ; j'ai trois stylos, et toi, tu as deux stylos.
OU Tu as moins de stylos que moi.
OU J'ai plus de stylos que toi.

1. Qui a le plus de stylos ?
2. Qui a le plus de livres ?
3. Qui a le plus de cahiers ?
4. Qui a le plus de crayons ?
5. Qui a le plus de devoirs ?
6. Qui a le plus d'argent ?
7. Qui a le plus de photos ?

4-23 Distribution des prix. In your French class, who excels in each of the following categories? Ask your classmates questions to find out. Can you get them to demonstrate their talents?

MODÈLE danser
É1 Qui danse le mieux ?
É2 Cindy danse le mieux.

1. danser
2. parler français
3. travailler
4. chanter
5. s'habiller
6. parler espagnol
7. écrire

Écrivons

Stratégie

Before composing your response to a casual note, such as an e-mail from a friend, be sure to refer back to the original message to organize your answer.

Implementation: Make sure that students focus carefully on the e-mail from Alexis and the questions that are raised. You may want to make this a whole-class activity.

4-24 La visite

A. Avant d'écrire. Imagine that your French friend Alexis, who is traveling in the United States, is planning to visit you for a long weekend and has sent you the following e-mail. Read Alexis's e-mail carefully and decide how you will respond:

1. Begin by listing the information Alexis is asking you to provide about your schedule and the plans you can make together.
2. Next, note down how you will answer each of Alexis's questions.
3. Finally, decide how you will organize your information. Will you answer Alexis's questions one by one, in the order in which they are raised? Or, will you be more systematic, describing first your Friday schedule and your weekend routine, then suggesting things the two of you can do together and when?

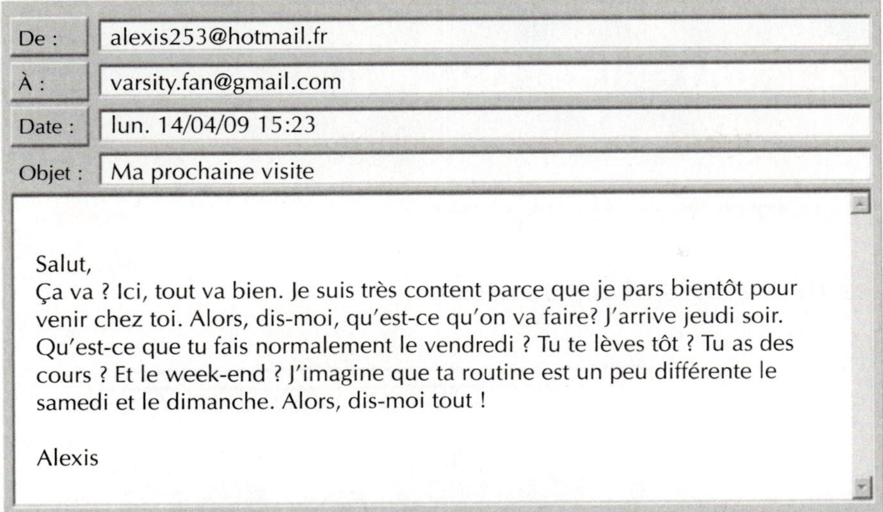

De :	alexis253@hotmail.fr
À :	varsity.fan@gmail.com
Date :	lun. 14/04/09 15:23
Objet :	Ma prochaine visite

Salut,
Ça va ? Ici, tout va bien. Je suis très content parce que je pars bientôt pour venir chez toi. Alors, dis-moi, qu'est-ce qu'on va faire? J'arrive jeudi soir. Qu'est-ce que tu fais normalement le vendredi ? Tu te lèves tôt ? Tu as des cours ? Et le week-end ? J'imagine que ta routine est un peu différente le samedi et le dimanche. Alors, dis-moi tout !

Alexis

B. En écrivant. Draft your e-mail, using the information you have noted down and organizing it carefully, as you have planned.

MODÈLE

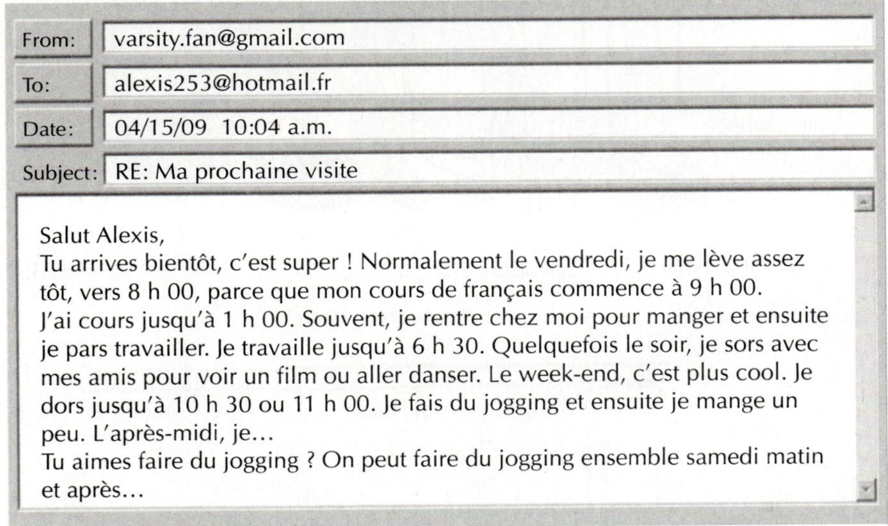

From:	varsity.fan@gmail.com
To:	alexis253@hotmail.fr
Date:	04/15/09 10:04 a.m.
Subject:	RE: Ma prochaine visite

Salut Alexis,
Tu arrives bientôt, c'est super ! Normalement le vendredi, je me lève assez tôt, vers 8 h 00, parce que mon cours de français commence à 9 h 00. J'ai cours jusqu'à 1 h 00. Souvent, je rentre chez moi pour manger et ensuite je pars travailler. Je travaille jusqu'à 6 h 30. Quelquefois le soir, je sors avec mes amis pour voir un film ou aller danser. Le week-end, c'est plus cool. Je dors jusqu'à 10 h 30 ou 11 h 00. Je fais du jogging et ensuite je mange un peu. L'après-midi, je...
Tu aimes faire du jogging ? On peut faire du jogging ensemble samedi matin et après...

C. En révisant. As you re-read your e-mail, think about the following questions and make any necessary changes.

1. Analyze the content: did you respond to Alexis's questions and describe your routine on Fridays and on the weekend? Did you suggest a few activities for the two of you to do during the visit? Have you stuck with your plan for organizing your information?
2. Analyze your description for style and form: do you use appropriate temporal expressions to describe your activities and to specify at what time of day each takes place?

D. Après avoir écrit. Exchange e-mails with a group of your classmates. Whose response(s) would probably be particularly appealing to Alexis? Why?

Leçon 3 Qu'est-ce qu'on met ?

Presentation: This vocabulary is best presented over two days. On day 1, present sportswear and outerwear along with colors and the accompanying cultural notes. Review and present more formal clothes on day 2. To test comprehension on day 1, use *la chasse à l'intrus : quel mot ne va pas avec les autres ? un polo, un jean, un pantalon ; des chaussettes, des baskets, des gants ; un manteau, un imperméable, un short*, etc. To provide simple productive practice, ask *Qui porte du rouge ?* and have students respond with, for example: *Moi, je porte un polo rouge.* Ex. 4-25 can also be used on day 1.

POINTS DE DÉPART

TEXT AUDIO
CD 2 TRACK 33

Les vêtements et les couleurs

Vêtements de sports

Presentation: Point out that when a color is paired with a noun, agreement is made, but when used alone, the color name takes the masculine form: *J'aime le* vert = "I like the color green" or "I like the green one." *Marron* and *orange* are unlike other color names. They are derived from the name of the fruit, *une orange*, and the nut, *un marron*, "chestnut." These two adjectives never vary in spelling; the same is not true of rose, which does add an *-s* in the plural. Point out the idiosyncratic spelling for *blanche*; the masculine oral form is derived in normal fashion from the feminine, i.e., by the loss of the final consonant sound. Model pronunciation for the colors, then test comprehension; ask, *Qu'est-ce qui est bleu ?* Students can name an item of clothing from the visuals or something in the classroom. To further practice colors, have students name the colors for: *le drapeau américain ; le drapeau français ; un pingouin ; une tulipe ; une banane ; une craie ; un éléphant ; un océan ; une plante ; un tigre ; un zèbre.*

Vêtements d'extérieur

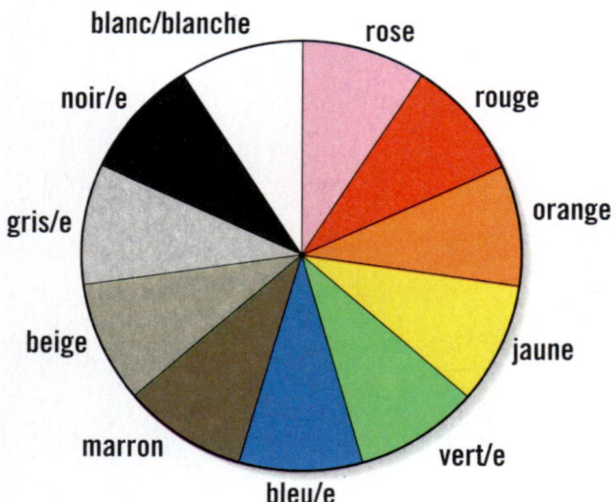

Vêtements pour hommes et femmes

Presentation: For day 2, you might bring in a suitcase filled with interesting clothing items, or encourage your students to "dress up" in interesting ways. For the initial presentation, describe the articles of clothing using visuals (MFL, Ch. 4). Present only a few items at a time before checking students' comprehension: have them come up to the overhead and point to the article that you name, using the unlabeled visual (MFL, Ch. 4) ; you may also ask, *Qui porte une robe ? une chemise ?*, etc. Exercises 4-26 and 4-27 can be used on day 2.

Deux amies regardent des vêtements dans la vitrine d'un grand magasin :

MANON : Je vais à un mariage, et je dois mettre une robe assez élégante pour la soirée. Regarde cette belle robe en soie. Elle est très chic, tu ne penses pas ?

AUDREY : Si, mais dis donc, elle est chère ; regarde le prix !

MANON : Ah oui ; mais j'ai envie d'être aussi belle que la mariée et de porter une robe magnifique.

AUDREY : Alors, achète la robe noire. Qu'est-ce que tu mets comme chaussures ?

MANON : Des chaussures à talons, bien sûr. J'ai des belles chaussures noires à la maison.

Presentation: In this mini-dialogue, point out the expression *avoir envie de* and ask students for a synonym in French (*vouloir, désirer*). Mention that it can be followed by a noun or a verb. (*J'ai envie d'une robe élégante en soie. J'ai envie d'être aussi belle que la mariée.*) Treat the verb *acheter* as a lexical item here; the conjugation will be introduced in Ch. 5, L. 2. Also point out the expression *tu ne penses pas* and encourage students to use it in their conversational exchanges.

METTRE *to put, to put on*

SINGULIER		PLURIEL	
je	mets	nous	mett**ons**
tu	mets	vous	mett**ez**
il / elle / on	met	ils / elles	mett**ent**

IMPÉRATIF : Mets tes bottes ! Mett**ez** un pull ! Mett**ons** un jean !

Presentation: The verb *mettre* is introduced in context as a lexical item; the conjugation is presented here for reference and students will use the verb in the **Points de départ** exercises. Show students that *mettre* is similar to verbs like *dormir* with two stems, four spoken forms, and a pronunciation difference in the third person that allows them to determine if someone is talking about one person or more than one person. You may wish to point out that *mettre* has a wide range of other meanings: *Mets ton sac dans ta chambre !* "Put your bag in your room!" *Tu peux mettre la table ?* "Can you set the table?" *On met une heure pour arriver au bureau.* "It takes us an hour to get to the office."

Vie et culture

Presentation: Students should notice that in each case, the response does not imply agreement with the compliment, but rather a modest acceptance or even a denial. Ask students whether they often compliment people on their appearance. Also, is a compliment perceived differently depending on whether it is made to a person of the same, or the opposite, sex?

Les compliments

The French do not usually compliment people they do not know well on their personal appearance. Among friends, the compliments and responses below are typical. What do you notice about the nature of the response in each case? How do you typically respond to compliments? Would you feel comfortable responding to compliments as the French do?

—Il est chic, ton pantalon !	—*Your pants are really stylish!*
—Tu trouves ?	—*Do you think so?*
—Elle est très jolie, ta robe !	—*Your dress is very pretty!*
—Oh, elle n'est pas un peu démodée ?	—*Oh, isn't it a little old-fashioned?*
—Tu parles très bien le français.	—*You speak French really well.*
—Ah ! pas toujours !	—*Oh! not always!*

La haute couture

Paris has long been an international fashion center with worldwide influence. When you think of French fashion, what images come to mind? Watch the video clip *La mode*, and see how many designers and styles you can recognize. Did you see the names of such great designers as Coco Chanel, Pierre Cardin, and Christian Lacroix?

Paris is not the only center of **la haute couture** in the Francophone world. Since 1998, **FIMA (le Festival International de la Mode Africaine)** has been held in Niger and features the largest fashion shows of African designers. In 1997 in Senegal, Oumou Sy launched **SIMOD (la Semaine Internationale de la Mode de Dakar)**, which has since become the annual Dakar Fashion Week. These events present the creations of designers such as Adama Amanda Ndiaye, Alphadi, Diouma Dieng Diakhaté, Ndiaga Diaw, and Oumou Sy, who showcase traditional African styles alongside European styles.

Un défilé de mode Lanvin à Paris, la haute couture

ET VOUS ?

1. Are you familiar with any the designers mentioned here? Who is your favorite designer?
2. What is the economic and cultural importance of fashion events such as these for the countries where they are held?

Presentation: Students may mention outrageous styles, high prices, top models, luxurious materials, and the names of specific designers when they think of French fashion. Women's fashion magazines, many men's magazines, and department store sales flyers will carry ads by some of the designers shown in the video montage and named here. Bring ads to class, or ask your students to bring them, to enrich the presentation visually. You might also link to designers' websites for additional visuals. Visit the *Chez nous* Companion Website for links to *le Festival International de la Mode Africaine*. Interesting photos and posters of the events can be found online.

Une création de Catherine Bizoux à Niamey au 5e Festival International de la Mode Africaine

À vous la parole

4-25 Comment s'habiller ? Tell how people normally dress for each of the following occasions.

MODÈLE Pour aller en classe, je...
Pour aller en classe, je mets un jean, un polo et des baskets.

1. Pour aller en classe, mes amis...
2. Pour courir dans un marathon, tu...
3. Pour faire des courses, ma mère...
4. Pour travailler dans le jardin, mes parents...
5. Pour faire du ski, je...
6. Pour nager, elles...
7. Pour manger au resto U, vous...
8. Pour sortir avec des amis, on...

4-26 Marier les vêtements. What goes well with each of the items mentioned? Work with a partner to decide.

MODÈLE avec une robe bleue en soie ?

É1 Avec une robe bleue en soie, on peut porter un foulard bleu et vert.
É2 Et des chaussures à talons.
É1 Oui, c'est bien.

1. avec une mini-jupe rouge
2. avec un costume bleu marine
3. avec un pantalon bleu
4. avec une veste noire
5. avec une belle jupe multicolore en soie
6. avec un tailleur marron
7. avec un jean
8. avec un pantalon noir en cuir

4-27 Préparez la valise. Imagine that you and the members of your group have just won a trip to one of the destinations indicated. Decide what items you will pack, and make a list.

MODÈLE huit jours à Tahiti
trois maillots de bain, deux paires de sandales, des baskets, cinq shorts, sept tee-shirts, des lunettes de soleil

1. un long week-end à Québec, en février pour le Carnaval de Québec
2. quatre jours à Lafayette, en Louisiane, en juillet
3. huit jours à Grenoble, dans les Alpes, en janvier
4. six jours à Cannes pour le Festival International du Film
5. cinq jours à Dakar, au Sénégal
6. huit jours à Paris, en avril

Sons et lettres

Les voyelles /ø/ et /œ/

To pronounce the vowel /ø/ of **deux**, start from the position of /e/ as in **des** and round the lips. The lips should also be tense and moved forward. It is important to lengthen the sound while continuing to keep the lips rounded, protruded, and tense. Typically, /ø/ occurs at the end of words and syllables and before the consonant /z/: **deux**, **jeu**, **peu**, **sérieuse**,

Initial practice: 4-25 Before completing this exercise with the verb *mettre*, begin practice with a discrimination drill: one person, or more than one? *Elle met un chapeau. Elles mettent des gants. Ils mettent une écharpe. Elle met ses nouvelles sandales. Elles mettent un pull. Ils mettent des lunettes de soleil. Il met une veste. Elles mettent le même jean*, etc. Follow with a simple substitution drill: *Je mets un pull ; vous. — Vous mettez un pull*, etc.

Additional activities: (1) Tell students: Find a partner, and take a minute to look at each other. Now stand back-to-back with your partner. (Wait until they have complied before continuing.) Describe what the other person is wearing today; no looking allowed! Provide a model such as:

É1 — Tu portes un tee-shirt bleu et blanc ?
É2 — Oui.
É1 — Et un pantalon noir ?
É2 — Non, mon pantalon est gris.

(2) Ask students to close their eyes. Describe someone in the class by the clothes that he/she is wearing and have the class guess whom you are describing. (3) Ask one student to leave the classroom and stand out in the hallway. While that person is gone, ask his/her classmates to describe what he/she is wearing. Bring the student back and compare the actual outfit to the students' recollections.

Implementation: 4-27 Divide the class into pairs or small groups and have each group decide what to pack for one of the locations given. Follow up by having each group share their list. As a variation, have groups of students prepare and read their lists, letting classmates guess their probable destination.

Presentation: This vowel distinction is often difficult for speakers of English to perceive and produce in isolation. You may wish to use the text audio to practice this distinction with your class. Stress the distribution facts, namely that [œ] occurs before a consonant and [ø] in open syllables. To differentiate /ø/ from /œ/, have students place their hand below their chin, pronounce /ø/ first, then drop the chin and pronounce /œ/. The downward hand movement makes the jaw movement more apparent.

vendeuse. When it is pronounced, the *mute e* (in words like **le**, **me**, **ce**, and **vendredi**) is usually pronounced with the vowel /ø/ of **deux**.

To pronounce the vowel /œ/ of **leur**, start from the position of /ø/ and drop your jaw so that your mouth is open wider. Both vowels are usually spelled as **eu**. The vowel /œ/ is also spelled as **œu**, as in **sœur**. The vowel /œ/ of **leur** occurs before a pronounced consonant, except for /z/ as mentioned above.

/ø/	/œ/
bl**eu**	la coul**eur**
il p**eu**t	ils p**eu**vent
la vend**eu**se	le vend**eur**
vendr**e**di	un taill**eur**

Initial practice: Begin practice with a discrimination drill; have students tell which of the two vowels they hear (the vowel of *deux* or that of *leur*) for words you read aloud such as *lieu, veulent, tailleur, bleu, jeudi, couleur, fleur, peu, vendeuse, ennuyeuse, sœur, neuf, monsieur.*

À vous la parole

4-28 Contrastes. Compare the vowels in each pair of words.

/y/ vs /ø/	/ø/ vs /œ/
du / deux	ne / neuf
lu / le	eux / sœurs
du jus / deux jeux	la chanteuse / le chanteur

4-29 Au féminin. Provide the appropriate feminine form.

MODÈLE le vendeur
→ la vendeuse

1. le chanteur
2. le chercheur
3. il est généreux
4. ils sont malheureux
5. il est paresseux

4-30 Phrases. Read each sentence aloud.

1. Des cheveux bleus ! Ce n'est pas sérieux !
2. Le neveu de Monsieur Meunier sort de l'immeuble (*building*) à neuf heures.
3. La sœur de Madame Francœur porte un tailleur à fleurs bleues.
4. Le vendeur suggère ces deux couleurs.
5. Depardieu est un acteur ; Montesquieu, un auteur.

FORMES ET FONCTIONS

1. *L'adjectif démonstratif*

Presentation: This treatment allows for recycling of adjective placement and prenominal adjective forms, taught in Ch. 3, L. 1. Review those before presenting this new material. Point out to students that adjectives like *belle* follow the same pattern as the demonstrative, with two spoken and three written forms in the singular: *belle/bel/beau ; cette/cet/ce.*

- The demonstrative adjective is used to point out specific people or things that are close at hand. The singular form corresponds to *this* or *that* in English, the plural, to *these* or *those.*

Tu aimes **les robes** ?	*Do you like dresses (in general) ?*
Tu aimes **cette** robe ?	*Do you like this dress?*

◆ Note the masculine singular form used before a noun beginning with a vowel sound. It is pronounced like the feminine form but has a different spelling.

Regarde **ce** blouson !	*Look at this jacket!*
Regarde **cet** anorak !	*Look at that ski jacket.*
Regarde **cette** veste !	*Look at that suit jacket!*
Regarde **ces** bottes !	*Look at these boots!*

◆ Here are the forms of the demonstrative adjective.

	FÉMININ	**MASCULIN**	
		devant voyelle	*devant consonne*
SINGULIER	**cette** jupe	**cet**‿anorak	**ce** manteau
PLURIEL	**ces**‿écharpes	**ces**‿imperméables	**ces** maillots

À vous la parole

4-31 Dans l'immeuble. Read the descriptions of people who work in Clément's building and decide in each case if it's a man or a woman.

	un homme	une femme
MODÈLE Ce comptable est sociable.	✓	______
1. Cette dentiste est sympa.	______	______
2. Ce secrétaire est conformiste.	______	______
3. Cet architecte est jeune.	______	______
4. Cette journaliste est dynamique.	______	______
5. Cette artiste est énergique.	______	______
6. Cet avocat est idéaliste.	______	______
7. Cet ingénieur est calme.	______	______
8. Ce fonctionnaire est timide.	______	______

Based on the information above, would you assume that more men or women work in Clément's building?

Initial practice: Begin practice with this comprehension-based activity, which helps students focus on the cues to gender provided by the written forms of the demonstrative adjective. Point out to students that cases like **cet architecte** and **cette artiste** are ambiguous in the oral form. Follow with a substitution drill, using vocabulary from this lesson: *Tu aimes cette jupe ? pantalon. — Tu aimes ce pantalon ? gants ; tailleur ; imperméable ; chaussettes ; chemise; écharpe*, etc.

4-32 Regarde ça ! Imagine that you are window shopping with a friend in an exclusive shopping center and point out the clothes that you see.

MODÈLE un tailleur violet
→ Regarde ce tailleur violet !

1. une belle chemise
2. des beaux mocassins
3. des chaussures à talons très hauts
4. des écharpes multicolores en laine
5. un jean en solde
6. des bottes magnifiques
7. un gros anorak
8. un beau pantalon marron

Implementation: 4-32, 4-33 These exercises can be cued with visuals, either actual items of clothing or pictures, if you have them available.

Variation: 4-33 Allow students to suggest other items of clothing that might be found in the closet being organized. Encourage students to be dramatic with their partner and to have fun with this activity.

Additional activity: In pairs, one student points out something that someone in the class is wearing; the other comments on it. Provide a model such as:

É1 Regarde le jean de Matt.
É2 Il est beau, ce jean !

Follow up by having various groups share their comments and see if the rest of the class is in agreement with their descriptions or not.

4-33 On s'organise. Imagine that you are helping a friend organize his or her closet. Based on the description, decide whether each item should be kept (**garder**) or thrown away (**jeter**).

Pour décrire les vêtements

long, longue	≠	court/e
large	≠	petit/e
fin/e		
à la mode	≠	démodé/e
chic		
cher, chère	≠	bon marché

MODÈLES un tee-shirt blanc avec le logo de l'université
É1 Tu dois garder ce tee-shirt.
É2 Oui, d'accord.

une robe démodée
É1 Tu dois jeter cette robe.
É2 Oui, d'accord.

OU Non, j'adore cette robe !

1. des bottes chic
2. une mini-jupe trop courte
3. des gants roses, violets et noirs
4. une chemise trop large
5. un pantalon trop court
6. une belle écharpe
7. des sandales fines à la mode
8. un gros anorak

Preparation: Before presenting this material, review the comparative of adverbs and nouns, treated in Ch. 4, L. 2. Use a meaning-based activity from the lesson, then have students summarize rules.

Presentation: Comparatives and superlatives can be presented inductively in class using appropriate visuals, or by having various students stand up, and then comparing them: *Sarah est plus grande que Julie*, etc. Be attentive, however, to students' sensitivity about their looks, especially with regard to their weight.

2. *Le comparatif et le superlatif des adjectifs*

- In the previous lesson, you learned to use the expressions **plus... que**, **moins... que**, and **aussi... que** with adverbs to make comparisons.

Je dors **plus** tard **que** lui.	*I sleep later than he does.*
Tu joues **aussi** bien **que** moi.	*You play as well as I do.*
Il sort **moins** souvent **que** toi.	*He goes out less often than you do.*
Elle s'habille **mieux que** nous.	*She dresses better than we do.*

- To compare the qualities of two people or things, use these same expressions with an adjective. The adjective you use agrees with the first noun.

La robe est **plus** élégante **que** le tailleur.	*The dress is more elegant than the suit.*
Le pantalon est **moins** cher **que** la jupe.	*The pants are less expensive than the skirt.*
Les bottes noires sont **aussi** larges **que** les bottes marron.	*The black boots are as roomy as the brown boots.*

- When comparing people, remember to use stressed pronouns after **que**:

Christiane est plus grande que **moi**.	*Christiane is taller than I am.*
Vous êtes moins sociables qu'**eux**.	*You are not as outgoing as they are.*
Je suis aussi grand que **lui**.	*I'm as tall as he is.*

- The adjective **bon** has an irregular comparative form **meilleur/e**, as shown below:

La qualité de cette robe est bonne.	*The quality of this dress is good.*
En fait, la robe est **meilleure** que la jupe.	*In fact, the dress is **better** than the skirt.*
La qualité de la jupe est moins bonne.	*The quality of the skirt is less good.*

- To express the superlative, use the definite article **le**, **la**, or **les** with **plus**, **moins**, or **meilleur/e**:

La jupe rose est **la moins** chère.	*The pink skirt is the least expensive.*
Les bottes marron sont **les plus** élégantes.	*The brown boots are the most elegant.*
Les gants noirs en cuir sont les **meilleurs**.	*The black leather gloves are the best.*

 À vous la parole 

4-34 Comparez les vêtements. Answer the questions, referring to the illustrations.

MODÈLE Quel pantalon est plus long ?
Le pantalon bleu est plus long que le pantalon noir.

1. Quelle robe est plus élégante ?
2. Quel blouson est plus large ?
3. Quelle jupe est plus courte ?
4. Quelles chaussures sont plus fines ?
5. Quelle chemise est plus à la mode ?

1.

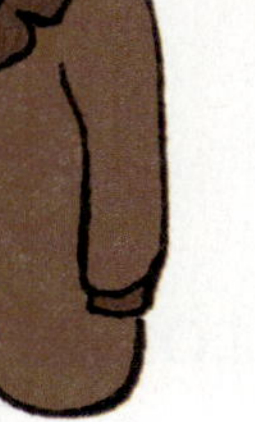

2.

3.

4.

5.

Initial practice: First test comprehension using a visual (a photo, image, or actual students) and questions to which students respond with a name: *Qui est moins grande, Brigitte ou Pauline ? — Brigitte. Qui est plus âgé, le prof ou Tom ?*, etc. Using names of famous people, you can also have students make simple comparisons using *plus* and *moins;* you might also suggest possible adjectives.

Implementation: 4-34 This can be completed using the illustrations of clothing (MFL, Ch. 4). For each item, ask which is better for a specific context: *Quel pantalon est le meilleur pour faire du jardinage ? Quelle robe est la meilleure pour un mariage ?*

Implementation: 4-35 Begin by having the class look at the picture and brainstorm as many adjectives as possible to describe the people in the picture. Ask them to speculate on the relationships among them, their likely professions, and the activities they like to do. You could impose a time limit and see which pair of students can come up with the most (properly formed) comparisons in the time given.

Additional activity: For an additional pair activity, perhaps for review: **Comparez-vous !** Tell your partner how you compare to each of the people listed.

MODÈLE votre mère et vous

É1 Ma mère est plus petite que moi, je suis plus grand qu'elle. Elle est plus patiente et plus généreuse que moi.

É2 Ma mère est beaucoup plus grande que moi, mais elle est plus forte. Elle est plus amusante, mais moins sportive que moi.

1. votre mère et vous
2. votre père et vous
3. votre frère ou votre sœur et vous
4. votre ami/e et vous
5. votre colocataire et vous
6. votre professeur et vous

Note: Further information about Alphadi, *FIMA*, and other events he has organized, including interesting photos and posters, can be found on the Web; see the *Chez nous* Companion Website for links. An exercise in the SAM also guides students to these Web sites and leads them to discover more about *FIMA*.

Seidnaly Alphadi, au centre, est un styliste nigérien qu'on surnomme « le magicien du désert ». C'est lui, le créateur du *Festival International de la Mode Africaine*.

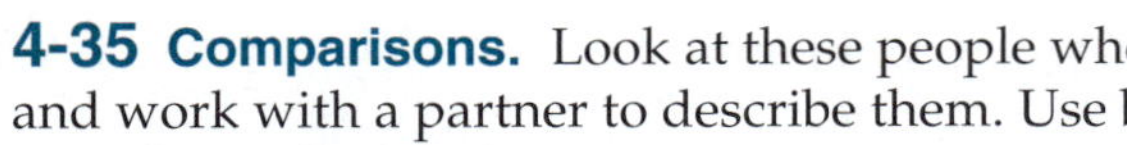

4-35 Comparisons. Look at these people who are waiting for the metro and work with a partner to describe them. Use both comparative and superlative descriptions.

MODÈLES É1 Sabrina est plus petite que Marie-Ange.
É2 Oui, mais Marie-Ange est plus chic.
É1 D'accord, mais Sabrina est la plus mignonne (*cute*).

4-36 Les stars. Compare yourself to your classmates in groups of three or four. Who is . . .

Implementation: 4-36 Provide a measuring tape in centimeters or a conversion chart to enable students to complete this exercise using the metric system.

MODÈLE le plus grand ?
É1 Qui est le plus grand de nous quatre ?
É2 Moi, je fais 1 m 75.
É3 Et moi, 1 m 80.
É1 Moi, je suis assez petite.
É4 Alors, Max est le plus grand.

1. le plus grand ?
2. le plus jeune ?
3. le moins sérieux ?
4. le plus sociable ?
5. le plus élégant ?
6. le moins doué pour le sport ?
7. le plus doué pour les langues étrangères ?
8. le meilleur musicien ?

Écoutons

TEXT AUDIO CD 2 TRACK 37

4-37 Boutique Mode-Afrique. Imagine that you are monitoring the customer service operations of a company that sells African designers' clothes. Listen in on the following telephone conversations to determine if the service representatives are performing their job properly.

A. Avant d'écouter. Before listening, answer the following questions.

1. Think about when you've ordered something on the phone. What did you say? What did the operator ask you? With a partner, make a list of expressions in French that one would probably hear in a conversation of this type.

Implementation: Complete the **Avant d'écouter** with students and help them think of appropriate expressions to use in this situation. Have students look at the photos as a way of anticipating the content of the conversations.

2. You will hear the conversations of two clients who are looking for information or placing an order for clothes designed by an African designer.
   a. What kinds of questions do you think they will ask?
   b. Look at the photos and make a list of the type of clothes they may wish to order.

Key: En écoutant 1) b 2) a 3) c 4) a 5)a: the three women; b: the man in the middle photo; c: the man on the left.

B. En écoutant. Listen to the two conversations and answer the following questions.

1. In the first call, what does the woman order?
   a. une veste b. une robe pagne c. un boubou brodé
2. How much is she going to pay?
   a. 95 euros b. 85 euros c. 115 euros
3. In the second call, what does the man wish to buy?
   a. une cravate et une chemise b. un costume c. un pantalon et une chemise
4. How much does the shirt cost?
   a. 53 euros b. 63 euros c. 43 euros
5. Look again at the photos and decide which corresponds to:
   a. un pagne b. un boubou c. une chemise batik

C. Après avoir écouté. Now discuss these questions with classmates.

1. Did the operators each handle their call in a satisfactory way? Why or why not?
2. Would you be interested in buying something from an African designer? Why or why not?

Note: A *boubou* is a long tunic worn by African men over pants. It is also a large, flowing dress worn by African women, often with fancy stitching.

Script: Écoutons

Appel 1

STANDARDISTE : Boutique Mode-Afrique, bonjour.

CLIENTE : Bonjour, madame. Je voudrais acheter une robe africaine. J'ai une amie qui a visité le Mali, où elle a acheté des très beaux vêtements.

S : Oui, Madame, voulez-vous une jupe, une robe pagne ou un boubou ?

C : Oh là là ! Je ne sais pas du tout. Un boubou, c'est quoi exactement ?

S : C'est une robe large à la mode africaine, parfois avec de la broderie.

C : Non, ce n'est pas ça. Ma copine a une robe en batik avec un grand carré de tissu de la même couleur qu'elle porte en chapeau. Je voudrais une robe comme ça.

S : Oh, je vois. Je crois que vous parlez d'une robe avec un pagne.

C : Un pagne ?

S : Oui, c'est un grand carré de tissu, souvent en batik, que les femmes africaines portent autour de la taille ou autour de la tête comme coiffe.

C : Ça doit être ça. Je voudrais une robe comme ça dans des couleurs très vives.

S : J'ai exactement ce qu'il vous faut. Une robe multicolore avec un joli pagne qui l'accompagne. Ça fait 95 euros.

C : C'est en batik ?

S : Bien sûr, madame.

Appel 2

STANDARDISTE : Allô.

CLIENT : Je voudrais acheter une chemise et un pantalon dans le style africain.

S : Oui ?

C : Est-ce que vous vendez des vêtements comme ça ?

S : Oui.

C : Ça coûte combien ?

S : Monsieur, je ne peux pas vous dire sans plus de précisions. Voulez-vous une chemise en coton, en soie ou en batik, par exemple ?

C : En coton batik.

S : Une chemise ça fait 53 euros.

C : Et le pantalon ?

S : Un pantalon pagne coûte 64 euros. Alors, vous allez commander quelque chose ou quoi ?

Venez chez nous ! La vie de tous les jours à travers le monde francophone

La journée commence avec un arrêt chez le boulanger.

All over the Francophone world, people follow a daily routine; they get up in the morning, get dressed, get ready for work, school, or play, and spend their days in a variety of activities that tend to seem repetitive. Of course, people's daily activities, choice of clothes, type of work, and leisure activities may differ dramatically depending on where in the Francophone world they live and work.

Note: See the SAM/MFL for activities related to two additional speakers from Morocco and Paris who describe typical clothing.

Observons

Note: Point out the use of the slang *boulot* for *travail* and the use of Canadian expressions such as *le soulier à talons* instead of *les chaussures à talons* and *la tuque* instead of *le bonnet.*

4-38 Mon style personnel

A. Avant de regarder. In this video clip, watch as two women from different parts of the world describe the ways they dress for different situations and the ways in which they express their own style through their choice of clothing. Do you dress the same each day of the week? Make a list in French of the things you normally wear in a work situation and in a more casual situation.

B. En regardant. As you watch, look for answers to the following questions.

1. Marie-Julie describes the clothes she typically wears in three different contexts; list the contexts and the articles of clothing she names:

   Context #1: _______________ clothing: ____________________________

   Context #2: _______________ clothing: ____________________________

   Context #3: _______________ clothing: ____________________________

2. What article of clothing does she most enjoy personalizing? How would you describe her choices for this item of clothing?
3. Honorine and her friend model typical women's clothing from Bénin. She specifies that women dressed like this are...

   a. stared at **b.** imitated **c.** respected

4. In her country, women do not typically wear...
5. She demonstrates how to use an item of clothing called...

   a. un pagne **b.** un boubou **c.** une chemise batik

C. Après avoir regardé. Now discuss the following questions with your classmates.

1. In this video clip Marie-Julie and Honorine model and talk about their clothing. Does either woman also make a personal statement through her clothing? How?
2. Is it more typical to dress like Marie-Julie or Honorine where you live? Do you ever see women dressed like Honorine? If so, where, and in what situations? What do you typically wear in such situations?

Script: Observons Note that the elements in brackets reflect standard usage and have been added to the written transcripts. They were not pronounced by the speaker(s) in question.

MARIE-JULIE : Pour le boulot, je préfère des vêtements beaucoup plus habillés : le tailleur, le chemisier, la jupe longue, le soulier à talons. Euh mais par contre, le week-end, je préfère [un style] un peu plus décontracté, c'est-à-dire, le pantalon ample, le jean, parfois même le tee-shirt, lorsqu'il fait un peu plus froid c'est le pull-over, mais surtout j'adore porter mes chaussettes rigolotes. Alors elles sont à braque et à bran, elles ont toutes sortes de petits motifs rigolos, et bon, quand je vais au Québec, il faut s'habiller un peu plus chaudement, il faut porter la tuque, les mitaines, le foulard, les bottes surtout et le manteau en duvet.

HONORINE : Et si on sort comme ça, on est [plus] respecté que de porter [des] pantalons comme ici, chez nous, on ne [les] porte pas. Les femmes ne portent pas [de] pantalon, c'est comme ça que nous nous habillons. Ici sur la tête, c'est un autre morceau de de ce pagne, là. On a beaucoup de manières pour [l']attacher. Voilà, je peux faire comme ça. Ça dépend de ce que tu veux. Voilà. C'est comme ça que nous nous habillons chez nous.

3. In French there is a proverb, **L'habit ne fait pas le moine** (*monk*). Do you know a similar proverb in English? How is it different from the French example?

Presentation: Avant d'écrire You may wish to have students describe the photos to each other in pairs or small groups as a prelude to the writing activity. Encourage students to find their own images via a Web search or their own personal collection of photos if they have visited parts of the Francophone world. If students select their own image, be sure that they turn a copy of the image in with their written description.

Note: Students who live in areas with African heritage communities may see women dressed like Honorine for special occasions, celebrations, and to attend religious services. Ask students how they dress for formal occasions. Does their ethnic heritage play a role in how they or people they know dress for such occasions? The corresponding English proverb is "Clothes make the man," which expresses the opposite idea. However, students often cite the proverb, "Don't judge a book by its cover," which corresponds nicely to the French saying. Students may also think of "First impressions are lasting ones," since this can be related to appearance.

Écrivons

4-39 Une journée typique

A. Avant d'écrire. Choose one of the photos below or an image of your own representing a slice of daily life in a Francophone country or region. Select one of the people shown in the photo and imagine what a typical day in his or her life is like. Before you begin to write, complete the following steps.

1. List the important details of the person's identity: name, age, marital status, children, work, favorite hobbies, personality traits, living situation, etc.
2. Make a list of the person's likely activities in the course of a typical day.
3. Put the activities you've listed in chronological order and indicate at what time of day each is carried out. Provide a few adverbs to describe how each activity is performed.

Stratégie

To write a convincing description of someone's daily activities, begin by conceptualizing the person very clearly. Decide first on the essential details of his or her life and personality, then you can focus on his or her everyday experience.

en France

au Maroc

un village au Sénégal

B. En écrivant. Now write your description, using the notes that you have prepared.

MODÈLE Cette femme habite dans un village au Sénégal. Elle s'appelle Amina et elle n'est pas du tout paresseuse. Elle se lève tôt le matin parce qu'elle a beaucoup de travail. Elle se lève plus tôt que son mari et ses cinq enfants pour préparer à manger. Son mari part pour travailler à six heures et demie, et les enfants vont à l'école à sept heures. À dix heures, elle retrouve ses amis du village pour chercher de l'eau (*water*) et pour discuter un peu . . .

Expansion: If many students selected images that were not in the book, you might display their images in the classroom. Have students take turns reading their descriptions, then ask the class to decide which image is being described.

C. En révisant. As you revise your description, think about the following questions and make any necessary changes.

1. Analyze the content: Does your description provide a convincing sense of who the person in your photo is and what he or she is like? Have you provided a coherent, well-sequenced description of his or her activities throughout the day?
2. Analyze the style and form: have you used a variety of adjectives and adverbs to describe the person and his or her activities?

D. Après avoir écrit. Share your description with your classmates. Whose day seems most interesting or agreeable? Why? Whose day is the most like your own?

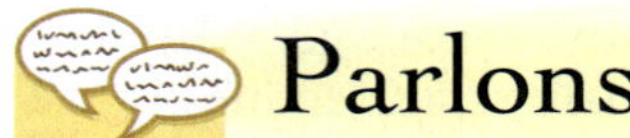

Parlons

4-40 Où aller pour faire du shopping?

Implementation: Avant de parler Each of the stores listed has a Web site; refer students to the *Chez nous* Companion Website for links. You may assign pairs or groups of students to research types of shopping establishments or individual stores during class time on a lab day or for homework; have them present what they learn to the class before completing the activity. You may also check to see whether students understand the main differences between the various options by supplying examples of similar types of shopping venues in North America. Note that many popular stores from North America are represented in France: Gap and Banana Republic, for example. You may wish to point out that in Canada the verb *magasiner* is used in place of the expression *faire du shopping*.

A. Avant de parler. Depending on where you live, you have different options for buying daily necessities as well as items such as books, clothing, electronic items, and music. Not everyone shops in exclusive boutiques. Note, however, that **boutique** in French does not necessarily imply an exclusive shop; it is used to describe any specialized store, so that one might shop in **une boutique de presse** as well as **la boutique Lanvin**. The French have many shopping options; here are a few:

un centre commercial	le Forum des Halles à Paris, la Part-Dieu à Lyon
des grands magasins	les Galeries Lafayette, le Printemps, la FNAC
des grandes surfaces	E.Leclerc, Carrefour, Monoprix
des boutiques	Promod, Maison de la Presse, Habitat
objets « recyclés »	les puces, les marchés
en ligne	laredoute.fr, alapage.com

Do a little research online to discover what types of things you can purchase in each of these shopping locations and to identify their North American counterparts.

Variation: Pairs or small groups of students could make presentations about what is available at each particular store and in particular, what they would like to purchase there. Encourage students to make printouts or slides of the various items that are available for purchase from the online ads and/or catalogues that many stores have.

B. En parlant. With a partner...

1. describe the shopping option you see in each photo and the types of things you could buy there;

MODÈLE Voilà un grand magasin, la FNAC. À la FNAC, on peut trouver des livres, des CD, des DVD, des ordinateurs et...

2. indicate where you prefer to do your shopping, and why.

MODÈLE J'aime bien les grandes librairies, mais habituellement, j'achète mes livres en ligne... parce que c'est plus pratique et moins cher. Et toi ?

La FNAC, un grand magasin de livres et de média

Le Forum des Halles, un centre commercial à Paris

Une boutique de vêtements à Paris

Un marché aux puces

C. Après avoir parlé. Compare your own answers and those of your partner with the answers of the class as a whole. What conclusions can you draw about your shopping preferences?

Lisons

4-41 Frère Jacques, dormez-vous ?

A. Avant de lire. Before reading this article about young people in France, answer the following questions.

1. Look at the title. What does it indicate that the article will be about?
2. Look at the subtitle: Have you yourself ever fallen into the "crazy rhythm" that is described (**se coucher tard, se lever tôt**)? If so, describe your experience.
3. Now, look at the photo that accompanies the article. Can you identify with the person depicted? Why or why not?

B. En lisant. As you read, answer the following questions.

1. What does Adèle say happens to her in the morning in class? According to the article, is she alone in this experience? Justify your answer.
2. How much sleep do 40 percent of young people get each night, according to the article? How does this compare with how much sleep they should be getting?
3. Paul says he gets tired at 11 P.M. Does he go to sleep then? Why or why not?

Stratégie

Before you read a text, think about the topic in terms of your own experience. This can help you better understand and respond to the ideas that are presented.

Implementation: Lisons Students will recognize the title from the traditional French song. Point out that "matins" in Catholic and some Protestant traditions is the early morning service ending at sunrise. To focus on students' experiences with the topic, begin with a general discussion of their sleeping habits: *À quelle heure est-ce que vous vous couchez ? À quelle heure est-ce que vous vous levez ? Combien d'heures est-ce que vous dormez par nuit ? Est-ce que vous êtes fatigué/e pendant la journée ? Est-ce que vous vous endormez en classe quelquefois ? Est-ce que vous vous endormez dans le bus, la navette, le métro ?* You could also have students conduct an in-class survey in small groups with these questions and tabulate the results before beginning the reading.

Key: En lisant 1) She falls asleep. No, she is not alone. In a survey, 50% of French youth aged 15–19 said they dozed off at least once a week. 2) Less than eight hours. It's about an hour less than the amount of sleep they need. 3) No. He wants to do something else like watch TV or play on the computer. 4) Biological changes associated with puberty and the schedule of young people, which includes homework. 5) Some people then become unable to go to bed at a reasonable hour and to wake up early. 8) Dr. Brun explains that the sleep patterns of these young people are normal in both quantity and quality if they are permitted to go to bed and wake up when they want, as opposed to when society dictates that they must. According to him, the problem is that the natural rhythms of these young people are not in sync with the schedule imposed by society, i.e., getting up early for school.

4. Name two reasons why almost half of all young people in France do not go to bed before 11 P.M.
5. According to the article, what is the consequence of constantly pushing back one's bedtime?
6. Dr. Brun says that these difficulties are not caused by insomnia. To what does he attribute the problem?

Frère Jacques, dormez-vous ?

« Je rêve[1] de dormir le matin quand je m'endors en cours », dit Adèle, 16 ans. Elle n'est pas la seule : d'après un sondage de TNS-Sofres, 50 % des 15-19 ans admettent qu'ils s'endorment au moins[2] une fois par semaine … dans le train, le bus ou le métro, ou même en classe. Ce n'est pas surprenant parce que 40% des jeunes dorment moins de huit heures par nuit ; c'est en moyenne une heure de moins que la quantité de sommeil[3] nécessaire pour être en forme.

Note: TNS-Sofres is the largest French marketing research and opinion polling firm.

Se coucher tard, se lever tôt… un rythme fou[4]

« Le soir vers onze heures, je suis fatigué, dit Paul, 19 ans. Mais je n'ai pas envie de dormir : je regarde la télé, je joue sur l'ordi… » Comme lui, 47% des 15-19 ans se couchent après 23 heures. Les modifications biologiques liées à la puberté expliquent en partie cette tendance, mais les causes sont aussi à chercher dans le rythme de vie[5] des jeunes. Après le travail scolaire, il reste très peu de temps pour les loisirs. Il est donc très tentant de réduire[6] le temps de sommeil en faveur d'autres activités plus intéressantes.

À force de différer[7] continuellement l'heure du coucher, certains sont incapables de s'endormir à une heure décente, et par conséquant de se lever tôt. « Ce syndrome fréquent chez l'adolescent et le jeune adulte s'appelle 'retard de phase'[8], explique le Docteur Georges Brun, spécialiste du sommeil. Ce n'est pas une insomnie, parce que le sommeil est normal en quantité et en qualité si la personne se couche et se réveille quand elle veut. C'est que la personne n'arrive[9] pas à s'adapter aux horaires imposés par la vie en société. »

[1] *dream about* [2] *at least* [3] *sleep* [4] *crazy* [5] *life* [6] *to reduce* [7] *to postpone* [8] *phase delay* [9] *manage*

C. En regardant de plus près. Now look more closely at the following features of the text.

1. You know that the expression **de taille moyenne** means of medium or average height. What do you think the expression **en moyenne** used in the text means?
2. Paul says that he likes to do other things besides sleep, such as **jouer sur l'ordi.** For which French word that you know is **l'ordi** an abbreviation?
3. Can you find a synonym in French for the expression **le travail scolaire**?
4. In the second and third paragraphs, there are several sophisticated expressions in French, such as « **les modifications biologiques liées à la puberté** » ; « **ce syndrome fréquent chez l'adolescent et le jeune adulte** » ; « **est normal en quantité et qualité** ». Use your knowledge of the reading topic and of cognates to determine what these expressions mean.

Key: En regardant de plus près 1) on average 2) *l'ordinateur* 3) *les devoirs* 4) biological modifications linked to puberty; this frequent syndrome in adolescents and young adults; is normal in quantity and quality.

D. Après avoir lu. Discuss the following questions with your classmates.

1. Is it common, in your experience, for young people in North America to doze off on the way to school and/or in class? Why or why not?
2. Is the conclusion reached by Dr. Brun that the sleep rhythms of adolescents and young adults are not well suited to the schedule imposed by society a point of concern in your community? In what ways?
3. After reading the article, do you think that the sleeping habits of French students and North American students are similar or different? Explain your response.

Variation: Provide additional models that allow students to talk about their own sleep habits: *Je me couche vers 1 heure du matin et je me lève normalment à 6 h 00. Donc je je ne dors pas assez* » or « *On me surnomme la marmotte... Quand je rentre chez moi, je mange, je me lave, je fais mes devoirs puis je me couche. Je m'endors avant 21 h 00* ». Ask students to write a short description of their own sleeping habits, or to compare their habits with a partner. Point out that *une marmotte* is a groundhog and is used to refer to a 'sleepyhead' in French.

Now that you have completed *Chapitre 4*, can you do the following in French?

- ☐ describe your daily routine?
- ☐ ask what time it is and tell time?
- ☐ make comparisons using adjectives and adverbs?
- ☐ talk about and describe clothing?
- ☐ talk about day-to-day life in some places where French is spoken?

Leçon 1

la routine de la journée	the daily routine
être debout	*to be up*
prendre une douche	*to take a shower*
se brosser les dents	*to brush one's teeth*
se coiffer	*to fix one's hair*
se coucher	*to go to bed*
se dépêcher	*to hurry*
se déshabiller	*to undress*
se doucher	*to shower*
s'endormir	*to fall asleep*
s'essuyer	*to dry off, wipe off*
s'habiller	*to get dressed*
se laver (les cheveux [m.], la figure [f.], les mains [f.])	*to wash (one's hair, one's face, one's hands)*
se lever	*to get up*
se maquiller	*to put on makeup*
se raser	*to shave*
se réveiller	*to wake up*
rentrer	*to return home*

les articles de toilette	toiletries
une brosse à dents/à cheveux	*toothbrush/hairbrush*
du dentifrice	*toothpaste*
un gant de toilette	*wash mitt*
du maquillage	*makeup*
un peigne	*comb*
un rasoir	*razor*
un savon	*soap*
une serviette de toilette	*towel*
du shampooing	*shampoo*

pour exprimer la fréquence	to express frequency
toujours	*always, still*
tous les... / toutes les...	*every . . .*
souvent	*often*
quelquefois	*sometimes*
rarement	*rarely*
ne... jamais	*never*
deux fois par jour	*twice a day*

autres mots utiles	other useful words
un appartement	*apartment*
une chambre	*bedroom*
déjà	*already*
de nouveau	*again*
être en train de (+ infinitif)	*to be busy (doing something)*
une journée	*day*
le lavabo	*bathroom sink*
la nuit	*at night*
tôt	*early*
tard	*late*
assez	*enough*

Leçon 2

pour parler de l'heure	to talk about the time
une horloge	*clock*
une montre	*watch*
un (radio-)réveil	*alarm clock (clock radio)*
être à l'heure	*to be on time*
être en avance	*to be early*
être en retard	*to be late*
Vous avez l'heure ?	*What time is it?*
pendant	*during, for*
jusqu'à	*until*
encore (un quart d'heure)	*another (quarter of an hour)*
entre	*between*
vers	*around, toward*
Il est une heure, huit heures.	*It is one o'clock, eight o'clock.*
et quart	*00:15*
et demi/e	*00:30*
moins vingt	*00:40*
moins le quart	*00:45*
du matin	*in the morning,* A.M.
de l'après-midi	*in the afternoon,* P.M.
du soir	*in the evening,* P.M.
midi	*noon*
minuit	*midnight*

quelques expressions utiles	some useful expressions
Mince !	*Shoot!*
Super !	*Great!*

Vocabulaire

Ouf !	*Whew!*
Zut (alors) !	*Darn!*

quelques verbes utiles	***some useful verbs***
chanter	*to sing*
commencer	*to begin*
courir	*to run*
dormir	*to sleep*
mentir	*to lie*
partir	*to leave*
quitter (ma chambre)	*to leave (my room)*
servir	*to serve*
sonner	*to ring, to alarm*
sortir	*to go out*
trouver	*to find*

pour comparer	***to compare***
aussi... que	*as . . . as*
autant de... que	*as many . . . as*
moins (de)... que	*less . . . than*
plus (de)... que	*more . . . than*
mieux que	*better than*
le mieux	*the best*

Leçon 3

les vêtements de sports et d'extérieur	***sportswear and outerwear***
un anorak	*ski jacket, parka*
un blouson	*heavy jacket*
un bonnet de laine	*knit/wool cap*
des bottes (f.)	*boots*
une casquette	*baseball cap*
un chapeau	*hat*
des chaussettes (f.)	*socks*
une écharpe	*scarf*
des gants (m.)	*gloves*
un gilet	*cardigan sweater*
un imper(méable)	*raincoat*
un jean	*jeans*
des lunettes (f.) (de soleil)	*(sun)glasses*
un maillot (de bain)	*swimsuit*
un manteau	*overcoat*
une (mini-)jupe	*(mini)skirt*
un pantalon	*slacks*
un parapluie	*umbrella*
un polo	*polo shirt*
un pull(-over)	*pullover sweater*
des sandales (f.)	*sandals*
un short	*shorts*
un tee-shirt	*T-shirt*
des baskets (f.)	*sports shoes*
une veste	*jacket, suit coat*

les vêtements (m.) pour femmes	***women's clothing***
des chaussures (f.) à talons	*high-heeled shoes*
un chemisier	*blouse*
un collant	*pantyhose*
un foulard	*silk scarf*
une jupe	*skirt*
une robe	*dress*
un sac	*purse*
un tailleur	*woman's suit*

les vêtements pour hommes	***men's clothing***
une chemise	*man's shirt*
un costume	*man's suit*
une cravate	*tie*
des mocassins (m.)	*loafers*

les tissus (m.) et les matières (f.)	***fabrics and materials***
le coton	*cotton*
le cuir	*leather*
la laine	*wool*
la soie	*silk*

les couleurs	***colors***
Voir à la page 164	*See page 164*

au (grand) magasin	***at the (department) store***
avoir envie de (+ nom, + infinitif)	*to want (something, to do something)*
mettre	*to put, to put on*
penser	*to think*
porter (une robe)	*to wear (a dress)*
le prix	*price*
les soldes (f.)	*sales*
la vitrine	*display window*

pour décrire les vêtements	***to describe clothing***
à la mode	*stylish, fashionable*
bon marché	*inexpensive*
cher/chère	*expensive*
chic (inv.)	*stylish*
court/e	*short*
démodé/e	*old-fashioned, out-of-date*
fin/e	*thin, elegant*
large	*big, large, roomy*
long/ue	*long*
magnifique	*magnificent*
(le/la/les) meilleur/e/s	*better (the best)*

5 Du marché à la table

Qui va au marché ? Qu'est-ce qu'ils cherchent ? Qu'est-ce que vous aimez trouver au marché ?

Leçon 1 Qu'est-ce que vous prenez ?

Leçon 2 À table !

Leçon 3 Faisons des courses

Venez chez nous ! Traditions gastronomiques

After completing this chapter, you should be able to:

- Order food and drink in a restaurant
- Talk about meals and a wide variety of dishes
- Shop for food
- Specify quantities
- Tell about past actions or events
- Describe the importance of cuisine and regional dishes in the Francophone world

Leçon  Qu'est-ce que vous prenez ?

POINTS DE DÉPART

Au café

Presentation: Examine the photo and treat the dialogue first, letting students listen to the recording. Test students' comprehension: *On va au McDo ou au café ?*, etc. Explain key expressions such as *avoir faim* and *avoir soif* using description, circumlocution, and examples. Treat the expression *je voudrais* as a lexical item; polite requests using the conditional will be presented in Ch. 8, L. 3. Point out the growing popularity of fast-food restaurants in France—see the **Vie et culture** notes for more details. The café continues to play a part in the life of most French people as a place to socialize. Ask students whether they can think of a place that plays a similar role in their life.

ROMAIN : J'ai faim. On va au McDo ?
HÉLÈNE : Des hamburgers, des frites et du coca, quelle horreur ! Allons au café, c'est plus sympa.

(au café)
LE SERVEUR : Qu'est-ce que je vous sers ?
HÉLÈNE : J'ai très soif. Je voudrais seulement quelque chose à boire. Euh, une limonade, s'il vous plaît.
ROMAIN : Moi, j'ai faim. Je prends un croque-monsieur et une bière.

(plus tard)
ROMAIN : Monsieur ! ... L'addition, s'il vous plaît.
LE SERVEUR : J'arrive... Voilà.
HÉLÈNE : C'est combien ?
ROMAIN : Seize euros. On partage ?
HÉLÈNE : Sans problème.

Presentation: Present the vocabulary on the following page using the visual of café fare (MFL, Ch. 5). Highlight the learning strategy and explain that it will be used throughout the chapter as students add to their vocabulary to name foods. Encourage them to develop additional groupings that they find meaningful and useful. Describe items in each semantic grouping to make meaning clear, for example: *un citron pressé, c'est du jus de citron avec de l'eau et du sucre.* Test comprehension (*Montrez le thé*, etc.), then have students repeat, using either/or questions: *C'est un café ou un chocolat chaud ?*

Des boissons chaudes

Des boissons rafraîchissantes

Des boissons alcoolisées

Des casse-croûte

Fiche pratique

To learn new vocabulary, such as the food-related vocabulary in this chapter, it is helpful to organize words and expressions into logically related groupings. For example, like the illustrations on this page, you can group together hot drinks, cold drinks, and snacks. Or, you can make lists of foods you typically eat at certain meals; foods you typically eat with certain courses; types of foods (for example, fruits, vegetables, and meats); foods you purchase in a particular type of container or amount (in a box, in a package, by the dozen, etc.).

Note: The French generally drink less coffee than Americans, but prefer a stronger coffee. You might give students some of the more specific terms: *un déca, un crème (un grand crème ou un petit crème), un expresso, une noisette (un expresso avec un peu de lait) ; un allongé (un expresso dilué avec de l'eau chaude), un café serré (un expresso très fort).* A customer may order *de l'eau minérale plate (Vittel, Évian) ou gazeuse (Perrier, Badoit). L'Orangina* and *la limonade* are also carbonated drinks. *Un croque-monsieur* is a grilled ham-and-cheese sandwich made with *pain de mie.* Most other sandwiches are made using *de la baguette.* Canadians refer to *un coca* as *un coke* and *une glace* as *une crème glacée.*

À vous la parole

5-1 Proposez des boissons. Proposez des boissons...

MODÈLE chaudes
un café, un thé, un chocolat chaud

1. rafraîchissantes
2. gazeuses (*carbonated*)
3. alcoolisées
4. qui contiennent du jus de fruit
5. qui contiennent de la caféine
6. à prendre avec le dîner

Implementation: 5-1 Display the café items (MFL, Ch. 5) as students complete the exercise. Note that all direction lines for the *À vous la parole* are in French beginning in Ch. 5.

5-2 Qu'est-ce que vous désirez ? Vous êtes au café avec un/e partenaire. Dites ce que vous préférez d'après la situation donnée.

MODÈLE Vous êtes au McDo.
É1 Pour moi, un cheeseburger et un coca.
É2 Un hamburger avec des frites et une limonade.

1. Vous êtes au café.
2. Vous n'avez pas faim.
3. Vous devez travailler très tard.
4. Il est 12 h 30.
5. C'est le matin.
6. Vous mangez une pizza et vous voulez boire quelque chose.
7. Vous avez très faim.
8. Vous avez très soif.

5-3 Au café. À tour de rôle, imaginez que vous êtes le serveur ou la serveuse. Vous prenez la commande de vos camarades qui sont les clients.

MODÈLE É1 Madame !
É2 Vous désirez ?
É1 Un café crème.
É2 Oui, et pour vous, mademoiselle ?
É3 Je voudrais un sandwich au jambon.
É2 C'est tout ?
É3 Non, une bière aussi, s'il vous plaît.
É2 Alors, pour monsieur, un café crème et pour mademoiselle un sandwich au jambon et une bière.

Implementation: 5-3 Use as a role-play activity. You may choose to act the part of the server. Use the photo from a café as a prompt, or bring in empty cups and bottles as props to enliven the activity. This exercise prepares students for the **Parlons** activity at the end of the lesson.

Vie et culture

La restauration à la chaîne

Aujourd'hui, les Français mangent moins souvent au restaurant. Les jeunes préfèrent les chaînes de restauration comme McDonald's (McDo), mais ils mangent plus de sandwichs que de hamburgers. Ils achètent leurs sandwichs surtout dans des chaînes spécialisées (**La Brioche Dorée, Paul, Point Chaud**) et pas nécessairement dans des cafés. Le nombre de cafés en France diminue, mais c'est encore un endroit agréable pour prendre un casse-croûte et discuter avec ses amis. Souvent, les cafés ont des terrasses où on aime prendre une boisson et regarder les gens passer.

Qu'est-ce que vous désirez ?

Implementation: Have students describe what they see in the photos; what would they most likely order?

Note: In 2006, there were 1060 McDonald's restaurants in France; in second place was Quick's, with about 315 restaurants. The number of traditional cafés has plummeted: from 200,000 in 1960 to fewer than 50,000 in 2003. They have been replaced to some degree by fast-food and specialized sandwich shops *à la française*, as described here in the cultural note.

ET VOUS ?

1. Est-ce qu'il y a beaucoup de cafés en Amérique du Nord ? Pourquoi ? Est-ce qu'il y a beaucoup de chaînes de restauration chez vous ?
2. Est-ce que vous allez habituellement au café pour discuter avec vos amis ? Expliquez votre réponse.

Sons et lettres

Les voyelles nasales

Both English and French have nasal vowels. In English, any vowel followed by a nasal consonant is automatically nasalized, as in *man*, *pen*, *song*. In French, whether the vowel is nasal or not can make a difference in meaning. For example:

beau	/bo/	*handsome*	vs.	bon	/bɔ̃/	*good*
ça	/sa/	*that*	vs.	cent	/sɑ̃/	*a hundred*
sec	/sɛk/	*dry*	vs.	cinq	/sɛ̃k/	*five*

There are four nasal vowels in French. Use this phrase to remember them:

un /œ̃/ bon /bɔ̃/ vin /vɛ̃/ blanc /blɑ̃/ *a good white wine*

Nasal vowels are always written with a vowel letter followed by a nasal consonant (**m** or **n**), but that consonant is not usually pronounced: **mon**, **dans**, **cinq**.

- The vowel /ɔ̃/ is usually spelled **on**: **jambon, des glaçons**
- The vowel /ɑ̃/ is spelled **an** or **en**: **sandwich, prendre**
- For /ɛ̃/there are several spellings: **le vin**, **l'examen**, **la faim, sympa**
- The vowel /œ̃/, which is rare and often pronounced like /ɛ̃/, is spelled **un**: **brun**, **lundi**
- Before **b** and **p**, nasal vowels are spelled with **m**: **combien**, **impossible**

  Note this exception: **le bonbon**

Note: The distinction between / œ̃ / and / ɛ̃ / is not generally made by speakers in the region of Paris, who tend to use / ɛ̃ / only. Because of that, and because / œ̃/ occurs in few words (*un, chacun, quelqu'un, lundi, parfum*) it is not useful to insist that students make this distinction.

À vous la parole

5-4 Contrastes. Répétez et faites bien entendre les différences de prononciation.

beau / bon	allô / allons	sec / cinq
fine / fin	Jeanne / Jean	américaine / américain

5-5 Quelle voyelle nasale ? Faites attention à bien faire entendre les différences de prononciation entre ces voyelles nasales.

1. le vin / le vent *(the wind)*
2. cent pages / cinq pages
3. c'est long / c'est lent *(slow)*
4. il vend / ils vont
5. il est blond / il est blanc

Initial practice: Begin practice with a discrimination drill. Have students raise their hand when they hear words with a nasal vowel: *bon, l'eau, chanter, Jeanne, beau, mon, cent, sec, ta, vent*, etc.
In another discrimination exercise, write the three vowels on the board as *in an on*, and have students indicate which you have pronounced: *Jean, jambon, faim, combien, orange, glaçons, vin, citron, sandwich*, etc.

5-6 Phrases. Répétez chaque phrase.

1. Voyons ! Pas de glaçons ?
2. On prend une boisson ? un thé au citron ?
3. Alain n'a pas faim, mais il prend du vin blanc.
4. On commande un sandwich au jambon.

FORMES ET FONCTIONS

1. *Les verbes* prendre *et* boire

Presentation: These irregular verbs have three stems. Introduce the verbs inductively, using questions and the vocabulary of the lesson; this should follow very naturally from the presentation and practice of the café fare, for example, as you follow up on Ex. 5-2. Ask students to tell how many different spoken forms they hear (four). Using the verb chart, start with the first-person plural and show how the vowel changes in the third-person plural: for *prendre*, from the vowel /ø/ in *prenons*, to the vowel /ɛ/ in *prennent*; for *boire*, from the vowel /y/ in *buvons*, to the sound /wa/ in *boivent*. Like other verbs with four spoken forms, the consonant heard in the third-person plural is dropped in the singular forms. Point out to students that when *boire* is used without a complement, it is understood that one is talking about drinking alcohol. *Ils boivent* means "They drink (alcohol)" or "They are drinkers."

The verbs **prendre** and **boire** are irregular.

PRENDRE *to take*			
SINGULIER		**PLURIEL**	
je	pren**ds**	nous	pren**ons**
tu	pren**ds**	vous	pren**ez**
il / elle / on	pren**d**	ils / elles	pre**nn**ent

IMPÉRATIF : **Prends** un café ! **Prenez** du vin ! **Prenons** une pizza !

BOIRE *to drink*			
SINGULIER		**PLURIEL**	
je	boi**s**	nous	**buv**ons
tu	boi**s**	vous	**buv**ez
il / elle / on	boi**t**	ils / elles	**boiv**ent

IMPÉRATIF : Ne **bois** pas ça ! **Buvez** de l'eau ! Ne **buvons** pas trop !

- The verb **prendre** is used with foods or beverages.

Je **prends** un citron pressé.	*I'm having lemonade.*
—Qu'est-ce que vous **prenez** ?	*—What are you having?*
—Un coca.	*—A Coke.*
On **prend** un sandwich au jambon et des frites.	*We're having a ham sandwich and fries.*

- **Prendre** also means *to take*.

On **prend** le bus ou un taxi ?	*Shall we take the bus or a taxi?*
Tu **prends** ton sac ?	*Are you taking your bag?*
Elle **prend** une douche.	*She's taking a shower.*

- **Apprendre**, *to learn*, and **comprendre**, *to understand*, are formed like **prendre**.

Tu **apprends** l'italien ?	*You're learning Italian?*
Ils **comprennent** l'arabe.	*They understand Arabic.*

◆ **Boire** means *to drink.*

Qu'est-ce que tu **bois** ?	*What are you drinking?*
On **boit** du vin rouge.	*We're drinking red wine.*
Je ne **bois** pas trop de café.	*I don't drink too much coffee.*

Initial practice: Begin practice with a discrimination drill: one person, or more than one? *Il prend une bière. Elles prennent du café. Prends une pizza ! Elles boivent du coca. Il boit beaucoup. Elle boit une limonade. Ils prennent des frites. Ils boivent le week-end. Il prend de l'eau minérale. Elle boit trop de café. Elles prennent le bus.* Follow with a simple substitution drill: *Je prends du café* (*nous, eux, lui,* etc.) ; *Qu'est-ce que tu bois* (*nous, vous, eux*) ?

À vous la parole

5-7 Quelle consommation ? Qu'est-ce que ces personnes prennent ou boivent ?

MODÈLE la dame âgée ?

Elle prend un café crème.

OU Elle boit un café crème.

1. et le jeune homme ?
2. et son amie ?
3. et les enfants ?
4. et le monsieur ?
5. et la petite fille ?
6. et ces hommes ?

5-8 C'est logique. Posez une question logique pour savoir quelles langues ces personnes comprennent ou apprennent. Voici la liste des langues :

l'allemand, l'espagnol, le français, l'italien, le portugais, le russe

Implementation: 5-8 Before completing the exercise, go over the list of languages, perhaps even matching languages to place names in the exercise.

MODÈLES Bruno habite au Portugal.

Alors il comprend le portugais ?

Je vais en Russie.

Alors tu apprends le russe ?

1. Isabella habite en Italie.
2. J'habite en Russie.
3. Franz habite en Allemagne.
4. Georges et moi, nous habitons en France.
5. Mes cousins habitent en Espagne.
6. Guillaume et Pierre vont à Moscou.
7. Paul et moi, nous allons au Mexique.
8. Mélanie va en Allemagne.
9. Je vais au Portugal.
10. Vous allez au Québec ?

Implementation: 5-9 This can be completed in pairs or small groups; then have students compare answers. You may wish to complete this exercise after introducing the partitive, since students may wish to use this structure (e.g., *je prends du café*).

5-9 Vos habitudes. Qu'est-ce que vous prenez dans ces situations ? Comparez votre réponse avec la réponse de votre partenaire.

MODÈLE le matin, avant (*before*) d'aller en classe ?
É1 Moi, je prends un café noir.
É2 Et moi, un jus d'orange.

1. pendant la journée ?
2. quand vous n'avez pas le temps de manger ?
3. le soir, quand vous ne pouvez pas dormir ?
4. quand vous regardez la télé ?
5. quand vous êtes au cinéma ?
6. quand vous sortez avec des amis ?
7. quand vous avez très soif ?

2. *L'article partitif*

Presentation: To present this topic inductively, provide additional examples similar to those found in the text in order to help students discover the differences between a) mass and count nouns; b) use of the indefinite versus the partitive articles with unspecified nouns; c) use of the definite article with presupposed nouns or nouns used in a general sense. Based on the examples, ask students to summarize when the partitive article is used.

- Look at the following examples:

J'aime le café, mais pas le thé.	*I like coffee, but not tea.*
J'adore les croissants, mais je déteste les bananes.	*I love croissants, but I hate bananas.*

Nouns are of two types in French and in English. *Count nouns* refer to things that can be counted, such as croissants and bananas. *Mass nouns* are things that normally are not counted, like coffee, tea, sugar, and water. Notice that, as in the examples above, count nouns can be made plural; mass nouns are normally used only in the singular.

- When you refer to a noun not previously specified, use the indefinite article if it is a count noun.

Il mange **un** sandwich.	*He's eating a sandwich.*
Je prends **une** pizza.	*I'm having a pizza.*
Elle achète **des** oranges.	*She's buying oranges.*

Use one of the three forms of the *partitive article* if it is a mass noun.

Tu veux **du** coca ?	*Do you want some Coke?*
Tu prends **de la** glace ?	*Do you want some ice cream?*
Je sers **de l'**eau minérale.	*I'm serving mineral water.*

Note: In French and English we sometimes use the singular indefinite article with mass nouns: *Je voudrais une bière,* "I'd like a beer." *Des* is the plural form of the indefinite article. The partitive article is used with mass nouns and the indefinite article with count nouns. Both of these articles contrast with the definite article. Depending on the verb, the definite article carries the meaning of generic or of previously identified, specified, or presupposed: *J'aime le vin* (generic), *Où est le vin ?* (presupposed), *Tu as acheté la pizza ?* (presupposed). The examples provided here, and the first exercises, emphasize these distinctions. Use the examples to illustrate these points as you explain.

- In the examples below, note the differences in meaning between the definite article on the one hand, and the indefinite and partitive articles on the other. Here the definite article denotes a specific or presupposed item. The indefinite or partitive article denotes an unspecified item.

Definite article	**Indefinite or partitive article**
Il prend l'orange. *He's taking the orange.* (*the specific orange*)	Il prend **une** orange. *He's taking an orange.* (*any orange*)
Vous voulez **les** sandwichs ? *Do you want the sandwiches?* (*these particular sandwiches*)	Vous voulez **des** sandwichs ? *Do you want sandwiches?* (*any sandwiches*)

Definite article	**Indefinite or partitive article**
Elle mange **le** pain.	Elle mange **du** pain.
She's eating the bread. (*this specific bread*)	*She's eating some bread.* (*any bread*)

- The definite article is also used when nouns are used in a general sense, to express preferences.

J'aime **le** vin, mais je n'aime pas **la** bière.	*I like wine, but I do not like beer.*

- In negative sentences, both the indefinite and the partitive articles are replaced by **de/d'**:

Il prend **un** Orangina ?	—Non, non, il ne prend pas **d'**Orangina.
Je peux avoir **des** glaçons ?	—On n'a pas **de** glaçons, mademoiselle.
Vous servez **du** thé ?	—Non, nous ne servons pas **de** thé, monsieur.

À vous la parole

5-10 Qu'est-ce que Chloé mange ? Regardez bien la liste des aliments suivants. Notez la forme de l'article dans chaque cas pour bien déterminer si Chloé prend les aliments suivants ou pas.

	Elle prend...	Elle ne prend pas...	
MODÈLE	______	✓	... de glace.
1.	______	______	... du thé nature.
2.	______	______	... de café crème.
3.	______	______	... de la salade.
4.	______	______	... de l'eau minérale.
5.	______	______	... de frites.
6.	______	______	... de sucre.
7.	______	______	... des fruits.

D'après les habitudes de Chloé, est-ce qu'elle va probablement maigrir ou grossir ? Expliquez votre réponse.

Implementation: 5-10 Begin practice with this comprehension-based activity, to help students recognize forms of the partitive. Help students figure out the meaning of the verbs *maigrir* and *grossir* based on context and the adjectives *maigre* and *gros/se*. For practice in producing forms, use simple substitution drills. Begin by having students manipulate familiar forms: *Vous voulez du café ? —Oui, j'aime le café*, etc. This allows them to hear multiple examples of the partitive used in context. Remind students of the importance of the verb in determining the choice of article. Next have students use the new partitive forms: *Vous aimez le café ? —Oui, donnez-moi du café*, etc. Drill the negative forms as well: *De la glace ? Je ne prends pas de glace ; de l'eau minérale ? du thé ?*, etc.

Additional activity: For another simple exercise, put realia or pictures depicting types of food and drink in a bag. A student holding the bag answers questions from others about the contents: *Il y a du coca dans le sac ? —Oui, voilà le coca. Il y a des sandwichs ? —Non, il n'y a pas de sandwichs*, etc.

5-11 Ce n'est pas logique ! Corrigez ces phrases illogiques.

MODÈLE Avec le café, je prends du vin blanc.
→ Avec le café, je ne prends pas de vin blanc ; je prends du sucre.

1. Comme dessert, je prends une pizza.
2. Avec une pizza, je prends du café.
3. Quand j'ai très soif, je prends du vin.
4. Généralement, je prends de la bière avec des glaçons.
5. Au mois de juillet, on prend souvent du chocolat chaud.
6. Dans un thé au lait, on met des frites.
7. Quand on veut manger quelque chose, on prend de la limonade.
8. Quand on veut boire quelque chose, on prend une pizza.

5-12 Au café. D'après les descriptions suivantes, imaginez ce que chaque personne prend au café.

MODÈLE Vincent n'a jamais assez de temps pour manger le matin.
Il prend seulement un café noir.

1. Mme Sauvert fait très attention de manger correctement.
2. Sophie voudrait un dessert.
3. Claire n'a pas très faim.
4. Rémi a très soif.
5. Antoine est végétarien.
6. Le petit Nicolas a très faim.
7. M. Berger mange souvent au McDo.

Implementation: 5-13 This contrasts the use of the non-definite (indefinite and partitive) articles to that of the definite article. As a follow-up, have students report back what their partner said.

5-13 Vos habitudes et préférences. Complétez chaque phrase et comparez votre réponse avec la réponse de votre partenaire.

MODÈLE Le matin, je prends toujours...

É1 Le matin, je prends toujours du café.
É2 Je déteste le café. Moi, je prends toujours du thé.

1. Le matin, je prends toujours...
2. Quand je vais au McDo, je prends toujours...
3. Le week-end, je prends...
4. Quand j'ai très soif, j'aime...
5. Quand je travaille très tard le soir, je prends souvent...
6. Ma boisson préférée, c'est...

Implementation: En parlant Model this activity before continuing in small groups. Alternatively, if you have a small class, you might act as the server. Add interest and humor by dressing in black and white and bringing in props: a tray, towel, and paper for creating receipts. Group students' chairs across the classroom, put up posters or slides of cafés for ambiance, and insist that students call you to their "table" when they are ready to order. Bring in bottles, glasses, cups, and plastic food as additional props if possible. You can also add interest by introducing variations: one person keeps changing his or her order; the server keeps making mistakes; the server is ill-tempered; everyone wants to leave, but one person keeps ordering more food and/or drink, etc.

Expansion: Après avoir parlé To follow up, you might also have groups perform for the class, then have the class vote on the best/funniest/most realistic exchange. If there is a French café, bakery, or restaurant in your area, this might offer an opportunity for a class field trip. You might arrange in advance so that the class has a French-speaking server.

Parlons

5-14 Allons au café !

Implementation: Avant de parler As students prepare for the role-play, you might review with them expressions for calling the server, asking for the bill, and paying. Students should not write out answers.

A. Avant de parler. Est-ce que vous allez souvent au café ? Qu'est-ce que vous prenez d'habitude comme boisson ou sandwich ? Discutez de ces questions avec deux camarades de classe.

B. En parlant. En groupes de trois, imaginez que vous êtes au café. Une personne est le serveur ou la serveuse. Appelez cette personne et donnez votre commande. Prenez votre boisson ou sandwich, discutez un peu avec votre camarade de classe et payez l'addition.

C. Après avoir parlé. Quels sont les boissons et les sandwichs les plus populaires ? Est-ce qu'il y a un café ou un restaurant français dans votre ville ? Pourquoi ne pas aller au café ou au restaurant avec votre professeur et vos camarades de classe un jour ? Fixez un rendez-vous avec eux !

Leçon 2 À table !

POINTS DE DÉPART

TEXT AUDIO
CD 3 TRACK 6

Les repas

Les Sangala habitent à Bordeaux ; ils prennent le petit-déjeuner vers huit heures.

Les Canadiens prennent souvent un petit-déjeuner copieux.

Presentation: Present the vocabulary scene by scene, using the visuals for meals (MFL, Ch. 5); you may want to treat this vocabulary over two days, for example, treating breakfast vocabulary on day 1 and the other meals on day 2. Show on a map where the various families live. Describe each meal, model pronunciation, then test comprehension by having students point to the item you name. Have students repeat the new words, using either/or questions: *C'est du beurre ou de la confiture ?*, etc. As you move from one group of words to the next, review the most useful words already presented.
Teach the superordinate terms *une entrée, un plat principal, un dessert*, as well as *une viande* and *un légume*. These words appear in the **Vie et culture** notes and throughout the lesson and are helpful in organizing the various food words into categories for practice and review, as outlined in the learning strategy in L. 1.

Review: To review the food vocabulary, have students compete in teams to see how many items each team can list for a specific category. This allows students to implement the learning strategy presented for vocabulary in L. 1. Send one member of each team to the board for each category, and give them a limited amount of time to write their lists. Sample categories: *les boissons rafraîchissantes ; les fruits ; les légumes ; les desserts.*

Les Dupuis habitent une ferme en Touraine ; ils déjeunent chez eux à midi et demi.

Marie-Christelle, Janique et Guillaume habitent en Belgique ; ils prennent le goûter vers quatre heures.

M. et Mme Haddad habitent en Algérie ; ils dînent vers huit heures.

Note: Cultural features include: times for meals, size of meals, choices of snacks. *Une rôtie (Can.)* is a type of toast. *Bacon* is pronounced /bekɔn/.
In Canada, the meals are: *le déjeuner, le dîner, le souper.* Small children often have an after-school snack, *le goûter*, or *le quatre heures* (*une collation* in Canada) around four o'clock, since dinner is typically served around eight o'clock. They may have *un pain au chocolat* (a chocolate croissant), or a portion of a *baguette* with a piece of chocolate inside (*du pain avec du chocolat*), *un fruit, un yaourt,* or *des tartines,* with juice or water to drink.

Implementation: Use the restaurant menu to illustrate the categories described in the note and to provide additional examples of *entrées, plats principaux*, and *desserts*. Remind students that *une entrée* is a starter or appetizer, and that *le plat principal* refers to the main course. Note the differences between the two menus offered, in terms of price and choice.

Vie et culture

Le déjeuner

Aujourd'hui beaucoup d'employés déjeunent au restaurant, près de leur travail. Regardez ces menus à l'entrée d'un petit restaurant : en quoi consiste un déjeuner typique ? D'abord[1], il y a une entrée ; indiquez une ou deux des entrées proposées. Ensuite[2], il y un plat principal (de la viande ou du poisson) servi avec un légume. Après, on peut prendre un fromage ou un dessert. À la fin du repas, on prend le café. Quel menu et quels plats est-ce que vous préférez et pourquoi ?

Le dîner

Le repas du soir, le dîner ou le souper, est normalement moins copieux. Il commence souvent par une soupe. Ensuite on peut avoir une omelette, des pâtes, de la viande ou du poisson avec un légume. Pour finir, il y a un peu de fromage, un yaourt ou des fruits. Le dîner en famille commence assez tard, vers huit heures. Souvent on regarde le journal télévisé[3] pendant le repas.

Qui va déjeuner chez ses grands-parents ? À votre avis, est-ce que c'est un repas ordinaire ou un repas de fête ? En France, le grand repas de la semaine est le déjeuner du dimanche. Souvent on invite des membres de la famille ou des bons amis. Ces déjeuners sont très animés et très longs : ils peuvent durer entre deux et trois heures.

ET VOUS ?

1. Est-ce que vos habitudes sont semblables aux habitudes des Français ou différentes ? Par exemple, quel est le repas principal de la journée chez vous ? Expliquez votre réponse.
2. Est-ce que vous dînez plus tôt ou plus tard que les Français le soir ? Pourquoi ? Est-ce que vous regardez la télé quand vous mangez ?

[1]*first* [2]*next* [3]*T.V. news*

Note: Saturday dinner is also a time when the French typically invite friends and family for a meal. Many French people enjoy entertaining in their homes for special occasions such as birthdays, baptisms, confirmations, etc., and the focus of the get-together is frequently an elaborate meal.

À vous la parole

Implementation: 5-15 Begin by having students identify the meal depicted in the photo. Personalize by having students describe one of their typical meals and let classmates guess which meal it is. Point out that M. Maisonneuve could be having breakfast in the restaurant pictured here and that since he's in Canada, his meal would be referred to as *le déjeuner*.

5-15 Quel repas ? Selon la description, identifiez le repas.

MODÈLE M. Maisonneuve prend des œufs sur le plat avec du jambon et des rôties.
Il prend le petit-déjeuner.

1. Mme Lopez donne des yaourts et des fruits à ses enfants.
2. Mme Leroux prend seulement du café et un croissant.
3. Nicolas prend un pain au chocolat et un jus de pomme.
4. M. et Mme Poirier prennent des œufs avec des rôties.
5. Il est une heure ; les Schumann mangent du poisson avec du riz.
6. Nous sommes à Montréal, le soir. Mme Ladouceur sert de la soupe.
7. Avant de retourner au bureau, Marion et Gaëlle prennent un hamburger et des frites au McDo.
8. Il est huit heures du soir, et les Deleuze mangent du rosbif et des pommes de terre.

Additional activity/Review: *Les bonnes combinaisons. Qu'est-ce qu'on prend avec la boisson ou l'aliment mentionné ? avec le café ? — du sucre ou du lait ; avec le thé ? avec le pain ? avec les œufs ? avec le poulet ? avec le poisson ? avec le fromage ? avec les hamburgers ?*

5-16 Quels ingrédients ? Avec quoi est-ce qu'on fait les plats suivants ? Avec un/e partenaire, mettez-vous d'accord sur les ingrédients.

MODÈLE une omelette ?

É1 Avec quoi est-ce qu'on fait une omelette ?
É2 On fait une omelette avec des œufs, du lait et du beurre.
É1 Et aussi avec du jambon et du fromage.

1. un citron pressé ?
2. une omelette ?
3. un sandwich ?
4. une salade de fruits ?
5. une tartine ?
6. un croque-monsieur ?
7. un café au lait ?
8. un pain au chocolat ?

5-17 Vos préférences. Qu'est-ce que vous prenez d'habitude dans les situations suivantes ? Comparez vos habitudes avec celles d'un/e camarade de classe.

MODÈLE comme boisson, au petit-déjeuner ?

É1 D'habitude, je prends du café avec du sucre.

É2 Moi, je ne prends pas de boisson au petit-déjeuner.

1. comme boisson, au petit-déjeuner ?
2. à manger, au petit-déjeuner ?
3. à manger, au déjeuner ?
4. comme goûter, l'après-midi ?
5. quand vous voulez prendre une boisson, l'après-midi ?
6. comme boisson, au dîner ?
7. quand vous êtes très occupé/e et vous dînez très tard le soir ?
8. quand vous êtes très stressé/e ?
9. comme boisson, quand vous avez des invités ?

Implementation: 5-17 Follow up by having several students report back their partners' preferences.

Sons et lettres

Les voyelles nasales et les voyelles orales plus consonne nasale

Compare the following pairs of words; the first ends with a final pronounced consonant (**-n** or **-m**) and the second ends in a nasal vowel. Only the second word contains a nasal vowel; notice the difference as you repeat after your instructor.

bonne/bɔn/	bon/bɔ̃/
ma cousine/kuzin/	mon cousin/kuzɛ̃/
ils prennent/prɛn/	il prend/prɑ̃/
Jeanne/ʒan/	Jean/ʒɑ̃/

For words containing a nasal vowel, pronounce each syllable slowly, and do not pronounce **-m** or **-n** when it follows the nasal vowel:

sans	un sand-wich	sans moutarde
Jean	le jam-bon	un sand-wich au jam-bon
en	une en-trée	une en-trée froide

Presentation: Demonstrate for students a careful articulation of the final /n/ for words in the left-hand column. To practice other pairs, use names such as *Simone/Simon, Adrienne/Adrien, Yvonne/Yvon.*

À vous la parole

5-18 Les groupes de mots. Attention de bien insister sur les voyelles nasales.

1. mon	mon-tagne
2. sans	sand-wich
3. camp	cam-ping
4. franc	fran-çaise
5. l'un	lun-di

Initial practice: Begin with an exercise that requires a change from masculine to feminine, and vice versa: *Il est bon. — Elle est bonne ; Il est brun ; Ils sont canadiens ; Il est américain ; C'est Jean ; mon cousin ; mes voisins ; Voilà Simon ; Ils sont bons.*

Implementation: 5-18 Have students pronounce the second word syllable-by-syllable several times, and then as a word: *mon, mon tagne, montagne.* Additional words with *n: rentrer, penser, chanter,* with *m: combien, la campagne, impossible.*

5-19 Les phrases. Lisez chaque phrase.

1. Il a faim ; donc, il mange un sandwich.
2. Le matin, on prend des croissants, du pain et de la confiture.
3. Au restaurant, on prend du poisson.
4. Jean et Jeanne vont en Bourgogne en juin.
5. Marianne va en Louisiane chez son oncle et ses cousins.

FORMES ET FONCTIONS

1. *Le passé composé avec* avoir

Presentation: This topic can be presented inductively in class. Begin by describing your own activities during, for example, the past weekend. Then ask students questions about their own weekend, using yes/no, either/or, and short-answer questions. Then ask students to tell you what time frame you are talking about, and whether they can tell how to form the *passé composé*. For students who are visual learners, you could display the text of your weekend activities on a transparency or slide with the forms in the *passé composé* highlighted.

- To express an action completed in the past, use the **passé composé**. The **passé composé** is a past tense composed of an auxiliary, or helping verb, and the past participle of the verb that expresses the action. Usually, the present tense of **avoir** is the helping verb.

J'**ai travaillé** hier au restaurant.	*I worked yesterday at the restaurant.*
Tu **as mangé** ?	*Did you eat?*
Il **a préparé** un sandwich.	*He made a sandwich.*
Nous **avons écouté** le serveur.	*We listened to the server.*
Vous **avez regardé** le menu ?	*Did you look at the menu?*
Ils **ont servi** une bonne soupe à l'oignon.	*They served a nice onion soup.*

- The specific meaning of the **passé composé** depends on the verb and on the context.

Hier on **a montré** un film à la télé.	*Yesterday they showed a film on TV.*
Mais j'**ai** déjà **fait** la vaisselle !	*But I have already done the dishes!*
La semaine dernière, il **a été** malade.	*Last week, he got sick.*
Mais j'**ai** beaucoup **travaillé** !	*But I did work a lot!*

- To form the past participle . . .
  - for **-er** verbs, add **-é** to the base (the infinitive form minus the **-er** ending):

achet**er**	Ils ont achet**é** du lait et des œufs.	*They bought milk and eggs.*

  - for **-ir** verbs, add **-i** to the base (the infinitive form minus the **-ir** ending):

serv**ir**	Tu as serv**i** le vin ?	*Did you serve the wine?*

  - for **-re** verbs, add **-u** to the base (the infinitive form minus the **-re** ending):

attend**re**	Ils ont attend**u** devant le café.	*They waited in front of the café.*

- Here are past participles for irregular verbs that you know.

avoir	J'ai **eu** une bonne note.	*I got a good grade.*
boire	On a **bu** un bon vin blanc.	*We drank a nice white wine.*
courir	Elle a **couru** cinq kilomètres.	*She ran five kilometers.*
devoir	Il a **dû** travailler hier soir.	*He had to work last night.*
être	On a **été** surpris.	*We were surprised.*
faire	Il a **fait** la vaisselle.	*He did the dishes.*
mettre	J'ai **mis** du sel et du poivre.	*I put in salt and pepper.*
ouvrir	Tu as **ouvert** le paquet ?	*Did you open the package?*
pouvoir	J'ai **pu** sortir.	*I was able to go out.*
prendre	Elle a **pris** le poisson.	*She had the fish.*
vouloir	Elles n'ont pas **voulu** partir.	*They refused to leave.*

- In negative sentences, place **ne** and **pas** around the conjugated auxiliary verb.

Note: Short adverbs such as *déjà* and *beaucoup* are placed after the helping verb.

Il **n'**a **pas** payé l'addition.	*He didn't pay the bill.*
Nos parents **n'**ont **pas** téléphoné.	*Our parents didn't call.*

- The following expressions are useful for referring to the past.

hier	*yesterday*
avant-hier	*the day before yesterday*
samedi dernier	*last Saturday*
l'année dernière	*last year*
il y a longtemps	*a long time ago*
il y a deux jours	*two days ago*
ce jour-là	*that day*
à ce moment-là	*at that moment*

À vous la parole

5-20 Qu'est-ce qu'on a mangé ? Selon la situation, qu'est-ce que les gens ont probablement mangé, bu ou servi ?

MODÈLE M. et Mme Jourdain ont fêté dix ans de mariage hier.
→ Ils ont bu du champagne.
OU → Ils ont servi du champagne à leurs invités.

1. Sébastien a pris un petit-déjeuner copieux ce matin.
2. Marie-Laure a rencontré son copain au café avant-hier.
3. Georges a fait la cuisine pour ses amis le week-end dernier.
4. Mme Sauvert a préparé un déjeuner très simple à midi.
5. Les enfants ont pris un goûter après l'école.
6. Suzanne et moi, nous avons invité nos grands-parents à déjeuner dimanche.
7. On a servi un très bon dessert.

Initial practice: Begin practice with a discrimination drill: *aujourd'hui ou hier ? Je vais au resto U. J'ai fait la soupe. J'ai regardé la télé. Il dîne. Nous avons travaillé. Tu regardes le menu. J'ai bien mangé.* Continue with simple substitution drills a) to practice the forms of the verb *avoir*: *Nous avons un problème ; Clarice. —Elle a un problème*, etc.; b) to practice negation: *Elle a mangé ; Elle n'a pas mangé*, etc.; c) to practice regular and irregular past participles: *Elle travaille —Elle a travaillé ; Elle fait la vaisselle —Elle a fait la vaisselle*, etc.

Implementation: 5-20 This exercise can also be completed quickly in pairs; give each pair of students a different item to complete, then compare notes.

Implementation: 5-21 Point out to students at the beginning that asking *Qu'est-ce que vous avez fait hier ?* does not necessarily require that the answer begin with the verb *faire*. It is simply a general question. It might help students to show the similarity with English, where the question "What did you do yesterday?" would not normally be answered by saying something like "I **did** watch television." Follow up by having students compare their answers.

5-21 Mais c'est logique ! Avec un/e partenaire, imaginez ce que ces gens ont fait à l'endroit mentionné. Combien de possibilités est-ce que vous pouvez trouver ?

MODÈLE Qu'est-ce que Julie a fait dans le magasin hier ?
Elle a trouvé une jolie robe.
OU Elle a travaillé ; c'est une vendeuse.

1. Qu'est-ce que vous avez fait au restaurant hier ?
2. Qu'est-ce que les Brunet ont fait à la piscine l'été dernier ?
3. Qu'est-ce que tu as fait au supermarché hier ?
4. Qu'est ce qu'on a fait en cours hier matin ?
5. Qu'est-ce que tu as fait chez toi hier soir ?
6. Qu'est-ce que David a fait au café avant-hier ?
7. Qu'est-ce que vos camarades ont fait chez eux le week-end dernier ?
8. Qu'est-ce que le prof a fait dans son bureau ce matin ?

Additional activity: Put students into small groups to describe their activities of the previous day. The group must then decide whether each student was *très actif/active, assez actif/active*, or *(assez) sédentaire* (put these categories on the board). Follow up by having each group tell what they decided, and have them justify their response.

5-22 Normalement, mais... Racontez à votre partenaire vos habitudes et aussi les exceptions !

MODÈLE dormir
Normalement, je dors jusqu'à sept heures, mais samedi dernier j'ai dormi jusqu'à dix heures.

1. dormir
2. manger
3. quitter la maison
4. travailler
5. jouer
6. regarder la télé
7. boire

2. *Les verbes comme* acheter *et* appeler

Preparation: Review regular *-er* verbs and verbs like *préférer* before treating this section: use quick substitution drills and have students summarize the number of spoken forms. Remind them of the alternation /e/ vs. /ɛ/ presented in Ch. 3, L. 1, and link this to the nature of the syllable: open syllables end in /e/, closed syllables in /ɛ/; this is the same alternation they will observe in the new verbs. Emphasize pattern similarities and the link to what students already know.

- You have learned that for verbs like **préférer** (*to prefer*), the second vowel in the singular forms and the third-person plural form of the present tense are spelled and pronounced like the **è** in **mère**:

  Je préf**è**re le poisson. Ils préf**è**rent le poulet.

- Verbs like **acheter** (*to buy*) and **appeler** (*to call*) similarly show changes in the singular forms and in the third-person plural. The final vowel in these forms is also pronounced like the /ɛ/ in **mère**.
  - This pronunciation change is reflected in the spelling by the use of the **accent grave** in verbs like **acheter**.

acheter	*to buy*	Qu'est-ce que tu **achètes** ?
se lever	*to get up*	Elle se **lève** à huit heures.

  - Verbs like **appeler** reflect the pronunciation change by doubling the final consonant of the base in the singular and the third-person plural forms:

appeler	*to call*	J'**appelle** le restaurant pour réserver ?
épeler	*to spell*	Il **épelle** son nom.
jeter	*to throw (out)*	Elle ne **jette** pas les bananes.

- The **nous** and **vous** forms for these verbs are two syllables long:

nous aché tons　　　　vous appé lez

ACHETER *to buy*

SINGULIER		PLURIEL	
j'	ach**è**te	nous	achetons
tu	ach**è**tes	vous	achetez
il / elle / on	ach**è**te	ils / elles	ach**è**tent

IMPÉRATIF : **Achète** des haricots !
Achetez une belle tarte !
Achetons des asperges !

PASSÉ COMPOSÉ : J'**ai acheté** des belles tomates.

APPELER *to call*

SINGULIER		PLURIEL	
j'	appe**ll**e	nous	appelons
tu	appe**ll**es	vous	appelez
il / elle / on	appe**ll**e	ils / elles	appe**ll**ent

IMPÉRATIF : **Appelle** le serveur !
Appelez le médecin !
Appelons ton copain !

PASSÉ COMPOSÉ : On **a appelé** leurs parents.

À vous la parole

5-23 Des achats. Quels produits est-ce qu'on achète ?

MODÈLE Je prépare un plateau de fromages.
J'achète du brie, du camembert et du chèvre *(goat cheese)*.

1. Nous, on prépare un petit-déjeuner copieux.
2. Mes amis vont faire un pique-nique.
3. David a envie d'un fruit.
4. Maryse n'aime pas le poisson comme plat principal.
5. Vous êtes invité chez des amis pour dîner.
6. Christiane cherche des épices.
7. Tu veux des légumes ?
8. Je voudrais un beau dessert.

Initial practice: Begin with a discrimination drill; have students write out the verb form they hear in sentences: *Il appelle le restaurant. Nous jetons les restes. Je me lève tard. Vous appelez le serveur ? Tu achètes une baguette ? Tu jettes les fruits ? Nous achetons des tomates. Il épelle son nom.* Since pronunciation differences are reflected in the spelling, written practice is appropriate. Follow with simple substitution drills to practice correct pronunciation: *J'appelle le restaurant ; vous ? — Vous appelez le restaurant*, etc.

Expansion: 5-24 Vary the form used by having students imagine they are speaking to more than one co-renter.

5-24 Mais pourquoi ?
Imaginez que vous avez un/e colocataire impossible. Demandez-lui pourquoi il/elle fait les choses suivantes.

MODÈLE jeter les bananes

É1 Pourquoi est-ce que tu jettes les bananes ?
É2 Je n'aime pas les bananes.

1. acheter tous ces biscuits
2. ne pas appeler tes parents
3. ne pas te lever avant midi
4. ne pas épeler correctement mon nom
5. acheter toujours des chips et du chocolat
6. jeter les tomates
7. appeler tous tes amis

Expansion: 5-25 As a follow-up, have students tell something they learned about their partner. This will encourage the use of the third-person singular form.

5-25 Une interview.
Interviewez un/e partenaire pour apprendre s'il ou si elle...

MODÈLE jette ses vieux tickets de concerts

É1 Est-ce que tu jettes tes vieux tickets de concerts ?
É2 Oui, je jette mes vieux tickets de concerts.

1. appelle ses parents tous les week-ends
2. achète beaucoup de légumes
3. achète des fruits
4. se lève toujours avant huit heures
5. jette ses vieux tickets de concerts
6. jette toujours ses devoirs et examens corrigés (*graded*)
7. ne se lève pas avant midi le week-end

Implementation: Avant de lire If you treated the earlier Prévert poem, *Familiale*, in Ch. 4, L. 1, you might use the following reading strategy for this new poem: Use your familiarity with a particular writer to predict the style and content of a new text. Ask students the following: Describe what you know about the way in which Prévert writes: is his language simple or complex? Does he tend to use description or narration? Will his subject likely be lighthearted or serious?

Lisons

TEXT AUDIO CD 3 TRACK 10

Stratégie

Use a poem's title to help you anticipate its focus and content. Consider as well that a title may have broader implications relating to the subjective as well as the literal meaning of a poem.

5-26 Déjeuner du matin

A. Avant de lire. The title of the poem that you are going to read is ***Déjeuner du matin***. What does it lead you to expect the poem will be about, at a literal and perhaps subjective level? How might a poem with this focus be organized? As you read, consider the series of events that comprise the **déjeuner du matin**. Try to determine why the poet, Jacques Prévert, is focusing on this simple meal.

B. En lisant. Ce poème est une narration. Un personnage décrit une série d'actions pendant le déjeuner du matin. Pour comprendre son histoire, considérez les questions suivantes.

1. Il y a combien de personnages dans le poème ? Qui sont ces personnes, à votre avis ?
2. Qui raconte cette histoire, et comment ? Notez que Prévert a commencé sa carrière dans le cinéma.
3. Résumez les activités. Par exemple, (a) le monsieur a bu une tasse de café, (b)...

Implementation: En lisant Mime the actions as students listen to the poem, or show one of the many versions available on online video-sharing sites. Have students guess the meaning of unfamiliar words based on their context: *tourné, allumé, des ronds, ma tête*. Point out related words: *les cendres/le cendrier, une parole/parlé*.

C. En regardant de plus près. Maintenant répondez aux questions suivantes.

1. Les personnages dans le poème n'ont pas de nom : ils sont simplement **il** et **je**. Qui sont ces personnages, à votre avis ?
2. Le poème décrit en général les actions d'un personnage masculin. Quels sont les actions et les sentiments de l'autre personnage ?
3. Quel est le ton du poème : gai, triste (*sad*) ? Quelles techniques est-ce que Prévert utilise pour communiquer cela ?

D. Après avoir lu. Maintenant que vous avez lu et discuté du poème :

1. Imaginez :
   a. les actions avant le début du poème
   b. les actions après la fin du poème
2. Le titre du poème est ***Déjeuner du matin***. Est-ce que le petit-déjeuner est en réalité le sujet du poème ? Pourquoi est-ce que Prévert a donné ce titre au poème ?

DÉJEUNER DU MATIN

Il a mis le café
Dans la tasse
Il a mis le lait
Dans la tasse de café
Il a mis le sucre
Dans le café au lait
Avec la petite cuiller
Il a tourné
Il a bu le café au lait
Et il a reposé la tasse
Sans me parler
Il a allumé
Une cigarette
Il a fait des ronds
Avec la fumée
Il a mis les cendres
Dans le cendrier
Sans me parler
Sans me regarder
Il s'est levé
Il a mis
Son chapeau sur sa tête
Il a mis son manteau de pluie
Parce qu'il pleuvait
Et il est parti
Sous la pluie
Sans une parole
Sans me regarder
Et moi j'ai pris
Ma tête dans ma main
Et j'ai pleuré.

Jacques Prévert, *Paroles*.

Implementation: En regardant de plus près Point out to students that the second character, *je*, appears very late in the poem. What effect does this have? You might have students pick out all the examples of the *passé composé*, noting the two examples of the *passé composé* with *être*. This grammatical feature will be taught in Ch. 5, L. 3.

Implementation: Après avoir lu Point out to students the ambiguities in the poem, which allow for multiple interpretations by the reader. The reader must actively create some of the meaning of the poem.

Expansion: As a more extended follow-up, ask students to recount one of their own daily activities using Prévert's style.

Leçon 3 Faisons des courses

POINTS DE DÉPART

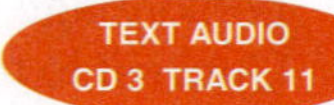

Allons au supermarché

Presentation: Present the vocabulary using the grocery store image (MFL, Ch. 5) and describing what one can find in each of the grocery store sections. Many of the products will be familiar to students, and some new items can be presented first for receptive control only. Note the spelling of *crèmerie* based on the 1990 orthographic reform and the dropping of *ne* in *C'est pas sur la liste*, which is characteristic of spoken French. Test students' comprehension by having them point to an item you name; have them repeat, using either/or questions: *Ce sont des petits pois ou des champignons ?*, etc. Then move on to the dialogue.

Presentation: Let students listen to the dialogue, then ask questions to check comprehension. Point out the expression *avoir besoin de* and compare it to *avoir envie de*, taught in Ch. 4, L. 3. Have students role-play, using parts of the dialogue and varying the vocabulary: *Qu'est-ce qu'on prend comme fruits ? — Des cerises ?* Be sure to provide a clear model. Use the **Vie et culture** notes to talk about where people shop for food.

Expansion: In conjunction with this section, you might wish to present the video clip *Pour faire une vinaigrette*, which includes key vocabulary and focuses on the ingredients needed and the process of preparing a simple recipe.

Variation: 5–27 Bring in a net bag of food items and have students guess where you would have bought them. For items that you wish to make part of students' productive vocabulary, play "Kim's Game": show students 8–10 articles that you then hide from view; they must write down a list of those articles.

C'est samedi. Les Mathieu font les courses à Super U. Ils se trouvent au rayon fruits et légumes.

M. MATHIEU : Qu'est-ce qu'on prend comme fruits ? Des cerises ? Elles sont belles !
MME MATHIEU : Mais elles sont trop chères. Sept euros le kilo !
M. MATHIEU : Alors, prenons des pommes !
MME MATHIEU : D'accord. Tu veux passer au rayon crèmerie ? On a besoin d'une douzaine d'œufs, d'une bouteille de lait, d'un morceau de cantal et aussi peut-être d'un bon camembert. Moi, je vais au rayon charcuterie pour chercher quelques tranches de jambon et du pâté. On se retrouve à la caisse ?

(*quelques minutes plus tard*)
M. MATHIEU : Regarde, chérie, j'ai trouvé cette boîte de sardines, un pot de moutarde à l'ancienne et ce paquet de chips bio.
MME MATHIEU : Tu es incorrigible ! C'est pas sur la liste, tout ça !

 À vous la parole 

5-27 Quel rayon ? On est au supermarché. Où est-ce que vous entendez cela ? Choisissez vos réponses dans cette liste.

au rayon crèmerie	au rayon boulangerie-pâtisserie
au rayon charcuterie	au rayon fruits et légumes
au rayon viandes et poissons	au rayon surgelés
	à la caisse

MODÈLE Je voudrais une demi-douzaine de petits pains, s'il vous plait.
→ C'est au rayon boulangerie-pâtisserie.

1. Je mets les croissants dans un sac ?
2. Qu'est-ce que tu préfères, le pâté de campagne ou le jambon ?
3. Vous avez des sardines ?
4. Comme dessert, on prend de la glace ou un sorbet ?
5. Je vous recommande le brie, madame.
6. Il y a des côtelettes d'agneau et du poulet.
7. La pâtissière fait des gâteaux délicieux !
8. Les melons sont beaux, mais ils sont chers.
9. Donne-moi mon sac, chéri ; on doit payer maintenant.

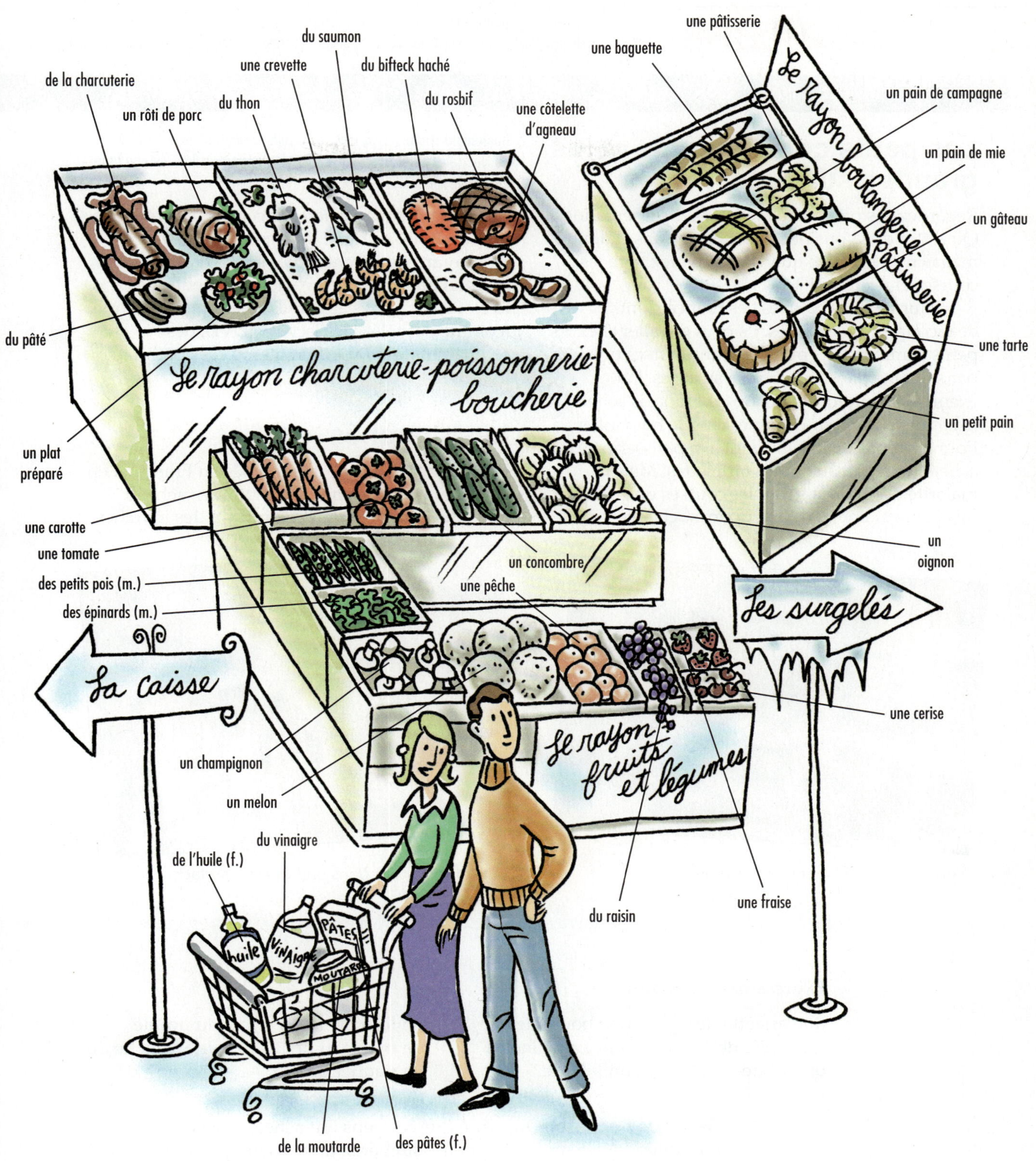
du saumon
une pâtisserie
une baguette
une crevette
du bifteck haché
de la charcuterie
du thon
du rosbif
un rôti de porc
une côtelette
d'agneau
un pain de campagne
Le rayon boulangerie-pâtisserie
un pain de mie
un gâteau
du pâté
une tarte
Le rayon charcuterie-poissonnerie-boucherie
un petit pain
un plat
préparé
une carotte
une tomate
un
oignon
un concombre
des petits pois (m.)
une pêche
Les surgelés
des épinards (m.)
La caisse
une cerise
Le rayon fruits et légumes
un champignon
un melon
du vinaigre
de l'huile (f.)
huile
VINAIGRE
PÂTES
MOUTARDE
du raisin
une fraise
de la moutarde
des pâtes (f.)

Vie et culture

Implementation: Use the photos to exploit the text and check for general comprehension: have students identify the various shops and summarize what items are generally purchased at each. Have them identify the main shopping options presented: neighborhood shops, supermarkets, and fresh markets. Ask them to

Les petits commerçants et les grandes surfaces

Regardez ces photos de magasins d'alimentation[1]. Qu'est-ce que vous pouvez acheter dans chaque magasin ? Où est-ce que vous préférez faire les courses et pourquoi ?

Pour faire les courses, les Français ont beaucoup de possibilités. Ils peuvent aller chez les petits commerçants ou faire leurs courses une fois par semaine dans les grandes surfaces. Par exemple, le matin, beaucoup de Français achètent la baguette du petit-déjeuner chez le boulanger. Pour les repas de fête, ils vont à la pâtisserie où ils achètent un gâteau ou des tartelettes. Mais la majorité des Français font les courses une ou deux fois par semaine dans les supermarchés comme Casino ou les hypermarchés comme Intermarché ou Carrefour. Comme les supermarchés, les hypermarchés offrent toutes sortes d'aliments. Mais en plus, on y trouve des vêtements, des livres, des CD, des appareils électroniques (comme des télés, des lecteurs DVD, des ordinateurs, etc.) et différentes choses pour la maison.

Implementation: As you make cross-cultural comparisons, suggest to students some possible reasons for shopping where they do: *C'est plus facile, c'est moins cher*, etc.

Les marchés

Regardez ces photos de marchés en France et en Guyane. Qu'est-ce que vous pouvez acheter dans ces marchés ? Est-ce qu'il y a des marchés

Voilà l'épicier devant son magasin.

On trouve de tout dans une grande surface.

Expressions de quantité

une assiette de	une bouteille de	un litre de	un pot de
une boîte de	une douzaine de	un morceau de	une tranche de
un bol de	un kilo de	un paquet de	un verre de

 **5-28 Des achats.** Qu'est-ce que ces gens ont acheté et en quelles quantités ? Avec un/e partenaire, suggérez un ou deux produits.

MODÈLE Pauline se trouve au rayon boulangerie.
É1 Elle a acheté une baguette.
É2 Et aussi une demi-douzaine de petits pains.

describe differences between markets in France and those in other parts of the Francophone world. Help students see the relationship between words such as *le boulanger* (a person) and *la boulangerie* (a place) and *une tarte* and *des tartelettes* (small tarts). Help them derive from context the meaning of the expressions *faire leur marché, marché couvert, marché en plein air.* Follow up with the cross-cultural questions.

Le fromager vend une grande variété de fromages.

Un marché en Guyane

là où vous habitez ? Si oui, est-ce que vous allez souvent au marché pour faire des achats ? Quels sont les avantages d'acheter certains produits au marché ?

Pour acheter des fruits et des légumes frais[2] ou biologiques, les Français aiment faire leur marché, en particulier le samedi et le dimanche. Il est vrai que les marchés sont moins pratiques que les supermarchés, en particulier au mois de janvier ! Alors pourquoi est-ce que les gens préfèrent les marchés ? C'est parce que les produits sont plus frais et les marchés sont plus animés. On y trouve une grande variété de couleurs, d'odeurs et de bruits[3].

[1]*food* [2]*fresh* [3]*noises*

Un marché en plein air à Nîmes

1. Nicolas a trouvé un beau dessert.
2. M. Dumas va faire une salade.
3. Mme Ducastel se trouve au rayon fruits et légumes pour acheter des fruits.
4. M. et Mme Camus veulent servir du jambon.
5. Matthieu a seulement pris des surgelés.
6. Gaëlle a été au rayon crèmerie.
7. Christophe va préparer des spaghettis.
8. Lucie veut faire une vinaigrette.

Implementation: 5-29 Before completing this activity, review with students the meaning of *l'entrée* and *le plat principal*, both of which were presented in the **Vie et culture** notes in L. 2. Remind students to use vocabulary they have already learned to complete this exercise. As a follow-up, have each group describe their menu and have the class vote on the best.

Presentation: Have students pick out the complete paradigm of the *passé composé* with *être* through the examples provided. You might show contrasts like *Je suis allé/e à la bibliothèque* vs. *J'ai trouvé le livre de Simenon* and ask students what type of expression follows the verb. Point out that verbs that form the *passé composé* with *être* do not take a direct object, only adverbial complements. In fact, if a direct object does follow, the verb *avoir* must be used: *Je suis sorti ce matin* vs. *J'ai sorti le chien ; Il est monté au bureau* vs. *Il a monté les ordinateurs au bureau.* Also, not all verbs of motion form the *passé composé* with *être: J'ai marché une heure ; Nous avons traversé la rue ; Tu as quitté l'université ?* The learning strategy focuses on mnemonic devices: display, explain, and distribute the illustration of the "house of *être*," included in the IRM; help students organize the list of verbs according to the "Dr. & Mrs. Vandertrampp" mnemonic. Remind students that they used this strategy in Ch. 3, L. 1, for the prenominal adjectives, where they learned the "BRAGS" mnemonic. Verbs conjugated like *venir* will be presented in Ch. 9, L. 2. Refer students to Appendix 5 for conjugations of *naître* and *mourir*.

5-29 Un grand dîner. Avec un/e partenaire, planifiez un grand dîner avec des amis. Quelle occasion est-ce que vous allez fêter ? Qu'est-ce que vous allez servir comme entrée ? comme plat principal ? comme légume ? comme fromage ? comme boisson ? comme dessert ?

MODÈLE É1 Comme entrée, on peut acheter du jambon et des crudités.
É2 Je déteste ça. Je préfère les crevettes.
É1 C'est cher, mais d'accord. Et comme plat principal ? …

FORMES ET FONCTIONS

1. *Le passé composé avec* être

- To tell what you did in the past, you have already learned that most French verbs form the **passé composé** with the present tense of **avoir**. However, some verbs use the present tense forms of **être** as an auxiliary. These are usually verbs of motion:

aller	*to go*	Tu **es allé** au restaurant ce week-end ?
arriver	*to arrive*	Je **suis arrivé** en ville vers 10 heures du matin.
venir	*to come*	Il **est venu** avec nous pour faire un pique-nique.
revenir	*to return*	Elle **est revenue** au bureau hier matin.
devenir	*to become*	Elle **est devenue** chef.
entrer	*to go/come in*	Anne **est entrée** dans le café.
rentrer	*to go/come back*	Nous **sommes rentrés** tard après le travail.
retourner	*to go back*	Elles **sont retournées** en France.
partir	*to leave*	Vous **êtes parties** ensemble à Lyon ?
sortir	*to go out*	Rémy **est sorti** avec Juliette pour voir un film.
passer	*to go/come by*	On **est passés** chez toi hier.
rester	*to stay*	Ils **sont restés** chez eux tout l'après-midi.
tomber	*to fall*	Elle **est tombée** dans le supermarché.
monter	*to go up*	Lucie **est montée** dans sa chambre.
descendre	*to go down*	On **est descendues** en ville pour dîner.
naître	*to be born*	Elle **est née** en 1988.
mourir	*to die*	Il **est mort** l'été dernier.

- For verbs that form the **passé composé** with **être**, the past participle agrees in gender and number with the subject.

Mon frère est arrivé hier.	*My brother arrived yesterday.*
Ma sœur est arrivé**e** ce matin.	*My sister arrived this morning.*
Ses cousins sont allé**s** au musée.	*Her cousins went to the museum.*
Ses cousines sont descendu**es** en ville aussi.	*Her cousins went downtown too.*

Fiche pratique

You have learned that you can use a mnemonic device to recall facts that must be memorized. The list of verbs conjugated with **être** in the **passé composé** is easy to remember if you use a mnemonic device such as the acronym "Dr. & Mrs. Vandertrampp" (each letter stands for a verb conjugated with **être**).

◆ Pronominal verbs also use **être** in the **passé composé**. Note, however, that when a noun follows the verb, no past participle agreement is made.

Il s'est endormi.	*He fell asleep.*
Ils se sont couché**s**.	*They went to bed.*
Elle s'est lavé**e**.	*She washed up.*
Elle s'est lavé les cheveux.	*She washed her hair.*

◆ To narrate a series of events or actions, use the following expressions.

D'abord elle s'est lavée et **ensuite** elle s'est habillée.	*First she washed up and then she got dressed.*
Puis, elle a pris un café et **enfin** elle est partie au travail.	*Then, she had coffee and finally, she left for work.*

Pour faire un récit

d'abord	ensuite	après	puis	enfin
first	*next*	*after*	*then*	*finally*

À vous la parole

5-30 La vie des serveurs. Il est difficile de travailler comme serveur dans un restaurant. Lisez attentivement les phrases suivantes pour déterminer si elles décrivent les serveurs maintenant ou au passé.

Initial practice: Begin practice with this comprehension-based activity. To practice forms orally, begin with a discrimination drill: tell a story in the past and have students raise their hands when they hear a verb conjugated with *être: Nous avons décidé de préparer une fête. J'ai téléphoné à Alain. Il est venu chez moi. On a téléphoné à nos amis. Patricia et Francine sont arrivées tout de suite. Aurélie est arrivée un peu plus tard. Nous avons écouté de la musique. Alain est allé au supermarché pour chercher du coca-cola. Nous avons dansé. Nos amis sont partis vers minuit,* etc. Review the forms of *être* with simple substitution drills: *Je suis parti ; nous ; eux,* etc. *; Je me suis réveillé ; toi ; vous,* etc. Follow with a transformation drill, present to past: *Je voyage. —J'ai voyagé ; Je pars. —Je suis parti/e.*

Les serveurs…

		maintenant	au passé
MODÈLE	… sont stressés.	✓	______
1.	… sont arrivés à l'heure.	______	______
2.	… sont énergiques.	______	______
3.	… sont entrés dans le bar.	______	______
4.	… sont assez jeunes.	______	______
5.	… sont devenus des amis.	______	______
6.	… sont fatigués.	______	______
7.	… sont sortis ensemble.	______	______
8.	… sont réservés.	______	______
9.	… sont allés au cinéma.	______	______

À votre avis, est-ce que c'est mieux d'être serveur maintenant ou dans le passé ? Pourquoi ?

5-31 L'après-midi de M. Dumont. Racontez l'après-midi de M. Dumont au passé.

Cet après-midi M. Dumont va sortir faire une promenade. Sa femme va rester à la maison pour préparer le dîner. Alors, M. Dumont va sortir avec son chien, Castor. Ils vont partir vers trois heures, et ils vont passer d'abord chez un ami de M. Dumont. Ensuite ils vont aller au parc, et ils vont entrer au zoo. Après, ils vont descendre par l'avenue principale et ils vont s'arrêter au café où M. Dumont va prendre un thé. Finalement, ils vont rentrer à la maison vers six heures.

MODÈLE Hier après-midi, M. Dumont est sorti faire une promenade.

Implementation: 5-32 To prepare for the narrative, review the useful adverbs *d'abord, ensuite, après, puis, enfin*, and have students first narrate in the present tense. You might have students work in pairs. You may also ask them to go beyond the pictures and imagine other logical activities. As a follow-up, have several pairs read their narratives and have the class vote on the best one.

5-32 Le samedi de Guillaume. Racontez comment Guillaume a passé la journée samedi. Utilisez les expressions pour faire un récit : **d'abord, ensuite, après, puis, enfin.**

MODÈLE D'abord, Guillaume a quitté sa chambre à huit heures. Ensuite, il...
OU D'abord, Guillaume est sorti à huit heures. Après, il...

a.

b.

c.

d.

e.

f.

g.

Variation: 5-33 Vary by having students tell about last weekend, last summer, etc.

 **5-33 Et vous ?** Qu'est-ce que vous avez fait hier ? Où est-ce que vous êtes allé/e ? Avec qui ? Qu'est-ce que vous avez fait ? Racontez à un/e partenaire.

MODÈLE Hier, dimanche, je ne suis pas allé/e à la fac. J'ai quitté mon appartement vers neuf heures et ensuite...

2. *Les expressions de quantité et le pronom* en

Presentation: To present inductively, show examples similar to those found here, and have students analyze the use and placement of *en*.

Note: The object pronoun *en* is placed after the conjugated verb in affirmative commands and joined to it by a hyphen: *Donnez-en à Suzanne ! En* is placed before the conjugated verb in negative commands: *N'en donnez pas à Paul !* The use of *en* with the imperative is not practiced here.

- The pronoun **en** replaces nouns used with the partitive article or the plural indefinite article **des**:

Vous avez acheté **de l'huile** ? —Oui, j'**en** ai acheté.	*Did you buy oil?* *—Yes, I bought some.*
Il n'y a pas **de sucre** ? —Si, il y **en** a.	*There isn't any sugar?* *—Yes, there is some.*
Qui veut **des fraises à la crème** ? —Jérémy **en** veut. Elles sont délicieuses.	*Who wants strawberries with cream?* *—Jeremy wants some. They're delicious.*

- The pronoun **en** can be used to replace nouns modified by an expression of quantity (including numbers). In this case, the expression of quantity is placed at the end of the sentence.

Il faut beaucoup de sucre pour cette recette? —Oui, il **en** faut beaucoup.	*Do you need a lot of sugar for this recipe?* *—Yes, you need a lot (of it).*
Tu as pris **du vin rouge** ? —Oui, j'**en** ai bu un verre.	*Did you have some red wine?* *—Yes, I drank a glass (of it).*
Combien de **melons** est-ce que vous allez prendre ? —Nous allons **en** prendre trois.	*How many melons are you going to take?* *—We'll take three (of them).*

As the examples above show, **en** is placed immediately before the conjugated verb of a sentence, unless there is an infinitive. In that case, it precedes the infinitive.

 À vous la parole 

5-34 Qu'est-ce qu'il a acheté ? David achète des provisions. D'après les indications, qu'est-ce qu'il a acheté ? Avec un/e partenaire, trouvez des possibilités.

Note: 5-34 This initial exercise helps students make the form-meaning link between the use of the pronoun *en* and the expressions of quantity.

MODÈLE Il en a acheté une douzaine.

É1 Il a acheté une douzaine d'œufs.
É2 Il a acheté une douzaine de citrons.

1. Il en a pris un pot.
2. Il en a acheté un morceau.
3. Il en a pris une douzaine.
4. Il en a acheté une bouteille.
5. Il en a pris deux paquets.
6. Il en a demandé deux.
7. Il en a pris beaucoup.
8. Il en a acheté un kilo.
9. Il en a demandé dix tranches.
10. Il en a acheté une boîte.

5-35 Elle en prend combien ? Voici la liste des provisions que Mme Serres achète pour sa famille. Quelles quantités est-ce qu'il lui faut ?

MODÈLE des carottes
Elle en achète un kilo.

- carottes
- oignons
- petits pains
- pâtes
- moutarde
- vin
- eau minérale
- lait
- œufs
- saumon

Note: No agreement of the past participle is made with *en*. Point out the useful expression *il faut*, used in the examples here and in exercises below. Compare to *avoir besoin de*, presented in the opening dialogue. The use of *il faut* with an infinitive will be presented in more detail in Ch. 8, L. 1.

Presentation: To review the expressions taught in Ch. 5, L. 1–3, have students tell: a) what items they would buy in the quantities specified: *une boîte ? —une boîte de sardines, une boîte de chocolats,* etc.; b) how much of a product they would normally buy: *Des carottes ? —un kilo de carottes. Des sardines ? —une boîte de sardines. Des tomates ? du vin ? des œufs ? du riz ? du brie ? des pommes de terre ? des champignons ? de l'huile ? des crevettes ? des petits pois ?*

Additional activities: a) Show a picture of a market (for example, MFL, Ch. 5) and ask students whether they can see certain items: *Il y a des carottes ? —Non, il n'y en a pas. / —Oui, il y en a.* b) Have students express their preferences as you point out various items: *Voici des carottes. —J'aime bien les carottes ; je vais en acheter un kilo. / —Je n'aime pas les carottes ; je ne vais pas en acheter.*
See the SAM/MFL for practice that mixes the various tenses.
For a more personalized activity, put students into groups of three or four to plan a meal. Have them write out their menu and grocery list. Give them five minutes to work, then let each group describe their meal.
Vous préparez un repas. Vous et vos amis, vous avez invité des gens à dîner. D'abord, décidez d'un menu. Ensuite, préparez une liste de choses à acheter. Enfin, distribuez les responsabilités : qui achète quoi, et où ?

MODÈLE É1 Comme entrée, on peut servir des crudités.
É2 Oui, c'est bon et ce n'est pas cher. Ensuite, du rosbif ou du poulet ?
É3 Moi, je préfère le poulet avec des haricots verts.
É1 Donc, on va au rayon boucherie pour acheter un gros poulet de deux kilos.
É2 Je vais au marché samedi matin pour acheter un kilo de haricots verts et...

SUGGESTIONS : un dîner d'anniversaire ; un pique-nique ; un petit-déjeuner copieux ; un repas pas cher.

5-36 Un pot-au-feu. Qu'est-ce qu'il faut pour faire un pot-au-feu ? Regardez l'image du « pot-au-feu géant » préparé pour un festival d'été en Bretagne. Avec un/e partenaire, décidez de quelle quantité il faut pour préparer un pot-au-feu pour votre famille.

MODÈLE É1 Pour un pot-au-feu géant, il faut 260 kg de viande ! Et pour ta famille ?
É2 Pour ma famille, il faut seulement un kilo de viande…
É1 On est huit chez moi, il en faut deux kilos.

5-37 Vous en avez combien ? Donnez une réponse logique et personnalisée, et comparez-la avec la réponse de votre partenaire. Ensuite, comparez vos réponses avec les autres étudiants dans votre cours.

MODÈLE des sœurs ?
É1 J'en ai une.
É2 Je n'en ai pas.

1. des sœurs ?
2. des frères ?
3. des amis ?
4. des problèmes ?
5. de l'argent ?
6. des devoirs ?
7. des responsabilités ?
8. des vacances ?

Écrivons

5-38 Vous avez bien mangé hier ?

A. Avant d'écrire. Qu'est-ce que vous avez mangé hier ? Quand ? Décrivez vos repas et vos casse-croûte et décidez si vous avez bien mangé.

1. Pour organiser vos idées, complétez ce tableau.

L'heure	Les aliments
MODÈLE *vers 9 h*	*un café et un croissant*
à midi	*un sandwich, de la soupe*

Stratégie

To narrate past events effectively, clearly establish the sequence in which they took place by using appropriate adverbial expressions.

Implementation: Avant d'écrire To complete the **Écrivons**, instruct students to keep track of what and when they eat during a 24-hour period.

2. Ensuite, évaluez ce que vous avez mangé : Est-ce que vous avez mangé très mal ? assez bien ? bien ? très bien ? Expliquez pourquoi : par exemple, est-ce que vous n'avez pas mangé assez de fruits et de légumes ? Est-ce que vous avez trop couru pendant la journée ?

B. En écrivant.

1. Expliquez ce que vous avez mangé et quand.
2. Dans votre description, utilisez des mots qui permettent d'indiquer une série d'actions : par exemple, **le matin, l'après-midi, le soir** ; ou **d'abord, ensuite, après.**
3. Faites une évaluation : comment est-ce que vous avez mangé ? Expliquez pourquoi vous pensez cela.

MODÈLE *Hier*, j'ai mangé très mal. *Le matin*, je n'ai pas déjeuné parce que j'ai dormi jusqu'à sept heures et demie et j'ai dû me dépêcher pour arriver à mon cours de huit heures. *Après* mon premier cours, vers dix heures, j'ai bu un café et j'ai pris un croissant. *Ensuite*, je suis allé(e) à un autre cours. *À midi*, je me suis arrêté(e) au restaurant universitaire ; j'ai pris seulement...

C. En révisant. Réfléchissez aux questions suivantes et puis faites tous les changements nécessaires.

1. Relisez votre paragraphe pour analyser le contenu : est-ce que vous avez décrit tout ce que vous avez mangé hier ? Est-ce que vous avez fait une évaluation ?
2. Relisez de nouveau votre paragraphe pour analyser le style et la forme : est-ce que vous avez bien indiqué une série d'actions avec une variété d'expressions ? Est-ce que les verbes au passé composé sont bien formés ?

D. Après avoir écrit. Échangez votre paragraphe avec quelqu'un dans votre classe. Qui a mangé le mieux ? Pourquoi ?

Expansion: Après avoir écrit To follow up, have students compare their eating habits: who eats best, and why?

Les Niçois et les touristes aiment prendre une bonne pizza en plein air dans ces deux pizzerias qui se trouvent face à face dans la rue Masséna à Nice.

Venez chez nous ! Traditions gastronomiques

Parlons

Preparation: Avant de parler To begin, show the video montage *Traditions gastronomiques* and ask students whether they recognize specific regional dishes or can identify ingredients.

Alternative activity: You may wish to identify the various dishes pictured and model pronunciation before students begin the exercise. In that case, students would be describing the dishes to each other and not matching the picture with the name.

5-39 Les plats régionaux

A. Avant de parler. Les Français ont la réputation de bien manger et boire. C'est une réputation bien méritée. La cuisine française est très variée. Chaque région a ses plats particuliers qui dépendent de son climat, de ses produits et de ses traditions culturelles. Voici une liste de quelques spécialités régionales en France :

- la bouillabaisse marseillaise
- la choucroute alsacienne
- la quiche lorraine
- les crêpes bretonnes
- le coq au vin bourguignon
- la fondue savoyarde

Est-ce que vous avez déjà goûté certains de ces plats ?

B. En parlant. Avec un/e partenaire, regardez ces images de spécialités et de plats régionaux. Décrivez chaque photo et identifiez le plat.

MODÈLE É1 Regarde cette image. C'est une soupe.
É2 Oui, une soupe de poisson. Il y a différents poissons.
É1 Oui, et aussi des tomates parce que la soupe est rouge.
É2 C'est la bouillabaisse marseillaise ?
É1 C'est possible. Oui, c'est ça.

C. Après avoir parlé. Est-ce que vous et votre partenaire avez identifié tous les plats ? Comparez vos réponses aux réponses de vos camarades de classe.

Implementation: Après avoir parlé Locate the various regions on a map and discuss why particular specialties might come from each region. For example, Marseille is a seaport city, hence the fish soup.

Observons

5-40 Voici des spécialités de chez nous

Additional activity: Additional activities related to the **Observons** can be found in the SAM/MFL.

Voici un buffet plein de spécialités du Bénin.

Un bon couscous. Est-ce que vous avez déjà mangé du couscous ? Où ?

A. Avant de regarder. Est-ce que vous avez déjà dîné dans un restaurant marocain ? africain ? Si oui, quelles sont les spécialités que vous avez goûtées ? Regardez la photo du buffet — est-ce que vous avez mangé certains de ces plats du Bénin ? Quels sont les ingrédients nécessaires pour préparer ces plats ? Regardez le couscous ; quels sont les ingrédients nécessaires ?

Script: Observons Note that the elements in brackets reflect standard usage and have been added to the written transcripts. They were not pronounced by the speaker(s) in question. The word *épinard* is usually used in the plural, *les épinards*, contrary to this speaker's usage here.

BIENVENU : Donc, chez nous, au Bénin, voici... euh... quelques-uns des plats que nous mangeons. Vous avez ici de l'épinard préparé avec du poulet, des crevettes. L'épinard est accompagné de, de pâte. Ça peut être de la pâte de maïs, ça peut être aussi de, du plantain pilé. Alors le plantain, c'est une forme de banane euh, que nous avons ici. Ça, c'est la banane plantain. On peut la piler, pour avoir une pâte comme celle-ci.

FADOUA : Alors, mon plat préféré, que l'on mange tous les vendredis au Maroc, c'est le couscous. Alors, le couscous, alors, déjà il faut un couscoussier. Alors un couscoussier, c'est une sorte de marmite avec un... un support au-dessus à trous. Donc en bas, on fait revenir les oignons avec les épices et de la viande, on met de l'eau, et dans l'eau on met euh des tomates, des carottes, des navets, euh [de] la citrouille, tous les légumes de saison. Une fois que la graine est bien cuite, c'est-à-dire qu'on, qu'on sent qu'elle est un peu moelleuse et plus craquante, alors on sert le couscous, c'est-à-dire que... on sert le couscous euh sur un plat, on fait un puits, où l'on met des... des légumes, et les légumes, on les met sur le couscous, et à côté on met deux bols, où on a un bouillon. Ça permet de mouiller le couscous, c'est-à-dire qu'on met le couscous dans l'assiette, et on met un peu plus d'eau selon notre goût.

LA SERVEUSE : À table, mesdames. C'est prêt.

Key: En regardant 1) b 2) a, c 3) b, c 4) c 5) a 6) b 7) a, c, d, e, f 8) c

B. En regardant. Deux personnes vont décrire des spécialités de leur région. Trouvez toutes les bonnes réponses à chaque question.

1. Bienvenu décrit des spécialités du...
   a. Mali. **b.** Bénin. **c.** Cameroun.
2. D'abord, c'est de l'épinard avec...
   a. du poulet. **b.** du porc. **c.** des crevettes.
3. L'épinard est accompagné de pâte faite de...
   a. riz. **b.** maïs. **c.** plantain.
4. Le plantain, c'est une forme de...
   a. céréales. **b.** légume. **c.** banane.
5. Fadoua décrit une spécialité du...
   a. Maroc. **b.** Tchad. **c.** Midi de la France.
6. Pour préparer ce plat, il faut...
   a. un grand four. **b.** un couscoussier. **c.** une casserole.
7. Comme ingrédients, on peut mettre...
   a. de la viande. **b.** du poisson. **c.** des tomates.
   d. des carottes. **e.** des oignons. **f.** des navets (*turnips*).
   g. des concombres.
8. Pour servir, on met un bol avec du bouillon pour...
   a. boire.
   b. mélanger (*mix*) les ingrédients.
   c. mouiller (*moisten*) le plat.

C. Après avoir regardé. Est-ce que vous avez déjà gouté un de ces plats ? Est-ce que vous avez aimé ce plat ? Pourquoi ? Quel plat est-ce que vous voulez essayer et pourquoi ?

Key: En lisant 1) a) une description qui indique le temps de préparation et la difficulté de la recette b) une liste d'ingrédients c) des instructions pour la préparation du plat 2) du sucre brun, du beurre, des œufs, du sel, de la farine, de la poudre à pâte, de la vanille, des pécans

Lisons

5-41 Une recette louisianaise

A. Avant de lire. When you think of Louisiana, what types of food come to mind? Jambalaya? Gumbo? Crayfish étouffé? These typical dishes are made with local products, using traditional methods of preparation. Look at the recipe on the following page and the photo that accompanies it: have you ever eaten pralines, another specialty of Louisiana? What will probably be among the main ingredients? Follow the text step-by-step, making sure you understand the procedures, the ingredients, and the quantities involved.

Stratégie

Read a text such as a recipe intensively: make sure you understand each step as it is outlined before you proceed.

B. En lisant. Trouvez les réponses aux questions suivantes.

1. La recette est divisée en trois parties — quelles sont ces trois parties ?
2. Dressez une liste des ingrédients, par exemple : du sucre brun clair, ...

Implementation: En lisant Help students figure out the various cooking terms and ingredients they may not be familiar with. Note cooking terms of Louisiana French origin: *une cuillerée à thé*, literally, a teaspoonful, rather than *une cuillerée à café ; de la poudre à pâte* (baking powder), rather than *de la levure ; du sucre brun*, rather than *du sucre roux*. Note the variable spelling of *pécans/pacanes*. In France, *la cassonade* is brown, unrefined sugar. The *beurre-cassonade* referred to in step three of the recipe is the mixture of ingredients from step one. Point out to students that directions in recipes (and in other contexts as well) are often written in infinitive form.

Pralines aux pacanes

Mark Thomas/Getty Images, Inc. – Foodpix

Temps de préparation : 5 minutes
Temps de cuisson: 30 minutes
Difficulté : très facile

Traditionnellement, les pralines sont faites avec des noix de pécans ou pacanes qui poussent abondamment dans le Sud des États-Unis.

Ingrédients pour 12 grandes pralines ou 48 morceaux

- 500 g de sucre brun clair
- 450 g de beurre fondu
- 2 œufs battus
- 1 pincée de sel
- 500 g de farine[1]
- 1 cuillerée à thé de poudre à pâte[2]
- 1 c. à thé de vanille
- 250 g de pécans

Préparation

1. dans un bol, mélanger le beurre, le sucre brun, les œufs battus et la vanille ;
2. dans un autre bol mélanger la farine, la poudre à pâte et le sel ;
3. incorporer le mélange de farine doucement au beurre-cassonade ;
4. incorporer les pacanes ;
5. déposer des cuillerées de ce mélange sur une plaque graissée et farinée ;
6. enfourner dans un four préchauffé à 160°C (325°F) pendant 30 min ;
7. laisser refroidir avant de servir.

[1] *flour* [2] *baking powder*

C. En regardant de plus près. Maintenant examinez quelques caractéristiques du texte.

1. Quand on prépare une recette, il est très important de bien mesurer les ingrédients. Quel est le sens exact des mots et des abréviations suivantes ?
   - **a.** g
   - **b.** une pincée
   - **c.** une cuillerée à thé
2. Les verbes suivants indiquent les méthodes de préparation. Quel est le sens de chaque verbe ?
   - **a.** mélanger
   - **b.** incorporer
   - **c.** déposer
   - **d.** enfourner
   - **e.** laisser refroidir
3. Les adjectifs expliquent aussi la préparation ; quel est le sens des expressions suivantes ?
   - **a.** du beurre **fondu**
   - **b.** un œuf **battu**
   - **c.** une plaque **graissée** et **farinée**

Implementation: En regardant de plus près Help students use the context and their knowledge of cooking and baking procedures to answer these questions.

Key: En regardant de plus près
1) gram, pinch, teaspoon 2) mix, combine, drop, bake, let cool 3) melted, beaten, greased and floured (note that these are all past participles).

Expansion: As a culminating activity for the chapter, you may wish to assign groups of students to prepare various *plats régionaux*. This could be in the context of either a school-wide or national French festival (for example the AATF's *La semaine du français* in November or the international weeks of *la Francophonie* during the last two weeks in March) or simply as an out-of-class activity for an honors section or motivated group of students. Check the *Chez nous* Companion Website for links to sites where students can access authentic French and Francophone recipes.

Implementation: Après avoir lu This is a good example of a regional dish because it highlights a product that is grown locally (pecans); this point is made at the beginning of the recipe. The **Écrivons** builds on this exercise by having students write their own recipe.

D. Après avoir lu. Discutez de ces questions avec vos camarades de classe.

1. Pourquoi est-ce que c'est un bon exemple d'un plat louisianais ?
2. Est-ce que vous connaissez une autre recette qui ressemble à celle-ci ? Quelle est cette recette ?
3. Essayez cette recette, et apportez des pralines à votre professeur et à vos camarades de classe !

Écrivons

5-42 Une spécialité de chez vous

A. Avant d'écrire. Écrivez la recette d'une spécialité de votre famille ou de votre région et notez les traditions associées à ce plat.

Voici un marché dans les Alpes où vous pouvez acheter du fromage à raclette.

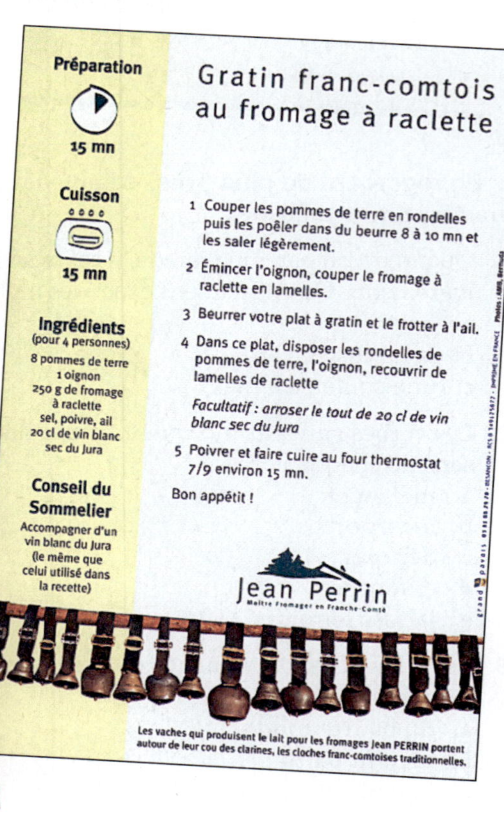

Gratin franc-comtois au fromage à raclette

Préparation
15 mn

Cuisson
15 mn

Ingrédients (pour 4 personnes)
8 pommes de terre
1 oignon
250 g de fromage à raclette
sel, poivre, ail
20 cl de vin blanc sec du Jura

Conseil du Sommelier
Accompagner d'un vin blanc du Jura (le même que celui utilisé dans la recette)

1 Couper les pommes de terre en rondelles puis les poêler dans du beurre 8 à 10 mn et les saler légèrement.
2 Émincer l'oignon, couper le fromage à raclette en lamelles.
3 Beurrer votre plat à gratin et le frotter à l'ail.
4 Dans ce plat, disposer les rondelles de pommes de terre, l'oignon, recouvrir de lamelles de raclette

Facultatif : arroser le tout de 20 cl de vin blanc sec du Jura

5 Poivrer et faire cuire au four thermostat 7/9 environ 15 mn.

Bon appétit !

Jean Perrin
Maître Fromager en Franche-Comté

Les vaches qui produisent le lait pour les fromages Jean PERRIN portent autour de leur cou des clarines, les cloches franc-comtoises traditionnelles.

1. D'abord, faites une petite liste des plats typiques de votre région ou des spécialités de votre famille. Quel plat est-ce que vous allez décrire ?
2. Ensuite, analysez la recette pour les **Pralines aux pacanes** ou la recette pour le **Gratin franc-comtois au fromage à raclette**. Comment est-ce que la recette est organisée ? Quels sont les mesures et les verbes importants pour expliquer comment préparer la recette ?
3. Notez les ingrédients nécessaires pour préparer votre plat.
4. Enfin, notez les traditions associées à ce plat. Est-ce qu'on mange ce plat pour une fête ? Avec qui est-ce qu'on le mange ?, etc.

Implementation: Avant d'écrire The **Lisons** provides a model for this writing activity. You might also use the recipe for *le Gratin franc-comtois* as a model; have the class as a whole analyze the recipe, then put students in small groups to complete the preparation for writing. Help the class generate a list of measures and useful verbs, as well as kitchen appliances they may need to complete their recipes: *un mixer, un robot de cuisine, un micro-ondes*, etc.

B. En écrivant. Maintenant écrivez la recette d'une spécialité régionale ou familiale.

1. Suivez l'organisation de la recette modèle ; numérotez les étapes à suivre ; précisez les quantités. Regardez le site Web de *Chez nous* pour un lien où vous pouvez convertir les mesures.
2. N'oubliez pas d'expliquer pourquoi cette recette est importante pour votre famille ou votre région.

Stratégie

Some texts, such as recipes, require a specific format and careful sequencing of the information. Be sure to keep these conventions in mind as you write.

C. En révisant. Réfléchissez aux questions suivantes et puis faites tous les changements nécessaires.

1. Relisez votre recette pour analyser sa forme. Est-ce que vous avez noté : le temps de préparation et de cuisson ; les ingrédients ; les quantités ; toutes les étapes à suivre ?
2. Trouvez une belle photo pour illustrer votre recette !

Implementation: En écrivant This can be completed as a group or whole-class writing activity, either as a prelude to, or instead of, individual writing.

D. Après avoir écrit. Avec vos camarades de classe, comparez vos recettes. Est-ce qu'il y a des recettes similaires, par exemple avec les mêmes ingrédients ou la même méthode de préparation ? Est-ce que les recettes sont typiques de votre région, ou est-ce qu'elles reflètent des traditions culinaires différentes ?

Implementation: Après avoir écrit Ask students how the recipes for pecan pralines from Louisiana and the *gratin* from the Comté region in France near the Swiss border reflect regional traditions.

Now that you have completed *Chapitre 5*, can you do the following in French?

- ☐ order something to eat and drink in a restaurant and ask for the bill?
- ☐ describe what you typically eat in a day?
- ☐ shop for food, specifying the quantities you need?
- ☐ read a recipe, or write one?
- ☐ relate a series of actions or events in the past?
- ☐ describe some regional French specialties and tell why they are typical of the region?

Leçon 1

au café ou au restaurant	in the cafe or in the restaurant
l'addition (f.)	*bill*
avoir faim	*to be hungry*
avoir soif	*to be thirsty*
boire	*to drink*
prendre	*to have (to eat or drink)*
des boissons chaudes	***hot drinks***
un café (crème)	*coffee (with cream)*
un chocolat chaud	*hot chocolate*
un thé (au lait)	*tea (with milk)*
des boissons rafraîchissantes	***cold drinks***
un citron pressé	*lemonade*
un coca(-cola)	*cola*
de l'eau (f.) (minérale)	*water (mineral water)*
un jus d'orange	*orange juice*
une limonade	*lemon-lime soft drink*
un Orangina	*orange soda*
des boissons alcoolisées	***alcoholic drinks***
une bière	*beer*
du vin (rouge, blanc, rosé)	*(red, white, rosé) wine*
des casse-croûte (m. inv.)	***snacks***
un croque-monsieur	*grilled ham-and-cheese sandwich*
des crudités (f.)	*cut-up raw vegetables*
des frites (f.)	*French fries*
une glace	*ice cream*
un *hamburger	*hamburger*
une pizza	*pizza*
une salade verte	*green salad*
un sandwich (au jambon, au fromage)	*(ham, cheese) sandwich*
quelques expressions utiles	***some useful expressions***
apprendre	*to learn*
une bouteille	*bottle*
une cannette	*(soda) can*
commander	*to order*
comprendre	*to understand*
des glaçons (m.)	*ice cubes*
une cuillère	*spoon*
je voudrais...	*I would like . . .*
partager	*to share*
quelle horreur !	*how awful!*
quelque chose (à manger, à boire)	*something (to eat, to drink)*
sans problème	*no problem*
seulement	*only*
du sucre	*sugar*
une tasse	*cup*
un verre	*glass*

Leçon 2

les repas	meals
le petit-déjeuner	*breakfast*
le déjeuner	*lunch; breakfast (Can.)*
le goûter	*afternoon snack*
le dîner	*dinner; lunch (Can.)*
le souper	*dinner (Can.)*
au petit-déjeuner	***at breakfast***
prendre le petit-déjeuner	*to have breakfast*
le bacon	*bacon*
le beurre	*butter*
un café au lait	*coffee with milk*
des céréales (f.)	*cereal*
la confiture	*jam*
un croissant	*croissant*
un œuf (sur le plat/au plat)	*(fried) egg*
du pain	*bread*
un pain au chocolat	*chocolate croissant*
une rôtie	*piece of toast (Can.)*
une tartine	*slice of bread*
une tranche de pain grillé	*slice of toast*
au déjeuner	***at lunch***
une entrée	*appetizer or starter*
un plat principal	*main dish*
un dessert	*dessert*
des aliments (m.)	***foods***
une asperge	*asparagus*
un biscuit	*cookie*
le fromage	*cheese*
les *haricots verts (m.)	*green beans*
un légume	*vegetable*
des pâtes (f.)	*pasta*
le poisson	*fish*
une pomme de terre	*potato*
le poulet	*chicken*
le riz	*rice*
une soupe	*soup*
une tarte aux pommes	*apple pie*
la viande	*meat*
un yaourt	*yogurt*
des fruits (m.)	***fruits***
une banane	*banana*

une poire	*pear*
une pomme	*apple*

des épices (f.)	***spices***
le poivre	*pepper*
le sel	*salt*

d'autres mots utiles	***other useful words***
un bol (de café au lait)	*bowl (of coffee with hot milk)*
une carafe (d'eau)	*carafe (of water)*

pour décrire	***to describe***
copieux	*copious, hearty*
grillé/e	*grilled, toasted*

pour parler du passé	***to talk about the past***
hier	*yesterday*
avant-hier	*the day before yesterday*
samedi dernier	*last Saturday*
l'année dernière	*last year*
il y a longtemps	*a long time ago*
il y a deux jours	*two days ago*
ce jour-là	*that day*
à ce moment-là	*at that moment*

quelques verbes utiles	***some useful verbs***
acheter	*to buy*
appeler	*to call*
épeler	*to spell*
faire la vaisselle	*to do the dishes*
jeter	*to throw, to throw away*
lever	*to raise*

Leçon 3

les rayons du supermarché	***supermarket aisles***
le rayon boulangerie-pâtisserie	*bakery/pastry aisle*
une baguette	*long, thin loaf*
un pain de campagne	*round loaf of bread*
un pain de mie	*loaf of sliced bread*
une pâtisserie	*pastry*
des petits pains (m.)	*rolls*
une tarte	*pie*
le rayon boucherie	*meat counter*
du bifteck haché	*ground beef*
une côtelette d'agneau	*lamb chop*
du rosbif	*roast beef*
le rayon charcuterie	*deli counter*
du pâté	*pâté*
des plats (m.) préparés	*prepared dishes*
un rôti (de porc)	*(pork) roast*
le rayon fruits et légumes	*produce aisle*
une cerise	*cherry*
une fraise	*strawberry*
un melon	*cantaloupe*
une pêche	*peach*
du raisin	*grapes*
une carotte	*carrot*
un champignon	*mushroom*
un concombre	*cucumber*
les épinards (m.)	*spinach*
les *haricots (m.)	*beans*
un oignon	*onion*
les petits pois (m.)	*peas*
une tomate	*tomato*
le rayon poissonnerie	*fish counter*
une crevette	*shrimp*
du saumon	*salmon*
du thon	*tuna*
le rayon surgelés	*frozen foods aisle*
les surgelés (m.)	*frozen foods*

des condiments	***condiments***
l'huile (f.)	*oil*
la moutarde	*mustard*
le vinaigre	*vinegar*

pour faire les courses	***to shop for food***
un/e commerçant/e	*shopkeeper, merchant*
une épicerie	*small grocery*
une grande surface	*superstore*

des quantités (f.)	***quantities***
une assiette de (crudités)	*plate of (crudités)*
une boîte de (sardines)	*can of (sardines)*
une douzaine d'(œufs)	*dozen (eggs)*
un kilo de (pommes)	*kilo of (apples)*
un litre de (lait)	*liter of (milk)*
un morceau de (fromage)	*piece of (cheese)*
un paquet de (riz, céréales, biscuits)	*package of (rice, cereal, cookies)*
un pot de (moutarde)	*jar of (mustard)*
une tranche de (pâté)	*slice of (pâté)*

quelques verbes conjugués avec *être* au passé composé	***some verbs conjugated with* être *in the passé composé***
Voir à la page 206	*See page 206*

pour faire un récit	***to construct a narrative***
d'abord	*first*
ensuite	*next*
après	*after, after that*
puis	*then*
enfin	*finally*

d'autres expressions utiles	***other useful expressions***
avoir besoin de	*to need*
J'ai besoin d'huile.	*I need (some) oil.*
il faut	*to need*
Il faut quatre oeufs.	*We need four eggs.*
biologique	*organic*
une tomate bio(logique)	*organic tomato*
la caisse	*cash register*
d'accord	*O.K., alright*
délicieux/-euse	*delicious*
demander	*to ask (for)*

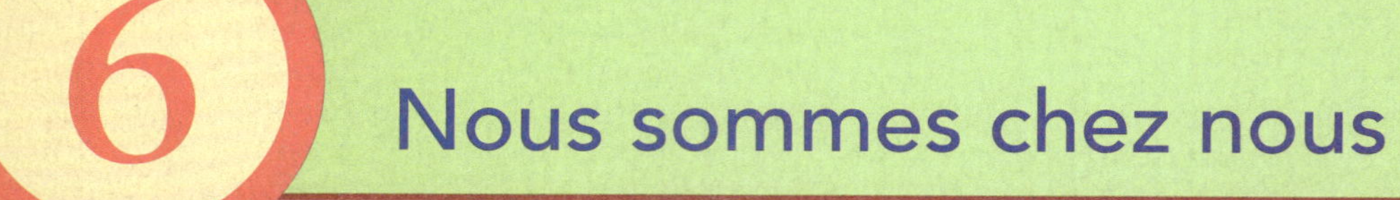

6 Nous sommes chez nous

Est-ce que cette maison est semblable aux maisons où vous habitez ? Pourquoi ?

Leçon 1 La vie en ville

Leçon 2 Je suis chez moi

Leçon 3 La vie à la campagne

Venez chez nous ! À la découverte de la France : les régions

After completing this chapter, you should be able to:

- Talk about where you live
- Specify dates, distances, and prices
- Identify geographical features
- Make suggestions
- Describe situations and settings in the past
- Understand concepts of home and regionalism in France

Leçon  La vie en ville

POINTS DE DÉPART

Chez les Santini

Les Santini habitent dans le dix-huitième arrondissement, près de Montmartre, un quartier animé de Paris. M. et Mme Santini ont deux enfants, Nicolas et Véronique. Ils habitent un bel immeuble dans une rue tranquille d'un quartier résidentiel.

L'appartement des Santini est au sixième étage — on peut prendre les escaliers ou l'ascenseur. C'est un cinq-pièces, avec une grande salle de séjour, une salle à manger et trois chambres. Chaque enfant a sa propre chambre. Il y a aussi une salle de bains, des toilettes (des W.-C.) et une grande cuisine. L'appartement a un grand balcon qui donne sur la rue, et dans la chambre de M. et Mme Santini il y a même un petit balcon qui donne sur la cour. Au sous-sol, il y a un garage où les Santini garent leur voiture. Ils ont des voisins sympathiques au cinquième étage.

Presentation: Use the photo and line drawings (MFL, Ch. 6) to present the vocabulary. Have students listen to the narrative as you show the visuals, elaborating where appropriate. Explain that Paris is divided into 20 *arrondissements* or neighborhoods. Explain the distinction between *salle de bains/toilettes, W.-C.* (from English *water closet*). In France, the kitchen and bath are not included when counting the number of rooms. Test comprehension by having students point to the feature you name, using the unlabeled art (MFL, Ch. 6) or by having them describe activities: *Dans la cuisine ? — On prépare le dîner, on mange*, etc. Next have students repeat key words and phrases: *C'est la cuisine ou le séjour ? — C'est le séjour*, etc.

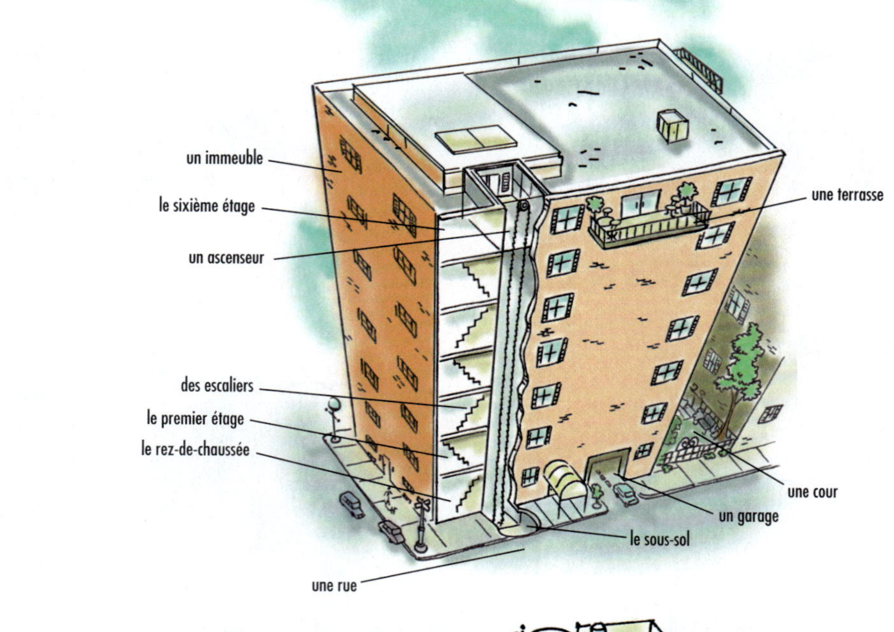

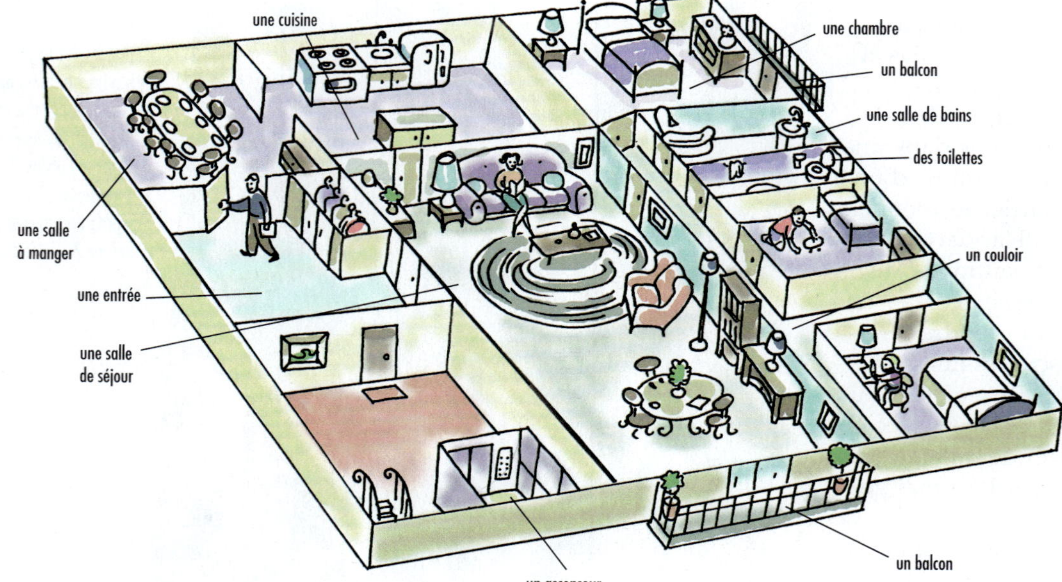

À vous la parole

Implementation: 6-1 This exercise can be completed with books closed. Read each description and have students indicate where the person is located. Students will not know the expression *frapper à la porte;* as you read this description, mime the action or knock on the classroom door or a table to help them understand. Remind students of the meaning of the verb *mettre* and ask them to guess what the expression *mettre la table* means.

6-1 Où est-ce qu'ils sont ? Expliquez où sont ces gens.

MODÈLE Nicolas fait ses devoirs.
Il est dans sa chambre.

1. Mme Santini prépare le dîner pour la famille.
2. Véronique met la table.
3. M. Santini regarde un film à la télé.
4. Nicolas prend une douche.
5. Les enfants jouent aux cartes.
6. M. Santini regarde les voitures qui passent.
7. Le voisin frappe à la porte.
8. M. Santini prépare le café.
9. Véronique fait la sieste.
10. Mme Santini gare la voiture.

6-2 Où allez-vous ? Où est-ce que vous préférez faire les choses suivantes ? Comparez vos préférences avec celles de vos camarades de classe.

MODÈLE faire la sieste

É1 J'aime aller dans ma chambre pour faire la sieste.
É2 Je préfère faire la sieste dans la salle de séjour, devant la télé.
É3 Moi, j'aime aller sur la terrasse.

1. faire la sieste
2. regarder un film
3. faire les devoirs
4. prendre le petit-déjeuner
5. écouter de la musique
6. travailler sur l'ordinateur
7. parler avec des amis

Implementation: 6-2 Have students report back to the class on their preferences and those of their classmates. Ask follow-up questions such as *Pourquoi est-ce que vous préférez faire la sieste dans la salle de séjour ?*

Presentation: Guide students to discover the meaning of key words such as *loyer, charges comprises, propriétaire,* and *locataire,* using cognates and context; these words are used in **6-3** and **6-4**, and should be added to productive vocabulary. Students may be unfamiliar with buying an apartment; this can be compared to condominium or co-op housing. You may wish to introduce the phrase *habiter en banlieue* (to live in the suburbs). Note that the expression *la banlieue* in French has a rather negative connotation and often refers to poorer neighborhoods, filled with subsidized housing, and in *la banlieue parisienne,* with immigrants. Use the photo to describe home construction in France and compare it with construction in North America.

Vie et culture

Où habitent les Français ?

Environ[1] 56 % des familles en France habitent une maison individuelle, mais dans les centres urbains les appartements sont plus nombreux. La majorité des Français (57 %) sont propriétaires de leur maison ou appartement ; 40 % sont locataires, c'est-à-dire qu'ils paient un loyer chaque mois. Quelquefois les charges (l'électricité et le gaz) sont comprises[2] dans le loyer et quelquefois c'est en supplément.

Dans les quartiers résidentiels des grandes villes, beaucoup de familles habitent un appartement dans un grand immeuble. En France, le nombre de pièces (sans compter la cuisine, la salle de bains ou les toilettes) détermine la classification des appartements et des maisons. Un studio est un appartement avec une seule pièce (plus éventuellement[3] cuisine, salle de bains et toilettes). Est-ce que la majorité des Américains habitent des maisons individuelles ou des appartements ?

Voici une maison typiquement française à Joinville-le-Pont près de Paris.

À quel étage ?

Regardez l'immeuble à la page 222 et surtout **le rez-de-chaussée** et **le premier étage**. Est-ce que c'est le même système où vous habitez ? En France, quand vous entrez dans un bâtiment ou un immeuble, vous êtes au **rez-de-chaussée** et **le premier étage** se trouve au-dessus[4]. Si vous descendez un étage, vous êtes au **sous-sol**.

RdeCh	rez-de-chaussée	11^{e}	onzième
1er	premier	12^{e}	douzième
2^{e}	deuxième	...	
3^{e}	troisième	20^{e}	vingtième
...		21^{e}	vingt-et-unième

[1]*approximately* [2]*included* [3]peut-être [4]*above*

Note: Homes in France are generally constructed of stone, brick, or block, considered more durable than wood. The majority of single-family homes in France, especially in towns and cities, are actually connected to one another, either as row houses (43%) or as duplexes (20%). Point out the presence of the wall and grill surrounding the house, and the tiled roof. According to the 2000 U.S. Census, the majority of households in each of the four census regions owned their homes: Midwest, 70.2%; South, 68.4%; Northeast, 62.4%; and West, 61.5%. In North America, apartments (and homes) are advertised based on the number of bedrooms. A two-bedroom apartment in the U.S. would be equivalent to *un appartement trois-pièces* in France.

Presentation: Point out the special forms *premier/première, second/e* (the latter term used when there are only two items in a series). You may wish to provide your students with a full list of ordinals to complement the examples given here. Practice by having students write down the ordinal you say: *treizième, vingt-et-unième,* etc. (Students write: 13e, 21e, etc.) Next have students read the ordinals you write. For additional practice and to recycle campus vocabulary, pick a familiar campus building (such as where your French class meets) and have students work in pairs to identify on which floor the following places can be found: *un snack-bar ; un amphithéâtre ; une bibliothèque ; un centre informatique ; un laboratoire ; des bureaux des profs ; des salles de classe.* Be sure to provide a model such as: *Il y a un snack-bar au rez-de-chaussée. / Il n'y a pas de bibliothèque dans notre bâtiment.*

Implementation: 6-3 Treat *Où habitent les Français* in the *Vie et culture* section before completing this activity to introduce needed vocabulary such as *un propriétaire, un deux-pièces,* and *un appartment de cinq pièces.*

 **6-3 Une comparaison.** Avec un/e partenaire, comparez l'endroit (*place*) où vous habitez avec l'appartement des Santini.

MODÈLE Les Santini habitent un appartement de cinq pièces.
É1 Moi, j'habite un deux-pièces.
É2 Moi, j'ai une chambre à la résidence.

1. Les Santini habitent une grande ville.
2. Ils habitent un quartier animé.
3. Ils habitent un bel immeuble.
4. Ils sont propriétaires.
5. Ils habitent au sixième étage.
6. Il y a un ascenseur et aussi des escaliers dans l'immeuble.
7. Les Santini habitent un appartement de cinq pièces.
8. Chez les Santini, il y a une grande cuisine.
9. Il y a trois chambres chez eux.
10. Ils ont deux balcons.

Expansion: 6-4 As a follow-up, have students draw and describe their current home or apartment; their ideal apartment.

 **6-4 Trois appartements.** Voici trois appartements. Avec un/e partenaire, décrivez chaque appartement et choisissez l'appartement que vous préférez.

MODÈLE Le premier appartement est un deux-pièces. Il y a une petite chambre et un séjour. Il y a une terrasse, etc. ... Je préfère... , parce que...

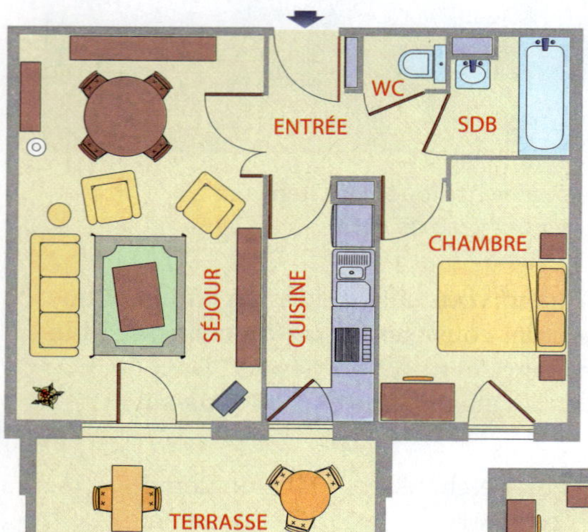

Appartement n° 1

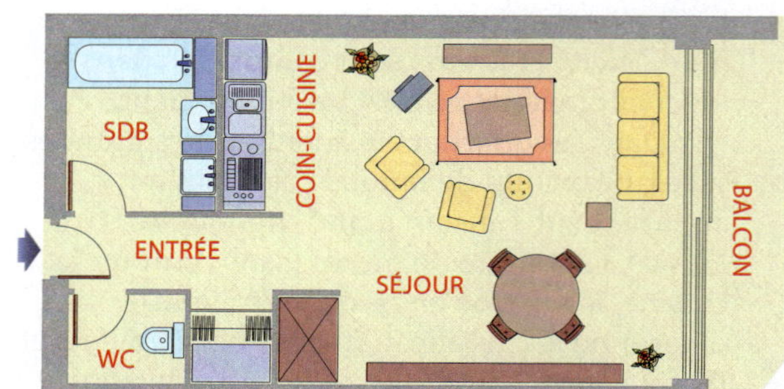

Appartement n° 2

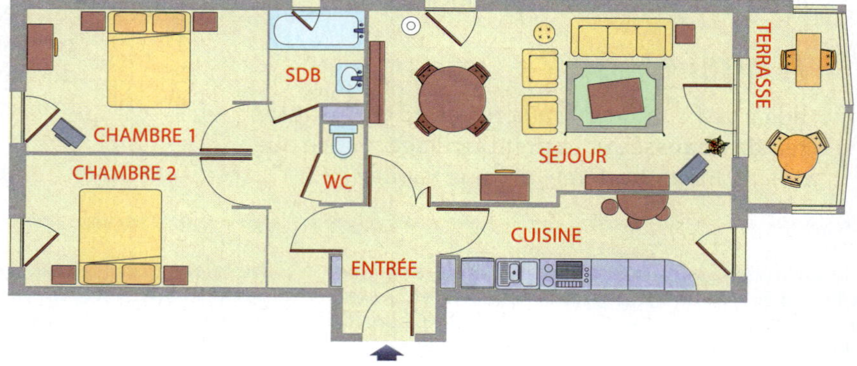

Appartement n° 3

Sons et lettres

La consonne *l*

Say the English word *little*. Notice how your tongue moves from the front to the back of your mouth. In English, we have two ways of producing the consonant **l**: a front **l**, with the tongue against the upper front teeth and a final **l**, pronounced with the tongue pulled back. To pronounce a French **l**, however, always keep your tongue against your upper front teeth, just like the English front **l**. Compare the differences in pronunciation of a final **-l** in English and French:

English	French
ill	il
bell	belle
bowl	bol

La prononciation de *-ill-*

The combination of letters **-ill-** has two pronunciations: with the /l/ sound of **il** or the /j/ sound at the end of **travail**. It is difficult to predict how that combination is to be pronounced in a given word; the pronunciation of individual words must be memorized. Compare:

/l/		/j/	
mille	un million	la fille	la famille
la ville	le village	se maquiller	elle se maquille
tranquille		s'habiller	il s'habille

Note: To help students remember some frequent words where **-ill-** is pronounced as [il], introduce this sentence as a mnemonic device: *Mille personnes habitent ce village tranquille ; dans la ville c'est un million.*

6-5 Répétitions. Répétez les mots et les groupes de mots suivants.

pas mal	résidentiel	la salle	la ville
un bel hôtel	elle s'appelle	tranquille	Jules
une ville calme	dans quelle salle	le journal idéal	

Initial practice: Begin practice with a discrimination drill: *anglais ou français ? Levez le doigt pour le français :* bell, *belle*, tell, *telle*, ill, *il*, *cool*, cool, ball, *balle*, *Paul*, Paul, pull, *pull*.

6-6 Des phrases. Lisez chaque phrase.

1. La famille de Cyril et Nicole Blondel habite en ville.
2. Clément Lemont, Gaëlle LeBrun et leurs deux filles habitent un village tranquille.
3. Paul et Emmanuelle Morel habitent un quartier résidentiel qui est idéal pour les enfants.
4. Amélie Lalonde s'excuse mille fois ; elle a oublié le journal dans la salle de classe.
5. M. et Mme Villeneuve sont descendus dans un hôtel élégant ; Michel s'habille et Camille se maquille pour leur grande soirée dansante.

Note: 6-7 The van Gogh painting suggests strong emotion and a swirling Milky Way. Translation of the poem:

What Beauty of the night in anger
Has thrown her pearl necklace up there,
Her celestial necklace of stars
In the Milky Way?

6-7 La lettre « L ». Voici un petit poème du livre *Comptines en forme d'alphabet* de Jo Hoestlandt. Répétez cette strophe.

Quelle Belle de nuit en colère,
A lancé son collier de perles là-haut,
Son céleste collier d'étoiles
Dans la Voie lactée ?

Vincent van Gogh (1853–1890), « La nuit étoilée » 1889.
Oil on canvas, 29 × 36 1/4″ (73.7 × 92.1 cm). Acquired through the Lillie P. Bliss Bequest. (472.1941). The Museum of Modern Art, NY, U.S.A. Digital Image © The Museum of Modern Art/Licensed de Vincent Van Gogh.

FORMES ET FONCTIONS

1. *Les verbes en* -ir *comme* choisir

Presentation: To present inductively, use pictures or floor plans of apartments and discuss your choices and those of the students: *Moi, je choisis ce studio, parce que c'est pratique et vous, quel appartement est-ce que vous choisissez ?* Then quickly review *-ir* verbs (*les enfants s'endorment dans leur chamber ; leur père s'endort dans le salon devant la télé*) and *-re* verbs (*il descend l'escalier ; ses parents descendent dans l'ascenseur*) and remind students that for all two-stem verbs, the spoken singular forms are derived by dropping the final consonant sound of the third-person plural form. Ask students to derive the forms for *choisir*, then for other verbs in the list.

- Like other **-ir** verbs, verbs like **choisir** have four spoken forms. The final /s/ of the plural form is dropped in the singular.

  ils **choisissent**/ʃwazis/le deux-pièces   il **choisit**/ʃwazi/le studio

  To form the present indicative of verbs like **choisir**, add **-iss-** to the base for the plural forms: **chois ir** → **chois -iss-**.

CHOISIR ***to choose***

SINGULIER		PLURIEL	
je	chois**is**	nous	chois**issons**
tu	chois**is**	vous	chois**issez**
il / elle / on	chois**it**	ils / elles	chois**issent**

IMPÉRATIF : Ne **choisis** pas ça ! **Choisissez** le studio ! **Choisissons** un appartement !

PASSÉ COMPOSÉ : J'ai déjà **choisi**.

- Some **-ir/-iss-** verbs are derived from common adjectives. They express the meaning that someone or something is becoming more like the adjective:

maigre	*thin, skinny*	**maigrir**	*to lose weight*
grosse	*large, fat*	**grossir**	*to gain weight*
grande	*large, tall*	**grandir**	*to grow taller, to grow up (for children)*
rouge	*red*	**rougir**	*to blush*
pâle	*pale*	**pâlir**	*to become pale*

- Some other common verbs conjugated like **choisir** are:

finir	*to finish*	Tu **as fini** la visite de l'appartement ?
obéir à	*to obey*	**Obéis à** ta mère ! Pas de chocolat dans le séjour !
désobéir à	*to disobey*	Ces enfants **désobéissent** toujours **à** leur père.
punir	*to punish*	Tu **punis** ton fils parce qu'il n'a pas bien garé la voiture ?
réfléchir à	*to think*	Je **réfléchis à** l'appartement que je préfère.
réussir à	*to succeed*	Elle ne **réussit** pas **à** appeler l'ascenseur.
	to pass	Il **a** bien **réussi à** son examen de maths. (OU Il **a réussi** son examen de maths.)

Note: You might also wish to point out the verb *mincir* (a near synonym to *maigrir*), which means to get slimmer. Other verbs in *-ir/-iss-* correspond to English verbs in "-ish": *finir, punir, établir, démolir.*

À vous la parole

6-8 Des enfants modèles ? Est-ce que ces enfants obéissent ou désobéissent à leurs parents ?

MODÈLE Delphine ne s'essuie pas quand elle sort de la douche.
Elle désobéit à ses parents.

1. Fabien mange du chocolat dans sa chambre.
2. Laetitia et Fabien font leurs devoirs devant la télé.
3. Tu manges bien tous les matins avant d'aller à l'école.
4. Fabien et Delphine jouent au basket sur la terrasse.
5. Laetitia ne mange jamais dans sa chambre.
6. Vous ne sortez pas quand vous avez un examen à préparer.
7. Delphine et vous, vous mettez la musique très fort.
8. J'aide mes parents à préparer le dîner.

Initial practice: Begin practice with a discrimination drill: one person, or more than one? *Elle grandit. Ils maigrissent. Ils finissent. Elle obéit. Elle choisit bien. Ils rougissent. Il réussit. Elles réfléchissent,* etc. Follow with one or two simple substitution drills: *Je maigris ; nous ; lui,* etc. You might also include a transformation drill, present to past or vice versa: *Nous choisissons un studio. — Nous avons choisi un studio,* etc.

6-9 Le choix est à vous ! Qu'est-ce que vous choisissez ? En groupes de trois ou quatre, comparez votre réponse avec la réponse de vos partenaires.

MODÈLE entre un appartement au rez-de-chaussée et un appartement au cinquième étage

É1 Moi, je choisis l'appartement au rez-de-chaussée ; c'est pratique pour sortir.

É2 Pas moi ! Je choisis l'appartement au cinquième, j'aime avoir une belle vue.

É3 Moi aussi, donc toi et moi, on choisit l'appartement au cinquième.

Expansion: 6-9 After completing, have students report back what they and their partners decided.

1. entre un appartement en centre-ville et un appartement dans un quartier tranquille
2. entre un grand studio et un petit deux-pièces
3. entre l'ascenseur et les escaliers
4. entre une grande cuisine et une grande salle de bains
5. entre une belle terrasse qui donne sur la rue et un petit balcon qui donne sur la cour
6. entre un appartement avec une grande chambre et un appartement avec deux petites chambres
7. entre un appartement avec un jardin et un appartement avec un garage

Implementation: 6-10 Use as a mixing activity. Have students ask only two questions of each person before moving on to someone else. Give students a limited amount of time to work, then follow up by having them ask questions about the items for which they did not find a response.

6-10 Trouvez une personne. Dans votre salle de classe, trouvez une personne qui...

MODÈLE finit toujours ses devoirs avant d'arriver en classe

É1 Est-ce que tu finis toujours tes devoirs avant d'arriver en classe ?

É2 Non, je ne finis pas toujours mes devoirs avant d'arriver en classe.

OU Oui, je finis toujours mes devoirs avant d'arriver en classe.

1. rougit toujours quand il/elle parle devant un groupe
2. finit toujours ses devoirs avant d'arriver en classe
3. grossit toujours en hiver
4. grandit toujours (*still*)
5. réfléchit toujours avant de répondre
6. réussit toujours à ses examens
7. maigrit quand il/elle est stressé/e
8. grossit quand il/elle est stressé/e
9. ne désobéit jamais à ses parents

2. *Les pronoms compléments d'objet direct* le, la, l', les

Fiche pratique

Use direct-object pronouns when you speak to avoid sounding repetitive. Remember, as you do so, not to translate directly from English, since direct-object pronouns usually precede rather than follow the verb in French.

- A direct object receives the action of a verb, answering the question *whom* or *what*. For example, **la voiture** is the direct object in the following sentence: **Elle gare la voiture**. A direct-object pronoun can replace a direct-object noun; it agrees in gender and number with the noun it replaces.

Elle gare **la voiture** ?	Oui, elle **la** gare.	*Yes, she is parking it.*
Elle regarde **le voisin** ?	Oui, elle **le** regarde.	*Yes, she is looking at him.*
Elle achète **l'appartement** ?	Oui, elle **l'**achète.	*Yes, she is buying it.*
Elle aime bien **les voisins** ?	Oui, elle **les**‿aime bien. /z/	*Yes, she likes them.*

Presentation: Use classroom objects to present the direct-object pronouns; for example, give a ruler to a student and say: *Donnez la règle à Susan.* After the student does it, you say: *Elle la donne à Susan.* Continue to demonstrate *le, les,* and *l'*. Ask students to summarize rules. Point out to students that use of object pronouns allows the speaker to avoid redundancy and repetition.

◆ Here are the forms of the direct-object pronouns. In the plural, liaison /z/ is pronounced before a vowel sound.

	SINGULIER	PLURIEL
masc	**le**	**les**
m/ f + voyelle	**l'**	**les‿** /z/
fém	**la**	**les**

◆ Normally, direct-object pronouns precede the conjugated verb:

—Vous aimez l'appartement en centre-ville ? — *Do you like the downtown apartment?*
—Oui, on **l'**aime bien. Ce n'est pas trop cher. — *Yes, we like it. It's not too expensive.*

—Où sont les escaliers ? — *Where are the stairs?*
—Je ne sais pas, je ne **les** ai pas remarqués. — *I don't know, I didn't notice them.*

◆ A direct-object pronoun precedes an infinitive:

—Tu vas payer les charges ? — *Are you going to pay the utilities?*
—Mais bien sûr, je vais **les** payer ; on doit **les** payer tous les mois. — *Well, of course I'm going to pay them; we have to pay them every month.*

◆ The negative **ne** never comes between an object pronoun and verb:

Les voisins, on ne **les** voit jamais. *... we never see them.*
L'appartement, je ne **l'**ai pas acheté. *... I didn't buy it.*
La voiture, je ne vais pas **la** garer. *... I'm not going to park it.*

◆ To point out people or objects, the direct-object pronouns precede **voilà**:

Sylvie ? **La** voilà. *Sylvie? There she is.*
Mes CD ? **Les** voilà. *My CDs? There they are.*

◆ Note the placement of direct-object pronouns in commands:
In negative commands, the object pronoun precedes the conjugated verb:

Cet appartement ? Ne **le** montrez pas ! *... Don't show it!*

In affirmative commands, an object pronoun is placed after the conjugated verb and is joined to it by a hyphen:

Le nouveau studio ? Montrez-**le** à Susan ! *... Show it to Susan!*

◆ In the **passé composé**, the past participle agrees in gender and number with a preceding direct-object pronoun:

J'ai donné **le CD** à Justine. Je **l'**ai donné à Justine.
J'ai donné **la lampe** à Yann. Je **l'**ai donné**e** à Yann.
J'ai donné **les livres** à Coralie. Je **les** ai donné**s** à Coralie.
J'ai donné **les affiches** à Thibaut. Je **les** ai donné**es** à Thibaut.

Fiche pratique

In French you cannot emphasize a word by adding stress to it, as in English: "Did you see *John* or *Bill*?" "I saw *John*." One way to emphasize a word or phrase in French is to place it at the very beginning of the sentence, and put a pronoun equivalent in its place: **Les voisins**, tu **les** aimes ?

Note: Dislocation, described here in the *Fiche Pratique*, is a frequent and useful conversational feature in spoken French and is practiced in Ex. 6-12.

Note: Past participle agreement affects only the pronunciation of participles that end with a consonant. The addition of the feminine marker *-e* causes the consonant to be pronounced. Compare *Le livre, je l'ai pris ; La lettre, je l'ai prise ; Les lettres, je les ai prises* with *Ce livre, je l'ai donné à Paul ; Cette lettre, je l'ai donnée à Karine ; Ces lettres, je les ai données au musée.* For that reason, past participle agreement is presented largely for recognition. You may also provide appropriate written practice. As this agreement is largely a spelling convention, it is no surprise that native speakers often omit it in writing or in casual speech.

À vous la parole

Initial practice: Begin practice with this activity to establish a form-meaning connection between the direct-object pronouns and their referents. Then have students supply possible nouns for the object pronouns in sentences such as: *Je l'ai regardé à la télé. — le film ; Elle l'a acheté en ville. Nous allons le choisir demain. Il l'appelle le soir. Ils la regardent beaucoup. Tu la gares toujours au parking ? Je les trouve très chers. Vous le préparez ? Elles les portent tous les jours.* Continue with simple substitution drills to practice forms: *Le crayon ? — Le voilà ; Les devoirs ? — Les voilà ; Le tableau ? La porte ? Les fenêtres ? Le professeur ? Les livres ? Les cahiers ? L'examen ? L'affiche ? Le stylo ?* etc. This leads into Ex. 6-13.

6-11 On joue à cache-cache. Cécile joue à cache-cache (*hide-and-seek*) avec sa sœur, son frère et ses chats. Pour chaque phrase, décidez si elle cherche (ou trouve) sa sœur, son frère ou ses chats.

Je...	sa sœur	son frère	ses chats
MODÈLE ... la cherche dans la cour.	✓	______	______
1. ... les cherche dans le séjour.	______	______	______
2. ... le cherche dans la cuisine.	______	______	______
3. ... la cherche sur la terrasse.	______	______	______
4. ... le cherche partout (*everywhere*).	______	______	______
5. ... les trouve sur le balcon.	______	______	______
6. ... la trouve dans sa chambre.	______	______	______
7. ... le cherche encore.	______	______	______

Qui a trouvé le meilleur endroit (*place*) pour se cacher ? Pourquoi ?

6-12 Les opinions sont partagées ! Décidez avec un/e partenaire si vous êtes d'accord ou non.

MODÈLES On les aime : les films ou les examens ?
É1 Les films, on les aime.
É2 Oui, et les examens, on ne les aime pas.

On les aide souvent : les amis ou les parents ?
É1 Les amis, on les aide souvent.
É2 Oui, mais les parents, on les aide souvent aussi.

1. On l'aime beaucoup : la danse ou le théâtre ?
2. On l'aime bien : le golf ou le football ?
3. On les écoute toujours : les parents ou les professeurs ?
4. On les déteste : les examens ou les essais ?
5. On les regarde souvent : les films ou les documentaires ?
6. On la visite souvent : la ville de New York ou la France ?
7. On l'adore : le français ou la musique ?
8. On les aime : les pique-niques ou les vacances ?

6-13 Où est-ce que c'est rangé ? David s'installe dans un nouvel appartement, mais il ne trouve plus rien ! Jouez les rôles de David et de son copain avec un/e partenaire.

MODÈLE É1 Où sont mes bols ?
É2 Les voilà dans la cuisine.

1. Où est ma télé ?
2. Où sont mes livres ?
3. Où sont mes verres ?
4. Où sont mes CD ?
5. Où est mon mixer ?
6. Où sont mes photos ?
7. Où est mon ordinateur ?
8. Où est mon affiche de Paris ?

6-14 Les occupations et les loisirs. Quels sont les occupations et les loisirs de vos camarades de classe ? Posez des questions à deux camarades, et ensuite comparez les réponses.

MODÈLE faire la cuisine
É1 Tu aimes faire la cuisine ?
É2 Oui, j'aime la faire. Et toi ?
É3 Non, je n'aime pas la faire.

1. faire la cuisine
2. faire les courses
3. mettre la table
4. faire les devoirs
5. inviter tes amis
6. préparer les repas
7. regarder la télé pendant le dîner
8. faire la vaisselle

Expansion: 6-14 Expand by having students state how often they do each activity:

É1 *Tu aimes faire la cuisine ?*
É2 *Oui, j'aime la faire ; je la fais souvent. Et toi ?*
É3 *Non, moi, je n'aime pas la faire ; je la fais rarement.*

Simplify by providing students with a scale of frequency adverbs: *ne... jamais ; rarement ; quelquefois ; souvent ; toujours.*

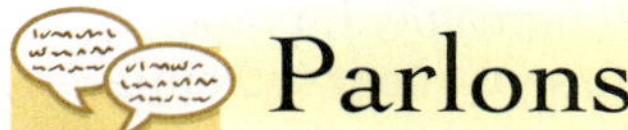

Parlons

6-15 À la recherche d'un appartement

A. Avant de parler. Imaginez que vous cherchez un appartement. Quelles sont les questions que vous posez à un agent immobilier (*real estate agent*) à propos d'un appartement à louer ? Si vous êtes un agent immobilier, comment persuader un/e client/e de prendre l'appartement ? D'abord, créez une liste de questions pour le/la client/e et une liste de commentaires possibles pour l'agent immobilier.

B. En parlant. Maintenant, jouez avec un/e partenaire les deux rôles : client/e et agent immobilier.

MODÈLE agent immobilier : J'ai un très bel appartement au cinquième étage.
client/e : Il a combien de pièces ? Je voudrais un deux-pièces...

Ensuite, échangez les rôles.

C. Après avoir parlé. Présentez votre dialogue aux autres.

Implementation: Divide the class in half: half will be clients, half real estate agents. Brainstorm a list of questions for clients and positive statements for agents. Have students complete the activity in pairs, or for an extended activity, have clients circulate among agents until they find an apartment they like.

Voici deux immeubles d'appartements à Nice et à Rennes. Quel appartement est-ce que vous choisissez ?

Leçon 2 Je suis chez moi

POINTS DE DÉPART

TEXT AUDIO
CD 3 TRACK 40

Chez Christelle

Voici l'immeuble où se trouve le studio de Christelle.

Christelle habite un vieil immeuble rénové dans le centre-ville de Nice. Son studio se trouve sous les toits : il n'est pas très chic, mais il est agréable. En plus, il n'est pas cher : son loyer est de seulement 480 euros par mois. Le studio est meublé : il y a une belle armoire ancienne pour ranger ses vêtements et une petite étagère pour ranger ses livres. Les autres meubles sont un peu abîmés, mais ils sont confortables, surtout le lit et le fauteuil. Par terre il y a un beau tapis, et il y a des rideaux neufs à la fenêtre. Il y a des affiches aux murs. Le coin cuisine est petit mais bien équipé : il y a un petit réfrigérateur à côté de l'évier, une cuisinière avec un petit four. Il y a aussi des grands placards — c'est très pratique pour mettre ses affaires. Il y a aussi une salle de bains moderne et des W.-C.

Have students listen to the description, and use the photo and the labeled drawing of Christelle's room (MFL, Ch. 6) to present this vocabulary. Test comprehension by having students point to items you name as you show the unlabeled room (MFL, Ch. 6), or ask what various items are used for: *Un lit ? — C'est pour dormir*, etc. Next have students repeat key terms and group descriptive words as opposites: *abîmée/neuve ; ancienne/moderne*, etc. All the prepositions are familiar except for *sous* and *sur*.

Vie et culture

Note: It is becoming more common for students or young professionals in France to share an apartment or house without being in a romantic relationship or having a family connection. This is referred to as *la colocation*. Visit the *Chez nous* Companion Website for links to sites with ads for people seeking *des colocataires* that you could use in class to practice key vocabulary linked to housing.

Le quartier

Dans les grandes villes, c'est le quartier qui donne un aspect plus personnel à la vie urbaine souvent trop impersonnelle. Chaque quartier est comme une petite communauté : il y a le café du coin[1] et les petits commerçants. On peut faire les courses tous les jours. Il y a souvent un marché certains jours de la semaine.

Regardez la séquence vidéo *Mon quartier*, où une jeune Parisienne décrit son quartier. Quels aspects de son quartier est-ce qu'elle aime en particulier ? Et vous, est-ce que vous habitez aussi dans un quartier ? Est-ce que vous avez aussi le sentiment de faire partie d'une petite communauté ? Pourquoi ?

Pauline achète son pain à la boulangerie du coin.

[1]*corner*

À vous la parole

6-16 Chez Christelle. Décrivez l'appartement où habite Christelle en choisissant un adjectif approprié.

Variation: 6-16 To provide review of prenominal adjective forms, have students reply with: *C'est un vieil immeuble.* Note that the adjective *neuf/neuve* is irregular in its formation.

MODÈLE L'immeuble est neuf ou vieux ?

  L'immeuble est vieux.

1. Le studio est spacieux ou petit ?
2. Le loyer est cher ou pas cher ?
3. Le fauteuil est confortable ou pas confortable ?
4. La salle de bains est ancienne ou moderne ?
5. L'armoire est neuve ou ancienne ?
6. Les rideaux sont neufs ou vieux ?
7. Le tapis est abîmé ou beau ?
8. La cuisine est bien équipée ou mal équipée ?

Implementation: 6-17 Before completing, review the prepositions students learned in Ch. 3, L. 1 and the contracted forms of the prepositions *à* and *de*. Point out that *sur* is used to talk about things placed on horizontal surfaces. Use the preposition *à* for items on vertical surfaces, for example, *L'affiche est au mur*. You might also have students indicate what is *not* in the room, e.g., *Il n'y a pas de tapis*, etc. As a follow-up, use other famous paintings of interiors to practice this vocabulary; allow students to work in pairs or groups.

6-17 La chambre de Van Gogh. Van Gogh (1853–1890), un artiste néerlandais bien connu, a habité en France. Voici un de ses tableaux ; c'est sa chambre en Provence. Décrivez cette chambre en cinq ou six phrases.

MODÈLE Dans cette chambre, il y a un petit lit. À côté du lit, il y a...

Vincent Van Gogh, « La chambre de Van Gogh à Arles », 1889. Oil on canvas. 57.5 × 74 cm. Musée d'Orsay, Paris, France. Erich Lessing/Art Resource, NY.

Variation: 6-18 Modify by having one student describe his/her room while the partner tries to draw it.

6-18 Ma chambre. Avec un/e partenaire, décrivez votre chambre à la résidence, dans votre maison ou votre appartement, ou chez vos parents. N'oubliez pas de parler de ce que vous avez fait pour rendre votre environnement plus personnel.

Des suggestions :

Quels meubles est-ce qu'il y a ?
Qu'est-ce qu'il y a aux murs ? par terre ?
Quels objets personnels — des photos, des plantes — est-ce qu'il y a ?
Quelles couleurs est-ce que tu as mises dans la chambre ?

MODÈLE
É1 J'habite une grande chambre dans la résidence universitaire. Dans ma chambre, il y a deux lits, deux bureaux et des étagères.
É2 Moi aussi, j'habite une chambre dans la résidence. Qu'est-ce que tu as fait pour rendre ta chambre plus personnelle ?
É1 J'ai mis des plantes ; j'adore les plantes. Et toi ?
É2 Moi j'ai mis un beau tapis par terre et beaucoup d'affiches aux murs. C'est très bien chez moi.

Sons et lettres

La consonne *r*

The French /r/ has no equivalent sound in English. To pronounce /r/ in French, begin by saying **aga**; then move your tongue up and back until you pronounce a continuous sound: **ara**. Practice by alternating the two sounds: **aga/ara**, **aga/ara**, etc.

Note the pronunciation of /r/ in **liaison** and linking across words (**enchaînement**).

Liaison :	le premier‿étage	le dernier‿immeuble
Enchaînement :	un séjour‿agréable	Il sort‿avec moi.

Note: The American *r* is a retroflex *r*; the tongue curves back. Tell students not to roll their tongue to produce the French r.

Note: Point out that liaison also involves *enchaînement*. Liaison is the pronunciation of a liaison (or latent) consonant before a vowel; *enchaînement* is the pronunciation of any consonant—whether latent or always pronounced—before words beginning with a vowel. The consonant is pronounced as if it were part of the next word.

À vous la parole

6-19 Répétitions. Répétez les mots suivants.

la rue	la route	la rose	la terrasse	arriver
Paris	la gare	première	servir	maigrir

Initial practice: Begin practice with a discrimination drill: *anglais ou français ? roux, rue*, Robert, *rat, Richard*, terrace, rose, *route*, etc.

6-20 La forme correcte. Donnez les formes de la troisième personne (singulier et pluriel) du présent de l'indicatif des verbes suivants.

MODÈLE servir
→ elle sert, elles servent

sortir partir dormir maigrir servir

6-21 Phrases. Répétez chaque phrase.

1. La terrasse donne sur la rue.
2. L'ascenseur s'arrête au dernier étage.
3. Marie achète l'autre appartement.

FORMES ET FONCTIONS

1. *Les pronoms compléments d'objet indirect* lui *et* leur

Presentation: Review the forms of the direct-object pronouns with a transformation drill before introducing the indirect-object pronouns: *Je regarde la télé. —Je la regarde ; les voisins—Je les regarde ; le toit ; les fenêtres ; l'ascenseur ; la cuisinière ; le balcon*, etc. Present the new forms with a narrative: *Aujourd'hui, j'ai rendez-vous avec un collègue ; je lui téléphone pour vérifier. J'ai cours avec mes étudiants à 10 h ; je leur rends les devoirs. Je déjeune avec une amie ; c'est son anniversaire, et je lui offre un cadeau*, etc. Present these examples both orally and in written form, and ask students to explain usage.

- You have learned that nouns that function as direct objects answer the question *whom?* or *what?*; they follow the verb directly and can be replaced by a direct-object pronoun.

Tu prends **cet appartement** ?	—Oui, je **le** prends.
Elle attend **le propriétaire** ?	—Oui, elle **l'**attend.
Vous aimez **ces appartements** ?	—Non, on ne **les** aime pas.

◆ In French, nouns that function as indirect objects are generally introduced by the preposition **à;** they often answer the question *to whom?* and always refer to a person:

Je donne le loyer **à la propriétaire.**	*I'm giving the rent* ***to the landlady.*** (OR *I'm giving* ***the landlady*** *the rent.*)
Tu as répondu **à tes parents** ?	*Did you answer* ***your parents?***

In the sentences above, the indirect-object pronouns **lui** (*to him, to her*) and **leur** (*to them*) can be substituted for **à la propriétaire** and **à tes parents**.

Je **lui** donne le loyer.	*I'm giving the rent* ***to him/her.***
Tu **leur** as répondu ?	*Did you answer* ***them?***

Presentation: Students should be able to summarize placement rules on their own, since the indirect-object pronouns function in the same way as the direct-object pronouns that they have already seen. Point out that in the *passé composé,* the past participle never agrees with a preceding indirect-object pronoun.

◆ Like other object pronouns, **lui** and **leur** are placed immediately before the conjugated verb, unless there is an infinitive. If there is an infinitive in the sentence, **lui** and **leur** precede the infinitive.

Je **lui** parle du loyer.	*I'm speaking* ***to him/her*** *about the rent.*
Nous **leur** avons téléphoné.	*We called* ***them*** *up.*
Tu vas **lui** donner l'argent pour les charges ?	*Are you going to give* ***him/her*** *the money for utilities?*
Elle peut **leur** expliquer combien ça coute par mois.	*She can explain* ***to them*** *how much it costs per month.*

◆ In affirmative commands, **lui** and **leur** are placed immediately after the verb and joined to it by a hyphen:

Donne**-lui** ta nouvelle adresse.	*Give her/him your new address.*
Téléphone**-leur** à propos de l'appartement.	*Call them about the apartment.*

In negative commands, **lui** and **leur** are placed immediately before the conjugated verb:

Ne **lui** prête pas l'appartement.	*Don't loan the apartment to him/her.*

Note: The full conjugation of the irregular verbs *dire* and *écrire* will be presented in Ch. 7, L. 1.

◆ Two main groups of verbs take indirect objects.

◆ Verbs of communication:

demander	*to ask*	On va **leur** demander l'adresse.
dire	*to tell*	Dites-**lui** la vérité !
écrire	*to write*	Vous **leur** écrivez souvent ?
expliquer	*to explain*	Tu peux **lui** expliquer le problème ?
montrer	*to show*	Qui va **lui** montrer la chambre ?
parler	*to speak*	Je **leur** parle souvent au téléphone.
répondre	*to answer*	Elle ne **leur** a pas répondu.
téléphoner	*to phone*	Nous **leur** avons téléphoné hier.

- Verbs of transfer:

acheter	*to buy*	Je **leur** ai acheté un petit appartement.
apporter	*to bring*	La propriétaire **lui** a apporté la lettre.
donner	*to give*	On peut **leur** donner l'adresse.
emprunter	*to borrow*	Je **lui** emprunte la voiture.
offrir	*to give (a gift)*	Elle **lui** offre un cadeau pour son anniversaire.
prêter	*to lend*	Tu **leur** prêtes ton appartement ?
remettre	*to hand in/over*	On **lui** a remis le loyer.
rendre	*to give back*	Je **lui** ai rendu le livre.

Note: This construction is ambiguous for the verb *acheter: Je lui achète un livre* (I'm buying a book for/from him). For greater clarity: *J'achète un livre pour mon frère.* Point out to students that *offrir*, like *ouvrir*, takes *-er* verb endings. A full conjugation can be found in Appendix 5.

À vous la parole 

6-22 À qui est-ce qu'on parle ? Romain parle de ses habitudes. Pour chaque phrase, décidez s'il parle à sa copine ou à ses parents.

Normalement, je...

	à sa copine	à ses parents
MODÈLE ... lui téléphone une ou deux fois par jour.	✓	______
1. ... leur téléphone le week-end.	______	______
2. ... lui parle quand je suis frustré.	______	______
3. ... lui parle quand je me lève le matin.	______	______
4. ... lui téléphone quand j'ai des problèmes.	______	______
5. ... leur parle quand j'ai besoin d'argent.	______	______
6. ... lui téléphone quand je veux sortir.	______	______
7. ... leur parle quand c'est bientôt les vacances.	______	______

D'après ces descriptions, à qui est-ce qu'il parle le plus souvent ?

Initial practice: Begin practice with this activity to establish a form-meaning connection between the indirect-object pronouns and their referents. For additional practice, ask students to find two logical possibilities for each of these sentences: *Je lui offre souvent des cadeaux — à mon petit frère ; à mon copain. Je leur téléphone souvent le week-end. Je lui ai rendu visite l'été passé. Je voudrais lui donner mon adresse. J'aime leur parler. Je lui prête mes affaires. Je leur explique mes problèmes. Je peux lui demander de l'argent. Je leur offre des cadeaux.* For productive practice, use a simple substitution drill: *Je réponds au prof. — Je lui réponds ; à mes parents ; à Suzanne ; à mes amis ; à mon frère ; à mes colocataires ; au serveur ; à mon meilleur ami ; à mes cousins.*

6-23 Qu'est-ce qu'on peut offrir ? Les personnes suivantes ont acheté un nouvel appartement. D'après les indications, qu'est-ce qu'on pourrait leur offrir comme cadeau ?

MODÈLE Ma sœur n'a pas grand-chose aux murs.
→ Je lui offre une belle affiche.

1. Mes parents ont un nouveau lecteur DVD.
2. Mon oncle adore faire la cuisine.
3. Ma tante adore les plantes et les fleurs (*flowers*).
4. Ma cousine aime les livres.
5. Mes grands-parents aiment la musique.
6. Mon cousin n'a pas de colocataire.
7. Mes amis ont une belle terrasse.

Variation: 6-23 This can be personalized by asking students about the interests of their family and friends and having others suggest suitable gifts.

Expansion: 6-24 Follow up by having students report back what they learned.

6-24 Rarement, souvent ou jamais ? Interviewez un/e camarade de classe pour savoir avec quelle fréquence il/elle fait les choses suivantes : **rarement**, **souvent** ou **jamais** ?

MODÈLE prêtes tes vêtements à ta/ton colocataire

É1 Est-ce que tu prêtes tes vêtements à ta colocataire ?
É2 Non, je ne lui prête jamais mes vêtements.
OU Oui, je lui prête souvent mes pull-overs.

1. rends les devoirs au professeur
2. expliques tes problèmes à tes parents
3. parles à tes parents
4. offres des cadeaux à tes amis
5. demandes de l'argent à tes parents
6. empruntes des vêtements à tes amis
7. achètes des bonbons pour tes nièces et tes neveux
8. empruntes de l'argent à tes amis

2. *Les nombres à partir de mille*

Note: Following the orthographic reform of 1990, all compound numbers, including dates, are written with hyphens. You may wish to point out that students will likely encounter examples of the traditional system in which numbers under one hundred are written with a hyphen (except for the forms *x et un*) while numbers above one hundred are not. The new system has the merit of reducing the exceptional forms that students (and speakers of French) must learn.

Presentation: Review numbers up to 999 before treating this topic. In treating large numbers, we focus here on their use in dates, prices (for housing), and distances.

To express numbers larger than 999, use the following terms:

1 000	mille	1 000 000	un-million
2 000	deux-mille	2 000 000	deux-millions
1 000 000 000	un-milliard	2 000 000 000	deux-milliards

- As the examples above show, add **-s** after **million** and **milliard** in the plural. No **-s** is ever added after **mille**.
- Dates prior to the twenty-first century can be expressed in either of two ways:

Note: The spelling *mil* may also be used in dates.

On a acheté la maison en mille-neuf-cent-quatre-vingt-neuf (1989). — *We bought the house in 1989.*

Ils louent cet appartement depuis dix-neuf-cent-quatre-vingt-dix-neuf (1999). — *They've been renting that apartment since 1999.*

Dates in the twenty-first century and beyond are expressed with **deux-mille**:

Elle habite là depuis deux-mille-neuf (2009). — *She's been living there since 2009.*

- A comma is used in French where we would use a decimal point.

Environ trente-sept virgule neuf pour cent (37,9 %) des Français sont locataires. — *About thirty-seven point nine percent (37.9%) of the French are renters.*

- Use a space or a period to separate out thousands and other large numbers.

De Lille à Ajaccio (en Corse), ça fait 1 061 kilomètres.	*From Lille to Ajaccio (in Corsica) is 1,061 kilometers.*
De Paris à Montréal, ça fait 5 511 kilomètres.	*From Paris to Montreal is 5,511 kilometers.*

- Use **de/d'** after **million**:

À Paris, il y a plus de 11 000 000 **d'**habitants.	*The city of Paris has more than 11,000,000 inhabitants.*

À vous la parole

6-25 Maisons de rêve. Regardez ces annonces pour des belles propriétés à vendre en France. Dites combien coûte chaque maison ou appartement.

Initial practice: Begin practice by having students write the number you say; say the number you write. For Ex. 6-25, use a map of France to show the location of the regions and departments. Note that *Normandie* and *Bretagne* refer to regions, while the other places listed are all departments.

MODÈLE Normandie : maison ancienne avec vue sur la mer ; Prix : 775.000 €
La maison en Normandie coûte sept-cent-soixante-quinze-mille euros.

1. **CÔTE D'OR :** une ferme restaurée ; **Prix : 371.650 €**
2. **BRETAGNE :** propriété de charme près de la mer ; **Prix : 636.000 €**
3. **LOIRE-ATLANTIQUE :** la vue sur l'océan ; **Prix : 768.000 €**
4. **ALPES-MARITIMES :** un charme fou ; **Prix : 1.280.000 €**
5. **CHARENTE-MARITIME :** grand appartement, excellent état ; **Prix : 247.850 €**
6. **TARN-ET-GARONNE :** maison ancienne, à rénover ; **Prix : 110.000 €**

6-26 Un peu d'histoire. Est-ce que vous êtes doué/e en histoire ? Avec un/e partenaire, trouvez la bonne date pour chaque évènement.

Key: 1066 : les Normands… ; 1492 : Christophe Colomb… ; 1776 : Jefferson écrit… ; 1789 : La Révolution française… ; 1804 : les Haïtiens… ; 1860 : la Guerre de Sécession… ; 1914 : la Première Guerre mondiale… ; 1939 : la Seconde Guerre mondiale… ; 1969 : les Américains vont sur la Lune ; 2001 : les attentats du 11 septembre.

MODÈLE 1804
En mille-huit-cent-quatre les Haïtiens déclarent leur indépendance.

1066	Les Haïtiens déclarent leur indépendance.
1492	La Révolution française commence.
1776	Les Normands arrivent en Angleterre.
1789	Les Américains vont sur la Lune.
1804	La Première Guerre mondiale commence.
1860	Les attentats du 11 septembre ont lieu.
1914	La Seconde Guerre mondiale commence.
1939	La Guerre de Sécession commence.
1969	Jefferson écrit la Déclaration d'Indépendance américaine.
2001	Christophe Colomb découvre l'Amérique.

Additional activity: To practice distances, ask students to imagine that they are traveling by train between two French cities and to compare the distance one-way and round-trip. Provide a model such as:

MODÈLE Rouen – Toulouse / 650 km

É1 De Rouen à Toulouse, ça fait six-cent-cinquante kilomètres.

É2 Donc, mille-trois-cents kilomètres aller-retour.

1. Caen – Nice / 840 km
2. Rennes – Marseille / 760 km
3. Strasbourg – Bordeaux / 760 km
4. Calais – Cannes / 910 km
5. Metz – Pau / 820 km
6. Paris – Menton / 700 km

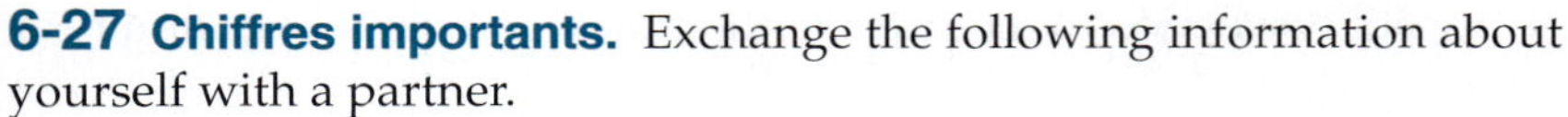

6-27 Chiffres importants. Exchange the following information about yourself with a partner.

MODÈLES date de naissance (*birth*)

É1 C'est le quatorze février, mille-neuf-cent-quatre-vingt-sept. (14/02/1987)

numéro de téléphone

É2 C'est le cinq-cent-cinquante-cinq, zéro huit, trente-sept. (555-0837)

Note: 6-27 Point out that the French read phone numbers as a series of two numbers. To say an American phone number, they will frequently read the first part as a three-number series followed by a series of two numbers.

1. date de naissance **2.** numéro de téléphone **3.** code postal

Écoutons

6-28 Deux appartements

Implementation: Avant d'écouter To prepare this activity, give students time to write their lists in French and then have them compare their ideas with a partner or the whole class.

Script: Écoutons Le premier appartement se trouve en centre-ville. C'est un grand studio neuf avec un coin cuisine très moderne, une petite salle de bains et des W.-C. Il y a des meubles, mais ils sont un peu abîmés, et il n'y a pas de placards. Le loyer est raisonnable ; c'est seulement 500 euros par mois, charges comprises.
Le deuxième appartement est à l'extérieur de la ville, mais avec le train, on est à une demi-heure seulement du centre-ville. J'aime cet appartement. C'est un très beau deux-pièces rénové, avec un grand séjour. Dans la chambre il y a un petit balcon avec une vue magnifique sur le parc. Il y a aussi une petite cuisine, des W.-C. et une douche dans la salle de bains. Mais ce n'est pas meublé, et je n'ai pas de meubles.

A. Avant d'écouter. Imaginez que vous cherchez un appartement. Faites une liste de vos critères de sélection, c'est-à-dire, ce que vous voulez trouver dans l'appartement.

B. En écoutant. Maintenant, écoutez Damien, qui décrit deux appartements qu'il a visités.

1. Pour chaque appartement, cochez les critères qu'il mentionne.

Appartement	n° 1	n° 2
en centre-ville		
deux pièces		
cuisine équipée		
salle de bains		
W.-C.		
balcon		
meublé		

2. Écoutez une deuxième fois pour vérifier que vous avez coché tous les détails que Damien a mentionnés.

C. Après avoir écouté. Discutez de ces questions avec vos camarades de classe.

1. D'après la description des deux appartements, est-ce que Damien va probablement louer le premier ou le second ? Pourquoi ?
2. Est-ce que Damien a les mêmes critères que vous pour un appartement ?
3. Et vous, quel appartement est-ce que vous préférez ? Pourquoi ?

Leçon 3 La vie à la campagne

POINTS DE DÉPART

TEXT AUDIO
CD 3 TRACK 45

Presentation: Using the photo that opens the lesson, describe the house, related activities, and surroundings. Have students listen to the dialogue, and test comprehension using simple questions: *La villa des Santini est située en ville ?*, etc. Point out the location of Haute-Normandie on a map of France; and ask students to speculate about why it might be an ideal location for a vacation home for Parisians (e.g., its location not too far from Paris and also not far from the English Channel).

Tout près de la nature

Les Santini possèdent une petite villa qui se trouve en Haute-Normandie. C'est loin de Paris et à une heure de la mer. Ils ont passé le week-end dernier là-bas. M. Santini en parle avec son collègue M. Deleuze.

M. DELEUZE : Qu'est-ce que vous avez fait le week-end dernier ?
M. SANTINI : On est allés à la campagne où nous avons une petite maison.
M. DELEUZE : C'était bien ?
M. SANTINI : Formidable ! C'était calme, j'ai bricolé, je suis allé à la pêche et avec les enfants, on s'est promenés dans le bois. Dimanche, on est allé à Honfleur et on a fait un pique-nique au bord de la mer.
M. DELEUZE : Vous avez un jardin aussi ?
M. SANTINI : Oh, on a un petit potager et quelques arbres fruitiers, c'est tout. C'est ma femme qui s'occupe de tout cela.
M. DELEUZE : Alors, il me semble que vous avez passé un week-end agréable.
M. SANTINI : En effet, on se détend toujours quand on est à la campagne.

La résidence secondaire des Santini en Haute-Normandie ; ils peuvent bricoler et faire du jardinage le week-end et pendant les vacances.

Note: About 10% of French families own a *résidence secondaire*; this statistic is down a bit from a few years ago, for both economic and sociological reasons: the French like to vary their vacation destinations. A house in a town or a village is *une maison*; in the suburbs, *un pavillon*; in a resort area or away from the city, *une villa*.

Presentation: Present the vocabulary by describing the drawing of natural sites (MFL, Ch. 6); you might use additional photos or slides to enrich the presentation. Test comprehension of key words by having students point to (using the unlabeled art, MFL, Ch. 6), or draw, the geographical features you name. Have them suggest activities appropriate for the places pictured. Repeat key words and phrases: *C'est un lac ou une rivière ?* then continue with the cultural notes and exercises. For honors or other advanced classes, there is a story from *Le Petit Nicolas et les copains* which would work quite well here: *Le chouette bol d'air.* Illustrations of a small country house with a vegetable garden and fruit trees accompany the story.

Vie et culture

Note: The **Venez chez nous** ! section of this chapter focuses on the regions in more depth with regard to languages, customs, and history.

La diversité géographique de la France

Pour les Français, la France a la forme d'une figure géométrique. Quand vous regardez la carte, quelle figure géométrique est-ce que vous voyez ? Oui, c'est un hexagone. C'est un hexagone équilibré, avec trois côtés bordés par des mers et trois côtés limités par d'autres pays[1]. Est-ce que vous pouvez nommer les mers et les pays qui bordent la France ? Regardez les huit villes de France qui sont indiquées sur la carte ; toutes ces grandes villes se trouvent à proximité de la mer ou d'un fleuve. Regardez bien et nommez ces huit villes et la mer ou le fleuve dans chaque cas. Regardez encore une fois la carte. Est-ce qu'il y a des montagnes ? Où ? Est-ce que vous pouvez les nommer ?

Pour un pays qui est un peu moins grand que l'état du Texas, la France a une variété géographique impressionnante. Chaque région a ses attractions : en Bretagne on trouve des côtes sauvages. En Auvergne, on peut descendre dans une grotte préhistorique ou monter au sommet d'un puy[2], site d'un ancien volcan. Sur la côte ouest, on peut se bronzer[3] sur les plages blanches de l'Atlantique. Dans les Alpes et les Pyrénées on trouve les plaisirs de la montagne : le ski en hiver, la marche et la pêche en été. Sur la côte méditerranéenne, on trouve des panoramas magnifiques et des belles plages. Si vous préférez la ville, la campagne, la montagne ou la mer, il y en a en France pour tous les goûts !

ET VOUS ?

1. Quelles sont les particularités géographiques de votre région ? Est-que vous devez aller loin pour trouver de la diversité géographique (par exemple, combien de temps est-ce qu'il vous faut pour aller à la montagne ou à la mer) ? Quels sont les avantages d'un pays comme la France où l'on trouve beaucoup de variation géographique dans un espace réduit ?
2. Est-ce que les villes principales en Amérique du Nord se trouvent près de la mer ou d'un fleuve ? Pourquoi à votre avis ?

[1] *country* [2] *mountaintop* [3] *to tan*

Variation: Assign pairs or groups of students to a particular region in France and ask them to present a brief in-class report with pictures (or slides) of the geographic features typical of that area.

Presentation: As you treat this passage, have students look at the map in their textbook or display the map of France (MFL, Ch. 6; MFL, Maps). Have them identify the water borders, the borders with neighboring countries, and the mountain ranges displayed. Ask students to point out on the map the various regions mentioned. To enliven the presentation, bring in images of the Brittany coasts, the volcanic peaks in the Massif Central, the Atlantic and Mediterranean beaches and coasts, the Alps in both winter and spring/summer, and pictures of flat, rural countryside in the central regions. Stress the large variety of geographical features that are found in France in a rather compact area. Explain that *un fleuve* is a river that leads directly to the sea; *une rivière* is a tributary (*un affluent*); for example, *le Mississippi est un fleuve, mais l'Ohio est une rivière. La Seine, la Loire, le Rhône et la Garonne sont des fleuves ; la Marne, un affluent de la Seine, est une rivière.*

À vous la parole

6-29 Où aller ? Suggérez le meilleur endroit pour chaque activité mentionnée.

MODÈLE pour faire de la pêche
Allons au bord d'une rivière.
OU Allons au bord de la mer.
OU Allons au lac.

1. pour faire du ski
2. pour faire un pique-nique
3. pour nager
4. pour se promener dans la nature
5. pour chercher des tomates et des carottes
6. pour faire du camping
7. pour faire du bateau

6-30 Projets pour une sortie. Avec deux ou trois camarades de classe, faites des projets pour une sortie le week-end. Choisissez une destination et des activités.

MODÈLE É1 On va à la montagne ?
É2 Je préfère aller au bord d'un lac.
É3 Moi aussi. On peut nager...

Implementation: 6-30 Put students into small groups to plan. You might impose certain constraints—time of year, distance they may travel, amount of money they may spend, etc.

6-31 Plaisirs de la ville, plaisirs de la campagne. Vous préférez habiter la ville ou la campagne ? Pourquoi ? Discutez de votre préférence avec un/e partenaire et dressez une liste des avantages et des inconvénients.

MODÈLE É1 Moi, je préfère habiter la ville ; il y a beaucoup de bons restaurants et de cinémas.
É2 Il y a trop d'activité et trop de voitures en ville ; je préfère le calme à la campagne...

la ville : avantages = les restaurants, les cinémas, ...
inconvénients = les voitures, ...
la campagne : avantages = le calme, ...

Implementation: 6-31 This can also be carried out as a whole-class activity, or students can be put into small groups as follows: advantages of the city, advantages of the country, etc. Circulate as groups prepare their lists and help out with ideas and vocabulary. Have groups report back, and summarize information orally and visually before students are polled to express their personal preference. As an additional follow-up, students can write about their personal preference.

6-32 La maison de vos rêves. Imaginez que vous pouvez acheter une résidence secondaire. Décrivez-la d'après vos préférences, et comparez vos idées avec celles d'un/e partenaire.

1. Elle se trouve au bord de la mer ? à la montagne ? à la campagne ?
2. C'est une grande ou une petite maison ? simple ou élégante ?
3. Qu'est-ce que vous faites quand vous allez dans votre résidence secondaire ?

MODÈLE Ma résidence secondaire se trouve à la montagne. C'est un petit chalet, très simple mais confortable. J'adore la nature. J'aime me promener et faire de la marche.

Variation: 6-32 Ask students to make a sketch of their dream house to share with the class. As students share their visions of their dream house, have the class decide on whose house is the most luxurious, the most practical, the most realistic, etc.

Note: This section focuses on the formation of the *imparfait*. For that reason, we use a function of the *imparfait* unrelated to the expression of past events. You might point out that the main use of the *imparfait* is to express certain types of past events and that this function will be taught in the next section, which you will want to treat on a subsequent day.

Presentation: Show students how the rule for formation of the *imparfait* works for irregular verbs they have learned: *faire* —> *nous faisons* —> *il faisait, nous faisions*, etc. Point out that the singular and third-person plural forms are pronounced alike. In pronouncing these endings, French speakers vary between /e/, as in *thé*, and /ɛ/, as in *cette*.

FORMES ET FONCTIONS

1. *Faire des suggestions avec l'imparfait*

- The imperfect **(l'imparfait)** is a tense that is used in a variety of ways. For example, it is used with **si** to make suggestions and to soften commands.

Si on **faisait** une promenade ?	*Shall we take a walk?*
Si tu **allais** à la pêche ?	*Why don't you go fishing?*
Si on allait à la montagne ?	*How about going to the mountains?*

- To form the **imparfait**, drop the **-ons** ending of the **nous** form of the present tense and add the **imparfait** endings. The only exception to this rule is the verb **être**, which has an irregular stem, **ét-**, as shown below.

L'IMPARFAIT					
INFINITIVE	jouer	partir	finir	descendre	être
NOUS FORM	jouons	partons	finissons	descendons	
IMPARFAIT STEM	**jou-**	**part-**	**finiss-**	**descend-**	**ét-**
je	jou**ais**	part**ais**	finiss**ais**	descend**ais**	ét**ais**
tu	jou**ais**	part**ais**	finiss**ais**	descend**ais**	ét**ais**
il / elle / on	jou**ait**	part**ait**	finiss**ait**	descend**ait**	ét**ait**
nous	jou**ions**	part**ions**	finiss**ions**	descend**ions**	ét**ions**
vous	jou**iez**	part**iez**	finiss**iez**	descend**iez**	ét**iez**
ils / elles	jou**aient**	part**aient**	finiss**aient**	descend**aient**	ét**aient**

Note: You might remind students to picture the "boot" shape (as discussed in the **Fiche pratique** in Ch. 1, L. 3 for regular **-er** verbs) as they imagine themselves writing out the various endings for the imperfect. The imperfect also displays the boot shape and has three spoken forms.

Fiche pratique

As you encounter a new verb tense, use several of your senses to help you learn the new forms. For example, practice repeating the **imparfait** forms of the verb **finir** out loud: **je finissais, tu finissais, elle finissait,** etc., while forming a picture in your mind of your hand writing out the endings **-ais, -ais, -ait,** etc., for each form.

À vous la parole

6-33 Un week-end à la campagne. Transformez ces ordres en suggestions.

MODÈLE Jouons au golf !
Si on jouait au golf ?

1. Faisons de la marche !
2. Travaille dans le jardin !
3. Descendez au bord du lac !
4. Organisons un pique-nique !
5. Faites une promenade dans la forêt !
6. Cherchons des tomates !
7. Fais du bricolage !
8. Allons à la pêche !

Initial practice: Begin practice with a substitution drill: *Si on allait à la piscine ?; nous, toi, vous*, etc. Follow with a transformation drill that allows students to practice multiple verbs: *On va au lac ? —Si on allait au lac ? On fait une promenade ? —Si on faisait une promenade ? On part à la campagne ? On attend les amis ? On finit les devoirs ?*, etc.

6-34 Pour une sortie. En groupes de trois personnes, organisez une petite sortie. Mettez-vous d'accord sur l'endroit et les distractions. Utilisez les verbes indiqués.

MODÈLE aller ; apporter ; faire
É1 Si on allait à la plage ? (ou chez Tracy ?, etc.)
É2 Si tu apportais ta guitare ?
É3 Si on faisait un pique-nique ?

1. aller
2. apporter
3. acheter
4. jouer
5. faire
6. inviter

6-35 Projets pour le week-end. Avec un/e partenaire, faites des projets pour un week-end dans la nature. Décidez de la destination et des activités.

MODÈLE É1 Si on allait dans la forêt ?
É2 Oui, et si on faisait des promenades le matin ?
É1 Bonne idée ! Si on faisait un pique-nique à midi ?, etc.

2. *L'imparfait : la description au passé*

Presentation: Treat this topic on day 2 of the lesson, and first review forms using a substitution drill: *Si tu jouais au tennis ; on, lui, vous,* etc.

- You have just learned to use the **imparfait** to make suggestions. You can also use this tense to describe situations and settings in the past.
  - To indicate the time:

    Il **était** une heure du matin. — *It was one o'clock in the morning.*
    C'**était** au mois de mai. — *It was during the month of May.*

  - To describe the weather:

    Il **faisait** beau. — *It was nice.*
    Il y **avait** du soleil. — *It was sunny.*

  - To describe people and places:

    C'**était** une belle maison. — *It was a nice house.*
    La dame **avait** les cheveux roux. — *The woman had red hair.*
    Elle **portait** un manteau noir. — *She was wearing a black coat.*

  - To express feelings or describe emotions:

    On **avait** faim. — *We were hungry.*
    Ils **étaient** contents. — *They were happy.*

Note: For the sake of completeness, we mention the use of the *imparfait* to describe the weather. However, weather vocabulary will not be formally presented until Ch. 8, L.1. Be sure to limit practice of weather and the *imparfait* to the two expressions presented here.

- Use the **imparfait** to express habitual actions in the past:

  Tous les week-ends on **faisait** une promenade dans les bois. — *Every weekend we would take (we took) a walk in the woods.*
  Quand j'étais petit, on **passait** les vacances chez mes grands-parents. — *When I was little, we used to spend vacations at my grandparents'.*

Here are some expressions often used with the **imparfait** to describe things that were done on a routine basis:

Presentation: Remind students that *le* used before a day of the week or a word like *week-end* changes the meaning to "every Monday" or "every weekend," for example.

quelquefois	*sometimes*
souvent	*often*
d'habitude	*usually*
toujours	*always*
le lundi, le week-end	*every Monday, every weekend*
tous les jours, tous les soirs	*every day, every evening*
toutes les semaines	*every week*

 À vous la parole 

6-36 Un après-midi en famille. Regardez l'image de cette famille à Biarritz et complétez les phrases pour décrire leur après-midi.

MODÈLE Ce / être le mois de juin
→ C'était le mois de juin.

1. les enfants / jouer dans le jardin
2. le grand-père / parle avec sa petite-fille
3. le fils / jouer au foot
4. leur mère et leur tante / boire un jus d'orange
5. les femmes / regarder les enfants et leur père
6. leur frère / préparer le repas
7. le chien et les chats / dormir

Implementation: 6-37 If this is the first language course for some students, suggest that they focus on the first few weeks of the semester and describe what things were like and how they felt at that point.

6-37 Votre premier cours de langue. Avec un/e partenaire, parlez de votre premier cours de langue. Est-ce que vous aviez des expériences semblables ou pas ?

MODÈLE le prof

É1 Mon premier prof de français s'appelait M. Dell. Il était grand et assez mince. Il était très dynamique et assez drôle. Et toi ?

É2 Mon premier prof d'espagnol s'appelait Señora Glatis. Elle était très sympa et très énergique. Je l'adorais !

1. l'heure du cours
2. l'endroit (le bâtiment, la salle de classe ou le campus...)
3. le prof
4. les autres étudiants ou élèves
5. vos émotions/sentiments
6. le travail
7. les activités habituelles

6-38 Votre enfance. Posez des questions à un/e camarade de classe pour savoir ce qu'il/elle faisait pendant son enfance.

MODÈLE habiter ici

É1 Est-ce que tu habitais ici ?

É2 Non, j'habitais à Chicago avec mes parents.

1. habiter ici
2. avoir des animaux
3. aimer aller à l'école
4. faire du sport
5. jouer d'un instrument
6. aller souvent chez des amis
7. partir souvent en vacances
8. avoir une résidence secondaire

Implementation: 6-38 Have students work in pairs; as they report back what they have learned, ask follow-up questions. This exercise can lead into the reading in **Lisons**.

Stratégie

To understand a narrative, identify the main characters and the nature of their relationship with each other. Then as you read and reread the passage, focus on defining the significance of each character and how he or she figures in the story.

Lisons

6-39 Quand j'étais toute petite

A. Avant de lire. J.M.G. Le Clézio, a well known and prolific French author, was awarded the Nobel Prize for Literature in 2008. The excerpt you are about to read is from ***Printemps et autres saisons,*** a collection of short stories. Each one is set in a different season and tells the story of a particular woman. In this excerpt, Zinna, a young woman who has left her home in Morocco for the South of France, describes her childhood home in the **Mellah** (the Jewish quarter). Before you begin reading, skim the text and make a list of all characters mentioned; take note especially of an essential character who figures prominently in the story: Zinna's elderly neighbor, **la tante Rahel**. Consider as you read why Rahel, whom Zinna never actually encounters in person, is very important to her narrative.

Presentation: Link this reading to the notion of place developed in the chapter by having students make the connection that Morocco is a place where French is spoken and that Zinna's description of her home and neighborhood are very specific to a particular place. Ask students to describe the image that accompanies the reading and to discuss the feelings/associations that it may evoke. As you work with the text, you might ask students what they know about Morocco and have them do some Internet research on *le Mellah.*

Key: Avant de lire Characters mentioned include: *Gazelle / Tomi ; Zinna ; le père de Zinna et son oncle Moché ; Khadija ; la (vieille) tante Rahel (une voisine).* Help students see that Gazelle is a nickname for *Tomi* and ask them why Tomi might be referred to as a "gazelle." The opening lines of the story explain: *« Il s'appelait Tomi, mais Zinna l'appelait Gazelle, à cause de son autre nom, Arzel, parce qu'elle disait que c'était ce que ça voulait dire, en arabe. C'était peut-être pour ça qu'il savait courir si vite.»*

B. En lisant. Répondez aux questions suivantes.

1. Ce texte est principalement une conversation. À qui est-ce que Zinna parle ? Quand est-ce qu'elle raconte son histoire ? Où ?
2. Zinna décrit deux maisons ; ce sont les maisons de qui ? Décrivez chaque maison : elles sont grandes ou petites ? Elles ont combien de pièces ? Combien d'étages ? Est-ce qu'il y a d'autres détails intéressants ?
3. Qui habite la deuxième maison ? Cette personne est comment ? Pourquoi est-ce que Zinna la trouve fascinante ?

Key: En lisant 1) Zinna parle à Gazelle / Tomi ; le matin ; à la plage 2) la maison de Zinna : vieille, petite, une pièce en bas, une chambre en haut, une échelle pour aller sur le toit (pour laver les vêtements) ; la maison de Rahel, la maison bleue : grande, il y a une grande porte bleue et des fenêtres bleues à l'étage ; il y a un balcon rond 3) Rahel habite la deuxième maison. Elle est riche. Elle est célibataire ; elle a toujours refusé le mariage. Une femme riche et indépendante qui habite seule n'est pas habituelle dans cette société.

« Tu sais, Gazelle, quand j'étais toute petite, il n'y avait pas de plus beau quartier que le Mellah. »

Zinna commençait toujours ainsi. Elle s'asseyait sur la plage, et Tomi se mettait à côté d'elle. C'était généralement le matin…

« Alors, nous habitions une maison très vieille, étroite, juste une pièce en bas où couchait mon père avec mon oncle Moché, et moi j'étais dans la chambre du haut. Il y avait une échelle[1] pour grimper[2] sur le toit, là où était le lavoir[3]. C'était moi qui lavais le linge, quelquefois Khadija venait m'aider, elle était grosse, elle n'arrivait pas à grimper l'échelle, il fallait[4] la pousser. À côté de chez nous, il y avait la maison bleue. Elle n'était pas bleue, mais on l'appelait comme ça parce qu'elle avait une grande porte peinte en bleu, et les fenêtres à l'étage aussi étaient peintes en bleu. Il y avait surtout une fenêtre très haute, au premier, qui donnait sur un balcon rond. C'était la maison d'une vieille femme qu'on appelait la tante Rahel, mais elle n'était pas vraiment notre tante. On disait qu'elle était très riche, qu'elle n'avait jamais voulu se marier. Elle vivait[5] toute seule dans cette grande maison, avec ce balcon où les pigeons venaient se percher. Tous les jours, j'allais voir sa maison. De son balcon, je rêvais[6] qu'on pouvait voir tout le paysage, la ville, la rivière avec les barques qui traversaient, jusqu'à la mer. La vieille Rahel n'ouvrait jamais sa fenêtre, elle ne se mettait jamais au balcon pour regarder… »

[1]*ladder* [2]*climb* [3]*washtub* [4]*it was necessary* [5]*lived* [6]*imagined*

Key: En regardant de plus près
1) l'emploi de l'imparfait et des adverbes comme *toujours, généralement* 2) Il y avait une échelle pour aller sur le toit. Zinna lavait les vêtements là. Khadija l'aidait quelquefois. Elle était grosse et Zinna devait la pousser parce qu'elle avait des difficultés pour monter. 3) Rahel n'ouvrait jamais sa fenêtre ; elle ne regardait jamais la vue de son balcon. Zinna imagine qu'on peut voir la campagne, la ville, la rivière, des bateaux et même la mer.

Key: Après avoir lu Zinna est jeune et sa famille n'a pas beaucoup d'argent. Ses activités sont routines (par exemple, laver les vêtements) et assez limitées. Rahel est vieille et riche, et Zinna imagine qu'elle a beaucoup de possibilités (par exemple qu'elle peut voir beaucoup de choses de son balcon). Ces possibilités évoquent la curiosité de la jeune Zinna et lui donne envie de découvrir d'autres choses que sa maison et son quartier.

C. En regardant de plus près. Maintenant, considérez la structure et la signification de ce texte.

1. Au début, comment est-ce que nous savons que Tomi (Gazelle) a l'habitude d'entendre des histoires de la vie de Zinna dans le Mellah ?
2. Zinna a un souvenir très précis du toit de sa maison d'enfance : décrivez les activités et les personnes qui font partie de cette mémoire.
3. Zinna compare le toit de sa maison avec le balcon de sa voisine, Rahel. Qu'est-ce que nous apprenons de la vie de Rahel ? Zinna n'a pas visité le balcon de la maison de Rahel. Quelles sortes de choses est-ce qu'elle imagine être possible du balcon de Rahel ?

D. Après avoir lu. Discutez de ces questions avec vos camarades de classe.

1. Quelles sont les différences entre Zinna et Rahel ? Pourquoi est-ce que ces différences sont importantes ?
2. Est-ce que vous avez le souvenir d'un endroit lié avec une personne qui a marqué votre imagination ? Quelle idée est-ce que vous associez à cet endroit ?

Venez chez nous ! À la découverte de la France : les régions

La naissance de la France

On ne peut pas donner une date précise à la naissance de la France. Les frontières de la France d'aujourd'hui ne sont pas des frontières naturelles. En fait, l'Hexagone est le résultat de guerres[1] et d'autres évènements[2] politiques qui ont réuni[3] peu à peu des peuples de langues et de cultures différentes, par exemple, les Alsaciens, qui parlent encore des dialectes allemands, et les Corses, qui parlent une langue proche[4] de l'italien.

Le royaume[5] de France s'est constitué aux XIe et XIIe siècles[6] autour de Paris. Ensuite, le royaume de France s'est étendu[7] vers le sud où l'on trouve encore des gens qui parlent des dialectes occitans[8]. Puis, d'autres régions ont été ajoutées[9] à ce nouvel ensemble[10] : la Bretagne en 1532 ; le Pays Basque en 1620 ; le Roussillon (la région autour de Perpignan) en 1659 ; la Flandre en 1713 ; l'Alsace en 1681 ; la Corse en 1768 ; la Savoie et la région de Nice en 1860.

La Flandre
L'Alsace
La Bretagne
pays de langue d'oïl
pays de langue d'oc
La Savoie
Nice
Le Roussillon
Le Pays Basque
la Corse

[1]*wars* [2]*events* [3]*brought together* [4]*close* [5]*kingdom* [6]*centuries* [7]*extended* [8]*dialects spoken in the South of France* [9]*added* [10]*entity*

Presentation: To introduce this lesson and provide an overview of the diversity of the French regions, show the **Venez chez nous !** video montage (*À la découverte de la France : les régions*). See whether students can identify various regions and/or specific sites. You might add slides and photos to enrich this presentation.

Presentation: As you work with this passage, ask students to point out on a map (MFL, Ch. 6; MFL, Maps) the various regions mentioned. Have them compare the development of modern-day France with the development of the U.S., from the thirteen original colonies to the addition of the Louisiana Purchase, to the additions of Florida, Texas, California, Alaska, etc.

Lisons

6-40 L'identité de la France : la pluralité culturelle

A. Avant de lire. This excerpt from a history-geography textbook for French high school students discusses the cultural diversity apparent in the various regions in France. Follow the progression of the passage by identifying the main idea of each paragraph; at the end, you should be able to articulate the essential points of this discussion. Then fill in the details about regional differences and similarities that complement the main ideas.

Stratégie

In a long passage, identify the main idea of each paragraph as you read. This will help you understand each paragraph's overall content and ultimately the progression and meaning of the passage as a whole.

Key: En lisant 1) b 2) a 3) b, c 4) a

B. En lisant. Trouvez la réponse (ou les réponses) à chaque question.

1. Quelle est l'idée principale du premier paragraphe ?
   a. La France est un pays uniforme et homogène.
   b. Chaque région de France est un peu différente à cause du contact entre les peuples qui sont arrivés plus récemment et les peuples qui étaient déjà là.
   c. Il faut respecter les habitudes et les coutumes des peuples qui sont originaires de chaque région.
2. Le deuxième paragraphe parle principalement des différences...
   a. linguistiques b. culturelles c. sociales
3. Selon le troisième paragraphe, les régions de France...
   a. sont toutes assez similaires.
   b. ont leurs propres identités.
   c. ont leurs propres coutumes.
4. Le dernier paragraphe conclut que la distinction principale en France actuelle peut se résumer à la différence entre...
   a. le Nord et le Sud.
   b. la langue d'oc et la langue d'oïl.
   c. l'Est et l'Ouest.

Un village aux toits de tuiles rondes à Roquebrune sur la Côte d'Azur.

Des maisons aux toits de tuiles plates en Normandie.

Un village aux toits d'ardoise en Bretagne.

La pluralité culturelle

Des apports multiples

La France est un creuset[1] humain et culturel.... Les peuples qui se sont installés dans une région y ont imposé certaines de leurs habitudes, mais ils ont aussi transformé leurs usages au contact des populations autochtones[2]...

Certains contrastes anciens ont aujourd'hui disparu.... Les divisions linguistiques se sont atténuées[3] et si quelques langues régionales comme le breton, le basque et le corse se maintiennent, la généralisation du français et le brassage[4] des populations ont minimisé l'opposition entre pays de langue d'oïl[5] et pays de langue d'oc[6].

France du Nord, France du Sud

La France forme une mosaïque complexe de provinces, qui ont une identité historique forte et des modes de vie assez homogènes. On identifie encore, à juste titre, les Normands, les Bourguignons, les Angevins, les Provençaux ou les Béarnais, et chacune de leurs régions a sa propre cuisine, son folklore, ses proverbes et ses coutumes pour les grands moments de la vie sociale (comme les baptêmes ou les mariages).

À l'échelle[7] nationale cependant[8], la division Nord-Sud semble s'imposer plus que toute autre.... On utilise toujours la tuile plate[9] dans la France du Nord, la tuile ronde[10] dans le Sud et l'ardoise[11] dans l'Ouest armoricain[12], mais plus importantes sont les différences de comportement[13] : par exemple, ... dans le domaine sportif : grandes villes exceptées, une France méridionale[14] du rugby s'oppose à une France septentrionale[15] du football ; et dans le domaine culinaire : une France du beurre au nord fait face à une France de l'huile au sud.

[1]*melting pot* [2]*indigenous* [3]*diminished* [4]*mixing* [5]*name given to the languages (where* oïl *meant* oui*) spoken in the North of France* [6]*name given to the languages (where* oc *meant* oui*) spoken in the South of France* [7]*scale* [8]*however* [9]*flat roofing tile* [10]*rounded roofing tile* [11]*slate roofing* [12]*Bretagne* [13]*behavior* [14]*du Sud* [15]*du Nord*

Extrait de: *Geographie 1er: La France en Europe et dans le monde.* Sous la direction de J.L. Mathieu.

C. En regardant de plus près. Maintenant examinez quelques caractéristiques du texte.

1. D'après le texte, quelles langues régionales est-ce qu'on parle toujours ? Identifiez la région de chaque langue sur la carte.
2. D'après le troisième paragraphe, qu'est-ce qui distingue les régions différentes ?
3. Complétez le tableau avec les principales différences entre le Nord et le Sud de la France.

	le Nord	**le Sud**
la langue		
la construction des maisons		
la cuisine		
le sport		

Key: En regardant de plus près 1) le breton [parlé en Bretagne], le basque [parlé dans le sud-ouest près de la frontière espagnole], le corse [parlé en Corse] 2) la cuisine, le folklore, les proverbes, les coutumes pour les baptêmes et les mariages 3) le Nord : les langues d'oïl ; tuiles plates ou l'ardoise ; le beurre ; le foot ; le Sud : les langues d'oc ; tuiles rondes ; l'huile ; le rugby

D. Après avoir lu. Discutez de ces questions avec vos camarades de classe.

1. Est-ce que vous pouvez identifier des caractéristiques particulières d'une ou de plusieurs régions aux États-Unis ou au Canada ? Trouvez des exemples avec un/e partenaire.
2. Est-ce qu'il y a aux États-Unis, comme en France, une division majeure entre le Nord et le Sud ? Expliquez votre réponse.

Key: Après avoir lu 1) Students may come up with differences in food, in accent, in climate, in sports (e.g., the importance of high school football in Texas or basketball in rural Indiana), in housing styles . . . 2) Students will probably answer that there are differences between the North and the South and may well link this to the Civil War, but that there are also differences between the East Coast and the West Coast; they may also mention regions like New England, the Midwest, the Pacific Northwest, the Gulf Coast, etc.

Les régions et les langues de France

Les habitants des régions françaises ont conservé une partie de leur culture à travers la musique, les fêtes et la cuisine régionales. La diversité culturelle se manifeste aussi par la langue. Dans ces régions, on entend encore parler les langues traditionnelles. Les communautés locales font un effort pour préserver ces langues, et on commence à enseigner les langues régionales à l'école. Voici quelques exemples de la langue de ces régions qui, tous, veulent dire : « Venez chez nous en... ! »

- En Bretagne, le breton : **Deit genomb é Breizh !**
- Dans la région de Dunkerque, le flamand : **Kom bij ons in Vlanders !**
- En Alsace et en Lorraine, des dialectes allemands : **Komme zü uns ens Elsass !**
- En Corse, le corse : **Venite in Corsica !**
- Dans le Roussillon, une variété de catalan : **Vine a veure'ns al Roselló !**
- Au Pays Basque, le basque : **Zatozte Euskal herrirat !**
- Dans tout le Midi, des dialectes occitans : **Venetz en Occitania !**

ET VOUS ?

1. Avec un/e partenaire, faites une liste des régions des États-Unis. Quelles sortes de spécialités (la cuisine, la musique, les fêtes) est-ce qu'on trouve dans ces régions ?
2. D'après vous, est-ce qu'il existe des langues régionales aux États-Unis comme en France ? Expliquez.

Note: The regional languages of France include four Romance languages: *le catalan, le corse, l'occitan, le franco-provençal;* three Germanic languages: *le flamand, l'alsacien, le lorrain* ; one Celtic language: *le breton* ; and one language of unknown origin: *le basque.* In 2001, the French government modified its language policy to recognize the internal linguistic diversity of the country as well as its overseas departments and collectivities; it now recognizes 76 different languages of France, spoken in France and the *Outre-mer.* See the *Chez nous* Companion Website for more information.

Note: Et vous ? The U.S. Census defines four regions: the Midwest, the South, the Northeast, and the West; students may identify others as well.

Un bel exemple du folklore régional : le « Mai » ou la fête de Nice, sur la Côte d'Azur ; en niçois (une variété de l'occitan) : lu « Mai » o lu festin de Nissa.

Combien de régions différentes est-ce que vous pouvez associer aux images sur ces beaux timbres ?

Implementation: Have students look at the stamps and see if they can identify the regions with which the various specialties illustrated on the stamps are associated. *Les mirabelles* are a type of plum grown in the regions of Alsace and Lorraine and used primarily in fine pastries and liqueurs; *le carnaval* occurs in Nice and in Martinique/ Guadeloupe; *le Roquefort* is a cheese from the *département* of Aveyron in the South of France between Toulouse and Montpelier; *l'huile d'olive* is used throughout the south as indicated in the reading; *les hortillonnages* refer to "floating" gardens built along a series of canals in Amiens in the North of France that date back to Gallo-Roman times.

Presentation: Show Seillans on a map of France. The *Chez nous* Companion Website has information about Seillans and about the other *villages classés*. See the SAM/MFL for additional activities related to the **Observons**.

Script: Observons

MONSIEUR LE MAIRE DE SEILLANS : Oui, eh bien, nous sommes dans un vieux village provençal. Euh, Seillans fait partie des 148 plus beaux villages de France. Il a été sélectionné parce qu'il a un patrimoine très ancien, qui a gardé tout son caractère, son authenticité et euh beaucoup de charme... . Ce village comprend aussi euh de nombreuses fontaines, des placettes ombragées. Euh, c'est un village typiquement provençal parce qu'il est perché, sur une colline. Et en cette saison, en automne, on a le plaisir de découvrir des paysages magnifiques... . C'est un village provençal aussi qui a son terroir, avec la culture de l'olivier, de la vigne... donc des produits locaux qui sont très appréciés.

GRAND-PÈRE ROUSTAN : C'est... C'est du vin. C'est du vin de Seillans. Château de Selves.

Observons

6-41 Visitons Seillans

A. Avant de regarder. Dans cette séquence vidéo, nous allons « visiter Seillans ». Seillans se trouve dans le Midi de la France, pas très loin de la Côte d'Azur. Regardez la photo de Seillans pour répondre à ces questions.

1. Qui est la personne qui va faire le guide dans la séquence vidéo, à votre avis ?
2. Seillans, c'est un centre urbain, une grande ville ou un petit village ?
3. À votre avis, quels aspects de Seillans est-ce que le guide va nous montrer ?

B. En regardant. Maintenant, regardez la séquence vidéo pour trouver la bonne réponse.

1. Seillans se trouve dans quelle région de la France ?
2. Seillans, c'est un village classé : pourquoi ?
3. À Seillans, vous allez remarquer (cochez les bonnes réponses) :

_____ des belles fontaines	_____ des églises romanes
_____ des villas magnifiques	_____ des collines boisées
_____ des petites places avec des arbres	_____ des paysages spectaculaires

4. Quels sont les produits locaux bien appréciés ?

_____ le vin	_____ les olives
_____ la lavande	_____ le coton

C. Après avoir regardé. D'après la description, est-ce que Seillans est un endroit que vous voudriez visiter ? Pourquoi ?

Écrivons

6-42 La ville de…

A. Avant d'écrire. Préparez une brochure publicitaire sur une ville de France qui vous intéresse. Pour commencer, identifiez les personnes pour qui vous allez préparer la brochure : est-ce qu'elles sont sportives, artistiques, gastronomes, adultes, étudiants, enfants… ? Ensuite, en fonction de leurs intérêts, répondez aux questions suivantes en consultant des guides, des vidéos touristiques et des sites Internet.

1. Où se trouve cette ville en France ? (près de la mer ? à côté de Paris ? à la montagne ?)
2. Quels sont les sites touristiques les plus intéressants dans cette ville ? Décrivez-les.
3. Quelles activités est-ce qu'on peut y pratiquer ? Est-ce qu'il y a des activités, par exemple, pour les personnes qui aiment le sport, les beaux-arts, l'histoire ? pour les enfants, les jeunes, les personnes âgées ?

B. En écrivant. Maintenant, utilisez vos informations pour rédiger un texte (quatre petits paragraphes) qui décrit la ville. N'oubliez pas les personnes pour qui vous préparez la brochure. Regardez comme modèle la brochure pour Marseille à la page suivante qui a comme public les sportifs et les gens qui aiment l'histoire. Pour élaborer votre projet, vous pouvez ajouter des images (photos, dessins, tableaux) de la ville. Donnez un titre à votre brochure.

C. En révisant. Réfléchissez aux questions suivantes et faites tous les changements nécessaires.

1. Relisez votre brochure pour analyser le contenu : est-ce que vous avez décrit des sites et des activités qui vont probablement intéresser votre public ?
2. Relisez de nouveau votre brochure pour analyser le style et la forme : est-ce que vous donnez une description vive et colorée de la région ? Est-ce que vous avez inclus des photos, des tableaux ou des dessins ?

D. Après avoir écrit. Présentez votre ville à vos camarades de classe et essayez de les persuader de la visiter.

Stratégie

When preparing a promotional brochure, think about who your readers will be and how best to reach them with well-chosen content and an enticing presentation.

Présentation: As an introduction to the writing activity, treat the brochure as a reading. Have students look at the pictures on the cover to get some ideas about where the city is located and what kinds of activities can be done there. Then have them look at the various subsections of the brochure and summarize the information that can be gleaned from each part. Ask them what type of additional information they would want to include about the city they will be presenting. Refer students to the *Chez nous* Companion Website for links to cities and regions in France.

Expansion: As an alternative follow-up, divide the class into two groups: one group staffs "tourist booths" to promote their city; the other group circulates to gain information about each city. Then switch roles.

Parlons

6-43 Un voyage en France. Imaginez qu'avec deux de vos amis, vous décidez de faire un voyage de quinze jours en France cet été. Mais dans le groupe, il y a des personnalités très différentes :

1. Une personne est très sportive. Il/Elle adore assister à des matchs de tennis et de foot et il/elle aime bien faire de la marche, du canoë et du kayak.
2. Une personne se spécialise en histoire de l'art. Il/Elle veut visiter tous les musées possibles.
3. Une personne est très pantouflarde. Il/Elle veut faire le moins possible et surtout se détendre au maximum.

Implementation: 6-43 Add variety to the **Parlons** activity by creating other "characters" or adding further specifications, for example, person A has mobility issues, person B dislikes museums, person C has a lot of food allergies, etc. Have students present their dialogues and/or itineraries to the class.

Lieu d'habitat prédestiné depuis 28000 ans, Marseille compte près d'un million d'habitants.

Paradis des plongeurs et des plaisanciers, les loisirs se pratiquent ici en pleine nature et toute l'année. Le bleu est sa couleur quotidienne.

À Découvrir, à Visiter

Les Monuments

Abbaye de Saint-Victor Bus 54, 55, 60, 61, 80 81 E5

Fondée au Ve siècle par Jean Cassien sur la sépulture de Saint-Victor, martyr romain mort au IIIe siècle.

Château d'If (point de vue) Métro 1 Vieux Port + Bateau C6

Ancienne forteresse construite sous François Ier en 1524… Le roman d'Alexandre Dumas, « le Comte de Monte Cristo » l'a rendu célèbre.

Les Musées

Musée des Beaux-Arts Métro 2, Avenue Longchamp ; Bus 81 D3

Musée des Docks Romains Métro 1 Vieux Port D5

Musée d'Histoire de Marseille de Jardin des Vestiges Métro 1 Vieux Port D4

Le Parc Balnéaire du Prado

Métro 1 Castellane + bus 19

– **Plages du Roucas Blanc** (graviers, sable) : Pistes de vélo-cross, jeux d'enfants, jeu de boules, jeu de volley-ball, radeaux et plongeoirs, solarium

– **Plages du David** (galets) : Jeux de sable, 2 solariums

– **Plage des Véliplanchistes** : Réservée aux planches à voile

Le phare de Ploumanach, sur la côte de granit rose en Bretagne.

Le château de Castelnaud, au-dessus de la Dordogne en Aquitaine.

A. Avant de parler. Choisissez le rôle que vous allez jouer, et réfléchissez à vos projets préférés. Faites une petite liste des possibilités.

MODÈLE É1 Il faut s'arrêter d'abord à Paris pour voir les musées et les monuments, par exemple, Le Louvre, ...

B. En parlant. En groupes de trois, jouez les rôles. Essayez de persuader vos amis de visiter les sites qui vous intéressent et de faire les activités que vous préférez. Créez un itinéraire qui plaît à tout le monde.

MODÈLE É1 On s'arrête d'abord à Paris où je peux assister au tournoi de tennis Roland-Garros.
É2 Oui, et quand tu es aux matchs, je visite les musées, par exemple, ...
É3 Et moi, je peux m'installer à la terrasse d'un café pour regarder les gens.
É1 Et après trois jours, nous allons à...

C. Après avoir parlé. Partagez votre itinéraire avec les autres étudiants. Qui a l'itinéraire le plus intéressant ? Qui visite le plus grand nombre de villes ? Qui fait le plus de kilomètres ?

Now that you have completed *Chapitre 6*, can you do the following in French?

- ☐ describe where you live?
- ☐ state dates, distances, and numbers over a thousand?
- ☐ use direct- and indirect-object pronouns to avoid repetition?
- ☐ make suggestions using the **imparfait**?
- ☐ describe situations and habitual actions in the past using the **imparfait**?
- ☐ describe the notion of regionalism in France and describe various geographical features of France?

Leçon 1

pour décrire un immeuble	***to describe a building***
un ascenseur	*elevator*
un bâtiment	*building*
une cour	*courtyard*
des escaliers (m.)	*staircase, stairs*
un étage	*floor (of a building)*
un garage	*garage*
garer la voiture	*to park the car*
le rez-de-chaussée	*ground floor*
le sous-sol	*basement*
un/e voisin/e	*neighbor*

pour situer un immeuble	***to situate a building***
animé/e	*lively, animated*
un quartier (résidentiel)	*(residential) neighborhood*
une rue	*street*
tranquille	*quiet, tranquil*

pour parler d'un appartement	***to talk about an apartment***
un balcon	*balcony*
une chambre	*bedroom*
les charges (comprises) (f. pl.)	*utilities (included)*
un cinq-pièces	*3-bedroom apartment with living room and dining room*
un couloir	*hallway*
une cuisine	*kitchen*
donner sur	*to look onto or lead out to*
une entrée	*entrance, foyer*
un/e locataire	*renter*
louer	*to rent*
le loyer	*the rent*
un/une propriétaire	*homeowner; landlord/landlady*
une salle à manger	*dining room*
une salle de bains	*bathroom*
un séjour, une salle de séjour	*living room*
un studio	*studio apartment*
une terrasse	*terrace*
des toilettes (f.), des W.-C. (m.)	*toilet, water closet*

verbes en *-ir* comme *choisir*	***verbs ending in* -ir *like* choisir**
choisir	*to choose*
désobéir à	*to disobey*
finir	*to finish*
grandir	*to grow taller, to grow up (for children)*
grossir	*to gain weight*
maigrir	*to lose weight*
obéir à	*to obey*
pâlir	*to become pale*
punir	*to punish*
réfléchir à	*to think*
réussir à	*to succeed/to pass*
rougir	*to blush*

autres mots utiles	***other useful words***
chaque	*each*
même	*even, same*
pâle	*pale*
propre	*own*

à quel étage ?	***on what floor?***
RdeCh rez-de-chaussée	*ground floor*
1er premier	*first*
2e deuxième	*second*
3e troisième	*third*
10e dixième	*tenth*
11e onzième	*eleventh*
12e douzième	*twelfth*
13e treizième	*thirteenth*
19e dix-neuvième	*nineteenth*
20e vingtième	*twentieth*
21e vingt-et-unième	*twenty-first*

Leçon 2

des meubles (m.)	***furniture***
une armoire	*armoire, wardrobe*
un canapé	*couch*
une cuisinière	*stove*
une étagère	*bookcase, (book)shelf*
un évier	*sink*
un fauteuil	*armchair*
un four	*oven*
une lampe	*lamp*
un lit	*bed*
des placards (m.)	*cupboards, kitchen cabinets*
un réfrigérateur	*refrigerator*

Vocabulaire

des rideaux (m.)	*curtains*
une table basse	*coffee table*
un tapis	*rug*

pour décrire un appartement ou un meuble	***to describe an apartment or a piece of furniture***
abîmé/e	*worn, worn-out*
agréable	*pleasant*
ancien/ne	*old, antique*
le centre-ville	*downtown*
avec coin cuisine	*with a kitchenette*
confortable	*comfortable (said of objects or places)*
équipé/e	*equipped*
meublé/e	*furnished*
moderne	*modern*
un mur	*wall*
neuf/neuve	*brand-new*
par terre	*on the floor*
pratique	*practical*
rénové/e	*renovated*
sous les toits	*in the attic*
sous	*under*
sur	*on top of*
le toit	*roof*

autres mots utiles	***other useful words***
des affaires (f.)	*belongings, things*
coûter	*to cost*
ranger	*to put up, to put away*
surtout	*above all*

quelques verbes de communication et de transfert	***some verbs of communication and transfer***
apporter	*to bring*
emprunter	*to borrow*
expliquer	*to explain*
offrir (un cadeau)	*to give (a gift)*
prêter	*to lend*
remettre	*to hand in/over*

Leçon 3

la vie à la campagne	***life in the country***
aller à la pêche	*to go fishing*
se détendre	*to relax*
faire un pique-nique	*to picnic*
une ferme	*farm*
un jardin	*garden, yard*
un potager	*vegetable garden*
se promener	*to take a walk*
une villa	*house in a residential area, villa*

la nature	***nature***
un arbre (fruitier)	*(fruit) tree*
un bateau (à voile)	*(sail) boat*
un bois	*woods*
un champ	*field*
une colline	*hill*
un fleuve	*river (leading to the sea)*
une forêt	*forest*
un lac	*lake*
la mer	*sea*
une montagne	*mountain*
une plage	*beach*
une rivière	*large stream or river (tributary)*
un sapin	*evergreen tree*
une vallée	*valley*

quelques mots utiles	***some useful words***
au bord (du lac)	*on the shore (of the lake)*
au bord de la mer	*at the seashore*
un endroit	*place*
en effet	*yes, indeed*
formidable	*great*
il me semble	*it seems to me*
là(-bas)	*there*
s'occuper de	*to take care of*
posséder	*to own*
les vacances (f. pl.)	*vacation*

pour parler des activités habituelles dans le passé	***to talk about habitual activities in the past***
d'habitude	*usually*
le lundi	*every Monday, on Mondays*
quelquefois	*sometimes*
souvent	*often*
toujours	*always*
tous les jours/les soirs	*every day/evening*
toutes les semaines	*every week*
le week-end	*on weekends, every weekend*

7 Les relations personnelles

Quels sont les rapports entre les personnes ici ? Pour quelle occasion est-ce qu'elles se réunissent ?

After completing this chapter, you should be able to:

- Describe and narrate past events
- Report what others say and write
- Express opinions
- Express emotions
- Understand and describe ethnic diversity, rites, and rituals in the Francophone world

Leçon  Les jeunes et la vie

POINTS DE DÉPART

TEXT AUDIO
CD 4 TRACK 1

Les jeunes parlent

 discussions  blogs  mes sujets  mes messages  mes favoris  mes blogues 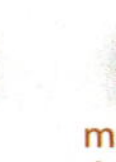 mon profil  messages échangés

Forum de discussion > Famille > Nos racines   Afficher réaction

Auteur	Message
Pierre **le mar. 7 avr. 09 à 15h08** 	Sur le temple d'Apollon à Delphes on trouve l'inscription « Connais-toi toi-même »[1]. Une façon de se connaître, c'est d'examiner ses racines. Quelles sont les expériences et les personnes qui vous ont influencées le plus ? Pour moi, mes parents ont divorcé quand j'avais cinq ans, et j'ai ressenti l'absence de mon père. Heureusement, mon grand-père était là. Ancien professeur, il m'a appris à aimer les livres, en particulier les livres d'histoire. Ma mère était toujours très autoritaire, très exigeante — et moi, j'étais un enfant rebelle. Mais aujourd'hui, à 22 ans, je prépare un diplôme en histoire et une carrière de professeur.
Sarah **le mar. 7 avr. 09 à 18h38** 	Je fais partie d'une famille assez « traditionnelle » : mon père travaille et ma mère, c'est une femme au foyer. J'ai des bons rapports avec mes parents. Ils m'ont donné une morale, une vision du monde, le goût du travail et une présence très sécurisante. Je n'ai pas de complexes ; je suis bien dans ma peau.
Alima **le mer. 8 avr. 09 à 9h10** 	Je suis franco-marocaine. J'ai commencé par refuser mes racines maghrébines, mais après j'ai compris que ces racines multiples (arabes, juives, françaises) sont une richesse fabuleuse. Par exemple, je ne suis pas vraiment pratiquante, mais je ne rate jamais le ramadan. Ce n'est pas une pratique imposée par ma famille, mais c'est une épreuve personnelle qui me permet de réfléchir, d'avancer dans la connaissance de ma personne. Être français, ce n'est pas se couler dans le moule[2] de la culture dominante. Tous avec nos racines, nous pouvons participer aux changements de la culture française et européenne.

[1]*Know thyself* [2]*to pour oneself into the mold*

Presentation: The entries provide students with models for talking about their own background and experiences. Have students discuss each entry. Point out that when *ancien* precedes the noun, it means "former." Also point out the expression *m'a appris à* and tell students that *apprendre* can be used to mean "to learn" or "to teach someone something" (*apprendre à quelqu'un à...*). Check students' comprehension of the following expressions by having them provide a paraphrase: *être autoritaire = dire aux autres ce qu'ils doivent faire ; une femme au foyer = une femme qui ne travaille pas hors de la maison ; avoir des bons rapports avec quelqu'un = bien s'entendre avec quelqu'un ; avoir le goût du travail = être travailleur / travailleuse ; être bien dans sa peau = avoir confiance en soi.* See the chart for logical groupings of the expressions. Using Ex. 7-1, have students provide definitions or explanations in French for the vocabulary highlighted in the box. Incorporate information from the **Vie et culture**. Ask students whether they can identify with the ideas expressed by any of the young people quoted here.

Vie et culture

Note: According to the 2000 U.S. Census, the majority of households consist of married couples (52%). The number of unmarried couples increased substantially from the 1990 census (from 3.2 to 5.5 million), but still represents only about 5% of the total number of households surveyed.

La famille à la carte

Qu'est-ce qu'une « famille » ? Avec ou sans enfants ? Deux parents, un seul, davantage[1] ? De quel sexe ? Nos idées sur la famille évoluent, et le vocabulaire le signale : on parle de familles monoparentales, de pères et de mères célibataires, de mères travailleuses et de pères absents, de familles recomposées, d'unions libres et de couples pacsés. En fait, le mariage « traditionnel », où la femme reste au foyer, est un phénomène devenu assez rare en France aujourd'hui : 80 % des Françaises de 25 à 49 ans travaillent. Et au lieu de[2] se marier, 15 % des couples en France choisissent de vivre ensemble en « union libre » ; c'est trois fois plus qu'il y a vingt ans. L'arrivée d'un enfant n'implique pas le mariage ; une naissance sur deux se produit hors du mariage.

À votre avis, est-ce que le mariage « traditionnel » est aussi rare en Amérique du nord qu'en France ? Justifiez votre réponse.

La diversité ethnique en France

Regardez à la page suivante quelques photos prises à Paris. Qu'est-ce qu'elles suggèrent sur l'origine des habitants de la capitale ? Il est difficile de préciser les chiffres[3] de l'immigration, mais la région parisienne, surtout les banlieues[4], accueille[5] un grand nombre d'étrangers et d'immigrés. Cette nouvelle réalité démographique est en même temps un défi[6] et une richesse pour la France. Un défi parce que ces populations ne s'intègrent pas toujours bien à la société française : le chômage[7] est en particulier un problème très grave pour les jeunes des banlieues. Une richesse aussi, parce que ces populations rajoutent leur cuisine, leur musique et leurs traditions à la culture de la France. On peut parler d'un « métissage culturel »[8] en France aujourd'hui, ce qui suggère l'image d'une tapisserie, tissée[9] de couleurs très variées.

[1]plus [2]*instead of* [3]les statistiques [4]*areas around Paris where recent immigrants live* [5]*welcome* [6]*challenge* [7]*unemployment* [8]*cultural mixing* [9]*woven*

Presentation: Use this note in conjunction with the vocabulary presentation. Have students examine the title and explain what it means to order "à la carte" in a restaurant; relate this notion to the concept of the family. Ask students to define the various terms included here (see Ex. 7-1). Help students link *pacsé* to *un pacs* (*Pacte civile de solidarité*), which was presented in the **Vie et culture** in L. 1 of Ch. 1. Point out the verb *vivre* and remind students that it refers to personal and quality-of-life considerations (*Ils vivent ensemble*) while *habiter* refers to physical location (*J'habite Paris*). The full conjugation for *vivre* is provided in Appendix 5. The video clip *Une famille, style marocain* features a young Moroccan woman living in Nice who describes her family in France and in Morocco.

Pour parler de la famille et des racines

un père/une mère célibataire
un homme/une femme au foyer
un père/une mère absent/e
une famille monoparentale/recomposée/étendue
un beau-père, une belle-mère, un beau-frère, une belle-sœur, les demi-frères et sœurs
les parents : être autoritaire, exigeant/e, indulgent/e
les enfants : être rebelle, être bien dans sa peau, avoir des complexes
avoir des bons rapports avec quelqu'un
avoir des racines multiculturelles

Un agent de police au Quartier latin.

Des élèves du lycée Charlemagne au Marais.

ET VOUS ?

1. Quelle est l'importance de l'immigration dans votre région ? Est-ce qu'on accueille un grand nombre d'immigrés ?
2. Est-ce que l'immigration constitue une richesse ou un défi pour votre région ? Quelles difficultés est-ce que les immigrés rencontrent chez vous ? Par exemple, est-ce qu'ils ont des difficultés à s'intégrer ou à trouver du travail ? Quels éléments culturels est-ce qu'ils apportent à votre région ?

Un couple au marché à St-Germain-des-Prés.

On fait des courses au marché Barbès (18e).

Implementation: The issue of immigration is politically charged, but the goal of this presentation is to recognize the challenges as well as the positive aspects of a diverse population, which is becoming the rule rather than the exception in societies today. Examine the photos, and encourage cross-cultural comparisons that invoke the history of the U.S. as a nation of immigrants and the challenges that immigration presents today.

À vous la parole

Implementation: 7-1 This exercise should be completed as the vocabulary is introduced.

7-1 Définitions. Trouvez une définition pour chaque expression.

MODÈLE une mère célibataire
C'est une mère qui n'a pas de partenaire.

1. une mère célibataire	a. un couple qui vit ensemble sans être marié
2. un homme au foyer	b. un père qui n'habite pas avec ses enfants
3. les racines	c. une famille avec un seul parent
4. un père absent	d. une famille avec des demi-frères ou sœurs
5. une famille monoparentale	e. une mère qui n'a pas de partenaire
6. une famille recomposée	f. les origines
7. l'union libre	g. un père qui reste à la maison et s'occupe de ses enfants

Implementation: 7-2 As you follow up, ask the class as a whole whether they agree or disagree with each statement.

7-2 D'accord ou pas d'accord ? Est-ce que vous êtes d'accord avec les assertions suivantes ? Parlez-en avec un/e partenaire et expliquez votre réponse.

MODÈLE Grandir dans une famille monoparentale, c'est une tragédie pour l'enfant.

É1 Si la famille étendue est là, ce n'est pas une tragédie.
É2 Voilà, et les amis peuvent aider la famille aussi. Donc, on n'est pas d'accord.

1. La famille exerce très peu d'influence sur les jeunes.
2. On apprécie toujours des parents autoritaires.
3. Les racines multiples, c'est une richesse.
4. Les jeunes veulent toujours être différents de leurs parents.
5. Une femme au foyer, c'est mieux pour les enfants.
6. Être français, c'est s'assimiler à la culture dominante.
7. Le divorce n'a pas d'impact sur les enfants.
8. Les enfants qui grandissent dans une famille monoparentale ont toujours des complexes.

Additional activity: For additional practice, use the following pair activity. To follow up, have students compare answers with the whole class.
Cause probable. Avec un/e partenaire, expliquez comment on est probablement arrivé à la situation décrite.

MODÈLE Fatima n'est pas pratiquante.
É1 Peut-être qu'elle a refusé ses racines.
É2 Ou peut-être que ses parents n'ont pas imposé leurs pratiques religieuses.

1. Lucie est bien dans sa peau.
2. Laurent a été un enfant rebelle.
3. C'est la mère de Julien qui a dû exercer l'autorité parentale.
4. Nathalie fait partie d'une famille recomposée.
5. Sandrine a le goût du travail.
6. Hervé fait partie d'une famille traditionnelle.
7. Hélène a ressenti l'absence de son père.

7-3 Et vous ? Avec un/e partenaire, complétez les phrases suivantes selon votre propre expérience.

MODÈLE Mes parents m'ont appris...

É1 Mes parents m'ont appris à aimer la musique classique.
É2 Et moi, mon père m'a appris à apprécier la nature.

1. Mes parents m'ont appris...
2. J'étais un enfant...
3. Ma famille, c'est une famille...
4. J'ai des bons rapports avec...
5. Mes racines sont...
6. Je suis bien dans ma peau parce que...

FORMES ET FONCTIONS

1. *Les verbes de communication* écrire, lire *et* dire

- Here are three useful verbs of communication: **écrire**, *to write*; **lire**, *to read*; **dire**, *to say, to tell.*

SINGULIER		PLURIEL	
je/j'	écris	nous	écriv**ons**
	lis		lis**ons**
	dis		dis**ons**
tu	écris	vous	écriv**ez**
	lis		lis**ez**
	dis		**dites**
il / elle / on	écrit	ils / elles	écriv**ent**
	lit		lis**ent**
	dit		dis**ent**

IMPÉRATIF :	Écris !	Écrivons !	Écrivez !
	Lis !	Lisons !	Lisez !
	Dis !	Disons !	**Dites** !
PASSÉ COMPOSÉ :	il a **écrit**	il a **lu**	il a **dit**

Presentation: To present the verb *dire*, demonstrate how one says *Bonjour !* in various countries: En Allemagne, ils disent *Guten Tag !* En Italie, on dit *Buon giorno !* et vous, vous dites *Hello !* Ask students to summarize the forms of this irregular verb, then compare the verb charts for all three verbs. Stress the importance of a clear release of the final consonant in the third-person plural: *écrit* vs. *écrivent ; lit* vs. *lisent ; dit* vs. *disent ;* point out the irregular form *dites*, and ask students what other verbs they know show this irregularity (*être/êtes ; faire/faites*).

- **Décrire**, *to describe*, is conjugated like **écrire**.
- All these verbs may take direct and indirect objects.

J'écris **une lettre à mes parents**.	*I'm writing a letter to my parents.*
Tu **leur** dis **bonjour** de ma part ?	*Will you say hello to them for me?*
Tu **lui** as écrit ?	*Did you write to him?*
Décris **ton cousin à Gabriel**.	*Describe your cousin to Gabriel.*
Vous écrivez **votre rapport** pour demain ?	*Are you writing your report for tomorrow?*
Elles ne mentent jamais ; elles disent toujours **la vérité**.	*They never lie; they always tell the truth.*
Elle lit **ses poèmes à ses amis**, mais elle ne **les** lit pas **à ses parents**.	*She reads her poems to her friends, but she doesn't read them to her parents.*

À vous la parole

Initial practice: Begin with a discrimination drill, singular vs. plural, for all three verbs. One person, or more? *Ils disent bonjour. Elle lit le journal. Il écrit une lettre. Ils lisent beaucoup. Elle ne dit pas grand-chose. Elles écrivent bien. Ils disent toujours « oui ». Il lit des articles. Elles lisent un magazine,* etc. Follow with substitution drills: *Elle écrit une lettre ; nous. —Nous écrivons une lettre,* etc.

Key: 7-4 1) *ja* 2) *oui* 3) *da* 4) *sí* 5) *oui, ja* 6) *yes* 7) *ja, oui, sì* 8) *yes*

7-4 Étudiants étrangers. Tout le monde est d'accord ! Comment est-ce que ces étudiants disent « oui » ? Choisissez un mot de la liste : **oui, da, ja, sì, sí, yes.**

MODÈLE Maria est espagnole.
Elle dit « sí ».

1. Peter et Helmut sont allemands.
2. Louis-Jean est haïtien.
3. Moi, je suis russe.
4. Isabel est mexicaine.
5. Michèle et moi, nous sommes belges.
6. Toi, tu es américaine.
7. Georges et toi, vous êtes suisses.
8. Alan, il est anglais.

Expansion: 7-5 The verb *lire* does not have its own exercise, but you could expand on Ex. 7-5 by asking students what these people read (e.g., #1, *Nous écrivons des programmes et nous lisons des livres d'informatique*). The verb *lire* will be recycled in Ch. 11, L. 3 with the presentation of various reading materials.

7-5 Qu'est-ce qu'ils écrivent ? Choisissez dans la liste ce qu'écrivent ces jeunes gens.

MODÈLE Marc travaille pour le journal de l'université.
Il écrit des articles.

des articles	des critiques	des essais	des lettres
des poèmes	des programmes	des recettes	

1. Amélie et moi, nous étudions l'informatique.
2. Maxime et toi, vous êtes bons correspondants.
3. Je suis étudiant en littérature.
4. Laetitia aime faire la cuisine.
5. Jessica et Florian sont poètes.
6. Tu travailles pour un magazine.
7. Adrien va souvent au théâtre.

Implementation: 7-6 Use as a mixing activity. Tell students to ask no more than two questions per person before moving on to another student. Limit time, and follow up by having students ask questions about the items they did not find. Synthesize the information gathered: how many people read a newspaper every day? How often do students write to their parents? What was the hardest category to get a positive response for?, etc.

7-6 Sondage. Trouvez une personne qui…

MODÈLE lit le journal tous les jours
É1 Est-ce que tu lis le journal tous les jours ?
É2 Oui, je lis le *New York Times*.
OU Non, je ne lis pas le journal.

1. lit le journal tous les jours
2. écrit souvent à ses parents
3. dit toujours la vérité
4. écrit pour le journal de l'université
5. a lu une biographie récemment
6. va écrire des e-mails ce soir
7. lit son horoscope tous les jours
8. a écrit un poème

2. *Imparfait et passé composé : description et narration*

Both the **passé composé** and the **imparfait** express past actions and states. They serve different functions in a narrative, however.

- The **passé composé** indicates that an event in the past has been completed. In a story or narrative, the **passé composé** is used to recount actions or events that move the story forward. In other words, the **passé composé** advances the plot; it answers the question, *What happened?* Consider the opening sentences of the following narrative:

Bruno **a terminé** ses études en juin. Il **a quitté** la fac.	*Bruno finished his studies in June. He left the university.*

- In contrast, the **imparfait** provides background information. It describes the setting or situation and answers the questions: *What were the circumstances? What was going on?* Compare the use of the **passé composé** and the **imparfait** as the narrative about Bruno's experience continues:

Bruno **était** fatigué. Il **voulait** prendre des vacances. Mais il n'**avait** pas d'argent. Il **devait** trouver un emploi. Alors il **a lu** les petites annonces. Et il **a écrit** des lettres. Enfin, un jour, il **a eu** une réponse. Il **était** très heureux.	*Bruno was tired. He wanted to take a vacation. But he didn't have any money. He needed to find work. So he read the newspaper ads. And he wrote letters. Finally one day he got a response. He was very happy.*

- Use the **imparfait** to describe time, weather, ongoing actions, physical characteristics, psychological states and feelings, intentions, and thoughts. The following verbs, when used in the past, will more often appear in the **imparfait**.

avoir	Elle **avait** vingt ans en 2009.
devoir	Elle **devait** travailler comme serveuse.
être	Ils **étaient** contents de terminer leurs études.
penser	Je **pensais** qu'elle avait des bons rapports avec ses parents.
pouvoir	Ils ne **pouvaient** pas trouver d'emploi.
vouloir	Il ne **voulait** pas habiter avec ses parents.

Presentation: Review the forms and uses of the *passé composé* and the *imparfait* before introducing this topic. This section contrasting the two tenses focuses on the functions of description and narration; the terms "background" and "foreground" can also be used. Have students study the examples in the second bulleted point to decide whether they involve description or narration; for visual impact, you might divide these examples into two columns.

Fiche pratique

Certain verbs, when used in the past, generally occur in the **imparfait**. When these verbs are used in the **passé composé**, they have a specific meaning. Compare, for example : **Elle avait dix ans.** *(She was ten years old.)* and **Elle a eu dix ans.** *(She turned ten / celebrated her tenth birthday.)*

Presentation: Provide additional examples related to the **Fiche pratique** : *Ils ont été à Paris* (They went to Paris); *Elle n'a pas voulu le faire* (She refused to do it.).

À vous la parole

7-7 Des excuses. Pourquoi est-ce que ces gens ne sont pas venus en classe ? Expliquez la situation ou l'évènement, selon le cas.

MODÈLE Vanessa : elle / être malade
→ Vanessa n'est pas venue parce qu'elle était malade.
David : il / tomber dans les escaliers
→ David n'est pas venu parce qu'il est tombé dans les escaliers.

1. Ben : sa mère / téléphoner
2. Adrien : il / rater l'autobus
3. Marie : elle / dormir
4. Guillaume : son chien / manger ses devoirs
5. Annick : elle / préparer un examen
6. Grégory : il / travailler à la bibliothèque
7. Claire : elle / avoir un accident
8. Koffi : il / devoir terminer un rapport

Note: 7-7 Students have seen the past participle of *venir* in Ch. 5, L. 3. The full conjugation will be presented in Ch. 9, L. 2.

Key: 7-7 1) *lui a téléphoné* 2) *a raté* 3) *dormait* 4) *a mangé* 5) *préparait* 6) *travaillait* 7) *a eu* 8) *devait terminer*

Expansion: After completing Ex. 7-7, have students give you their own excuses for not coming to class, not doing their homework, etc.

Key: 7-8 1) *faisait* 2) *avait* 3) *allais* 4) *est passée* 5) *j'ai essayé, ne pouvais pas* 6) *j'ai heurté* 7) *sont sortis* 8) *n'étaient pas* 9) *j'étais, n'a été blessé* 10) *j'ai téléphoné* 11) *sont arrivés.*

7-8 Un accident de voiture.

Racontez cette histoire au passé ; employez le passé composé ou l'imparfait, selon le cas.

MODÈLE Il est huit heures du soir.
Il était huit heures du soir.

(1) Il fait très froid. (2) Il y a du verglas (*ice*) sur la route. (3) Je vais un peu vite (*fast*). (4) Soudain, une autre voiture passe devant moi. (5) J'essaie de m'arrêter, mais je ne peux pas. (6) Je heurte (*hit*) l'autre voiture. (7) Deux hommes sortent de cette voiture. (8) Ils ne sont pas contents. (9) Mais moi, je suis content parce que personne n'est blessé (*injured*). (10) Je téléphone à la police. (11) Ils arrivent tout de suite après.

Key: 7-9 *Hier, c'était samedi. Adrien s'est réveillé à huit heures. Il n'avait pas de cours. Adrien était à table. Le téléphone a sonné. C'était Julie. Elle voulait jouer au tennis. Adrien a dit « oui ». L'après-midi, ils ont joué au tennis. Adrien est tombé. Julie était anxieuse. Ils sont allés à l'hôpital. Le médecin a dit que ce n'était pas sérieux.*

Implementation: 7-9 To simplify, lead students through the story by asking questions as you display the drawings (MFL, Ch. 7). Then have students use the key expressions provided (plus others, if you like) to describe their day yesterday. Use your own day as a model. Let students work in pairs and report back what they learned about their partner's day.

7-9 Racontez une histoire.

Racontez la journée d'Adrien d'après les dessins et en utilisant les mots-clés.

MODÈLE Hier, c'était samedi. Adrien s'est réveillé à huit heures, etc.

A. être samedi, se réveiller, ne pas avoir cours

B. être à table, le téléphone/sonner, être Julie, vouloir jouer au tennis, dire oui

C. l'après-midi, jouer au tennis, tomber, être anxieuse

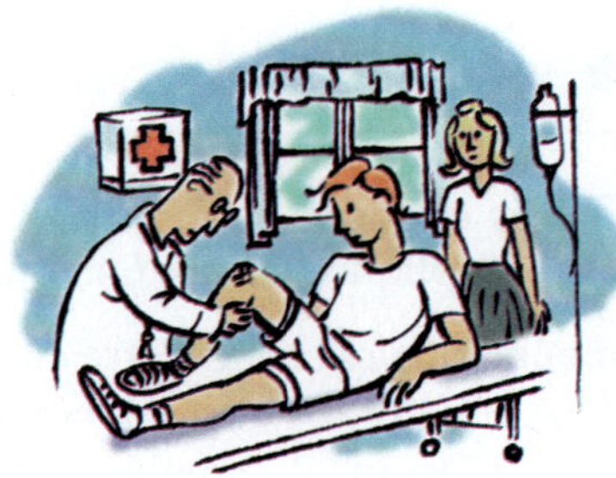

D. aller à l'hôpital, le médecin / dire / ne pas être sérieux

Maintenant, racontez votre journée d'hier à un/e partenaire.

7-10 Vérifier des alibis. On a volé (*stole*) le gâteau d'anniversaire du professeur entre midi et treize heures ! Avec un/e partenaire, préparez un alibi. Mettez-vous d'accord sur tous les détails. Attention ! Vos camarades de classe vont vous séparer et ensuite essayer de casser votre alibi en vous posant des questions très détaillées !

MODÈLE É1 Où étiez-vous hier à midi ?
É2 Mon copain et moi, nous étions au gymnase.
É3 Qu'est-ce que vous faisiez ?
É2 Moi, je jouais au basket et lui aussi.

Implementation: 7-10 To help students prepare their alibis, list questions they might be asked: *Entre midi et treize heures, où est-ce que vous étiez ? Qu'est-ce que vous faisiez ? Quels vêtements est-ce que vous portiez ? De quoi est-ce que vous parliez ? Qui est-ce que vous avez vu ? Qu'est-ce que vous avez mangé ?*, etc. Give the class a few minutes to prepare their alibis, then for each pair, send one student into the hallway while the class questions his/her partner. Everyone must take notes, then try to break the alibi by asking the same questions of the second student when he/she re-enters the classroom. The first group to have their alibi broken is declared guilty!

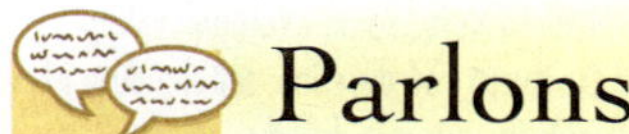

Parlons

7-11 Notre famille

A. Avant de parler. Pensez à votre famille et réfléchissez à cette question : Quelle est l'importance de la famille pour vous ? Utilisez le schéma pour prendre des notes avant de parler. Regardez bien le modèle.

ma famille	**Modèle** *ma mère, mon père, mes deux sœurs*
nos rapports	*on s'entend bien*
nos activités ensemble	*passer des vacances à la plage*
mes parents m'ont appris à...	*aimer la nature et les voyages*

B. En parlant. Maintenant, à l'aide de vos notes, parlez de votre famille.

MODÈLE É1 Je suis d'une famille nombreuse ; nous sommes cinq personnes. Et toi ?
É2 Moi non ; je suis fille unique — je n'ai pas de frères ou sœurs. Tu as de la chance d'avoir des frères et des sœurs. Tu t'entends bien avec eux ?
É1 J'ai deux sœurs. Je m'entends bien avec ma grande sœur, mais je me dispute souvent avec ma petite sœur. ...

Implementation: Go over the model with students and show how it picks up on vocabulary from the **Points de départ**. Discuss the use of the *passé composé* and the *imparfait* in answering the questions.

C. Après avoir parlé. Comparez vos idées sur l'importance de la famille avec celles de vos camarades de classe. Est-ce que vous avez des expériences et des opinions différentes ?

Leçon 2 Les grands évènements de la vie

Presentation: Use the photographs to tell the story of important events in Sophie's life. Point out cultural information conveyed by the photos and captions: Catholic customs and holidays, the civil and religious wedding ceremonies. Include information contained in the **Vie et culture** notes. Encourage cross-cultural comparison by asking what major childhood events students' own family albums contain that are not pictured here. Some examples might include: first day of school, rituals related to other faith traditions, graduation, prom. Test comprehension by having students point to the event you describe; tell the date of Sophie's birthday and of their own birthday. Have students repeat key words. Adapt by creating your own slide show of noteworthy events in your own family.

POINTS DE DÉPART

TEXT AUDIO
CD 4 TRACK 2

Les grands évènements

La mère de Sophie regarde son album de photos.

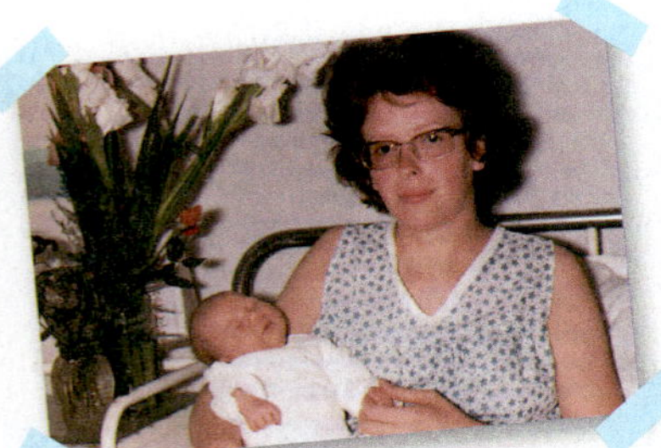

Le 9 mai 1980, Sophie est née ; elle était adorable !

Le jour de Noël 1982 ; Sophie avait 2 ans. Que de cadeaux !

L'été 1995, Sophie a passé les grandes vacances à la plage avec son amie Virginie.

Voilà Sophie à son baptême, avec sa marraine et son parrain.

C'était l'anniversaire de Sophie : 6 bougies sur le gâteau !

Le mariage de Sophie et Arnaud. La cérémonie civile a eu lieu à la mairie et ensuite la cérémonie religieuse, à l'église ; la mariée était en blanc, le marié en smoking !

Implementation: Create a chart to summarize, with columns for students to fill in: *Nom de la fête ; Date ; Activités spécifiques.* Let students add in American holidays (Halloween, Thanksgiving, and 4th of July, for example), to discuss similarities and differences. Show the video montage *Les rites et les rituels,* which features various national and religious holidays and rituals. See if students can match events they see in the clip to holidays and events mentioned here. Point out the following vocabulary: *jour férié, galette, cacher, œuf en chocolat, muguet, bal populaire, feu d'artifice, défilé, fleur.* Students will need these words to complete the exercises and will find them useful to talk about holidays in general. Captions have not been provided for the photos; encourage students to identify the holiday illustrated in each: *Maintenant que vous connaissez les fêtes françaises, trouvez la fête qui correspond à chaque photo ! Pâques, le premier mai, la Chandeleur.*

Vie et culture

Les fêtes religieuses et officielles

Certains jours fériés en France sont des fêtes traditionnelles catholiques et d'autres sont des fêtes nationales.

Noël est la plus grande fête de l'année. On décore le sapin et on échange des cadeaux. Le soir du 24 décembre, on prépare un grand repas, le réveillon.

Le jour de l'An est précédé par le réveillon de la Saint-Sylvestre, la nuit du 31 décembre.

Le jour des Rois (l'Épiphanie) a lieu le 6 janvier. On partage un gâteau, la galette des rois, dans lequel on a caché la fève — un petit personnage en plastique ou en céramique. La personne qui trouve la fève dans sa part de galette est nommée le roi ou la reine[1] et porte une couronne en papier.

La Chandeleur, c'est le 2 février. Traditionnellement, on mange des crêpes. Si vous faites sauter[2] une crêpe et si elle retombe dans la poêle[3], vous allez avoir de la chance toute l'année.

Pâques. Pour Pâques, en France on peut voir des œufs et des poules[4] en chocolat dans les vitrines de toutes les pâtisseries et les confiseries. Le lundi de Pâques est un jour férié.

La fête du Travail. Le premier mai, on organise des défilés et l'on offre du muguet[5] aux membres de sa famille. C'est aussi un jour férié.

La fête nationale. Cette grande fête célèbre le début de la Révolution le 14 juillet 1789. Le matin, les Parisiens assistent au grand défilé militaire sur les Champs-Élysées, retransmis en direct à la télévision. Le soir, toutes les villes organisent un bal populaire et l'on tire un feu d'artifice.

La Toussaint. Le 1er novembre, on honore les morts de la famille en mettant des fleurs, surtout des chrysanthèmes, sur leurs tombes.

ET VOUS ?

1. Regardez la séquence vidéo, *Les rites et les rituels.* Quelles occasions est-ce qu'on fête ?
2. Est-ce que vous célébrez certaines de ces fêtes dans votre région ? Est-ce que vos traditions sont différentes des traditions des Français ? Expliquez pourquoi.
3. À votre avis, est-ce que les fêtes nationales sont plus importantes chez vous que chez les Français ? Et les fêtes religieuses ?

[1]*king or queen* [2]*flip* [3]*frying pan* [4]*hens* [5]*lily of the valley*

Expansion: Suggest that students get more information about unfamiliar holidays that interest them by looking them up on the Internet and reporting to the class. See the *Chez nous* Companion Website for links. Or, put students into small groups to discuss a) their favorite holiday and how they celebrate it; b) the most significant holiday for North Americans, and why. Note that the **Venez chez nous !** lesson provides more information on celebrations across the Francophone world.

Les vœux

Meilleurs vœux !	*Best wishes!*	Bonne année !	*Happy New Year!*
Félicitations !	*Congratulations!*	Bon voyage !	*Have a good trip!*
Bon/Joyeux anniversaire !	*Happy Birthday!*	Bonnes vacances !	*Have a good vacation!*
Joyeux Noël !	*Merry Christmas!*		

Presentation: Read the expressions aloud and model pronunciation. Go back to the events in Sophie's life and have students decide which would be the most appropriate greeting/s in each case; follow up with Ex. 7-12.

À vous la parole

Variation: 7-12 Recycle forms of *dire* by suggesting a different subject for each item: *Vos amis ont eu un enfant ; vous. — Vous dites, « Félicitations ! »*

7-12 Qu'est-ce qu'on dit ? Qu'est-ce que vous dites dans les situations suivantes ?

MODÈLE C'est l'anniversaire de votre mère.
Je dis, « Bon anniversaire, maman ! »

1. Vos amis ont eu un enfant.
2. C'est le 25 décembre.
3. C'est la Saint-Sylvestre.
4. Vous assistez à un mariage.
5. Votre ami fête ses 20 ans.
6. Vos parents fêtent leurs 25 ans de mariage.
7. C'est le jour de l'An.
8. Vos cousins partent en voyage.

Implementation: 7-13 Since multiple responses are possible, you might have each group make a list and compare answers at the end. The video montage (*Les rites et les rituels*) could accompany Ex. 7-13, since many of the items listed can be seen in the clip.

7-13 Jeu d'association. À quelle occasion est-ce que vous associez ces choses ou ces personnes ? Parlez-en avec un/e partenaire.

MODÈLE un voyage
É1 Ce sont les grandes vacances.
É2 C'est un mariage.

1. un gâteau
2. des cadeaux
3. un document officiel
4. un grand dîner
5. un défilé militaire
6. des fleurs
7. la marraine
8. le maire (*mayor*)
9. le prêtre (*priest*), le pasteur, le rabbin, l'imam
10. un bébé

7-14 Tous les éléments. Quels sont les éléments importants pour une fête ? Avec un/e partenaire, décrivez une fête d'après les éléments suivants : **l'endroit**, **les gens importants**, **les vêtements/les accessoires**, **les activités.**

MODÈLE un anniversaire

É1 On peut fêter un anniversaire à la maison ou dans un restaurant, par exemple.

É2 Normalement, la famille et les amis sont présents. Il y a presque toujours un gâteau avec des bougies.

É1 Oui, on chante et on offre des cadeaux.

1. Noël
2. un mariage
3. un baptême
4. la fête nationale
5. les grandes vacances

Sons et lettres

La semi-voyelle /j/

When the letter **i** immediately precedes a vowel sound, it is pronounced /j/, as in the English word *yes*. It forms a single syllable with the following vowel. Compare:

le mari / le marié   étudie / étudiez   bougie / changiez

Note that when **i** is preceded by a group of consonants and followed by a vowel sound, it is pronounced /i/ and forms a separate syllable. Compare:

le lien / le cli-ent   bien / ou-bli-er

The letter **y** is often pronounced /j/:

joyeux   foyer   Lyon

Note: In *étudie* and *bougie*, the final *-e* is not pronounced. Remind students that the sequence *-ill* is often pronounced /j/ as well. This was presented in Ch. 6, L. 1. Note the intervocalic glide in the second example: *client* /klijã/, *oublier* /ublije/

À vous la parole

7-15 Imitation. Répétez ces mots ou expressions qui contiennent la semi-voyelle /j/ devant une voyelle orale.

mieux	le mariage	officiel	la mariée
l'union	traditionnelle	génial	monsieur
la société	un-million	vous chantiez	nous voulions

7-16 Contrastes. Comparez les deux mots ou expressions.

1. la vie / les vieux   le mari / le mariage
2. l'ami / le mieux   elle étudie / elle va étudier
3. le cri / crier   c'est une bougie / c'est génial

7-17 Phrases. Maintenant lisez ces phrases.

1. La cérémonie officielle pour le mariage a lieu le 3 février.
2. Ces étudiantes étudiaient les sciences économiques à Lyon l'an dernier.
3. Dans la société actuelle, il y a des familles traditionnelles avec des femmes au foyer mais aussi des couples qui vivent en union libre.

Implementation: Begin with a discrimination drill contrasting the first- and second-person plural of the present versus the corresponding forms of the imperfect. Have students raise their hand when they hear the imperfect (and therefore the glide /j/): *nous lisons, nous lisions, vous écrivez, vous écriviez, nous disions, nous disons, vous fêtez, vous fêtiez, nous célébrons, nous célébrions, nous jouions, nous jouons, vous chantez, vous chantiez.* You may also wish to add a drill in which students transform from the present to the imperfect: *vous écrivez* → *vous écriviez ; nous dansons, vous mangez, vous passez, nous faisons, nous allons, vous achetez, vous finissez, nous préférons.*

Note: Remind students that in *millier, million,* and *milliard, ll* represents /l/, not /j/. These are derivatives of *mille.*

FORMES ET FONCTIONS

1. *L'imparfait et le passé composé : d'autres contrastes*

Implementation: Review uses of the *passé composé* and *imparfait* as presented in Ch. 6, L. 3 and Ch. 7, L. 1. First, have students brainstorm to list uses of each tense; use this summary as a point of departure for review practice before presenting the new information. A narrative such as that provided in Ex. 7-8 or 7-9, or in the corresponding section of the SAM/MFL, would offer a good basis for review. This section focuses on adverbial cues to one-time versus habitual actions in the past and the use of the *imparfait* for ongoing actions as opposed to punctual actions. Review the various adverbial cues to repeated/habitual action, including use of the definite article with days of the week: *dimanche* (Sunday) vs. *le dimanche* (on Sundays).

As you have seen, the choice of the **imparfait** or the **passé composé** to express an action in the past often depends on the context and the speaker's view of the action or situation.

- Use the **passé composé** to express:
  - an action or state that occurred at a specific point in time:

    Elle est née **le jeudi 9 mai 1991**. — *She was born on Thursday, May 9, 1991.*

  - an action or state that occurred a specified number of times:

    Elle a visité le Canada **deux fois**. — *She visited Canada twice.*

- Use the **imparfait** to express:
  - enduring states in the past:

    Cécile était une enfant très sérieuse. — *Cécile was a very studious child.*

  - habitual actions in the past:

    D'habitude la famille allait au parc **le dimanche**. — *Usually the family would go to the park on Sundays.*

- Use the **imparfait** to express an ongoing action or state interrupted by another action, which is expressed by the **passé composé**.

  Sophie **regardait** la télé quand sa marraine **a téléphoné**. — *Sophie was watching TV when her godmother called.*
  Ils **quittaient** l'église quand elle **est arrivée.** — *They were leaving the church when she arrived.*

- Finally, some actions or states can be expressed either in the **passé composé** or the **imparfait**, depending on what the speaker means to say.

  Elle était malade pendant les vacances. — *She was sick during the vacation.* (emphasis on her state of being sick)

  Elle a été malade pendant les vacances. — *She got sick during the vacation.* (emphasis on the act of getting sick)

  Il avait peur. — *He was afraid.*
  Il a eu peur. — *He got scared/Something scared him.*

Fiche pratique

The **imparfait** can often be translated as "used to . . .," "would . . .," "was [doing something]", or "was feeling . . ." When in doubt about whether to use the **imparfait** or the **passé composé**, try substituting these expressions in the sentence to see whether they fit the context.

À vous la parole

7-18 Hier, ça n'allait pas ! Chloé a eu des problèmes hier. Les choses n'ont pas marché comme d'habitude. Expliquez !

MODÈLE arriver en avance
- D'habitude, elle arrivait en avance.
- Mais hier elle n'est pas arrivée en avance.

1. quitter la maison à 8 h
2. arriver la première
3. apporter son cahier
4. réviser sa leçon
5. finir ses devoirs
6. apporter ses livres
7. travailler à la bibliothèque
8. appeler ses amis

Initial practice: Begin with a discrimination drill: have students decide whether you are describing a one-time or habitual action. *J'allais souvent au cinéma. Un jour, j'ai vu un film extraordinaire. Je partais souvent en vacances avec ma famille. On est allé au Canada deux fois. L'été dernier, on a visité le Rocher percé et l'île Bonaventure.*

Note: 7-18 This exercise contrasts one-time events with habitual actions in the past.

7-19 Qu'est-ce qu'ils faisaient ? Décrivez ce que ces gens faisaient quand Solange est arrivée à la fête.

MODÈLE Quand Solange est arrivée, Marc travaillait dans sa chambre.

Note: 7-19 This exercise contrasts ongoing actions interrupted by punctual actions in the past. Use the house visual (MFL, Ch. 7) to cue.

 **7-20 Mes quinze ans.** Avec un/e partenaire, parlez de vos quinze ans. Comment étiez-vous ? Qu'est-ce que vous faisiez ? Qu'est-ce que vous avez fait ?

MODÈLES le caractère

É1 Moi, à quinze ans, j'étais très timide.
É2 Moi, à quinze ans, j'étais très indépendant et individualiste.

les voyages

É1 À quinze ans, je suis allée à Washington, D.C. visiter les monuments et les musées.
É2 Et moi, je suis allé en Floride avec ma famille.

1. le caractère
2. le physique
3. les amis
4. le sport
5. les voyages
6. les études
7. la musique
8. les projets d'avenir

Implementation: 7-20 This exercise mixes ongoing states, habitual actions, and one-time events in the past. To simplify and allow students to focus on the verb forms, brainstorm with students or supply a list of adjectives and verb infinitives for them to choose from.

2. *Les pronoms complément d'objet* me, te, nous *et* vous

Presentation: Use the first two bulleted points as a point of departure for a systematic review of the third-person direct- and indirect-object pronouns. Practice using substitution drills (*Je regarde les enfants. — Je les regarde ; le prof, Suzanne, etc. ; Je parle aux étudiants. — Je leur parle ; le prof, Marc, etc.*). Follow up with a meaning-based activity, such as Ex. 6-12 or 6-24. Next present the new information using numerous examples and having students summarize rules.

- You have learned that nouns that function as direct objects answer the question *whom?* or *what?*; they follow the verb directly and can be replaced by a direct-object pronoun.

  Tu entends **les enfants** ? — Oui, je **les** entends.

- Nouns that function as indirect objects are generally introduced by the preposition **à**; they often answer the question *to whom?* and they generally refer to a person.

  Tu donnes des chips **aux enfants** ? — Oui, je **leur** donne des chips.

- The pronouns **me/m'**, **te/t'**, **nous**, and **vous** function as direct-object pronouns, corresponding to **le**, **la**, **l'**, and **les**. They also serve as indirect-object pronouns, corresponding to **lui** and **leur**.

Direct-object pronouns

Tu **m'**attends devant l'église ? — *Will you wait for me in front of the church?*

Je vais **vous** inviter à dîner. — *I'm going to invite you to dinner.*

Indirect-object pronouns

Je **te** souhaite un bon anniversaire. — *I wish you a Happy Birthday.*
Il **nous** a offert un cadeau. — *He gave us a gift.*

- Here is a summary of object pronouns:

	PERSONNE	DIRECT	INDIRECT
SINGULIER	1ère	me/m'	me/m'
	2e	te/t'	te/t'
	3e *m.*	le/l'	lui
	f.	la/l'	lui
PLURIEL	1ère	nous	nous
	2e	vous	vous
	3e	les	leur

À vous la parole

7-21 Esprit de contradiction ou pas ? Vous allez proposer quelque chose. Un/e de vos partenaires va donner son accord, l'autre va refuser.

Initial practice: Begin with substitution drills: *Il les regarde ; nous, toi,* etc. *Elle lui parle ; vous, eux,* etc.

Variation: 7-21 Modify to practice plural forms: *Vous allez nous aider ?,* etc.

MODÈLE É1 Tu m'attends ?
É2 Oui, je t'attends.
É3 Non, je ne t'attends pas.

1. Tu vas m'aider à préparer le dîner ?
2. Tu me téléphones ce soir ?
3. Tu m'invites chez toi ce week-end ?
4. Tu me prêtes ton beau pull ?
5. Tu vas me répondre rapidement ?
6. Tu vas me montrer tes cadeaux ?
7. Tu vas m'accompagner à la fête ?

7-22 Du chantage. Répondez à votre partenaire que vous êtes d'accord.

MODÈLE Je t'invite à dîner si tu me prêtes de l'argent.
Alors, je te prête de l'argent.

1. Je t'envoie une carte postale si tu me donnes ton adresse.
2. Je te téléphone si tu me donnes ton numéro de téléphone.
3. Nous t'invitons au réveillon si tu nous accompagnes à l'église.
4. Nous t'offrons une bouteille de vin si tu nous prépares un pique-nique.
5. Je t'invite au cinéma si tu me prêtes ta voiture demain.
6. Je t'accompagne au défilé militaire si tu m'accompagnes au bal.
7. Nous te prêtons de l'argent si tu nous offres du muguet.

7-23 Qu'est-ce qu'ils font ? Qu'est-ce que ces gens font pour vous ? Parlez-en avec un/e camarade, et ensuite comparez vos réponses avec celles des autres étudiants.

Implementation: 7-23 Conduct as a paired activity; students will use *te* and *me* with each other. Have them report back, using *me, lui, nous ;* then summarize by listing generalities for each category: *Vos parents, ils vous prêtent de l'argent ; ils vous écoutent,* etc.

MODÈLE vos parents
É1 Qu'est-ce que tes parents font pour toi ?
É2 Ils me téléphonent le week-end ; ils me prêtent de l'argent pour payer mes études ; ils m'offrent des cadeaux.

1. votre frère ou sœur
2. votre colocataire
3. votre meilleur/e ami/e
4. votre copain/copine ou votre mari/femme
5. vos professeurs
6. vos parents

Écrivons

7-24 Un souvenir marquant

Stratégie

As you write a narrative in the past, consider in each instance whether you are describing a situation or advancing the plot by telling what happened. This will help you decide whether to use the **imparfait** or the **passé composé** for each verb.

A. Avant d'écrire. Pensez à un souvenir très marquant. Pour vous aider à organiser vos pensées, réfléchissez aux questions suivantes. Attention au temps du verbe : passé composé ou imparfait ?

Quelle **était** l'occasion ?	
C'est un souvenir heureux ou triste ?	
Qui **était** là ?	
Qu'est-ce que vous **avez fait** ?	
Quelles **étaient** vos émotions ?	

Implementation: To prepare students for the writing task, have them analyze the model for its use of the *passé composé* and *imparfait*. Show how the information contained in the paragraph would fit into the chart. You might also review forms briefly, and refer students back to the sections that outline the uses of the two tenses—Ch. 6, L. 3; Ch. 7, L. 1 and 2.
As a prelude to writing, have students discuss their experience in class. As a variation, have students describe a person from their past, telling who the person was, what the person was like physically and personality-wise, and why that person was memorable.
This activity can also be completed as a whole-class writing task, giving students additional practice and preparation for writing on their own.
You might have students share their story with classmates, either orally or by distributing copies of stories (with the author's permission).

B. En écrivant. Maintenant, composez votre texte sous forme de paragraphe(s) :

MODÈLE Mon souvenir le plus marquant, c'est un souvenir heureux. J'avais cinq ans, et j'étais fille unique. Un jour, mes parents m'ont dit qu'ils allaient à l'hôpital me chercher un petit frère ou une petite sœur. Ma grand-mère est venue à la maison pour rester avec moi. Deux jours après, quand j'ai entendu la voiture de mon père, j'ai crié, « Voici notre bébé ! Voici notre bébé ! ». C'était ma petite sœur. Et maintenant, c'est toujours ma meilleure amie.

C. En révisant. Réfléchissez aux questions suivantes et puis faites tous les changements nécessaires.

1. Relisez votre paragraphe pour analyser le contenu : est-ce que vous avez décrit une expérience marquante, en expliquant la situation et les évènements ?
2. Relisez de nouveau votre paragraphe pour analyser le style et la forme : est-ce que votre narration a une introduction et une conclusion ? Est-ce que vous avez employé le passé composé et l'imparfait dans des contextes appropriés ? Est-ce que les verbes sont bien formés ?
3. Donnez un titre à votre texte, par exemple « L'arrivée de ma sœur ».

D. Après avoir écrit. Comparez votre paragraphe avec celui de vos camarades de classe. Quelles sortes d'expériences est-ce que vous avez décrites ?

Leçon 3 Les émotions

POINTS DE DÉPART

TEXT AUDIO
CD 4 TRACK 7

Presentation: Begin by having students listen to the dialogue as they look at the photo and text. Then use mime and description to present the vocabulary list in the shaded box. Finally, use the illustrations of emotions (MFL, Ch. 7) to model typical phrases; describe the situations by re-using the key vocabulary. Test comprehension by having students point to a picture of the attitude you describe or mime the emotion. Have students repeat key words and phrases: *Elle est heureuse ou elle est furieuse ?*, etc.

Pour exprimer les sentiments et les émotions

MÉLANIE : Tu as l'air content, toi !

ANTOINE : En effet, je suis ravi. Écoute la bonne nouvelle : mon frère s'est fiancé. Il va se marier au mois de juin.

MÉLANIE : C'est super. Elle est comment, sa fiancée ?

ANTOINE : Elle est très sympa ; on s'entend bien. Mais dis-moi, qu'est-ce que tu as, toi ? Tu n'as pas l'air heureuse. Tu te fais du souci ?

MÉLANIE : Eh bien, je suis assez inquiète ; je n'ai pas de nouvelles de ma sœur. Elle a eu un bébé le mois dernier et elle se dispute beaucoup avec son mari. Elle doit se reposer, mais c'est elle qui fait tout le travail.

ANTOINE : Calme-toi. Elle est probablement trop occupée pour t'appeler. Téléphone-lui.

Les sentiments

être heureux/-euse, content/e, ravi/e
être inquiet/inquiète, anxieux/-euse
être furieux/-euse, fâché/e, en colère
être amoureux/-euse ; tomber amoureux/-euse
être sensible
être triste, malheureux/-euse
être surpris/e
être embarrassé/e, gêné/e
être jaloux/-ouse

Presentation: Relate the exclamations to the emotions presented earlier. Provide formal and familiar forms where appropriate. Have students repeat the phrases. Demonstrate the proper intonation patterns, including the *accent d'insistance émotionnelle : **Fo**rmidable ! **Cré**tin !*, etc. Many terms of endearment are based on names for animals: *ma puce, ma biche*, etc.

Vie et culture

Les Français s'expriment

Il y a beaucoup d'expressions fixes que les Français utilisent pour exprimer les émotions. (L'accent et l'intonation sont très importants aussi !) Est-ce que vous pouvez marier les expressions de la colonne de droite aux émotions de la colonne de gauche ? **Key:** 1) b 2) h 3) e 4) f 5) c 6) a, g 7) d 8) a

1. la joie →	**a.** Mon Dieu ! Oh, là, là !
2. la colère	**b.** Super ! Sensationnel ! Formidable !
3. l'indifférence	**c.** Excusez-moi ! Oh, pardon ! Je suis désolé/e !
4. la tendresse	**d.** Oh, zut ! Mince !
5. l'embarras	**e.** Bof ! Ça m'est égal.
6. la surprise	**f.** Ma chérie/mon chéri, mon cœur, ma puce
7. la frustration	**g.** C'est pas vrai ! Pas possible ! Incroyable !
8. l'inquiétude	**h.** Espèce d'imbécile ! Crétin ! Quel idiot !

Expansion: Have students work in pairs to make up their own situations and reactions. They might create a short scene based on their scenario and then act it out in front of the class.

Qu'est-ce qu'on dit quand on perd son sang-froid ?

ET VOUS ?

Le mot juste. Qu'est-ce que vous dites dans les situations suivantes ?

1. Vous avez perdu vos devoirs.
2. Vous avez eu une bonne note à un examen très difficile.
3. Vos amis hésitent entre le cinéma ou un DVD ; vous n'avez pas d'opinion.
4. Vous regardez un enfant adorable, votre nièce ou votre neveu.
5. Votre colocataire a emprunté votre livre de français et l'a perdu.
6. Vous avez fait tomber un vase chez la grand-mère de votre ami.
7. Vous apprenez que votre ami/e a eu un accident de voiture.

À vous la parole

7-25 Lire les expressions du visage. Est-ce que vous et votre partenaire savez lire les émotions peintes sur le visage d'une personne ?

MODÈLE É1 Cette dame a l'air malheureuse ; peut-être qu'elle a entendu des mauvaises nouvelles.

É2 Je pense qu'elle est anxieuse parce qu'elle n'a pas de nouvelles de son ami.

Implementation: 7-25, 7-26 Students may work in pairs or groups. Have them come up with as many alternatives as possible, then compare notes with the class as a whole.

Alternate activity: 7-25, 7-26 For each item, have students choose an appropriate expression from the list in **Vie et culture**.

1. 

2. 

3. 

4. 

7-26 Des conseils. Quels conseils est-ce que vous et votre partenaire pouvez donner aux personnes suivantes ?

MODÈLE Votre colocataire a des soucis.
Ne t'en fais pas ! Ça va s'arranger.

1. Une amie est très anxieuse avant un examen.
2. Votre ami est furieux parce qu'il pense qu'on l'a insulté.
3. Un monsieur se fâche parce qu'il n'y a pas de place dans l'autobus.
4. Votre amie a tendance à être un peu jalouse.
5. Votre petit frère pleure parce qu'il ne trouve pas son DVD préféré.
6. Une femme est furieuse et elle crie très fort.
7. Vos copains sont anxieux avant un match de tennis.
8. Vos camarades s'inquiètent de leurs notes d'examens ce semestre.

Implementation: 7-27 Nouns are for recognition only. Help students discover their meanings by associating them with the adjectives they know. For example, knowing *heureux* and *malheureux* helps to understand *le bonheur*.

Additional activities: Conduct a mixing activity where students interact with three other people. Provide a model: *Ça va aujourd'hui ? —Pas vraiment. J'ai un examen important, et je suis un peu anxieux. —Ne t'en fais pas ! Tu vas réussir à cet examen.* Follow up by having students tell what they learned about the people they spoke to. As a variation, perhaps on another class day, have students tell each other what's new and react to the news: *Quoi de neuf ? —Eh bien, je vais bientôt me marier. Ah bon ? C'est formidable !* Have students act out their conversations for the class.

Note: When the combination *ou* occurs before a vowel, it may be pronounced as the semivowel /w/ or the corresponding vowel /u/: *louer* /lwe/ (one syllable) or /lue/ (two syllables). Most of these cases involve verb forms (stem plus ending): *jouer, nous jouons, vous jouez.* However, it is preferable for students to pronounce forms like *un souhait* or *un jouet* with /w/. But note, as was the case for *i*, when *ou* occurs after consonant groups, the pronunciation of /u/ is obligatory. Compare: *louer* /lwe/ or /lue/ versus *trouer* /true/. However, the combination *oi* is pronounced /wa/ in this context: *trois.* The same principle applies to *u* before vowels: *nuage, tuer.*

7-27 Les sentiments. Expliquez à votre partenaire dans quelle/s situation/s vous ressentez les sentiments suivants.

MODÈLE la tristesse
Je suis triste quand mes parents se disputent.

1. le bonheur
2. la jalousie
3. l'inquiétude
4. l'anxiété
5. la colère
6. la surprise
7. la frustration

Sons et lettres

Les semi-voyelles /w/ et /ɥ/

The semivowel /w/ is always followed by a vowel, and that vowel is very often /a/. To pronounce /w/, start from the word "tweet" in English: *tweet* / **toi**.

When followed by the sound /a/, the semivowel is usually spelled **oi**, as in **moi**, **trois**. It can also be spelled **ou**, as in **oui** or **jouer**. The spelling **oy** represents the sound /waj/, as in **employé** or **royal**. The semivowel /w/ also occurs in combination with the nasal vowel /ɛ̃/. In this case, it is spelled **oin**: **loin** or **moins**.

To pronounce the semivowel /ɥ/, as in **lui**, start from the /y/ of **du** but pronounce it together with the following vowel: **lu** / **lui**.

The sound /ɥ/ is frequently followed by the vowel /i/: **huit**, **je suis**, **la nuit**, **bruit**, but not exclusively: **nuage**, **ennuyeux**, **s'essuyer**. It is always spelled with the letter **u** followed by another vowel.

À vous la parole

7-28 Contrastes. Comparez les paires de mots suivantes.

la j**oi**e	j**oy**eux	un m**oi**s	m**oin**s
le r**oi**	r**oy**al	la l**oi**	l**oin**
l'empl**oi**	empl**oy**er		

Maintenant, comparez les mots avec /w/ et /ɥ/.

oui	h**u**it	L**ou**is	l**u**i
j**o**int	j**u**in	le s**o**ir	ess**u**ie

7-29 Poème. Lisez ce petit poème.

Le Ver Luisant

Ver l**ui**sant°, tu l**ui**s° à min**ui**t
Tu t'allumes sous les ét**oi**les°
Et quand tout dort, tu t'introd**ui**s°
Dans la lune° et ronge sa m**oe**lle°.

—Robert Desnos, *Chantefables et Chantefleurs*. Librairie Grund, 1970.

glowworm; shine
stars
penetrate
moon; gnaw its marrow

Note: The distinction between /w/ and /ɥ/ is a difficult one for American speakers to perceive and to articulate, partly due to the difficulty with the pairs /u/ and /y/. You may wish to use the audio program to present this exercise in class and/or to assign as homework in addition to the activities in the SAM/MFL.

Implementation: When treating the poem, point out the difference in the pronunciation of *oe* in *moelle, poème,* and *Noël.*

FORMES ET FONCTIONS

1. *Les verbes pronominaux idiomatiques*

- Certain verbs change meaning when combined with a reflexive pronoun:

appeler	J'appelle mon chien.	*I'm calling my dog.*
s'appeler	Je **m'appelle** David.	*My name is David.*
entendre	J'entends un bruit.	*I hear a noise.*
s'entendre avec	Je **m'entends** bien **avec** eux.	*I get along well with them.*

- Here are some additional idiomatic pronominal verbs:

s'amuser	Ils **se sont** bien **amusés**.	*They had a lot of fun.*
s'arranger	Ça va **s'arranger** !	*It will be all right!*
se calmer	**Calmez-vous**, voyons !	*Look here, calm down!*
se dépêcher	Il ne **se dépêchait** jamais.	*He never hurried.*
se détendre	Tu devrais **te détendre**.	*You should relax.*
se disputer	Ils **se disputent** tout le temps.	*They argue all the time.*
s'ennuyer	Je **m'ennuie** !	*I'm bored!*
se fâcher	Elle **se fâche** contre lui.	*She's getting angry at him.*
s'inquiéter	Ne **t'inquiète** pas !	*Don't worry!*
s'intéresser à	Tu **t'intéresses à** la musique ?	*Are you interested in music?*
s'occuper de	Tu **t'occupes de** lui ?	*Are you taking care of him?*
se passer	Qu'est-ce qui **se passe** ?	*What's happening?*
se promener	Elle **se promène** souvent.	*She often takes a walk.*
se rappeler	Je ne **me rappelle** pas.	*I don't remember.*
se reposer	On **se repose**.	*We're resting.*
se retrouver	On **se retrouve** ici ?	*Shall we meet here?*

Presentation: Before treating this topic, review reflexive pronominal verbs presented in Ch. 4, L. 1. Treat the verbs in this **Formes et fonctions** as new vocabulary. Remind students that several of these were presented in the **Points de départ** for L. 2 and L. 3. Review stem and spelling changes for *s'appeler/se rappeler, s'ennuyer, s'inquiéter, se promener.* Conjugations are provided in Appendix 5.

◆ Many verbs can be used with a reflexive pronoun to show that the action is mutual, or reciprocal. In English we sometimes use the phrase *each other* to express this idea.

Note: There is no agreement of the past participle of *se téléphoner* because this verb takes an indirect object.

se téléphoner	Nous **nous** sommes téléphoné.	*We phoned each other.*
se rencontrer	On **s'**est rencontrés cet été.	*We met this summer.*
s'embrasser	Ils **se** sont embrassés.	*They kissed.*
se fiancer	Ils **se** sont fiancés.	*They got engaged.*
se marier	Ils **se** sont mariés.	*They got married.*
se séparer	Ils **se** sont séparés.	*They separated.*

 À vous la parole 

Initial practice: Begin with a discrimination drill: have students raise their hand when they hear a verb used pronominally: *Ils se reposent. Il essuie la table. Elle s'appelle Stéphanie. J'entends un bruit. Ils s'entendent bien. Elle embrasse son fiancé. Je m'ennuie. On va se promener. Vous passez chez moi demain ? Ils se séparent ?*, etc. Follow up with a substitution drill to review forms: *Je m'amuse ; toi. — Tu t'amuses*, etc.

7-30 À la maternelle. Christophe se rappelle sa classe à l'école maternelle. Pour compléter ses descriptions, choisissez un verbe qui convient dans la liste ci-dessous.

MODÈLE La maîtresse était toujours calme.
Elle ne se fâchait jamais.

s'amuser	se dépêcher	s'ennuyer	s'entendre
se fâcher	s'occuper de	se rappeler	se reposer

1. Pendant la récréation, les enfants jouaient ensemble.
2. À midi, on n'avait pas beaucoup de temps pour aller à la cantine.
3. Une vieille femme préparait le déjeuner.
4. Après le déjeuner, tout le monde faisait la sieste.
5. Jacques et moi, nous étions des bons amis.
6. Je trouvais nos activités en classe très intéressantes.
7. Jacques n'oubliait jamais ses leçons.

Variation: 7-31 Vary by suggesting that students present the love stories of famous couples of their choosing (e.g., Marc Antony and Cleopatra, Romeo and Juliet, Bill and Hillary Clinton, Angelina Jolie and Brad Pitt) or even of friends and/or family members. Point out that not all verbs are used pronominally. Students may work in pairs or groups to complete this adaptation.

7-31 Histoire d'amour. Racontez cette histoire d'amour en vous servant des verbes indiqués.

MODÈLE se rencontrer
Ils se sont rencontrés au cinéma.

1. se parler de
2. tomber amoureux
3. se fiancer
4. se marier
5. s'entendre bien
6. se disputer
7. se séparer
8. divorcer

7-32 Trouvez une personne. Trouvez une personne qui...

MODÈLE s'entend bien avec ses parents
É1 Est-ce que tu t'entends bien avec tes parents ?
É2 Non, je ne m'entends pas bien avec eux.
OU Oui, je m'entends bien avec eux.

1. s'entend bien avec ses parents
2. se rappelle son premier jour à l'école
3. s'amuse quelquefois pendant le cours de français
4. s'occupe toujours du dîner le soir
5. ne se fâche jamais
6. s'est dépêchée ce matin
7. va se détendre ce week-end
8. se rappelle les heures de bureau du professeur

Implementation: 7-32 Use as a mixing exercise; let students ask each other a maximum of two questions before moving on to someone else. After a few minutes, have students compare notes, asking questions about items they did not find. Take the opportunity to ask follow-up questions.

7-33 Quand ? Avec un/e partenaire, expliquez quand cela vous arrive de...

MODÈLE vous fâcher
É1 Quand est-ce que tu te fâches ?
É2 Je me fâche quand ma sœur emprunte mes affaires.

1. vous fâcher
2. vous inquiéter
3. vous amuser
4. vous dépêcher
5. vous reposer
6. vous ennuyer
7. vous détendre

Expansion: 7-33 Follow up by comparing answers with the whole class.

2. *Les verbes* voir *et* croire *et la conjonction* que

- Here are the forms of the irregular verbs **croire** and **voir**.

CROIRE	*to believe*	VOIR	*to see*		
SINGULIER			PLURIEL		
je	crois	vois	nous	croy**ons**	voy**ons**
tu	crois	vois	vous	croy**ez**	voy**ez**
il / elle / on	croit	voit	ils / elles	croi**ent**	voi**ent**

IMPÉRATIF : **Crois**-moi ! **Croyez**-nous ! **Croyons** aux jeunes ! **Voyons** !
PASSÉ COMPOSÉ : J'ai **cru** qu'il partait. J'ai **vu** ce film.

Presentation: Point out that these verbs have three spoken forms and follow the "boot" pattern. The third-person singular and plural forms sound alike: *il croit/ils croient ; elle voit/elles voient.* The *nous-* and *vous-* forms contain the sound /j/, as in English "yes." The sound /j/ is reflected by the letter *y*: *croyons, voyez.*

- Use the verb **croire**:
  - to indicate that you believe someone or something:

Je **crois** Jean.	*I believe John.*
Cette histoire ? Nous la **croyons**.	*This story? We believe it.*

  - to indicate that you believe in something. In this case, use **croire** along with the preposition **à**.

Nous **croyons à** l'avenir.	*We believe in the future.*
Ils **croient au** Père Noël.	*They believe in Santa Claus.*

  - Note, however, the following expression.

Nous **croyons en** Dieu.	*We believe in God.*

- Here are some common expressions using **croire**:

Je crois. / Je crois que oui.	*I think so.*
Je ne crois pas. / Je crois que non.	*I don't think so.*

- To express an opinion, use a verb such as **croire** or **penser** plus the conjunction **que**. Notice that the conjunction is not always expressed in English but must be present in French.

Je **pense que** Suzanne est furieuse.	*I think (that) Suzanne is furious.*
Je **crois que** tu as raison.	*I think (that) you are right.*

- Use the verb **dire** plus the conjunction **que** to report what someone says.

Elle dit **qu'**elle se fait du souci.	*She says (that) she's worried.*
Il dit **que** son frère va se fiancer.	*He says (that) his brother is getting engaged.*

Note: We avoid the use of past tense with *dire que* in order to avoid agreement of tenses. If you wish to present this feature, provide multiple examples: *Elle a dit que ce film était excellent*, etc. You might point out that the verb *voir* can also be used with the conjunction *que* : *Je vois qu'ils sont déjà partis.*

Initial practice: Practice *croire* first using a substitution drill: *Je crois au Père Noël ; vous. — Vous croyez au Père Noël*, etc.

Implementation: 7-34 Make sure students understand all the possible responses before beginning.

À vous la parole

7-34 Les croyances. À quoi croient ces personnes ? Pour chaque phrase, choisissez dans la liste suivante la réponse qui convient.

MODÈLE Mme Martin achète des billets de LOTO chaque semaine.
→ Elle croit à la chance.

Réponses possibles :

l'amour	Dieu	le Père Noël
l'avenir	la discipline	le plaisir
la chance	la médecine	

1. Je voudrais avoir beaucoup d'enfants.
2. Anne a six ans, son frère a quatre ans.
3. Geoffrey est un jeune homme sentimental.
4. M. Leblanc va à l'église toutes les semaines.
5. Nous sortons jusqu'à trois heures du matin tous les soirs.
6. M. Gervais a trois enfants et il est très autoritaire.
7. Quand ça ne va pas bien, Alex va tout de suite voir le médecin.

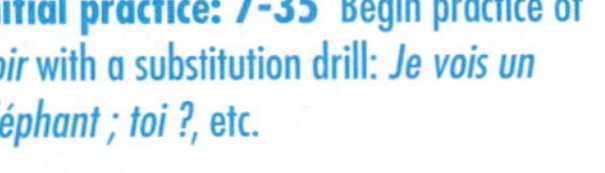

Initial practice: 7-35 Begin practice of *voir* with a substitution drill: *Je vois un éléphant ; toi ?*, etc.

7-35 Que de choses à voir ! Expliquez ce que chaque personne voit—attention au temps du verbe !

MODÈLES Nous avons visité Paris.
→ Nous avons vu la tour Eiffel.

Les Davy allaient souvent au zoo.
→ Ils voyaient souvent des lions, des tigres et des éléphants.

1. Je vais aller à Nice pour les vacances.
2. Vous êtes allés au Québec ?
3. Ils vont visiter Washington.
4. Tu visites la Guadeloupe ?
5. Elles allaient souvent à Paris.
6. Nous sommes allés à New York le mois dernier.
7. Ma copine va aller au centre-ville.

7-36 Dialogue des générations. Est-ce que la vie est meilleure aujourd'hui qu'à l'époque (*time*) de vos parents ? Discutez-en avec un/e partenaire. Ensuite, comparez vos idées avec les idées des autres étudiants de votre classe.

Implementation: 7-36 Go over the model with students before putting them in pairs to consider the topics. To help frame the discussion, you might have students express each item as a question: *Est-ce que les adolescents sont plus heureux ou moins heureux qu'au temps de vos parents ?*, etc.

MODÈLE le bonheur et les adolescents

É1 Je crois que les ados sont moins heureux aujourd'hui qu'à l'époque de mes parents. Ils sont plus stressés par les examens et le travail.

É2 Je ne pense pas. Mes parents disent qu'ils travaillaient très dur et qu'ils avaient plus de responsabilités à notre âge. Je crois que nous avons beaucoup de chance parce que nous avons plus de temps libre pour nous amuser.

1. le bonheur et les adolescents
2. le problème de la drogue
3. les études universitaires
4. la musique
5. les rapports familiaux

Stratégie

Put yourself in the writer's place to better understand his/her point of view. Consider whether there may be aspects of the writer's background or experience that have shaped his or her perspective, reactions, and focus.

Lisons

TEXT AUDIO CD 4 TRACK 11

7-37 Je suis cadien

Preparation: Ask students what they know about the history of Louisiana and the French heritage there. Ancelet is wearing a costume for *Mardi gras*. More information about this event can be found in the **Venez chez nous !**

A. Avant de lire. The title of this poem, ***Je suis cadien***, gives you essential information about the identity of the poet, Barry Ancelet (who takes the pen name Jean Arceneaux). He speaks **le français cadien**, and he is a descendent of French speakers who fled to Louisiana in the eighteenth century from the former French colony of **Acadie** (the present-day Canadian provinces of Nova Scotia and New Brunswick). After **Acadie** was ceded to England, the Acadians refused allegiance to the British crown. Since the poet has announced his Cajun French identity at the outset, are you surprised, looking at the first lines of his poem, to see that they are in English? Why do you think the poem is written in two languages, French and English? Can you put yourself in the poet's place, identifying with his feelings as a Louisiana schoolboy? What message do you think he will attempt to convey?

Voici le poète, Barry Ancelet. Pourquoi, à votre avis, est-ce qu'il est habillé ainsi ?

Implementation: The poem is written in *le français cadien* and departs from Standard French in the following ways: 1) general deletion of *ne* in the negative, *On sait jamais* 2) no elision in *que eux* 3) deletion of *il* before *faut*. Most of these features are also found in the variety of everyday spoken French called *le français familier*.

Key: En lisant 1) les enfants doivent écrire la phrase au tableau pendant leur temps de recess (en français standard, pendant la récréation) ; c'est pour punir les enfants parce qu'ils parlent français à l'école 2) il exprime l'attitude des enfants quand ils sont punis 3) c'est plus facile, on n'a pas besoin du français, et on est vraiment américain si on parle anglais 4) l'enfant demande, quelle langue est-ce qu'il faut utiliser pour rire, pour pleurer, pour crier, pour chanter, pour aimer, pour vivre ? You might discuss with students the issue of voice in the poem: go through the text and help them determine at what points the poet is speaking, at what points it is the child, and at what points others are speaking to the child.

B. En lisant. Le poète exprime les pensées et les émotions d'un enfant cadien qui va à l'école publique en Louisiane. En lisant un extrait de ce poème, répondez aux questions suivantes.

1. Pourquoi est-ce que le poète répète la première phrase plusieurs fois ? À quelle punition pendant « leur temps de recess » est-ce qu'il fait référence ?
2. Le poète écrit au vers (*line*) 9, « Ça fait mal ; ça fait honte ». Quelle situation est-ce qu'il décrit ?
3. Dans les vers 25 à 42, on explique à l'enfant pourquoi il doit parler anglais. Est-ce que vous pouvez résumer les arguments ?
4. L'enfant n'est pas convaincu. Comment est-ce que les derniers vers (52 à 57) montrent cela ?

JE SUIS CADIEN (*suite poètique*)

I will not speak French on the school grounds.
I will not speak French on the school grounds.
I will not speak French...
I will not speak French...
I will not speak French...
Hé ! Ils sont pas bêtes, ces salauds°.
Après mille fois, ça commence à pénétrer
Dans n'importe quel esprit°.
Ça fait mal ; ça fait honte°.
Et on ne speak pas French on the school grounds
Et ni anywhere else non plus.
Jamais avec des étrangers.
On sait jamais° qui a l'autorité
De faire écrire ces sacrées° lignes
À n'importe quel âge.
Surtout pas avec les enfants.
Faut jamais que eux, ils passent leur temps de recess
À écrire ces sacrées lignes.

I will not speak French on the school grounds.
I will not speak French on the school grounds.

Faut pas qu'ils aient besoin° d'écrire ça
Parce qu'il faut pas qu'ils parlent français du tout.
Ça laisse voir° qu'on est rien que° des Cadiens.
Don't mind us, we're just poor coonasses,
Basse classe, faut cacher ça°.
Faut dépasser ça.
Faut parler en anglais.
Faut regarder la télévision en anglais.
Faut écouter la radio en anglais
Comme de bons Américains.
Why not just go ahead and learn English,

° salauds: *bastards*
° esprit: *anybody's head*
° fait honte: *makes you ashamed*
° On sait jamais: *You never know*
° sacrées: *damned*
° Faut pas qu'ils aient besoin: *They shouldn't have to*
° laisse voir; rien que: *It shows; nothing but*
° faut cacher ça: *gotta hide it*

Don't fight it, it's much easier anyway,
No bilingual bills, no bilingual publicity.
No danger of internal frontiers.
Enseignez l'anglais aux enfants.
Rendez-les tout le long°,
Tout le long jusqu'aux discos,
Jusqu'au Million Dollar Man.
On a pas réellement besoin de parler français quand même°.
C'est les États-Unis ici.
Land of the Free.
On restera toujours° rien que des poor coonasses.

I will not speak French on the school grounds.
I will not speak French on the school grounds.

Coonass, non, non, ça gêne pas°.
C'est juste un petit nom.
Ça veut rien dire.
C'est pour s'amuser, ça gêne pas.
On aime ça, c'est cute.
Ça nous fait pas fâchés°.
Ça nous fait rire°.
Mais quand on doit rire, c'est en quelle langue qu'on rit ?
Et pour pleurer, c'est en quelle langue qu'on pleure ?
Et pour crier ?
Et chanter ?
Et aimer ?
Et vivre ?

—Jean Arceneaux, de « Je suis Cadien », *Suite du loup*, Éditions Perce-Neige, 1998.

Take them all the way

anyway

will always be

that doesn't bother us

That doesn't make us mad.

laugh

Key: En regardant de plus près 1) pour montrer les différents points de vue et la tension entre les anglophones et les francophones 2) il dit, « c'est cute, ça nous gêne pas, c'est juste un petit nom » ; mais pour le lecteur, c'est choquant et très péjoratif. Here is what Ancelet has to say about the use of this term: « L'auteur essaie de montrer que ce terme, qui a été en effet adopté par un certain segment de la population cadienne comme « terme valorisant », est en fait un terme qui reflète l'internalisation de l'américanisation brutale qu'on a subie. Mais le narrateur ne l'utilise pas pour s'adresser à quelqu'un d'autre ; il l'utilise malheureusement pour s'adresser à lui-même. Le poème finit par mettre en question la valeur du terme dans une sorte de catharsis. » 3) Le poète montre que la langue française, c'est très important pour sa vie, c'est son identité.

C. En regardant de plus près. Le poète permet au lecteur (*reader*) de s'identifier avec l'enfant cadien.

1. Pourquoi est-ce que le poème mélange (*mix*) l'anglais et le français ?
2. Dans le texte, on utilise un nom péjoratif : quelle est la réaction de l'enfant quand il entend ce nom ? Quelle est votre réaction quand vous le lisez ? Quelle réaction est-ce que le poète cherche, à votre avis ?
3. Le poème finit par une série de questions ; quel est l'effet de ces questions sur le lecteur ?

D. Après avoir lu. Discutez de ces questions avec vos camarades de classe.

1. Est-ce que vous pouvez vous identifier avec le point de vue et les émotions exprimés dans ce poème ? Pourquoi ?
2. Est-ce que vous connaissez un peu l'histoire des immigrés qui sont arrivés aux États-Unis à la fin du XIXe et au début du XXe siècle ? Est-ce que l'expérience de l'enfant cadien décrite dans ce poème ressemble à l'expérience des enfants de ces immigrés, ou non ?

Expansion: Après avoir lu You might share your own cultural heritage with students, and ask: Does your family or your community recognize a particular cultural heritage? Do members make an effort to learn about and honor their cultural roots? In what ways do they do this?

Venez chez nous ! Les rites et les rituels

Après la cérémonie de mariage en France, il y a souvent du champagne à boire et une pièce montée à déguster.

Implementation: Use the video montage to provide an overview of the lesson. Have students identify the various events they see and perhaps provide an appropriate reaction/expression of emotion: *Félicitations !*, etc.

Chaque culture exprime ses valeurs à travers ses rites et ses rituels. Voici quelques exemples de rituels du monde francophone.

Observons

7-38 Rites et traditions

Implementation: Avant de regarder You might work with students to develop this list and put the expressions on the board. See the SAM/MFL for activities that accompany the third speaker, a young woman who discusses her experiences with the rites of baptism and communion in the Catholic Church.

A. Avant de regarder. Vous allez écouter des personnes qui parlent d'évènements importants dans leur vie. Quels sont les évènements les plus importants dans la vie d'une personne ? Préparez une liste avec vos camarades de classe.

MODÈLE la naissance (*birth*) d'un enfant, le baptême, la bar et bat mitsva...

B. En regardant. Pour chaque personne, répondez aux questions.

Marie-Julie

1. Marie-Julie explique qu'au Québec, lorsqu'elles se marient, les femmes doivent garder…
   a. leur nom de jeune fille
   b. le nom de leur mari
   c. les deux noms
2. C'est…
   a. une vieille coutume
   b. une loi récente
   c. une tradition dans certaines familles

Monsieur le maire de Seillans et Barbara

3. Pour le maire de Seillans, le mariage est un acte…
   a. de foi (*faith*). **b.** familial. **c.** officiel.
4. Les participants à la cérémonie sont : le maire, les mariés, et…
   a. leurs parents. **b.** leurs amis. **c.** leurs témoins (*witnesses*).
5. Pour Barbara, son mariage était un peu spécial parce que… était le maire.
   a. sa mère
   b. sa future belle-mère
   c. son futur mari

Key: En regardant 1) a 2) b 3) c 4) c 5) b

C. Après avoir regardé. Maintenant discutez des questions suivantes avec vos camarades de classe.

1. Est-ce que les femmes qui se marient chez vous peuvent choisir leur nom ? Quelles sont les traditions dans votre communauté ?
2. En quoi est-ce que les mariages chez vous sont semblables aux mariages en France ? En quoi est-ce qu'ils sont différents ?

Script: Observons

MARIE-JULIE : Je m'appelle Marie-Julie Kerharo, mais à toutes les fois où* je rentre au Québec, c'est Marie-Julie Lavoie parce qu'au Québec, les femmes doivent préserver leur nom de jeune fille tout le reste de leur vie. C'est une loi qui date des années 80, si je ne m'abuse pas, c'est 1986. Et depuis lors, les femmes n'ont pas le choix, elles doivent garder leur nom de jeune fille, même si elles sont mariées.

MONSIEUR LE MAIRE DE SEILLANS : Bonjour, j'ai le plaisir de vous accueillir dans la salle des mariages de la commune de Seillans. Je suis le maire et en cette qualité, je célèbre les mariages des habitants de la commune. C'est une cérémonie officielle, qui consiste à recueillir le consentement des mariés, en présence de deux ou quatre témoins.

BARBARA : Bonjour, bonjour Monsieur le Maire.

M. LE MAIRE : Bonjour, Barbara.

BARBARA : Voilà, je m'appelle Barbara Roustan, je suis, euh, j'habite à Seillans. Il ne faut pas oublier aussi, je me suis mariée en 1988 dans cette salle de mariage. Et c'était un petit peu original parce que ma future belle-mère à l'époque était le maire de Seillans en 1988 et donc, elle était très émue à l'issue de ce mariage, de nous marier, et c'était magnifique, parce que c'était très familial et en même temps, c'était un mariage, voilà, un petit peu spécial.

*In Standard French, *mais toutes les fois que…*

Les rituels du mariage dans le monde francophone

Les rituels du mariage varient d'un pays[1] à l'autre. Comme vous le savez, en France on se marie d'abord à la mairie et après lors d'une cérémonie religieuse si les mariés le désirent. Les robes que les mariées portent en France et au Québec sont souvent blanches et ressemblent aux robes de mariée que vous avez sans doute vues aux États-Unis. En Afrique francophone, les mariées de familles aisées[2] dans les grandes villes peuvent s'habiller de la même façon[3] ou elles peuvent se vêtir[4] de robes plus traditionnelles. Quelquefois, il y a même deux mariages : un mariage à l'européenne et un mariage traditionnel à l'africaine. Au Maroc, il y a un rituel précis pour la mariée : les femmes décorent les mains de la future mariée avec du henné pour la protéger du mal[5] et pour lui porter bonne chance[6] et lui apporter de la fertilité.

[1]*country* [2]riches [3]*the same way* [4]s'habiller [5]*protect from evil* [6]*luck*

Implementation: Treat the text as a short reading; relate the information here to the photos.

Variation: You may want to ask students to bring in pictures of a wedding of a friend or family member before completing the **Parlons** activity in class. As a variation, you could display all the pictures in the front of the room and have students take turns describing the picture they brought. The other students in the class can then guess which wedding is being described. If you feel comfortable doing so, you may also want to share a picture from your own wedding or from the wedding of one of your friends or family members. You will most likely have students from a variety of ethnic and religious backgrounds in your class. Encourage students to discuss the cultural aspects of the weddings they have participated in (for example, a Greek wedding often includes a certain type of dancing at the reception, and in a traditional Scottish wedding the groom might wear a kilt) and to compare them with the experiences of their classmates.

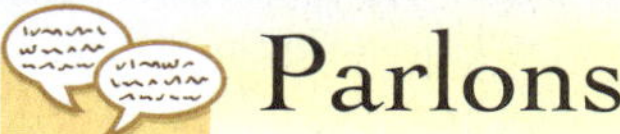

Parlons

7-39 Le mariage

A. Avant de parler. Examinez les photos de mariage dans le monde francophone et lisez les légendes (*captions*). N'oubliez pas la photo d'un mariage en France au début de la leçon **Venez chez nous !** à la page 288.

Au Maroc, on décore les mains de la mariée au henné.

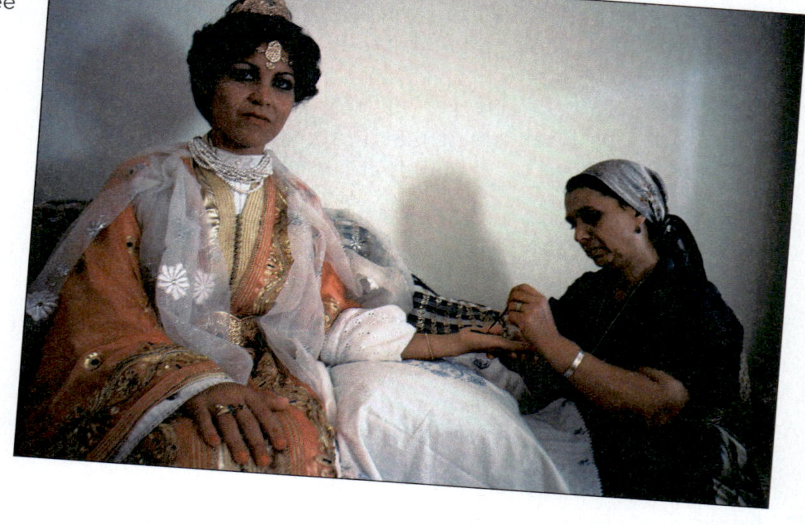

Un mariage au Mali, où la mariée et le marié arrivent sur le dos d'un dromadaire.

À la fin d'une cérémonie juive en Bourgogne, le marié brise un verre.

B. En parlant. Avec un/e partenaire, décrivez chaque image. Par exemple, qui sont ces personnes ? Qu'est-ce qu'elles font ? Qu'est-ce qu'elles portent ?

MODÈLE Sur cette photo, je pense que la femme se prépare pour aller à son mariage. Elle porte…

C. Après avoir parlé. À quel mariage est-ce que vous voudriez assister ? Qu'est-ce qui vous intéresse en particulier sur ces photos ? Comparez vos réactions à celles de vos camarades de classe.

Lisons

TEXT AUDIO CD 4 TRACK 12

7-40 L'Enfant noir

Sur le chemin du village.

Stratégie

Draw on your personal experience to better understand and respond to the events and emotions expressed by a writer. For example, when you know the topic of a reading passage, think about it, before you read, in terms of your own memories and associations.

A. Avant de lire. *L'Enfant noir*, published in 1954, was written by Camara Laye at the age of 25 while he was studying in Paris. This autobiographical novel recounts his experiences growing up in **la Guinée** in Sub-Saharan Africa. The following excerpt recounts an important "coming of age" experience: Baba, the main character, who is fifteen years old, is getting ready to leave home to live with his uncle and attend school in the distant city of Conakry. He is saying his good-byes, thinking about the implications of his departure, and experiencing a range of powerful emotions. Can you identify with Baba at this moment of transition? Have you had a similar experience—perhaps when you finished high school and went on to college? How did you feel about saying good-bye to friends and family and leaving behind a familiar setting? If you can draw on your own experience

Implementation: Avant de lire You might find photos from the film online; these help illustrate the point that Baba is very young when he leaves home. Before they read the passage, have students describe their own experiences on leaving home for the first time. Remind them that as they read, they should not expect to understand every word of the text, but instead should study the questions carefully and focus on finding the information specified.

to help you understand the events and feelings evoked by Camara Laye, you will be better able to grasp and respond to them.

The writer mainly uses two past tenses to tell his story: the **imparfait** and the **passé simple**. The latter is a literary tense that has generally the same meaning as the **passé composé**. Here are some examples you will see in the text; find their equivalent:

Ma mère me réveilla →	Je suis revenu
Je me levai	Elle m'a fait signe
Je revins	Ma mère m'a réveillé
Je me mis	j'ai fait (= j'ai dit)
Elle me fit signe	Je me suis levé
fis-je	Je me suis mis

Implementation: En lisant Once students have identified the two parts of the excerpt, have them listen to each section read aloud and then answer the corresponding questions. Ask students whether they can relate to the scene where the parents give gifts to Baba; did their own parents give them a family keepsake or a Saint Christopher's medal, for example, when they left home?

Key: En lisant 1) la première partie correspond aux deux premiers paragraphes ; la deuxième partie commence par : *— Cours vite* 2) sa mère lui donne une bouteille d'eau magique pour développer son intelligence ; son père lui donne une corne de bouc remplie de talismans pour le défendre contre les mauvais esprits 3) la référence à Kankan, une ville « très musulmane » ; la croyance à la magie et aux mauvais esprits ; l'usage des talismans 4) Baba dit adieu aux vieilles gens de son village, avec le cœur gros ; il dit adieu à sa mère et à son père avec des larmes. Sa mère ne l'accompagnera pas à la gare, parce que ce serait trop difficile pour elle et pour lui.

Key: En regardant de plus près frappé de cette incertitude; en larmes; je me mis à pleurer; Mère ne pleure pas; j'étais sans courage; je sanglotais.

Expansion: Après avoir lu Show in class the scene from the film that corresponds to the text. Have students explain which version they prefer, and why.

B. En lisant. Répondez à ces questions.

1. Ce passage peut être divisé en deux parties : (1) Le matin du départ et les cadeaux et (2) Les adieux. Est-ce que vous pouvez identifier ces deux parties ?
2. Dans la première partie, les parents offrent des cadeaux à Baba :

sa mère lui donne :
pour :
son père lui donne :
pour :

3. Dans cette partie, quels sont les éléments de la religion islamique et des traditions africaines que vous remarquez ?
4. Dans la deuxième partie, Baba doit faire ses adieux. À qui ? Quelle est sa réaction à chaque fois ?

C. En regardant de plus près. Dans ce passage Baba et sa famille expriment leurs émotions. Relevez les expressions qui servent à exprimer des émotions.

MODÈLE avoir le cœur gros, ...

D. Après avoir lu. Enfin, discutez de ces questions avec vos camarades de classe.

1. Baba éprouve des fortes émotions quand il dit adieu à ses voisins et à sa famille. Est-ce que vous avez eu une expérience semblable ? Est-ce que Baba décrit une situation universelle, à votre avis, ou est-ce que ce récit reflète sa situation particulière en Guinée ?
2. Est-ce que vous avez eu une expérience qui a complètement changé votre vie ? Décrivez cela à un/e partenaire.

Ma mère me réveilla à l'aube[1], et je me levai sans qu'elle dût insister. ... Mes bagages étaient en tas[2] dans la case[3]. Soigneusement[4] calée[5] et placée en évidence, une bouteille y était jointe.

—Qu'y a-t-il dans cette bouteille ? dis-je.

—Ne la casse[6] pas ! dit ma mère.

—J'y ferai attention[7].

—Fais-y grande attention ! Chaque matin, avant d'entrer en classe, tu prendras une petite gorgée[8] de cette bouteille.

—Est-ce l'eau destinée à développer l'intelligence ? dis-je.

—Celle-la même ![9] Et il n'en peut exister de plus efficace[10] : elle vient de[11] Kankan !

J'avais déjà bu de cette eau : mon professeur m'en avait fait boire, quand j'avais passé mon certificat d'études. C'est une eau magique qui a nombre de pouvoirs et en particulier celui de développer le cerveau[12]. ... Acheté dans la ville de Kankan, qui est une ville très musulmane et la plus sainte de nos villes, et manifestement acheté à haut prix[13], le breuvage[14] devait être particulièrement agissant[15]. Mon père, pour sa part, m'avait remis, la veille, une petite corne de bouc[16] renfermant des talismans ; et je devais porter continuellement sur moi cette corne qui me défendrait contre les mauvais esprits[17].

—Cours vite[18] faire tes adieux maintenant ! dit ma mère.

J'allais dire au revoir aux vieilles gens de notre concession[19] et des concessions voisines, et j'avais le cœur gros[20]. Ces hommes, ces femmes, je les connaissais depuis ma plus tendre enfance[21], depuis toujours je les avais vus à la place même où je les voyais, et aussi j'en avais vu disparaître[22] : ma grand-mère paternelle avait disparu ! Et reverrais-je[23] tous ceux auxquels[24] je disais à présent adieu ? Frappé[25] de cette incertitude, ce fut comme si soudain je prenais congé[26] de mon passé même. Mais n'était-ce pas un peu cela ? Ne quittais-je pas ici toute une partie de mon passé ?

Quand je revins[27] près de ma mère et que je l'aperçus[28] en larmes[29] devant mes bagages, je me mis à pleurer à mon tour. Je me jetai dans ses bras[30] et je l'étreignis[31]. ...

—Mère, ne pleure pas ! dis-je. Ne pleure pas !

Mais je n'arrivais pas moi-même à refréner[32] mes larmes et je la suppliai[33] de ne pas m'accompagner à la gare, car il me semblait qu'alors je ne pourrais jamais m'arracher[34] à ses bras. Elle me fit signe qu'elle y consentait. Nous nous étreignîmes une dernière fois, et je m'éloignai presque en courant[35]. ...

Mon père m'avait rapidement rejoint et il m'avait pris la main[36], comme du temps où j'étais encore enfant. Je ralentis le pas[37] : j'étais sans courage, je sanglotais éperdument[38].

—Père ! fis-je.

—Je t'écoute, dit-il.

—Est-ce vrai que je pars ?

—Que ferais-tu d'autre ?[39] Tu sais bien que tu dois partir.

—Oui, dis-je.

[1]le lever du soleil [2]*piled up* [3]*hut* [4]*Carefully* [5]*wedged* [6]*break* [7]*I'll be careful.* [8]*sip* [9]*Precisely!* [10]*effective* [11]*comes from* [12]*brain* [13]*at a high price* [14]*beverage* [15]*effective* [16]*ram's horn* [17]*spirits* [18]*Run quickly* [19]*property* [20]*a heavy heart* [21]*from my earliest childhood* [22]*I had seen some pass on* [23]*would I see again* [24]*those to whom* [25]*struck* [26]*was leaving* [27]*came back* [28]*saw* [29]*in tears* [30]*arms* [31]*held her tightly* [32]*stop* [33]*begged* [34]*tear myself away* [35]*walked away hurriedly* [36]*took my hand* [37]*slowed my steps* [38]*was sobbing uncontrollably* [39]*What else would you do?*

Les rites religieux et les fêtes populaires

Le ramadan

Le ramadan est un rituel pratiqué par les musulmans, les gens qui croient en la religion islamique. Ils sont environ cinq millions en France, où l'islam est la deuxième religion après le catholicisme. Au Maghreb (au Maroc, en Algérie et en Tunisie), les musulmans sont en vaste majorité.

Le ramadan, le neuvième mois de l'année lunaire du calendrier islamique, est une période de jeûne[1]. Pendant ce mois, les musulmans ne peuvent ni manger, ni[2] boire pendant la journée. Mais au coucher du soleil, les familles et les amis partagent des grands repas. Il y a aussi des fêtes foraines[3] où les gens s'amusent à la tombée de la nuit. À la fin du ramadan, il y a trois jours de fête qui s'appellent **Aïd-el-fitr** (qui veut dire **la fête de la rupture du jeûne**).

La fête de Aïd-el-fitr marque la fin de ramadan.

Le carême : Carnaval et Mardi gras

Les Chrétiens ont aussi un rituel de jeûne, la période du Carême[4] (les quarante jours qui précèdent Pâques). Avant cette période assez stricte, il y a des fêtes importantes. En France, le Carnaval de Nice a lieu au mois de février. En Louisiane, à la Nouvelle-Orléans, on fête le Mardi gras avec de la musique, de la danse et des déguisements[5]. Dans les petites villes comme Eunice, Basile et Mamou, on participe au « Courir de Mardi Gras », où les gens vont de maison en maison en demandant des ingrédients pour faire un gombo communal. Ces fêtes, à l'origine des fêtes religieuses, sont maintenant célébrées de façon[6] séculaire.

Le Courir de Mardi Gras à Basile, en Louisiane.

[1]*fasting* [2]*neither, nor* [3]*traveling fairs* [4]*Lent* [5]*costumes, disguises* [6]*in a way*

Implementation: You may have students who are Muslim and who celebrate Ramadan. If they are willing, you may ask them to share their experiences. Ask students if they have ever participated in *Mardi gras* or any other pre-Lenten ritual (such as eating pancakes on Shrove Tuesday). Help students make the connection that *Mardi gras* refers to a Tuesday, and that it is the Tuesday prior to Ash Wednesday, which marks the beginning of the forty days of Lent. The central point here is not to teach students about Christian holidays, but rather to make the point that what was once a religious celebration has now become a popular holiday for all. Some questions you could ask include: *Est-ce que vous connaissez quelqu'un qui fête le ramadan ? Vous avez participé à un carnaval ? Où ?*

Masked participants in the *Courir de Mardi Gras* are traditionally led by *le Capitaine*, who asks permission to come onto private property, where the maskers sing, dance, and beg for ingredients for a communal meal. Sometimes a farm owner will throw out a live chicken that the maskers chase. At the end of the day, participants parade downtown to the location where the communal feast is prepared.

Écrivons

7-41 Une tradition importante

A. Avant d'écrire. Lisez les textes au sujet du rituel islamique, le ramadan et les fêtes du Carnaval et de Mardi gras. Pensez maintenant aux rituels que vous pratiquez. Est-ce qu'il y a des rituels importants dans votre famille ? votre religion ? votre région ? votre université ? Choisissez un rituel avec des traditions que vous voulez décrire et faites une liste des éléments importants de ce rituel. Pensez à la dernière fois que vous avez participé à ce rituel, et indiquez des détails essentiels.

MODÈLE La fête de *Homecoming*

Éléments importants	Détails
un match de football américain	*L'année dernière notre équipe a gagné contre l'université X.*
des chars décorés avec des fleurs	*Le char préparé par mes amis et moi était un désastre. Les fleurs n'étaient pas bien fixées sur le char.*
un bal	*1. Je suis allé au bal avec Samantha, ma copine.*
	2. Nous avons dansé jusqu'à une heure du matin.

B. En écrivant. Maintenant, écrivez un paragraphe pour décrire la dernière fois que vous avez participé à ce rituel. N'oubliez pas de donner des détails et d'utiliser le passé composé et l'imparfait !

MODÈLE La fête de *Homecoming*

Une des traditions sur mon campus, c'est la fête de *Homecoming*. L'année dernière je me suis bien amusé avec mes amis. Notre équipe de football américain a bien joué et elle a gagné le match ! Mais, le corso de chars pendant la mi-temps était un désastre pour mes amis et moi. Les fleurs n'étaient pas bien fixées sur le char et elles ont toutes commencé à tomber. Le soir, il y avait un grand bal et j'ai dansé avec ma copine Samantha jusqu'à une heure du matin.

C. En révisant. Réfléchissez aux questions suivantes et puis faites tous les changements nécessaires.

1. Relisez votre paragraphe pour analyser le contenu : est-ce que vous avez choisi trois ou quatre éléments importants ? Est-ce que vous avez décrit chacun de ces éléments ?
2. Relisez de nouveau votre paragraphe pour analyser le style et la forme : est-ce que vous avez utilisé un vocabulaire simple ? Est-ce que vous avez bien utilisé le passé composé et l'imparfait pour exprimer les évènements au passé ?

D. Après avoir écrit. Échangez votre texte avec un/e camarade de classe pour comparer vos expériences. Est-ce que certaines personnes ont choisi de décrire le même évènement ?

Stratégie

When describing a culturally distinctive event, use precise, familiar details to give your reader an immediate feel for the occasion.

Implementation: 7-41 Students will ask for help with vocabulary, as they are unlikely to know words specific to some holidays and North American traditions. Brainstorm with them to find simple ways of conveying complex ideas. Emphasize that they should rely on familiar words and phrases to tell their stories, as outlined in the writing strategy. Use the model as an example of how to do this. Ask students to exchange first drafts with a classmate and have the classmate suggest where more detail could be added to make the paragraph more interesting. Following revisions, have students exchange papers again with the same classmate for feedback before turning in their description.

Now that you have completed *Chapitre 7*, can you do the following in French?

- ☐ Talk about your family background, beliefs, and values?
- ☐ Describe significant holiday celebrations and events?
- ☐ Construct a coherent narrative in French, using the **passé composé** and **imparfait**?
- ☐ Express your own opinions and report what others say and believe?
- ☐ Express your emotions appropriately?
- ☐ Describe rites and rituals across the Francophone world?

Leçon 

pour parler de la famille	***to talk about the family***
un beau-frère	*brother-in-law*
une belle-sœur	*sister-in-law*
un demi-frère	*half-brother, step brother*
une demi-sœur	*half-sister, step sister*
divorcer	*to divorce*
une famille étendue	*extended family*
une famille monoparentale	*single-parent family*
une famille recomposée	*blended family*
une femme/un homme au foyer	*stay-at-home mother/father*
un père/une mère célibataire	*single father/mother*
l'union libre (f.)	*cohabitation*

pour décrire une personne	***to describe a person***
absent/e	*absent, missing*
ancien/ne	*former (placed before the noun)*
autoritaire	*authoritarian*
avoir des bons rapports avec quelqu'un	*to get along well with someone*
avoir des racines (f.)	*to have roots*
juives	*Jewish*
maghrébines	*North African*
multiculturelles	*multicultural*
avoir des complexes	*to have issues*
avoir une vision du monde	*to have a worldview*
être bien dans sa peau	*to have confidence in oneself*
être pratiquant/e	*to practice a faith*
exigeant/e	*strict, demanding*
indulgent/e	*indulgent, lenient*
rebelle	*rebellious*
sécurisant/e	*reassuring*
traditionnel/le	*traditional*
travailleur/-euse	*working; hardworking*

pour parler des études et du travail	***to talk about studies and work***
apprendre à	*to teach, to learn*
avoir le goût du travail	*to have a strong work ethic*

verbes de communication	***verbs of communication***
décrire	*to describe*
dire	*to say, to tell*
écrire	*to write*
lire	*to read*

autres mots utiles	***other useful words***
la connaissance	*knowledge, understanding*
une épreuve	*test*
faire partie de	*to belong to*
heureusement	*fortunately*
permettre (de + inf)	*to allow (to + verb)*
rater	*to miss*
ressentir	*to feel, be affected by*
terminer	*to end*
la vérité	*truth*
vivre	*to live*

Leçon 

les grands évènements de la vie	***major life events***
un anniversaire	*birthday, anniversary*
un baptême	*baptism*
une bougie	*candle*
un cadeau	*gift*
une cérémonie civile	*civil ceremony*
une fête religieuse	*religious holiday*
un gâteau	*cake*
les grandes vacances (f.)	*summer vacation*
un mariage	*wedding*
un/e marié/e	*groom/bride*
une marraine	*godmother*
un parrain	*godfather*

des vœux	***wishes***
un vœu	*wish*
Meilleurs vœux !	*Best wishes!*
Félicitations !	*Congratulations!*
Bon/Joyeux anniversaire !	*Happy Birthday!*
Joyeux Noël !	*Merry Christmas!*
Bonne année !	*Happy New Year!*
Bon voyage !	*Have a good trip!*
Bonnes vacances !	*Have a good vacation!*

Vocabulaire

pour parler des fêtes	***to talk about holidays***
avoir lieu	*to take place*
un bal populaire	*a street dance*
cacher	*to hide*
un défilé	*parade*
fêter	*to celebrate*
un feu d'artifice	*fireworks*
une fleur	*flower*
une galette	*type of cake*
un jour férié	*public holiday*
le muguet	*lily of the valley*
un œuf en chocolat	*chocolate egg*

Leçon 

les sentiments	***feelings***
avoir l'air (d'être) + adj.	*to seem, to appear (to be) + adj.*
Qu'est-ce que tu as ?	*What's wrong?*
amoureux/-euse	*in love*
tomber amoureux/-euse	*to fall in love*
anxieux/-euse	*anxious*
content/e	*happy*
embarrassé/e	*embarrassed*
en colère	*angry*
fâché/e	*angry*
furieux/-euse	*furious*
gêné/e	*bothered, embarrassed*
heureux/-euse	*happy*
inquiet/inquiète	*uneasy, anxious, worried*
jaloux/-ouse	*jealous*
malheureux/-euse	*unhappy*
ravi/e	*delighted*
sensible	*sensitive*
surpris/e	*surprised*
triste	*sad*

pour exprimer les sentiments	***to express feelings***
crier	*to yell*
perdre son sang-froid	*to lose one's composure*
pleurer	*to cry*

quelques verbes pronominaux	***some pronominal verbs***
s'amuser	*to have fun*
s'appeler	*to be named, called*
s'arranger	*to work out, to be all right*
se calmer	*to calm down*
se disputer	*to argue*
s'ennuyer	*to become bored*
s'entendre (avec)	*to get along (with)*
se fâcher (contre)	*to get angry (at, with)*
se faire du souci	*to worry*
Ne t'en fais pas !/ Ne vous en faites pas !	*Don't worry!*
s'inquiéter	*to worry*
s'intéresser à	*to be interested in*
se passer	*to happen*
se rappeler	*to remember*
se reposer	*to rest*
se retrouver	*to meet*
se téléphoner	*to phone each other*

dans la vie sentimentale	***in one's emotional life***
se disputer	*to argue, to fight*
s'embrasser	*to kiss*
se fiancer	*to get engaged*
se marier	*to get married*
se rencontrer	*to meet (for the first time)*
se séparer	*to separate*

autres verbes utiles	***other useful verbs***
croire (à)	*to believe (in)*
voir	*to see*

quelques expressions utiles	***some useful expressions***
Ce n'est pas grave.	*It's not serious.*
fort (adv.)	*loudly*
Je crois. / Je crois que oui.	*I think so.*
Je ne crois pas. / Je crois que non.	*I don't think so.*
Je crois que...	*I think / believe that . . .*
une nouvelle	*piece of news*
si	*whether, if*
Soyez calme !	*Be calm!*
Ne sois pas furieuse !	*Don't be angry!*
Voyons !	*See here!*

8 Activités par tous les temps

Regardez ces deux personnes : où sont-elles, à votre avis ? Qu'est-ce qu'elles vont probablement faire aujourd'hui ?

After completing this chapter, you should be able to:

- Talk about the weather
- Ask for specific information
- Extend, accept, and refuse invitations
- Give advice
- Identify vacation spots and cultural activities in places where French is spoken

Leçon 1 Il fait quel temps ?

Presentation: Provide an overview of this chapter by showing the video montage *Vive les vacances !* See whether students can identify the various places, activities, and seasons. Use the weather visuals (MFL, Ch. 8) and brief descriptions to present the new vocabulary. Once you have presented a few items, show an image without labels (MFL, Ch. 8) and test comprehension by having students point to a picture that illustrates the weather you describe. Next, have students repeat key expressions. Emphasize the use of *il fait* for most expressions, except for *il pleut* and *il neige*. Point out that the pronoun *il* is used in an impersonal way and does not refer to a person. Point out near-equivalent expressions, for example, *il y a des nuages/le ciel est couvert.*

POINTS DE DÉPART

TEXT AUDIO
CD 4 TRACK 27

Le temps à toutes les saisons

En été, il fait chaud et lourd.

Il fait beau. Il y a du soleil et le ciel est bleu.

Le ciel est couvert ; il y a des nuages. Il va pleuvoir.

Au printemps, il fait frais et il y a du vent.

En automne, il fait mauvais. Il pleut et il y a du brouillard.

Finally, treat the **Vie et culture** notes and check comprehension: *Il fait 30°C. —Il fait très chaud.* We suggest that you review this new vocabulary on day 2 of the lesson and then present the seasons, continuing with the exercises that follow. If you live in the Snow Belt, you may wish to introduce some Québec French weather expressions such as *neigeasser* 'to be snowing lightly,' *une poudrerie* 'blowing snow,' *de la sloche* 'slush.'

Il y a un orage : il y a des éclairs et du tonnerre.

En hiver, il gèle ; il y a du verglas.

Il fait froid et il neige.

Implementation: Help students discover the meaning of the proverb *En avril ne te découvre pas d'un fil* by using the clues in the sub-headline: *gelées tardives, froid, masse d'air froid, Scandinavie* combined with their world knowledge that the weather is often unpredictable in April and not yet summer-like. A literal translation of this proverb would be something like: "In April, do not take off so much as a stitch of clothing." You may wish to introduce other French proverbs or brainstorm with students to create a list of English proverbs that evoke the weather. See the SAM/MFL for an exercise matching near-equivalent proverbs in French and English. Examples of other weather-related proverbs in French are: *Autant en emporte le vent* (said of insincere or unkept promises); *Une hirondelle ne fait pas le printemps ; En mai, fais ce qu'il te plaît.* Visit the *Chez nous* Companion Website for links to Web sites with weather proverbs in French and English.

Vie et culture

Proverbes

En avril, ne te découvre pas d'un fil

Gare aux gelées tardives. Des records de froid ont été battus en raison de l'arrivée d'une masse d'air froid venue de Scandinavie

Michel BARELLI, Nice-Matin, 9 avril 2003, p.30, Tous droits réservés

Regardez ce titre du journal **Nice-Matin** ; c'est un proverbe pour présenter un article sur le temps. La plupart des langues ont des proverbes qui parlent du temps ; mais comme vous l'avez découvert pour d'autres aspects de la langue française, on ne peut pas traduire les proverbes mot à mot. Pour comprendre ce proverbe, examinez bien le contexte. Le journal a été publié en quel mois ? Regardez les mots en dessous du titre « **En avril, ne te découvre pas d'un fil** »; quels mots indiquent le temps prévu ? Avec toutes ces informations, est-ce que vous pouvez trouver le sens du proverbe ?

ET VOUS ?

1. Est-ce que vous pouvez donner un exemple d'un proverbe en anglais qui parle du temps ?
2. Pourquoi, à votre avis, est-ce qu'il y a beaucoup de proverbes qui parlent du temps ?

Key: Et vous ? 1) Students may mention proverbs such as "Every cloud has a silver lining," "April showers bring May flowers," or "March comes in like a lion and goes out like a lamb." 2) Everyone experiences weather, and many proverbs go back to a more agrarian form of society that was dependent on weather.

Implementation: Practice these expressions using the weather art (MFL, Ch. 8); for each image, have students decide which would be more appropriate: *j'ai chaud/j'ai froid.*

Fiche pratique

In Francophone countries and throughout much of the world, temperature is measured in degrees Celsius. To make things easy, just remember a few key expressions that correspond to certain temperatures. For example, look at the thermometer and these expressions:

To indicate that a person feels cold or hot, use the verb **avoir**:

Il fait 30°C ; j'**ai** très **chaud**.	*It's 86 degrees; I'm very hot.*
Il commence à neiger ; nous **avons froid**.	*It's starting to snow; we're cold.*

Note: In case students are interested in the formula: To convert from Celsius to Fahrenheit, divide by 5, multiply by 9 and add 32. To convert from Fahrenheit to Celsius, subtract 32, multiply by 5 and divide by 9.

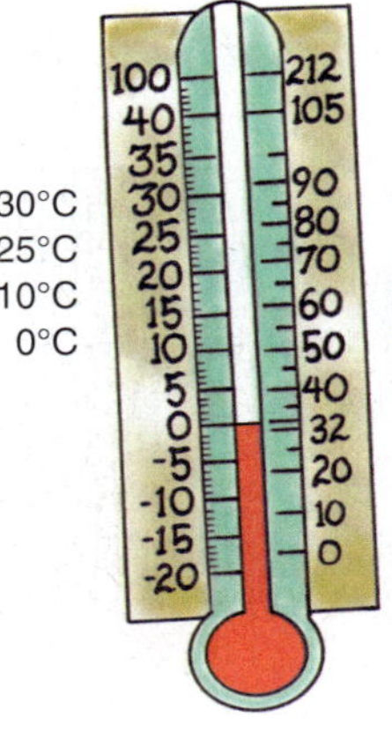

30°C très chaud.
25°C bon.
10°C frais.
0°C froid.

À vous la parole

8-1 Quel temps fait-il ?

D'après le journal, dites quel temps il fait dans ces villes francophones.

MODÈLE Paris
À Paris, il fait assez frais et le ciel est couvert.

1. Cayenne
2. Alger
3. Dakar
4. Montréal
5. Nice
6. La Nouvelle-Orléans
7. Papeete
8. Fort-de-France
9. Tunis

PRÉVISIONS POUR LE 2 AVRIL

Ville par ville, les minima/maxima de température et l'état du ciel.
S : soleil ; C : couvert ; P : pluie ; V : vent fort ; O : orages ; N : neige

AMÉRIQUES		
BRASILIA	19/28	S
CHICAGO	7/21	S
MEXICO	10/24	S
MONTRÉAL	−6/0	N
NEW YORK	5/14	C
LA NOUVELLE-ORLÉANS	10/26	S
TORONTO	2/13	C

FRANCE métropole		
AJACCIO	9/19	S
BIARRITZ	8/16	P
CAEN	3/10	C
LILLE	3/11	C
NICE	9/16	S,V
PARIS	3/12	C

FRANCE d'outre-mer		
CAYENNE	23/27	P
FORT-DE-FR.	23/28	S
PAPEETE	25/31	P

AFRIQUE		
ALGER	13/21	S
DAKAR	20/26	O
KINSHASA	23/29	P
LE CAIRE	16/27	S
TUNIS	15/26	P

Implementation: 8-1 Use a map (for example, MFL, Maps) to show the location of cities. Note the distinction between *la France métropole* and *la France d'outre-mer*. You may also wish to display the newspaper weather forecast (MFL, Ch. 8). To expand and review, have students describe what clothing they would wear in each city.

8-2 Prévisions météorologiques.

Voilà le temps qu'on annonce pour la France. Demandez à votre partenaire quel temps il va faire et la température.

MODÈLE à Lyon

É1 Quel temps est-ce qu'il va faire à Lyon ?
É2 À Lyon, il va pleuvoir.
É1 Et la température ?
É2 Il va faire onze degrés, donc il va faire assez frais.

1. à Paris
2. à Bordeaux
3. à Perpignan
4. à Brest
5. à Nice
6. à Grenoble
7. à Lille
8. à Strasbourg
9. à Bastia

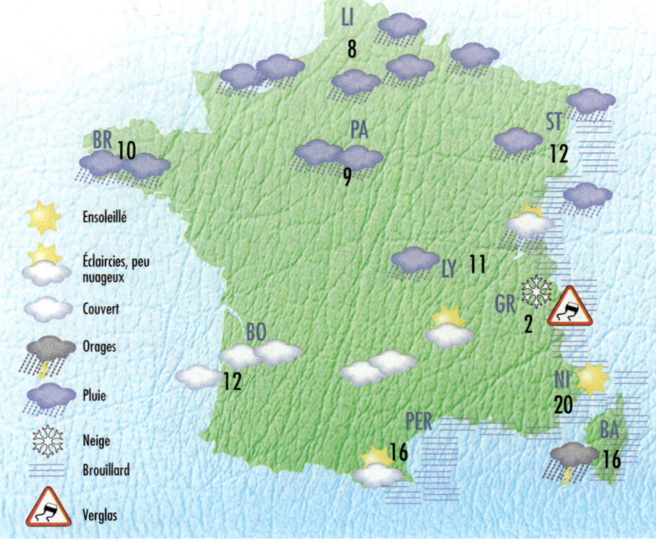

Implementation: 8-2 Show the weather map (MFL, Ch. 8) and go over the city codes and weather symbols before completing the exercise. You may also substitute a current weather map; see the *Chez nous* Companion Website for links to sites where you can download a current weather forecast for France or show it live in your classroom.

Variation: As an alternative to Ex. 8-2, have students (in pairs or small groups) describe the weather in famous paintings you display as posters or slides. Some examples of good paintings to use include: *Rue de Paris, jour de pluie ; Toits sous la neige, Paris*, Gustave Caillebotte ; *La neige à Louveciennes ; Printemps aux environs de Paris, pommiers en fleurs*, Alfred Sisley ; *Coquelicots ; Promenade près d'Argenteuil ; Effet de vent, série des Peupliers ; Le Déjeuner*, Claude Monet ; *Les Boulevards extérieurs, effet de neige ; Arbres en fleurs*, Pissarro ; *La Méridienne ou La Sieste (d'après Millet)*, Vincent Van Gogh ; *Les parapluies*, Renoir.

Implementation: 8-3 Follow up by having the class compare responses for each item.

8-3 Vos préférences.

Avec un/e partenaire, posez les questions suivantes pour découvrir quand votre partenaire préfère faire ces activités. Ensuite, comparez vos réponses avec celles de vos camarades de classe.

MODÈLE É1 Quand est-ce que tu n'aimes pas aller en classe ?
É2 Je n'aime pas aller en classe quand il pleut ou quand il y a un orage.

Presentation: You may wish to present this vocabulary on day 2. Have students describe the weather in each photo. Ask what month they think it is, and present the seasons. Point out that the preposition *en* is used with all months of the year and all seasons except *le printemps* (*au printemps*).

1. Quand est-ce que tu aimes rester dans le jardin ?
2. Quand est-ce que tu aimes faire du shopping ?
3. Quand est-ce que tu aimes faire du sport ?
4. Quand est-ce que tu préfères rester chez toi ?
5. Quand est-ce que tu aimes aller au cinéma ?
6. Quand est-ce que tu n'aimes pas voyager ?

Les saisons de l'année

le printemps (au printemps) : mars, avril, mai

l'été (en été) : juin, juillet, août

l'automne (en automne) : septembre, octobre, novembre

l'hiver (en hiver) : décembre, janvier, février

8-4 Nous sommes en quelle saison ? Pour chaque phrase, décidez avec un/e partenaire de quelle saison on parle.

MODÈLE En Bretagne le ciel est souvent couvert, il y a souvent de la pluie, mais il fait bon. On peut jouer au tennis ou au golf.

É1 C'est le printemps ou peut-être l'automne.
É2 Je pense que c'est le printemps parce qu'il y a beaucoup de pluie.

1. En France, on célèbre la fête nationale. Mais c'est la saison des orages : il y a des éclairs et du tonnerre.
2. Il y a souvent du brouillard en Bourgogne. Il gèle et il y a du verglas.
3. À Paris, c'est la rentrée et le temps est variable. Souvent, il y a du vent et le ciel est gris.
4. À la Martinique, il fait très chaud et lourd et il y a des nuages. Il pleut souvent.
5. On est sûr d'avoir du soleil et un temps chaud en France. Voilà pourquoi les Français partent en vacances.
6. Il y a beaucoup de soleil à Tahiti. On porte un maillot de bain.
7. Partout en France c'est la belle saison. Le ciel est bleu et il fait très beau. Mais les étudiants sont stressés parce que les examens vont bientôt commencer.
8. Il fait beau à la Guadeloupe. Il ne fait pas trop chaud. C'est le temps parfait pour aller à la plage.

Key: 8-4 *l'automne* = 3, 4 ; *l'hiver* = 2, 6 (from the point of view of the northern hemisphere) ; *le printemps* = 7, 8 ; *l'été* = 1, 5.
Ask students to give specific months when appropriate 1 = *juillet*, 3 = *septembre/octobre*, 5 = *juillet/août*, 7 = *mai/juin*. This exercise introduces cultural information and additional useful vocabulary; explain unfamiliar terms. Remind students that seasons are relative to the hemisphere; southern and northern hemispheres experience seasons at opposite times of the year. As a personalized follow-up, ask students *Quelle saison préférez-vous ? Pourquoi ?*

8-5 Quel est le climat chez vous ? Posez des questions à votre partenaire pour découvrir quel temps il fait d'habitude chez elle/lui et chez les membres de sa famille, pendant la saison indiquée.

Implementation: 8-5 Conclude by having students tell what type of climate they prefer and why.

MODÈLE en hiver, chez ses parents

É1 Quel temps fait-il en hiver chez tes parents ?
É2 Chez mes parents, en Louisiane, il fait assez frais et le ciel est souvent couvert en hiver.

1. en été, chez elle/lui
2. en hiver, chez elle/lui
3. au printemps, chez ses parents
4. en automne, chez ses grands-parents

L'été en Bretagne. Il fait chaud et il y a du soleil.

Quel temps fait-il ? Téléphonez pour savoir !

Presentation: Examine the poster and have students look at the weather symbols and read the sequences out loud to discover what they mean: *Il fait beau ? Il (ne) fait pas beau ?* What can one do in France to hear the weather report? —call 32-50.

Note: When the letter *e* is in non-final position, many French speakers produce a vowel ranging between [e] and [ɛ]. The *e instable* (also referred to as *e muet, e caduc, schwa*, etc.) is pronounced variably: as zero (no sound) or a vowel ranging between /œ/ and /ø/. That vowel is often represented by the symbol [ə]. We propose that, when retained, unstable *e* should be pronounced as /ø /; in this way, the definite articles can be clearly distinguished, for example *le livre* vs. *la livre* or *le chat* vs. *les chats*. In addition to the cases presented here, note that in the prefix *re-* the letter e is pronounced [ø], *ressentir, refaire.*

Sons et lettres

La prononciation de la lettre *e*

You know that the letter **e** at the end of a word is usually not pronounced; it tells you that the consonant it follows is pronounced. Compare:

un anglais vs. un**e** anglais**e**

However, final **e** may be pronounced in one-syllable words such as the pronouns **je**, **me**, **te**, **se**, and **le**, the definite article **le**, the preposition **de** and the negative marker **ne**.

Within a word, the letter **e** is pronounced in several different ways:

- Like the sound in **deux** [ø]
  - when followed by a single consonant letter:

    un semestre premier une partenaire vous prenez
  - when followed by a consonant plus **r** or **l**:

    regretter un secret degrés
- Like the sound in **mère** [ɛ]
  - in the final syllable of a word, when it is followed by one or more pronounced consonants:

    sert couvert hiver lunettes de soleil cet
  - in a non-final syllable, when it is followed by two consonants (but see the exception below for double consonants):

    du verglas mercredi quelque
  - in a non-final syllable, when followed by an **x** (that letter represents the consonant groups **gz** or **ks**)

    un exemple expliquer un examen
- Like the sound in **thé** [e]
  - when it is followed by a double consonant or the combination **sc** in a non-final syllable of a word:

    pressé un effort descendre
  - in one-syllable function words such as **les**, **des**, **ces**, **ses**, **tes**.
- Sometimes, in one-syllable function words like **je**, **te**, **le**, **de**, **ce**, etc., and in words like **samedi** and **mademoiselle**, the letter **e** in the middle of the word is not pronounced; it is *elided*. For this reason a letter **e** pronounced with the vowel of **deux** is called an **unstable e**.

Compare the following two words. Look especially at the number of consonants before the unstable **e**:

vendredi samedi

An unstable **e** is usually dropped within words when it comes after only one pronounced consonant. In **samedi**, it comes after a single consonant, /m/, so it is dropped. But in **vendredi**, it comes after two pronounced consonants /dr/, so it is retained.

À vous la parole

8-6 Comparez. Comparez la prononciation du **e** dans chaque colonne.

[ø] **comme dans *deux***	[ɛ] **comme dans *mère***
1. prenez	prennent
2. demain	hier
3. devoir	détester
4. petit	exemple
5. degrés	verglas
6. demande	accepte

8-7 Contrastes. Comparez la chute et le maintien du **e** instable. Répétez :

samedi	vendredi
rarement	quelquefois
achetez	prenez

8-8 Quel son ? Lisez les phrases suivantes en faisant attention à la lettre **e** prononcée comme la voyelle de **thé**, ou de **mère**, ou de **deux**. Faites tomber aussi les **e** instables. Les **e** instables qui ne tombent pas sont prononcés comme la voyelle de **deux**.

1. Vous mettez vos tennis ? Il fait beau dehors cet après-midi.
2. Il fait moins deux degrés et il y a du verglas. Mettez ce bonnet, mademoiselle !
3. Restons à la maison : le ciel est couvert et il va y avoir du tonnerre.
4. Je dois faire un effort demain pour me lever tôt ; j'ai un examen à huit heures.
5. Appelez mercredi ou vendredi, jamais le samedi.
6. Elle explique les prévisions météorologiques à sa partenaire allemande.

Initial practice: Begin with a discrimination drill :
Levez le doigt quand vous entendez le son indiqué :
[ø] *comme dans* peu *en syllabe initiale : demander ; service ; degrés ; lever ; quelque ; devoir ; hier ; restaurant*
[ɛ] *comme dans* mère *en syllabe initiale : question ; derrière ; petit ; mettre ; descendre ; verglas ; retour*

Note: 8-7 If the question comes up, point out that unstable *e* is retained at the beginning of sentences (*Venez ! Je sors demain*) and in proper names like *Denise* and *Lefranc*. A full treatment of unstable **e** is provided in Ch. 11, L. 1 and L. 2.

FORMES ET FONCTIONS

1. *Les questions avec* quel *et* lequel

- The interrogative adjective **quel** is used to ask *which?* or *what?* Although **quel** agrees in number and gender with the noun it modifies, it is always pronounced the same, unless a plural form, **quels** or **quelles**, modifies a noun beginning with a vowel and liaison occurs.

Quel écrivain est-ce que tu préfères ?	*Which writer do you prefer?*
Quelle musique est-ce qu'il préfère ?	*What type of music does he prefer?*
Quels cours est-ce que tu suis ?	*Which courses are you taking?*
Quelles‿affiches est-ce que tu vas acheter ?	*Which posters are you going to buy?*

Presentation: You might use this as an opportunity to review question formation and prepare for the interrogative forms to be presented in L. 2. Use a variation on Ex. 2-12 on p. 77 to review question formation in a communicative context. To present *quel*, use the sentence examples and ask students to explain the differences in spelling; point out *enchaînement* and *liaison* before nouns beginning with a vowel, in the singular and plural, respectively. Additional practice is provided in the SAM/MFL.

Note: Since many of these examples involve inversion, focus on having students learn them as fixed phrases; do not teach or stress inversion here.

- **Quel** is used in a number of fixed interrogative expressions:

Quel temps fait-il ?	*What's the weather like?*
Quelle heure est-il ?	*What time is it?*
Quelle est la date aujourd'hui ?	*What's today's date?*
Quel âge est-ce que tu as ?	*How old are you?*

- **Quel** can also be used before a form of the verb **être**, followed by the noun it modifies:

Quelle est ta saison préférée ?	*What's your favorite season?*
Quelles sont les meilleures résidences ?	*Which are the best residence halls?*

- Use a form of the interrogative pronoun **lequel** to ask about someone or something that has already been mentioned. **Lequel**—which asks *which one?* or *which?*—agrees in number and gender with the noun it replaces.

—Tu as cours cet après-midi ?	*—Do you have class this afternoon?*
—Oui.	*—Yes.*
—**Lequel** ?	*—Which one?*
—Il sort avec l'une des sœurs de Sophie.	*—He's going out with one of Sophie's sisters.*
— Ah bon ? Avec **laquelle** ?	*—Really? With which one?*
Il fait froid. Voici des gants noirs, des gants rouges et des gants marron. **Lesquels** est-ce que tu préfères ?	*It's cold. Here are some black gloves, some red gloves, and some brown gloves. Which (ones) do you prefer?*

À vous la parole

Initial practice: Begin with a quick drill: *Tu vois le parapluie ? — Quel parapluie ? ; Tu vois le monsieur ? les enfants ? le chat ? les vélos ? la montagne ? les chiens ? les CD ?*

8-9 Petite épreuve. Posez des questions à un/e partenaire, qui doit répondre correctement !

MODÈLE les jours de la semaine
É1 Quels sont les jours de la semaine ?
É2 Lundi, mardi,...

1. les jours de la semaine
2. les mois de l'année
3. les saisons de l'année
4. la date de la fête nationale française
5. la date de ton anniversaire
6. ta saison préférée

8-10 Une interview. Interviewez un/e partenaire pour découvrir ses préférences.

MODÈLE la saison
É1 Quelle saison est-ce que tu préfères ?
É2 Je préfère l'automne. Et toi, quelle est ta saison préférée ?
É1 Moi, j'adore le printemps.

1. la saison
2. la ville
3. l'artiste
4. les acteurs
5. le sport
6. la musique
7. les écrivains

Variation: 8-10 If you wish for students to have written practice, you might ask them to write out their questions. Additional practice is provided in the SAM/MFL.

8-11 Préférences alimentaires. Discutez de vos préférences alimentaires avec un/e partenaire, en utilisant des questions avec **lequel**.

MODÈLES les fruits
É1 Je mange beaucoup de fruits.
É2 Lesquels est-ce que tu préfères ?
É1 Je préfère les fraises et les pêches. Et toi ?

1. les fruits
2. les légumes
3. les desserts
4. les boissons
5. les jus de fruits
6. les casse-croûte

Initial practice: Begin practice of *lequel* with a quick drill that also recycles clothing vocabulary: *Donne-moi un tee-shirt ! —Lequel ? ; une écharpe ; des gants ; un foulard ; une veste ; un bonnet ; des tennis ; des chaussettes.* Continue with a drill focusing on the use of prepositions: *Je vais au ciné avec une de mes sœurs. Ah bon ? Avec laquelle ? ; avec un de mes cousins ; avec des copains ; avec des étudiants dans mon cours de français ; avec une copine ; avec un ami ; avec un prof d'histoire ; avec un de mes frères ; avec une de mes filles.*

2. *Les expressions de nécessité*

- You have learned to use a form of the verb **devoir** plus an infinitive to describe what one *must* or *should* do.

Pour maigrir, tu **dois suivre** un régime.	*To lose weight, you must go on a diet.*
Elle **doit travailler** plus si elle veut réussir.	*She must work more if she wants to succeed.*

- The following expressions that include the impersonal subject **il** can be used with an infinitive to express obligation in a more general way:

il faut	*you have to/must*
il ne faut pas	*you must not*
il est nécessaire de	*it is necessary to*
il est important de	*it is important to*
il est utile de	*it is useful to*

Il faut porter des gants et un bonnet quand il fait moins de zéro degré Celsius.	*You must wear gloves and a hat when the temperature is below zero degrees Celsius.*
Il ne faut pas sortir sous la pluie sans son parapluie.	*You mustn't go out in the rain without an umbrella.*
En été, **il est important de porter** des lunettes de soleil.	*In summer, it's important to wear sunglasses.*

Note: This section allows students to gain familiarity with impersonal expressions before their use is presented in complex sentences with the subjunctive in Ch. 10, L. 1. In particular, the simple structures *il faut* and *il ne faut pas* followed by an infinitive are quite useful for students to express a range of meanings and should be targeted during classroom practice.

À vous la parole

8-12 Bien s'habiller pour le temps qu'il fait. Quand est-ce qu'il faut mettre ces vêtements ? Précisez le temps ou la saison.

MODÈLE un anorak ?
Il faut le mettre quand il fait froid.

une mini-jupe ?
Il faut la mettre en été.

1. des chaussettes en laine ?
2. un pull-over ?
3. des gants ?
4. des sandales ?
5. un imperméable ?
6. des lunettes de soleil ?
7. des bottes ?
8. une écharpe ?

Variation: 8-13 Vary by presenting an alternative scenario with the same questions, for example *quand il fait beau et vous avez fini tous vos devoirs.*

8-13 Oui ou non ? Quand il fait beau et on a un examen et des devoirs importants à préparer, est-ce qu'il faut faire les choses suivantes ?

MODÈLE aller à la plage ?
Non, il ne faut pas aller à la plage. Il faut aller à la bibliothèque.

1. travailler sérieusement ?
2. appeler les copains pour sortir ?
3. faire un pique-nique avec des amis ?
4. aller au parc pour se promener ?
5. bien manger ?
6. sortir avec ses amis ?
7. se coucher tôt ?

Implementation: 8-14 Begin by having students brainstorm as a whole class about possible problems faced by new students on campus and potential solutions. Follow up by comparing solutions.

8-14 S.O.S. étudiants ! Avec un/e partenaire, à tour de rôle, imaginez que vous donnez des conseils aux nouveaux étudiants sur le campus.

MODÈLE É1 Je travaille tout le temps et je suis assez stressé.
É2 Est-ce que tu te détends quelquefois ?
É1 Pas beaucoup.
É2 Ah, il est important de te détendre. Il faut sortir un peu avec tes amis ou écouter de la musique pour te changer les idées (*for a change*).

1. Je ne peux pas me lever tôt pour aller à mon cours de neuf heures du matin.
2. Je n'ai pas beaucoup d'amis ici.
3. Je vais grossir si je mange au resto U.
4. Je n'ai pas assez de temps pour finir tous mes devoirs.
5. Je ne m'entends pas bien avec mes colocataires.
6. Il fait trop froid ici. Ce n'est pas comme chez moi.

Lisons

TEXT AUDIO
CD 4 TRACK 32

8-15 Il pleure dans mon cœur

A. Avant de lire. The poet Paul Verlaine (1844–1896) believed that the music of language is more important than the actual words, and that suggestion is more important than statement. The effect of his poetry is like that of Impressionist art or music, and his poems are often compared with the paintings of Claude Monet or the music of Claude Debussy (who set sixteen of Verlaine's poems to music).

Verlaine often used free verse (that is, unrhymed lines of unequal length) and the sounds and rhythms of French to create richly musical poems, like ***Il pleure dans mon cœur***, which even listeners who do not know French can appreciate. Listen as the poem is read aloud and think about how its sounds and rhythm suggest the poet's melancholy sadness on a rainy day. Next, read the poem and complete the related work.

Ce tableau de Claude Monet, « Impression : soleil levant », a donné son nom au mouvement impressionniste.

B. En lisant. Cherchez les réponses à ces questions.

1. Dans ce poème, la nature reflète les sentiments du poète. Expliquez comment.
2. Dans les deux premières strophes (*verses*), le poète parle du temps et aussi de ses propres sentiments. Quelles expressions est-ce qu'il emploie pour le faire ?
3. Dans les dernières strophes, le poète parle plus de ses propres sentiments. Il est surtout…

   a. confus **b.** triste **c.** fâché
4. Résumez l'action du poème en une ou deux phrases.

Stratégie

Discover by reading aloud how sounds and rhythm affect the musicality of a poem. Consider in turn what the music of language may be suggesting about a poem's meaning, and what the impact is on your own reactions.

Presentation: In his *Art poétique*, Verlaine proclaimed, *« De la musique avant toute chose »*. Emphasize to students that the message of Verlaine's poem is conveyed largely through its sounds and its rhythm. The reference to Rimbaud is a reprise of a line written by this fellow poet, with whom Verlaine had an unhappy romantic relationship. Be sure to point out to students that the Monet painting shown here was the source of the name for the Impressionist movement, which was much ridiculed when these artists began to show their work. You might show students additional examples of Monet's paintings and play part of Debussy's *Après-midi d'une faune* to illustrate Impressionism in art and music.
Have students listen as you read aloud or play the recording of the poem. This is a good poem for students to memorize. Learning and reciting poetry is a culturally authentic activity, helps improve pronunciation, and can serve for extra credit and as the basis for a recitation competition. See the Instructor's Resource Manual for a list of poems that students might select from.

Key: En lisant 1) Il y a de la pluie et la pluie est comme les larmes (*teardrops*). 2) *il pleut/il pleure* 3) b 4) Il pleut. Le poète est triste, et il ne sait pas pourquoi.

IL PLEURE DANS MON CŒUR...

Il pleut doucement sur la ville.
Arthur Rimbaud

Il pleure° dans mon cœur°
Comme il pleut sur la ville ;
Quelle est cette langueur
Qui pénètre mon cœur ?

Ô bruit doux° de la pluie
Par terre° et sur les toits !
Pour un cœur qui s'ennuie°
Ô le chant° de la pluie !

Il pleure sans raison
Dans ce cœur qui s'écœure°.
Quoi ! nulle trahison° ?...
Ce deuil° est sans raison.

C'est bien la pire peine°
De ne savoir° pourquoi
Sans amour et sans haine°
Mon cœur a tant de° peine !

Paul Verlaine

It's crying; heart
soft sound
ground
is troubled
song
is discouraged
no betrayal
sadness
worst pain
not knowing
hate
so much

Key: En regardant de plus près 1) *il pleure/il pleut*—demonstrate for students the slight difference between these two phrases, the simple change of one vowel: /œ/ vs. /ø/. This distinction was presented in Ch. 4, L. 3., but it is a difficult one for beginning students to perceive and produce. Note also the repetition of the initial consonant *p*- throughout the poem. 2) *cœur, pleure, langueur* ; il y a beaucoup de rimes avec ce son ; cela contribue au sens mélancolique du poème.

C. En regardant de plus près. Maintenant, examinez les aspects suivants du poème.

1. Trouvez deux phrases répétées dans le poème qui ont presque la même prononciation et qui ont une signification semblable. Comment est-ce que ces phrases communiquent le message du poète ?
2. Notez la répétition de certains sons dans le poème, surtout de la voyelle dans le mot **cœur**. Trouvez tous les mots avec ce son ; est-ce que ces mots sont importants pour les rimes ? Quel effet est-ce que la répétition de cette voyelle produit ? Quel sentiment est-ce qu'elle évoque ? Si vous voulez, écoutez de nouveau le poème.

Key: Après avoir lu 1) Le poème et le tableau sont semblables parce qu'ils donnent une impression au lieu de représenter quelque chose de concret. Le poète ne raconte pas directement ses sentiments ; il les suggère. De même, l'artiste ne peint pas un tableau réaliste (comme une photographie) ; il représente une scène d'une façon imprécise. 2) avec des accords mineurs et un tempo lent.

D. Après avoir lu. Discutez de ces questions avec vos camarades de classe.

1. Regardez le tableau de Monet à la page précédente. Est-ce que ce tableau est semblable au poème de Verlaine ? Comment ? Par exemple, est-ce que le tableau et le poème suggèrent un sentiment concret ou plutôt une impression ? Comment est-ce que vous pourriez caractériser l'approche de l'artiste et du poète ?
2. Ce poème a un ton très mélancolique. Comment est-ce qu'on peut produire les effets de mélancolie dans la musique : avec des accords majeurs ou mineurs (*major or minor keys*) ? avec un tempo rapide ou lent ?

Leçon 2 On part en vacances !

POINTS DE DÉPART

TEXT AUDIO
CD 4 TRACKS 33–34

Des activités par tous les temps

Preparation: You might show the video montage for **Venez chez nous !** (*Vive les vacances !*) in conjunction with this vocabulary since it provides examples of vacation activities at different times of the year. Ask students to identify locations (*la plage, la montagne, la ville*), seasons, weather, and activities that they see. The video clip *La Côte d'Azur : destination de rêve* can also be used in L. 2. In this clip, a young woman describes attractions of the *Côte d'Azur*. See SAM/MFL for a complete treatment.

Presentation: Show the vacation activities (MFL, Ch. 8) to present the new vocabulary. Describe each scene briefly; display each image without labels (MFL, Ch. 8), and test comprehension by having students point to the activity you name. As a prelude to Ex. 8-16, have students associate each activity with a place, a season, and weather conditions. Have students repeat the new vocabulary, using either/or questions: *On fait du ski nautique ou de la voile ?*, etc. Complete Ex. 8-16 before presenting the dialogue.

À la plage, on peut faire...
du ski nautique
du surf
de la voile
de la planche à voile,
et on peut se bronzer.

À la campagne, on peut faire...
des pique-niques
du cheval
du vélo
de la moto.

À la montagne, on peut faire...
du camping
de l'alpinisme
des randonnées
du ski
du surf des neiges
de la motoneige.

En ville, on peut faire...
du tourisme
un tour dans le quartier
un tour au parc
des courses
des achats,
et on peut visiter des musées
et des monuments.

Note: The locations mentioned in the dialogue — *les Antilles, Tahiti, la Réunion* — are *collectivités d'outre-mer* (former French colonies), so all are logical choices for a French family. Locate each place on a map. The **Venez chez nous !** lesson provides more information on these territories.

Note: This dialogue introduces some typical exclamations used in French and features colloquial speech one would tend to hear in conversations between family members and friends. For example, *on va pas aux sports d'hiver* instead of the more formal *nous n'allons pas aux sports d'hiver*. In normal conversational style, negative *ne/n'* is usually dropped by native speakers of French. However, point out that it is better for students learning French to pronounce the *ne/n'*, as its loss by non-native speakers may be perceived negatively by many French speakers. Thus, students should say *Ce n'est pas vrai !* Have students listen to the dialogue. Check comprehension by having students pick out the preferred activities of each person. You can use this exchange as a point of departure for discussing *les vacances de février*. Follow up with Ex. 8-17 through 8-19.

Projets de vacances

M. KELLER : Cette année, on va pas aux sports d'hiver.
MAX : Ah, non, c'est pas vrai ! Zut alors !
M. KELLER : Si, cette année vous n'allez pas faire du ski en février, mais du ski nautique.
CAROLINE : Chouette ! Alors on va aux Antilles ? À Tahiti ?
M. KELLER : Pas tout à fait, ma grande. J'ai des billets d'avion pour aller à la Réunion, dans l'Océan Indien.
MAX : Bravo ! Vive la Réunion !
CAROLINE : Et la voile, la planche à voile !
M. KELLER : Et vive la pêche et le repos !

À vous la parole

8-16 Qu'est-ce qu'on peut faire ? Suggérez des activités logiques.

MODÈLE à la montagne, quand il y a de la neige ?
É1 Qu'est-ce qu'on peut faire à la montagne, quand il y a de la neige ?
É2 On peut faire du ski ou du surf des neiges.

1. à la plage, en été ?
2. à la campagne, quand il fait beau ?
3. à la plage, quand il y a un beau soleil ?
4. à la montagne, au printemps ?
5. au lac, quand il y a du vent ?
6. en ville, quand il fait très chaud ?
7. en ville, quand il fait beau ?
8. en ville, quand il fait mauvais ?

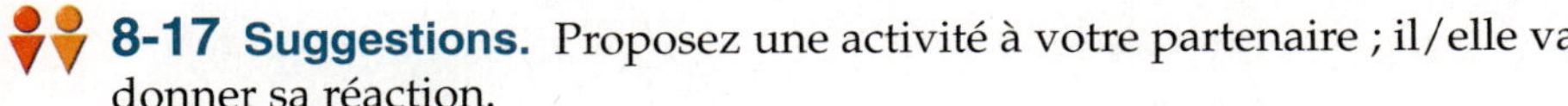

8-17 Suggestions. Proposez une activité à votre partenaire ; il/elle va donner sa réaction.

MODÈLE Vous êtes à la montagne.
É1 On va faire une randonnée.
É2 Super ! J'adore la nature !
Zut alors ! Je n'ai pas de bonnes chaussures !

1. Vous êtes à la montagne.
2. Vous êtes à la plage.
3. Vous êtes à la campagne.
4. Vous êtes en ville.

Implementation: 8-17 Let students take turns suggesting an activity. Note that the reactions come from the dialogue *Projets de vacances.* Encourage students to be dramatic as they react with an appropriate expression to suggestions from their partner.

8-18 À l'Office de Tourisme. En parlant avec un/e partenaire, expliquez ce que les vacanciers peuvent faire dans votre région.

MODÈLE É1 J'habite à Asheville, en Caroline du Nord. Nous sommes à la montagne. Il fait beau en été et on peut faire du camping et des randonnées. En hiver, il neige et on peut faire du ski. Et toi ?
É2 Moi, j'habite à Baltimore, dans le Maryland. C'est près de la mer. Il y a un port et un grand aquarium,...

Implementation: 8-18 Note that students may need additional vocabulary to complete this activity, as shown in the model, depending on what city or region they describe. You might start by brainstorming with students about things to do in the region in which your school is located as a model.

8-19 Les vacances idéales. Demandez à un/e camarade quelles sont ses vacances idéales, et ensuite dites ce que vous préférez.

MODÈLE É1 Moi, je préfère aller à la plage, où il fait chaud. J'aime bien nager et jouer au volley-ball. Et toi ?
É2 Pour moi, les vacances idéales, c'est la montagne en hiver. J'adore faire du ski et du surf des neiges. Mon copain aime bien la motoneige.

Implementation: 8-19 Follow up by having students report back on their ideal vacations.

Vie et culture

Presentation: Use the school calendar to review important cultural concepts such as *la rentrée* and holiday periods in France. Establishing zones makes it possible to avoid major traffic difficulties when everyone leaves on vacation and overcrowding at the most popular destinations.

Les vacances des Français

Regardez ce calendrier des vacances scolaires pour les élèves des écoles primaires, des collèges et des lycées. La France est divisée en trois zones, et pour certaines périodes de vacances, les dates sont différentes selon la zone. Est-ce que vous pouvez donner une explication possible pour ces différences ? Par exemple, quand est-ce que ces vacances ont lieu ? Qu'est-ce que les Français pourraient faire pendant ces périodes ?

Depuis 1982, tous les employés en France ont le droit[1] à cinq semaines de congés payés[2] tous les ans. Depuis l'arrivée de la semaine de 35 heures en 2000, les Français commencent à partir pour des vacances plus fréquentes et plus courtes, par exemple, pour un voyage de week-end qui dure trois ou quatre jours. Cependant, si vous êtes en France pendant l'été, vous

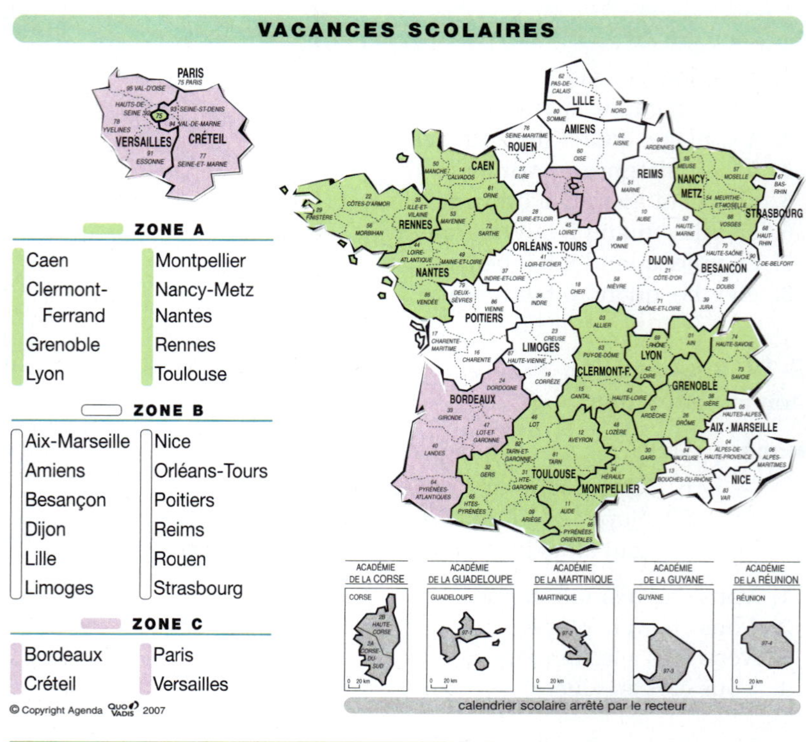

Presentation: Review question formation from Ch. 2, L. 1 and Ch. 8, L. 1. Ask questions using the new expressions and have students answer logically. Then present the new information using examples. Show examples of *qui, qui est-ce que,* and *qu'est-ce qui* in minimal pairs: *Qu'est-ce qui est sur la photo ? / Qui est sur la photo ? ; Qu'est-ce que vous attendez ? / Qui est-ce que vous attendez ?* You can stress the difference between questions using *qui* or *quoi* with the following questions and answers: *Avec **qui** est-ce que tu joues au tennis ? —Avec ma sœur. Avec **quoi** est-ce que tu joues au tennis ? —Avec ma nouvelle raquette.*

FORMES ET FONCTIONS

1. *Les questions avec les pronoms interrogatifs :* qui, que, quoi

- To ask *what*, use **qu'est-ce qui** and **qu'est-ce que**:
  - **Qu'est-ce qui** is used as the subject of a question and is followed by a verb:

Qu'est-ce qui se passe ?	*What's happening?*
Qu'est-ce qui est sur la photo ?	*What's in the photo?*

  - **Qu'est-ce que** is used as the direct object and is followed by the subject of the sentence:

Qu'est-ce que vous faites ?	*What are you doing?*
Qu'est-ce que tu as mis dans la valise ?	*What did you put in the suitcase?*

Note: You may want to discuss the following quote from *Francoscopie 2007* about changing patterns in French vacation practices as another source of cross-cultural comparisons:*... on pourrait... parler des trois D : détente, divertissement, développement. Si les Français cherchent évidemment à se reposer et à se faire plaisir, beaucoup profitent en effet des vacances pour développer leurs connaissances et leurs capacités physiques ou intellectuelles, leurs compétences professionnelles* (p. 494). How does this vision of vacation compare to the typical American one?

ZONE A
Caen, Clermont-Ferrand, Grenoble, Lyon, Montpellier, Nancy-Metz, Nantes, Rennes, Toulouse

Rentrée scolaire des élèves	Toussaint	Noël	Hiver	Printemps	Début des vacances d'été
le mercredi 02-09-09	du samedi 24-10-09 au jeudi 05-11-09	du samedi 19-12-09 au lundi 04-01-10	du samedi 13-02-10 au lundi 01-03-10	du samedi 10-04-10 au lundi 26-04-10	le vendredi 02-07-10

ZONE B
Aix-Marseille, Amiens, Besançon, Dijon, Lille, Limoges, Nice, Orléans-Tours, Poitiers, Reims, Rouen, Strasbourg

Rentrée scolaire des élèves	Toussaint	Noël	Hiver	Printemps	Début des vacances d'été
le mercredi 02-09-09	du samedi 24-10-09 au jeudi 05-11-09	du samedi 19-12-09 au lundi 04-01-10	du samedi 06-02-10 au lundi 22-02-10	du samedi 03-04-10 au lundi 19-04-10	le vendredi 02-07-10

ZONE C
Bordeaux, Créteil, Paris, Versailles

Rentrée scolaire des élèves	Toussaint	Noël	Hiver	Printemps	Début des vacances d'été
le mercredi 02-09-09	du samedi 24-10-09 au jeudi 05-11-09	du samedi 19-12-09 au lundi 04-01-10	du samedi 20-02-10 au lundi 08-03-10	du samedi 18-04-10 au lundi 03-05-10	le vendredi 02-07-10

Le départ en vacances a lieu après la classe, la reprise des cours le matin des jours indiqués.

allez remarquer qu'un certain nombre d'établissements (des restaurants, des salons de coiffeur, des petits magasins, des boulangeries, par exemple) ferment pour trois ou quatre semaines pendant les mois de juillet et d'août.

ET VOUS ?

1. Aux États-Unis, en général, les employés et les ouvriers ont combien de semaines de congés payés ? Comparez cette situation avec la France. Comment est-ce que vous pouvez expliquer ces différences ?
2. Le droit aux congés payés a souvent été très important dans les négociations des syndicats[3] en France. Qu'est-ce que cela nous dit sur l'importance des vacances pour les Français ? Est-ce que vous pensez que les Américains donnent autant d'importance aux vacances ? Pourquoi ?

[1] *have the right to* [2] *paid vacation* [3] *labor unions*

Note: As the examples illustrate, questions in informal, spoken English often feature preposition stranding, that is, the preposition can fall at the end of the question. The same is not true in French. Point out to students that the preposition must be at the beginning of the question, before the interrogative pronoun.

- To ask *who* or *whom*, use **qui**:
  - When **qui** is the subject, it is followed directly by the verb:

Qui va à la plage ?	*Who's going to the beach?*
Qui n'aime pas partir à la montagne ?	*Who doesn't like going to the mountains?*

  - When **qui** is the direct object, use **est-ce que** before the subject of the sentence:

Qui est-ce que tu aimes ?	*Who do you like?*
Qui est-ce qu'ils regardent ?	*Who are they looking at?*

  - When a verb requires a preposition, that preposition precedes **qui**:

À qui est-ce que tu parles ?	*Who are you talking to?*
Avec qui est-ce que tu pars en vacances ?	*Who are you going on vacation with?*

- After prepositions, use **quoi** to ask *what*:

Avec quoi est-ce qu'on écrit ?	*What are we writing with?*
De quoi est-ce qu'il va parler ?	*What is he going to speak about?*

Fiche pratique

To help learn whether to use **qu'est-ce qui/ qu'est-ce que** or **qui/qui est-ce que** to ask a question, practice repeating simple questions with short answers out loud. For example, **Qu'est-ce qui est sur la table ? —un livre ; Qui est sur la table ? —le prof ! Qu'est-ce que tu regardes ? —le tableau. Qui est-ce que tu regardes ? —la prof.**

À vous la parole

Initial practice: 8-20 Begin with this comprehension-based activity that helps students recognize and understand the forms before they are asked to produce questions.

8-20 La curieuse. La petite sœur d'Élodie est très curieuse et lui pose beaucoup de questions. Pour chaque question, indiquez si elle parle d'une chose ou d'une personne.

	une chose	une personne
MODÈLE Qu'est-ce que tu fais ?	✓	______
1. Qu'est-ce que tu regardes ?	______	______
2. Qui est-ce que tu préfères ?	______	______
3. Qui est-ce que tu attends ?	______	______
4. Qui est-ce que tu vois ?	______	______
5. De quoi est-ce que tu parles ?	______	______
6. Avec qui est-ce que tu vas partir ?	______	______
7. Qu'est-ce que tu veux voir ?	______	______
8. De qui est-ce que tu parles ?	______	______

À votre avis, est-ce que la sœur d'Élodie s'intéresse plus aux personnes ou aux objets ? Pourquoi ?

8-21 Projets de vacances. La famille Dupont part en vacances. Mme Dupont est très anxieuse et n'arrête pas de poser des questions pour avoir tous les détails. Avec un/e partenaire, suivez le modèle et jouez les rôles de Mme Dupont et de son mari.

MODÈLES É1 Dis, chéri, *Damien* a acheté les billets ?
É2 Mais non.
É1 Alors, *qui* a acheté les billets ?

É2 Dis, chéri, on va dîner *chez ta cousine* ?
É1 Mais non, ma chérie.
É2 Alors, *chez qui est-ce qu'*on va dîner ?

1. On a demandé *à Suzanne* de garder le chien ?
2. *Damien* va porter nos sacs ?
3. Stéphane va inviter *sa fiancée* ?
4. On va acheter *des cartes postales* comme souvenirs ?
5. On va faire *du vélo* ?
6. *Ta secrétaire* va téléphoner à l'hôtel ?
7. On va payer *avec la carte de crédit* ?

Implementation: 8-22 Put students on teams to play this popular game. Or, to simplify, have students volunteer responses at random.

8-22 Jéopardy ! Avec deux partenaires, jouez au Jéopardy. La première personne va donner une réponse au hasard. Les deux autres vont consulter la liste des verbes pour pouvoir poser une question logique. La première à poser sa question peut donner la réponse suivante.

admirer	écouter	manger	parler	regarder	réviser	téléphoner

MODÈLES É1 de la musique classique
É2 Qu'est-ce que vous écoutez ?
É1 C'est bon. Alors, c'est à toi.

É2 à mes parents
É3 À qui est-ce que tu téléphones ?
É2 Oui, à toi alors !

la télévision	la sociologie
Bill et Melinda Gates	le manuel de français
de la pizza	de politique
à mon copain	Carrie Underwood

Note: Bill Gates is the founder of Microsoft and (with his wife) the Bill and Melinda Gates Foundation; according to its web site, the foundation is dedicated to bringing innovations in health and learning to the global community. Carrie Underwood is a young country music star.

 **8-23 On va tout savoir.** Interviewez un/e partenaire pour connaître tous les détails de sa vie universitaire.

Implementation: 8-23 Model for students how to ask and answer questions before putting them to work in pairs. Follow up by having students report what they learned about their partners.

MODÈLES habiter
➤ Où est-ce que tu habites ? Avec qui est-ce que tu habites ?

faire comme études
➤ Qu'est-ce que tu fais comme études ?

1. habiter
2. faire comme études
3. manger le matin
4. sortir le soir
5. faire le week-end

2. *Les verbes* connaître *et* savoir

The irregular verbs **connaître** and **savoir** both mean *to know*, but they are used in somewhat different ways.

- **Connaître** means *to be acquainted with* or *to be familiar with* and usually refers to places and persons; **connaître** is always followed by a noun:

Je **connais** bien sa famille.	*I know his/her family well.*
Il ne **connaît** pas les Antilles.	*He is not familiar with the West Indies.*
Vous **connaissez** ce poème ?	*Are you familiar with this poem?*

- When used in the **passé composé** with persons, **connaître** means *to have met.*

J'**ai connu** mon copain l'été dernier. *I met my boyfriend last summer.*

CONNAÎTRE *to know, to be familiar with*			
SINGULIER		**PLURIEL**	
je	connais	nous	connaiss**ons**
tu	connais	vous	connaiss**ez**
il / elle / on	connaît	ils / elles	connaiss**ent**

PASSÉ COMPOSÉ : J'**ai connu** Jamila l'été dernier.

Note: The present-tense forms of *connaître* are predictable, like regular *-ir/-iss-* verbs: beginning with the base *connaiss-*, the final consonant is lost in the singular forms. You might want to call attention to the use of the past participle as an adjective — *connu/e, inconnu/e* because of its frequent use.

- **Savoir** generally means *to know facts, information*, or *how to do something*. It can be used in five types of constructions:
  - Followed by an infinitive:

Tu **sais** faire de la voile ?	*Do you know how to sail?*
Ma mère ne **sait** pas se détendre.	*My mother doesn't know how to relax.*

Note: In cases where the complement is a noun, native speaker usage is nuanced: one can say *Je connais le code de la route ; son adresse ; ses opinions.* But for things that are learned by rote memory, native speakers use *savoir : il sait mon numéro de téléphone ; elle sait sa leçon.*

  - Followed by a noun:

Il **sait** sa leçon par cœur.	*He knows his lesson by heart.*
Je ne **sais** pas tout.	*I don't know everything.*
Nous **savons** la réponse.	*We know the answer.*

  - Followed by a sentence introduced by **que**:

Je **sais qu'**ils préfèrent la mer.	*I know that they prefer the seashore.*
Elle **sait qu'**on adore les pique-niques.	*She knows that we love picnics.*

  - Followed by a sentence introduced by a question word or **si** (*whether*).

Je ne **sais** pas **comment** sa copine s'appelle.	*I don't know his girlfriend's name.*
Tu **sais si** elle va venir ?	*Do you know if she's coming?*

  - Used alone:

Qu'est-ce qu'elles **savent** ?	*What do they know?*
Je **sais**.	*I know.*

- When used to talk about the past, **savoir** in the **imparfait** means *knew*.

Elle **savait** que nous faisions du camping.	*She knew that we were camping.*

- When used in the **passé composé**, **savoir** means *to have learned* or *found out*.

J'**ai su** qu'elle est partie à la montagne.	*I found out that she went to the mountains.*

Note: In the present tense of *savoir*, the irregularity consists of the change in vowel /sa/ to /se/ (or for some speakers, /sɛ/) and the corresponding spelling change. As the final consonant of the stem, the loss of /v/ in the singular forms is predictable.

SAVOIR *to know*

SINGULIER		PLURIEL	
je	sais	nous	sav**ons**
tu	sais	vous	sav**ez**
il / elle / on	sait	ils / elles	sav**ent**

PASSÉ COMPOSÉ : J'**ai su** qu'ils ont acheté un appartement au bord le la mer.

À vous la parole

8-24 Les connaissances de famille. Avec un/e partenaire, précisez qui vous connaissez et qui vous ne connaissez pas dans la famille des personnes indiquées.

MODÈLE votre beau-frère/belle-sœur
Je connais la sœur de mon beau-frère, mais je ne connais pas sa mère.

1. votre beau-frère/belle-sœur
2. votre colocataire
3. vos voisins
4. votre prof de français
5. votre meilleur/e ami/e
6. votre ami/e
7. votre femme/mari/fiancé/e

Initial practice: Begin with a discrimination drill: one person, or more than one? *Ils savent nager. Elle sait danser. Il connaît mon frère. Elles connaissent bien Paris. Elles savent parler français. Il sait bien parler. Il connaît ses voisins. Ils connaissent cette ville. Elle sait tout*, etc. Follow with simple substitution drills for each verb: *Je sais nager ; vous ; lui*, etc., and *Je connais Paris ; toi ; nous*, etc.

8-25 L'espion international. L'Interpol recherche Claude Martin, un grand espion. Est-ce que vous le connaissez ? Qu'est-ce que vous savez à son sujet ? Faites des phrases en employant **connaître** ou **savoir**.

MODÈLES où il travaille
Je sais où il travaille.

la ville où il est né
Je connais la ville où il est né.

1. M. Martin
2. qu'il parle portugais
3. les noms de ses camarades
4. sa femme
5. quand il est parti d'Italie
6. qu'il parle allemand
7. où M. Martin habite
8. pourquoi il est allé en Belgique
9. ses amis à Liège
10. quand il va repartir

Implementation: 8-25 Students may play the role of an Interpol inspector and question their classmates: *Est-ce que vous savez où il travaille ?* Students answer appropriately. Help students discover the meaning of *espion* through context and perhaps an example: *James Bond, c'est un espion.*

Additional activity: For simple practice, ask students what the following people know how to do. Be sure to provide a model: *les membres de l'équipe « Les Canadiens » de Montréal ? — Ils savent bien jouer au hockey sur glace. Fred Astaire et Ginger Rogers ; Placido Domingo ; Serena Williams ; J.K. Rowling ; votre prof de français ; votre frère ou sœur ; votre meilleur/e ami/e ; vous.* Have students suggest other famous people and expand on the second half of the exercise by having several students provide their own personalized responses.

8-26 Trouvez une personne. Trouvez quelqu'un parmi vos camarades de classe qui sait/connaît... Comparez vos notes à la fin pour bien connaître vos camarades de classe !

MODÈLE jouer de la guitare
Est-ce que tu sais jouer de la guitare ?

1. parler italien
2. une personne célèbre
3. le président de l'université
4. faire du ski
5. la ville de Washington, D.C.
6. la Belgique
7. jouer d'un instrument
8. le prénom du professeur
9. combien d'étudiants il y a à l'université

Implementation: 8-26 Use as a mixing exercise. Give students a limited amount of time to circulate, asking a maximum of two questions of each person before moving on to someone else. Follow up by having students ask about the items they did not find: *Qui sait jouer de la guitare ?* Ask additional questions to find out more information as appropriate.

Écrivons

Implementation: Have students write on an actual postcard or on one of their own design. This will impose a limit on the amount written. Postcards can be exchanged among class members or with another class. This activity can also be completed as a group or whole class writing project.

Stratégie

A postcard calls for a brief, informal communication: begin with an appropriate greeting, share a few interesting or amusing details about what you are doing, and close informally.

8-27 Une carte postale

A. Avant d'écrire. Quand vous êtes en vacances, est-ce que vous écrivez des cartes postales ? À qui est-ce que vous écrivez ? Qu'est-ce que vous décrivez ? Faites une liste en français de trois ou quatre choses que vous écrivez normalement sur une carte postale.

B. En écrivant. Choisissez quelqu'un dans votre classe à qui vous allez envoyer votre carte postale.

1. Utilisez la liste que vous avez préparée dans l'exercice A pour rédiger votre message.
2. Commencez votre carte postale avec une salutation comme **Cher papa** ou **Chère Suzanne** ou utilisez une expression moins formelle comme **Salut** ou **Bonjour de Paris !** Pour terminer, choisissez une de ces formules: **Amitiés, Bisous, Gros bisous, À bientôt**.

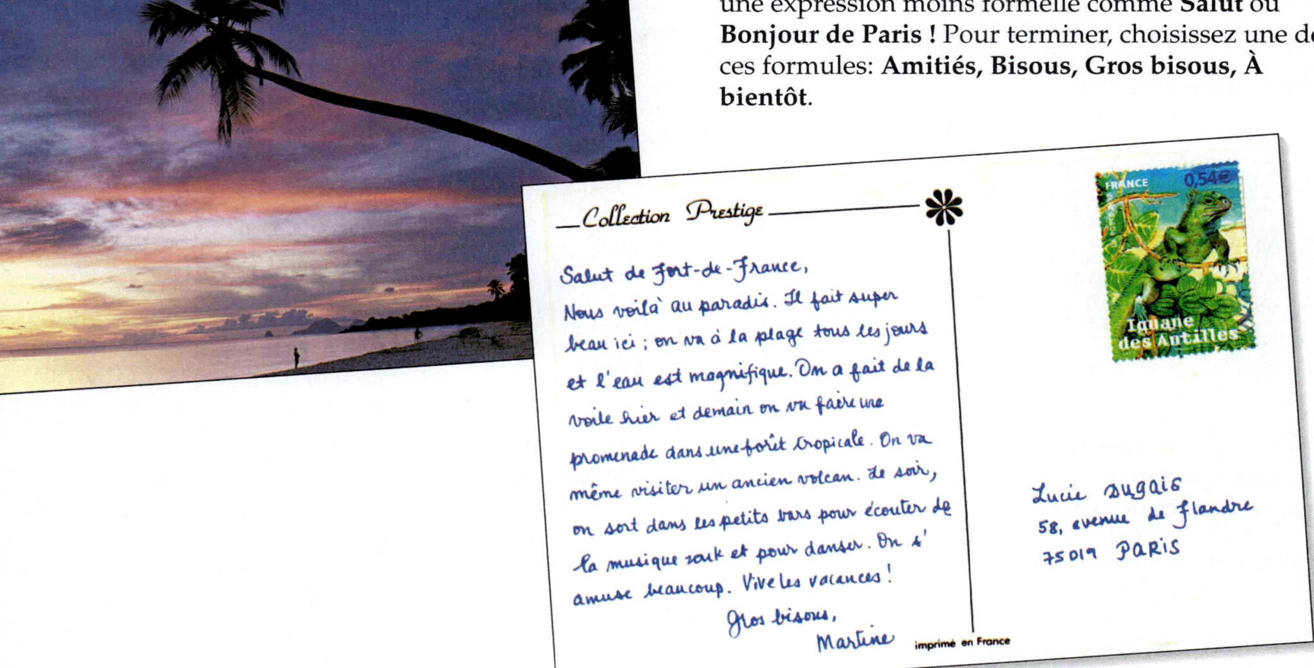

Collection Prestige

Salut de Fort-de-France,
Nous voilà au paradis. Il fait super beau ici ; on va à la plage tous les jours et l'eau est magnifique. On a fait de la voile hier et demain on va faire une promenade dans une forêt tropicale. On va même visiter un ancien volcan. Le soir, on sort dans les petits bars pour écouter de la musique zouk et pour danser. On s'amuse beaucoup. Vive les vacances !
Gros bisous,
Martine

Lucie Dugais
58, avenue de Flandre
75019 PARIS

C. En révisant. Réfléchissez aux questions suivantes et puis faites tous les changements nécessaires.

1. Relisez votre carte postale pour analyser le contenu : est-ce que vous avez décrit quelques activités intéressantes ou amusantes ?
2. Relisez de nouveau votre carte pour analyser le style et la forme. Est-ce que vous avez commencé et terminé la carte avec une salutation appropriée ? Est-ce que vous avez utilisé des mots appropriés pour parler du temps et de vos activités ?

D. Après avoir écrit. « Envoyez » votre carte postale à un/e camarade de classe ou à votre professeur. Si vous avez de la chance, vous allez recevoir une carte postale aussi.

Leçon 3 Je vous invite

POINTS DE DÉPART

TEXT AUDIO
CD 4 TRACK 35

Qu'est-ce qu'on propose ?

Presentation: Display the cultural activities (MFL, Ch. 8) and describe them; ask for examples of ballets, plays, concerts, and exhibitions that students have seen. Test comprehension by showing a numbered list of the unlabeled illustrations (MFL, Ch. 8) and reading the mini-dialogues aloud and asking students to tell you which image is being referenced. Find out which of these cultural activities your students prefer, using either/or questions, so that students repeat key vocabulary. Use the mini-dialogues to introduce formulas for inviting, accepting, and refusing.

—On organise une petite fête samedi soir ; tu es libre ?
—Non, désolée, je ne peux pas.

—Vous êtes libres samedi ? J'ai des places pour un ballet, « Coppélia » de Delibes.
—Ah oui, c'est très gentil à vous !

—On ne joue pas au tennis à cause de la pluie, alors, je peux t'accompagner à l'exposition.
—Super ; on se retrouve devant le musée ?

—Alors, rendez-vous au Palais des Congrès pour voir le concert de rock ?
—Oui, à 19 h 30.

—Tu veux nous accompagner au théâtre ? On va voir une pièce de Molière.
—Volontiers ! J'adore le théâtre.

—Il pleut, donc qu'est-ce qu'on fait cet après-midi ?
—Il y a un bon film à la Cinémathèque.
—Super ! On y va ensemble ?

—On va passer une soirée tranquille chez nous.
—Je regrette, je ne peux pas venir. Je dois travailler.

Pour inviter quelqu'un

Tu es/vous êtes libre/s ?
On y va ensemble ?
Tu veux/voudrais m'accompagner ?/Vous voulez/voudriez nous accompagner ?

Pour accepter une invitation	**Pour refuser une invitation**	
Oui, je suis libre.	Je suis désolé/e...	je ne suis pas libre.
(J'accepte) Avec plaisir.	Je regrette...	je suis pris/e.
C'est gentil à toi/vous.	C'est dommage,...	j'ai déjà un rendez-vous.
Je suis ravi/e.		
Volontiers.		

Vie et culture

Les pratiques culturelles

Ce document présente les résultats d'un sondage récent du Ministère de la Culture en France. Les résultats indiquent le nombre de Français qui ont participé à des activités culturelles au cours des douze mois précédents. Regardez le titre : est-ce qu'on décrit les pratiques culturelles des adultes ? des ados ? des enfants ? Ensuite, regardez les chiffres donnés dans le tableau (qui sont des pourcentages) et répondez aux questions suivantes :

1. Quelles sont les trois activités les plus populaires pour les Français ?
2. Quelle est l'activité la moins populaire ?
3. Pensez aux activités culturelles de vos amis et des membres de votre famille ; est-ce qu'elles ressemblent aux activités des Français ? Pourquoi ? Quelles sont les différences ?

PRATIQUES CULTURELLES

Sur 100 Français de 15 ans et plus, au cours des douze derniers mois :

58	ont lu au moins un livre
46	ont lu au moins un magazine
87	ont écouté la radio
75	ont écouté des disques
99	ont regardé la télévision
47	sont allés au cinéma
39	ont visité un musée ou une exposition
31	sont allés au concert ou spectacle musical
16	sont allés au théâtre ou café-théâtre

Source : Ministère de la Culture, *mini-chiffres clés 2008*

Les Français aiment bien aller aux concerts, au cinéma et aux expositions avec des amis et la famille pendant le week-end et aussi pendant leurs vacances. Est-ce que vous participez à ce genre d'activités avec votre famille pendant les vacances ?

Presentation: Students may be surprised to learn that a Ministry of Culture exists in France. The document shows the percentages of French people over age 15 participating in various cultural activities over a period of twelve months. You may wish to point out the link between "percent" in English and *pourcentage* and illustrate how a percentage is literally something out of 100; see if students can come up with other words in English where "*cent*" stands for one hundred, i.e., century, centennial. To test comprehension, ask the class to rank these activities in popularity on a scale from 1 to 10. Students can work in pairs or small groups to answer the questions; follow up with class as a whole.

À vous la parole

8-28 Qu'est-ce qu'on peut faire ? Le Centre Pompidou est un musée à Paris qui a aussi des salles de cinéma, de conférences et de spectacles. Avec un/e partenaire, regardez le programme à droite et décrivez les activités possibles.

MODÈLE É1 Le cinq mai, il y a un concert de musique contemporaine.

É2 Et regarde, du 5 mars au 2 juin, il y a une exposition à la Galerie d'art graphique.

Implementation: 8-28 Treat the schedule first as a short reading; have students identify the main categories of activities taking place, then describe some of the specific events. Once students are familiar with the schedule, go on to complete the exercise. If you teach in a smart classroom, you may also have students visit the Centre Pompidou Web site to see what the most current events are.

Note: 8-29 The brief exchanges prepare students for the more extended and open-ended activities in Ex. 8-30 and 8-31.

8-29 Oui ou non ? Avec un/e camarade de classe, imaginez les situations suivantes. Qu'est-ce que vous allez dire ?

MODÈLE On vous invite à aller au musée demain. Vous ne voulez pas y aller.

É1 Tu veux aller au musée avec moi ? Il y a une bonne exposition.

É2 Je regrette (OU Désolé), je ne suis pas libre.

1. On vous invite à un concert. Vous êtes ravi/e d'y aller.
2. On vous invite à aller au théâtre. Vous demandez quelle pièce on joue.
3. On vous invite à faire une randonnée, mais vous n'aimez pas les promenades.
4. On cherche quelqu'un pour jouer au bridge. Vous aimez ce jeu.
5. On a des places pour un concert de rock. Vous aimez ce type de musique, mais vous avez un rendez-vous ce jour-là.
6. On a deux places pour un ballet. Vous demandez, « C'est pour quel soir ? », et puis vous acceptez.

AGENDA

TOUTES LES MANIFESTATIONS

CENTRE POMPIDOU – Art, culture, musée, expositions, cinémas, conférences, débats, spectacles, concerts.

EXPOSITIONS

Louise Bourgeois
Cette exposition présente plus de 200 œuvres, sculptures, peintures, dessins, gravures, de 1940 à 2007, en insistant sur les dix dernières années de création de cette artiste de 96 ans qui ne cesse de renouveler son langage artistique.

5 mars – 2 juin
11 h 00 – 21 h 00
Galerie d'art graphique Niveau 4

Accrochage « Histoire de l'Atelier Brancusi »
Une reconstitution de l'atelier parisien, où vécut l'un des maîtres de la sculpture moderne.

7 mars – 6 octobre
14 h 00 – 18 h 00
Galerie de l'Atelier Brancusi

VISITES COMMENTÉES

Promenades urbaines
Des parcours en compagnie d'architectes, d'urbanistes, de créateurs, de conservateurs, d'universitaires et d'acteurs de la vie associative.

29 mars – 29 juin

CINÉMAS

Vers l'Olympe, Être fan des Rolling Stones
Cinéma documentaire

10 – 12 avril
20 h 30 – 14 h 30 (90 mn)
Cinéma 1 Niveau 1

Kijû Yoshida, Visions de la beauté

26 mars – 19 mai
Cycle – « Seuls les corps parviennent à raconter des histoires vraies parce qu'ils font apparaître tout le refoulé d'un pays à la surface de la peau. Cherchant à enregistrer les angoisses de ses contemporains, Yoshida s'est ainsi fait le cinéaste de l'extrême corps. »
Antoine de Baecque
19 h 00 – *Beauté de la beauté : Goya*, Kijû Yoshida, 1974–1978–Cinéma 2
20 h 30 – *Promesse*, Kijû Yoshida, 1986–Cinéma 1

SPECTACLES–CONCERTS

Olivia Grandville, My Space
Danse-performance
Accompagnée des musiciens Jérôme Noetinger et Tom Mays, la chorégraphe Olivia Grandville explore grâce à un dispositif informatique de capture du geste les interactions entre les mouvements et le son. Dans My Space, il s'agit d'« écouter ce que l'on a l'habitude de voir, voir ce qu'on a l'habitude d'entendre. Matérialiser ce qu'est réellement l'espace : une architecture de temps, une géométrie turbulente. » Olivia Grandville

24 – 26 avril

Mot(et)s Cachés, Ensemble Vocal Exaudi
Musique contemporaine
Pour sa première apparition en France, l'ensemble vocal anglais Exaudi réunit Brian Ferneyhough et Thomas Tallis.

5 mai

Implementation: 8-30 Use as a mixing activity. Impose a time limit, and tell students to ask no more than two questions of any one person before moving on. When time is up, have students ask questions about the items they did not find: *Qui a organisé une fête ?*

8-30 Les distractions du week-end dernier. Découvrez comment vos camarades de classe ont passé le week-end dernier. Faites le tour de la classe pour obtenir les renseignements suivants et essayez d'obtenir quelques détails supplémentaires. Après, faites un compte-rendu.

MODÈLE organiser une fête

É1 Est-ce que tu as organisé une fête ?
É2 Oui, j'ai organisé une fête avec ma colocataire.
É1 Tu as invité beaucoup de personnes ?
É2 Seulement cinq ou six amis.

plus tard:

É1 Julie a organisé une petite fête avec sa colocataire. Elle a invité quelques amis…

1. aller à un concert ou au théâtre
2. faire une randonnée ou du camping
3. aller à un évènement sportif
4. aller au musée ou aller voir une exposition
5. inviter quelqu'un
6. organiser ou aller à une fête

Implementation: 8-31 Have students work individually to prepare their lists of people to invite and activities to suggest. Once students have their lists prepared, they should circulate and everyone should invite three people in the class. You can follow up by asking students who they invited and if anyone accepted.

8-31 Des invitations. Vous allez inviter des camarades de classe. Ils vont accepter ou refuser selon leurs préférences.

1. D'abord, faites une liste de trois activités que vous voulez proposer et une liste de trois personnes que vous voulez inviter. N'oubliez pas le professeur !
2. Ensuite, proposez vos activités à trois personnes différentes qui vont accepter ou refuser vos invitations selon leurs préférences. Bien sûr, vos camarades de classe vont vous inviter aussi et vous devez accepter ou refuser à votre tour.
3. Pour terminer : Qui est-ce que vous avez invité ? Pour quelle activité ? Est-ce qu'on a accepté ou refusé ?

Sons et lettres

Le *h* aspiré et le *h* muet

Presentation: Point out that most words written with *h* contain "mute h." Most dictionaries mark "aspirate h" words: the *Larousse* dictionaries use the asterisk, as do we; the *Robert* provides the phonetic transcription and uses the symbol ['].

In French the letter **h** does not represent any sound. Most words beginning with **h** behave as if they began with a vowel, in other words *elision* and *liaison* are normally made. These words are said to contain **un h muet**.

l'hiver	l'histoire	
le**s**‿hommes /z/	le**s**‿habitudes /z/	avan**t**‿hier /t/
pas d'huile	s'habiller	

Other words beginning with **h** behave as if they began with a consonant: there is neither *elision* nor *liaison*. These words contain **un h aspiré**. In the glossary at the end of this textbook and in the vocabulary lists in each chapter, these words are preceded by an asterisk (*).

un *hamburger	la *Hollande	le *huitième mois
les *haricots verts	le *hockey	

Some words that begin with a vowel letter, in particular **un** and **onze**, also behave as if they contain **un h aspiré**.

le nombre *un　　　le *onze novembre

 À vous la parole

8-32 Contrastes. Comparez les deux mots ou expressions.

1. les *haricots verts	les hommes
2. la *Hollande	l'habitude
3. un *hamburger	un hôpital
4. en *haut	en hiver

8-33 Phrases. Répétez chaque phrase.

1. J'aime les haricots verts avec de l'huile d'olive et du citron.
2. Hier et avant-hier, il a neigé ; c'est parfait pour les sports d'hiver.
3. On part à la mer le onze juillet à huit heures.
4. D'habitude, je ne mange pas au fast-food, mais j'aime bien les hamburgers.

FORMES ET FONCTIONS

1. *La modalité :* devoir, pouvoir *et* vouloir

- You saw in **Chapitre 3**, **Leçon 3**, that the verbs **devoir**, **pouvoir**, and **vouloir** can be used to soften commands and make suggestions. Compare:

Attendez-moi devant le café !	*Wait for me in front of the café!*
Vous **devez** m'attendre devant le café.	*You must wait for me in front of the café.*
Vous **pouvez** m'attendre devant le café.	*You can wait for me in front of the café.*
Vous **voulez** m'attendre devant le café ?	*Will you wait for me in front of the café?*

- The conditional forms of the three verbs make orders or suggestions sound even more polite. The conditional forms are generally equivalent to *should*, *could*, and *would like to*.

Vous **devriez** voir cette pièce.	*You should see that play.*
Ils **pourraient** réserver des places.	*They could reserve tickets.*
Tu **voudrais** nous accompagner au spectacle ?	*Would you like to go with us to the show?*

Note: We present this use of the conditional first because it is the most frequent use of that mood. We limit usage here to the three modal verbs. We recycle and expand on uses of the conditional in Ch. 11, L. 2.

Presentation: Students may notice that the conditional endings are the same as those for the imperfect. Point out that there are three spoken forms; the singular and third-person plural forms are pronounced alike, following the "boot" pattern. In pronouncing these endings, French speakers vary between /e/, as in *thé*, and /ɛ/, as in *mère*.

◆ Here are the conditional forms for **devoir**, **pouvoir**, and **vouloir**.

SINGULIER		PLURIEL	
je	dev**rais** pour**rais** voud**rais**	nous	dev**rions** pour**rions** voud**rions**
tu	dev**rais** pour**rais** voud**rais**	vous	dev**riez** pour**riez** voud**riez**
il elle on	dev**rait** pour**rait** voud**rait**	ils elles	dev**raient** pour**raient** voud**raient**

À vous la parole

Initial practice: 8-34 Begin practice with this comprehension-based exercise. To practice the forms, follow with a transformation drill, such as present tense to conditional: *Elle doit aller au théâtre. — Elle devrait aller au théâtre ; Ils ne veulent pas voir ce film. — Ils ne voudraient pas voir ce film*, etc.

8-34 Une soirée élégante. Mme Élaguais organise une soirée très chic chez elle. Décidez si les instructions qu'elle donne à ses enfants, à son mari et aux serveurs sont du style « ordre direct » ou « suggestion / conseil ».

	ordre direct	suggestion/ conseil
MODÈLE Mets cette plante près de la porte !	✓	______
1. Tu devrais bien t'habiller chéri !	______	______
2. Apportez ces plats à la cuisine !	______	______
3. Cherchez les jolies assiettes !	______	______
4. Vous pourriez servir le vin ici.	______	______
5. Tu voudrais montrer le salon à cette dame ?	______	______
6. Mettez les manteaux ici !	______	______
7. Tu pourrais aider Loïc dans la cuisine ?	______	______
8. Vous devriez servir les hors-d'œuvre maintenant.	______	______

À votre avis, est-ce que Mme Élaguais donne plus de suggestions, ou plus d'ordres ?

Expansion: 8-35 You might repeat the exercise, having students offer advice directly to the person(s), using the *tu* or *vous* form and the conditional.

8-35 Qu'est-ce qu'on devrait faire ce week-end ? Offrez une suggestion à chaque personne selon le cas.

MODÈLE Stéphanie aime bien la danse.
→ Elle devrait aller voir un ballet.
OU → Elle pourrait voir un spectacle de danse.

1. Mathieu n'aime pas le théâtre.
2. Nous adorons les concerts en plein air.
3. Jessica est très sociable.
4. M. et Mme Dulac voudraient voir cette exposition.
5. Je voudrais voir un bon film.
6. On n'aime pas le rock.
7. Jonathan et Ben vont à la campagne.
8. Je vais au bord de la mer.

8-36 Bonnes résolutions. Avec un/e partenaire, comparez vos bonnes résolutions pour ce semestre.

Implementation: **8-36** Survey students afterward to find out what the most popular resolutions are.

MODÈLE finir tous les devoirs avant les cours
É1 Est-ce que tu finis tous tes devoirs avant les cours?
É2 Pas toujours, mais ce semestre je voudrais finir tous mes devoirs avant les cours. Et toi ?
É1 Moi aussi, je devrais les finir avant les cours.
É2 C'est bien. On va avoir des bonnes notes ce semestre !

1. finir tous les devoirs avant les cours
2. travailler à la bibliothèque
3. assister régulièrement aux cours
4. manger des repas équilibrés
5. faire régulièrement du sport
6. se détendre de temps en temps
7. regarder la télévision
8. dormir toujours assez

2. *Les expressions indéfinies et négatives*

Presentation: The expressions *quelquefois* and *ne... jamais* were presented in Ch. 4, L. 1; here they are treated more systematically along with other indefinite and negative expressions. Present using these examples and others, which provide a context for understanding meaning and usage. Have students describe placement for *rien* and *personne* in the various tenses when they function as the subject.

- Look at the following exchanges:

—Tu fais **quelque chose** ce week-end ?	—*Are you doing something this weekend?*
—Non, je **ne** fais **rien**.	—*No, I'm not doing anything.*
—Il y a **quelqu'un** à la porte ?	—*Is there someone at the door?*
—Non, il **n'**y a **personne**.	—*No, there's no one there.*
—Tu vas **quelquefois** au musée ?	—*Do you go to the museum sometimes?*
—Non, je **ne** vais **jamais** au musée.	—*No, I never go to the museum.*

As you can see in the exchanges above, the negative expressions are composed of two parts: **ne...** plus another element carrying the specific meaning.

- These negative expressions may also be used alone:

—Qu'est-ce que tu as ?	—**Rien**.
—Qui vient ce soir ?	—**Personne**.
—Tu es allé voir un ballet ?	—**Jamais**.

- **Rien** and **personne** may be used as the subject of a sentence; **ne** still precedes the verb:

Rien ne s'est passé hier.	*Nothing happened yesterday.*
Personne n'est venu.	*No one came.*

The following chart summarizes indefinite and negative expressions referring to time, things, and persons:

indéfini	**négatif**
quelquefois	ne... jamais
quelque chose	ne... rien
quelqu'un	ne... personne

- Note the placement of negative and indefinite expressions in the **passé composé** and **futur proche**:

—Tu **n'**as **rien** vu ? —Si, j'ai vu **quelque chose**.

—Tu **n'**a **jamais** dîné ici ? —Si, j'ai mangé ici **quelquefois**.

—Tu **n'**as vu **personne** ? —Si, j'ai vu **quelqu'un**.

—Il **ne** va **rien** acheter ? —Si, il va acheter **quelque chose**.

—Il **ne** va **jamais** nous accompagner ? —Si, il va nous accompagner **quelquefois**.

—Il **ne** va inviter **personne** ? —Si, il va inviter **quelqu'un**.

À vous la parole

Implementation: 8-37 First complete the exercise by having students respond only with the negative expression. Then repeat the exercise, having students respond with a full sentence.

8-37 Au négatif. Répondez avec une expression négative.

MODÈLE Qu'est-ce que tu regardes ?
Rien. Je ne regarde rien.

1. Qu'est-ce que tu écoutes ?
2. Qui nous invite à dîner?
3. Quand est-ce qu'ils sont venus à la soirée ?
4. Qu'est-ce qu'il y a dans ton sac ?
5. Qui est-ce que tu écoutes ?
6. Qu'est-ce que tu prends ?
7. Quand est-ce que tu vas au cinéma ?
8. Qui est-ce que tu accompagnes ?

8-38 Une petite contradiction. Dites le contraire dans vos réponses !

MODÈLE Est-ce qu'il y a quelqu'un au théâtre ?
Non, il n'y a personne.

Vous ne vous détendez jamais ?
Si, je me détends quelquefois.

1. Il y a quelque chose sur la table ?
2. Est-ce qu'elle invite quelqu'un ?
3. Vous achetez quelque chose ?
4. Vous ne mangez rien ?
5. Personne n'a téléphoné ?
6. Il ne va jamais au musée ?
7. Vous allez quelquefois aux concerts ?
8. Il y a quelqu'un à la porte ?

8-39 Des situations. Pour chaque situation, discutez avec un/e partenaire de ce que vous faites. Utilisez **ne… jamais**, **ne… personne**, **ne… rien** et leurs contraires **quelquefois**, **quelqu'un** et **quelque chose**.

MODÈLE quand vous allez au cinéma

É1 Qu'est-ce que tu fais quand tu vas au cinéma ?
É2 Je n'achète jamais de pop-corn parce que je ne l'aime pas. Je regarde toujours les publicités avant le film, etc. Et toi ?
É1 Moi, je ne regarde jamais les publicités. C'est ennuyeux. Et je n'achète rien à manger au cinéma parce que c'est trop cher.

1. quand vous allez au cinéma
2. quand vous allez au musée
3. quand vous sortez avec des amis le week-end
4. quand vous partez en vacances en famille
5. quand vous avez beaucoup de travail à la fac
6. quand vous organisez une fête pour des amis
7. quand vous êtes en cours de français
8. quand vous n'avez pas beaucoup d'argent

Implementation: 8-39 Follow up by having students report something they learned about their partner; or, solicit multiple answers for each item.

Implementation: En écoutant Remind students that it is normal to listen to answering machine messages more than once, even in one's native language, to get all the details. Encourage them to complete the chart progressively by listening to the messages several times. You can demonstrate this strategy if you complete the activity in class.

Script: Écoutons Salut, c'est Sylvain à l'appareil. J'appelle pour t'inviter à une fête chez Patrick et Delphine samedi soir. C'est à huit heures et demie. C'est une soirée dansante assez élégante. Je sais que tu aimes danser, donc je me demande si tu veux m'accompagner. Rappelle-moi ce soir pour me dire oui ou non.
Bonjour, c'est moi, Cécile. J'ai eu ton message et c'est très sympa de m'inviter à ce concert de jazz la semaine prochaine. Mais je suis désolée. Je ne peux pas. Je dois travailler ce soir-là. Ça sera peut-être pour une autre fois. Je vais te rappeler.
Bonjour, c'est Florian. J'ai des détails pour ce soir. On a rendez-vous à 19 h 30 devant le théâtre municipal. J'ai déjà acheté ton billet et les billets pour Paul et Catherine. Tu peux leur téléphoner ? Si non, rappelle-moi au 03-23-92-20-15 avant cinq heures. Ciao.
Bonjour chérie. C'est ta maman. Papa et moi acceptons avec plaisir de venir manger chez toi dimanche prochain. Mais qui va être là ? Et qu'est-ce que tu vas servir ? Je veux bien t'aider avec tout cela. Appelle-moi. Je suis à la maison tout l'après-midi.

Écoutons

8-40 Des invitations

Aurélie a beaucoup d'amis et elle sort beaucoup. Écoutez les messages sur son répondeur.

A. Avant d'écouter. Quand vous écoutez vos messages sur le répondeur, quel type d'informations est-ce que vous pensez entendre ?

B. En écoutant. Complétez le tableau avec les détails importants de chaque message.

1. La première fois que vous écoutez ces messages, décidez pourquoi chaque personne a appelé : **pour inviter Aurélie, pour accepter une invitation, pour refuser une invitation, pour confirmer un rendez-vous.**
2. Écoutez encore et notez les détails pour **Activité**, **Quand** et **Où**.
3. Écoutez une dernière fois et notez d'autres détails importants pour chaque message.

Qui	**Sylvain**	**Cécile**	**Florian**	**Maman**
Pourquoi	*pour inviter*		*pour confirmer*	
Activité				
Quand				
Où	*chez Patrick et Delphine*			
D'autres détails importants				

C. Après avoir écouté. Imaginez que vous êtes Aurélie. À qui est-ce que vous allez téléphoner d'abord ? Pourquoi ? Et ensuite ? Comparez vos réponses avec les réponses de vos camarades de classe.

Venez chez nous ! Vive les vacances !

Presentation: As suggested in the photo caption, ask students to locate the various places that make up *la France d'outre-mer* on a map (MFL, Maps) and speculate about what the climate would be like — *Quel temps fait-il à la Martinique ? Il fait chaud ?* — and what activities would be likely. Finally, ask students to find out what languages are spoken in these regions. Then complete the questions in *Et vous ?* in small groups or as a whole class activity. You may also assign students or small groups of students to do Web research to discover more information about these overseas territories.

Note: Formerly referred to as *les DOM-TOM* (*départements d'outre mer* et *territoires d'outre mer*), the status of the overseas French territories has been evolving over time. After the constitutional revision in March 2003 and corresponding legislation passed in July 2003, the former TOM (la Mayotte, St-Pierre-et-Miquelon (which was a DOM between 1976 and 1985), Wallis-et-Futuna, la Polynésie francaise, la Nouvelle-Calédonie and les Terres australes et antarctiques françaises (TAFF) were reclassified as *collectivités d'outre-mer*, although the status of the last two territories was in fact a bit more nuanced. Since *la loi du 21 février 2007*, neither of these two territories is considered a COM ; *la Nouvelle-Calédonie* is in a transitory phase, heading for a vote in 2014 on its eventual independence or autonomous government. *Les TAFF* are in the unique position of being the only remaining TOM, even after the official status no longer exists; they are officially referred to as *un territoire situé outre-mer*. Additionally, in 2007, both St-Martin and St-Barthélemy, formerly considered as part of Guadeloupe, received the status of independent *collectivités d'outre-mer*. For further information, visit the *Chez nous* Companion Website for links to the *Ministère de l'intérieur, de l'outre-mer et des collectivités territoriales*.

La Réunion, un département d'outre-mer. Regardez la carte du monde francophone au début de votre livre et trouvez les quatre départements et les six collectivités d'outre-mer.

La France d'outre-mer

« Où vont les Français pour trouver du soleil au mois de février ? » Attention ! La bonne réponse n'est pas « sur la Côte d'Azur » car [1] en hiver dans le Midi de la France il ne fait pas assez chaud pour se bronzer à la plage ou nager dans la mer. Une meilleure réponse, c'est « aux Antilles, à la Réunion ou à Tahiti ». Ce sont des bonnes destinations touristiques si vous voulez trouver le soleil en hiver et des plages, et si vous voulez entendre parler français !

En fait, vous pouvez voyager aux quatre coins du globe et rester toujours en contact avec la France car ce pays comprend des départements, des régions et des territoires **d'outre-mer**. Ce sont des anciennes colonies françaises qui continuent à être associées administrativement et politiquement à la France. Depuis 1946, la Guadeloupe, la Martinique, la Guyane et la Réunion ont le statut de **Départements d'outre-mer** (DOM) et depuis 1982 de **Régions d'outre-mer** (ROM). À ce titre, elles ont la même organisation administrative que les départements et régions de la France métropolitaine, et leurs habitants sont des citoyens français. À la Réunion, à la Martinique et en Guadeloupe on parle créole et français, en Guyane française, créole, français et des langues amérindiennes. Il y a également [2] six **collectivités d'outre-mer** (COM) ; ce sont les îles de St-Pierre-et-Miquelon (à l'est du Canada), Saint-Barthélemy et Saint-Martin (aux Antilles), la Mayotte (à l'est de l'Afrique) et deux archipels [3] dans l'océan Pacifique : la Polynésie française (où se trouve l'île de Tahiti) et Wallis-et-Futuna. Ces territoires ont une plus grande autonomie administrative que les départements/régions d'outre-mer.

[1] parce que [2] aussi [3] *archipelago, group of islands*

Et vous ?

1. Est-ce que les États-Unis possèdent des territoires d'outre-mer comme la France ?
2. Comme vous l'avez remarqué sur la carte, la France a des territoires partout (*everywhere*) dans le monde. Est-ce que c'est un avantage pour la France ? Expliquez.
3. Est-ce que c'est un avantage pour les départements/régions et les collectivités d'outre-mer ? Expliquez.
4. Pour quelles raisons historiques est-ce que la France a développé des liens (*ties*) avec ces territoires ?

Presentation: Compare France's overseas departments and territories with the status of Hawaii and Alaska versus Puerto Rico and the American Virgin Islands. Note the influences of colonial practices and the slave trade in the history of both France and the U.S.

Lisons

8-41 Martinique : Guide pratique

La baie de St-Pierre, à la Martinique

Stratégie

Use the title and subtitles of a text as clues to understanding its focus and organization. You can learn what kind of information is likely to be included and what the major subsections are. With this approach, you will know a great deal about the content even before you read the passage as a whole.

A. Avant de lire. The following passage is excerpted from a travel guide written by **le Comité Martiniquais du Tourisme**. Before reading, look at the title and the various subtitles to get a sense of the focus and organization of this passage.

1. The title of the booklet is **Martinique : Guide pratique**. Who do you think is the intended audience for a **Guide pratique**? What kind of information would you expect to be included in a "practical guide"?
2. Now look at the two major subtitles that appear in red type. They establish the two major divisions of this text. What is the focus of each?
3. Finally, look at the eight black subheadings. These indicate the topic of each paragraph. Considering these subheadings together with what you have determined about the focus and organization of the text, summarize what you know already about its content.

Key: Avant de lire 1) the intended audience is those who are planning to travel there; brainstorm a list with students; this might include: information about visas, climate, what to visit, and so forth 2) general information and practical concerns 3) students' answers will vary, but should include the main topics listed in the subheadings

Key: En lisant 1) Fort-de-France 2) 7 000 kilomètres 3) il fait bon et assez chaud avec une température moyenne de 27° (environ 80°F) 4) le rhum, le sucre, l'ananas, la banane 5) le français, le créole, l'anglais dans les endroits touristiques 6) Non, un visa n'est pas nécessaire pour une visite de moins de trois mois ; il faut une pièce d'identité 7) les vêtements d'été, un gilet et des lunettes de soleil

B. En lisant. Trouvez les réponses aux questions suivantes.

1. Quelle est la capitale de la Martinique ?
2. Il y a combien de kilomètres entre la Martinique et la France ?
3. Quel est le climat à la Martinique ?
4. Quelles sont trois ressources naturelles martiniquaises ?
5. Quelles langues sont parlées à la Martinique ?
6. Est-ce qu'il est nécessaire pour les voyageurs d'Amérique du Nord d'avoir un visa pour entrer en Martinique ? Qu'est-ce qu'il leur faut ?
7. Quels vêtements est-ce qu'il faut apporter pour une visite à la Martinique ?

Martinique : Guide pratique

Informations générales

Histoire et administration

Christophe Colomb débarqua à la Martinique en 1502 et depuis 1635, excepté de courtes périodes d'occupation anglaise, elle partage les destinées de la France. Département français depuis 1946 et région depuis 1982, sa structure administrative et politique est identique à celle des départements de la métropole. Siège[1] de la préfecture, Fort-de-France est la capitale administrative, commerciale et culturelle de la Martinique.

Géographie

La Martinique fait partie du groupe des petites Antilles ou « Îles au vent ». Elle est baignée à l'Ouest par la Mer des Antilles et à l'Est par l'Océan Atlantique. Elle se trouve à environ 7.000 km de la France et 440 km du continent américain.

Climat

Le climat est relativement doux à la Martinique et la chaleur n'y est jamais insupportable. La température moyenne se situe aux environs de 27°C, mais sur les hauteurs, il fait plus frais. De l'Est et du Nord-est, des brises régulières, les alizés, rafraîchissent l'atmosphère en permanence.

Ressources économiques

Principales ressources naturelles de l'île : le rhum, le sucre, l'ananas, la banane. La Martinique produit également des conserves de fruits, des confitures et des jus de fruits locaux. Le tourisme connaît un essor[2] remarquable et tend à devenir le secteur économique de pointe.

Langue

Le français est parlé et compris par toute la population mais on entend beaucoup le créole. Bien entendu, l'anglais est également parlé surtout dans les lieux touristiques.

Informations pratiques

Formalités d'entrée

Les Français peuvent entrer en Martinique avec leur carte nationale d'identité ou leur passeport. Les ressortissants des États-Unis et du Canada sont admis sans visa pour un séjour inférieur à trois mois. Une pièce d'identité est toutefois requise.

Conseils vestimentaires

Au pays de l'éternel été, vous porterez des vêtements légers et décontractés pour vos excursions : maillot de bain, short et sandales pour la plage. Les femmes s'habillent généralement le soir davantage[3] que les messieurs pour lesquels veste et cravate ne sont exigés que[4] très rarement. Toutefois, n'oubliez pas un lainage et vos lunettes de soleil.

Monnaie

La monnaie légale est l'Euro. Le dollar américain est accepté ainsi que tout autre paiement par chèque de voyage ou carte de crédit.

[1]*Seat* [2]*development* [3]*more* [4]*are only required*

Key: En regardant de plus près 1) le verbe : *sortir ;* quelqu'un qui sort ou quitte un endroit, ici ce sont les touristes américains et canadiens qui quittent l'Amérique du Nord pour aller à la Martinique 2) le mot : *vêtements ; conseils vestimentaires* veut dire des suggestions pour les vêtements 3) le mot : *laine ;* un synonyme : un gilet ou un pull-over.

C. En regardant de plus près. Maintenant examinez de plus près les aspects suivants du guide.

1. Regardez le nom **les ressortissants** dans la section **Formalités d'entrée**. Est-ce que ce mot ressemble à un verbe en **-ir** que vous connaissez ? Lequel ? D'après la signification du verbe et le contexte, quelle est la signification du mot **ressortissants** ?
2. Le mot **vestimentaires** dans la section **Conseils vestimentaires** est lié à un autre mot en français que vous connaissez. Quel mot ? D'après le contexte, quelle est la signification de l'adjectif **vestimentaires** ?
3. Dans la même section, vous voyez le mot **un lainage**. Quel mot en français est-ce que vous voyez dans ce mot ? Quel est un synonyme en français pour **un lainage** ?

D. Après avoir lu. Discutez de ces questions avec vos camarades de classe.

1. Avant de lire **le Guide**, vous avez fait un résumé du texte en considérant les titres et les sous-titres. Est-ce que ce résumé vous a aidé à comprendre le texte ? Qu'est-ce que vous avez appris même avant de lire ? Qu'est-ce que vous avez appris de plus en lisant le texte lui-même ?
2. Est-ce que vous pouvez suggérer d'autres informations importantes qu'on devrait ajouter au **Guide** pour les visiteurs à la Martinique ?
3. Après avoir lu **le Guide**, est-ce qu'une visite à la Martinique vous intéresse ? Pourquoi ?

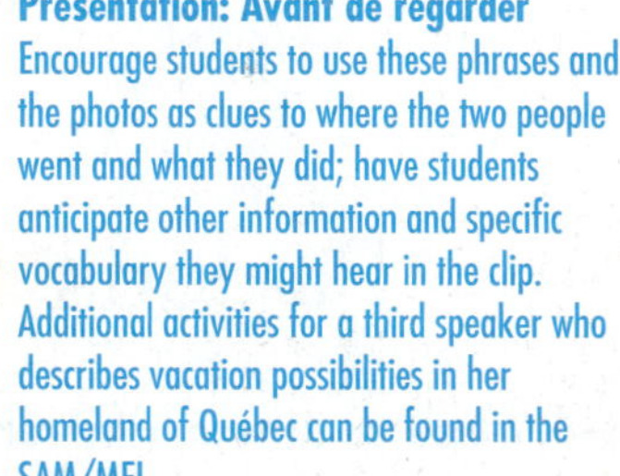

Presentation: Avant de regarder
Encourage students to use these phrases and the photos as clues to where the two people went and what they did; have students anticipate other information and specific vocabulary they might hear in the clip. Additional activities for a third speaker who describes vacation possibilities in her homeland of Québec can be found in the SAM/MFL.

Observons

8-42 Des superbes vacances

A. Avant de regarder. Dans cette séquence vidéo, Corinne et Édouard parlent de leurs superbes vacances. D'après les photos ainsi que les phrases et expressions suivantes, où est-ce qu'ils sont allés ? Qu'est-ce qu'ils ont fait ?

Corinne :

J'ai pu voir des crocodiles...

...ils ont un beau hamac.

...j'en ai profité pour faire des photos avec Mickey, Daisy, Donald...

Édouard :

...je suis parti en croisière en bateau à voile.

...on a découvert... toutes les îles italiennes.

B. En regardant. Regardez et écoutez la séquence pour répondre aux questions suivantes.

1. Pour chaque personne, indiquez les endroits mentionnés :

Corinne :

____ la Californie	____ les États-Unis	____ les Everglades	____ la Floride
____ Miami	____ New York	____ Orlando	____ Paris

Édouard :

____ Antibes	____ la Corse	____ la France	____ la Grèce
____ l'île Maurice	____ Naples	____ Nice	____ Rome

2. Avec qui est-ce que Corinne et Édouard ont passé leurs vacances ?
3. Qu'est-ce qu'ils ont vu pendant leur voyage ?

Script: Observons

CORINNE : En septembre 2001, j'étais aux États-Unis en Floride chez ma famille. Et ils m'ont fait un petit peu visiter euh le la la région. Donc, ils m'ont amenée aux Everglades. J'ai pu voir des crocodiles et euh... cette photo me plaît beaucoup parce que... la première fois que je tenais un petit crocodile qui a failli me manger les doigts d'ailleurs.

Et sinon, les familles ont des belles villas avec des très beaux jardins ce que je n'ai pas la chance d'avoir ici. Et ils ont un beau hamac. J'étais très contente de pouvoir... poser dedans avec mes petites cousines et mes petits cousins.

Évidemment j'ai pas... je suis allée à Orlando je pouvais pas éviter. J'adore Disney donc vu que je connaissais celui en France je voulais absolument voir le Walt Disney américain et donc j'en ai profité pour faire des photos avec Mickey, Daisy, Donald et visiter tout le parc.

ÉDOUARD : Donc cet été j'ai eu un été très sympathique puisque je suis parti en croisière euh en bateau euh... à voile. Je suis parti de... Antibes euh jusqu'à Naples durant trois semaines avec trois autres amis euh et on a découvert euh la Corse, euh euh toutes les îles italiennes jusqu'à arriver à Naples euh où je suis resté trois jours et je suis revenu en train en France. Et c'est vraiment des, vraiment des vacances très très bonnes.

C. Après avoir regardé. Discutez de ces questions avec vos camarades de classe.

1. Pourquoi, à votre avis, est-ce que Corinne et Édouard considèrent que ce sont des superbes vacances ?
2. Est-ce que vous avez visité les endroits mentionnés par Corinne ou Édouard ? Si oui, qu'est-ce que vous avez vu et qu'est-ce que vous avez fait ?
3. Pour vous personnellement, qu'est-ce que c'est des superbes vacances ?

Parlons

Variation: 8-43 As an alternative, have each student (or small group of students) choose a vacation spot in the Francophone world and prepare a small exposé on it, presenting the climate, activities, clothes one should bring, and languages spoken there. This allows students to practice the presentational mode of the *National Standards*. As each student (or group) presents, the others can guess which spot is being described and/or vote on the destination that sounds the most interesting.

8-43 Les vacances d'hiver

A. Avant de parler. Comme vous le savez, beaucoup de Français prennent des vacances d'une ou deux semaines au mois de février. Imaginez que vous avez des vacances vous aussi en février. Où est-ce que vous voudriez aller ? Pensez à vos vacances idéales et partagez vos idées avec un/e partenaire. Regardez les images pour avoir des idées.

On fait du ski à Chamonix dans les Alpes françaises.

On visite le Musée d'Orsay à Paris.

Musée D'Orsay, Paris, interior, main floor. Gae Aluenti architect, 1986. John Brooks/Liaison Agency, Inc./ Getty Images

On fait du bateau à l'île Curieuse aux Seychelles.

B. En parlant. En groupes de quatre ou cinq personnes, parlez de vos vacances d'hiver idéales. Expliquez aux membres de votre groupe le climat que vous préférez, les vêtements que vous voulez porter et les activités que vous voulez faire. Les autres vont vous suggérer des endroits possibles pour ce voyage dans le monde francophone.

C. Après avoir parlé. Comparez les vacances proposées dans votre groupe avec les autres groupes dans la classe. Est-ce que vous voulez tous aller au même endroit ou est-ce que vous avez des camarades de classe qui veulent aller partout dans le monde francophone ?

Écrivons

8-44 Mes meilleurs souvenirs de vacances

A. Avant d'écrire. Racontez des vacances mémorables que vous avez passées.

1. Répondez à ces questions générales avant d'écrire :
   Où est-ce que vous êtes allé/e ? Avec qui ? Quand ?
   Quel temps est-ce qu'il faisait ?
   Comment était cet endroit ? *tropical, pittoresque, tranquille, calme, animé...*
2. Maintenant, pensez à ce que vous avez fait. Quels sont les deux ou trois évènements les plus mémorables ? Faites une liste.

B. En écrivant. Utilisez vos réponses aux questions générales et la liste que vous avez préparée dans l'exercice A, et rédigez deux ou trois paragraphes pour décrire vos vacances. N'oubliez pas d'utiliser le passé composé et l'imparfait.

MODÈLE L'été dernier, je suis allée au Québec avec ma famille. La ville de Québec était très pittoresque ; il y avait des petits magasins avec des fleurs, des cafés et des restaurants en plein air et beaucoup d'animation... Un jour, nous avons fait une promenade en bateau pour voir des baleines (*whales*). Il faisait frais sur le bateau, mais on a vu plusieurs baleines. C'était super. On s'est bien amusés au Canada.

C. En révisant. Réfléchissez aux questions suivantes et puis faites tous les changements nécessaires.

1. Relisez votre description pour le contenu. Est-ce que vous avez inclus une description générale pour situer votre récit : l'endroit, le temps, les dates ? Est-ce que vous avez décrit deux ou trois évènements mémorables ?
2. Maintenant, relisez votre description pour le style et la forme. Soulignez tous les verbes. Vérifiez que vous avez fait le bon choix entre le passé composé et l'imparfait pour chaque verbe. Vérifiez aussi que vous avez fait un bon choix entre les auxiliaires **être** et **avoir** pour les verbes au passé composé et que vous avez utilisé la forme correcte des verbes à l'imparfait.

D. Après avoir écrit. Échangez votre travail avec vos camarades de classe. Qui a passé les vacances les plus intéressantes ?

Now that you have completed *Chapitre 8*, can you do the following in French?

- ☐ discuss and ask about the weather?
- ☐ describe the four seasons and seasonal activities at the seashore, in the mountains, or in the city?
- ☐ ask questions to find out specific information?
- ☐ extend an invitation to a French-speaking person and politely accept or refuse an invitation?
- ☐ make suggestions and give orders in an indirect manner, using the conditional of the verbs **vouloir/pouvoir/devoir**?
- ☐ describe various French-speaking vacation destinations?

Stratégie

When you write an account of an event in the past, set the scene first, and then focus on narrating a few exciting or interesting things that happened.

Implementation: Review the use of the *passé composé* vs. the *imparfait* in narratives. Students should use the *imparfait* to set the scene, describe the weather, talk about feelings and emotions; and the *passé composé* to indicate punctual actions that advance the narrative.

Expansion: As a follow-up, have students exchange their descriptions, read silently, then summarize the trip they read about in two or three sentences.

Vocabulaire

Leçon 1

le temps à toutes les saisons (f.)	***the weather in all seasons***
Quel temps fait-il ?	*What's the weather like?*
Il fait beau.	*It's beautiful weather.*
Il y a du soleil.	*It's sunny.*
Le ciel est bleu.	*The sky is blue.*
Il y a du brouillard.	*It's foggy.*
Il y a des nuages (m.).	*It's cloudy.*
Le ciel est couvert.	*The sky is overcast.*
Le ciel est gris.	*The sky is gray.*
Il y a du vent.	*It's windy.*
Il fait mauvais.	*The weather's bad.*
Il fait lourd.	*It's humid.*
Il neige. (neiger)	*It's snowing. (to snow)*
Il y a du verglas.	*It's icy, slippery.*
Il y a un orage.	*There is a (thunder)storm.*
Il y a des éclairs (m.).	*There is lightning.*
Il y a du tonnerre.	*There is thunder.*
Il pleut. (pleuvoir) (la pluie)	*It's raining. (to rain) (rain)*

pour parler de la température	***to talk about the temperature***
Il fait 10 degrés (m.).	*It's 10 degrees.*
Il fait bon.	*It's warm (weather).*
Il fait chaud.	*It's hot (weather).*
Il fait frais.	*It's cool (weather).*
Il fait froid.	*It's cold (weather).*
Il gèle. (geler)	*It's freezing. (to freeze)*
J'ai chaud/froid.	*I'm hot/cold.*
la météo(rologie)	*weather, weather report*

les saisons (f.)	***the seasons***
au printemps (m.)	*in the spring*
en été (m.)	*in the summer*
en automne (m.)	*in the fall*
en hiver (m.)	*in the winter*

pour poser une question	***to ask a question***
lequel/laquelle/ lesquels/lesquelles	*which one/s*
quel/s, quelle/s	*which*
Quelle est votre saison préférée?	*What is your favorite season?*

expressions de nécessité	***expressions of necessity***
il faut	*you have to/must*
il ne faut pas	*you must not*
il est important de	*it is important to*
il est nécessaire de	*it is necessary to*
il est utile de	*it is useful to*

Leçon 2

les vacances (f. pl.)	***vacation***
partir en vacances	*to go on vacation*
un billet (d'avion)	*(plane) ticket*
une carte postale	*postcard*
des destinations (f.)	*destinations*
la campagne	*countryside*
la mer	*sea*
la montagne	*mountains*
l'océan	*ocean*
la plage	*beach*
la ville	*city*
des projets (m.) de vacances	*vacation plans*
le repos	*rest*
les sports (m.) d'hiver	*winter sports*

des activités (f.)	***activities***
faire…	
des achats (m.)	*to shop*
de l'alpinisme (m.)	*to go mountain climbing*
du camping	*to camp, to go camping*
du cheval	*to go horseback riding*
de la moto	*to ride a motorcycle*
de la motoneige	*to go snowmobiling*
de la planche à voile	*to windsurf*
une randonnée	*to take a hike*
du ski	*to ski*
du ski nautique	*to water ski*
du surf	*to go surfing*
du surf des neiges	*to go snowboarding*
du tourisme	*to go sightseeing*
de la voile	*to go sailing*
se bronzer	*to sunbathe*
visiter des musées ou des monuments	*to visit museums or monuments*

quelques expressions utiles	***some useful expressions***
Bravo !	*Great! Well done!*
C'est pas vrai !	*It can't be!*
Chouette !	*Neat!*
Pas tout à fait !	*Not quite!*
Vive... (les vacances) !	*Hurray for . . . (vacation)!*

pour poser une question	***to ask a question***
qu'est-ce que/qui...?	*what . . .?*
qui ?	*who?*
quoi ?	*what?*

des verbes utiles	***some useful verbs***
connaître	*to know, be familiar with*
savoir	*to know*

Leçon 3

pour inviter quelqu'un	***to invite someone***
Tu es/Vous êtes libre(s) ?	*Are you free?*
On y va ensemble ?	*Shall we go (there) together?*
Tu veux/voudrais m'accompagner ?	*Would you like to come with me?*
Vous voulez/voudriez m'accompagner ?	*Would you like to come with me?*

pour accepter une invitation	**to accept an invitation**
Oui, je suis libre.	*Yes, I am free.*
(J'accepte) Avec plaisir.	*(I accept) With pleasure.*
C'est gentil à toi/vous.	*That's kind (of you).*
Je suis ravi/e.	*I am delighted.*
Volontiers.	*With pleasure, gladly.*

pour refuser une invitation	***to refuse an invitation***
Je suis désolé/e...	*I am sorry . . .*
C'est dommage...	*It's too bad . . .*
Je regrette...	*I'm sorry . . .*
Je ne suis pas libre.	*I'm not free.*
Je suis pris/e.	*I'm busy.*
J'ai déjà un rendez-vous.	*I already have a meeting/date/appointment.*

des distractions (f.)	***amusements/diversions***
aller à un concert	*to go to a concert*
voir/jouer une pièce	*to watch/perform a play*
passer une soirée tranquille	*to spend a quiet evening*
une place	*seat, place*

quelques expressions indéfinies et négatives	***some indefinite and negative expressions***
quelque chose	*something*
quelquefois	*sometimes*
quelqu'un	*someone*
ne... jamais	*never*
ne... personne	*no one*
ne... rien	*nothing*

une expression utile	***a useful expression***
à cause de	*because of*

9 Voyageons !

Pourquoi est-ce que ces deux amoureux se quittent sur le quai de la gare de Lyon à Paris ? Partir, c'est mourir un peu !

After completing this chapter, you should be able to:

- Describe future plans
- Make travel plans
- Make arrangements for lodging
- Describe places and people
- Describe some major French cities, especially Paris

Leçon 1 Projets de voyage

POINTS DE DÉPART

TEXT AUDIO
CD 5 TRACK 1

Comment y aller ?

M. et Mme Mathieu partent en vacances en Tunisie. Ils prennent un taxi pour aller à la gare, et puis le train pour aller à l'aéroport pour prendre leur vol. Ils ont beaucoup de valises.

MME MATHIEU : Tu as tout ? On n'a rien oublié ?

M. MATHIEU : Voyons. On a besoin de nos passeports et de nos billets. Tout est là. Non, je n'ai rien oublié. Et toi, tu n'as rien oublié ?

MME MATHIEU : Mais si ! J'ai laissé mon appareil photo sur la table dans la cuisine, zut !

M. MATHIEU : Ne t'en fais pas. J'ai mon nouvel appareil photo numérique ; je te le prête si tu veux.

MME MATHIEU : Merci, mon chéri, c'est très gentil.

Presentation: Use the drawing of the taxi (MFL, Ch. 9) as you describe the Mathieus' trip. Let students listen to the dialogue, then ask simple comprehension questions: *Comment est-ce que les Mathieu voyagent ? Quelle est leur destination ? Qu'est-ce que M. Mathieu emporte ? Qu'est-ce que Mme Mathieu a oublié ? Quelle est la solution proposée par M. Mathieu ?* Point out the expression *avoir besoin de* taught in Ch. 5, L. 3. Tell students to imagine that the class is taking a trip to Paris and that there are things you must bring because you need them. Start off with *Nous avons besoin de nos passeports* and ask students to provide other examples. You may also wish to review the conjugation of the verb *avoir* with students and remind students of a complementary expression they learned in Ch. 4, L. 3: *avoir envie de.*

Presentation: Use the visual of the hand luggage (MFL, Ch. 9) to present the vocabulary of travel items; provide a description for each item. Note that *un appareil photo numérique* is a digital camera and uses *une carte mémoire ; un appareil photo* requires *une pellicule*. You may wish to teach the vocabulary for both types of cameras. Tell students that they will also see *appareil numérique* for a digital camera. Test comprehension by having students 1) point to the items you name; 2) identify an item by repeating its name: *C'est un passeport ou un permis ?* Note that the French refer to their driver's license as *le papier rose*. You might also use objects to enliven this presentation. Then complete Ex. 9-1.

Presentation: Use visuals (for example, magazine ads) or verbal cues (*Air France, c'est des avions*, etc.) to convey the meaning for means of transportation. Explain the difference between *un bus* (operating within a city) and *un car* (operating between cities). Then move on to Ex. 9-2 and 9-3.

Les moyens de transport

l'avion (m.)	le car	la moto	le tramway
le bateau	le métro	le taxi	le vélo
le bus	la mobylette	le train	la voiture

When specifying a means of transportation, use . . .

- **prendre** plus the means of transportation preceded by an article or possessive:

Je prends **le** métro.	*I'm taking the subway.*
Ils prennent **un** taxi.	*They're taking a taxi.*
Elle prend **son** vélo.	*She's taking her bike.*

- verbs of travel such as **aller**, **partir**, or **voyager** followed by the preposition **en** or **à**, as specified below. In these cases, no article is used.

en avion, **en** bateau, **en** bus, **en** car, **en** métro, **en** taxi, **en** train, **en** tram, **en** voiture, **à** mobylette, **à** moto, **à** pied, **à** vélo

Nous partons **en** avion pour le Mali.	*We're leaving by plane for Mali.*
Moi, je vais au travail **en** métro, mais Christine va au travail **à** pied.	*I take the subway to work, but Christine goes to work on foot.*
Ils préfèrent voyager **en** train.	*They prefer to travel by train.*

Additional practice: Put students in groups and ask: *Est-ce que vous avez un sac, un sac à dos ou un pantalon ou une jupe avec des poches ? Qu'est-ce qu'il y a à l'intérieur ? Comparez ce que vous avez avec un/e partenaire. Qui a les objets les plus intéressants ?* Provide a model: *Voilà mon sac. Voyons, j'ai un portefeuille avec mon permis de conduire et ma carte bancaire, j'ai des lunettes, un carnet d'adresses et un stylo. —Moi, je n'ai pas de sac. Dans mes poches, j'ai mon portefeuille avec un peu d'argent et mon permis, et voilà mes clés.*

À vous la parole

9-1 Qu'est-ce qu'il faut ? De quoi est-ce que les touristes ont besoin ?

MODÈLE pour trouver les monuments dans une grande ville ?
Ils ont besoin d'un plan de la ville.

1. pour payer l'hôtel ?
2. pour louer une voiture ?
3. pour ranger leur argent ?
4. pour prendre des photos ?
5. pour aller dans un pays étranger ?
6. pour rentrer dans leur chambre d'hôtel ?

9-2 Quel moyen de transport ? D'après les indications, quel/s moyen/s de transport est-ce que les personnes suivantes vont probablement utiliser ?

MODÈLE Adeline habite près de Paris ; elle va faire des courses à Paris.
Elle va prendre le train pour aller à Paris, et ensuite le métro ou l'autobus pour faire ses courses.

1. Mme Duclair habite à Paris ; elle va rendre visite à sa grand-mère à Lyon.
2. Les Lefranc vont quitter la France pour passer des vacances aux Antilles.
3. La petite Hélène va à l'école primaire près de chez elle.
4. Robert habite une ville moyenne ; il va au centre-ville pour faire des courses.
5. M. Rolland doit traverser Paris pour aller au travail.
6. Maxime et Amélie vont faire un pique-nique à la campagne.
7. Mme Antonine voyage pour son travail : elle va à Lyon, à Rome et à Berlin.
8. Les Leclair vont visiter les îles grecques pendant les vacances.

Key: 9-2 1) le train, l'avion, la voiture 2) l'avion 3) à pied 4) à pied, à vélo, à mobylette, en tram 5) le métro, le bus, la mobylette, le tram 6) la voiture, le vélo 7) le train, l'avion 8) l'avion, le bateau

Vie et culture

Implementation: Show the brief video clip (*On prend le train*) and help students identify locations and activities pictured and mentioned in the voice-over. Make sure students understand the importance of the TGV and the Chunnel. Some of your students may have traveled by train in Europe and even via the Chunnel; ask them to share their impressions.

Voyager en train en France

Regardez la séquence vidéo, *On prend le train*. Comment sont les trains français ? Pourquoi, à votre avis, est-ce que les Français, et les Européens en général, voyagent plus souvent en train que les Nord-Américains ?

En France, le système ferroviaire[1] est nationalisé. Tous les trains sont sous le contrôle de la Société nationale des chemins de fer français (la SNCF). Le TGV (Train à grande vitesse) est un des trains les plus rapides au monde. Par exemple, il parcourt[2] les 400 kilomètres qui séparent Lyon de Paris en seulement deux heures. Regardez la carte du réseau TGV: quelles sont les régions desservies par le train rapide ? Où est-ce que vous voudriez voyager en TGV ?

Depuis 1994, on peut traverser la Manche entre la France et l'Angleterre en train, en passant par le « Chunnel ». Ce tunnel est important parce qu'il relie l'Angleterre au continent européen. Ainsi, au départ de Lyon il faut seulement cinq heures pour arriver à Londres.

[1]*railway* [2]*covers*

Implementation: 9-3 Give students a limited amount of time to work in pairs, then bring the class together to compare responses.

9-3 Comment y aller ? Avec un/e partenaire, discutez de ces questions. Ensuite, comparez vos réponses et vos conclusions avec les conclusions de vos camarades de classe.

1. Comment est-ce que vous allez à vos cours ? Comment est-ce que vous faites vos courses ?
2. Est-ce qu'il y a un service de bus dans votre ville ? Un métro ? Comment est-ce que les habitants de votre ville vont au travail habituellement ?
3. Comment est-ce que vous rentrez chez vous pour les vacances ?
4. Est-ce que vous avez une voiture ? Si oui, quelle sorte de voiture : une voiture française, japonaise, américaine ? Est-ce que c'est une voiture hybride ?
5. Est-ce que le train passe par votre ville ? Où est-ce qu'on peut aller en train en partant de votre ville ?
6. Comment sont les trains américains comparés aux trains français ? Est-ce qu'il existe un TGV aux États-Unis ?
7. Pour voyager aux États-Unis, quel est votre moyen de transport préféré ? Pourquoi ?

Sons et lettres

La liaison obligatoire

Presentation: Show that *liaison* implies *enchaînement* by inserting a pause after the first syllable and overarticulating the liaison consonant: *un gros‿homme = /gro zɔm/, ils‿ont = /il zɔ̃/.*

You will recall that liaison consonants are pronounced only when the word that follows begins with a vowel. The pronunciation of these consonants is called **liaison**. Liaison is always accompanied by **enchaînement**: the liaison consonant is pronounced as part of the following word: **nous allons** /nu za lɔ̃/.

Liaison is not always made. In addition to occurring before a vowel, liaison depends on grammatical factors. Cases where liaison must always be made are called **liaisons obligatoires**. They are relatively limited. In this lesson and in Lesson 2 we list the cases of **liaisons obligatoires**.

Liaison /z/ is the most common liaison consonant because it indicates the plural. It is usually spelled **-s**, but in some cases it is spelled **-x**. Always pronounce liaison /z/:

- After the plural form of articles and adjectives that precede the noun:

  le**s**‿hôtels /z/ — de**s**‿autos /z/ — ce**s**‿étages /z/
  le**s**‿ancienne**s**‿églises /z/ /z/ — les grand**s**‿immeubles /z/ — ces beau**x**‿avions /z/

- After the singular adjectives **gros** and **mauvais**:

  un gro**s**‿homme /z/ — un mauvai**s**‿hôtel /z/

- After numerals:

  troi**s**‿heures /z/ — quatre-vingt**s**‿ans /z/ — le si**x**‿avril /z/

- After the plural subject pronouns **nous**, **vous**, **ils**, **elles**:

  nou**s**‿habitons /z/ — vou**s**‿utilisez /z/ — il**s**‿ont payé /z/ — elle**s**‿adorent /z/

- After the plural possessive adjectives **mes, tes, ses, vos, nos, leurs**:

mes‿amis /z/ leurs‿enfants /z/ nos‿itinéraires /z/

- After one-syllable adverbs and prepositions (**pas, plus, très** ; **dans, sans, sous**) and the combination of the preposition **à** and **de** with the plural definite articles (**aux, des**):

très‿intéressant /z/ dans‿un appartement /z/ aux‿Antilles /z/ sans‿argent /z/

À vous la parole

9-4 Contrastes. Remplacez le premier nom par le second.

MODÈLE un gros bateau / avion

É1 Tu as dit un gros bateau ?
É2 Non, un gros avion.

1. un mauvais quartier / endroit
2. deux trains / avions
3. les billets / appareil photos
4. des villes / îles
5. les belles Françaises / Américaines
6. les belles rues / avenues
7. ces beaux musées / hôtels
8. nous louons / achetons
9. ils partent / arrivent

Initial practice: *Liaison obligatoire* is relatively limited, so encourage students to memorize where it occurs. Use substitution drills to practice: 1) determiners and adjectives, singular to plural: *l'homme > les hommes ; une amie > des amies ; cet enfant > ces enfants ; son ami > ses amis ; un petit appartement > des petits appartements ; la vieille église > les vieilles églises* 2) the adjectives *gros* and *mauvais*, feminine to masculine: *une grosse auto > un gros avion ; une mauvaise architecte > un mauvais architecte* 3) numerals: *deux immeubles* [3] > *trois immeubles ; six étages* [10] > *dix étages* 4) pronouns, singular to plural: *elle a les billets > elles ont les billets ; j'achète des lunettes > nous achetons des lunettes* 5) prepositions, *très* + adjective: *Il est très petit (amusant) > très amusant ;* other vowel-initial adjectives include: *énergique, optimiste, idéaliste, indiscipliné, individualiste, élégante, intelligente, ambitieuse, âgé, égoïste.*

9-5 Phrases. Répétez chaque phrase.

1. Vous allez aux Antilles ou en Afrique ?
2. Mes autres amis habitent aux États-Unis.
3. Cet avion part à trois heures et arrive à six heures.
4. C'est un mauvais endroit pour construire des grands immeubles.
5. En Italie, il y a des très anciennes églises et des beaux hôtels.

Implementation: 9-5 Suggest that students first mark the *liaisons obligatoires* and then repeat.

FORMES ET FONCTIONS

1. *Le futur*

- One may express future events in French using the **futur proche** or the **futur**. The two grammatical structures do not carry precisely the same meaning for French speakers. Compare:

a. Ma tante **va avoir** un enfant.	*My aunt's going to have a baby.*
b. Ils vont se marier et ils **auront** beaucoup d'enfants.	*They're going to get married, and they'll have lots of kids.*

In **a.** we assume that the aunt is expecting. In **b.** it is not certain that the couple to be married will have *any* children, let alone many.

Note: In view of its link with intentionality, it is also appropriate to refer to *le futur proche* as *le futur défini*, and to the so-called *futur simple* as *le futur indéfini*. The exercises stress the semantic and pragmatic distinctions between the two structures. Students can also express the notion of the future by using the present tense plus an adverbial expression: *Ils partent demain.*

- The difference between the **futur proche** and the **futur** is not primarily one of nearness or remoteness of the future event, but of its degree of certainty or definiteness. Compare:

Je **ferai** la cuisine plus tard.	*I'll do the cooking later (perhaps).*
Je **vais faire** la cuisine.	*I'm going to cook (right away).*
L'été prochain je **vais aller** en Suisse.	*Next summer I'm going to Switzerland (definite).*
Un jour, j'**irai** en Afrique.	*Someday I'll go to Africa (indefinite).*

- Use the **futur** to soften instructions and emphatic commands.

Vous **traverserez** l'avenue et vous **tournerez** à gauche dans la rue Colbert.	*You cross the avenue and turn left at Colbert Street.*

Note: The future stem is the same as the infinitive, except that: a) the final *-e* of *-re* verbs is dropped: *apprendre, j'apprendrai* b) the *-e* of *-er* verbs is an unstable *e* and may or may not be pronounced, depending on the number of consonant sounds that follow or precede: *tu chantéras, tu parleras.*

- To form the future tense, add the future endings to the future stem. The future stem of regular verbs is the infinitive (for verbs ending in **-re**, remove the final **-e** from the infinitive).

LE FUTUR

INFINITIVE ENDING:	-ER	-IR	-RE
FUTURE STEM:	CHANTER-	PARTIR-	VENDR-
je	chanter**ai**	partir**ai**	vendr**ai**
tu	chanter**as**	partir**as**	vendr**as**
il / elle / on	chanter**a**	partir**a**	vendr**a**
nous	chanter**ons**	partir**ons**	vendr**ons**
vous	chanter**ez**	partir**ez**	vendr**ez**
ils / elles	chanter**ont**	partir**ont**	vendr**ont**

- The following verbs have irregular future stems:

acheter	j'**achèter**ai	devoir	je **devr**ai	pleuvoir	il **pleuvr**a
aller	j'**ir**ai	être	je **ser**ai	pouvoir	je **pourr**ai
appeler	j'**appeller**ai	faire	je **fer**ai	savoir	je **saur**ai
avoir	j'**aur**ai	préférer	je **préfèrer**ai	vouloir	je **voudr**ai

Note: *Amener, (se) lever,* and *(se) promener* show the same irregular future stem change as *acheter. Épeler* and *jeter* show the same stem change as *appeler.* In both cases, the pronunciation of the vowel [ɛ] is indicated by the *accent grave* or the double consonant. *Préférer*-type verbs (*préférer, espérer, répéter, suggérer*) are included here based on the 1990 Orthographic reform (règle 3a): «*On accentue sur le modèle de **semer** les futurs et conditionnels des verbes du type céder: **je cèderai, je cèderais**...*» As with the *acheter*-type verbs, the *accent grave* here clearly indicates the pronunciation of [ɛ]. For formation of the conditional, see Ch. 11, L. 2.

À vous la parole

9-6 C'est sérieux ou pas ? Adèle parle de ses projets. Pour chaque activité décrite, notez si c'est sûr qu'elle va la faire, ou non.

Adèle...	sûr	pas sûr
MODÈLE va téléphoner à sa copine.	✓	______
fera ses devoirs.	______	✓
1. terminera son projet.	______	______
2. préparera son exposé oral.	______	______
3. va sortir avec des amis.	______	______
4. va regarder la télé.	______	______
5. ira à la B.U. pour travailler.	______	______
6. va dîner en ville.	______	______
7. aura une bonne note en chimie.	______	______

Est-ce qu'Adèle est une étudiante sérieuse ou pas ? Pourquoi ?

9-7 Préparatifs de voyage. La famille Meunier part en voyage. Mme Meunier organise les taches à accomplir. Qu'est-ce qu'elle dit à chaque personne ?

MODÈLE acheter les billets, Thomas
Thomas, tu achèteras les billets !

1. réserver une chambre, Thomas
2. préparer la voiture, Thomas
3. faire les valises, les enfants
4. ranger la salle à manger, Fred
5. fermer les fenêtres, Hélène
6. mettre un beau pantalon, Fred
7. prendre cette valise, Fred
8. appeler un taxi, Thomas

9-8 Prévisions météo. Voici les prévisions météo pour le Canada et pour le monde entier. Quel temps est prévu pour les villes indiquées ?

Au Pays		Demain	Le monde		Demain
Vancouver	Averses	14/8	Berlin	Ensoleillé	14/3
Victoria	Averses	13/8	Bruxelles	Ensoleillé	16/5
Edmonton	P/Nuageux	15/2	Buenos Aires	Nuageux	15/11
Calgary	P/Nuageux	19/3	Honolulu	P/Nuageux	29/23
Saskatoon	Ensoleillé	12/1	Lisbonne	Ensoleillé	27/14
Régina	P/Nuageux	11/2	Londres	P/Nuageux	19/8
Winnipeg	Nuageux	12/5	Los Angeles	Ensoleillé	23/12
Ottawa	Ensoleillé	18/6	New Delhi	P/Nuageux	34/23
Québec	Ensoleillé	18/5	New York	P/Nuageux	17/11
Moncton	Ensoleillé	17/6	Paris	Ensoleillé	19/6

MODÈLE à Ottawa
Demain, il fera beau. La température sera de 18 degrés. Ce soir, elle descendra jusqu'à 6 degrés.

1. à Québec
2. à Winnipeg
3. à Calgary
4. à Vancouver
5. à Paris
6. à Bruxelles
7. à Londres
8. à Honolulu

Initial practice: Begin with the comprehension-based activity, Ex. 9-6. Next use discrimination drills to practice other distinctions: have students raise their hand when they hear a future event described: *Ils sont allés en Grèce l'été dernier. Ils iront en Espagne l'été prochain. Je prendrai l'avion pour aller en Belgique. Nous voyageons souvent en train. Elle attend le bus devant chez elle. Tu partiras vraiment toute seule en Europe ? Vous avez oublié les billets ? Je n'oublierai pas mon appareil cette fois-ci. Elles vont en ville en car tous les vendredis. Elle achètera son billet la semaine prochaine.* One person, or more than one? *Il sera en retard. Ils feront le travail. Elle prendra le bus. Il louera une voiture. Ils voyageront en première classe. Elles feront le tour du monde en avion. Elle prendra beaucoup de photos. Ils rendront visite à des amis. Elles achèteront des souvenirs à Paris.* Practice with transformation drills to emphasize future stems: *Je suis (Je serai) ; Je regarde (Je regarderai) ; Je dors (Je dormirai)*, etc. Continue with substitution drills for each regular verb group: *Je travaillerai beaucoup ; nous. — Nous travaillerons beaucoup*, etc. *Il sortira ce week-end ; nous. — Nous sortirons ce week-end*, etc. *Elle attendra à l'aéroport ; moi. — J'attendrai à l'aéroport.*

Implementation: 9-8 Before beginning the exercise, you may wish to review weather terms. This could be accomplished simply by asking students what the weather is like currently and what the forecast is for the coming weekend or days. Note that P stands for *pluie*.

Note: Typically the *futur* (*indéfini*) is used in weather forecasts, since weather is anything but fully predictable and certain: *Mardi sera marqué par une crête de haute pression qui apportera du soleil à l'ensemble des régions.*

Implementation: 9-9 Pretend you are the fortune teller and act the role! Vary the exercise by having students take either the optimist's or the pessimist's point of view.

Additional practice: Use this pair activity for further practice:
L'an 2050. Parlez de vos prédictions pour l'an 2050 avec un/e partenaire.

MODÈLE travailler dans les usines (*factories*)
É1 Personne ne travaillera dans les usines.
É2 Tout le travail sera fait par des robots.

1. utiliser des ordinateurs
2. lire des livres
3. voyager en train
4. parler anglais
5. explorer la planète Mars
6. habiter sur la Lune ou dans l'espace
7. choisir une femme comme présidente

Help students discover the meaning of the words *lune* and *espace* through the cognates "lunar, space" and the context. See whether they can come up with additional examples of how things might be in 2050 using verbs they know.

Presentation: Start with examples and see whether students can derive the meaning and rules. Alternatively, you can tell a story about your travels, using *y* and asking students questions about whether they have been to the various places. For example: *L'été dernier, je suis allée en Angleterre avec ma famille. On y est allé en avion. D'abord on a visité Liverpool. Ma nièce y habite et fait ses études à l'Université de Liverpool. Est-ce que vous avez déjà visité l'Angleterre ? Comment est-ce que vous y êtes allé/e ? En avion ? Et Londres ? Vous y êtes allé/e aussi ? Comment ?*, etc.

9-9 Boule de cristal. Imaginez que vous allez chez une voyante. Voici ses prédictions. Avec un/e partenaire, tirez-en des conclusions. Voyons si vous avez compris la même chose.

MODÈLE Je vois que beaucoup d'argent passe entre vos mains.
É1 Alors je serai très riche.
É2 Alors je travaillerai dans une banque.

1. Je vois que vous voyagez beaucoup à cause du travail.
2. Je vois beaucoup d'enfants dans votre avenir.
3. Je vous vois devant une grande maison.
4. Je vous vois en compagnie d'une belle femme/d'un bel homme.
5. Je vois que vous avez beaucoup d'amis.
6. Je vois que vous êtes très célèbre.

2. *Le pronom* y

- The pronoun **y** means *there*. It refers back to the name of a place, which can be introduced by a preposition such as **à**, **en**, **chez**, **devant**, or **à côté de**, for example.

—Tu es allé **en** Provence l'été dernier ?	—*You went to Provence last summer?*
—Oui, j'**y** suis allé avec mes parents.	—*Yes, I went there with my parents.*
—Tes cousins habitent **au** Canada ?	—*Your cousins live in Canada?*
—Non, ils n'**y** habitent plus.	—*No, they don't live there anymore.*
—Qui va aller **chez** Cécile ?	—*Who's going to Cécile's house?*
—Pas moi ; je n'aime pas **y** aller.	—*Not me; I don't like going there.*

- Like the other object pronouns, **y** is placed immediately before the conjugated verb, unless there is an infinitive. When there is an infinitive, the pronoun goes immediately in front of it.

Tu **y** vas ?	*Are you going there?*
Cet hôtel est abominable. Je ne peux plus **y** rester.	*This hotel is awful. I can't stay here any longer.*
Paris ? Oui, nous **y** sommes allés l'été dernier.	*Paris? Yes, we went there last summer.*

À vous la parole

9-10 C'est logique. De quelle ville francophone est-ce qu'on parle probablement ? Il y a souvent plusieurs possibilités.

En Afrique : Dakar, Abidjan, Bamako
En Amérique du Nord : Québec, Montréal, La Nouvelle-Orléans
Les DOM : Fort-de-France (Martinique), Pointe-à-Pitre (Guadeloupe), Cayenne (Guyane)
En Europe : Paris, Genève, Bruxelles, Nice

MODÈLE On y va pour les sports d'hiver.
À Genève.
ou À Montréal.

1. On y trouve des belles plages.
2. Les gens y parlent créole.
3. On y parle anglais et français.
4. On y parle wolof et français.
5. On y parle flamand et français.
6. On y va pour le Carnaval.
7. Les Américains y vont pour parler français sans quitter l'Amérique du Nord.

Implementation: 9-10 This tests students' understanding of the use of the pronoun *y*; to simplify, have students answer with the location only.

Key: 9-10 Answers include: 1) Nice, Martinique, Guadeloupe 2) Fort-de-France, Pointe-à-Pitre, La Nouvelle-Orléans 3) Montréal, Québec, La Nouvelle-Orléans 4) Dakar 5) Bruxelles 6) La Nouvelle-Orléans, Nice 7) Québec, Montréal, La Nouvelle-Orléans.
Continue with quick substitution drills to practice placement of the pronoun *y* : *J'y suis allé/e ; nous. —Nous y sommes allés*, etc. ; *Je vais y aller ; toi. —Tu vas y aller*, etc.

9-11 Les voyageurs. En choisissant l'expression appropriée dans la colonne B, dites pourquoi les personnes suivantes visitent les endroits indiqués. Attention au temps du verbe !

MODÈLE Arnaud va aller à Paris.
Il va y aller pour visiter la tour Eiffel.

A	B
1. Les Kerboul sont allés à La Nouvelle-Orléans.	**a.** acheter du bon vin
2. Les Dupuis vont aller dans les Alpes.	**b.** voir le Carnaval
3. Raymond veut aller à la Guadeloupe.	**c.** visiter les pyramides
4. Arnaud va aller à Paris.	**d.** visiter la tour Eiffel
5. Les Brunet sont allés sur la Côte d'Azur.	**e.** apprendre l'espagnol
6. Christiane voudrait aller au Mexique.	**f.** apprendre le créole
7. Les Santini vont en Égypte.	**g.** nager et se bronzer
8. M. Lescure va aller dans la région de Bordeaux.	**h.** faire du ski

Expansion: 9-12 Have students suggest other places.

 **9-12 Vos habitudes.** Demandez à votre partenaire s'il ou si elle va aux endroits suivants pendant les vacances. Il/Elle doit vous donner une raison pour justifier sa réponse.

MODÈLE dans des bons restaurants

É1 Tu vas quelquefois dans des bons restaurants ?
É2 Non, je n'y vais jamais.
É1 Pourquoi ?
É2 Parce qu'ils sont très chers et je n'ai pas assez d'argent pour y aller.

1. au théâtre
2. à des concerts
3. à Disneyland Paris
4. au musée
5. en Louisiane
6. en Europe
7. aux Antilles
8. dans un pays francophone

Fiche pratique

When listening to an announcement, you may find it difficult to understand every word. Use the context and key words to make intelligent guesses about the content of the announcement. Also, don't panic! In an airport or train station, announcements are usually repeated so you can listen more than once for information you may have missed.

Écoutons

9-13 Votre attention, s'il vous plaît !

A. Avant d'écouter. Quand on voyage, on entend souvent des annonces à l'aéroport, à la gare, à la station de métro, dans le métro ou le tram. Regardez les photos. Où sommes-nous ? Quelles sortes d'annonces est-ce que vous entendez typiquement dans ces endroits ?

B. En écoutant. Écoutez ces annonces adressées aux voyageurs et complétez le tableau suivant.

1. La première fois que vous écoutez, dites où se trouvent les gens qui entendent l'annonce — **à l'aéroport**, **à la gare**, **à la station de métro**, **dans le métro** — et complétez la première colonne.
2. Ensuite, complétez la deuxième colonne. Déterminez si le message est adressé aux gens qui sont déjà dans l'avion ou le train, ou qui attendent un vol ou un train.
3. Dans la troisième colonne, indiquez ce que les gens qui entendent l'annonce doivent faire.
4. Enfin, notez dans la quatrième colonne, d'autres détails importants pour chaque annonce.

On se dépêche pour prendre le train.

	Où	Pour qui ?	Action à prendre	Autres détails importants
1.	*la gare*	*les voyageurs dans le train*	*descendre*	*deux minutes d'arrêt*
2.				
3.			*s'éloigner du quai*	
4.				
5.			*faire attention*	
6.				

C. Après avoir écouté. Est-ce que vous avez déjà entendu des annonces de ce style ? Où ? Est-ce que vous les écoutez attentivement ? Pourquoi ?

Script: Écoutons

1. Mesdames et messieurs, dans quelques instants, nous allons arriver en gare de Cannes. Cannes. Deux minutes d'arrêt.
2. Tous les passagers pour le vol Air France 342 à destination de Nouméa sont priés de se présenter à la porte 34 pour un départ immédiat.
3. Dans quelques instants, le train arrivera en gare. Éloignez-vous du bord du quai, s'il vous plaît.
4. Les passagers Dupont, Smith et Labonté sont priés de se présenter au comptoir Air France dans le Hall B.
5. Par mesure de sécurité (en accord avec la loi vigipirate) tout bagage suspect ou abandonné sera immédiatement détruit.
6. Terminus du train. Tous les passagers sont priés de descendre du train. Faites attention de ne rien oublier dans le train.

On attend le métro à Paris.

Une bouche de métro, style art nouveau, dans le Quartier latin à Paris.

Leçon 2 Destinations

POINTS DE DÉPART

TEXT AUDIO
CD 5 TRACK 5

Presentation: The photos and introductions provide an overview of countries, nationalities, and languages. Have students find the places mentioned on a world map (MFL, Maps or the textbook endpages). Ask students to use these brief introductions as a model for introducing themselves.

Où est-ce qu'on va ?

Je m'appelle David Diouf. Je suis du Sénégal et j'étudie à Paris. Ma langue maternelle, c'est le wolof, mais je parle aussi français. Je vais bientôt prendre l'avion pour aller à Dakar. Je vais passer les vacances chez moi, au Sénégal, cet été.

Je suis Denise Duclos. Je suis suisse. J'habite à Lausanne. Je parle allemand aussi bien que français. Je prends l'avion pour aller à Bruxelles pour une réunion de travail. Je vais rentrer en Suisse ce soir.

Mon nom, c'est Pierre Piron. Je suis belge et j'habite à Bruxelles. Je retourne au Mali, où je vais reprendre mon travail pour Médecins sans Frontières.

Continents	*Pays*	*Adjectif de nationalité*
L'Afrique	l'Algérie	algérien/algérienne
	le Cameroun	camerounais/e
	la Côte d'Ivoire	ivoirien/ivoirienne
	le Maroc	marocain/e
	le Sénégal	sénégalais/e
L'Asie	la Chine	chinois/e
	la Corée	coréen/coréenne
	l'Inde	indien/indienne
	le Japon	japonais/e
	le Vietnam	vietnamien/vietnamienne
L'Océanie	l'Australie	australien/australienne
L'Amérique	le Canada	canadien/canadienne
...du Nord	les États-Unis	américain/e
	le Mexique	mexicain/e
...du Sud	l'Argentine	argentin/e
	le Brésil	brésilien/brésilienne
	la Colombie	colombien/colombienne
L'Europe	l'Allemagne	allemand/e
	l'Angleterre	anglais/e
	l'Autriche	autrichien/autrichienne
	la Belgique	belge
	l'Espagne	espagnol/e
	la France	français/e
	l'Italie	italien/italienne
	les Pays-Bas	néerlandais/e
	le Portugal	portugais/e
	la Suisse	suisse

Note: Whereas North Americans think of seven continents: *L'Afrique, l'Asie, l'Australie, l'Amérique du Nord, l'Amérique du Sud, l'Europe,* and *l'Antarctique*, the French divide the world into five continents: *l'Afrique, l'Asie, l'Amérique, l'Europe,* and *l'Océanie.* According to the composition of your class, you may wish to introduce the names of other countries and nationalities. See the *Chez nous* Companion Website for additional resources.

Note: The name of the inhabitants of a country is usually derived from the adjective of nationality, but is written with a capital letter: *un Chinois, une Anglaise, les Ivoiriens.* The name of the language is often derived from the masculine form of the adjective of nationality: *les Portugais parlent portugais.* There are many exceptions, however: *en Algérie, on parle arabe, berbère et français ; en Suisse, on parle allemand, français, italien et romanche.*

À vous la parole

9-14 C'est quel pays ? Décidez quel pays on visite, d'après la description.

MODÈLE On visite le palais de Buckingham et le *British Museum.*
C'est l'Angleterre.

1. On s'installe à la terrasse d'un café pour admirer la tour Eiffel.
2. On boit un cappuccino et on regarde les gondoles qui passent.
3. Il y a des pyramides aztèques.
4. On peut visiter les souks (*les marchés*) de Marrakech.
5. On visite le château Frontenac à Québec.
6. Là-bas, il y a l'administration centrale de la Communauté Européenne.
7. C'est le seul pays d'Europe où l'on parle espagnol.

Initial practice: Name a country and have students tell on which continent it is found: *le Vietnam ? —Le Vietnam est en Asie ; le Sénégal ? —Le Sénégal est en Afrique ; le Mexique ; les Pays-Bas ; le Brésil ; le Maroc ; la Chine ; l'Italie ; le Canada ; le Cameroun ; la Suisse ; l'Australie ; la Côte d'Ivoire,* etc. Here country names can be for recognition only.

Variation: 9-14 To include cities, give students two possibilities and let them choose the correct response: *Le palais de Buckingham, c'est à Londres ou à Bruxelles ?*

Key: 9-14 1) la France 2) l'Italie 3) le Mexique 4) le Maroc 5) le Canada 6) la Belgique 7) l'Espagne. Have students suggest additional items, perhaps using simple one-word associations: *le chocolat —la Belgique ou la Suisse,* etc.

Vie et culture

Implementation: See the *Chez nous* Companion Website for links to the official Web sites for these organizations. **MSF** was created in response to the situation in Biafra in 1971. Since the organization is politically active and does not remain neutral, its stands are sometimes controversial. Members have been active in politics; for example, Bernard Kouchner, a founder of **MSF**, served as health minister for Mitterrand and foreign affairs minister for Sarkozy. It is estimated that more than 20 million individuals benefited from the actions of **PSF** in 2006–2007 alone. See the organizations' official Web sites for details on recent projects. Students may be familiar with the Peace Corps, a federal agency founded in 1961, whose volunteers live and work in 139 countries all over the world.
In your discussion, you might emphasize that all these organizations allow volunteers to use their specialized skills to make a difference in the world while enriching their own lives.

Les organisations internationales humanitaires

CICR

MEDECINS SANS FRONTIERES

PHARMACIENS SANS FRONTIERES®

Comité International

Certaines organisations non gouvernementales internationales à but humanitaire ont été créées dans des pays francophones. En voici quelques-unes :

Le Comité international de la Croix-Rouge, créé en 1863, est une organisation indépendante et neutre qui apporte une protection et une assistance humanitaires aux victimes de la guerre[1] ou de la violence armée. Le CICR intervient de manière impartiale en faveur des prisonniers, des blessés[2] et des malades, ainsi que[3] des civils[4] touchés par un conflit armé. Le CICR, qui a son siège[5] à Genève (en Suisse), est présent dans environ 80 pays et compte plus de 12 000 collaborateurs. Le CICR est à l'origine du Mouvement international de la Croix-Rouge et du Croissant-Rouge ainsi que du droit international humanitaire, en particulier des Conventions de Genève.

Médecins sans frontières a été créé en 1971 par des médecins français. L'organisation offre une assistance médicale d'urgence[6] dans des cas de conflits armés, de catastrophes naturelles, d'épidémies et de famine. À la différence de la Croix-Rouge, **MSF** estime que la politique de neutralité est une erreur ; cette association allie[7] aide humanitaire et actions de sensibilisation[8] auprès des médias et des institutions politiques.

Pharmaciens sans frontières, créé en 1985, est la plus grande association humanitaire pharmaceutique mondiale. **PSF** aide certains pays en développement[9] à mettre en place un système d'approvisionnement[10] et de distribution de médicaments essentiels de qualité. **Pharmaciens sans frontières** a ses bureaux à Bordeaux ; depuis sa création, elle a opéré dans plus de 43 pays.

ET VOUS ?

1. Qu'est-ce que vous savez sur les bonnes actions des organisations décrites ici ?
2. Quelles sont les organisations internationales humanitaires créées aux États-Unis ? Est-ce que vous connaissez des gens qui ont fait partie d'une de ces organisations ? Quelles ont été leurs expériences ?

[1]*war* [2]*injured* [3]*as well as* [4]*civilians* [5]*headquarters* [6]*emergency* [7]*combines* [8]*consciousness raising* [9]*developing* [10]*supply*

9-15 Présentations. Selon l'endroit où chaque personne habite, indiquez sa nationalité et des langues possibles.

MODÈLE Luc Auger habite à Québec.
➤ Il est canadien. Il parle français et probablement un peu anglais.

1. Maria Garcia est de Buenos Aires.
2. Sylvie Gerniers habite à Bruxelles.
3. Chantal Dupuis est de Genève.
4. Paolo Dos Santos habite à Rio de Janeiro.
5. Helmut Müller est de Berlin.
6. Maria Verdi habite à Milan.
7. Jin Lu ? Elle est de Pékin.

9-16 Un voyage. Avec un/e partenaire, imaginez que vous partez visiter un pays lointain. Quel pays est-ce que vous choisirez ? Qu'est-ce que vous y ferez ?

MODÈLE É1 Je visiterai la Suisse, parce que j'ai des cousins là-bas. Je ferai du ski dans les Alpes.
É2 Et moi, je visiterai l'Égypte. J'irai voir les pyramides.

Sons et lettres

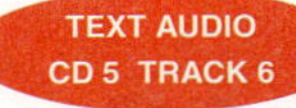

La liaison avec *t*, *n* et *r*

After /z/, the next most common liaison consonant is /t/. It is usually spelled **-t**, but in some cases it is spelled **-d**.

- Pronounce liaison /t/ after the adjectives **petit** and **grand**, the form **cet**, and the numbers **huit**, **vingt**, **cent**:

un peti**t**‿animal /t/ un gran**d**‿immeuble /t/ ce**t**‿hiver /t/
il a hui**t**‿ans /t/ ving**t**‿heures /t/ cen**t**‿appartements /t/

- Liaison /t/ must also be pronounced in certain fixed phrases:

Quel temps fai**t**‿-il ? /t/ Quelle heure es**t**‿-il ? /t/ Commen**t**‿allez-vous ? /t/

- Although it is not obligatory, liaison is often made after the verb forms **ont**, **sont**, **vont**, and **font**. These are cases of optional liaison:

ils son**t**‿ici /t/ elles fon**t**‿un voyage /t/ elles von**t**‿en Afrique /t/

- Liaison /t/ is *never* pronounced after the word **et**:

Pierre et Alain ving**t**‿-et-un /t/

Liaison /n/ occurs in the following cases:

- after **un** and the possessives **mon**, **ton**, **son**:

u**n**‿hôtel /n/ mo**n**‿église /n/ to**n**‿auto /n/ so**n**‿itinéraire /n/

Key: 9-15 1) argentine ; espagnol 2) belge ; français, flamand 3) suisse ; français, allemand, italien 4) brésilien ; portugais 5) allemand ; allemand 6) italienne ; italien 7) chinoise ; chinois

Implementation: 9-16 Introduce by asking students if they have relatives or friends in other countries. Follow up by asking about trips students may have already made overseas.

Additional practice: As a culminating exercise, have students assume a new identity (with a name indicative of the target language they choose) and introduce themselves. Classmates can take notes and then be asked to recall the new identity of each student. This can become a fun game; you may want to give students a day to prepare.

Note: Except for the cases of the verbs pointed out here—*ont*, *sont*, *font*, and *vont*—beginning students should not be encouraged to make optional liaisons. Liaison should be avoided after other verb forms, for example: *vous faites une excursion, elles prennent un TGV.*

- after the pronouns **on** and **en**, and the preposition **en**:

on‿y va /n/	il **en**‿a /n/	**en**‿octobre /n/

- after the adjectives **bon, certain, prochain**:

un **bon**‿avion /n/	un **certain**‿itinéraire /n/	le **prochain**‿arrêt /n/

Liaison /R/ occurs in **dernier** and **premier**:

le premier‿étage /R/	le dernier‿avion /R/

Presentation: Point out the accompanying vowel change for *bon* (/bɔ̃/ to /bɔn/ and for *certain* and *prochain* (/ɛ̃/ to /ɛn/). Some speakers maintain the nasal vowel in the latter two adjectives. In *premier* and *dernier* there are alternations between /e/ and /ɛ/.

À vous la parole

Note: The use of prepositions with country names will be presented in the following **Formes et fonctions** section. Here all countries are feminine and the preposition *en* is used consistently.

9-17 Des beaux voyages. Indiquez quel pays on visitera. Faites bien la liaison avec **on** et **en**.

MODÈLE Le Caire
On ira en Égypte.

1. Londres
2. Madrid
3. Alger
4. New Delhi
5. Berlin
6. Sydney
7. Rome
8. Buenos Aires

9-18 Pardon ? Vous n'entendez pas bien ? Votre partenaire va vous corriger.

MODÈLE le prochain bateau / avion
É1 Tu as dit le prochain bateau ?
É2 Non, le prochain avion.

1. le dernier train / avion
2. le premier juin / août
3. le prochain taxi / arrêt
4. un certain voyage / itinéraire
5. un grand restaurant / hôtel
6. le petit bateau / avion
7. un mauvais lecteur CD / appareil photo
8. un gros monsieur / homme

FORMES ET FONCTIONS

1. *Les prépositions avec des noms de lieux*

Presentation: Review the forms and uses of the prepositions *à* and *de* introduced in Ch. 2, L. 2 as you begin this presentation. Explain that a few city names contain the definite article, for example, *La Nouvelle-Orléans, Le Havre, La Haye, Le Mans,* and *Les Eyzies.* These will form the contractions *au* and *du* if they are masculine, and the contractions *aux* and *des* if they are plural. Point out the contrast *à Québec/au Québec* (the city vs. the province).

- You have learned to use the prepositions **à** (meaning *to, at,* or *in*) and **de** (meaning *from*) with the names of cities.

Elle arrive **à** Paris.	*She's arriving in Paris.*
Nous allons **à** Lille.	*We're going to Lille.*
Ils viennent **de** Québec.	*They're coming from Quebec City.*

- To express *to*, *at*, *in*, or *from* with the name of countries and continents, use the following prepositions in French:

	FEMININE COUNTRY OR CONTINENT	MASCULINE COUNTRY BEGINNING WITH A VOWEL	MASCULINE COUNTRY BEGINNING WITH A CONSONANT	PLURAL COUNTRY
to, at, in	**en** Suisse	**en** Haïti	**au** Maroc	**aux** Pays-Bas
from	**de** Belgique **d'**Afrique	**d'**Iran	**du** Canada	**des** États-Unis

- The names of all the continents are feminine. As a general rule, country names that end in **-e** are feminine, but you should note the following exceptions: **le Mexique**, **le Mozambique**. In general, names of countries that end in any letter other than **-e** are masculine: **le Canada**, **le Brésil**, **les États-Unis**, **les Pays-Bas**.

Ils habitent **en** Amérique latine.	*They live in Latin America.*
Nous sommes allés **en** Australie.	*We went to Australia.*
Sakiko a fait ses études **au** Canada.	*Sakiko studied in Canada.*
Mon collègue va **aux** Pays-Bas.	*My colleague is going to the Netherlands.*
Je viens **du** Sénégal.	*I'm from Senegal.*

Note: There are numerous exceptions to these general rules, for example: *le Zimbabwe* and *le Belize*. See the *Chez nous* Companion Website for a complete list.

À vous la parole

9-19 Vos connaissances en géographie. Dites dans quel continent sont situés ces pays.

MODÈLE le Brésil
C'est en Amérique.

1. le Mexique
2. la Corée
3. le Nigéria
4. la Suisse
5. le Canada
6. l'Afrique du Sud
7. la Chine
8. les États-Unis

9-20 Escales. Quelquefois il n'y a pas de vol direct entre deux villes. Dites dans quel pays les personnes suivantes doivent s'arrêter pour arriver à leur destination.

MODÈLE Mlle Schmidt : Berlin–Madrid–Lisbonne
Elle doit s'arrêter en Espagne.

1. M. Ducret : Paris–Lisbonne–Abidjan
2. M. Thompson : Londres–Montréal–Chicago
3. Mme Smith : Londres–Paris–Barcelone
4. Mme Marconi : Marseille–Genève–Casablanca
5. Mlle Schmidt : Berlin–Londres–Québec
6. Mlle Bordes : Paris–New York–Mexico
7. M. Noyau : Marseille–Rome–Moscou

Initial practice: Begin with simple substitution drills: *Je vais en France ; Canada ; Belgique ; Mexique ; Brésil ; Inde ; Suisse ; Pays-Bas ; Japon ; Côte d'Ivoire ; Italie ; Chine ; Portugal*, etc. *Je suis des États-Unis ; Pays-Bas ; France ; Portugal ; Sénégal ; Angleterre ; Colombie ; Maroc ; Espagne ; Australie ; Brésil ; Algérie ; Canada*, etc. Follow with an exercise where students match capitals and countries: *Dakar ? — Dakar est au Sénégal ; Tokyo ? (Japon) ; Paris ? (France) ; Lisbonne ? (Portugal) ; Bruxelles ? (Belgique) ; Ottawa ? (Canada) ; Rabat ? (Maroc) ; Hanoï ? (Vietnam) ; Buenos Aires ? (Argentine) ; Amsterdam ? (Pays-Bas) ; Canberra ? (Australie) ; Madrid ? (Espagne) ; Alger ? (Algérie) ; Pékin ? (Chine) ; Yaoundé ? (Cameroun) ; Delhi ? (Inde) ; Bogota ? (Colombie) ; Berne ? (Suisse) ; Brasilia ? (Brésil).*

Key: 9-19 1) en Amérique [Centrale] 2) en Asie 3) en Afrique 4) en Europe 5) en Amérique [du Nord] 6) en Afrique 7) en Asie 8) en Amérique [du Nord]

Implementation: 9-21 Students may need to use names of U.S. states. Here are the basic rules: use *en* for states whose name ends in *-e* (and are therefore feminine) and before masculine states beginning with a vowel: *en Floride, en Indiana.* For other masculine states, use *dans le: dans le Vermont.* Exceptions: *au Texas, dans le Maine.* Refer students to the *Chez nous* Companion Website for complete list of U.S. state names in French.

9-21 Vos origines. Beaucoup d'Américains ont des parents ou des grands-parents qui sont nés dans un pays étranger. Est-ce que certains membres de votre famille ou certains de vos camarades sont nés à l'étranger ?

MODÈLE É1 Tes parents ou tes grands-parents sont nés dans un pays étranger ?
É2 Oui, ma grand-mère. Elle est née en Chine. Et toi, où est-ce que tu es né ?
É1 Moi, je suis né aux États-Unis, en Californie...

2. *Le verbe* venir

Presentation: Present this verb inductively by providing many oral examples and asking questions that model the various forms: *Je viens de Chicago ; et vous, vous venez de Chicago aussi ? Et vos parents, ils viennent de...*, etc. Ask students to summarize forms and display the verb chart.
The main irregularity of this verb is the change from *ven-* /vən/ to *vienn-* /vjɛn/. The change to a nasal vowel in the singular forms is predictable from the loss of the final /n/ (it is analogous to the alternation *italienne/italien*, for example). The unstable *e* of *venons, venez,* and *venu* is usually dropped.

- The verb **venir** means *to come* or *to come from*:

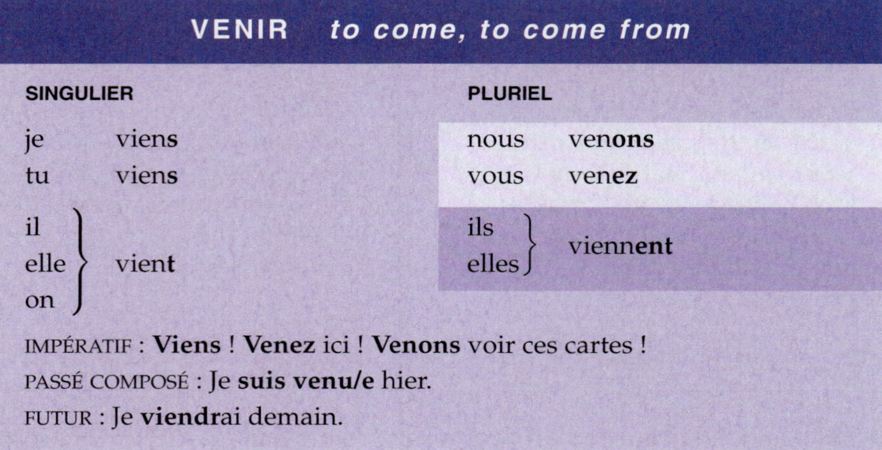

VENIR ***to come, to come from***

SINGULIER		PLURIEL	
je	viens	nous	ven**ons**
tu	viens	vous	ven**ez**
il / elle / on	vient	ils / elles	vienn**ent**

IMPÉRATIF : **Viens** ! **Venez** ici ! **Venons** voir ces cartes !
PASSÉ COMPOSÉ : Je **suis venu/e** hier.
FUTUR : Je **viendr**ai demain.

- **Devenir** (*to become*), **revenir** (*to come back*), **tenir** (*to hold*), **retenir** (*to hold, to book*), **maintenir** (*to affirm, to uphold*), **soutenir** (*to support*), and **obtenir** (*to obtain*) are conjugated like **venir**:

Qu'est-ce que vous **devenez** maintenant ?	*What's new with you these days?*
Quand est-ce que tu **reviens** de Genève ?	*When are you coming back from Geneva?*
Il **tenait** son billet à la main.	*He held his ticket in his hand.*
On va **retenir** des places dans l'avion.	*We're going to book plane tickets.*
Je **maintiens** que c'est vrai.	*I affirm that it's true.*
Le Sénat **soutient** le Président.	*The Senate is supporting the President.*
J'ai **obtenu** mon diplôme.	*I got my degree.*

- To express an event that has just occurred, use **venir de** plus an infinitive.

Le train **vient de partir**.	*The train has just left.*
Nous **venons d'acheter** nos billets.	*We've just purchased our tickets.*

À vous la parole

Initial practice: Begin with a discrimination drill: one person or more than one? *Il vient demain. Elles viennent d'Autriche. Viens ici ! Ils retiennent des places. Elle vient de partir. Elles tiennent leurs billets. Ils viennent avec moi. Il obtient un visa. Elles viennent de Paris. Ils deviennent fatigués. Elle soutient sa sœur,* etc. Follow up with a simple substitution drill: *Je viens ce soir ; nous, lui,* etc.

Key: 9-22 1) d'Italie 2) d'Espagne, des pays d'Amérique du Sud, du Mexique 3) des États-Unis, d'Angleterre, d'Australie 4) de Corée 5) d'Allemagne, de Suisse, d'Autriche 6) de Chine 7) de France, de Belgique, de Suisse, du Québec, des pays de l'Afrique francophone.

9-22 L'apprentissage des langues. Dites d'où ces personnes reviennent.

MODÈLE Elles ont appris le portugais.
→ Elles reviennent du Portugal ou du Brésil.

1. Elle a appris l'italien.
2. Il parle bien espagnol.
3. Nous avons appris l'anglais.
4. Je parle coréen.
5. Ils ont appris l'allemand.
6. Elles parlent chinois.
7. Il a appris le français.

9-23 Changement de caractère. Comment est-ce que ces gens changent ? Choisissez l'adjectif qui convient dans la liste :

adorable	désagréable	discipliné	égoïste
paresseux	populaire	sociable	

MODÈLE J'ai de plus en plus d'amis.
→ Je deviens populaire.

1. Tu ne travailles pas beaucoup ces jours-ci.
2. Roger écoute de plus en plus ses parents.
3. Nous sommes furieux.
4. Mes chats sont plus gentils aujourd'hui.
5. Je ne donne rien aux autres. Cela suffit !
6. Vous parlez à plus de gens maintenant.

9-24 Avant de venir en classe. Qu'est-ce que vous venez de faire, juste avant d'arriver en classe ? Expliquez-le à un/e partenaire.

MODÈLE É1 Moi, je viens de déjeuner au resto U. Et toi ?
É2 Moi, je viens de travailler au labo de langues. Je viens de terminer mes devoirs.

Stratégie

Use your knowledge of the historical context to better understand a narrative that takes place in another era. What characteristics of the period and what events might color or shape the story? What historical realities might distinguish the various places described?

Lisons

Implementation: Avant de lire Put students in small groups to discuss these questions, along with the reading strategy.

9-25 Le Tour du monde en quatre-vingts jours

A. Avant de lire. Connaissez-vous ce roman populaire, écrit au XIXe siècle par l'écrivain français Jules Verne ? Le personnage principal, Phileas Fogg, est un Anglais flegmatique et excentrique qui mène une vie réglée comme une montre. Le mercredi 2 octobre 1872, dans son Reform-Club, il soutient qu'avec les moyens de transport modernes, on peut maintenant parcourir la Terre en quatre-vingts jours seulement. Il lance un pari (*makes a wager*) : s'il n'est pas de retour le samedi 21 décembre à huit heures quarante-cinq du soir, il perd tout. Avant de lire le passage que nous reproduisons ici, réfléchissez aux questions suivantes :

1. Cette histoire se passe en 1872. Quels moyens de transport est-ce que Phileas Fogg va probablement utiliser pendant son voyage ? Faites-en une liste.

Phileas Fogg, dessiné par Alphonse de Neuville pour l'édition de 1873 du *Tour du monde en 80 jours*.

Note: **Note:** The goal in introducing the *passé simple* is for students to recognize the meaning of the verbs and understand that the *passé simple* expresses events in the past; there is no need to present the verb paradigm or to drill forms.

2. À votre avis, comment est-ce que Phileas Fogg pourra prouver à ses amis qu'il aura fait le tour du monde ?
3. Est-ce que Phileas Fogg est une personne à prendre des risques ? Comment va-t-il probablement organiser son voyage autour du monde ?
4. Dans l'extrait que vous allez lire, vous verrez quelques verbes au **passé simple**, un temps littéraire. Le **passé simple** exprime une action au passé, comme le **passé composé**. Pour chaque verbe indiqué au **passé simple**, trouvez son équivalent au **passé composé** :

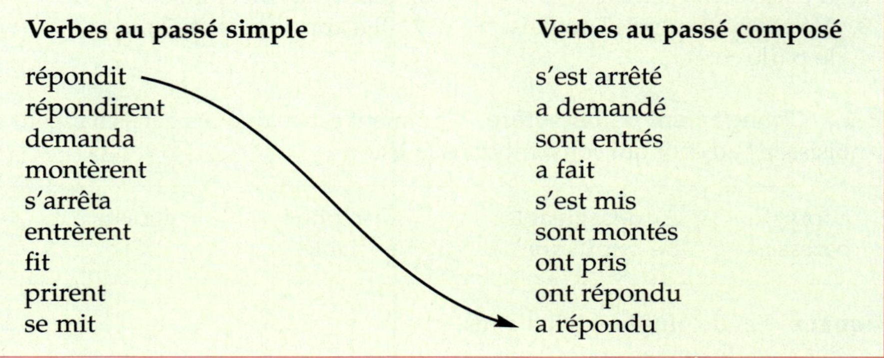

Verbes au passé simple	Verbes au passé composé
répondit	s'est arrêté
répondirent	a demandé
demanda	sont entrés
montèrent	a fait
s'arrêta	s'est mis
entrèrent	sont montés
fit	ont pris
prirent	ont répondu
se mit	a répondu

Key: En lisant 1) 1920 heures, 115 200 minutes 2) le mercredi 2 octobre à 8 h 45 du soir 3) un cab et puis le train 4) le samedi 21 décembre à 8 h 45, dans le salon du Reform-Club 5) son domestique, Jean Passepartout 6) à Paris 7) en montrant les visas apposés sur son passeport 8) à 8 h 45 du soir

B. En lisant. Trouvez les réponses aux questions suivantes.

1. Phileas Fogg parie qu'il fera le tour du monde en quatre-vingts jours, c'est-à-dire, en combien d'heures ? combien de minutes ?
2. Quand est-ce qu'il partira ?
3. Quels moyens de transport est-ce qu'il prendra au départ ?
4. Quand est-ce qu'il sera de retour et où ?
5. Qui l'accompagnera ?
6. Où est-ce qu'ils s'arrêteront d'abord ?
7. Comment est-ce que Phileas Fogg propose de prouver qu'il a bien fait le tour de la Terre ?
8. À quelle heure est-ce que les voyageurs quittent la gare de Charing-Cross ?

LE TOUR DU MONDE EN QUATRE-VINGTS JOURS

—Un bon Anglais ne plaisante[1] jamais, quand il s'agit d'une chose aussi sérieuse qu'un pari[2], répondit Phileas Fogg. Je parie vingt-mille livres contre qui voudra que je ferai le tour de la terre en quatre-vingts jours ou moins, soit[3] dix-neuf-cent-vingt heures ou cent-quinze-mille-deux-cents minutes. Acceptez-vous ?

—Nous acceptons, répondirent MM. Stuart, Fallentin, Sullivan, Flanagan et Ralph, après s'être entendus.

—Bien, dit Mr. Fogg. Le train de Douvres part à huit heures quarante-cinq. Je le prendrai.

—Ce soir même ? demanda Stuart.

—Ce soir même, répondit Phileas Fogg. Donc, ajouta-t-il en consultant un calendrier de poche, puisque c'est aujourd'hui mercredi 2 octobre, je devrai être de retour à Londres, dans ce salon même du Reform-Club, le samedi 21 décembre, à huit heures quarante-cinq du soir… [Phileas Fogg retourne à la maison pour se préparer et chercher son domestique Jean Passepartout.]

Une station de voitures se trouvait à l'extrémité de Saville-row. Phileas Fogg et son domestique montèrent dans un cab, qui se dirigea rapidement vers la gare de Charing-Cross… À huit heures vingt, le cab s'arrêta devant… la gare. Passepartout sauta à terre[4]…

Mr. Fogg et lui entrèrent aussitôt dans la grande salle de la gare. Là, Phileas Fogg donna à Passepartout l'ordre de prendre deux billets de première classe pour Paris. Puis, se retournant, il aperçut[5] ses cinq collègues du Reform-Club.

« Messieurs, je pars, dit-il, et les divers visas apposés sur un passeport que j'emporte à cet effet vous permettront, au retour, de contrôler mon itinéraire…

—Vous n'oubliez pas que vous devez être revenu ? … fit observer Andrew Stuart.

—Dans quatre-vingts jours, répondit Mr. Fogg, le samedi 21 décembre 1872, à huit heures du soir. Au revoir, messieurs. »

À huit heures quarante, Phileas Fogg et son domestique prirent place dans le même compartiment. À huit heures quarante-cinq… le train se mit en marche.

Source : Jules Verne, *Le tour du monde en quatre-vingts jours*

[1]raconte des histoires drôles [2]*a bet, a wager* [3]*in other words* [4]est descendu [5]a vu

C. En regardant de plus près. Examinez le texte plus en détail.

1. Phileas Fogg est accompagné de son domestique, Jean « Passepartout ». Pourquoi est-ce que c'est un nom amusant ?
2. Le texte nous indique quelle sorte de personne est Phileas Fogg ; dans chaque cas, trouvez un exemple qui illustre la description.

MODÈLE Phileas Fogg est un homme riche.
Il prend des billets de train de première classe.

a. Il habite un beau quartier de Londres.
b. Il est très ponctuel.
c. Il aime la précision.
d. Il prend rapidement des décisions.

Key: En regardant de plus près
1) « Passepartout » veut dire, « aller partout » et le domestique va accompagner Fogg partout où il va 2) a. Il habite Saville Row ; b. Il arrive dans son compartiment à 8 h 40 et le train part à 8 h 45 ; c. Il précise le nombre de jours, le nombre d'heures et le nombre de minutes de son voyage ; d. Il décide de partir le jour même.

D. Après avoir lu. Discutez des questions suivantes avec vos camarades de classe.

1. Voici l'itinéraire de Phileas Fogg publié dans le journal britannique *The Morning Chronicle*. Est-ce que vous pensez qu'il est vraiment possible pour Fogg d'accomplir son voyage en l'espace de quatre-vingts jours ? Pourquoi ?

LE TOUR DU MONDE EN QUATRE-VINGTS JOURS

De Londres à Suez par le Mont-Cenis et Brindisi, railways et paquebots	7 jours
De Suez à Bombay, paquebot	13 jours
De Bombay à Calcutta, railway	3 jours
De Calcutta à Hong-Kong (Chine), paquebot	13 jours
De Hong-Kong à Yokohama (Japon), paquebot	6 jours
De Yokohama à San Francisco, paquebot	22 jours
De San Francisco à New York, railroad	7 jours
De New York à Londres, paquebot et railway	9 jours
Total	80 jours

Expansion: Après avoir lu In 1988 Michael Palin attempted to duplicate Fogg's journey in a BBC documentary miniseries called *Michael Palin: Around the World in 80 Days*, returning to London with mere hours to spare. The best-known film version is the 1956 film starring David Niven and Cantinflas; the movie earned five Oscars. A 1989 TV miniseries starred Pierce Brosnan as Fogg, Eric Idle as Passepartout, and Peter Ustinov as Detective Fix. You might show a clip from one of these versions to enrich the presentation.

2. Est-ce que vous avez lu en traduction anglaise un roman de Jules Verne ou vu un film basé sur un de ses romans ? Parmi ses romans on trouve : *Vingt mille lieues sous les mers, L'île mystérieuse, Voyage au centre de la Terre*, et *De la Terre à la Lune*. Si vous en connaissez un, discutez-en avec vos camarades de classe.
3. Si vous aimez la science-fiction, cherchez un de ces romans à la bibliothèque ou louez un DVD—peut-être même une adaptation du *Tour du monde en quatre-vingts jours* !

Note: These titles are given in their original spelling and do not follow the orthographic reform of 1990. Point out to students that they will see compound numbers such as *vingt-mille* with and without the hyphen.

Leçon 3 Faisons du tourisme !

POINTS DE DÉPART

Le logement et les visites

La place Plumereau à Tours.

Presentation: You may wish to present this material over two days. If so, then treat the dialogue, directions, and the **Vie et culture** note on lodgings on day 1, completing Ex. 9-26 and 9-27; treat historical and cultural sites on day 2, and complete Ex. 9-28.
To present, let students listen to the exchange. Ask simple questions to test comprehension. *Qui cherche un logement ? Pour combien de personnes ? Combien de temps est-ce que les Francard vont passer en Touraine ? Quel type de logement est-ce qu'on leur propose ? Où se trouve l'hôtel ?* Using the detail map of *Tours* (MFL, Ch. 9), have students trace the route the Francard family will take to their hotel; have them find the *place Plumereau,* shown in the photo. Illustrate the meaning of each of the expressions in the shaded box, using the detail map.

Les Francard, une famille de touristes belges, viennent d'arriver à Tours. Ils rentrent dans l'Office de Tourisme pour chercher des renseignements et trouver un logement.

LA RÉCEPTIONNISTE : Bonjour, monsieur. Bonjour, madame.
M. FRANCARD : Bonjour, madame. Nous cherchons un logement pas trop cher pour trois nuits.
LA RÉCEPTIONNISTE : Oui, vous êtes combien ?
M. FRANCARD : Quatre personnes, donc nous aurons besoin de deux chambres.
LA RÉCEPTIONNISTE : Je peux vous proposer un petit hôtel deux étoiles en centre-ville. C'est 75 euros par chambre.
M. FRANCARD : Ça nous convient très bien.
LA RÉCEPTIONNISTE : Bon, alors, je vais faire une réservation sur Internet pour les deux chambres pour trois nuits.

...

LA RÉCEPTIONNISTE : Bon, vous serez à l'Hôtel Château Fleuri ; ce n'est pas très loin d'ici.
M. FRANCARD : L'hôtel se trouve où exactement ?

LA RÉCEPTIONNISTE :	Tenez, voici un plan du centre-ville. En sortant d'ici, vous allez prendre le boulevard. Ensuite vous tournez à droite dans la rue de Buffon. Continuez tout droit ; vous allez traverser la rue Émile Zola et ensuite prendre la rue de la Scellerie à gauche. L'hôtel se trouve au 7, rue de la Scellerie.
M. FRANCARD :	Alors, à droite dans la rue de Buffon et à gauche dans la rue de la Scellerie. Merci, madame, et au revoir.
LA RÉCEPTIONNISTE :	Je vous en prie, monsieur, au revoir.

Tours, le centre-ville

Implementation: As you discuss the map of Tours, point out streets and squares named for well-known writers (Voltaire, Émile Zola, Néricault Destouches); artists/composers (François Sicard, Bernard Palissy, Béranger); statesmen (Jules Simon, Colbert, Jean Jaurès); scientists (le Baron Heurteloup le Comte de Buffon).

Pour indiquer le chemin

prendre la rue, l'avenue, le boulevard, la première/la deuxième à droite...

traverser la place...

tourner à droite/à gauche dans le boulevard...

continuer tout droit jusqu'à la rue...

Vie et culture

Le logement

Si vous cherchez un logement pas cher en France, vous avez différents choix selon vos désirs et votre budget. Quels sont les avantages et les inconvénients de chaque option ? Quel type de logement est-ce que vous préférez et pourquoi ? Est-ce que vous avez les mêmes possibilités de logement dans votre pays ?

Pendant l'été en France, les campings sont pleins de gens qui voyagent avec des caravanes, des camping-cars ou simplement une tente.

Si on est jeune, on peut rester dans une auberge de jeunesse.

Implementation: Be sure to treat the **Vie et culture** before completing Ex. 9-26.

To expand the cultural content of the lesson, point out to students that the *Office de Tourisme* is an important resource for the French as well as for foreign travelers in France. You may want to display the home page of the Web site for the *Fédération Nationale des Offices de Tourisme.* As you show it, ask: *Quels services sont proposés aux voyageurs ? Quels services vous semblent les plus importants pour un Français ? pour un Américain qui voyage en France ?* and explain: *Un Office de Tourisme existe dans beaucoup de lieux touristiques en France, donc c'est l'endroit où il faut aller pour commencer à planifier un séjour.*

Une autre possibilité est de rester chez l'habitant, dans un gîte rural à la campagne. C'est surtout une bonne option si on veut établir un contact avec les gens du pays.

Implementation: You may wish to present historical and cultural sites on day 2 of the lesson. If so, this presentation can be enriched with slides, photos, or postcards of various locations in France. Use the drawing (MFL, Ch. 9) to introduce the basic vocabulary: model pronunciation and describe each location. Test comprehension by having students point to the place you name. Have them repeat key terms by identifying: *C'est une cave ou une abbaye ?*, etc. Follow up with Ex. 9-28.

Des sites historiques et culturels

un village perché
une abbaye
un château fort
un château
une cathédrale
un village médiéval
un spectacle son et lumière
une grotte préhistorique
une cave
un théâtre romain

À vous la parole

9-26 Où est-ce qu'ils vont loger ? D'après la description des touristes suivants, dites où ils vont probablement loger.

MODÈLE Les Merten voudraient établir un contact avec les gens de la région.
Ils vont loger dans un gîte rural.

1. Les Martini voudraient une chambre avec minibar, télévision et téléphone.
2. Christelle va passer trois jours à Bordeaux, mais c'est une étudiante et elle a un budget modeste.
3. Les Garcia voyagent avec leur caravane.
4. Max et ses copains veulent passer plusieurs semaines en Suisse sans dépenser (*spending*) trop d'argent.
5. Sébastien aime la nature ; il voyage avec son vélo et sa tente.
6. Les Smith aiment la campagne, et ils voudraient pratiquer leur français.
7. Les Bénini voyagent en train et voudraient rester en ville.

Expansion: Have students discuss their answers to the following questions in pairs and then share with the class: *Est-ce que vous préférez loger dans un hôtel chic ou un logement qui coûte moins cher ? Est-ce que vous préférez un hôtel qui se trouve au centre-ville ou dans un quartier plus calme ? Est-ce que vous aimez les villes où il y a beaucoup de touristes ? Pourquoi ?* You may also use these questions as a lead-in for an inductive presentation of the relatives *qui* and *où* in the **Formes et fonctions** of this lesson.

Implementation: 9-27 Display the detail map of Tours (MFL, Ch. 9) and have students take turns giving directions to their partner. Treat the **Fiche pratique** as you model the activity, and show how the dialogue at the beginning of the lesson illustrates this strategy.

Fiche pratique

When someone gives you directions, it is helpful to confirm that you have understood by repeating or summarizing briefly what you have been told.

Additional activity: To practice giving directions, put students in pairs and give each pair a slip of paper with a starting point and a destination. Using the detail map of Tours, they develop a set of directions, providing only the starting point and not the destination. Have each group exchange papers with another pair, who then try to follow the directions. See how many groups are successful. Suggested departure points/destinations: *de la gare à la cathédrale ; de la gare à l'Hôtel de Ville ; de l'Hôtel de Ville à la Faculté des lettres ; de la cathédrale à la poste ; de la place Plumereau à l'Hôtel de Ville ; du musée des Beaux-Arts à la place Plumereau.* As an alternative, use the map of Richelieu found in Ch. 2, L. 3 to pratice giving directions.

Additional practice: The following activity provides a review of the future tense. **Rêvons aux vacances.** Avec un/e partenaire, imaginez un voyage dans la ville ou l'endroit indiqué. Qu'est-ce que vous ferez ?

MODÈLE à Strasbourg
É1 Nous nous promènerons dans la vieille ville. Nous visiterons la cathédrale.
É2 Nous mangerons également une bonne choucroute.

1. en Touraine
2. à la Martinique
3. à La Nouvelle-Orléans
4. au Maroc
5. à Tahiti
6. au Québec
7. en Suisse
8. à Paris

9-27 Les bonnes indications. Imaginez que vous êtes devant la gare de Tours. Suivez les indications données et dites où vous arrivez. Choisissez votre destination dans la liste suivante.

MODÈLE É1 Vous tournez à gauche dans le boulevard Heurteloup, ensuite à droite dans la rue Nationale et à droite dans la rue de la Scellerie. Vous arrivez au coin (*corner*) de cette rue et de la rue Voltaire.
É2 À gauche dans le boulevard Heurteloup ? et ensuite à droite dans la rue Nationale ?
É1 Oui, c'est ça. Et après, à droite dans la rue de la Scellerie.
É2 C'est le Grand Théâtre ?
É1 Voilà.

Key: 9-27 1) le musée des Beaux-Arts 2) la poste 3) la Basilique Saint-Martin 4) la place Plumereau 5) la préfecture 6) les Halles

la cathédrale	la Basilique Saint-Martin
le Grand Théâtre	les Halles
le musée des Beaux-Arts	la place Plumereau
la préfecture de police	la poste

1. Vous traversez le boulevard Heurteloup. Vous prenez la rue Bernard Palissy et vous continuez tout droit. À la place François Sicard, vous tournez à droite.
2. Vous tournez à gauche dans le boulevard Heurteloup et vous traversez la place Jean-Jaurès. C'est sur votre droite à côté du Palais de Justice.
3. Vous tournez à gauche dans le boulevard Heurteloup, vous traversez la rue Nationale et vous continuez tout droit. Vous prenez la deuxième rue à droite. Vous arrivez dans la rue Néricault Destouches. C'est là, en face de vous.
4. Le plus facile, c'est de suivre la rue Nationale jusqu'à la Loire et de prendre la rue des Tanneurs juste avant le quai de Pont-Neuf. Ensuite, vous tournez à gauche en face de la fac dans une petite rue piétonnière (*pedestrian street*).
5. Traversez le boulevard Heurteloup et prenez la rue de Buffon. Tournez à droite à la place de la Préfecture et continuez tout droit. C'est au coin de la rue Bernard Palissy sur votre droite.
6. Traversez le boulevard Heurteloup, prenez la rue de Buffon, tournez à gauche dans la rue de la Scellerie et continuez tout droit. Traversez la rue Nationale. Suivez la rue des Halles. C'est au bout (*at the end*) sur votre gauche.

Implementation: 9-28 To follow up, have the class compare answers to see which pair came up with the most exciting things to do.

9-28 À l'Office de Tourisme. Avec un/e partenaire, quelles visites est-ce que vous recommandez à ces touristes ?

MODÈLE Jérôme et Camille sont très sportifs et ils aiment les beaux paysages.
É1 Ils peuvent faire du cyclotourisme.
É2 Oui. Comme ça, ils se promèneront dans la nature et ils visiteront tous les petits villages.

1. Les Martin sont fascinés par la préhistoire.
2. Sophie aime tout ce qui est spectacle.
3. Mme Francard s'intéresse aux arts décoratifs.
4. M. Francard aime surtout l'architecture de la Renaissance.
5. Pierre a étudié l'histoire des religions.
6. M. Dupin voudrait goûter les meilleurs vins de la région.
7. Audrey se passionne pour la peinture et la sculpture.
8. Vincent voudrait découvrir la France profonde.

FORMES ET FONCTIONS

1. *Les relatifs* où *et* qui

- A relative allows you to introduce a clause, called a subordinate clause, that provides additional information about a person, place, or thing. The relative connects the subordinate clause to the main clause of the sentence. In the examples below, the subordinate clause, introduced by the relative pronoun **qui**, is set off by brackets.

David est un guide [**qui** a beaucoup de talent].	*David is a tour guide [who is very talented].*
Rome est une ville [**qui** est connue pour son architecture].	*Rome is a city [that is known for its architecture].*

In these examples the relative pronoun **qui**, which refers to a guide or a city, respectively, is the subject of the subordinate clause. **Qui**, the equivalent of the English *who* or *which/that*, always functions as the subject of the clause it introduces and is always followed by a verb.

- **Où** is used to introduce a place or a time; it is equivalent to the English *where* or *when*.

C'est une ville [**où** il y a beaucoup de monuments historiques].	*It's a city [where there are many historical monuments].*
L'automne en France, c'est la saison [**où** il commence à faire froid].	*Autumn in France is the season [when it starts to get cold].*

Presentation: Introduce the relatives through examples. Meaning is fairly straightforward; however, students will need to pay particular attention to the use of *où* with expressions of time, since English uses the relative "when." Ex. 9-29 treats this feature. Analyzing complex sentences as two independent clauses helps students understand the fact that relatives have a double function: 1) linking two clauses; 2) replacing a co-referential noun.

Additional activities: Other simple exercises to practice relatives include: a) recycling professions: *Un acteur ? — C'est un homme qui joue dans des pièces ou des films. Une serveuse ? — C'est une femme qui travaille dans un restaurant/sert des boissons. Un médecin ? Un professeur ? Un avocat ? Une comptable ? Un guide touristique ? Un/e réceptionniste à l'Office de Tourisme ? Un/e réceptionniste à l'hôtel ? Un agent de voyage ?* etc.; b) a guessing game — students describe a classmate and let others guess who they're describing: *C'est un étudiant qui joue de la guitare ; C'est une étudiante qui porte une jupe bleue ;* etc.

À vous la parole

9-29 En quelles saisons ? En quelles saisons est-ce qu'on peut faire les activités suivantes ?

MODÈLE On va à la campagne chercher des pommes.
L'automne est la saison où on va à la campagne chercher des pommes.

1. On peut faire un pique-nique à la montagne.
2. On peut faire du ski.
3. On va souvent au bord de la mer.
4. On fait des randonnées dans la forêt.
5. On commence à faire du jardinage.
6. On admire les fleurs à la campagne.
7. On va voir les matchs de football américain.
8. On a envie de voyager dans les pays chauds.

Implementation: 9-29 Before beginning, review the four seasons quickly. As a variation, ask students to describe typical activities during each season, or typical activities on a particular holiday: *Noël ? — C'est un jour où on offre des cadeaux*, etc. Note that more formal usage would prefer *C'est un jour où l'on offre des cadeaux*, or for the model in the textbook, *L'automne est la saison où l'on va à la campagne chercher des pommes*, but this is not necessary in conversational style.

Variation: 9-30 Have students describe the town/city where your university is located, or another city of their choice.

9-30 Les grandes villes. Avec un/e partenaire, est-ce que vous pouvez décrire ces grandes villes ?

MODÈLE New York

É1 New York est une ville où il y a beaucoup de grands magasins.

É2 New York est aussi une ville qui a beaucoup de théâtres et de cinémas.

1. San Francisco
2. Paris
3. La Nouvelle-Orléans
4. Los Angeles
5. Washington D.C.
6. Dakar
7. Québec
8. Genève

Follow-up: 9-31 At the end, bring the class together as a group to compare responses.

9-31 Quelles sont vos préférences ? Pour le logement, les vacances, les gens ? Discutez de cela avec un/e partenaire.

MODÈLE J'aime les hôtels...

É1 J'aime les hôtels qui sont très modernes.

É2 Moi, j'aime surtout les hôtels où il y a une piscine.

1. J'aime les hôtels...
2. Je préfère les villes...
3. Je n'aime pas les musées...
4. J'aime les vacances...
5. J'aime surtout visiter les endroits...
6. J'aime les gens...
7. Je n'aime pas beaucoup les gens...

2. *Le pronom relatif* que

- As you have just learned, a relatives enables you to introduce a clause, called a subordinate clause, that provides additional information about a person, place, or thing. The relative pronoun **qui** functions as the subject of the clause it introduces and is followed by the verb of the subordinate clause.

Le guide [**qui** nous a fait visiter le château] était bien informé.	*The guide [who gave us a tour of the château] was well-informed.*

Note: With stylistic inversion, the subject may not follow directly: *Montréal est une ville qu'apprécient beaucoup les touristes.*

- **Que** is used when the relative is the direct object of the subordinate clause. Use **qu'** before words beginning with a vowel. The subject of the subordinate clause usually follows **que/qu'**.

C'est une ville. J'aime beaucoup cette ville.	
C'est une ville [**que** j'aime beaucoup].	*It's a city [that I like a lot].*

Like **qui**, the relative pronoun **que/qu'** can refer either to a person or a thing.

Le guide **que** j'ai eu était très enthousiaste.	*The guide whom/that I had was very enthusiastic.*
Nous avons visité le musée **que** Mme Lerond a recommandé.	*We visited the museum (that) Mrs. Lerond recommended.*

> Be careful! In English the words *whom* or *that* may be left out, but in French, **que** must always be used.

- When you use the **passé composé**, the past participle agrees in number and gender with the preceding direct-object pronoun. In both examples below, **que/qu'** refers to a feminine plural noun, and the feminine plural form of the past participle is used.

Voilà les cartes postales **que** j'ai écrit**es**.	*Here are the postcards (that) I wrote.*
Vous connaissez les musiciennes **qu'**ils ont invit**ées** à jouer ?	*Do you know the musicians (that) they invited to play?*

Note: Remind students that this is the case for any direct object that precedes the verb in the *passé composé*. In practice, however, many French speakers and writers do not make the agreement, so we consider this a minor point. This point was also addressed in Ch. 6, L. 1. The SAM/MFL includes writing activities that focus on placement with the various tenses and rules of agreement.

À vous la parole 

9-32 Un bibliophile à Paris. Complétez ces phrases avec le relatif qui convient : **qui**, **que** ou **où**.

Key: 9-32 1) où 2) qui 3) que 4) que 5) qui 6) qui 7) qui 8) qu'

MODÈLE La Maison de la Presse _______ je connais le mieux se trouve boulevard Auguste Blanqui à Paris et ouvre à 6 h 30 du matin.
La Maison de la Presse que je connais le mieux se trouve boulevard Auguste Blanqui à Paris et ouvre à 6 h 30 du matin.

1. Quand je visite Paris, je vais toujours à la FNAC _______ on peut trouver beaucoup de livres et de CD pas chers.
2. Pour acheter des journaux, les Français _______ habitent une grande ville peuvent aller à un kiosque.
3. Gibert Jeune est une librairie _______ les étudiants visitent régulièrement pour trouver des livres pour leurs cours à la fac.
4. Chez Gibert Jeune, on peut également trouver beaucoup de livres d'occasion (*used*) _______ les étudiants aiment acheter parce qu'ils sont moins chers.
5. À Paris, on peut trouver une librairie anglophone _______ s'appelle Shakespeare & Company.
6. Les bouquinistes _______ se trouvent au bord de la Seine près de Notre Dame sont très populaires avec les touristes.
7. La bibliothèque municipale _______ est ouverte de mardi à samedi est un bon endroit pour emprunter des livres et même des DVD.
8. À la bibliothèque universitaire, vous trouverez beaucoup d'ouvrages de référence _______ on peut consulter sur place.

Expansion: 9-33 This includes all the relatives introduced thus far; you might extend practice by asking students to provide additional examples of travel vocabulary to be defined.

9-33 Le mot juste. Le voyageur a besoin d'un vocabulaire précis. Dans les définitions, on emploie souvent des propositions relatives. Est-ce que vous et votre partenaire pouvez définir les choses suivantes ?

MODÈLES un lecteur DVD

É1 C'est un appareil qu'on utilise pour regarder un DVD.

un théâtre

É2 C'est un endroit où on joue des pièces de théâtre.

un guide

É1 C'est une personne ou un livre qui explique l'histoire des monuments.

1. un appareil photo numérique
2. un lecteur CD
3. un ordinateur portable
4. un musée
5. un office de tourisme
6. une agence de voyages
7. une réceptionniste
8. un agent de police

Additional practice: The following activity can serve as a logical model for the **Écrivons** activity, although it is a description in a different time frame.

Souvenirs de voyage. Quels sont vos souvenirs d'un voyage que vous avez fait ? Discutez de cela avec un/e partenaire.

MODÈLE le jour du départ

É1 C'était un jour que j'attendais avec beaucoup d'impatience.

É2 C'était un jour où il a fait très beau.

1. l'endroit visité
2. les transports
3. le logement
4. les activités
5. le dernier jour des vacances
6. le retour

Implementation: 9-34 Before beginning, explain to students the meaning of the verb *connaître* in this specific context: that one has actually visited the place mentioned.

9-34 Vous connaissez ? Est-ce que vous connaissez ces villes ou ces sites ? Parlez-en avec un/e partenaire.

MODÈLE la statue de la Liberté

É1 C'est un monument que je connais.

É2 Moi aussi, c'est un monument que j'ai visité avec mes parents.

1. New York
2. la statue de la Liberté
3. Washington D.C.
4. le Smithsonian
5. Paris
6. la tour Eiffel
7. Londres
8. le *British Museum*

Écrivons

Implementation: Brainstorm as a class possible destinations and a basic outline of areas students might wish to research. You might wish to have students work in pairs to complete this activity.

9-35 Projets pour un voyage

A. Avant d'écrire. Présentez des projets de voyage dans un pays francophone. Tout d'abord, préparez un plan. Quels détails est-ce qu'il faudra planifier ? Organisez vos idées. Ensuite, faites les recherches nécessaires pour détailler votre voyage et prenez des notes.

MODÈLE I. La destination : la ville de Québec
  A. une ville historique : ...
  B. ...

II. Les moyens de transport
  A. l'avion (jusqu'à Montréal)
  B. le car (jusqu'à Québec)

Stratégie

When you need to research and present a topic, prepare a basic outline before you begin, then fill it in as you gather information. This will provide you with a complete, orderly plan to follow when you begin to write.

III. Le logement et les repas
   A. un petit hôtel dans le centre-ville : …
   B. …

IV. Activités
   A. …
   B. …

B. En écrivant. Maintenant, utilisez votre plan pour écrire la description de vos projets de voyage.

MODÈLE Je voudrais visiter Québec, une ville francophone qui n'est pas très loin de chez moi. C'est une ville historique et très pittoresque. La ville de Québec a plus de 400 ans, et la vieille ville est entourée par un grand mur. Pour aller à Québec, je prendrai l'avion jusqu'à Montréal et ensuite le car jusqu'à Québec. Je pourrai obtenir les billets d'avion en ligne ; c'est moins cher. À Québec, on logera dans un petit hôtel dans la vieille ville. L'auberge J.A. Moisan se trouve dans la rue St-Jean. C'est un petit hôtel charmant qui offre le petit-déjeuner. Il y aura beaucoup de choses à faire : par exemple, …

C. En révisant. Réfléchissez aux questions suivantes et puis faites tous les changements nécessaires.

1. Relisez votre paragraphe pour analyser le contenu : est-ce que vous avez utilisé les informations que vous avez trouvées pour détailler vos projets de voyage ?
2. Relisez de nouveau votre paragraphe pour analyser le style et la forme : est-ce que vous avez bien suivi votre plan ? Est-ce que les verbes au futur sont bien formés ?

D. Après avoir écrit. Partagez votre description avec vos camarades de classe. Après la discussion, quels endroits est-ce que vous avez envie de visiter ? Pourquoi ?

Je voudrais visiter le Maroc. Je ferai un circuit des villes impériales. Le premier jour, j'irai à Marrakech et je logerai dans un hôtel quatre étoiles, l'hôtel le Marrakech. Ensuite j'irai à Meknes et à Fes.

Implementation: Begin this lesson with a think-pair-share brainstorm activity. Ask each student to take out a piece of paper and write down the first three things that come to mind when you say "Paris." Then have students compare their list with that of a partner. Finally, make a list on the board with input from the whole class. As you write their responses on the board, group the answers together into categories, but without using titles (e.g., *les monuments, les musées, la cuisine, le shopping, l'histoire*, etc.). After you've finished, ask students to identify and label each group. You could also ask if any students have visited Paris and have them share their experiences and/or bring in any souvenirs they collected.

Venez chez nous ! Paris, ville lumière

La tour Eiffel et le Sacré-Cœur

Notre-Dame de Paris

Implementation: Use the video montage (*Paris, ville lumière*) to provide an overview of this lesson; see how many monuments students recognize. You might replay this montage after having treated the lesson; students should then recognize more landmarks. Treat the opening segment in the book by having students look for main ideas: what will they find in Paris? Why is Paris known as the "City of Light"? Students may also have heard of the "Gay Nineties," an expression used in the United States for this same period.

Paris, comme vous le savez, est la capitale de la France. C'est aussi la ville la plus visitée du monde. C'est une belle ville remplie[1] d'histoire, de monuments intéressants, d'églises, de bons restaurants et de grands magasins et de petites boutiques de spécialités. Il y en a pour tous les goûts.

Paris est connue sous le nom de *Ville Lumière*. D'où cette désignation vient-elle ? C'est parce qu'à la fin du dix-neuvième siècle et au début du vingtième, Paris était le centre artistique et culturel du monde et la capitale de l'élégance, du luxe et des plaisirs. Beaucoup d'écrivains, de musiciens et d'artistes passaient au moins un an dans la *Ville Lumière* pour apprendre leur métier ou trouver de l'inspiration. Voilà pourquoi on appelle la fin du dix-neuvième siècle en France *la Belle Époque*.

[1] *full*

Observons

Note: 9-36 Two additional interviews are treated in SAM/MFL.

9-36 Mes impressions de Paris

A. Avant de regarder. Même si vous n'avez jamais visité Paris, quelle idée est-ce que vous avez de cette ville célèbre ? Dans cette séquence, vous allez entendre deux Niçois qui décrivent leurs impressions de Paris.

B. En regardant. Trouvez la réponse (ou les réponses) à chaque question.

1. Fabienne dit qu'il y a toujours un petit conflit entre...
   a. les Français et les Américains.
   b. les Parisiens et les Niçois.
   c. les hommes et les femmes.
2. Pour elle, ce n'est pas un problème parce qu'elle...
   a. est mariée avec un Parisien.
   b. adore les Américains.
   c. est née à Paris.
3. À Paris, elle aime surtout...
   a. la tour Eiffel.
   b. le climat.
   c. le shopping.
4. Édouard est allé à Paris pour...
   a. voir sa famille.
   b. travailler.
   c. passer des vacances.
5. Il a découvert beaucoup de monuments, par exemple :

____ l'Opéra de Paris ____ l'arc de Triomphe ____ la place de la Concorde
____ le Louvre ____ la tour Eiffel ____ la Bibliothèque François-Mitterrand

Key: 1. b 2. a 3. c 4. b, c 5. l'Opéra, la Concorde, la tour Eiffel, la Bibliothèque

La Bibliothèque nationale de France, site François-Mitterrand.

C. Après avoir regardé. Maintenant discutez de ces questions avec vos camarades de classe.

1. Fabienne remarque qu'il y a un petit conflit entre les gens du Nord (les Parisiens) et les gens du Sud (les Niçois). Comment pourriez-vous expliquer ce conflit ? Est-ce qu'il existe des tensions ou de la concurrence (*competition*) entre les gens de régions différentes chez vous ? Si oui, pourquoi ?
2. Fabienne n'est pas très impressionnée quand elle voit la tour Eiffel pour la première fois. Pourquoi ? Est-ce que vous avez déjà eu cette expérience, de voir un monument ou une œuvre d'art célèbre pour la première fois et puis d'être déçu/e (*disappointed*) ?
3. Est-ce que les impressions de Fabienne et Édouard vous étonnent (*surprise*) ? Pourquoi ? Est-ce qu'elles diffèrent de vos propres impressions de Paris ?

Script: Observons

FABIENNE : Alors je suis niçoise, mais je vais vous parler un petit peu de Paris. Nous, nous sommes dans le Sud de la France, Paris est beaucoup plus dans le Nord de la France. Nous avons entre les Niçois et les Parisiens toujours un petit conflit, qui ne se dit pas toujours, mais je suis mariée avec un Parisien, donc, j'ai dû faire mon deuil de cela. J'ai visité Paris un petit peu contrainte et forcée, et finalement cette ville m'a beaucoup plu, je... je dois le reconnaître. Peut-être pas la tour Eiffel, parce que c'est un monument qui m'a pas vraiment étonnée, peut-être à force de le voir en photo. Maintenant j'ai adoré vraiment toutes les activités, le shopping à Paris, chose que nous n'avons pas à Nice, peut-être. Nous avons à Nice le climat, à Paris ils ont toutes les activités. Et euh... j'aime bien les Parisiens, finalement.

ÉDOUARD : J'aime beaucoup Paris, c'est un lieu où je vais souvent et où j'ai travaillé notamment. Et j'ai pu découvrir beaucoup d'endroits cet été, notamment la Bibliothèque François-Mitterrand, qui est un endroit très... très intéressant, je trouve. Mais il y a d'autres endroits, comme l'Opéra, qui est... bon, que tout le monde connaît et qui est... que je trouve magnifique. Euh, et sinon, euh bien, évidemment tous les grands monuments, comme la Concorde, la tour Eiffel. Et, euh... c'est un lieu où j'aime bien aller, euh... en vacances, ... pour travailler...

Parlons

9-37 La visite d'un monument

Une façon agréable de voir les monuments de Paris est de prendre un bateau-mouche. Ces bateaux font des circuits touristiques avec des commentaires sur tous les monuments qui se trouvent au bord de la Seine. Regardez ce détail d'un plan de Paris et identifiez les monuments que vous reconnaissez.

Expansion: If you have a collection of maps (e.g., from the department stores in Paris), you could bring them to class and have students work in groups to find the monuments on the *bateau-mouche* map and label them. You might also assign this as homework and have students go to the *Chez nous* Companion Website to find links to maps and tourist guides of Paris.

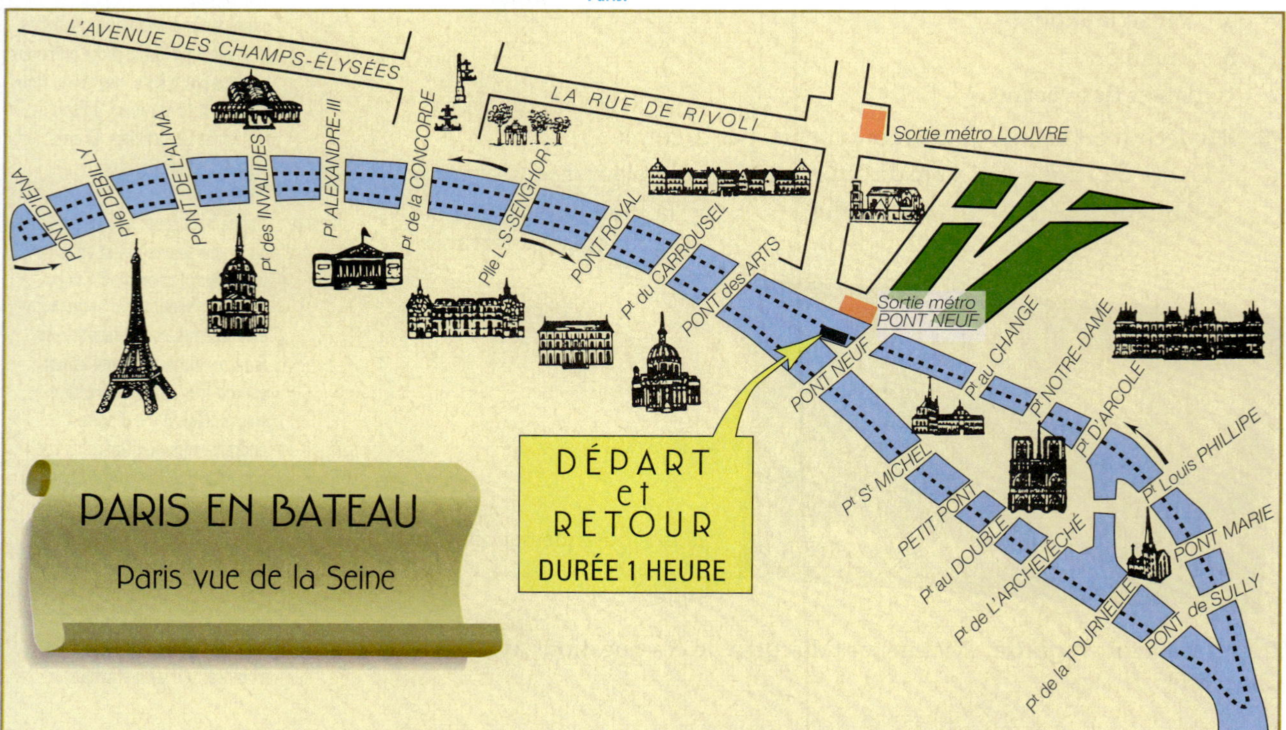

Note: *Plle* is the abbreviation for *passerelle*, a footbridge. The footbridge, *la passerelle Léopold-Sédar-Senghor*, was formerly known as *la passerelle Solferino.*

A. Avant de parler. Maintenant, c'est à vous de jouer le rôle d'un/e guide à bord d'un bateau-mouche à Paris. D'abord, choisissez un monument. Voici quelques possibilités :

1. l'Hôtel de Ville
2. la Conciergerie
3. les jardins des Tuileries
4. le musée d'Orsay
5. l'obélisque de la Concorde
6. le Pont Neuf
7. la tour Eiffel
8. Notre-Dame de Paris
9. les Invalides
10. le Louvre
11. le Grand Palais
12. l'Institut de France

Ensuite, préparez une description de votre monument ; considérez les questions suivantes :

1. Où se trouve ce monument ? Dans quel arrondissement ? Dans quelle rue ? À côté de quels autres sites importants ? Est-ce qu'il y a une station de métro à proximité ?
2. Quand est-ce que ce monument a été construit ? Par qui ? Pourquoi est-ce que ce monument est important aujourd'hui ?

Pour trouver des renseignements, consultez le site Web de ***Chez nous*** pour ce chapitre, des encyclopédies et des guides touristiques.

B. En parlant. Présentez votre monument à vos camarades de classe. N'oubliez pas d'apporter des images (des photos, des affiches, etc.) de votre monument !

C. Après avoir parlé. Quelles sont les présentations les plus intéressantes ? Quels monuments est-ce que vous voudriez visiter maintenant ?

Implementation: Avant de parler This speaking activity gives students the opportunity to practice presentational speaking skills, consistent with Standard 1.3 in the National Standards for Foreign Language Learning. If you wish, you may expand the activity to include monuments not visible from *les bateaux-mouches* such as: *l'arc de Triomphe, les Champs-Élysées, Montmartre et le Sacré-Cœur, la Sorbonne, le Centre Pompidou (Beaubourg), le cimetière du Père-Lachaise, le Moulin Rouge, le Panthéon, la Bibliothèque François-Mitterrand, les Catacombes.* Students may work independently or with a partner for this activity. Allow students a few days to prepare their presentations. Consider giving a model presentation so students know what you expect of them. Following the presentations, discuss and summarize the information conveyed. As a follow-up, you might have students work with a partner to plan an itinerary for the monuments they would most like to visit in one day. In addition to encyclopedias and the Internet, useful resources for this activity include: Applefield, David. *Paris Inside Out: The Insider's Handbook to Life in Paris.* Guilford, CT: Insiders' Guides, 2005; Mroue, Haas. *Frommer's Memorable Walks in Paris.* Hoboken, NJ: Frommer's, 2006; Tillier, Alan. *Paris, DK Eyewitness Travel Guides.* New York: DK Publications, 2007.

Lisons

9-38 Un détective à Paris

A. Avant de lire. Le Commissaire Jules Maigret est un des détectives fictifs les plus connus au monde. Son créateur est Georges Simenon (1903–1989), un écrivain belge. Les 75 romans et 28 nouvelles qui racontent les aventures de Maigret ont été traduits en 50 langues et vendus à plus de 500 000 millions d'exemplaires ; plusieurs ont été adaptés à des films.

Le Commissaire Maigret a son bureau au 36, Quai des Orfèvres à Paris. Il travaille donc au cœur de cette ville, dans le 1er arrondissement. C'est un homme patient, qui observe les lieux et les suspects pour trouver les éléments qui clochent (*that aren't quite right*) et les trous (*holes*) dans leur histoire.

Rupert Davies joue le rôle de Maigret dans la série BBC.

Note: Avant de lire Simenon was one of the twentieth century's most prolific authors, sometimes writing 60–80 pages per day. The Maigret novels were published at a rate of 2.5 books per year. Simenon is often credited with having created the modern detective novel.

Maigret, the son of a farmer, came to Paris to study medicine but joined the police instead, rising in rank from a uniformed bicycle patrolman to superintendent. His method is to study the settings where the victim and suspects operate, and patiently observe until he finds elements that don't quite fit logically, or until a suspect makes a misstep that reveals his or her guilt.

See the *Chez nous* Companion Website for links to sites that have additional information on, and photos of, Simenon and Maigret.

Dans le roman intitulé **La Folle de Maigret** (*Maigret and the Madwoman*), Maigret reçoit dans son bureau Quai des Orfèvres une vieille dame, Léontine Antoine. Elle pense que son appartement a été cambriolé (*broken into*). Mais elle est assassinée pas longtemps après, et c'est à Maigret de faire une enquête sur le meurtre. Il se rend aux jardins des Tuileries, où la vieille dame avait l'habitude de se promener.

Qu'est-ce que vous savez sur les jardins des Tuileries ? Regardez la photo, et faites des recherches sur Internet pour en apprendre plus. Quelles sont les activités typiques dans un jardin public ?

Stratégie

Use your knowledge of the setting of a story to help you understand what takes place there and how it fits into the overall narrative.

Implementation: Show students where the garden is located, using the *Paris en Bateau* map from this lesson, where the garden is indicated by three trees and the *Arc de Triomphe du Carrousel.* Catherine de Medici had the Tuileries Palace built in the sixteenth century, and Louis XIV lived there during the construction of Versailles. The name was derived from the existence of tile kilns on the site. Le Nôtre laid out the gardens in the seventeenth century, and during the same period, the palace was linked to the Louvre. In 1871, the palace was destroyed by arsonists. The gardens cover about 63 acres and are a favored location for Parisians and tourists alike. To help students better imagine the activities in the *jardins,* see the *Chez nous Companion Website* for links to sites with additional photos.

Les jardins des Tuileries.

Key: En lisant 1) Il veut se mettre à la place de la vieille dame 2) des clochards, des couples amoureux, des vieilles gens, des jeunes mamans, des enfants, un homme d'une trentaine d'années 3) les clochards dorment, les couples amoureux s'embrassent, les vieilles gens donnent à manger aux oiseaux, les jeunes mamans surveillent leurs enfants, les enfants jouent dans le bassin, un homme d'une trentaine d'années lit un livre de biologie 4) il fait du soleil et il fait beau, parce qu'il y a des vieilles gens, des enfants et des oiseaux 5) Il trouve que c'est reposant, et que la vie semble simple et sans histoires.

B. En lisant. Lisez le texte et ensuite répondez aux questions suivantes.

1. Maigret va aux jardins des Tuileries avec sa femme ; pourquoi ?
2. Qui sont les personnes qui fréquentent les jardins ? Regardez bien l'extrait, et faites une liste.
3. Quelles sont les activités de toutes ces personnes ? Rajoutez cela à votre liste.
4. À votre avis, quel temps fait-il aux jardins ce jour-là ? Pourquoi ?
5. Quelle est l'impression que le temps, les gens et les activités donnent à Maigret ?

Léontine Antoine « profite du moindre[1] rayon de soleil » pour passer « une partie de ses après-midi sur un banc[2] des Tuileries ». Soucieux[3] de se mettre à la place de cette vieille dame qui a été assassinée, Maigret se rend à son tour[4] aux Tuileries avec son épouse[5]:

—Si on s'asseyait un moment ? proposa-t-il.

Il se passait ainsi une envie[6] qu'il avait depuis la veille au soir. Il ne se souvenait pas s'être jamais assis sur un banc public. Il n'aurait pas été loin de penser[7] qu'ils ne servaient à rien, sinon de lits aux clochards[8] ou de refuge pour les amoureux.

Or, ils mirent[9] un long moment avant de trouver un banc libre. Tous les autres étaient occupés, et pas seulement par de vieilles gens. Il y avait beaucoup de jeunes mamans qui surveillaient[10] leur enfant. Un homme d'une trentaine d'années lisait un livre de biologie.

—On est bien, non ?

Des petits bateaux à voiles blanches croisaient sur l'eau limpide du bassin.

—Ne te mouille[11] pas, Hubert. Si tu te penches[12] ainsi, tu vas tomber à l'eau !

N'était-ce pas reposant ? La vie, vue d'ici, paraissait simple et sans histoires.

La vieille dame y venait chaque jour, quand le temps le permettait. Comme le faisait une autre vieille dame devant eux, elle devait donner des miettes de pain[13] aux oiseaux, qui se rapprochaient toujours davantage.

[1]plus petit [2]*bench* [3]anxieux [4]va aussi [5]femme [6]désir [7]*might have thought* [8]*homeless people* [9]ont regardé [10]observaient [11]*get wet* [12]*lean over* [13]*breadcrumbs*

C. En regardant de plus près. Maintenant examinez quelques caractéristiques du texte.

1. Dans cet extrait, il y a trois citations directes (*direct quotes*). Pour chaque citation, expliquez qui le dit et pourquoi :
   a. —Si on s'asseyait un moment ?
   b. —On est bien, non ?
   c. —Ne te mouille pas, Hubert. Si tu te penches ainsi, tu vas tomber à l'eau !
2. Avant cette visite, Maigret ne s'était jamais assis (*had never sat*) sur un banc public. Pourquoi, à votre avis ?

D. Après avoir lu. Discutez des questions suivantes avec vos camarades de classe.

1. D'après le texte que vous avez lu, décrivez une journée typique pour Léontine Antoine ; pour le Commissaire Maigret.
2. Est-ce que les jardins des Tuileries ressemblent aux jardins publics chez vous, ou est-ce qu'ils sont très différents ? Pourquoi ?

Key: En regardant de plus près
1) a) Maigret, parce qu'il veut observer les activités b) Maigret, ou peut-être sa femme, parce qu'il/elle trouve que c'est agréable dans les jardins c) une maman, parce que son fils joue dans le bassin 2) Peut-être parce qu'il n'a pas grandi en ville, et que c'est un homme qui est toujours occupé et qui ne prend pas le temps de se détendre.

Expansion: In the 1960s, the BBC produced a 51-episode television series, starring Rupert Davies as Maigret. Jean Gabin played the part of Maigret in several French films. Clips can be found on various online video-sharing sites. You might want to show a clip in class to enrich this presentation.

Stratégie

When writing a historical or biographical sketch, it is appropriate in French to use the present tense; this gives a sense of immediacy to your description.

Écrivons

9-39 Des Américains à Paris

C'est Thomas Jefferson qui a dit : « *Every man has two countries, his own and France.* » Jefferson, comme tant d'autres Américains, était fasciné par la France et par la ville de Paris. Nommé Ambassadeur des États-Unis en France, il y va en 1784, succédant à Benjamin Franklin, et il y reste cinq ans. Depuis longtemps, Paris attire non seulement des diplomates, mais aussi des artistes, des ingénieurs, des écrivains et des chanteurs. À Paris, ils trouvent une certaine liberté, personnelle et artistique, qui manque à leur vie américaine. Ils découvrent aussi une autre façon de voir le monde, une autre ouverture culturelle.

Benjamin Franklin est Ambassadeur des États-Unis en France de 1776 jusqu'en 1785.

Joséphine Baker, une vedette des Folies Bergères pendant les années vingt et trente.

A. Avant d'écrire. Préparez une description de la vie parisienne d'un/e Américain/e. D'abord, choisissez une personne dans une des catégories indiquées. Ensuite, cherchez des renseignements sur son séjour (ou ses séjours) à Paris. Pour trouver des renseignements, consultez le site Web de ***Chez nous*** pour ce chapitre, des encyclopédies et des biographies.

Implementation: Avant d'écrire This writing activity gives students the opportunity to practice presentational writing skills, consistent with Standard 1.3 in the National Standards for Foreign Language Learning. We suggest you model a text, using presentational software and a famous American not included in this list (for example, Mary Cassatt).

Refer students to the introduction about Thomas Jefferson for an example of the use in French of the historic present. Note the passage begins in the past, then shifts to the present to begin the narration, which gives a sense of immediacy. Use of the historic present is much more common in French than in English.

Students may work individually or with a partner to write brief biographies. Allow them a few days to prepare, and ask them to include a photo of the person. In addition to encyclopedias and the Internet, another useful resource is: Morton, Brian. *Americans in Paris: An Anecdotal Street Guide.* Ann Arbor, MI: The Olivia and Hill Press, 1984.

Diplomates	Ingénieurs/Aventuriers	Écrivains	Musiciens	Danseurs/Comédiens
John Adams	*Thomas Edison*	*e.e. cummings*	*Louis Armstrong*	*Fred Astaire*
Benjamin Franklin	*Robert Fulton*	*Ernest Hemingway*	*Aaron Copland*	*Joséphine Baker*
Thomas Jefferson	*Charles Lindbergh*	*Katherine Anne Porter*	*Duke Ellington*	*Ada 'Bricktop' Smith*
Franklin Roosevelt	*Samuel Morse*	*Gertrude Stein*	*George Gershwin*	*Isadora Duncan*
Woodrow Wilson	*Orville & Wilbur Wright*	*Mark Twain*	*Cole Porter*	*Buster Keaton*

Pour préparer votre description, répondez aux questions suivantes :

1. Quand et pourquoi est-ce que cet/te Américain/e va à Paris ?
2. Combien de temps est-ce qu'il/elle y reste ? Pourquoi ?
3. Qu'est-ce qu'il/elle fait à Paris ?
4. Quelles sont ses impressions de Paris ?

B. En écrivant. Rédigez deux paragraphes qui expliquent le séjour à Paris de cet/te Américain/e. Dans le premier paragraphe, donnez des détails sur son séjour (questions 1–3). Dans le deuxième paragraphe, parlez de ses impressions de Paris (question 4), et terminez votre texte avec une phrase qui résume l'importance du séjour parisien dans la vie de cette personne.

C. En révisant. Réfléchissez aux questions suivantes et puis faites tous les changements nécessaires.

1. Relisez vos paragraphes pour analyser le contenu : est-ce que vous avez bien répondu aux questions dans la partie A ? Est-ce que vous avez bien résumé l'importance de Paris pour cet individu ?
2. Relisez de nouveau votre paragraphe pour analyser le style et la forme : est-ce que vous avez mis les verbes au présent, en mettant des dates pour indiquer la période historique ? Est-ce que vous avez respecté l'ordre chronologique des évènements ?

D. Après avoir écrit. Lisez votre texte à vos camarades de classe. Qui sont les individus les plus intéressants qui ont visité Paris, à votre avis ? Pourquoi ?

Implementation: Après avoir écrit
Have students exchange descriptions for the purposes of peer editing. Then have them compare the experiences of their historical figures. Which people had similar experiences? Speculate on why this might be so.

Now that you have completed *Chapitre 9*, can you do the following in French?

- ☐ talk about various means of transportation, travel destinations, and lodgings?
- ☐ talk about your future plans?
- ☐ describe your travel experiences?
- ☐ follow and give directions in a city?
- ☐ describe train travel in France?
- ☐ describe some tourist destinations in the cities of Paris and Tours?

Vocabulaire

TEXT AUDIO CD 5 TRACKS 8–19

Leçon 1

moyens de transport (m.)	*means of transportation*
à pied	*on foot*
un avion	*plane*
un bus	*city bus*
un car	*excursion bus, intercity bus*
un métro	*subway*
une mobylette	*moped, motorscooter*
une moto	*motorcycle*
un taxi	*taxi*
un tram(way)	*tram*
un train	*train*

pour faire un voyage	*to take a trip*
un aéroport	*airport*
un appareil photo	*camera*
un appareil (photo) numérique	*digital camera*
un carnet d'adresses	*address book*
une carte bancaire	*debit card*
une carte de crédit	*credit card*
une clé, une clef	*key*
un passeport	*passport*
un permis de conduire	*driver's licence*
un plan de ville	*city map*
un portefeuille	*wallet*
un porte-monnaie *(inv.)*	*change purse*
un sac à dos	*backpack*
une valise	*suitcase*
un vol	*flight*

d'autres mots utiles	*other useful words*
un billet	*(train, plane) ticket*
un ticket	*(subway) ticket*
tout	*everything*
Voyons...	*Let's see . . .*

Leçon 2

les continents (m.)	*continents*
l'Afrique (f.)	*Africa*
l'Amérique (f.) du Nord	*North America*
l'Amérique (f.) du Sud	*South America*
l'Asie (f.)	*Asia*
l'Europe (f.)	*Europe*
l'Océanie (f.)	*Pacific*

des pays (m.)	*countries*
Voir à la page 351	*See page 351*

des nationalités	*nationalities*
Voir à la page 351	*See page 351*

d'autres mots utiles	*other useful words*
aussi bien que	*as well as*
une frontière	*border*
une langue maternelle	*native language*
une réunion	*meeting*

quelques verbes utiles	*some useful verbs*
devenir	*to become*
maintenir	*to affirm, to uphold*
obtenir	*to obtain*
retenir	*to hold, to book*
revenir	*to come back*
soutenir	*to support*
tenir	*to hold*
venir	*to come*
venir de + *inf.*	*to have just done something*

Leçon 

le logement	*lodgings*
aller sur Internet	*to go online*
une auberge (de jeunesse)	*inn, (youth) hostel*
un camping	*campground*
un camping-car	*recreational vehicle*
une caravane	*trailer*
Cela vous convient ?	*Does this suit you?*
un gîte (rural)	*(rural) bed and breakfast*
loger (dans un hôtel)	*to stay (in a hotel)*
une étoile	*one star*

pour se renseigner	*to get information*
un guide	*guide (tour guide or guide book)*
Je vous en prie.	*You're welcome.*
un office de tourisme	*tourism office*
des renseignements (m.)	*information*

pour indiquer le chemin	***to give directions***
une avenue	*an avenue*
un boulevard	*a boulevard*
le chemin	*the way*
continuer (tout droit)	*to keep going (straight ahead)*
tourner à (droite/ gauche)	*to turn (right/left)*
traverser	*to cross*

des sites (m.) historiques et culturels	***historical and cultural sites***
une abbaye	*abbey*
une cathédrale	*cathedral*
une cave	*wine cellar*
un château	*chateau*
un château fort	*fortress*
une grotte préhistorique	*prehistoric cave*
un spectacle son et lumière	*sound and light historical production*
un théâtre romain	*Roman theater*
un village médiéval	*medieval village*
un village perché	*village perched on a hillside*

10 La santé et le bien-être

Qu'est-ce que cette femme fait ? Pourquoi ?

Leçon 1 La santé

Leçon 2 Sauvons la planète

Leçon 3 Le bien commun : la politique et le civisme

Venez chez nous ! L'écologie

After completing this chapter, you should be able to:

- Discuss health and well-being
- Give advice
- Express emotions
- State opinions
- Discuss civic engagement and the political process in France
- Discuss environmental and ecological concerns in the Francophone world

Leçon 1 La santé

POINTS DE DÉPART

Santé physique et morale

Baptiste et Charlotte font très attention à leur santé. Ils n'ont pas beaucoup de temps libre parce qu'ils travaillent beaucoup, mais ils essayent de bien manger et de faire régulièrement de l'exercice. Charlotte aime bien les cours de fitness. Son mari est handicapé ; il doit se servir d'un fauteuil roulant, mais il est très sportif. Il fait souvent de la musculation, et il joue au basket-fauteuil avec des copains.

les cheveux (m.)
le dos
la tête
une oreille
les yeux (un œil)
les dents (f.)
le cou
le nez
la figure
la langue
la bouche
la gorge
les lèvres (f.)
l'épaule (f.)
la taille
le poignet
le ventre
la main
le bras
les doigts (m.)
le coude
la poitrine
le genou
la jambe
le pied
la cheville

Presentation: Present the parts of the body using the visual (MFL, Ch. 10), naming and describing the body parts: *Voici les yeux ; vous avez deux yeux ; c'est pour regarder. Au singulier, c'est un œil*, etc. Have students repeat the new vocabulary by identifying parts of the body: *C'est une oreille ou un œil ?* Then have them name parts of the body that come in twos — *les oreilles, les yeux, les bras, les jambes, les mains ;* then those for which they have only one: *un cœur, une tête, un estomac.* Alternatively, present this vocabulary using TPR: *Touchez le bras, la main, la jambe, les yeux*, etc., and test student comprehension by playing "Simon says" (*Jacques a dit...*).

To present this vocabulary over two days, begin with parts of the body, the expression *avoir mal*, and Ex. 10-1. On day 2, present *Êtes-vous en forme ?*, the **Vie et culture**, and Ex. 10-2 and 10-3.

Note: A limited number of terms relating to physical disabilities are presented in this lesson. You may wish to present more specific terms relating to disabilities: *quelqu'un qui ne voit pas est aveugle ou non-voyant ; si on ne peut pas entendre, on est sourd ou malentendant ; si on a des problèmes à marcher, on peut utiliser une canne ou un déambulateur ; des gens qui ont perdu une jambe ou un bras sont des amputés et ils peuvent se servir de prothèses ou de béquilles. Il ne faut pas oublier non plus les animaux : les aveugles peuvent se servir des chiens guides et d'autres personnes handicapées peuvent être aidées par des chiens d'assistance.*

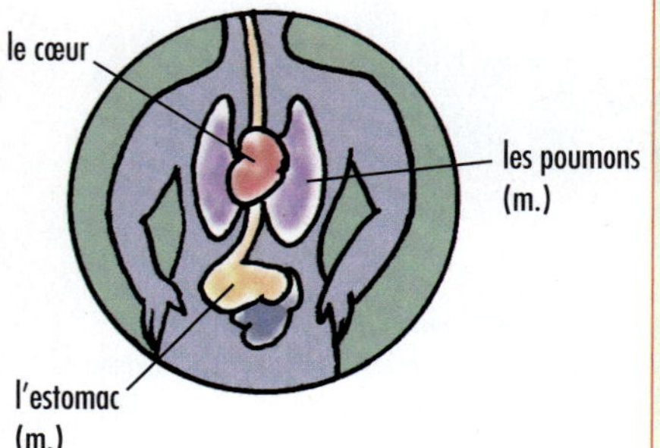

Presentation: Choose a "victim" from among the students, and use a toy hammer or bat to pretend you are inflicting pain on that person. Have students answer the question, *Où est-ce qu'il/elle a mal ?* You might focus on body parts not mentioned in the exercises. Follow up with Ex. 10-1.

Implementation: 10-1 Use the image of the hikers (MFL, Ch. 10) to complete the exercise.

Vous avez mal ?

To indicate the location of body pains in French, use the expression **avoir mal à** plus the definite article and the body part. Remember that the preposition **à** contracts with the definite article **le, la, les,** in some cases:

J'ai **mal à la** tête.	*I have a headache.*
Il **a mal au** cœur.	*He's nauseated.*
Elle **a mal aux** pieds.	*Her feet hurt.*
Tu **as mal au** ventre ?	*Do you have a stomachache?*
J'ai **mal partout**.	*I hurt everywhere.*

À vous la parole

10-1 J'ai mal ! Dites où ces personnes ont mal.

MODÈLE Christiane
Christiane, elle a mal au dos.

Presentation: Present this vocabulary by having students take the quiz individually or in pairs. Follow up by comparing profiles as a class and asking students which habits they might want to work on improving to be in better health.

Êtes-vous en forme ?
Faites le test pour le savoir.

1. **Je consulte régulièrement le médecin.** ☐ vrai ☐ faux
2. **Je fais souvent du sport ou de l'exercice.** ☐ vrai ☐ faux
3. **Je ne fume pas.** ☐ vrai ☐ faux
4. **Je mange des repas équilibrés.** ☐ vrai ☐ faux
5. **Je ne saute jamais de repas.** ☐ vrai ☐ faux
6. **Je me détends de temps en temps.** ☐ vrai ☐ faux
7. **Je ne suis pas de régimes trop stricts.** ☐ vrai ☐ faux
8. **Je bois de l'alcool avec modération.** ☐ vrai ☐ faux
9. **Je grignote peu entre les repas.** ☐ vrai ☐ faux
10. **Je dors huit heures par nuit.** ☐ vrai ☐ faux

Pour découvrir votre profil, comptez un point pour chaque « vrai ».

8 à 10 points :	Bravo ! Vous êtes en super bonne forme.
5 à 7 points :	Ça va, mais vous pouvez mieux faire !
3 à 4 points :	Franchement, vous avez du travail pour retrouver la forme !
0 à 2 points :	Oh là là, la crise ! Il faut passer à l'action.

Note: Medical care in France is ranked first worldwide. Life expectancy for the French is rising: in 2005, it reached 84 years for women, 77 years for men, among the highest averages in the world. Cardiovascular disease causes one in three deaths, cancer one in four. Mental illness is on the rise in France, but illicit drug and alcohol consumption are down (*Francoscopie 2007*). Why are the French such heavy consumers of medicines? One reason may be the relatively low cost of prescription drugs, which are subsidized by *la Sécu*. Point out that whereas Social Security in the U.S. concerns primarily pensions, and Medicaid/Medicare provide medical benefits to the poor and elderly, *la Sécu* in France is a more comprehensive and universal system of health coverage.

Vie et culture

La médecine en France

Quels aspects de la vie contribuent à notre sens du bien-être ? Un facteur important, c'est l'accès aux soins médicaux[1]. Les Français ont un excellent système médical. Ils sont assurés[2] par un système de Sécurité sociale qui couvre les dépenses[3] médicales de presque toute la population. Les malades doivent payer le médecin et le pharmacien, mais la plupart[4] des frais[5] médicaux sont remboursés. La vaste majorité (89 %) des Français se disent en bonne santé, mais paradoxalement, les Français sont les plus gros consommateurs de médicaments en Europe. Comment est-ce que le système médical chez vous diffère du système français ?

Le stress

Regardez la séquence vidéo *On se stresse et on se détend*.

1. Quelles sont les sources de stress mentionnées ? Quelles sont les méthodes employées par les gens que vous observez pour réduire le stress ?
2. Est-ce que vous pensez que le stress se manifeste en Amérique du Nord de la même façon qu'en France ? Pourquoi ?

Presentation: As students watch the video clip, have them make two lists: one for the sources of stress presented and one for the ways in which people try to counteract these stresses. Ask them if what they see and hear is comparable to the situation in their own living environment.

[1]*medical care* [2]*insured* [3]*expenses* [4]la majorité [5]*fees*

10-2 Des bons conseils. Avec un/e partenaire, offrez des conseils à chaque personne.

MODÈLE J'ai grossi de cinq kilos.
É1 Il faut suivre un régime.
É2 Et il ne faut pas grignoter entre les repas !

1. Je suis toujours fatigué.
2. J'ai très mal au dos.
3. Je voudrais maigrir un peu.
4. Je suis très stressé.
5. J'adore les chips et le coca, mais j'ai tendance à grossir.
6. J'ai très mal aux dents.
7. Je fume un paquet de cigarettes par jour.
8. Je n'ai pas le temps de manger le matin.

10-3 Pour combattre le stress. Avec un/e partenaire, dressez une liste de choses qui sont sources de stress pour vous. Ensuite, établissez une autre liste de solutions pour combattre le stress. Comparez vos listes avec celles de vos camarades de classe. Qu'est-ce qui cause le stress chez les étudiants en général ? Quelles sont les solutions les plus efficaces pour combattre le stress, selon vous ?

MODÈLE les causes du stress
É1 Pour moi, ce sont les examens qui causent du stress.
É2 Et pour moi, c'est la famille et...

les solutions
É1 Moi, pour réduire le stress, je fais du sport.
É2 Et moi, j'écoute de la musique et...

Qu'est-ce qu'elles font pour combattre le stress ?

Sons et lettres

Note: This first rule covers most of the vocabulary presented in *Chez nous*. The pronunciation of *-s* after a nasal vowel is somewhat more complex. For example, in the prefix *trans-*, *-s* is pronounced /z/ before a vowel. Compare: *transporter* vs. *transiter*.

Les consonnes *s* et *z*

The letter **s** may represent either the sound /s/ or the sound /z/. A number of word pairs are distinguished by these two consonant sounds. In the middle of words, **-ss-** is pronounced as /s/ and **-s-** as /z/:

le dessert	*dessert*	le désert	*desert*
le coussin	*cushion*	le cousin	*cousin*
le poisson	*fish*	le poison	*poison*

At the beginning of words, the letter **s** is pronounced /s/; in liaison it is pronounced /z/. Compare:

ils **s**ont/il**s**‿ont   vous **s**avez/vou**s**‿avez

After a nasal vowel written with **n**, the letter **s** is pronounced /s/:

con**s**ervation   pen**s**er   en**s**emble

Next to a consonant, **s** is pronounced /s/:

rembour**s**er   re**s**ter   l'e**s**tomac   re**s**pirer

But note the exception **Alsace**, where **s** is pronounced /z/.

The letter **c** is also pronounced /s/ before the letters **e** and **i** or when spelled with a cedilla.

cent   **c**igarette   **ç**a   gar**ç**on

Note: In France the *-x* of *Bruxelles* is usually pronounced /ks/. Make sure students understand that the *-x* of *six* is only pronounced /s/ when the word is pronounced alone or at the end of a phrase: *—Tu as combien de frères et de sœurs ? —J'en ai six ; —On est le combien aujourd'hui ? —Le six.* In liaison, the *-x* is pronounced /z/: *six‿hommes*.

The letter **x** is pronounced:

- /s/ in: si**x**   soi**x**ante   Bru**x**elles
- liaison /z/ in: si**x**‿hommes   di**x**‿aspirines
- /gz/ in: l'e**x**amen   e**x**agérer   e**x**actement
- /ks/ in: le ta**x**i   l'e**x**périence   e**x**cellent

Initial practice: Begin with a discrimination drill: are the two words or expressions the same or different? *le poisson/le poison ; le coussin/le coussin ; le dessert/le désert ; ils ont/ils sont ; le poison/le poison ; le cousin/le coussin ; ils ont/ils ont.* Students might also be amused by the following tongue twister: *Un chasseur sachant chasser sait chasser sans son chien.*

Expansion: Have students work in pairs to come up with English equivalents for these proverbs. They might suggest some variants on the following: Fish without drink is not fit to eat; it's better to be healthy than rich; youth is wasted on the young.

À vous la parole

10-4 Contrastes. Prononcez chaque groupe de mots.

pa**ss**é / ba**s**é
les Éco**ss**aises / les Anglai**s**es
soi**x**ante / e**x**acte
ils pa**ss**ent / ils se tai**s**ent
Al**c**este / l'Al**s**ace
e**x**otique / di**x**

10-5 Proverbes. Répétez ces proverbes.

1. Poisson sans boisson, c'est poison.
2. Santé passe richesse.
3. Si jeunesse savait, si vieillesse pouvait.

FORMES ET FONCTIONS

1. *Le subjonctif des verbes réguliers avec les expressions de nécessité*

- You have learned to use the indicative mood to state facts and ask questions, the imperative to express commands, and the conditional (with **devoir**, **pouvoir**, and **vouloir**) to make suggestions. When you wish to express obligation, wishes, emotions, or doubt in a complex sentence—a sentence that has two parts, or clauses, each with a different subject—you will need to use the *subjunctive* mood in the second clause. Compare the use of the present indicative and the present subjunctive in the sentences below. Note that the second clause is always introduced by **que/qu'**.

Tu **dors** six heures par nuit.	*You sleep six hours a night.*
Il est important que tu **dormes** huit heures par nuit.	*It is important that you sleep eight hours a night.*
Vous **consultez** rarement le médecin.	*You rarely see a doctor.*
Il vaut mieux que vous **consultiez** le médecin régulièrement.	*It's best that you see the doctor on a regular basis.*

Presentation: Point out that complex sentences contain two clauses, each with its own inflected verb, connected by the conjunction *que.* Have students identify the main and the subordinate clauses of several types of complex sentences. Make it clear that the verb in the main clause is in the indicative; the verb in the subordinate clause in the subjunctive. You may wish to point out that similar constructions such as *Je crois que...*, which were introduced in Ch. 7, L. 3, do not take the subjunctive in the second clause. This point will be elaborated upon in L. 3 of this chapter.

- Some common expressions of obligation or necessity used with the subjunctive include:

il faut que	*you have to/must*
il ne faut pas que	*you must not*
il est nécessaire que	*it is necessary that*
il est important que	*it is important that*
il est utile que	*it is useful that*
il est urgent que	*it is urgent that*
il vaut/vaudrait mieux que	*it is/would be better (best) that*

- Remember that impersonal expressions of obligation can also be used with an infinitive in sentences with a single subject.

Il est important de se détendre.	*It's important to relax.*
Il ne faut pas grignoter entre les repas.	*You must not snack between meals.*

Note: Many of these expressions must be followed by *de* plus the infinitive: *Il est important de...*, *il est utile de...*, etc. as presented in Ch. 8, L. 1.

- All verbs take the same set of present subjunctive endings. These endings are added to the present stem, which is found by dropping the present indicative ending **-ent** from the **ils/elles** form.

Presentation: Point out that the endings for singular and third-person plural forms of the present subjunctive are the same as the endings for the present indicative of *-er* verbs and that, for the *nous* and *vous* forms, the present subjunctive endings are the same as those of the imperfect. Contrast corresponding forms of the present indicative and the present subjunctive of the singular forms so that students clearly hear the final consonant present in the present subjunctive forms: *je dors/il faut que je dorme, tu sors/il vaut mieux que tu sortes.*

LE SUBJONCTIF				
INFINITIVE ENDING:	**-er**	**-ir**	**-ir/-iss-**	**-re**
ILS/ELLES FORM:	**mang**ent	**dorm**ent	**finiss**ent	**descend**ent
Il faut que...				
je	mang**e**	dorm**e**	finiss**e**	descend**e**
tu	mang**es**	dorm**es**	finiss**es**	descend**es**
il / elle / on	mang**e**	dorm**e**	finiss**e**	descend**e**
nous	mang**ions**	dorm**ions**	finiss**ions**	descend**ions**
vous	mang**iez**	dorm**iez**	finiss**iez**	descend**iez**
ils / elles	mang**ent**	dorm**ent**	finiss**ent**	descend**ent**

À vous la parole

Initial practice: Begin with a discrimination drill: subjunctive or infinitive? *Il faut manger de la soupe. Il faut que vous mangiez assez. Il faut qu'on parte. Il faut partir. Il est nécessaire de continuer. Il est nécessaire que vous continuiez. Il vaut mieux appeler le médecin. Il vaut mieux que tu appelles le médecin. Il est urgent que tu finisses ce travail. Il est urgent de finir ce travail. Il est important de bien manger. Il est important que vous mangiez bien, etc.* Continue with substitution drills for all regular verb conjugations: *Il est important que je dorme ; vous. — Il est important que vous dormiez ; etc.*

Implementation: 10-6 As a follow-up, have students compare their answers. Point out that the verb *payer* can either be conjugated as a regular *-er* verb *je paye, nous payons,* etc. or with *ai : je paie, tu paies, il paie* vs. *nous payons.* See Appendix 5 for the full conjugation.

10-6 C'est logique. Qu'est-ce qu'on dit dans chaque cas ? Travaillez avec un/e partenaire, et choisissez des verbes dans la liste suivante.

MODÈLE une mère à son enfant

É1 Il faut que tu manges tes carottes !

É2 Il ne faut pas que tu joues dans la rue !

arrêter	finir	jouer	manger	parler
payer	rendre	réserver	téléphoner	travailler

1. un professeur à ses élèves
2. une étudiante à sa colocataire
3. un agent de police à un automobiliste
4. une sœur à son petit frère
5. un médecin à un patient
6. une jeune femme à son mari
7. une patronne (*boss*) à son employée
8. un agent de voyage à son client

10-7 Pour être en meilleure santé. Avec un/e partenaire, dites à ces gens ce qu'il faut faire.

MODÈLE Mes filles veulent sortir, mais elles n'ont pas fini leurs devoirs.
É1 Mais il ne faut pas qu'elles sortent.
É2 Tu as raison (*You're right*), il vaut mieux qu'elles ne sortent pas.

1. On ne fait pas beaucoup d'exercice.
2. Pierre ne maigrit pas.
3. Fatmah ne veut pas manger de légumes.
4. Nous ne consultons jamais le médecin.
5. Je ne consulte pas le dentiste.
6. Ma sœur continue à grossir.
7. Mon fils a mal au ventre, mais il mange beaucoup de chocolat.

Implementation: 10-7 As a follow-up, compare answers and have students suggest other possibilities.

10-8 Obligations. Qu'est-ce que vous avez à faire ? Pour chaque verbe de la liste, précisez vos obligations en discutant avec un/e partenaire. Ensuite, comparez vos responsabilités avec celles de vos camarades de classe.

MODÈLE lire
É1 Il faut que je lise un article pour mon cours de philo.
É2 Et moi, il faut que je lise trois chapitres pour mon cours d'anglais.

1. lire
2. préparer
3. rendre
4. finir
5. téléphoner
6. sortir

2. *Le subjonctif des verbes irréguliers*

- A small number of verbs have a special stem for the subjunctive.

faire	**fass-**	Il vaut mieux qu'elle **fass**e un régime.
pouvoir	**puiss-**	Il faut qu'il **puisse** dormir.
savoir	**sach-**	Il est important qu'elles **sach**ent le nom du médecin.
pleuvoir	**pleuv-**	Il vaut mieux qu'il ne **pleuv**e pas le week-end.

- **Avoir** and **être** show many irregularities:

	AVOIR	ÊTRE
j'/je	**aie**	**sois**
tu	**aies**	**sois**
il / elle / on	**ait**	**soit**
nous	**ayons**	**soyons**
vous	**ayez**	**soyez**
ils / elles	**aient**	**soient**

Note: In her 1997 book, *Patterns Across Spoken and Written French: Empirical Research on the Interaction Among Forms, Functions and Genres*, O'Connor Di Vito reports that 78% of occurring subjunctives consist of regular *-er* verbs and the irregular verbs *avoir, être, faire,* and *pouvoir*. The percentage rises to 94% if the verbs *attendre, dire, finir, prendre,* and *venir* are added to the list. The more frequent irregulars are presented here; additional irregular verbs and *-er* verbs showing vowel changes are treated in L. 3.
Point out to students that the subjunctive forms of *avoir* and *être* are frequently used in commands: *Soyez raisonnable ! Aie de la patience !*

À vous la parole

Initial practice: Begin by having students identify the irregular verb used in the examples you provide: *Il est important que je puisse consulter le médecin (pouvoir). Il est essentiel que tu sois raisonnable (être). Il faut que tu fasses un régime (faire). Il est nécessaire que tu saches son adresse (savoir). Il vaut mieux que tu aies du temps pour te détendre (avoir)*, etc. Continue with transformation drills, indicative to subjunctive: *Il fait beau. —Il faut qu'il fasse beau ; Il peut voir le médecin ; Il est raisonnable ; Il fait un régime ; Il peut se coucher de bonne heure*, etc. For Ex. 10-9, encourage students to provide suggestions using the verbs *avoir, être, faire, pouvoir,* and *savoir*.

Implementation: 10-10 This exercise contrasts the infinitival construction with the subjunctive. To vary, have students offer advice to a friend: *Il faut que tu aies du temps libre.*

10-9 Prendre des bonnes habitudes. Expliquez comment Thomas doit changer certaines de ses habitudes pour améliorer sa santé.

MODÈLE Il n'est pas raisonnable.
→ Il vaut mieux qu'il soit raisonnable.

1. Il ne fait pas de repas équilibrés.
2. Il ne dort pas assez.
3. Il ne fait pas de sport.
4. Il ne sait pas son taux (*level*) de cholestérol.
5. Il n'a pas de vacances.
6. Il ne sait pas se détendre.
7. Il n'est pas très énergique.
8. Il ne fait pas attention à sa santé.

10-10 Pour combattre le stress. Imaginez que vous conseillez une personne qui voudrait combattre le stress. Regardez le modèle et donnez vos conseils d'une manière plus personnelle.

MODÈLE Il est important d'avoir du temps libre.
→ Il est important que vous ayez du temps libre.

1. Il faut avoir des loisirs.
2. Il faut être plus relax.
3. Il est utile de faire du yoga.
4. Il est important de savoir comment se détendre.
5. Il vaut mieux être patient/e.
6. Il est important d'avoir des amis.
7. Il vaut mieux faire du sport aussi.
8. Il faut pouvoir dormir sept ou huit heures par nuit.

Implementation: 10-11 Divide the class into groups of three or four students and give each one a scenario. Groups could then present their advice to the class, who could guess what their problem was.

10-11 Solutions. Comment est-ce qu'on pourrait résoudre les problèmes suivants ? Discutez des solutions possibles avec des camarades.

MODÈLE
É1 Je ne réussis pas dans mes études ; j'ai toujours des mauvaises notes.
É2 Il faut que tu fasses plus d'efforts, et que tu en parles avec tes profs.
É3 Oui, et il est important que tu sois toujours en classe et que tu lises les textes.

1. Je ne réussis pas dans mes études ; j'ai toujours des mauvaises notes.
2. J'ai des mauvaises relations avec mes parents.
3. Je ne suis pas en forme ; je suis toujours fatigué/e.
4. Je suis très stressé/e par tous mes problèmes.
5. J'ai besoin de maigrir, mais j'ai beaucoup de difficulté à le faire.

Lisons

10-12 Le Malade imaginaire

A. Avant de lire. Vous allez lire un extrait d'une pièce de théâtre, ***Le Malade imaginaire***, écrit par Molière en 1673. « Molière » est le nom de plume de Jean-Baptiste Poquelin, né en 1622 à Paris d'une famille bourgeoise. Les comédies de Molière sont toujours très appréciées et continuent à être jouées en France et dans le monde entier. Molière observait de manière précise les gens, et il a créé des personnages types comme l'avare (*the miser*), l'hypocrite et l'aristocrate arrogant. Par contre, il célèbre les gens de condition modeste qui sont souvent représentés dans ses pièces par le domestique qui est plus intelligent que son maître. Dans cette scène, le malade imaginaire (*hypochondriac*), Argan, parle avec sa domestique, Toinette, qui s'est déguisée en médecin. Avant de lire la scène, répondez à ces questions.

1. Dressez une liste des différences qui existent entre une pièce de théâtre et un texte littéraire.
2. D'après le titre de la pièce, ***Le Malade imaginaire***, et le fait que c'est une comédie, qu'est-ce que vous imaginez comme scénario ?

B. En lisant. Examinez quelques aspects comiques de cet extrait en répondant aux questions suivantes.

1. Quelles sont les maladies préférées du « docteur » ?
2. Complétez le schéma avec les symptômes d'Argan et le diagnostic correspondant de Toinette. Pourquoi est-ce que cet échange est amusant ?

Les symptômes	Le diagnostic
des lassitudes par tous les membres	

3. Comment est-il possible qu'Argan ne reconnaisse pas sa servante Toinette ?

Stratégie

Use your familiarity with a particular literary genre to help you predict the content and structure of a text. What might you expect, for example, in reading a scene from a play as opposed to a prose passage? How can you adjust your own approach to the text accordingly?

Presentation: Find out whether students are familiar with any of Molière's works; you might display photos or posters of stage productions. Go over the questions with students and help them generate ideas before tackling the text.

Key: En lisant 1) les maladies sérieuses comme les fièvres, les pestes, les pleurésies 2) les symptômes : maux de tête, les yeux voilés, maux de cœur, *lassitudes des membres*, mal au ventre/coliques ; le diagnostique : les poumons. C'est amusant parce que le diagnostique est toujours le même et ne semble pas avoir un grand rapport avec les symptômes. 3) Toinette s'est déguisée, probablement avec une longue robe noire, un chapeau et une barbe. Elle parle avec une voix d'homme.

Scène X.— TOINETTE, en médecin ; ARGAN

TOINETTE : Vous ne trouverez pas mauvais, s'il vous plaît, la curiosité que j'ai eue de voir un illustre malade comme vous êtes ; et votre réputation qui s'étend[1] partout, peut excuser la liberté que j'ai prise.

ARGAN : Monsieur, je suis votre serviteur....

TOINETTE : Je suis médecin passager, qui vais de ville en ville, de province en province, de royaume en royaume, pour chercher d'illustres matières à ma capacité, pour trouver des malades dignes[2] de m'occuper.... Je veux des maladies d'importance, de bonnes fièvres continues..., de bonnes pestes[3], ... de bonnes pleurésies[4], avec des inflammations de poitrine ; c'est là que je me plais[5], c'est là que je triomphe.... Donnez-moi votre pouls. Allons donc, que l'on batte comme il faut. Ah ! Je vous ferai bien aller comme vous devez. Ouais ! Ce pouls-là fait l'impertinent[6] ; je vois bien que vous ne me connaissez pas encore. Qui est votre médecin ?

ARGAN : Monsieur Purgon.

TOINETTE : ... De quoi dit-il que vous êtes malade ?

ARGAN : Il dit que c'est du foie[7], et d'autres disent que c'est de la rate[8].

TOINETTE : Ce sont tous des ignorants. C'est du poumon que vous êtes malade.

ARGAN : Du poumon ?

TOINETTE : Oui. Que sentez-vous ?

ARGAN : Je sens de temps en temps des douleurs[9] de tête.

TOINETTE : Justement, le poumon.

ARGAN : Il me semble parfois que j'ai un voile[10] devant les yeux.

TOINETTE : Le poumon.

ARGAN : J'ai quelque fois des maux de cœur.

TOINETTE : Le poumon.

ARGAN : Je sens parfois des lassitudes par tous les membres.

TOINETTE : Le poumon.

ARGAN : Et quelquefois il me prend des douleurs dans le ventre, comme si c'était des coliques.

TOINETTE : Le poumon. Vous avez appétit à ce que vous mangez ?

ARGAN : Oui, Monsieur.

TOINETTE : Le poumon. Vous aimez à boire un peu de vin ?

ARGAN : Oui, Monsieur.

TOINETTE : Le poumon. Il vous prend un petit sommeil après le repas, et vous êtes bien aise de dormir ?

ARGAN : Oui, Monsieur.

TOINETTE : Le poumon, le poumon, vous dis-je.

[1]*reaches* [2]*worthy* [3]*plagues* [4]*lung diseases* [5]j'aime [6]*is acting impertinent* [7]*liver* [8]*spleen* [9]des maux [10]*a curtain*

Extrait de : Molière, *Le Malade imaginaire*, Acte III, Scène X.

C. En regardant de plus près. Maintenant examinez les aspects suivants du texte.

Key: En regardant de plus près 1) elle prendra la main d'Argan 2) b 3) c

1. Toinette dit en bon médecin, **Donnez-moi votre pouls**. Qu'est-ce qu'elle va faire ensuite ? (Pensez à un mot en anglais qui ressemble au mot français, **pouls**.)
2. Ensuite, Toinette dit, **Ouais !** Cette prononciation correspond au mot…
   a. où **b.** oui **c.** une
3. Argan ressent « des lassitudes par tous les membres ». Qu'est-ce que ça signifie, « les membres » ?
   a. les yeux **b.** les oreilles **c.** les bras et les jambes

D. Après avoir lu. Discutez des questions suivantes avec vos camarades de classe.

Variation: To simplify, let students don costumes and mime the actions as the class listens to the recorded version of the scene. The costumes and actions should be amusing, bordering on slapstick.

1. Molière a écrit beaucoup de pièces comiques au dix-septième siècle. Dans cette pièce, il se moque (*makes fun of*) des médecins de son époque. Pourquoi est-ce que nous trouvons aujourd'hui que c'est toujours amusant ?
2. Quelles techniques rendent ce dialogue comique, à votre avis ?
3. Imaginez comment les acteurs peuvent jouer cette scène. Avec un/e partenaire, jouez les rôles de Toinette et d'Argan vous-mêmes !

Argan discute de ses problèmes médicaux avec son frère. Toinette écoute attentivement.

Leçon 2 Sauvons la planète

POINTS DE DÉPART

TEXT AUDIO
CD 5 TRACK 25

Pour protéger la Terre

Presentation: Begin by asking students to describe the photo and to discuss how it corresponds to their own experiences. As you work with the text, discuss local, regional, and national environmental concerns with students. Much of the vocabulary involves cognates. Have students identify as many cognates as they can and offer definitions or synonyms wherever possible (*atmosphère* ; synonym *air*). Global warming is also referred to in French as le *réchauffement global* ou *planétaire;* CO_2 is either referred to as *le dioxyde de carbone* or pronounced [se o dø]. Additional environmental vocabulary is presented in Ex. 10-13.

La planète va mal

Le réchauffement climatique est un problème sérieux, et les humains ont une grande part de responsabilité. La température augmente à cause des gaz à effet de serre, surtout le dioxyde de carbone, ou CO2.

Quelques problèmes et leurs causes :

La pollution atmosphérique

- les gaz carboniques rejetés par des usines
- les gaz d'échappement des voitures et des avions
- la déforestation (lorsqu'on brûle le bois)

La pollution sonore

- le bruit des moteurs, des sirènes
- le bruit de la musique trop fort

La pollution de l'eau et du sol

- les déchets industriels
- les déchets domestiques
- la déforestation (à cause de l'érosion)

Quelques conséquences graves

- Les glaciers fondent au Groenland et dans l'Antarctique.
- Il y a de plus en plus d'ouragans, de tornades, de pluies abondantes, d'inondations.
- Les écosystèmes sont menacés, par exemple, les ours blancs et le corail sont en péril.

La circulation sur le Périphérique à Paris.

Qu'est-ce qu'on peut faire pour sauver la Terre ?

- réduire son empreinte écologique* : consommer moins et de préférence des produits locaux, recycler, réutiliser
- utiliser des sources d'énergie renouvelables : le soleil, le vent, les vagues, les ordures
- se déplacer autrement : les vélos en libre-service, la marche à pied, les transports en commun, le covoiturage, les tramways électriques, les voitures hybrides

* une estimation des ressources naturelles que chaque personne consomme selon son mode de vie.

Presentation: Have students look at the pictures and decide how each picture illustrates an ecological improvement. Ask them to pick out from the text the various lifestyle choices that have led to France consuming less energy than the United States. Refer students to the *Chez nous* Companion Website for links to sites with more information about the concept of "ecological footprint" and calculators to determine one's individual ecological footprint. The Companion Website also includes links to sites with more updated information about the progress of the French national debate on the environment, named *le Grenelle de l'Environnement.* You may wish to introduce the well-known slogan: *En France, on n'a pas de pétrole, mais on a des idées.* This slogan was part of an advertising campaign by the French government in the 1970s to promote its alternative energy proposals, especially the use of nuclear energy during the oil crisis. At the current time, almost 80% of France's electricity is produced by nuclear power plants.

Vie et culture

La France et l'environnement

En France on réfléchit aux problèmes de l'environnement depuis longtemps. Regardez ces images avec un/e partenaire, et expliquez comment chaque photo représente une mesure écologique. En général, les Français ont des voitures plus petites qui consomment moins d'essence[1], se servent plus souvent des transports en commun et utilisent moins d'électricité que les Américains.

Dans plusieurs villes en France, on peut se déplacer[2] en tramway électrique ou en vélo avec les nouveaux services de location de vélo en libre-service. Vous prenez un abonnement[3] et puis vous pouvez prendre un vélo à une station et le retourner dans une autre. Ce n'est pas étonnant[4] que l'empreinte écologique du Français moyen soit presque la moitié[5] de l'empreinte écologique de l'Américain moyen.

En juin 2007, le président Nicolas Sarkozy a créé le ministère de l'Écologie, de l'Énergie, du Développement durable[6] et de l'Aménagement[7] du territoire. En juillet 2007 il a lancé un grand débat national au sujet de l'environnement. Cette initiative a regroupé des représentants du gouvernement, des industriels, des militants écologistes et des scientifiques pour discuter des problèmes et des projets qui concernent l'environnement pour les cinq ans à venir.

Note: Both *à vélo* and *en vélo* are widely used in France.

ET VOUS ?

1. Qu'est-ce qu'on fait dans votre ville ou sur votre campus pour réduire l'empreinte écologique ?
2. Les Américains consomment le plus de ressources naturelles et produisent le plus de pollution sur le plan mondial. Quelles en sont les raisons, à votre avis ? Qu'est-ce qu'on peut faire pour changer cette situation ?

[1]*gas* [2]voyager [3]*subscription* [4]*surprising* [5]*half* [6]*sustainable development* [7]*management*

Le tramway à Montpellier

« Vélib » à Paris

« Une Smart »

Note: In 2005, a Charter for the Environment was added to the French constitution. According to an information sheet published by *le Ministère de l'Écologie et du Développement Durable* in March 2007, *« La Charte reconnaît notamment à chacun le droit de vivre dans un environnement équilibré et respectueux de la santé, le droit d'accéder à l'information détenue par les autorités publiques et le droit de participer à l'élaboration des décisions publiques ayant une incidence sur l'environnement. Si ce texte accorde des droits à chacun, il impose aussi des devoirs. Chacun doit ainsi contribuer à la préservation et à l'amélioration de l'environnement et, le cas échéant, contribuer à la réparation des dommages qu'il a causés. »*

À vous la parole

Implementation: 10-13 This exercise uses realia both to present new vocabulary and to work with it in context. Before beginning, go over the poster with the students and have them identify cognates and near-cognates: *économiser, non biodégradable, huile usagée, recycler, sac en plastique.* Illustrate other vocabulary with pictures, drawings, or realia (bring in examples of *un panier, un emballage en plastique, une boîte de conserve, une bouteille en verre*). Have students figure out the meaning of words like *éteindre, gaspiller, laisser les lumières allumées, ampoules, trier,* and *covoiturage* (carpooling) through context. Have students describe additional sources of pollution. As you work with the text, ask students to evaluate the suggestions: are they all as relevant in North America as in France? Do any seem inappropriate?

10-13 Contre chaque nuisance, il y a des solutions ! Pour chaque problème indiqué, trouvez une solution sur le poster suivant en travaillant avec un/e partenaire. Attention ! Quelquefois il y a plus qu'une solution.

DES ÉCO-GESTES POUR LA CONSOMMATION ET LE DÉVELOPPEMENT DURABLE

- Ne jetez pas tous les déchets domestiques à la poubelle ; triez-les et recyclez les emballages en plastique, les boîtes de conserve, le papier, le carton, les bouteilles en verre.
- Privilégiez les transports en commun, le vélo, le covoiturage.
- Utilisez au maximum la lumière naturelle et les ampoules basse consommation.
- Ne laissez pas les lumières allumées et les appareils électriques en veille[1] ; éteignez-les !
- Prenez une douche rapide au lieu d'un bain pour ne pas gaspiller l'eau ; économisez entre 150 et 200 litres d'eau ! Coupez l'eau du robinet quand vous vous brossez les dents, vous rasez ou vous lavez les mains.
- Utilisez des paniers ou des sacs réutilisables pour faire vos courses ; refusez des sacs en plastique et des emballages non biodégradables.
- Utilisez le papier recyclé et n'imprimez[2] pas tous vos e-mails.
- Ne jetez pas les huiles de cuisine ou de moteur usagées dans l'évier ; elles empêchent[3] l'oxygénation de la faune et de la flore. Apportez-les à la déchèterie.

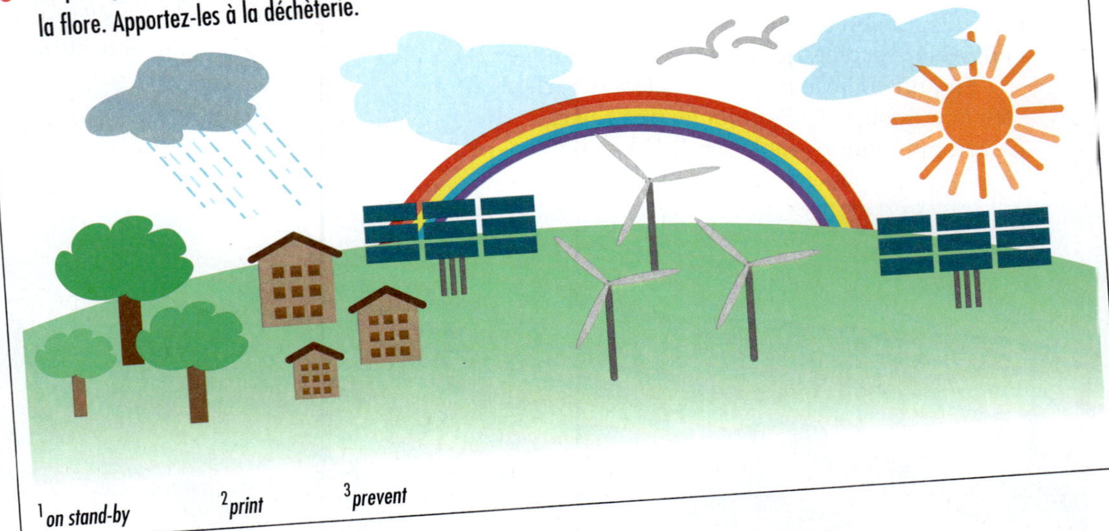

[1] on stand-by   [2] print   [3] prevent

MODÈLE É1 La déforestation est un problème sérieux.
É2 Utilisez du papier recyclé !

1. La température continue à augmenter.
2. Il y a trop de sacs en plastique et d'emballages non biodégradables.
3. Nous gaspillons l'électricité.
4. Nous utilisons trop d'eau. Bientôt il n'y aura plus d'eau potable.
5. Il y a trop de gaz carbonique dans l'atmosphère ; l'air de la ville est vraiment pollué.
6. Nous produisons trop de déchets.
7. L'eau devient très polluée.

10-14 Changeons le comportement des gens. Avec un/e partenaire, suggérez des alternatives moins polluantes. Voici quelques verbes utiles : **économiser**, **gaspiller**, **recycler**, **trier**, **utiliser**.

MODÈLE Je prends ma voiture pour aller en ville.
É1 Mais non ! Il faut prendre les transports en commun !
É2 Ou bien, il faut y aller à vélo.

1. Je prends ma moto pour aller à la bibliothèque.
2. Je vais prendre un bon bain très chaud.
3. J'ai besoin d'un nouveau cahier et de papier pour mes cours.
4. Jetons l'huile usagée dans l'évier.
5. Mettons ces emballages et ces boîtes de conserve à la poubelle.
6. J'utilise toujours des sacs en plastique pour mes courses.

Implementation: 10-14 As a follow-up, see which group generated the most answers for each item.

10-15 Les soucis écologiques chez vous. Quels sont les problèmes liés à l'environnement chez vous et qu'est-ce qu'on fait pour les réduire ? Parlez-en avec un/e partenaire.

MODÈLE la pollution atmosphérique
É1 Chez moi, il y a beaucoup de pollution atmosphérique, surtout l'été quand il fait chaud et lourd. Certains jours, les jeunes et les personnes âgées ne doivent pas sortir. Je crois qu'on devrait utiliser plus de transports en commun.
É2 Je suis d'accord. Il faut réduire notre consommation d'énergie et surtout les émissions de gaz produits par les voitures.

1. la pollution atmosphérique
2. les écosystèmes menacés
3. la déforestation
4. le gaspillage d'énergie
5. les déchets non biodégradables

Additional activity: Have students work with a partner to determine the advantages of each of the following measures: *faire du compost ; remplacer les autobus par des tramways ; interdire les voitures individuelles en ville ; faire du jardinage ; se promener dans la forêt à vélo ; planter des arbres.*

MODÈLE faire du compost
É1 On peut utiliser certains déchets domestiques dans le jardin.
É2 Oui, comme ça, on peut améliorer la qualité de la terre.

Sons et lettres

La consonne *gn*

The consonant /ɲ/, as in **campagne** or **oignon**, is pronounced with the tip of the tongue placed against the lower front teeth with the tongue body touching the hard palate. It is as if you were pronouncing /n/ and /j/ simultaneously. It is always spelled **gn**.

Note: There is a tendency for some speakers to pronounce the orthographic sequence **gn** as the nasal consonant /n/ followed by the palatal glide /j/, rather than with the palatal nasal /ɲ/.

 À vous la parole 

10-16 Répétition. Répétez chaque mot.

le si**gn**e	il ga**gn**e	ga**gn**er	l'Espa**gn**e	les Espa**gn**oles
le poi**gn**et	la monta**gn**e	la bai**gn**oire	l'Allema**gn**e	les oi**gn**ons

Initial practice: Begin with a discrimination drill: have students raise their hand when they hear you pronounce a word containing /ɲ/, for example: *montagne, monter, camper, campagne, oignon, Espagne, santé, poignet.*

Point out the exceptional pronunciation of *diagnostic* [djagnɔstik] which does not follow the general rule of *gn* = palatal nasal.

10-17 Phrases. Maintenant, répétez les phrases suivantes.

1. Il y a beaucoup de vignes magnifiques en Champagne et en Bourgogne.
2. Digne, Cagnes et Cannes sont en Provence.
3. Les Montaigne vont en Allemagne et en Espagne.
4. Diagnostic : votre nièce a mal au poignet.
5. Renseigne-toi ! L'omelette, c'est aux champignons ou aux oignons ?

FORMES ET FONCTIONS

1. *Le subjonctif avec les expressions de volonté*

- When the main verb of a sentence expresses a desire or wish, the verb of the following subordinate clause is usually in the subjunctive.

Elles souhaitent qu'il **parte**.	*They wish that he would leave.*
Il exige qu'on **attende** jusqu'à demain.	*He demands that we wait until tomorrow.*

Note: *Espérer*, which will be presented in Ch. 12, L. 1, is an exception and is followed by the future tense: *J'espère qu'il viendra demain.*

Here are some verbs used to express desires or wishes that are followed by the subjunctive:

aimer	désirer	souhaiter
aimer mieux	exiger	vouloir
demander	préférer	

- When the subject is the same for both parts of the sentence, use an infinitive construction instead of the subjunctive. Compare the following examples.

Il voudrait **rester** ici.	*He'd like to stay here.*
Il voudrait **que ses enfants restent** ici.	*He'd like his children to stay here.*
Moi, je voudrais **dormir** et je veux **que** toi, **tu te couches** bientôt aussi.	*As for me, I'd like to sleep, and I'd like for you to go to bed soon as*

 À vous la parole

Note: 10-18 This exercise provides practice with using the infinitive when the subject is the same in both clauses.

10-18 Une soirée tranquille. Vous avez prévu de passer la soirée avec votre colocataire, mais il/elle rentre tard après une journée très stressante. Imaginez ses réponses à vos questions.

MODÈLE Alors, qu'est-ce qu'on fait ? On pourrait sortir ce soir ou rester chez nous.

Je voudrais rester chez nous.

OU Je voudrais qu'on sorte.

1. On invite des amis ou on passe une soirée tranquille ?
2. Et pour manger ? On prépare des pâtes ou on commande une pizza ?
3. Et après, tu veux finir tes devoirs ou tu veux regarder la télé ?
4. Il y a un match de foot et un film à la télé. Qu'est-ce que tu préfères regarder ?
5. On attend le film de 21 h 30 ou on regarde *Star Academy* tout de suite ?
6. Tu as soif ? Tu veux prendre un thé ou un jus de fruit ?

10-19 Les désirs écologiques d'Olivier. Olivier est un père de famille très écolo, mais ses enfants ont des mauvaises habitudes. Avec un/e partenaire, imaginez les réponses d'Olivier à ses enfants.

MODÈLE Le recyclage est trop difficile ; ça prend trop de temps.
→ Mais moi, je veux que tu fasses du recyclage.

1. Je n'aime pas prendre le bus pour aller à la fac ; je veux prendre ma voiture.
2. Je n'aime pas aller à l'école avec les voisins dans leur voiture.
3. C'est inutile de recycler le plastique.
4. Je ne veux pas éteindre les lumières dans ma chambre.
5. Ce n'est pas juste. Je ne veux pas baisser (*turn down*) ma chaîne stéréo. Je ne peux rien entendre comme ça.
6. Je n'aime pas les douches. C'est plus agréable de prendre un bon bain.
7. Je ne vais pas prendre ces sacs réutilisables quand je vais au supermarché, c'est trop compliqué.
8. Je mets les boîtes de conserve dans la poubelle. C'est plus facile et je ne dois pas les rincer.

Expansion: 10-19 Have students suggest other environmentally friendly practices that Olivier might support and that his children might disagree with.

10-20 Harmonie ou conflit. Parlez-en avec un/e partenaire : pour chaque catégorie, dites si vous et vos parents partagez les mêmes souhaits, désirs, etc.

MODÈLE votre future profession : votre souhait
É1 Je souhaite être actrice. Mes parents veulent que je sois médecin.
É2 Mes parents veulent que je sois architecte et moi aussi. J'adore dessiner et je veux travailler comme architecte.

1. vos études : votre souhait
2. vos projets pour l'été prochain : votre préférence
3. votre prochaine voiture : votre désir
4. votre futur/e mari ou femme : votre préférence
5. vos futurs enfants : votre souhait
6. votre lieu de résidence éventuel : votre désir

Implementation: 10-20 Follow up by comparing answers for the class as a whole.

2. *D'autres verbes irréguliers au subjonctif*

- A few verbs have two stems in the subjunctive: one for the singular forms and the third-person plural, the other for the **nous**- and **vous**-forms. The second stem is based on the **nous**-form of the present indicative. The regular subjunctive endings are used for all of these verbs.

Il faut que tu **boives** de l'eau.	*You must drink some water.*
C'est dommage que vous ne **preniez** pas plus souvent le bus.	*It's a shame that you don't take the bus more often.*
Il faut que tu **ailles** au centre de recyclage.	*You must go to the recycling center.*
Elle veut que vous y **alliez**.	*She wants you to go there.*

Presentation: Point out to students that for these verbs, the singular and third-person plural forms are derived according to the rule. The *nous* and *vous* forms are exceptional, but they are identical to the imperfect forms. As was the case for the regular *-ir* and *-re* verbs, provide examples for the singular forms in which you stress the presence of the final consonant in the present subjunctive contrasting with its absence in the corresponding form of the present indicative: *il apprend/il faut qu'il apprenne.* Provide sample conjugations, as well as examples from compounds of *prendre* (*apprendre, comprendre*, etc.) and *venir* (*devenir, revenir*).

LE SUBJONCTIF DE QUELQUES VERBES IRRÉGULIERS						
	BOIRE	DEVOIR	PRENDRE	VENIR	ALLER	VOULOIR
Il faut que...						
je	boive	doive	prenne	vienne	**aille**	**veuille**
tu	boives	doives	prennes	viennes	**ailles**	**veuilles**
il / elle / on	boive	doive	prenne	vienne	**aille**	**veuille**
nous	**buv**ions	**dev**ions	**pren**ions	**ven**ions	**all**ions	**voul**ions
vous	**buv**iez	**dev**iez	**pren**iez	**ven**iez	**all**iez	**voul**iez
ils / elles	boivent	doivent	prennent	viennent	**aillent**	**veuillent**

Presentation: Review the list of verbs showing a vowel change (*préférer, acheter, appeler, jeter*) and those showing the change *oy/oi* or *ay/ai* (*essuyer, ennuyer, nettoyer, essayer, payer*). Provide a sample conjugation for each of the two subtypes, *acheter* and *appeler*. Remind students that these verbs still fit the "boot" pattern, with three spoken forms, and encourage them to visualize the pattern as mentioned in the **Fiche pratique**.

- Verbs in **-er** that have two stems in the present indicative show the same pattern in the subjunctive. As is the case for all **-er** verbs, only the **nous** and **vous** forms of the subjunctive are different from the indicative forms.

Il faut que nous **achetions** du papier recyclé.	*We have to buy recycled paper.*
Il vaut mieux qu'ils **appellent** un journaliste.	*It's best they call a reporter.*
Il est urgent que vous **nettoyiez** cette rivière polluée.	*It's urgent that you clean up this polluted river.*

LE SUBJONCTIF DES VERBES EN –ER AVEC DES CHANGEMENTS ORTHOGRAPHIQUES				
	PRÉFÉRER	ACHETER	APPELER	NETTOYER
Il faut que...				
je	**préfère**	**achète**	**appell**e	**nettoie**
tu	**préfère**s	**achète**s	**appell**es	**nettoie**s
il / elle / on	**préfère**	**achète**	**appell**e	**nettoie**
nous	**préfér**ions	**achet**ions	**appel**ions	**nettoy**ions
vous	**préfér**iez	**achet**iez	**appel**iez	**nettoy**iez
ils / elles	**préfèr**ent	**achèt**ent	**appell**ent	**nettoi**ent

Fiche pratique

To learn irregular verb forms, try writing them down or repeating them out loud. Whichever technique works best for you, focus both on exceptional forms and on any patterns that you see.

À vous la parole

10-21 C'est important ! Pour sauver la planète, qu'est-ce qu'il est important de faire ?

MODÈLE les employés de la ville / nettoyer les rivières
Il est essentiel que les employés de la ville nettoient les rivières.

1. les familles / prendre des douches rapides et pas de bains
2. la ville / pouvoir établir un programme de recyclage
3. nous / aller apporter les huiles usagées à la déchèterie
4. vous / acheter des produits recyclables
5. les étudiants / ne pas venir sur le campus en voiture individuelle
6. nous / prendre les transports en commun
7. tu / devenir plus écologique
8. nous / aller régulièrement au centre de recyclage
9. vous / maintenir vos bonnes habitudes écologiques
10. les jeunes / vouloir sauver la planète

Initial practice: Begin with substitution drills: *Il faut que je prenne le bus ; nous*, etc. Use the activities to review the uses of the subjunctive as well as forms.

Implementation: 10-21 This exercise practices the subjunctive in the context of expressions of necessity. You might provide a list of expressions for students to choose from as they complete the exercise.

Pour sauver la planète, faites du compost !

10-22 Nos préférences. Avec un/e partenaire, décidez si vos préférences sont les mêmes que les préférences de votre professeur. Comparez vos réponses avec les réponses de vos camarades de classe.

MODÈLE parler toujours en français en classe
É1 Je n'aime pas parler toujours en français.
É2 Moi ça va. Et le prof préfère que nous parlions toujours en français.

1. faire les devoirs
2. acheter un bon dictionnaire
3. prendre des notes
4. aller au labo de langues
5. venir en classe tous les jours
6. faire des crêpes
7. aller voir des films français
8. ne pas boire de vin
9. apprendre tout le vocabulaire
10. vouloir parler comme des Français

Implementation: 10-22 This allows students to practice the use of the infinitive as well as the subjunctive in appropriate contexts with expressions of preference. Provide a list of expressions for students to choose from.

Écoutons

10-23 Micro-trottoir sur le réchauffement climatique

A. Avant d'écouter. Un micro-trottoir est une technique journalistique où on pose la même question à plusieurs personnes dans la rue pour avoir leurs réponses spontanées. Avant d'écouter, dressez une liste de deux ou trois questions qu'un journaliste pourrait poser au sujet de l'environnement.

B. En écoutant. Écoutez le micro-trottoir et répondez aux questions suivantes.

1. D'abord, notez **en anglais** les questions que le journaliste pose dans la première colonne.
2. Pour chaque question, complétez le tableau avec les réponses des gens interviewés.

	Jeune femme	Homme	Femme
Question n° 1 :	*C'est un problème ; il faut réagir*		
Question n° 2 :			
Question n° 3 : *What will happen in twenty years?*			

3. Qui est le plus optimiste ? le plus pessimiste ? Pourquoi ?

C. Après avoir écouté. Discutez de ces questions avec vos camarades de classe.

1. Posez ces trois questions à vos camarades de classe. Est-ce que vous avez d'autres opinions et d'autres solutions ? Lesquelles ?
2. Avec quelle personne interviewée est-ce que vous êtes d'accord ? Pourquoi ?

Key: En écoutant 1) What do you think of global warming? What can we do to fight global warming? 2) Jeune femme : prenez le vélo, les transports en commun, limitez l'eau et l'électricité, recyclez ; Homme : c'est exagéré, on va trouver des solutions ; la marche à pied ; tout le monde doit faire des efforts ; Femme : une inquiétude, elle pense aux enfants ; on ne peut pas faire grand-chose, c'est trop tard ; elle n'est pas optimiste 3) le plus optimiste : l'homme ; le plus pessimiste : la deuxième femme

Variation: Après avoir écouté Put students in small groups to carry out *micro-trottoirs* in class. If you have video or recording equipment, have students record each other's answers and play them back for the class.

Presentation: Avant d'écouter
Videotaped *micro-trottoirs* on a variety of subjects are available online. See the *Chez nous* Companion Website for links or simply use a search engine to locate a few to share with the class. Ask students what the last *micro-trottoir* they listened to on the radio or saw on television was about.

Script: Écoutons

JOURNALISTE : Qu'est-ce que vous pensez du réchauffement climatique ?

JEUNE FEMME 1 : C'est un vrai problème. C'est dangereux pour la planète. Il faudrait qu'on réagisse maintenant. Il faut vraiment moins de pollution.

HOMME : Je pense franchement que c'est exagéré et puis on va trouver des solutions ; on finit toujours par trouver des solutions.

FEMME 2 : C'est vraiment une inquiétude réelle. Je pense à l'avenir et aux enfants. Quelle planète est-ce qu'on va leur laisser ?

JOURNALISTE : Qu'est-ce qu'on peut faire pour lutter contre le réchauffement climatique ?

JEUNE FEMME 1 : Plus de vélo, moins de voiture, et plus de transports en commun. Limitez l'électricité et l'eau et faites plus de recyclage.

HOMME : Utilisez le moins possible les véhicules... et voilà, moi je suis à pied... plutôt que de tourner en rond pour trouver un parking et utiliser plein de pétrole.

FEMME 2 : Vous savez, on peut pas faire grand-chose pour l'arrêter maintenant, même si on arrête de polluer et tout ça, le réchauffement est déjà en route. Ça va quand même se réchauffer.

JOURNALISTE : À votre avis, qu'est-ce qui va nous arriver dans une vingtaine d'années ?

JEUNE FEMME 1 : Si tout le monde fait des efforts, on va y arriver. Ça commence déjà. Les gens font plus attention.

HOMME : Tout sera réglé. On aura trouvé d'autres sources d'énergie renouvelable et des nouvelles technologies pour résoudre ces problèmes.

FEMME 2 : Je sais pas, mais il va pas nous arriver de bonnes choses. Je ne suis pas optimiste.

Leçon  Le bien commun : la politique et le civisme

POINTS DE DÉPART

TEXT AUDIO
CD 5 TRACK 30

On s'engage

Presentation: Have students listen to the text as they look at the pictures. Ask them to describe what they see in each picture and whether they have ever participated in the various activities depicted. Help students extract a list of key vocabulary and provide additional examples.

Note: *Les Restaurants du Cœur* is a charity in France founded by the French comedian Coluche in 1985. *Les Restos du Cœur* started out as a way to provide food to families and individuals struggling in the winter months. It has developed into a year-round service providing food, nutrition counseling, and other types of aid for families with new babies, the homeless, and others in difficulty, with over 100 local branches serving the 96 metropolitan *départements*. Other similar humanitarian organizations that operate in France include *l'Armée du salut* and *Emmaüs*.

Ce sont les élections étudiantes pour les représentants aux conseils universitaires. Tous les étudiants inscrits sur la liste électorale ont le droit de voter. Ils se rendent au bureau de vote, prennent un bulletin de vote et votent pour leurs candidats préférés. Les étudiants élus ont un mandat de deux ans.

Note: There is an important distinction in French between the words *bénévole/bénévolat* and *volontaire/volontariat.* The former refers to unpaid volunteer work and is the closest to the American sense of the word "volunteer"; students should be encouraged to use this word rather than the false-cognate *volontaire. Le volontariat* is associated with a specific legal status; *les volontaires* are covered by *la sécurité sociale* (and hence receive health and other benefits) and often receive a stipend or coverage of minimal living expenses. This is comparable to Americans volunteering for the Peace Corps, Americorps, City Year, the Jesuit Volunteer Corps, or Teach for America. For more information about *le volontariat* and *le bénévolat* and the ways students can become involved, visit the *Chez nous* Companion Website for helpful links.

Ces citoyens se mobilisent dans les rues de Paris contre les reformes proposées par le gouvernement français ; c'est une journée de grèves et de manifestations partout en France pour protester contre la réduction de postes dans le secteur public y compris les hôpitaux.

Gisèle travaille comme bénévole dans un centre de distribution pour « Restaurants du Cœur ». C'est une association humanitaire qui distribue de la nourriture et sert des repas chauds aux personnes en difficulté.

Presentation: Treat the following information in a game-like fashion by assigning one point to each question to which students can answer "yes" and award a prize to the student who knows the most about the French political system. Using the vocabulary presented in the *Points de départ* and here, ask students about their own experiences with voting in local and presidential elections.

Vie et culture

Les Français face à leurs responsabilités civiques

Dans un pays démocratique, une des principales responsabilités civiques est de voter aux élections.

Savez-vous…

- que le Président de la République française est élu pour cinq ans ?
- qu'il y a deux tours dans la plupart des élections en France, le premier tour servant à déterminer les deux candidats qui vont se battre lors du second tour ?
- que les Français votent toujours le dimanche ?
- que le taux de participation aux élections présidentielles françaises du 2007 était de 84 % ?
- qu'il y a une loi sur la parité politique en France qui date de l'an 2000 et qui précise qu'il faut avoir autant de candidats du sexe féminin que du sexe masculin ?

Est-ce que vous connaissez la moyenne du taux de participation aux élections présidentielles récentes aux États-Unis ? Il se situe autour de 60 %. À votre avis, quelles sont quelques raisons pour cette différence de participation dans la vie civique des Français et des Américains ?

Les associations bénévoles

La notion de solidarité est très importante pour les Français, et il y a beaucoup d'associations humanitaires qui s'occupent de donner du soutien aux personnes en difficulté. Il y a des banques alimentaires pour aider les gens qui n'ont pas les moyens de se nourrir et plusieurs associations comme S.O.S. Amitié où des bénévoles répondent aux coups de téléphone des gens avec des problèmes divers qui ont besoin d'une écoute sympathique. Il y a aussi des associations qui s'occupent des visites à domicile pour les personnes âgées ou handicapées. Si vous étudiez en France, une bonne façon de vous intégrer dans votre communauté d'accueil[1] est de devenir bénévole. Visitez le site Web *Chez nous* pour découvrir des liens utiles pour apprendre comment.

ET VOUS ?

1. Est-ce que les Américains font beaucoup de bénévolat ? Dans quels domaines ?
2. À votre avis, est-ce que la notion de solidarité joue un rôle dans la culture nord-américaine ? Comment ?

[1]*host*

Note: The majority of French elections follow the system of having two rounds: a first round to narrow the field and a second round where the majority candidate wins. As mentioned in the text, the French vote on Sundays and by law, electoral campaigns must end by midnight of the preceding Friday. Candidates are not allowed to appear on TV after that time and no polls are to be released. Election results or exit polls are also not permitted until the close of voting on Sunday evening. For more information about the various elections at the local, national, and European level in France, see the IRM.

Des jeunes Français se mobilisent contre la guerre (*war*).

À vous la parole

10-24 La vie civique. Trouvez l'expression qui correspond le mieux à chaque définition.

MODÈLE pour voter, il faut vous y inscrire
→ la liste électorale

1. pour voter, il faut vous y inscrire
2. un endroit où on stocke et distribue les aliments aux personnes qui en ont besoin
3. un arrêt de travail pour protester
4. une personne qui est née dans un pays et qui y a le droit de voter
5. la période du temps pendant laquelle un élu garde son poste
6. une personne qui fait don de ses services pour aider les gens ou les animaux
7. le papier sur lequel on marque son vote
8. une démonstration collective organisée pour exprimer une opinion

a. une manifestation
b. la liste électorale
c. un bulletin de vote
d. une banque alimentaire
e. un/e bénévole
f. un citoyen/une citoyenne
g. une grève
h. un mandat

Implementation: 10-24 This activity can be used while presenting the vocabulary in the **Points de départ** and **Vie et culture** or as the first quick exercise.

10-25 Vous êtes engagé/e ? En groupes de trois ou quatre, parlez de votre niveau d'engagement dans la vie politique et dans la vie de votre communauté en comparant vos réponses aux questions suivantes.

MODÈLE Est-ce que vous avez déjà voté ? Quand ? Où ? Pour quelles élections ?

É1 Moi, j'ai voté pour la première fois dans les élections présidentielles de 2008. Je me suis inscrite sur la liste électorale quand j'ai eu 18 ans. Et toi ?

É2 Je n'ai jamais voté. Je n'avais pas 18 ans pendant les dernières élections présidentielles, et les élections locales ne m'intéressent pas.

É3 C'est dommage que tu ne participes pas aux élections municipales. Je trouve que la politique locale est très importante pour notre qualité de vie. Moi, je vote toujours.

1. Est-ce que vous avez déjà voté ? Quand ? Où ? Pour quelles élections ?
2. Est-ce que vous vous êtes présenté/e comme candidat/e pour des élections (peut-être comme délégué/e de classe, par exemple) ? Lesquelles ? Est-ce que vous avez gagné ?
3. Est-ce que vous avez travaillé dans une campagne électorale ? Pour qui ? Quand ? Est-ce que votre candidat a gagné ?
4. Est-ce que vous avez participé ou assisté à une manifestation ? Pour quelle cause ? Quand ?
5. Quelles sont vos expériences avec le bénévolat ? Est-ce que vous avez été obligé/e de faire du bénévolat quand vous étiez au collège ou au lycée ? Si oui, est-ce que cette expérience a été positive ou négative ?

Variation: 10-25 Assign one or two questions to each group of students and have them share information during an all-class follow-up.

Note: The expression *C'est dommage que...* is formally introduced in the **Formes et fonctions** of this lesson.

Implementation: 10-26 Demonstrate the rhythmic chanting typical of slogans:

À bas les grosses voitures !

. . . .

where each bullet represents a syllable and the double bullet the final stressed syllable. Treat this exercise as a contest. The group that comes up with the best slogan for each item might be given some prize or recognition. You might ask students to create posters and post them on campus or on a Web site.

10-26 Posters et slogans. Imaginez que vous préparez un poster ou un slogan pour une manifestation sur le campus. Les posters et les slogans prennent souvent la forme d'une phrase impérative ou alors ils contiennent les expressions **À bas**... (*Down with* . . .), **Plus de**... (*No more* . . .), **Vive**..., **Non à**... . Organisez-vous en groupes de trois ou quatre et trouvez des slogans intéressants pour protester contre les situations indiquées ou pour encourager les gens à changer leur comportement.

MODÈLES l'utilisation des transports en commun

- Vive le tramway et le métro !
- Oui au covoiturage !
- À bas les grosses voitures !

1. la construction de nouvelles résidences avec l'énergie solaire
2. la réduction de nombre de postes de professeurs dans votre université
3. le développement d'un programme de recyclage sur le campus
4. le gaspillage de papier
5. l'augmentation des frais de scolarité dans votre université
6. le remplacement des cours avec des profs par des cours en ligne
7. les semestres plus longs et les vacances plus courtes

FORMES ET FONCTIONS

1. *Le subjonctif avec les expressions d'émotion*

Presentation: Many of these expressions were introduced in Ch. 7, L. 3 and Ch. 8, L. 3. You may wish to review them with an activity from that lesson before presenting their use in the subjunctive. Provide examples as in the text and have students analyze. Let students create additional examples using the expressions in the list.

- When the main clause of a sentence expresses an emotion, such as anger, fear, joy, or sadness, the verb of the subordinate clause is always in the subjunctive.

Je regrette que vous **partiez** si tôt.	*I'm sorry (that) you're leaving so soon.*
Elle est contente que tu **viennes** avec nous.	*She's happy (that) you're coming with us.*

Here are some verbs and expressions that convey emotion and are followed by the subjunctive:

avoir peur	être fâché/e	être triste
être content/e	être furieux/-euse	Il est/C'est dommage que
être déçu/e	être heureux/-euse	Il est/C'est étonnant que
être désolé/e	être inquiet/inquiète	Il est/C'est malheureux que
être enchanté/e	être ravi/e	regretter
être étonné/e	être surpris/e	

- When the subject is the same for both parts of a sentence, use an infinitive construction preceded by **de** instead of the subjunctive. Compare the following examples.

Elle est contente **de voter** dans ces élections.	*She's happy to vote in these elections.*
Elle est contente **que vous votiez** dans votre première élection présidentielle.	*She's happy (that) you are voting in your first presidential election.*
Je regrette **de ne pas pouvoir** participer.	*I'm sorry to not be able to participate.*
Je regrette **que tu ne puisses pas** participer.	*I'm sorry (that) you will not be able to participate.*

À vous la parole

10-27 Votre réaction. Exprimez votre réaction face à ces situations.

MODÈLES Souvent, les jeunes ne votent pas en grand nombre.
Je suis déçue que les jeunes ne votent pas en grand nombre.

Vous travaillez comme bénévole pour une campagne électorale.
Je suis ravi de travailler comme bénévole pour une campagne électorale.

1. Vous faites du bénévolat.
2. Vos voisins sont très engagés dans la politique locale.
3. Vous n'avez pas le temps d'aider votre association humanitaire préférée ce semestre.
4. Vos parents font beaucoup d'éco-gestes.
5. Vos amis ne participent jamais aux manifestations sur le campus.
6. Votre ami/e se présente aux élections comme délégué/e de classe.
7. Votre voisin/e n'est pas inscrit/e sur la liste électorale.

Implementation: 10-27 Display the list of expressions of emotion requiring the subjunctive to provide students with ideas for the exercise. To expand, elicit multiple reactions to each statement. For the model sentences, have students identify which was spoken by a man and which by a woman.

10-28 Que d'émotions ! Avec un/e partenaire, réagissez à ces annonces de votre professeur. Comparez vos réactions avec les réactions de vos camarades de classe.

MODÈLES Il n'y a pas de devoirs ce soir.
É1 Je suis surpris qu'il n'y ait pas de devoirs.
É2 Je suis contente qu'il n'y ait pas de devoirs.

Vous aurez un examen vendredi.
É1 C'est dommage qu'on ait un examen vendredi.
É2 Oui, je suis étonnée d'avoir un autre examen.

1. Il n'y aura pas cours demain.
2. Tout le monde ira au restaurant ensemble ce week-end.
3. Je vous achèterai un souvenir en France cet été.
4. Vous n'aurez pas d'examen final.
5. Les résultats du dernier examen sont excellents.
6. Vous faites beaucoup de progrès en français.

Implementation: 10-28 Have students identify which student in the model is a male and which a female. Follow up by calling on groups at random to give their reactions.

Implementation: 10-29 Model a few items with the class as a whole before having students work in groups. Remind students that when there is only one subject, they need to use *de* plus an infinitive. You may wish to review the appropriate expressions to use for each answer (for example, *je suis triste que…, j'ai peur que…, je regrette que…*).

10-29 On va tout savoir. Comparez vos réponses avec celles de vos camarades de classe.

MODÈLE Nommez une chose qui vous rend heureux/-euse.

É1 Je suis heureuse que ma petite sœur vienne me voir ce week-end. Et toi ?

É2 Je suis heureux que mon cours de biologie finisse la semaine prochaine. Et toi ?

É3 Je suis heureux d'avoir une bonne note pour l'examen de français !

1. Nommez une chose qui vous rend heureux/-euse.
2. Nommez une chose qui vous inquiète.
3. Nommez une chose qui vous surprend.
4. Nommez une chose qui vous rend triste.
5. Nommez une chose que vous regrettez.
6. Nommez une chose qui vous fait peur.
7. Nommez une chose qui vous fâche.

2. *Le subjonctif avec les expressions de doute*

Fiche pratique

One way to be sure that you have learned something well is to teach it to someone else. Try to explain the various uses of the subjunctive and the rules for its formation to a classmate or roommate. If you have trouble explaining certain aspects, go back to the textbook and look over the explanations and examples until you can explain it clearly.

Note: Use of the subjunctive with the verbs *penser, estimer, trouver,* and *être sûr/e* when these verbs are used in the interrogative or negative is optional, based on style or the speaker's attitude. We advocate a pedagogical norm of always using the subjunctive in this instance to make it simpler for the learner. Point out that the verb *estimer* and the expression *il est clair que* are never used in the negative.

- As you've learned, the subjunctive is used in the subordinate clause of a sentence after expressions of obligation, emotion, and desire. It is also used in the subordinate clause when the main verb expresses doubt or uncertainty. The verb most often used to indicate doubt is **douter**:

Je doute que ce candidat **ait** une solution réaliste à ce problème.	*I doubt that this candidate has a realistic solution for this problem.*

- Doubt can also be expressed by verbs of opinion, such as **croire, penser, estimer, trouver, être sûr/e,** and impersonal expressions, such as **il est évident, il est sûr, il est vrai,** when they are used in questions or negative statements. These expressions of doubt are followed by the subjunctive in the subordinate clause.

Est-ce que vous pensez toujours qu'il **puisse** gagner cette élection ?	*Do you still think he can win this election?*
Je ne pense pas que ce **soit** possible.	*I don't think that's possible.*
Est-ce que vous trouvez que le problème du réchauffement climatique **soit** une priorité ?	*Do you believe that the problem of global warming is a priority?*
On n'est pas sûrs que ce **soit** la meilleure solution.	*We are not sure that this is the best solution.*
Il n'est pas évident que les gens **soient** prêts à changer leurs	*It is not obvious that people are ready to change their habits.*

- To indicate certainty or to express an opinion, use the indicative with verbs like **penser, croire, trouver, estimer, être sûr/e** and impersonal expressions such as **il est clair que, il est évident que, il est vrai que, il est sûr que**.

Il est vrai que nous **devons** changer nos habitudes pour résoudre ce problème.	*It is true (that) we must change our habits to resolve this problem.*
Je pense que vous **avez** raison.	*I think (that) you are right.*

À vous la parole

10-30 Débat politique. Imaginez un débat entre deux candidats qui ne sont pas d'accord ; répondez donc avec une phrase qui dit le contraire.

MODÈLE Je pense que c'est une bonne solution sur le plan économique.
Je ne pense pas que ce soit une bonne solution sur le plan économique.

1. Je trouve que nous pouvons réduire le nombre de voitures en ville.
2. Je suis sûr que nous trouverons une solution.
3. Je pense que la parité politique est une bonne idée.
4. Il est évident que les individus sont prêts à modifier leurs comportements.
5. Je suis sûre que le gouvernement peut établir un règlement efficace.
6. Il est évident qu'on doit interdire la circulation des voitures en centre-ville.
7. Nous devons réduire le budget pour résoudre la crise économique.

Initial practice: Review the forms of the subjunctive with simple substitution drills using the *tu* and *vous* forms before completing these exercises. *Il faut venir. —Il faut que tu viennes ; Il est important de dormir. Il faut être à l'heure. Il faut prendre le tram. Il est urgent de partir ; etc. Il faut boire plus d'eau. —Il faut que vous buviez plus d'eau ; Il est important de faire un effort. Il faut prendre votre temps. Il faut manger des fruits,* etc.

10-31 Interview. Imaginez que vous interviewez un/e candidat/e, et posez-lui des questions d'après vos notes. Avec un/e partenaire, jouez les rôles du journaliste et du candidat.

MODÈLE É1 Madame, est-ce que vous pensez que le rôle de la femme dans la politique soit plus important aujourd'hui que dans le passé?
É2 Mais oui, il est évident que le rôle de la femme dans la politique est plus important aujourd'hui.
OU É2 Non, je ne pense pas que le rôle de la femme dans la politique soit plus important aujourd'hui que dans le passé. Elles ont toujours joué un rôle important.

1. Le rôle de la femme dans la politique est plus important aujourd'hui que dans le passé ?
2. L'environnement est une question de première importance ?
3. Le gouvernement peut résoudre tous les problèmes sociaux ?
4. Les soins médicaux doivent être gratuits pour tout le monde ?
5. Les entreprises sont responsables pour le nettoyage des rivières ?
6. Les différences entre les pays pauvres et les pays riches grandissent ?
7. La biogénétique peut réduire la faim dans le monde ?

Implementation: 10-31 Encourage students to use a variety of expressions of doubt by brainstorming all the possibilities with them or by posting a list of expressions before beginning.

Implementation: 10-32 Divide students up into groups of three to four to discuss these topics. Follow up by comparing the answers of the various groups and then asking the class which problem they consider to be the single most important problem in the world today. Alternatively, provide students with (or ask them for) problems that have local relevance, on campus or in the city or state where they live.

10-32 Le plus grand problème. Quel est, pour vous, le plus grand problème dans les domaines suivants ? Comparez votre opinion avec celle de vos camarades de classe.

MODÈLE l'environnement

É1 Je pense que le plus gros problème, c'est le réchauffement climatique. Si les glaciers fondent, le niveau de la mer va augmenter et nous aurons plus d'inondations. En fait, certains pays peuvent disparaître.

É2 Tout à fait d'accord. Mais je ne suis pas très optimiste. Je ne pense pas que les gens soient prêts à changer leurs mauvaises habitudes.

É3 Il est évident que le gouvernement doit prendre des mesures pour réduire les émissions de gaz à effet de serre.

1. l'environnement
2. la situation économique
3. l'aide aux personnes en difficulté
4. la situation politique

Parlons

Implementation: 10-33 This exercise guides students in preparing a discussion which will involve the whole class. Split the class in half, being careful to include a few strong students in each group, and work with students to select the group leader and recorder. During the preparation phase, students should work together to prepare notes and to organize an outline of their presentation. Remind students that they need to argue the point of view that they have received, even if they do not necessarily agree with it, and that they must listen carefully to what the other side has to say in order to understand and evaluate the other team's arguments. A few topics are suggested below; you may also wish to create your own to reflect local or national current events and/or relevant campus issues.

Selected topics:

Le campus doit faire plus pour réduire son empreinte écologique.
Les étudiants ne devraient pas avoir le droit de venir sur le campus en voiture.
Il ne faut plus donner le droit de vote aux jeunes de 18 ans ; 21 ans est plus raisonnable.
Chaque étudiant devrait être obligé/e de faire 20 heures de bénévolat par semestre avant de recevoir son diplôme.
Il faut interdire l'utilisation de toutes les voitures fabriquées avant 1985.

10-33 Les opinions sont partagées

Est-ce que vous avez déjà participé à un débat ? Il faut donner des arguments pour ou contre une affirmation. Le professeur va vous diviser en deux groupes, donner à chaque groupe une affirmation et vous dire si vous êtes « pour » ou « contre ».

A. Avant de parler. Dans vos groupes, élisez une personne pour être le responsable du groupe et une personne pour être secrétaire et prendre des notes. Le responsable lira votre affirmation et votre position « pour » ou « contre ». Ensuite, tous les membres du groupe travailleront ensemble pour trouver tous les arguments possibles pour soutenir votre position. Faites une liste de ces arguments et décidez ensemble de l'ordre de vos arguments.

MODÈLE Affirmation : Il faut interdire l'utilisation des voitures sur le campus. POUR

- il y a trop de circulation sur le campus
- le campus est dangereux pour les piétons (*pedestrians*)
- il faut un campus avec moins de pollution et plus d'espaces verts
- ...

B. En parlant. Après dix minutes de préparation, les membres de chaque équipe donnent leurs arguments devant la classe.

MODÈLE Nous estimons qu'il faut interdire l'utilisation des voitures sur le campus parce que le campus est devenu dangereux pour les étudiants qui essayent d'aller à leurs cours à pied. Nous avons peur qu'un accident sérieux ait lieu un de ces jours...

C. Après avoir parlé. Après avoir entendu tous les arguments, le professeur et la classe décident quel groupe avait les meilleurs arguments et les a présentés de la manière la plus convaincante.

Presentation: Use the video montage (*L'écologie*) to provide an overview for this lesson; have students describe the forms of pollution and the remedies they see.

Note: The Environmental Performance Index is a tool developed by researchers at Yale and Columbia to evaluate sanitation, greenhouse gas emissions, agricultural policies, air pollution, and 20 other measures in countries worldwide. According to the 2008 report, Switzerland is the most greenhouse gas efficient economy in the developed world, largely due to its use of hydroelectric power and its system of mass transit.

Venez chez nous ! L'écologie

Dans le monde entier, des gens font des efforts pour protéger l'environnement, pour sauver les écosystèmes et les animaux menacés et pour lutter contre le réchauffement climatique. Par exemple, en Suisse, des initiatives ont été prises pour réduire la pollution atmosphérique et pour encourager les gens à utiliser les transports en commun au lieu de la voiture individuelle. Ces efforts ont porté leur fruit, et selon l'Indice de performance environnementale, la Suisse a été classée en janvier 2008 comme le premier pays du monde. En Afrique, au Sénégal et en Côte d'Ivoire, il y a de nombreux parcs naturels pour la protection des animaux sauvages. Ces parcs servent aussi de centres de recherche pour l'histoire naturelle et la conservation de la nature. Voici donc des exemples, dans le monde francophone, de réponses face aux problèmes écologiques actuels.

Ce Québécois écolo fait pousser des légumes dans un jardin sur le toit de son immeuble à Montréal.

Note: Additional interviews are treated in the SAM/MFL.

Observons

10-34 L'environnement et nous

A. Avant de regarder. Vous allez entendre deux personnes parler de l'environnement.

1. Fabienne travaille dans une grande ville, mais elle habite à la campagne. Pourquoi, à votre avis, est-ce qu'elle a pris cette décision ?
2. Jean-Claude est de Madagascar. Il trouve que c'est dommage que les habitants de cette île détruisent le paysage. Pourquoi est-ce qu'ils font cela, à votre avis ?
3. Maintenant écoutez et regardez pour trouver les réponses.

Key: En regardant 1. b, 2. a, 3. c, 4. b, 5. b, 6. c, 7.a, b

B. En regardant. Entourez toutes les bonnes réponses.

1. Fabienne dit…
   a. qu'elle a trouvé la bonne solution contre la pollution.
   b. qu'elle n'a pas de leçon à donner.
   c. que c'est le gouvernement qui devrait s'occuper du problème.
2. Elle habite à la campagne parce qu'elle…
   a. adore la nature. b. déteste la ville. c. a des animaux.
3. Elle trouve qu'en ville, il y a trop de…
   a. circulation. b. gens. c. bruit.

Script: Observons Note that the elements in brackets reflect standard usage and have been added to the written transcripts. They were not pronounced by the speaker(s) in question.

FABIENNE : Je crois que l'environnement aujourd'hui nous concerne tous. Je n'ai pas de… leçon à donner à qui que ce soit. J'ai euh… j'habite, moi, en ce qui me concerne, à la campagne. J'adore la nature et… je n'échangerais jamais ma vie à la campagne pour une vie en ville. Je crois qu'on travaille toute la semaine dans un milieu très pollué où nous avons beaucoup de nuisances sonores et j'ai besoin de me retrouver. Je suis vraiment très* ravie d'être à l'extérieur malgré un petit peu la distance. Et je crois que aujourd'hui il est temps que nous nous mobilisions tous pour étudier un petit peu tout ce qui se passe et que nous soyons euh plus ouverts à tous les aspects de l'environnement.

JEAN-CLAUDE : Je suis né au nord… au nord de, de Madagascar, ça s'appelle Diégo-Suarez. C'est une île qui… qui est magnifique. Il y a une faune, une flore, qui euh qui qui qui est grandiose. Et c'est dommage que le pays est [soit] euh est détruit par les, les habitants qui habitent là-bas, parce que bon, ils ont pas de… de… beaucoup d'argent à [pour] subvenir à leurs besoins et tout ça, ainsi de suite, ils sont en train de saccager la… la faune.

*Note that *très* is not usually used with the adjective *ravi/e*.

4. Le seul inconvénient d'habiter la campagne, c'est...
   a. le manque d'activités. **b.** la distance. **c.** la solitude.

5. Jean-Claude est né à Madagascar. Il dit que c'est...
   a. une grande ville.
   b. une île magnifique.
   c. une région montagneuse.

6. Selon lui, il faut surtout protéger...
   a. l'eau des rivières.
   b. la terre.
   c. les plantes et les animaux.

7. Les habitants détruisent leur environnement pour avoir...
   a. de l'argent. **b.** des maisons. **c.** des usines.

C. Après avoir regardé. Est-ce que les problèmes mentionnés par Fabienne et Jean-Claude sont les mêmes problèmes écologiques que chez vous ? Dans quelles autres régions du monde est-ce que ces problèmes existent ? Quelles sont les solutions possibles à ces problèmes ?

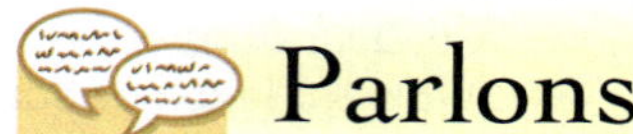

Parlons

10-35 Quelques problèmes écologiques et des solutions

Implementation: 10-35 You may wish to develop this **Parlons** activity into a more formal oral presentation project, either in small groups or as individuals. This topic lends itself easily to research on the Web and would be ideal as the subject of an *exposé oral.* Encourage students to visit the *Chez nous* Companion Website for links to Francophone sites dealing with ecological problems and solutions. You might also suggest that students consult magazines or publications such as *National Geographic, Sierra Magazine, Natural History, Smithsonian* in English or *Géo, Terre Sauvage, Sciences et Nature,* or the French version of *National Geographic* for pictures.

A. Avant de parler. Dans la Leçon 2 et dans *Venez chez nous !*, il y a quelques photos de problèmes écologiques et/ou de leurs solutions possibles. En groupes de deux ou trois, choisissez une de ces photos ou trouvez une autre photo qui illustre un problème écologique ou une solution dans le monde francophone.

B. En parlant. Identifiez et décrivez le/s problème/s représenté/s sur votre image. Ensuite proposez quelques solutions possibles. Enfin, considérez d'une façon critique vos solutions : ont-elles une portée (*reach*) universelle ou sont-elles plutôt limitées à une certaine région ou à un certain pays ? Expliquez pourquoi.

MODÈLE Cette photo montre une réserve naturelle à Madagascar. Ces réserves offrent une solution au problème de la déforestation. À Madagascar, on perd une partie des forêts tous les ans. Cette destruction cause des problèmes d'érosion mais aussi la disparition de plusieurs types d'animaux et de plantes. Le gouvernement et des organismes internationaux ont créé un certain nombre de réserves naturelles qui sont protégées. Ces réserves sont importantes pour sauvegarder les plantes et les animaux locaux. Nous pensons que c'est une bonne solution qui peut s'appliquer à d'autres pays. Mais, dans certains pays où il n'y a pas assez de terre pour toute la population, cette solution peut être difficile.

La déforestation à Madagascar.

Une chercheuse malgache étudie les lémurs dans une réserve naturelle à Madagascar.

C. Après avoir parlé. Maintenant, partagez votre image et vos solutions avec vos camarades de classe. Quel groupe a le problème le plus difficile à résoudre ? Quel groupe a trouvé la meilleure solution à son problème ?

Lisons

TEXT AUDIO CD 5 TRACK 31

10-36 L'arbre nourricier

A. Avant de lire. Dans les contes folkloriques, les animaux peuvent parler et ressemblent beaucoup aux êtres humains. Ce conte présente deux personnages bien connus dans le folklore de l'Afrique et des Caraïbes, Oncle lièvre (*hare*) et Oncle hyène. Oncle hyène n'est pas très intelligent et il est goulu (*gluttonous*) ; Oncle lièvre par contre représente l'intelligence. La cupidité (*greed*) d'Oncle hyène le rend vulnérable aux ruses d'Oncle lièvre, et cela mène à sa fin. Est-ce que ces personnages vous font penser à d'autres personnages de contes folkloriques que vous connaissez ?

Stratégie

Use your familiarity with the folktale genre to understand the style and purpose of folktales from another culture. For example, do you know any tales in your own language in which animals are the main characters? How are the animals presented and what role do they have?

Presentation: Avant de lire Lead students to draw the parallel between the purpose and literary style of this African folktale and the fables of Aesop (*Ésope* in French) and La Fontaine. Ask them to provide examples: *The Tortoise and the Hare*, *The Fox and the Crow*, etc. Students may also be familiar with the *Uncle Remus Stories*, which feature animal characters, including Brer (*Brother*) Rabbit who regularly outwits Brer (*Brother*) Bear. See whether students can re-tell the story of the goose that laid the golden eggs, since its moral is similar to that of the tale recounted here. Refer students to the *Chez nous* Companion Website for more information about the Soninke people and their oral literary culture as well as for other examples of African folktales translated into French.

L'adaptation de ce conte du peuple soninké au Sénégal s'adresse au problème de la déforestation dans la région aride du Sahel, entre le désert du Sahara et les forêts équatoriales. Dans la tradition soninké, ce sont les personnes plus âgées qui racontent les contes aux jeunes, surtout à la tombée de la nuit. Ces contes sont souvent interactifs ; il faut que le public réponde aux questions rituelles d'une façon bien déterminée. Voici la raison pour laquelle ce conte commence avec le conteur qui dit « **Xay** » (prononcé comme le mot *Hi* en anglais) ; le public répond « **Xay** » et le conteur commence à raconter son histoire.

Note: Point out that the term *oncle* is always used before the name of the animal characters as a way of teaching the young listeners that as a sign of respect they should never directly address their elders by their names.

Key: En lisant 1a) Oncle Hyène ne trouve rien ; Oncle Lièvre trouve l'arbre nourricier. b) ses feuilles, son écorce, sa sève (*sap*) c) c'est le mot magique qui fait ouvrir l'arbre 2a) Que ton ombre est bonne ! b) Il décide de prendre l'arbre avec lui jusqu'à son village. 3a) Il a besoin de leur aide parce qu'il ne peut pas faire descendre l'arbre de sa tête. b) Il est écrasé par le poids de l'arbre et il meurt. c) L'arbre retourne à la forêt.

B. En lisant. Cherchez les réponses aux questions suivantes.

1. Dans la première partie du conte :
   a. Oncle Hyène et Oncle Lièvre vont chercher de la nourriture pour leurs familles : qu'est-ce qu'ils trouvent ?
   b. À quelles parties de l'arbre est-ce qu'Oncle Lièvre goûte ?
   c. Quelle est l'importance du mot magique « dunwari » ?
2. Dans la deuxième partie du conte :
   a. Qu'est-ce qu'Oncle Hyène doit dire quand il arrive sous l'arbre ?
   b. Qu'est-ce qu'Oncle Hyène décide de faire avec l'arbre ?
3. Dans la troisième partie du conte :
   a. Pourquoi est-ce qu'Oncle Hyène appelle sa famille et puis la moitié du village ?
   b. Comment est-ce qu'Oncle Hyène meurt ?
   c. Qu'est-ce qui se passe avec l'arbre ?

C. En regardant de plus près. Maintenant, examinez les aspects suivants du texte.

1. En étudiant le contexte, expliquez le sens des expressions suivantes :
   a. il a mangé à sa faim
   b. mettre un coussinet sur sa tête
   c. cet arbre merveilleux
2. Vous connaissez sans doute le premier mot dans chaque paire de mots apparentés ci-dessous. Quel est le sens du deuxième mot dans chaque cas ?
   a. porter / un porteur
   b. appeler / un appel
   c. parler / la parole

Key: Après avoir lu 1) la question du conteur au début et la réponse du public, la répétition, et la dernière phrase où on voit de nouveau la présence du conteur 2) Les animaux représentent des personnages typiques, le lièvre intelligent, l'hyène avare, et en même temps évoquent la nature humaine et ses faiblesses. 3) On doit faire attention à conserver les ressources naturelles, sinon, on participe à leur — et à notre — destruction.

D. Après avoir lu. Discutez des questions suivantes avec vos camarades de classe.

1. Un conte, c'est surtout un texte oral ; il faut l'écouter. Quelles caractéristiques d'un texte oral est-ce que vous remarquez dans ce conte ?
2. Quel est le rôle des animaux dans ce conte ? Pourquoi, à votre avis, est-ce que le narrateur a choisi ces animaux comme personnages principaux ?
3. Quelle est la morale du conte ?
4. Comparez le message écologique donné dans ce conte avec celui de la liste de recommandations que vous trouvez dans la Leçon 2. Quel message est le plus efficace ? Pourquoi, à votre avis ?

L'arbre nourricier

Dites-moi « xay » !

–Xay !

Il y avait la famine au village. Oncle Hyène et Oncle Lièvre ont décidé d'aller chercher de la nourriture pour leurs familles. Oncle Hyène est parti mais n'a rien trouvé. Oncle Lièvre s'est mis aussi en route[1]. Après avoir marché longtemps il a rencontré un arbre. Il s'est arrêté sous son ombre[2] et a dit :

–Arbre, que ton ombre est fraîche !

–Tu as goûté mon ombre mais tu n'as pas goûté mes feuilles[3].

Alors Lièvre a pris plusieurs feuilles et les a goûtées.

–Arbre, que tes feuilles sont bonnes !

–Tu as goûté mes feuilles mais tu n'as pas encoure goûté mon écorce[4].

Lièvre a pris un bout d'écorce et l'a mis dans sa bouche. Il a dit :

–Arbre, que ton écorce est bonne !

–Tu as goûté mon écorce mais tu n'as pas goûté ce qu'il y a dans mon ventre.

–Comment faire pour en avoir ?

–Si tu dis « dunwari », je m'ouvrirai.

Lièvre a dit « dunwari » et l'arbre s'est ouvert. Il y est entré et a mangé à sa faim. Quand il avait assez mangé, il a pris de la nourriture pour sa famille.

De retour au village, Oncle Lièvre a dit à Oncle Hyène qu'il avait rencontré un arbre, qu'il avait mangé à sa faim et qu'il avait rapporté de la nourriture à sa famille. Oncle Hyène lui a dit :

–Montre-moi où tu as trouvé cet arbre merveilleux. J'irai à mon tour demain matin. Quand j'aurai mangé à ma faim, je rapporterai de la nourriture à ma famille.

–D'accord, lui a répondu Lièvre, demain matin je te montrerai cet arbre.

Il se sont mis en route le lendemain[5], et Lièvre a indiqué le chemin à Hyène :

–Tu marcheras, marcheras jusqu'à cet arbre là-bas. Tu t'arrêteras dessous et tu diras « que ton ombre est bonne ! »

Hyène est allé jusqu'à l'arbre, et il lui a dit :

–Arbre, que ton ombre est bonne !

–Tu as goûté mon ombre mais tu n'as pas goûté mes feuilles.

Hyène a pris plusieurs feuilles et les a goûtées.

–Arbre, que tes feuilles sont bonnes !

–Tu as goûté mes feuilles mais tu n'as pas goûté mon écorce.

Hyène a pris un bout d'écorce et l'a mis dans sa bouche. Il a dit :

–Que ton écorce est bonne !

–Tu as goûté mon écorce mais tu n'as pas goûté ce qu'il y a dans mon ventre.

–Comment faire pour en avoir ?

–Si tu dis « dunwari », je m'ouvrirai.

Hyène a dit « dunwari » et l'arbre s'est ouvert. Il y est entré et a mangé à sa faim. Quand il avait assez mangé, il a pris de la nourriture pour sa famille.

Oncle Hyène s'est dit alors : « Ah ! Si j'avais quelqu'un pour m'aider je rapporterais cet arbre au village. » L'arbre lui a répondu :

–Tu n'as pas besoin de porteurs, je peux t'aider moi-même. Mets ton coussinet[6] sur la tête.

Hyène a mis son coussinet sur la tête, puis a porté l'arbre sur sa tête, et l'a emporté au village. Arrivé là, il a appelé :

–Venez vite ! J'ai rapporté quelque chose de la forêt ! Venez m'aider à déposer ce lourd fardeau[7] !

Sa femme et ses enfants sont venus mais n'ont pas réussi à déposer l'arbre.

–Eh bien ! Appelez la moitié du village !

La moitié du village est venue mais sans résultat.

–Alors, appelez tout le village !

Le village entier est venu mais sans succès.

Écrasé[8] sous le poids[9] de l'arbre, Hyène est mort. Alors l'arbre est parti et est retourné à sa place dans la forêt. Je remets le conte là où je l'ai trouvé.

[1]est parti [2]*shade* [3]*leaves* [3]*bark* [5]le jour suivant [6]*small cushion* [7]*burden* [8]*crushed* [9]*weight*

Écrivons

Stratégie

To write persuasively—to inspire people to take action for the public good, for example—it is very effective to come up with an attention-getting slogan. Use the slogan to attract attention, then present your message.

Note: Avant d'écrire Help students figure out the meaning of *le tri* based on the verb *trier*.

Implementation: En écrivant Students can work on this writing project with a partner or in small groups. Encourage them to think up creative solutions to the problems they identify.

10-37 Une brochure

A. Avant d'écrire. Le gouvernement québécois publie souvent des brochures qui contiennent des conseils pour préserver l'environnement. Imaginez que vous faites partie d'une équipe qui doit préparer une de ces brochures. Voici quelques sujets possibles :

1. l'utilisation des transports en commun
2. le tri et le recyclage des déchets
3. la conservation des ressources énergétiques
4. la conservation des forêts et des rivières
5. la consommation des produits locaux

D'abord, choisissez votre sujet et trouvez un slogan qui va attirer l'attention du lecteur. Ensuite, notez deux ou trois aspects du problème et deux ou trois solutions possibles.

B. En écrivant. Maintenant, rédigez votre brochure.

1. Utilisez les notes que vous avez préparées et incorporez votre slogan.
2. Pensez à la présentation de votre brochure : des couleurs, des graphiques, des illustrations, etc.

MODÈLE

Réduire pour un Québec plus propre !

Savez-vous que les Québécois produisent assez de déchets pour remplir 5 millions de sacs poubelles chaque jour ?

Recyclons ensemble pour une meilleure qualité de vie au Québec !

Il faut réduire nos déchets !

Pensez à recycler le papier, le plastique, le verre, le carton et les boîtes de conserve.

C. En révisant. Réfléchissez aux questions suivantes et puis faites tous les changements nécessaires.

1. Relisez votre brochure pour analyser le contenu : est-ce que vous avez bien placé votre slogan ? Est-ce que vous avez inclus des statistiques et une brève description des problèmes et des solutions possibles ?
2. Relisez de nouveau votre brochure pour analyser le style et la forme : est-ce que votre brochure va attirer l'attention des gens ? Est-ce que vous avez inclus de la couleur, des dessins ou des illustrations pour la rendre plus attirante ? Est-ce que vous avez utilisé des phrases à l'impératif ou au subjonctif, et est-ce que ces phrases sont bien formées ?

D. Après avoir écrit. Imprimez votre brochure et distribuez-la à vos camarades de classe. Qui a la brochure avec le meilleur slogan ? Quelle brochure explique le mieux le/s problème/s ? Quelle brochure propose les solutions les plus innovatrices ? les mieux adaptées au problème ?

Now that you have completed *Chapitre 10*, can you do the following in French?

- ☐ discuss issues of physical and emotional well-being?
- ☐ give advice about improving one's health or environment?
- ☐ state opinions and express desires and emotions using the subjunctive when necessary?
- ☐ describe in simple terms the civic life of the French?
- ☐ describe environmental problems and potential solutions in the Francophone world and beyond?

Leçon 1

le corps humain	the human body
la bouche	*mouth*
le bras	*arm*
la cheville	*ankle*
le cœur	*heart*
le cou	*neck*
le coude	*elbow*
les doigts (m.)	*fingers*
le dos	*back*
l'épaule (f.)	*shoulder*
l'estomac (m.)	*stomach*
le genou	*knee*
la gorge	*throat*
la jambe	*leg*
la langue	*tongue*
les lèvres (f.)	*lips*
le nez	*nose*
l'œil (m.) (les yeux)	*eye (eyes)*
l'oreille (f.)	*ear*
le pied	*foot*
le poignet	*wrist*
la poitrine	*chest*
les poumons (m.)	*lungs*
la taille	*waist*
la tête	*head*
le ventre	*belly, abdomen*

des maux, un mal	ache/s and pain/s
avoir mal à (la tête)	*to hurt (to have a headache)*
avoir mal partout	*to hurt everywhere*
avoir mal au cœur	*to be nauseated*
avoir mal au ventre	*to have a stomachache*

pour parler des *handicaps	to talk about handicaps
le basket-fauteuil	*wheelchair basketball*
être *handicapé/e	*to be handicapped*
un fauteuil roulant	*a wheelchair*

pour rester en forme	to stay in shape
consulter le médecin	*to see a doctor*
essayer (de bien manger)	*to try (to eat well)*
faire de l'exercice	*to exercise*
faire de la musculation	*to do strength/resistance training/lift weights*
faire/suivre un régime	*to (be on a) diet*
un repas équilibré	*well-balanced meal*
réduire le stress	*to reduce stress*
la santé	*health*

choses à éviter pour rester en forme	things to avoid to stay in shape
l'alcool (m.)	*alcohol*
fumer	*to smoke*
grignoter	*to snack*
sauter (un repas)	*to skip (a meal)*

expressions de nécessité	expressions of necessity
Il est important que	*It is important that*
Il est nécessaire que	*It is necessary that*
Il est urgent que	*It is urgent that*
Il est utile que	*It is useful that*
Il faut que/Il ne faut pas que	*You must/must not*
Il vaut/vaudrait mieux que	*It is/would be better (best) that*

Leçon 2

bon pour l'environnement	good for the environment
une ampoule basse consommation	*energy-saving lightbulb*
couper l'eau du robinet	*to turn off the running water (from the faucet)*
le covoiturage	*carpooling*
un éco-geste	*ecological act or gesture*
économiser	*to save, economize*
l'énergie renouvelable (l'énergie solaire)	*renewable energy (solar power)*
éteindre (les lumières)	*to turn off (the lights)*
nettoyer (les rivières)	*to clean (the rivers)*
un panier	*basket*
protéger	*to protect*
le recyclage	*recycling*
recycler	*to recycle*
sauver, sauvegarder	*to protect*
les transports (m.) en commun	*public transportation*
trier	*to sort*
utiliser	*to use*

Vocabulaire

mauvais pour l'environnement	***bad for the environment***
le bruit	*noise*
le CO_2 (dioxyde de carbone)	*carbon dioxide*
la déchèterie	*waste collection center*
les déchets (m.) domestiques/industriels	*household/industrial waste, refuse*
la déforestation	*deforestation*
gaspiller	*to waste*
un gaz (à effet de serre)	*(greenhouse) gas*
le gaz (m.) carbonique	*carbon gas*
les gaz (m. pl.) d'échappement	*exhaust fumes*
l'huile (f.) usagée	*waste (used) oil*
laisser les lumières allumées	*to leave the lights on*
non biodégradable	*nonbiodegradable*
les ordures (f.)	*trash, waste*
polluer	*to pollute*
la pollution (atmosphérique/sonore)	*(air/noise) pollution*
le réchauffement climatique	*global warming*
un sac en plastique	*plastic sack/bag*
une usine	*factory*

des choses menacées par la pollution	***things threatened by pollution***
l'air (m.)	*air*
l'eau (f.) potable	*drinking water*
un écosystème	*ecosystem*
l'environnement (m.)	*environment*
un glacier	*glacier*
un ours blanc	*polar bear*
la planète	*planet*
une ressource naturelle	*natural resource*
la terre (la Terre)	*earth (the Earth)*

autres mots utiles	***other useful words***
un appareil électrique	*electrical appliance*
augmenter	*to increase*
brûler	*to burn*
consommer	*to consume*
se déplacer	*to get around, to travel*
une empreinte écologique	*ecological footprint*
un emballage	*packaging*
fondre	*to melt*
une inondation	*flood*
un moteur	*engine*
un ouragan	*hurricane*
une poubelle	*trash can*
une tornade	*tornado*
une vague	*(ocean) wave*

quelques verbes de volonté qui exigent le subjonctif (voir aussi à la page 396)	***some verbs of volition that require the subjunctive***
aimer mieux	*to prefer*
désirer	*to desire, to want*
exiger	*to require, to demand*
souhaiter	*to hope, to wish*

Leçon 3

pour s'engager	***to get involved***
un bulletin de vote	*ballot*
un bureau de vote	*polling station*
un/e candidat/e	*candidate*
un/e citoyen/-enne	*citizen*
élire	*to elect*
le gouvernement	*government*
s'inscrire sur la liste électorale	*to register to vote*
un mandat	*term (of office)*
voter	*to vote*

les manifestations (f.)	***protests***
une grève	*strike*
se mobiliser (contre)	*to organize (against)*
protester	*to protest*
une réduction	*reduction*

le bénévolat	***volunteering***
une association humanitaire	*humanitarian association*
une banque alimentaire	*food bank*
un/e bénévole	*volunteer*

quelques expressions d'émotion qui exigent le subjonctif (voir aussi à la page 404)	***some expressions of emotion that require the subjunctive***
avoir peur que	*to be afraid*
être déçu/e que	*to be disappointed*
être désolé/e que	*to be sorry*
Il est/C'est dommage que	*It's too bad, a shame*
être étonné/e que	*to be surprised*
Il est/C'est étonnant que	*It's surprising*

d'autres mots utiles	***other useful words***
douter	*to doubt*
estimer	*to consider, believe, judge*
résoudre	*to solve*
y compris	*including*

11 Quoi de neuf ? cinéma et médias

Steve Martin joue le rôle de l'Inspecteur Clouseau dans le film *La Panthère rose*, tourné à Paris.

Leçon 1 Le grand et le petit écran

Leçon 2 Êtes-vous branché ?

Leçon 3 On s'informe

Venez chez nous ! Le cinéma

After completing this chapter, you should be able to:

- Express opinions about the media
- Express hypothetical situations and possible results
- Describe simultaneous and sequential events in the past, present, and future
- Describe and narrate events in the past
- Discuss cinema, television, and computer use in the French-speaking world

Leçon 1 Le grand et le petit écran

POINTS DE DÉPART

Note: As you begin this lesson, ask students what they know about Francophone TV, film, and the press. The *Chez nous* Companion Website provides useful links to French television channels, periodicals, and online news media.

Qu'est-ce qu'il y a à la télé ?

Presentation: You may wish to teach this vocabulary over two days; if so, then present television vocabulary and the **Vie et culture** and complete Ex. 11-1 and 11-2 on day 1; continue with film vocabulary and the remaining exercises on day 2.

TF1

20.50
La main blanche
Série de suspense.
Épisode 3, Saison 1
Avec Ingrid Chauvin, Bruno Madinier, Frank Geney. 0h52mn

21.40
La main blanche
Série de suspense. 1h00mn

22.40
Grey's Anatomy
Série hospitalière.
Épisode 2, Saison 2
Donnant donnant.
Avec : Patrick Dempsey, Ellen Pompeo, Katherine Heigl, Justin Chambers. 0h52mn

France 2

20.50
Retrouver Sara
Téléfilm dramatique de Claude d'Anna. 2005.
Avec : Sophie de la Rochefoucauld, Maher Kamoun, Agathe Bouissières, Liliane Rovère. 1h30mn

22.20
FBI : portés disparus
Série policière
Épisode 5, Saison 5
Le mauvais exemple.
Avec : Anthony LaPaglia, Poppy Montgomery, Mark Pellegrino, Mireille Enos, Eric Close, Roselyn Sanchez, Enrique Murciano. 0h52mn

France 3

20.55
La santé polluée : vos questions, nos réponses
Magazine de la santé. Présenté par Marina Carrère d'Encausse, Michel Cymes, Jamy Gourmaud, Nicolas Angel. 2h00mn

23.00
Soir 3
Journal. Présenté par Marie Drucker. 0h25mn

M6

20.50
Armageddon
Film d'action de Michael Bay. 1998. États-Unis. VF. Avec Bruce Willis, Billy Bob Thornton, Liv Tyler, Ben Affleck, Will Patton, Steve Buscemi, William Fichtner. 2h40mn

23.30
Highlander Endgame
Film d'action de Douglas Aarniokoski. 2000. États-Unis. VF. Avec : Christophe Lambert, Adrian Paul, Bruce Payne, Lisa Barbuscia, Donnie Yen, Ian Paul Cassidy, Peter Wingfield. 1h45mn

CHRISTELLE : Qu'est-ce qu'il y a à la télé ce soir ?

THOMAS : Attends, je vais regarder le programme. ... Bon, sur TF1, il y a deux épisodes d'une série française. Sur France 2, il y a un téléfilm français à 8 h 50 et une série policière à 10 h 20. Sur France 3, il y a un magazine qui a l'air intéressant sur l'effet de la pollution sur la santé.

CHRISTELLE : Bof ! Il n'y pas d'autres films ? J'ai plutôt envie de voir un bon film ce soir.

THOMAS : Si, sur M6 il y a deux films américains, *Armageddon* à 8 h 50 et *Highlander Endgame* à 11 h 30. Lequel est-ce que tu préfères ?

CHRISTELLE : Tu rigoles ? Tu sais bien que je n'aime pas les films d'action. Et en plus, tous les films américains qui passent sur M6 sont doublés. J'aime pas ça ; je préfère les regarder en V.O. pour pratiquer mon anglais.

THOMAS : Pas moi. J'ai horreur des sous-titres. Alors, si on regardait le téléfilm sur France 2 ? C'est un film français. Tu peux allumer la télé ?

CHRISTELLE : Mais, c'est toi qui as la télécommande !

Presentation: Treat the TV listings first as a reading. As an overview, have students describe TV listings and programming in general: typical format, types of programs shown at particular times of the day, etc. Note: the use of the 24-hour clock; that programs do not always begin on the hour or half-hour; general programming tendencies. Selected listings are provided. You can easily obtain current TV listings on the Web; consult the *Chez nous* Companion Website for helpful links. You may want to display a current listing as you present this vocabulary. Show the dialogue as students listen. Have students match information in the dialogue to information in the listings provided. Use the dialogue as a model for the role-play activity in Ex. 11-2. Point out the expressions *Bof !* and *Tu rigoles ?* and help students figure out their meaning. A less familiar way of saying *Tu rigoles ?* would be *Tu plaisantes ?* Note also the *ne*-deletion characteristic of spoken French.

Presentation: The vocabulary allows students to name and describe types of programs, make choices or suggestions, and express an opinion about a program or programming in general. Describe the types of programs. To test comprehension, have students give examples of program types; these may be taken from the listings or given in English. Follow with simple repetition drills, using a specific example: *« Grey's Anatomy » c'est un documentaire ou une série ?* Let students make logical groupings of the programs: *pour s'informer, pour s'amuser,* etc.

Des genres d'émissions

un dessin animé	un film
un divertissement	un jeu télévisé
un documentaire	le journal télévisé (le JT), les informations (les infos)
une émission de musique	un magazine
une émission sportive	un reportage
une émission de téléachat	une série
une émission de téléréalité	
un feuilleton	

À vous la parole 

Implementation: 11-1 This exercise requires students to use contextual clues to identify program types. As an alternative, check online listings for French or French Canadian television programming and, based on the titles, have students identify the program types.

Key: 11-1 1) une émission de musique 2) un documentaire 3) le journal télévisé 4) un jeu télévisé 5) une série 6) une émission sportive 7) une émission de cuisine. Additionally, have students tell what kind of program they associate with specific people: *Michael Moore ? — un documentaire ; Charles Gibson ou Brian Williams ? — le journal télévisé*, etc. Ask students to generate examples on their own.

11-1 Quel genre d'émission ? Imaginez que vous lisez un magazine télé. Selon ces descriptions partielles, déterminez avec un/e partenaire le genre de chaque émission.

MODÈLE dernier épisode
É1 C'est peut-être une série.
É2 S'il y a des épisodes, c'est probablement un feuilleton.

1. avec notre invitée, la chanteuse…
2. l'astrologie face à la science
3. le journal de la semaine
4. à gagner cette semaine : un voyage à Tahiti
5. série américaine
6. Coupe de France. Quart de finale.
7. des recettes : ris de veau, fumet aux vieux cèpes, galette de pommes de terre

Variation: 11-2 Give students a specific time and have them choose a program from the listings. Consult the *Chez nous* Companion Website for links to sites with program guides.

11-2 Les émissions d'aujourd'hui. Qu'est-ce qu'on peut regarder aujourd'hui ? Avec un/e partenaire, jouez les rôles de deux amis. Consultez le magazine télé à la page suivante et discutez de vos choix.

MODÈLE É1 J'ai envie de regarder un documentaire.
É2 Si on regardait le documentaire sur France 2 ?

1. J'aime bien les films étrangers.
2. J'adore les séries américaines.
3. Il n'y a pas de magazine sur France 3 ce soir ?
4. Pourquoi pas un film ce soir ?
5. J'ai envie de regarder quelque chose de différent.
6. J'ai mal à la tête, alors rien de sérieux pour moi ce soir !
7. Il y a une série policière ce soir ?
8. J'aime bien les émissions de téléréalité.

TF1

14.55 Ma recette pour l'amour. Téléfilm américain d'Andy Wolk (2005). Avec Shiri Appleby. Avec Eyal Podell. **16.30** Méthode Zoé. Zoé voit rouge. **17.25** Ugly Betty. Amies amies ? **18.15** Secret Story. **19.05** Une famille en or. ■ **20.00** Journal.

20.50 Une famille formidable
Téléfilm français de Joël Santoni (2005). L'enfer au paradis. Avec Anny Duperey, Bernard Le Coq.

22.40 Grey's Anatomy
Série hospitalière. Code noir (Saison 2, 16/27). Avec Christina Ricci, Ellen Pompeo.

France 2

14.25 Tour de France 2008 : le direct. 3e étape : Saint-Malo - Nantes (208 km). EN DIRECT. **17.25** L'après Tour. **18.15** 26 minutes pour rire. **18.50** N'oubliez pas les paroles. ■ **20.00** Journal.

20.50 Rendez-vous en terre inconnue
Documentaire de Pierre Stine (2007). Adriana Karembeu chez les Amharas.

22.35 La Crim'
Série policière. Camarade P38 (Saison 7, 5/12). Avec Jean-François Garreaud, Sabine Haudepin.

France 3

14.50 Soko, section homicide. Le sourire du traître. **16.30** Duo de maîtres. **17.15** C'est pas sorcier. Les cités englouties d'Egypte. **17.50** Des chiffres et des lettres. **18.25** Questions pour un champion. **19.05** Le 19/20. ■ **20.25** Plus belle la vie.

20.55 Intervilles Jeu. Tarbes/Pau.
Présenté par Julien Lepers, Tex, Nathalie Simon et Olivier Alleman, avec la participation de Philippe Corti et Alessandro di Sarno.

23.40 Soir 3.
0.10 Carnets des festivals.
0.20 L'heure de l'opéra
Magazine. Carmen. Présenté par Alain Duault. Invitée : Béatrice Uria-Monzon.

14.55 Jeremiah Johnson. Western de Sydney Pollack (1972). **16.50** C'est le Pérou dans l'assiette ! **17.35** Tout le monde à la plage. Tarquinia/Italie. **18.05** Vénus et Apollon. Soin éternel. **18.30** Top of the Pops. **19.00** L'envol de l'ibis. **19.45** Arte info. **20.00** Le journal de la culture. **20.15** Un billet de train pour... Le Tibet.

21.00 Rocco et ses frères
Drame italo-français de Luchino Visconti (1960). 2h50. NB. Avec Alain Delon (Rocco), Katina Paxinou (Rosaria), Rocco Vidolazzi (Luca), Annie Girardot (Nadia).

23.50 Heitor Villa-Lobos, l'âme de Rio Documentaire d'Eric Darmon (2007).

M6

15.30 Le bonheur à nouveau. Téléfilm. **17.15** Le rêve de Diana. **17.55** Un dîner presque parfait. **18.50** 100% Mag. **19.50** Six. **20.00** Pas de secrets entre nous. **20.35** I love...

20.50 L'amour est dans le pré
Téléréalité. Présenté par Véronique Mounier. La découverte de la vie à la ferme continue pour les prétendants potentiels dans les diverses exploitations.

22.20 Recherche appartement ou maison
Téléréalité. "Eloa et Olivier" : Ce jeune couple doit trouver un appartement en location, impérativement dans Paris.

France 5

14.45 Tant qu'il y aura des rêves. Chine. **15.35** S.O.S. maison. **15.45** Echappées belles. Corée du Sud. **16.50** Question maison. **17.45** C dans l'air. Lire notre article. **19.00** Le magazine de la santé. **19.55** Bonsoir les zouzous.

20.40 Einstein: 1905, année lumière
Documentaire de Philippe Tourancheau (2005).

21.30 A visage découvert
Documentaire de Ludovic Fossard et Catherine Berthillier (2006). Romano Prodi.

Note: NB means *noir et blanc.*

Presentation: Discuss the availability (or unavailability) of international programming in the United States, and have students find out the possibilities for watching French-speaking TV in your area. Is TV5 available by satellite, for example? Compare typical times when TV news, films, game shows, etc., are aired. The statistical information provided here is based on *Francoscopie 2007*, as well as a study by the TDF Group (a French media and telecommunications conglomerate) reported in May 2008. Have students compare TV programming, viewing habits, and attitudes in France and North America. According to the A.C. Nielsen Co. the average American watches 3 hours and 46 minutes of TV each day, and according to census data from 2004, Canadians watch an average of 21.4 hours of television per week. Students can access French TV schedules and actually watch a number of French broadcasts online through links on the *Chez nous* Companion Website. As a follow-up activity, have students examine TV listings in detail to see what types of American films and programs are popular in France and discuss the image this may convey of the United States.

Vie et culture

La télévision en France

Les Français passent en moyenne trois heures et 26 minutes par jour devant la télé, et 51 % des ménages[1] ont accès à la télévision numérique. La TNT (Télévision numérique terrestre) permet aux Français de recevoir gratuitement 18 chaînes avec un adaptateur spécial ; les autres services (câble, satellite ou ADSL) proposent plus de 200 chaînes.

Regardez l'extrait du magazine télé pour répondre à ces questions : Quelles sont les six chaînes accessibles à tous ? À quelle heure est-ce que le journal télévisé passe ? Quels genres d'émissions est-ce qu'on peut voir pendant l'après-midi ? la soirée ?

L'influence de la télé américaine est très répandue[2] en France. On y trouve un grand nombre de films et séries américains doublés en français. Trouvez quelques exemples dans cet extrait. Avec la télé numérique et les émissions en V.M. (version multilingue), les Français peuvent regarder des émissions internationales en V.F. (version française), en V.O. (version originale) ou en V.O.S.T.F. (version originale sous-titrée en français).

ET VOUS ?

1. Est-ce que ce les Français regardent les mêmes genres d'émissions que vous ?
2. Même avec plus de 200 chaînes, 53 % des téléspectateurs français sont insatisfaits. Est-ce que vous êtes satisfait/e de la télévision chez vous ? Pourquoi ?

[1]*households* [2]*widespread*

Presentation: Present the various types of films using the descriptions and, if you wish, photos from magazines, newspapers, or Web sites for films. See the *Chez nous* Companion Website for useful links. Have students help you elaborate on descriptions provided. Point out to students that *comédie* often means drama in French (for example, *La comédie française*) and that *une comédie musicale* therefore refers to any kind of musical, not just musical comedy.
Find out whether students know famous actors, actresses, and directors: *Nicole Kidman ? — C'est une actrice australienne. Elle est très belle et elle joue souvent dans des drames psychologiques.* Other possibilities: Halle Berry, Audrey Tautou, Leonardo DiCaprio, Isabelle Adjani, Denzel Washington, Jean-Luc Godard, Eddie Murphy, Kate Hudson, Gérard Depardieu. Have students suggest others.

Des genres de films

une comédie	raconte les mésaventures amusantes des gens
une comédie dramatique	raconte une histoire pleine de drames mais avec des moments assez drôles
une comédie musicale	raconte une histoire dansée et chantée
une comédie romantique	raconte les histoires d'amour des personnages
un dessin animé	est fait surtout pour les enfants à partir d'images dessinées et puis filmées ; il met en vedette, par exemple, des animaux qui parlent
un documentaire	est un reportage sur la société, l'histoire, la nature, la science, la religion, etc.
un drame	raconte une histoire sérieuse
un drame psychologique	examine les relations entre les gens
un film d'action	raconte une histoire avec beaucoup de scènes d'action, quelquefois avec de la violence
un film d'animation	n'est pas fait avec des acteurs mais avec des effets spéciaux, des images dessinées, des images faites sur ordinateur, etc.
un film d'aventures	raconte les aventures d'un personnage courageux
un film d'espionnage	est plein de suspense, avec des agents secrets qui partent en mission
un film historique	raconte des évènements historiques ou la vie d'un personnage historique
un film d'horreur	doit faire peur aux gens ; il y a des monstres, des fantômes, des vampires ou bien des psychopathes
un film policier	raconte un crime et l'enquête (*investigation*) pour retrouver le criminel
un film de science-fiction	raconte des évènements futuristes et imaginaires
un western	est un film d'aventures avec des cow-boys dans le Far West

Presentation: Ask students if they have seen or heard of either of the movies in the photos on these two pages. Briefly discuss the information provided in the captions. *La vie en Rose* won two Academy Awards in 2007: Best actress in a Leading Role and Makeup. It is the third-highest-grossing French-language film in the United States in recent decades. *Bienvenue chez les Ch'tis* was released in February 2008 and became a runaway hit. It is the highest-grossing French-language film in French history and is poised to overtake *Titanic* as the highest-grossing film of any kind in France. Clips of both *La vie en Rose* et *Bienvenue chez les Ch'tis* are widely available online. *Ch'ti* is a shortened form of *Ch'timi*, which is a local name given to the dialect of Picard spoken in the North of France; it has come to refer to all things referring to Northerners.

En 2008, Gérard Depardieu et Marion Cotillard jouent dans le film *La Vie en Rose*. Ce film raconte la vie de la célèbre chanteuse française Édith Piaf. Cotillard a remporté l'Oscar de la meilleure actrice pour ce rôle.

Dany Boon, le réalisateur de *Bienvenue chez les Ch'tis*, devant une affiche du film. Kad Merad joue le rôle de Philippe, un fonctionnaire provençal qui est muté (*transferred*) dans le Nord de la France. Dany Boon est Antoine, un facteur local avec lequel Philippe devient ami. Ce film comique traite les différences entre les gens du Nord et les gens du Sud. Il a battu tous les records en France du plus gros succès au box-office pour un film français.

11-3 Films préférés. Quels genres de films est-ce que vous préférez ? Classez ces films par ordre de préférence et parlez-en avec un/e camarade de classe.

Implementation: 11-3 Time permitting, have each group compare their results with those of the other groups and summarize results for the class as a whole.

MODÈLE

moi	mon partenaire
1. comédies romantiques	**1.** films d'aventure
2. films historiques	**2.** westerns
3. drames psychologiques	**3.** films policiers

É1 J'aime surtout les comédies romantiques. Mais je regarde aussi des films historiques et des drames psychologiques. Et toi ?

É2 J'aime les films d'aventure, surtout les westerns. J'aime aussi les films policiers. Je regarde des séries policières toutes les semaines.

Initial practice: Begin practice with a recognition exercise: *Donnez-moi un exemple d'un film d'aventures.* Follow with either-or questions: *« James Bond » est-ce que c'est un film d'aventures ou un film d'espionnage ?* Then have students identify the genre of various films: *Agents secrets* [film d'espionnage] ; *Wall-E* [film d'animation] ; *Mama Mia* [comédie musicale] ; *Je t'aime, moi non plus* [drame psychologique] ; *La planète bleue* [documentaire] ; *Massacre à la tronçonneuse* [film d'horreur] ; *La forêt enchantée* [dessin animé] ; *Harry Potter et le Prince de Sang-Mêlé* [film d'aventures, film de science-fiction] ; *Il était une fois au Mexique Desperado 2* [western] ; *Frida* [film historique]. Check the *Chez nous* Companion Website for this chapter for links to French film pages.

11-4 Ça dépend des jours. Quelquefois on préfère un type de films, d'autres fois on préfère un autre type. Quel type de films est-ce que vous et votre partenaire préférez voir dans les situations suivantes ?

MODÈLE quand vous êtes triste ?

É1 Moi, je préfère les drames psychologiques.

É2 Moi non ; j'aime plutôt les comédies.

1. quand vous êtes heureux/heureuse ?
2. quand vous avez un problème que vous voulez oublier ?
3. quand vous venez de passer un examen ?
4. quand vous êtes avec votre petit frère ou un autre petit garçon ?
5. quand vous êtes avec votre petite sœur ou une autre petite fille ?
6. quand vous êtes avec vos parents ?
7. quand vous êtes avec votre copain/copine ?

Expansion: 11-4 Ask students to explain why they like or do not like certain types of movies at certain times. Compare results for the class.

Sons et lettres

Note: We present a simpler version of what is referred to as *la loi des trois consonnes* that takes into account only the number of consonants preceding unstable *e*. Even the *loi des trois consonnes* is an approximation: an important factor is the nature of the consonants involved. For example, compare: *nous montrerons*, where unstable *e* is always retained, to *nous regarderons*, where it may be deleted even though this results in three consonants coming together. To train students to be aware of the "two-consonant" principle, it would be useful to review the contrastive examples and have students count the number of consonants that precede the unstable *e*.

Le *e* instable et les groupes de consonnes

In Chapitre 8 you learned that, generally speaking, an unstable **e** is dropped within words when it occurs after only one pronounced consonant **(un feuilleton)** but that it is retained when it occurs after two pronounced consonants **(le gouvernement)**. This general rule also applies across words in phrases. Compare:

dans ce film	avec c**e** film
On peut regarder.	Elles peuvent r**e**garder.
C'est le journal télévisé.	On préfère l**e** journal télévisé.
beaucoup de chaînes	quelqu**e**s chaînes

Within words, unstable **e** is retained when it occurs after a group of consonants ending in /r/ or /l/. Compare:

nous monterons	nous montr**e**rons
facilement	simpl**e**ment

Unstable **e** occurs in many one-syllable function words: the pronouns **je**, **te**, **me**, **se**, **le**; the negative particle **ne**; the determiners **le**, **ce**; the preposition **de**; the conjunction **que**. In these words, the unstable **e** is usually retained when it occurs at the beginning of a phrase. Compare:

je peux	Mais je peux sortir.
Ne fais rien.	On ne fait rien.
ce documentaire	C'est ce documentaire.

This principle also applies to combinations of two one-syllable words. Note that when two unstable **e**'s occur in succession, one of them is generally deleted.

Je ne sais pas.	On ne **le** veut pas.
Ne le regarde pas.	**De** ne pas le faire est triste.

Implementation: 11-5 After checking answers, have students pronounce the phrases with the correct deletion and retention of unstable *e*'s.

Key: 11-5
1. le petit écran
2. une vedette
3. le festival de Cannes
4. une série de films
5. l'autre chaîne
6. Arrête de parler.
7. J'aime ce magazine.
8. Tu ne regardes pas ?
9. Pas de sous-titres.

11-5 Comptons les consonnes ! Indiquez les **e** instables qui devraient être prononcés.

MODÈLES nous devons nous montrerons

1. le petit écran
2. une vedette
3. le festival de Cannes
4. une série de films
5. l'autre chaîne
6. Arrête de parler.
7. J'aime ce magazine.
8. Tu ne regardes pas ?
9. Pas de sous-titres.

 **11-6 Comptine.** Écoutez cette comptine et puis lisez-la à haute voix.

Pomme **de** reinette et pomme d'api,
D'api d'api rouge.
Pomme **de** reinette et pomme d'api,
D'api d'api gris.
C'est à la halle°
Que **je** m'installe
C'est à Paris qu**e** je vends mes fruits.
Pomme **de** reinette et pomme d'api,
D'api d'api gris.

° *marché*

Implementation: 11-6 Begin by having students cross out the unstable *e's* that will not be retained and have them listen to the recording of the nursery rhyme. Then ask them to repeat it. *Une pomme reinette* is a variety of apple; *une pomme d'api* is a type of apple, red on one side, that no longer exists.

FORMES ET FONCTIONS

1. *L'emploi des temps avec certaines conjonctions*

- To talk about two events that occur at the same time, use the following conjunctions:

quand, lorsque	*when*
dès que, aussitôt que	*as soon as*
pendant que	*while*

- To describe ongoing or habitual actions, both verbs are in the present:

Je mets le DVD **pendant qu**'il cherche ses lunettes.	*I'm putting in the DVD while he's looking for his glasses.*
Quand j'ai du temps libre le week-end, je vais toujours au cinéma.	*When I have free time on the weekend, I always go to the movies.*

- To talk about future events that will occur at the same time, French uses the future tense in both clauses. Note that this is different from English usage.

On verra ce film français **quand** il **passera** à Washington.	*We'll see that French film when it is shown in Washington.*
Dès que l'émission **commencera,** tu m'appelleras, non ?	*As soon as the show starts, you'll call me, won't you?*

Note that with the imperative, either the present or the future tense can be used:

C'est tard. Éteins la télé **dès que** le documentaire **se terminera**.	*It's late. Turn off the TV as soon as the documentary is over.*
Quand ils **arrivent** à la gare, faites-moi signe.	*When they arrive at the train station, let me know.*

Presentation: Point out the use of the future tense in both clauses, which is unlike English usage. Note that *pendant que* can be followed by either the present or the future tense: *Pendant que tu lis/liras le programme, j'irai acheter les billets.* To express a sequence of events in the future, the *futur antérieur* refers to an event that will have happened before the event indicated by the *futur simple*: *Quand elle sera partie, je te téléphonerai.* The *futur antérieur* is presented, along with practice activities, in Appendix 3; you may wish to incorporate it here.

Note: Although both verbs express past events, it is not necessary that both be in the same past tense (i.e., one verb may be in the *passé composé* and the other in the *imparfait*).

- When talking about simultaneous events in the past, use a past tense for both verbs:

On a regardé une émission intéressante l'autre soir **quand** ils étaient chez nous.	*We watched an interesting show the other evening when they were at our house.*

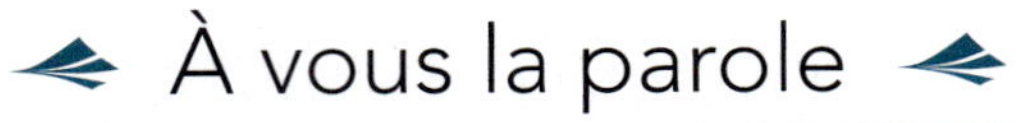

À vous la parole

Initial practice: Each of the exercises in **À vous la parole** focuses on one particular time frame. Begin with an exercise including multiple tenses, and ask students to identify the time frame: *Quand tu sortiras, je te donnerai un parapluie : futur ; Je bois du café pendant que je fais mes devoirs : présent ; Quand elle était petite, elle jouait de la flûte : passé ; Je te téléphonerai quand je saurai quelque chose de plus : futur.* Alternatively, you could produce only the first part of the sentence and ask students to complete it in an appropriate manner.

11-7 D'une pierre deux coups. On est tous pressés. Pour gagner du temps, suggérez des activités que ces personnes peuvent faire pendant qu'elles font autre chose.

MODÈLE Pendant qu'elle lit le journal, ma mère...
→ boit son café.

1. Pendant qu'elle regarde la télé, ma sœur...
2. Quand je fais du sport...
3. Pendant que mon professeur déjeune...
4. Quand je parle au téléphone...
5. Pendant que je vérifie mon e-mail...
6. Quand mes parents sont dans la voiture, ils...
7. Pendant que mon colocataire fait ses devoirs...
8. Quand je suis dans l'avion ou dans le train...
9. Pendant qu'il prend sa douche, mon frère...

Implementation: 11-8 Review the formation of the *imparfait* before completing this exercise. Remind students that sentences may include both the *passé composé* and the *imparfait*.

11-8 Les vacances du passé. Complétez les phrases pour parler de vos vacances dans le passé. Comparez vos souvenirs avec un/e partenaire.

MODÈLE Quand j'étais petit/e, ...

É1 Quand j'étais petit/e, nous passions toujours l'été dans le Maine.
É2 Tu avais de la chance. Moi, je devais rester chez moi et souvent je suivais des cours d'été.

1. Quand j'étais petit/e, ...
2. Quand j'allais au lycée, ...
3. Quand les vacances arrivaient, ...
4. Pendant que je m'amusais, ...
5. Pendant que mes parents travaillaient, ...
6. Quand il faisait très chaud, ...
7. Quand les vacances se sont terminées, ...

Implementation: 11-9 Review the formation of the *futur simple* before completing this exercise.

11-9 Des projets. Qu'est-ce que vous ferez dans les situations suivantes ? Avec un/e partenaire, parlez de vos projets.

MODÈLE quand tu seras en vacances ?

É1 Qu'est-ce que tu feras quand tu seras en vacances ?
É2 J'irai en Californie pour travailler. Et toi ?
É1 Pas moi, je resterai chez mes parents.

1. quand tu seras en vacances ?
2. quand tu auras ton diplôme ?
3. quand tu auras un emploi ?
4. quand tu seras riche ?
5. quand tu auras 50 ans ?

2. *Quelques prépositions avec les expressions de temps*

- There are two distinct prepositions in French, **pour** and **pendant**, which correspond to the English preposition *for* followed by a time expression.
  - **Pendant** is used to express *for* when it expresses a specific time duration and has the meaning of *during*. It is most often used with verbs in the past tense but can be used with verbs in the present or the future tense, as illustrated in the following examples:

Elles ont regardé la télé **pendant** cinq heures d'affilée hier après-midi.	*They watched television for five straight hours yesterday afternoon.*
Ma grand-mère regarde ses feuilletons **pendant** une heure et demie tous les jours.	*My grandmother watches her soap operas for an hour and a half every day.*
Elle sera au cinéma **pendant** deux heures.	*She will be at the movie theater for two hours.*

  - **Pour** is used when *for* refers to some period of time to come in the future. It is most often used with present or past tense forms of verbs such as **aller, partir, sortir, venir**.

Ils vont en France **pour** trois semaines et demie cet été.	*They are going to France for (a period of) three and a half weeks this summer.*
Agathe vient chez nous **pour** le week-end.	*Agathe is coming to our house for the weekend.*
Elle est partie faire des études à Nice **pour** un semestre.	*She left to study in Nice for a semester.*

- Likewise, two distinct prepositions in French, **dans** and **en**, correspond to the English preposition *in* followed by an expression of time.
  - **En** is used to express the amount of time needed to accomplish an action, while **dans** is used to express when a future action will take place.

Le dernier candidat de *Star Academy* a interprété cette chanson **en** trois minutes vingt-cinq secondes.	*The last contestant on Star Academy performed this song in three minutes twenty-five seconds.*
Je vais le faire **dans** cinq minutes. Un peu de patience, voyons !	*I'm going to do it in five minutes. Be patient!*

Note: This section introduces several prepositions used with time expressions that can cause difficulties for students, given that a single preposition in English corresponds to two different prepositions in French. Present the examples in the text as well as others to show the contexts in which the various prepositions are used.

Fiche pratique

When two French words correspond to a single English word, such as *in* used with a time expression, create contrasting examples to help remember which French word to use. For example, you might use the sentences: **J'ai terminé les devoirs de maths en vingt minutes. Je vais commencer les devoirs de français dans cinq minutes.**

À vous la parole

Key: 11-10 1) e 2) h 3) d 4) f 5) b 6) a 7) c 8) g

11-10 Le Festival de Cannes. Complétez ces phrases qui parlent du Festival international de film à Cannes.

MODÈLE Les grandes stars partiront à Cannes...
e. pour quinze jours.

1. Les grandes stars partiront à Cannes...
2. Cette actrice ne se presse pas ; elle se maquille et s'habille pour la grande soirée...
3. Le réalisateur parle aux journalistes...
4. Ce jeune acteur sans argent est allé à Cannes...
5. Il restera chez des amis...
6. Les professionnels du cinéma visionnent énormement de films...
7. Les invités d'honneur sortiront après la projection du film...
8. Quand il fait beau, les stars se promènent quelquefois sur la plage...

a. pendant les douze jours du Festival.
b. pendant deux nuits.
c. pour toute la soirée.
d. pendant trente-cinq minutes.
e. pour quinze jours.
f. pour seulement trois jours.
g. pendant l'après-midi.
h. pendant deux heures et des heures.

Implementation: 11-11 The model shows fairly naturalistic speech featuring object pronouns to avoid repetition. To simplify, provide alternative models such as... *je vais appeler le médecin dans dix minutes* or... *j'ai fini mes devoirs en 20 minutes.*

11-11 Chez Sophie et Guy. Sophie est une jeune fille dynamique qui accomplit tout assez rapidement. Par contre, son papa Guy est très occupé en ce moment et il remet (*puts off*) tout à plus tard. Imaginez leurs réponses aux situations suivantes en jouant les rôles de Sophie et de Guy avec un/e partenaire.

MODÈLES Guy : appeler le médecin pour fixer un rendez-vous

É1 (Sophie) « Papa, tu as appelé le médecin pour me fixer un rendez-vous ? »
É2 (Guy) « Non, chérie, mais je vais l'appeler dans dix minutes. »

Sophie : finir tes devoirs

É2 (Guy) « Sophie, tu as fini tes devoirs ? »
É2 (Sophie) « Oui, papa, je les ai finis en 20 minutes. »

1. Sophie : mettre la table
2. Sophie : promener le chien
3. Guy : préparer le dîner
4. Sophie : ranger ta chambre
5. Guy : écrire un mot pour le prof
6. Guy : signer l'autorisation parentale pour la sortie à l'école
7. Sophie : préparer une salade

Implementation: 11-12 Encourage students to come up with other possibilities as well or suggest others yourself.

11-12 Projets de vacances. C'est bientôt la fin du semestre. En groupes de trois ou quatre, parlez de vos projets. Voici quelques idées pour vous aider.

Quelques possibilités :

aller à la plage/à la montagne
faire du bénévolat
partir à l'étranger
partir en vacances
rendre visite à la famille/aux amis
se reposer
suivre des cours
travailler

MODÈLE É1 Moi, je vais me reposer pendant quelques jours et ensuite je dois travailler. Et toi, Rachel ?

É2 Moi, je compte me reposer pendant une semaine et ensuite, je vais travailler pendant trois semaines. Et toi, Nathan ?

É3 Je ne suis pas paresseux comme vous deux ! Je ne vais pas me reposer du tout. Je vais partir étudier en France pour trois semaines et après je voyagerai en Europe pendant dix jours avant de retourner aux États-Unis.

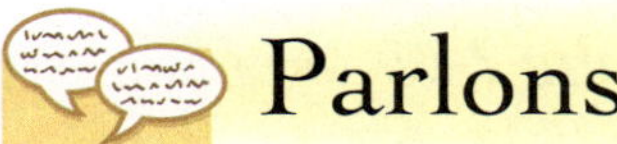

Parlons

11-13 Opinions sur la télévision. Quelles sont vos opinions et les opinions de vos camarades de classe au sujet de la télévision dans notre société ?

A. Avant de parler. Mettez-vous en groupes de quatre ou cinq et choisissez dans cette liste un sujet de discussion. Avant de discuter, réfléchissez sur vos opinions et écrivez les points essentiels.

- **La télé doit informer les gens et les enrichir au niveau culturel.**
- **Les émissions violentes à la télé poussent les gens à la violence quotidienne.**
- **La télé joue un rôle dans le problème de l'obésité chez les enfants et les adultes.**
- **Les séries américaines donnent une image fausse (*false*) de la vie américaine.**
- **Tout le monde devrait avoir un accès gratuit à la télé numérique.**
- **Les émissions de téléréalité ont baissé (*lowered*) la qualité de la télévision en général.**

Implementation: You may allow groups to select their own topic, assign topics to groups, or have groups pick a topic at random (e.g., by selecting a topic out of a hat). You may wish to begin with a whole-class activity, asking students for their general opinions or impressions of television. This could lead to the addition of a few new topics.

B. En parlant. Maintenant, partagez vos opinions avec les autres membres de votre groupe pour découvrir ce qu'ils pensent. Voici quelques expressions utiles.

Pour exprimer votre opinion	Pour réagir aux opinions des autres
Je pense/Je crois/Je trouve que...	Je (ne) suis (pas) (tout à fait) d'accord...
À mon avis, ...	Au contraire...
Pour moi, ...	D'un autre côté, ...

MODÈLE É1 Je crois qu'à cause de la télévision on accepte de plus en plus la violence dans la vie de tous les jours.

É2 Je suis tout à fait d'accord avec Kathleen. On voit de la violence non seulement pendant le journal télévisé, mais aussi dans tous les feuilletons et séries les plus populaires. Même les émissions pour enfants…

É3 Je ne suis pas tout à fait d'accord avec vous. À mon avis, ce n'est pas parce que les gens regardent la violence qu'ils deviennent violents.

C. Après avoir parlé. Est-ce que les membres de votre groupe étaient tous d'accord ou est-ce qu'il y avait des différences d'opinion ? Faites un résumé de votre discussion pour vos camarades de classe.

Leçon 2 Êtes-vous branché ?

Presentation: Have students take the quiz individually, with a partner, or as a whole class. Go over any difficult words or expressions. Students will most likely be familiar with most of this vocabulary since it is heavily based on cognates. Go over the pronunciation with them and point out, for example, that *un iPod* is pronounced [ipɔd] and *MP3* as [ɛmpetrwa]. If you are teaching in a technology classroom or can bring a portable computer and some computer peripherals with you to class, you may wish to begin by pointing out and having students repeat the names for the various parts of the computer and computer peripheries. Your might ask students to watch the supplemental video clip for Chapter 11 which features Fabienne showing off her computer with its flat screen monitor and wireless keyboard and mouse.

POINTS DE DÉPART

Êtes-vous technophile ou technophobe ?

Voulez-vous savoir où vous en êtes dans la révolution informatique ? Alors, répondez aux questions suivantes pour découvrir si vous êtes technophile ou technophobe.

Première partie :

1. Qu'est-ce que vous faites pour acheter vos livres au début du semestre ?

a. Je fais de la recherche en ligne pour voir où je peux trouver les livres les moins chers et je les commande avec une carte bancaire sur un site Web.

b. Je fais de la recherche en ligne pour découvrir les livres qu'il me faut et je vais les acheter à la librairie.

c. Je vais à la librairie et je demande de l'aide au libraire.

2. Qu'est-ce que vous faites quand vous devez faire un exposé devant la classe ?

a. Je surfe sur Internet pour trouver des informations et je prépare une présentation multimédia avec de la musique, du texte et des clips vidéo. Bien sûr, je sauvegarde une copie sur ma clé USB et je m'envoie une copie par e-mail en pièce jointe avant l'exposé. En classe, j'ouvre mon courrier électronique pour retrouver mon fichier et je fais mon exposé avec un ordinateur portable.

b. Je prépare un beau poster avec des jolies images que j'ai scannées et imprimées à la maison avec mon imprimante multifonction. J'y mets aussi quelques photos numériques que j'ai retouchées avec un logiciel sur ordinateur.

c. J'écris mon plan et les idées importantes dans mon cahier. Je fais ma présentation à l'oral devant la classe.

3. Comment est-ce que vous communiquez avec vos parents et vos grands-parents ?

a. On a un blog où on affiche les dernières nouvelles et des photos. Pour parler, on se sert des webcams et de nos ordis pour se voir en même temps qu'on se parle. C'est génial et ça ne coûte pas cher.

b. On échange souvent des messages instantanés et des e-mails. Quelquefois je leur envoie des liens pour des sites intéressants où ils peuvent télécharger de la musique ou même des logiciels utiles.

c. Je leur téléphone quelquefois, et je reçois régulièrement des lettres de ma mère.

4. Qu'est-ce que vous faites pour vous détendre ?

a. Je télécharge de la musique sur mon iPod ou mon baladeur MP3, je surfe sur Internet et je mets à jour mon profil sur Facebook.

b. Je joue aux jeux en ligne sur Internet avec des joueurs de pays différents.

c. Je lis un roman ou des bandes dessinées et quelquefois, je me promène s'il fait beau.

Comptez vos points pour la première partie : Les réponses a = 2 points ; b = 1 point ; c = 0

Deuxième partie :
Maintenant, ajoutez un point pour chaque item de la liste ci-dessous que vous possédez.

- ❑ un baladeur MP3
- ❑ un clavier sans fil
- ❑ une clé USB
- ❑ un disque dur externe
- ❑ une imprimante
- ❑ un iPod
- ❑ un lecteur/graveur CD
- ❑ un lecteur/graveur DVD
- ❑ un lecteur CD/DVD
- ❑ un moniteur avec un écran plat
- ❑ un ordinateur
- ❑ un ordinateur portable
- ❑ un PDA
- ❑ un réseau sans fil
- ❑ un scanner
- ❑ une souris optique sans fil
- ❑ une webcam

Maintenant, additionnez les points pour la première et la deuxième partie.

Votre score ?

20–25 *Vous êtes vraiment technophile. Vous adorez les nouveaux gadgets et vous êtes parmi les premiers à essayer chaque nouvelle technologie. Mais vous passez peut-être un peu trop de temps devant l'écran. Pensez à sortir un peu respirer l'air frais.*

15–19 *Vous aimez bien la technologie et vous savez vous en servir pour vous faciliter la vie. Attention de ne pas devenir trop dépendant/e de ces nouvelles technologies.*

6–14 *Vous semblez avoir trouvé le bon équilibre entre le virtuel et le réel. Vous vous servez de la technologie mais vous n'oubliez pas non plus qu'il y a plus que la technologie et la nouveauté dans la vie.*

0–5 *Oh là là, vous n'êtes vraiment pas dans la révolution technologique. Vous ne comprenez pas pourquoi tout le monde semble adorer ces ordinateurs et cet Internet auxquels vous résistez toujours. Mais attention ! Il y a des bons éléments de la technologie qui pourraient vous simplifier la vie. À vous de les trouver.*

À vous la parole

11-14 Définitions. Trouvez le mot qui correspond à chaque définition.

MODÈLE C'est un appareil qu'on utilise pour imprimer un texte.
C'est une imprimante.

1. C'est très pratique pour sauvegarder votre travail et le transporter.
2. C'est un ordinateur qu'on peut facilement transporter.
3. C'est sur cette partie de l'ordinateur qu'on tape (*types*).
4. C'est un message qu'on reçoit par Internet.
5. C'est ce qu'on regarde lorsqu'on utilise l'ordinateur.
6. On l'utilise pour sauvegarder un fichier sur l'ordinateur lui-même.
7. C'est ce que vous faites quand vous sauvegardez la musique d'un site Internet.
8. Cela permet de reproduire une photo ou un texte.

Key: 11-14 1) une clé USB 2) un ordinateur portable 3) un clavier 4) un e-mail 5) un écran 6) un disque dur 7) télécharger 8) un scanner

Variation: 11-14 Have students work in pairs to create their own definitions with which to test classmates.

Avec un ordinateur portable, on peut travailler n'importe où ; même dans un canoë en Polynésie française.

Note: In 2006, 52% of French households had a PC, and nearly 50% of the French had an Internet connection at home. Among European countries, France has the highest proportion of households having a high-speed connection to the Internet; 8 out of 10 users, and France boasts the third-largest Wi-Fi network after the U.S. and Great Britain. Internet users in France also have the distinction of connecting more often (36 times per month) than users anywhere else in the world; Australia at 35 times and the U.S. at 33 times a month come in second and third place, respectively. As might be expected, Internet users in France tend to be young (86% of 13–24 year-olds compared to 24% of those 50 and older). These and many other interesting facts about computer usage in France can be found in *Francoscopie 2007*. Note that contrary to English usage, the proper noun **Internet** does not take an article in French.

Vie et culture

Les Français et Internet

Combien d'heures par jour est-ce que vous passez devant un ordinateur ? Quand vous avez du temps libre, est-ce que vous aimez surfer sur le Web, télécharger de la musique ou communiquer avec vos amis avec la messagerie instantanée ou des e-mails ? Est-ce que vous pensez que les jeunes Français passent autant de temps que vous sur Internet ? Pour découvrir leurs habitudes concernant Internet, consultez ce tableau.

Ces étudiants travaillent à la terrasse d'un café avec un ordinateur portable. Est-ce qu'ils ont une connexion sans fil ?

ET VOUS ?

1. Est-ce que vous remarquez des différences entre l'usage d'Internet chez les jeunes de 15 à 19 ans et les jeunes adultes de 20 à 29 ans ? Pouvez-vous expliquer ces différences ?
2. Comment est-ce que vous avez utilisé Internet quand vous étiez au lycée ? Est-ce que vos pratiques ont changé depuis ce temps ? Est-ce que cela correspond aux différences d'usage chez les jeunes Français ?

Usages d'Internet (octobre 2005, en % des 15 ans et plus ayant utilisé Internet au moins une fois)

	Utiliser la messagerie électronique	Communiquer par messagerie instantanée	Obtenir des informations administratives	Rechercher des informations sur la santé	Accéder à son compte bancaire	Acheter des biens et services	Écouter, voir ou télécharger de la musique ou des films	Jouer ou télécharger des jeux	Télécharger des logiciels
15 à 19 ans	67	62	28	22	12	15	60	34	28
20 à 29 ans	76	47	61	30	46	41	42	27	33

Source : INSEE

Implementation: 11-15 This allows recycling of vocabulary for other technological devices. Have students work in pairs, then compare responses for the class as a whole.

11-15 La technologie et vous. Combien de ces appareils est-ce que vous savez utiliser ? Comment est-ce que vous les utilisez ? Comparez vos réponses avec les réponses d'un/e partenaire.

MODÈLE un lecteur DVD

É1 Mon ordinateur portable a un lecteur DVD. Je regarde beaucoup de DVD, et quelquefois je télécharge des films.

É2 Moi aussi, j'aime les DVD. Je les regarde avec mon lecteur DVD et souvent je regarde des émissions de télévision sur Internet.

1. une clé USB
2. une souris sans fil
3. une webcam
4. un lecteur DVD
5. un baladeur MP3 (ou un iPod)
6. un scanner
7. un appareil photo numérique
8. un graveur CD

11-16 Internet et vous. Faites un sondage dans votre classe pour déterminer les pourcentages de gens qui utilisent Internet pour les activités suivantes.

MODÈLE Pour envoyer et recevoir des e-mails

É1 Qui utilise Internet pour envoyer des e-mails ?
É2 Un, deux, trois, quatre, cinq. Cinq personnes dans notre groupe envoient et reçoivent des e-mails.

(plus tard)
É3 Cinq personnes ou 100 % des membres de notre groupe envoient des e-mails. Trois personnes ou 60 % utilisent la messagerie instantanée.

1. Pour envoyer et recevoir des e-mails.
2. Pour utiliser la messagerie instantanée.
3. Pour obtenir des informations administratives.
4. Pour accéder à votre compte en banque.
5. Pour acheter des livres, des CD ou des vêtements.
6. Pour télécharger de la musique ou des films.
7. Pour jouer ou télécharger des jeux.
8. Pour téléphoner.
9. Pour voir des films.
10. Pour faire de la recherche pour vos cours.

Implementation: 11-16 To complete the survey, divide the class into four or five groups; each group should select a leader, a recorder, and a spokesperson. The leader begins by asking the first question. The recorder counts the number of students who respond "yes" to each question. You may wish to prepare a simple worksheet as a handout on which students can record the answers for their group. The spokesperson for each group will provide the figures for how many do each activity. Sum up the figures on the board or on a transparency. Finish by comparing the class responses with those from the French survey presented in the **Vie et culture**.

À l'aéroport Orly à Paris, on se sert du réseau Wi-Fi pour se connecter.

Sons et lettres

Le *e* instable et les groupes consonne + /j/

TEXT AUDIO
CD 6 TRACK 5

Unstable **e** is pronounced when it occurs before groups consisting of a consonant plus the semivowel /j/. Compare the corresponding present indicative versus imperfect or present subjunctive **nous** and **vous** forms:

nous appelons	nous app**e**lions
vous devez	vous d**e**viez
vous achetez	il faut que vous ach**e**tiez
nous jetons	il est nécessaire que nous j**e**tions

These groups also occur in the conditional **nous** and **vous** forms. Compare the corresponding future and conditional forms:

nous mangerons	nous mang**er**ions
vous trouverez	vous trouv**e**riez

Recall that **i** is pronounced as the vowel /i/ rather than the semivowel /j/ after consonant groups ending with /r/ or /l/, for example: **le client**, **crier**. Such combinations occur especially in the **nous** and **vous** forms of the conditional of **-re** verbs. Compare:

vous prendrez	vous prendr**i**ez
nous nous détendrons	nous nous détendr**i**ons

Presentation: Treat this topic after presenting the conditional in this lesson or in conjunction with that presentation.

Implementation: 11-17 and 11-18 Have students mark off the unstable *e*'s in the present and future forms that are not pronounced before they repeat these words. Then, ask them to underline the unstable *e*'s that will be retained in the imperfect and conditional forms before they actually produce these forms.

À vous la parole

11-17 Plus ça change. Mettez chaque verbe à l'imparfait.

MODÈLE vous jetez
→ vous j**e**tiez

1. nous amenons
2. vous achetez
3. vous devez
4. nous épelons
5. nous appelons
6. vous vous rappelez

11-18 Ce n'est pas sûr. Mettez chaque verbe au conditionnel.

MODÈLE nous accepterons
→ nous accept**e**rions

1. nous regarderons
2. nous passerons
3. vous ferez
4. nous aiderons
5. vous porterez
6. vous voyagerez
7. vous vous fâcherez
8. nous nous laverons

FORMES ET FONCTIONS

1. *Le conditionnel*

Presentation: Use an activity from Ch. 8, L. 3 to review the forms and use of these verbs in the conditional before going on to the new information. Use examples similar to those in the text to introduce additional uses of the conditional.

- You have used the conditional forms of **devoir**, **pouvoir**, and **vouloir** to express obligation, to soften commands, and to make suggestions.

Tu **pourrais** lui envoyer un e-mail.	*You could send him an e-mail.*
On **devrait** acheter une webcam.	*We should buy a webcam.*

- Here are some additional uses of the conditional:
  - to express events or situations that are hypothetical or conjectural:

J'**aimerais** acheter un ordinateur portable, mais c'est cher.	*I'd like to buy a laptop, but it's expensive.*
Tu **vendrais** vraiment ton iPod ?	*Would you really sell your iPod?*
Nous **voudrions** être riches !	*We would like to be rich!*

  - to express future events or situations in relation to the past. Compare the uses of the future with the present and the conditional with the **passé composé** in the following pair of sentences:

Future event with relation to the present:

Il **dit** qu'il n'**achètera** jamais d'ordinateur.	*He says that he will never buy a computer.*

Future event with relation to the past:

Il **a dit** qu'il n'**achèterait** jamais d'ordinateur.	*He said that he would never buy a computer.*

- The conditional is formed by adding the imperfect endings to the future stem.

SINGULIER		PLURIEL	
je	donner**ais**	nous	donner**ions**
tu	donner**ais**	vous	donner**iez**
il / elle / on	donner**ait**	ils / elles	donner**aient**

Note: The endings of the singular and third-person plural forms are pronounced the same, with /ɛ/ in Standard French. However, there is wide variation, and many speakers pronounce these endings with /e/. In Standard French, the first-person singular forms of the future and the conditional differ: *je donnerai* /e/ vs. *je donnerais* /ɛ/. Because of the variation among native speakers, this distinction should not be emphasized in the beginning levels.

Here are the conditional forms of the main verb groups.

VERB GROUP	INFINITIVE	CONDITIONAL
-er	parler	je **parlerais**
-ir	partir	je **partirais**
-re	vendre	je **vendrais**

Verbs that have an irregular future stem use that same stem in the conditional: **j'irais, j'aurais, je serais, je me lèverais, je jetterais, je préfèrerais**, etc.

Note: Refer to the list of irregular future stem changes in Ch. 9, L. 1. See the **Sons et lettres** section for rules concerning the loss and retention of "unstable *e*." *Préférer*-type verbs (*préférer, espérer, répéter, suggérer*) are included here based on the 1990 Orthographic reform (règle 3a): *« On accentue sur le modèle de* ***semer*** *les futurs et conditionnels des verbes du type* ***céder*** *: je* ***cèderai****, je* ***cèderais****... »* Similar to the *acheter*-type verbs, the *accent grave* here clearly indicates the pronunciation of [ɛ].

À vous la parole

11-19 Projet ou rêve. Julien a beaucoup de projets pour l'avenir et beaucoup de rêves (*dreams*). Pour chacune de ses idées, indiquez si c'est un rêve ou un projet d'avenir.

	rêve	projet d'avenir
MODÈLE J'irais en Suisse.	✓	______
1. J'irais au Festival de Cannes.	______	______
2. Je regarderai le Festival à la télé.	______	______
3. J'achèterai un ordinateur portable.	______	______
4. Je ferais le tour du monde.	______	______
5. Je travaillerai beaucoup.	______	______
6. Je travaillerais avec Steve Jobs.	______	______
7. J'achèterais une imprimante laser couleur.	______	______

Est-ce que Julien est plus rêveur ou plus réaliste ? Pourquoi ?

Initial practice: 11-19 This meaning-based activity focuses students' attention on differences in verb endings between the conditional and the future. Continue with a simple substitution drill to practice these endings: *Je parlerais français ; vous. — Vous parleriez français*, etc. Review irregular stems: *Je suis riche. — Je serais riche ; J'ai une grande maison. — J'aurais une grande maison*, etc.

Implementation: 11-20 Have several students reply for each item, elaborate on their answers, or suggest other possibilities.

11-20 Vous aussi ? Avec plus d'argent, qu'est-ce que vous feriez ? Êtes-vous d'accord avec ces gens ?

MODÈLE Je m'achèterais une nouvelle voiture.

Moi aussi, je m'achèterais une nouvelle voiture.

OU Moi non, je m'achèterais un grand bateau.

1. Je voyagerais tout le temps.
2. Je ne travaillerais plus.
3. Je partagerais l'argent avec ma famille.
4. Je prêterais de l'argent à mes amis.
5. Je m'achèterais un château en France.
6. J'irais dîner dans les meilleurs restaurants.
7. Je donnerais de l'argent aux personnes en difficulté.

Avec plus d'argent, je m'achèterais un bateau et une maison secondaire dans le sud de la France.

Implementation: 11-21 Follow up by comparing responses for each item.

11-21 Des bons conseils. Quel conseil est-ce que vous et votre partenaire donneriez à ces personnes ?

MODÈLE Je ne suis pas très bien informé.

É1 À ta place, je regarderais les infos en ligne tous les jours.

É2 Tu devrais surfer sur Internet plus souvent.

1. Ma fille regarde trop la télé.
2. J'ai envie de me détendre ce soir.
3. Nous partons bientôt en vacances.
4. Dans ma famille, on se dispute toujours pour se servir de l'ordinateur portable.
5. J'ai envie de voir un bon film ce week-end.
6. J'ai du mal à choisir un candidat au moment des élections.

Implementation: 11-22 Have students name other important positions and ask their classmates to say what they would do if they occupied those positions.

11-22 Vous avez le pouvoir ! Avec un/e partenaire, imaginez que vous êtes dans les situations suivantes. Qu'est-ce que vous feriez ? Ensuite, comparez vos idées avec celles de vos camarades de classe.

MODÈLE Vous êtes le professeur de votre cours de français.

É1 Je donnerais moins de devoirs.

É2 Je ne permettrais pas aux étudiants de parler anglais.

1. Vous êtes le professeur de votre cours de français.
2. Vous êtes le président/la présidente de votre université.
3. Vous êtes un acteur/une actrice célèbre.
4. Vous êtes le directeur/la directrice d'une grande chaîne de télévision.
5. Vous êtes le maire de votre ville.
6. Vous êtes le président/la présidente des États-Unis.

Presentation: These expressions provide students with a means of ordering events that will allow them to avoid multiple-tense clauses. To present, provide multiple examples such as those found in the text and have students order the events: 2, 1 or 1, 2.

2. *L'ordre des évènements*

- To order events in time, you can use the expression **avant de** plus an infinitive. This expression can be used whether the time frame is past, present, or future.

Avant d'aller au travail, je vérifie mon courrier électronique.	*Before going to work, I check my e-mail.*
Avant de me coucher, j'ai lu un peu.	*Before going to bed, I read a little.*
Le ministre va y réfléchir **avant de répondre** aux journalistes.	*The minister will think about it before responding to the journalists.*

◆ The expression **après avoir/après être** plus the past participle can be used in a similar way to order events. Choose **avoir** or **être** based on how the particular verb is conjugated in the **passé composé**. Remember that when verbs are conjugated with **être,** the past participle must agree in number and gender with the subject.

Après avoir entendu la nouvelle, j'ai téléphoné à ma sœur.	*After hearing the news, I called my sister.*
Le soir, je surfe sur Internet **après avoir dîné**.	*In the evening, I surf the Internet after eating.*
Après s'être installée, la sénatrice se réunira avec son personnel.	*After getting settled in, the senator will meet with her staff.*

À vous la parole

11-23 Une journée typique. Déterminez l'ordre des évènements décrits.

Initial practice: 11-23 This comprehension-based activity asks students to order the two events.

MODÈLES Après avoir mangé, je me brosse les dents.
1. manger ; 2. me brosser les dents

Avant de me brosser les dents, je bois mon café.
1. boire mon café ; 2. me brosser les dents

1. Avant de m'habiller, je prends une douche.
2. Après être sortie, je mets mes gants et mon foulard.
3. Je vais acheter un journal avant d'arriver au bureau.
4. Après avoir travaillé un peu, j'ai déjeuné avec des amis.
5. Avant de quitter le bureau, j'ai téléphoné au chef de section.
6. Après avoir quitté le bureau, je suis allé au supermarché.
7. Avant de préparer à manger, j'ai cherché une recette sur Internet.
8. J'ai regardé un film sur mon ordi avant de me coucher.

11-24 Vos activités. Avec un/e partenaire, parlez de vos activités passées, actuelles et futures.

Implementation: 11-24 To prepare the exercise, you might first ask students to identify the time frame for each item (past/present/future); then put them to work in pairs.

MODÈLE Avant de venir en classe aujourd'hui, ...

È1 Avant de venir en classe aujourd'hui, j'ai travaillé à la B.U.
È2 Et moi, avant de venir en classe, j'ai déjeuné au resto U.

1. Avant de venir en classe aujourd'hui, ...
2. Après avoir fait les devoirs hier soir, ...
3. Avant de me coucher, normalement...
4. Avant de sortir avec mes amis le week-end, ...
5. Après avoir passé mes examens ce semestre, ...
6. Après avoir terminé mes études, ...
7. Avant de prendre ma retraite (*to retire*), ...

Variation: 11-25 You might assign this activity for written practice or ask students to put the various sentences together to create a pseudo-news report.

11-25 Dernières nouvelles. Imaginez le reportage d'un journaliste, qui doit utiliser un style plus sophistiqué.

MODÈLE Le président a parlé avec le ministre. Ensuite, il a donné une conférence de presse.

Après avoir parlé avec le ministre, le président a donné une conférence de presse.

OU Avant de donner une conférence de presse, le président a parlé avec le ministre.

1. Le ministre a parlé devant le Sénat, mais d'abord il a lu la proposition.
2. L'ambassadeur a annoncé la nouvelle, mais d'abord il a téléphoné au président.
3. Le sénateur se réunira (*will meet*) avec son personnel et ensuite il annoncera son plan économique.
4. Le ministre annoncera sa réforme éducative, mais d'abord il va prévenir (*to inform*) la presse.
5. Le journaliste a interviewé le président et ensuite il a écrit son article.

11-26 Narration. Expliquez à votre partenaire ce que vous avez fait hier, et ce que vous allez faire demain. Voici quelques expressions utiles.

d'abord	avant de + infinitif	après avoir } + participe passé
ensuite	enfin	après être } + participe passé

MODÈLE Hier, c'était dimanche. Je me suis levé très tard. D'abord, j'ai pris mon petit-déjeuner. Après avoir mangé, j'ai pris une douche. Avant de sortir, j'ai passé une ou deux heures sur Facebook…

Stratégie

Familiarize yourself with the conventions of the genre in which you are writing. For example, if you will be writing a futuristic piece, you may want to look at some typical examples of science fiction writing before you begin.

Note: Refer students to excerpts of some of Jules Verne's novels such as *De la terre à la lune* or *Autour de la Lune*.

Écrivons

11-27 Ma vie en 2040

A. Avant d'écrire. Imaginez votre vie en 2040 et écrivez deux ou trois paragraphes qui décrivent une journée typique pour vous. Pour rendre cette description plus intéressante, n'oubliez pas de parler des innovations technologiques qui feront partie de votre vie de tous les jours. Faites du remue-méninges (*brainstorming*) avec des camarades de classe pour imaginer les innovations futures. Pour vous donner quelques idées, consultez des œuvres de science-fiction ou futuristes.

B. En écrivant. Maintenant, rédigez quelques paragraphes qui décrivent votre journée typique dans l'avenir et les innovations technologiques qui vous entourent. N'oubliez pas d'écrire une phrase d'introduction et de terminer avec une brève conclusion.

MODÈLE Nous voilà en l'an 2040. Voici une journée typique pour moi. Comme tous les jours en semaine, je me lève à sept heures du matin quand je sens l'odeur du café préparé par mon robot domestique. Je prends mon PDA Génération-Six qui est aussi grand qu'une carte bancaire ! Mon empreinte digitale (*thumbprint*) sert de mot de passe et le PDA se met en marche (*starts up*). Pendant que je bois mon café, j'écoute les infos et mon PDA me précise quelle route je devrais prendre ce matin pour éviter les accidents de route et les embouteillages (*traffic jams*). Avant de quitter la maison, je règle les contrôles de l'ordinateur qui s'occupe de toutes les tâches (*chores*) domestiques pour indiquer que je dînerai à sept heures et demie ce soir et que j'amènerai une amie qui n'aime pas les haricots...

C. En révisant. Réfléchissez aux questions suivantes et puis faites tous les changements nécessaires.

1. Relisez votre description pour analyser le contenu : est-ce que vous avez décrit une journée typique en 2040 ? Combien d'innovations technologiques est-ce que vous avez mentionnées ?
2. Relisez de nouveau votre texte pour analyser le style et la forme : est-ce que la description de votre journée contient des éléments fantastiques ou futuristes ? Avez-vous inclus suffisamment de détails pour rendre votre description intéressante ? Est-ce que vous avez inclus des phrases d'introduction et de conclusion ? Vérifiez que vous avez bien utilisé le vocabulaire nécessaire pour décrire la technologie.

D. Après avoir écrit. Partagez votre description avec vos camarades de classe. Qui a la vision la plus futuriste ? la plus réaliste ? la moins probable ?

Variation: Ask students to illustrate their imagined descriptions. Collect all students' work and "publish" it together on a course Web site or in hard copy.

Leçon 3 On s'informe

Presentation: To introduce the new vocabulary, have students complete the *questionnaire*. To check comprehension, total the responses for the group. Have students repeat key words and phrases.

POINTS DE DÉPART

TEXT AUDIO
CD 6 TRACK 6

La lecture et vous

Qu'est-ce qu'elle lit ?

Quelles sont vos habitudes de lecture ? Complétez le questionnaire pour en savoir plus ! D'après vos résultats, est-ce que vous êtes un lecteur sérieux, un lecteur occasionnel ou un lecteur pragmatique ? Comparez vos réponses aux réponses de vos camarades de classe.

Indiquez vos trois types de lecture préférés :

- ☐ les journaux (nationaux, régionaux, spécialisés — sport, économie)
- ☐ les magazines (d'information, de télévision, féminins ou familiaux)
- ☐ les romans (d'amour, historiques, policiers, de science-fiction)
- ☐ les livres de loisirs (de cuisine, de sport, de bricolage, de jardinage)
- ☐ les livres d'art (sur la peinture, l'architecture, le cinéma)
- ☐ les livres d'histoire ou les biographies
- ☐ les blogs, les forums de discussion et les journaux en ligne
- ☐ les poésies
- ☐ les bandes dessinées (les BD)
- ☐ les ouvrages de référence (le dictionnaire, l'atlas, l'encyclopédie)

Comment choisissez-vous un livre ?

- ☐ les recommendations des critiques dans la presse ou en ligne
- ☐ les recommendations d'amis
- ☐ la réputation de l'auteur
- ☐ la publicité

Comment obtenez-vous les livres ?

- ☐ vous les empruntez à une bibliothèque
- ☐ vous les empruntez à des amis
- ☐ vous les achetez dans une librairie
- ☐ vous êtes abonné/e à un club lecture
- ☐ vous les téléchargez en ligne

Pourquoi lisez-vous ?

☐ pour vous détendre ☐ pour vous instruire ☐ pour vous distraire

Quand lisez-vous ?

- ☐ en vacances
- ☐ en voyage
- ☐ dans les transports en commun
- ☐ à la bibliothèque
- ☐ chez vous
- ☐ en écoutant de la musique
- ☐ au lit pour vous endormir
- ☐ devant l'ordinateur

Fiche pratique

To remember new words or expressions that may cause some confusion, associate a meaningful example with each one. For example: **une bande dessinée** : ***Astérix*** ; **un dessin animé** : ***Les 101 Dalmatiens*** ; **un film d'animation** : ***Wall-E.***

Note: Prompt students to find other word pairs that may also cause confusion, such as *une bibliothèque et une librairie, un/e volontaire et un/e bénévole, un magazine et un magasin, un chemisier et une chemise*, and to think about how they could apply this same technique.

À vous la parole

11-28 De la lecture pour tout le monde. Quel type de livre, de magazine ou de site Web est-ce qu'on pourrait conseiller à chaque personne décrite ici ?

Variation: 11-28 Have students suggest various Web sites and/or blogs that correspond to the interests of the people listed.

MODÈLE un enfant

On pourrait lui suggérer une histoire d'enfants ou une bande dessinée.

1. un étudiant qui prépare son diplôme en journalisme
2. quelqu'un qui adore l'art mais qui n'a pas souvent l'occasion d'aller au musée
3. quelqu'un qui aime bricoler
4. quelqu'un qui apprend l'anglais
5. quelqu'un qui regarde souvent la télévision
6. quelqu'un qui s'intéresse à l'histoire
7. quelqu'un qui adore la science-fiction
8. quelqu'un qui fait beaucoup de sport

Presentation: Further activities for use with this clip can be found in the SAM/MFL. To check students' comprehension of the cultural notes, use a recognition exercise: *Donnez-moi un exemple d'un magazine américain à caractère familial. —Better Homes and Gardens, Family Circle.* Point out that the French tend to buy newspapers and magazines at *un tabac* or *un kiosque*. In contrast, Americans tend to receive home delivery of newspapers and to subscribe or buy magazines at the supermarket.

The chart indicates the number of readers in thousands (as indicated in the legend) as determined by a survey carried out by AEPM (*Audiences, études sur la presse magazine*). More information can be obtained from their Web site (see the *Chez nous* Companion Website for links). Check the latest version of *Francoscopie* for interesting information on the French press, which can be found in the section on *Loisirs* under *Les Médias*. The French spend half their leisure time in front of the TV, hence the large number of TV magazines. Ask students to identify the most popular magazines in the U.S. According to the Audit Bureau of Statistics, the top ten U.S. periodicals for the period from July to December 2006 are: *1. AARP: The Magazine 2. Readers' Digest 3. Better Homes and Gardens 4. National Geographic 5. Good Housekeeping 6. Ladies' Home Journal 7. Time 8. Women's Day 9. Family Circle 10. People.* Note that in contrast to the French figures, which only pertain to weekly and bimonthly magazines, the U.S. figures also include monthly periodicals.

Vie et culture

La presse française

Regardez la séquence vidéo, *Je lis la presse*, où Pauline montre et décrit ses journaux et magazines préférés. D'après sa description, qu'est-ce qu'un quotidien ? un hebdomadaire ? un mensuel ?

Pauline achète *Le Monde*, mais elle est abonnée[1] au quotidien *Libération*. Comment est-ce qu'elle décrit son magazine préféré, *Le Nouvel Observateur* ? Quel autre hebdomadaire est-ce qu'elle achète, et pourquoi ? Pauline a acheté un mensuel, *Géo* ; pourquoi ?

Voici la liste des dix hebdomadaires et bimensuels les plus lus en France pour la période allant de janvier à décembre 2007. Pour chaque magazine, identifiez son genre : par exemple, est-ce que c'est un magazine féminin ? un magazine télé ? Qu'est-ce que vous pouvez déduire des priorités ou des goûts des gens qui les achètent ?

[1] *subscribes*

Le Top Ten des hebdomadaires les plus lus

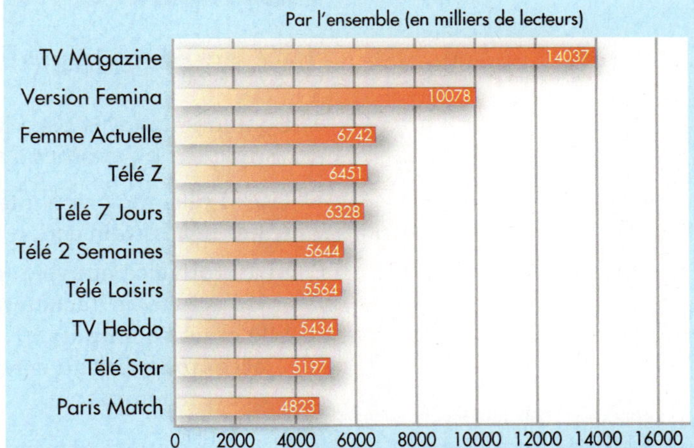

Implementation: 11-29 As a follow-up to this exercise, ask students 1) which of the books and magazines listed they would choose for themselves, and why 2) what type of book or magazine they would buy for a friend or family member. Have students role-play a situation in which they ask a bookseller's advice.

Note: *Télérama* includes a guide to TV programming, reviews of current films, and book reviews. It is popular with well-educated readers and is purchased even by people who have no television.

Implementation: 11-30 This can be carried out in pairs, in small groups, or as a whole-class exercise; summarize results at the end of group discussion. If you have a wide age range of students in your class, it might be interesting to compare current reading practices (for example, printing online articles to read versus reading them on screen) of the various age groups.

11-29 D'après le titre. D'après le titre, c'est quel genre de livre, de journal ou de magazine ?

MODÈLE *Marie Claire Maison*
C'est probablement un magazine féminin.

1. *Télérama*
2. *Info-Matin*
3. *Elle*
4. *Cahiers du Football*
5. *Bien-Être & Santé*
6. *Lucky Luke dans le Far West*
7. *Le Guide Pratique du Droit*
8. *Cuisine Minceur*

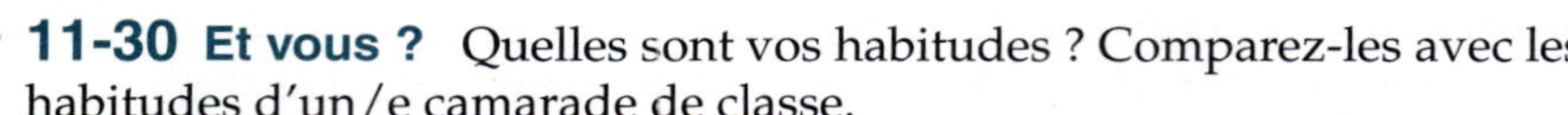

11-30 Et vous ? Quelles sont vos habitudes ? Comparez-les avec les habitudes d'un/e camarade de classe.

1. Qu'est-ce que vous lisez tous les jours ? — le journal, des magazines ? quels journaux ou magazines ? les infos en ligne ? les profils de vos amis sur Facebook ?
2. Quels ouvrages de référence est-ce que vous consultez chez vous ? à la bibliothèque ? en ligne ?
3. Qu'est-ce que vous lisez pour vos cours ? Est-ce que vous avez beaucoup de lectures en ligne à faire ?
4. Qu'est-ce que vous lisez pour vous informer ? pour vous détendre ?
5. Qu'est-ce que vous lisez quand vous êtes en vacances ?
6. Quel est le dernier livre que vous avez lu ? Est-ce que vous êtes en train de lire un livre maintenant ? Lequel ?
7. Quel est votre auteur préféré ? Est-ce que vous avez un journaliste ou un bloguer préféré ? Qui ?

FORMES ET FONCTIONS

1. *Les phrases avec* si...

The conjunction **si** is used in a clause that expresses a condition. It is often accompanied by another clause that expresses the result.

- Use **si** plus the present tense to express a condition that, if fulfilled, will result in a certain action (stated in the present or future).

Si je **trouve** ce nouveau roman, je l'**achète**/je l'**achèterai**.	*If I find this new novel, I'm buying it/I will buy it.*
Elle nous **accompagne**/**accompagnera** au cinéma **si** elle **a** le temps.	*She is going/will go with us to the movies if she has the time.*

Note: Point out that the clauses may be ordered in either way, as in the examples provided.

- Use **si** plus the imperfect if the situation is hypothetical; the result clause will then be in the conditional.

Si j'**avais** assez d'argent, je m'**achèterais** un nouvel ordinateur portable.	*If I had enough money, I would buy myself a new laptop.*
Ils **pourraient** répondre plus rapidement **s'**il leur **envoyait** un e-mail.	*They could respond more quickly if he sent them an e-mail.*

À vous la parole

11-31 Pour vous informer et vous distraire en ligne. David explique à son amie Céline comment se servir plus d'Internet. Terminez chaque phrase d'une façon logique.

MODÈLE Si tu achètes un ordinateur portable avec une connexion Wi-Fi, ...
Si tu achètes un ordinateur portable avec une connexion Wi-Fi, tu pourras travailler n'importe où.

1. Si tu as besoin de lire un article en ligne, ...
2. Si tu veux rester en contact avec tes amis, ...
3. Si tu veux écouter de la musique, ...
4. Si tu cherches un numéro de téléphone, ...
5. Si tu veux avoir les dernières nouvelles, ...
6. Si tu as le temps de jouer, ...
7. Si tu veux regarder un film, ...

Variation: 11-31 and 11-32 To vary or provide review, change the tense/mode: *Si tu achetais un portable, ... ; Si tu deviens journaliste, tu écriras...*, etc.

11-32 Choix de profession. Quelques jeunes gens ne peuvent pas décider quelle profession choisir. Qu'est-ce qu'ils feraient s'ils choisissaient une profession dans les arts ou dans les médias ?

MODÈLE journaliste
Si vous étiez journaliste, vous pourriez écrire des articles pour un journal ou un magazine.

1. présentateur/présentatrice à la télé
2. acteur/actrice
3. réalisateur/réalisatrice
4. chanteur/chanteuse
5. photographe
6. informaticien/ne
7. musicien/ne
8. écrivain

Implementation: 11-32 Have students suggest other professions and answers.

Additional activity: Recycle food vocabulary with the following type of exercise:

Quels plats ?

MODÈLE des œufs et des champignons
Si j'avais des œufs et des champignons, je ferais une omelette.

1. des carottes, des tomates et des oignons
2. des fruits de saison
3. du poisson et des légumes
4. du lait, des œufs et du sucre
5. du chocolat et du lait
6. du jus de citron, du sucre et de l'eau

11-33 Des rêves et des projets. Qu'est-ce que vous ferez ou feriez dans les situations suivantes ? Avec un/e partenaire, parlez de vos projets et de vos rêves (*dreams*).

MODÈLE être une actrice/un acteur célèbre
É1 Si tu étais une actrice célèbre, qu'est-ce que tu ferais ?
É2 Je serais très riche et j'habiterais à Hollywood.

1. avoir ton diplôme demain
2. être millionnaire
3. trouver un emploi aujourd'hui
4. aller en Suisse
5. être en France
6. être le président/la présidente des États-Unis
7. avoir 50 ans

Presentation: Point out that *Depuis combien de temps ?* is the preferred question to use when asking about duration of an event or activity, and *Depuis quand ?* is used when the speaker wants to know specifically when the event began. In actual conversation, however, a person may respond by specifying either the beginning or the duration of the event. The use of *depuis* with an expression referring to *heure(s)* is ambiguous and may refer to a period of time or a specific point in time: *Je t'attends depuis une heure.* (I've been waiting for you for an hour/since one o'clock.)

2. *Les expressions* depuis *et* il y a... que

Depuis and **il y a... que** are used with an expression of time and the present tense to indicate that an event that began in the past is still going on in the present.

- **Depuis** is used with an expression of time to indicate how long an event has been going on. To ask how long something has been going on, use **depuis combien de temps ?**

—**Depuis combien de temps** est-ce que tu écris des poèmes ?	—*How long have you been writing poems?*
—J'écris des poèmes **depuis** trois ans.	—*I've been writing poems for three years.*

- **Depuis** can also be used to indicate specifically when an event began. Use **depuis quand ?** to ask when an event started.

—**Depuis quand** est-ce que tu travailles ici ?	—*Since when have you been working here?*
—Je travaille ici **depuis** 2008.	—*I've been working here since 2008.*

- To emphasize the length of time that something has been going on, use **il y a**, plus a time expression, plus **que**.

—**Il y a combien de temps que** tu as cet ordinateur ?	—***How long*** *have you had this computer?*
—**Il y a deux mois.**	—*For two months.*

À vous la parole

11-34 Ça fait longtemps ! Mettez l'accent sur la durée en utilisant **il y a... que**.

MODÈLE Julie est à la fac depuis trois ans.
→ Il y a trois ans que Julie est à la fac.

1. Elle étudie les sciences de l'information depuis deux ans.
2. Elle fait un stage à la B.U. depuis trois mois.
3. Elle a un ordinateur portable depuis dix semaines.
4. Elle a un blog depuis un mois.
5. Elle lit l'autobiographie d'Eleanor Roosevelt depuis quelques semaines.
6. Elle cherche un article pour son cours de journalisme depuis quarante-cinq minutes.

Variation: 11-35 To introduce a cultural element to this activity, have students or groups of students research the biography of a well-known Francophone writer, actor, or director online and prepare a brief outline of some major events in his or her life. Students can then exchange biographies and ask each other questions using **11-35** as a model.

11-35 La biographie d'un journaliste. Avec un/e partenaire, parlez de la carrière de David en précisant depuis quand ou depuis combien de temps il fait les choses suivantes.

MODÈLE 1994 David devient photographe.
É1 Depuis quand est-ce que David est photographe ?
É2 Il est photographe depuis 1994.
OU É1 Depuis combien de temps est-ce que David est photographe ?
É2 Il est photographe depuis [seize] ans.

1994	David devient photographe.
1996	David étudie l'anglais.
1998	David travaille pour un magazine.
2000	David voyage pour le travail.
2001	David gagne des prix pour ses reportages.
2004	David a son bureau à Londres.
2006	David visite les États-Unis tous les ans.
2008	David est chef de bureau.

11-36 Et vous ? Posez des questions à un/e partenaire pour savoir s'il/si elle fait les choses suivantes, et si oui, depuis combien de temps.

Implementation: 11-36 Follow up by having students tell something they learned about their partner.

MODÈLES pratiquer un sport

É1 Est-ce que tu pratiques un sport ?
É2 Oui, je joue au basket.
É1 Depuis combien de temps est-ce que tu joues au basket ?
É2 Depuis sept ans.

1. pratiquer un sport
2. jouer d'un instrument
3. lire le journal
4. habiter la résidence ou un appartement
5. travailler
6. avoir un blog
7. avoir un ordi portable
8. être fiancé/e ou marié/e ou divorcé/e

Écoutons

Note: Students can listen to a *revue de presse* on the Internet; see the *Chez nous* Companion Website for links. You may wish to use the daily version of *la revue de presse* from the morning show *Télématin*. It can be downloaded from the Web. Although the French would be too complicated for students to follow without help, this *revue* has the advantage of showing headlines and articles as they are mentioned, which aids in comprehension. You may also choose to download for later use the *revue de presse* on a day when American news or international news with which American students would be familiar would be featured.

11-37 Revue de presse

A. Avant d'écouter. En France, vous pouvez entendre régulièrement à la radio ou même à la télévision le matin, une revue de presse. Dans ces émissions, un journaliste résume et commente des articles récents qu'il a sélectionnés. Dans cette revue de presse, vous allez entendre un journaliste qui parle de quatre thèmes différents : **le sport**, **la politique**, **les régions** et **la culture**. Avec un/e partenaire, pensez aux mots-clés que le journaliste pourrait employer pour parler de chaque thème. Par exemple, pour le thème **de la politique**, on pourrait entendre des mots comme **élections**, **président**, **parti politique**. Quand vous écoutez cette revue de presse, utilisez les mots-clés que vous avez identifiés pour vous aider à comprendre.

Key: En écoutant 1) la politique, le sport, les régions, la culture 2) *Libération, La Nouvelle République ; La Montagne, L'Équipe ; Le Point ; Première* 3) Answers include: Il y a des élections européennes dans deux semaines. Les Français ne s'intéressent pas beaucoup à ces élections ; L'équipe du Paris St-Germain a gagné la Coupe de France. Le match n'a pas été très intéressant ; La région de la Bretagne a créé des réserves naturelles ; Le Festival de Cannes est fini. Il y aura un festival du cinéma américain à Deauville.

B. En écoutant. Complétez le tableau en écoutant la revue de presse.

1. Pendant la première écoute, indiquez dans la première colonne, le thème (**sport**, **politique**, **région**, **culture**) pour chaque partie.
2. Écoutez de nouveau et entourez les magazines ou journaux mentionnés dans chaque partie. Il peut y avoir plusieurs sources pour chaque thème. (Attention : pour le premier thème, seulement un des journaux mentionnés a été sélectionné comme modèle. C'est à vous de trouver les autres.)
3. Écoutez une dernière fois et complétez la troisième colonne avec un fait intéressant que vous avez appris pour chaque thème.

Thème	Source(s)		Un fait intéressant
1. *la politique*	Le Figaro Libération Le Monde	Le Parisien La Nouvelle République	*Les élections européennes sont dans deux semaines.*
2.	La Montagne Les Echos	La Voix du Nord L'Équipe	
3.	L'Express Le Nouvel Observateur	Le Point	
4.	Géo Prima	Première Marie Claire	

Script: Écoutons

MALE VOICE 1: Vous écoutez France Inter. Il est 8 h 30. [Music.] 8 h 30. L'heure de la revue de presse d'Éric Richard. Bonjour Éric.

MALE VOICE 2: Bonjour. Comme vous le savez tous, c'est le moment des élections européennes et tous les journaux en parlent. Ce matin, à la une du *Figaro*, il y a un long article qui présente les candidats et leurs positions. Dans *Libération*, il y a un sondage qui indique que 32 % des Français ne connaissent pas les candidats et ne s'intéressent pas particulièrement à ces élections. À ce propos, vous trouverez dans *La Nouvelle République* un éditorial qui dit que la classe politique française ne semble pas très préoccupée par l'avenir de l'Union Européenne. Histoire à suivre en tout cas. Les élections sont dans deux semaines.

Tournons-nous vers le sport. Le journal *La Montagne* écrit ce matin en première page que le Paris St-Germain a gagné la Coupe de France de football. Malheureusement, le match n'a pas été très intéressant avec un seul but. Comme le dit le journal *L'Équipe* : « Hier soir au stade de France, on s'est un peu ennuyé. Un match sans panache. »

Cette semaine, l'hebdomadaire *Le Point* se tourne vers la Bretagne avec un reportage sur les charmes de cette région et ses efforts pour protéger son patrimoine avec la création de réserves naturelles régionales.

Dans le mensuel *Première*, tout un dossier consacré aux festivals de cinéma. C'est fini pour cette année le Festival de Cannes, mais pour les amateurs de l'Amérique, le Festival du Cinéma Américain de Deauville arrive dans quelques mois.

Allez bonne journée et bonne lecture à tous.

C. Après avoir écouté. Maintenant, répondez aux questions suivantes avec vos camarades de classe.

1. Après avoir écouté cette revue de presse, est-ce que vous avez envie de lire un de ces articles ? Quel(s) article(s) vous intéresse(nt) particulièrement ? Pourquoi ?
2. Est-ce que vous aimeriez écouter une revue de presse chez vous ? Pourquoi ?

Quels journaux et magazines est-ce que vous reconnaissez dans ce kiosque qui se trouve à Marrakech au Maroc ?

Venez chez nous ! Le cinéma

Les Français ont joué un grand rôle dans le développement du cinéma. C'est en 1895 à Lyon que les frères Lumière inventent le cinématographe, une machine qui permet de produire les premiers films. Deux ans après, le premier studio cinématographique est construit à Montreuil, près de Paris. Depuis, le film français est devenu un véhicule important de la culture francophone.

Presentation: Introduce this lesson by asking students what they know about the early film industry. How many have heard of *les frères Lumière*? You might show one or more of the Lumière brothers' first films, which are very short but include some interesting features, such as traveling shots and dissolves. Another interesting early film to show is Méliès' *Voyage dans la Lune*, which includes many special effects (Méliès was first and foremost a magician). Clips of these films are available for free viewing and download online. See the *Chez nous* Companion Website for links.

Louis et Auguste Lumière ont présenté le premier film de l'histoire du cinéma en 1895 : *la Sortie des usines Lumière.*

Voyage dans la Lune, tourné en 1902 par Georges Méliès, est le premier film de science-fiction. Georges Melies/The Metropolitan Museum of Art, New York, NY, U.S.A. Image copyright © The Metropolitan Museum of Art.

Observons

11-38 Réflexions sur le cinéma

A. Avant de regarder. Si vous habitiez les environs de Cannes, qu'est-ce que vous pourriez faire au moment du Festival International du Film ? Faites une liste d'activités possibles. Vous allez entendre une Niçoise qui décrit sa propre expérience, puis un étudiant à l'Université de Nice qui décrit ses préférences cinématographiques.

Note: This activity makes use of the first two interviews in the **Observons** clip; two additional interviews are treated in the SAM/MFL.

Implementation: Avant de regarder Help students generate a list of things they could see and do during the festival.

Script: Observons

FABIENNE : Vous savez que sur la Côte d'Azur nous avons Cannes, qui est pas très loin de Nice. Vous avez un tas de célébrités, de toutes nationalités qui euh viennent pour la promotion de leurs films. Je suis um très souvent aussi sur la ville de Cannes, donc j'aperçois souvent le Festival de Cannes et j'ai eu l'occasion de côtoyer quelques petites célébrités — un petit coucou, comme ça de, de quelques minutes. Voilà.

ÉDOUARD : Donc j'aime beaucoup le cinéma. Euh, j'y vais autant que je peux, ce qui est pas beaucoup, en tant que... parce que je suis étudiant. Euh mais dès que je peux, par contre, je loue un un DVD et je regarde ça avec des amis. Les derniers films que j'ai vus, c'est *Harry, un ami qui vous veut du bien*, euh un film français. Ou sinon, *L'auberge espagnole*. Je vous conseille de le voir, d'ailleurs. Euh sinon, ben, les grands classiques, comme euh *Le Seigneur des anneaux*, ou *Matrix*. Et euh, j'espère bientôt en voir un autre, ce soir peut-être.

Key: 1) a, d 2) b 3) a 4) a 5) c 6) c, d

Implementation: Après avoir regardé As a follow-up, have the class create a list of classic films, then develop a description in French for each of them. See the *Chez nous* Companion Website for links to French cinema sites.

B. En regardant. Trouvez toutes les bonnes réponses possibles à chaque question.

1. Selon Fabienne, des célébrités viennent à Cannes...
   a. de tous les pays.
   b. à tous les moments.
   c. pour les vacances.
   d. pour la promotion de leurs films.
2. Fabienne... à Cannes au moment du festival.
   a. ne va jamais
   b. est souvent
   c. va tous les ans
3. Elle a eu l'occasion... quelques célébrités.
   a. de voir
   b. de dîner avec
   c. d'interviewer
4. Édouard va au cinéma...
   a. aussi souvent que possible.
   b. très souvent.
   c. tous les soirs.
5. Le dernier film qu'il a vu, c'était un film...
   a. américain.
   b. espagnol.
   c. français.
6. Pour lui, un grand classique du cinéma, c'est...
   a. *Harry, un ami qui vous veut du bien.*
   b. *L'auberge espagnole.*
   c. *Le Seigneur des anneaux.*
   d. *Matrix.*

C. Après avoir regardé. Maintenant discutez des questions suivantes avec vos camarades de classe.

1. Est-ce qu'il est possible pour les gens chez vous de côtoyer (*to get close to*) des célébrités comme le fait Fabienne à Cannes ? Pourquoi est-ce que les gens aiment cela, à votre avis ?
2. Est-ce que vous êtes d'accord avec Édouard quand il nomme des « grands classiques » ? Quels sont les grands films classiques pour vous ?

Les festivals internationaux de films

Il y a de nombreux festivals de films chaque année. Un des plus connus est en France, à Cannes. Tous les ans, pendant quinze jours au mois de mai, la charmante ville touristique de Cannes devient la capitale cinématographique du monde. Le Festival International du Film est surtout un congrès professionnel : producteurs, réalisateurs et vedettes y viennent pour se rencontrer, pour échanger des idées, pour essayer de vendre leurs nouveaux films et pour distribuer des « Palmes » pour les meilleurs films de l'année.

Le Palais des Festivals à Cannes.

Pour savoir quels sont les meilleurs films canadiens, vous pouvez regarder Le Gala des Jutra. C'est le festival cinématographique qui a lieu chaque année au mois de mars au Québec. Pour le cinéma africain, le FESPACO (le Festival Panafricain du Cinéma et de la Télévision de Ouagadougou) a lieu tous les deux ans à Ouagadougou, au Burkina Faso. Ce grand festival a pour objectif de favoriser la diffusion de toutes les œuvres du cinéma africain. Est-ce que vous connaissez des films africains ? Lesquels ?

Une femme à mobylette devant une affiche qui annonce le Festival Panafricain du Cinéma et de la Télévision de Ouagadougou.

Presentation: Show the video montage *Le cinéma* to preview discussion of the Cannes film festival. Once students have read and discussed the text, see whether they can narrate the various events shown in the montage. Ask students if they enjoy watching the Oscars and if so, why, and whether they are familiar with any other film festivals. See the *Chez nous* Companion Website for links to Francophone film festivals.

Lisons

Stratégie

Considering the type of text you are reading and its conventions can help you to approach it knowledgeably. For example, your expectations about style and content can alert you as to what you should be watching for when you read reviews of a book or film.

Implementation: Avant de lire Complete this activity in class. Make a list of the expectations students have about what they are about to read, then see how this list compares with the information asked for in **En lisant.** Elements frequently found in movie reviews include title, name of director/producer, names of lead actors, a brief summary, a comparison of the film with other similar films, and a statement of the author's opinion of the film. Note that this reading activity serves as a model for the writing activity that follows.

Note: Point out the distinction between *la critique* (review) and *le critique* (reviewer).

Key: En lisant 1) Il y a trois critiques positives et une critique négative. 2) Les critiques de Christine et de Richard donnent des résumés du scénario. 3) Le fils, Thomas (Marc Paquet), ses parents et sa copine, Audrey (Catherine de Léan). 4) Stéphane Lapointe. La critique de Cassandra l'identifie et les renseignements généraux qui précèdent les critiques. 5) Un scénario magnifique, des bons acteurs ; ce film a une touche québécoise, des bons acteurs 6) C'est ennuyeux et trop long ; les personnages ne sont pas crédibles.

11-39 Critiques d'un film

Regardez cette photo du film franco-canadien *La vie secrète des gens hereux*. Qu'est-ce qui se passe dans le film. à votre avis ?

A. Avant de lire. De nos jours, on peut visiter plusieurs sites Web où les cinéphiles affichent leurs opinions sur les films récents. Voici quatre critiques du film québécois *La vie secrète des gens heureux*. Avant de les lire, pensez aux critiques de film que vous avez lues récemment.

1. Quels types de renseignements est-ce que vous y avez trouvés ? Par exemple, dans chacune de ces critiques, on parlera probablement de l'intrigue et des personnages et il y aura aussi une appréciation du film. Quelles autres conventions seront respectées dans ces critiques ?
2. Étant donné que ces critiques se trouvent sur un site Web, comment est-ce qu'elles seront différentes des autres critiques ?

B. En lisant. Cherchez les réponses aux questions suivantes.

1. En général, est-ce que les critiques de ce film sont positives ou négatives ? Qu'est-ce qui a influencé votre réponse ?
2. Trouvez un extrait dans une des critiques qui résume le scénario du film.
3. Identifiez les personnages principaux et les acteurs principaux.
4. Qui est le réalisateur du film ? Comment est-ce que vous le savez ?
5. Pour Cassandra, quels sont les points forts du film ? Et pour Richard ?
6. Pour Marie-Ange, quels sont les points faibles du film ?

la vie secrète des gens heureux

☆☆☆ **3.27**

Canada, 2006

De Stéphane Lapointe

Avec Marc Paquet, Gilbert Sicotte, Catherine de Léan, Marie Gignac, Gilles Renaud, Anne Dorval

Drame, 1 h 42, Général

Note: This film was nominated for several awards for the Jutra in 2007. You might show a portion of the film in class to elicit students' reactions. The film has been compared to the American film *American Beauty*. Ask if any students have seen this movie and how they think it might compare with the Quebec film reviewed here.

Critique de **Cassandra**

Stéphane Lapointe...réalisateur et scénariste brillant ! ☆☆☆☆☆

J'ai adoré ce film. Stéphane Lapointe a écrit un scénario absolument magnifique. Je suis passée par la colère, la tristesse, le rire, la joie...franchement c'est très bien réussi.
Marc Paquet et Catherine de Léan sont beaux à voir et ce sont de tellement bons acteurs. Et c'est bien de revoir Gilbert Sicotte au cinéma ! Il tient bien sa place.
J'ai beaucoup aimé.

Critique de **Marie-Ange**

Une déception ! ☆☆

Un des films québécois les plus décevants[1] que j'aie vu ces dernières années.
Non seulement il est ennuyeux, mais en plus il dure trop longtemps. En plus, les personnages ne sont pas crédibles et leur profil psychologique est un peu trop simpliste.

Critique de **Richard**

Beauté québécoise ! ☆☆☆☆

D'après le réalisateur Stéphane Lapointe *La vie secrète des gens heureux* est inspirée du film Oscarisé American Beauty. Eh oui mais avec cette touche québécoise ce film devient très original. C'est l'histoire de Thomas, mal dans sa peau, qui habite chez ses parents qui lui mettent (de) la pression[2] pour qu'il réussisse. Il a l'impression d'être un raté par rapport à son père prospère et sa mère enseignante qui sait tout. Comment peut-on réussir quand on sait qu'on est rien à côté d'eux ? Le film va nous montrer que le chemin de la réussite n'est pas toujours si simple et que les apparences peuvent être trompeuses[3]. Merveilleux film magnifiquement interprété par un groupe d'excellents acteurs. Bravo à ce film qui est une grande réussite à tous les points de vue ! Bravo au cinéma québécois...

Critique de **Christine**

Le bonheur total ☆☆☆

Le gazon est toujours plus vert chez le voisin, surtout quand ce voisin semble mener une vie parfaite, avec une famille parfaite. C'est le cas des Dufresne et leur fils adulte, Thomas (Marc Paquet). Celui-ci étudie l'architecture et n'a malheureusement pas de copine, car il est d'une timidité extrême. Ne voulant pas que leur fils abandonne tout juste avant la remise de son diplôme, les parents Dufresne décident d'engager une certaine Audrey (Catherine de Léan) pour lui redonner la motivation nécessaire pour finir ses études. Elle aura tout l'effet souhaité, et même plus, parce que sa présence viendra peu à peu bouleverser[4] la vie de tous les membres de la famille. Comme quoi la vie nous réserve parfois des mauvaises surprises.

[1]*disappointing* [2]*pressure* [3]*deceiving* [4]*completely disrupt*

Key: En regardant de plus près 1) Ils donnent une opinion 2) Marie-Ange : son évaluation ; Richard : une comparaison avec un film américain, un résumé, une évaluation ; Christine : un résumé 3) Cassandra : j'ai adoré ce film ; Marie-Ange : une déception ; Richard : Bravo à ce film.

C. En regardant de plus près. Maintenant examinez les aspects suivants de ces critiques.

1. Quels sont les éléments communs à ces quatre critiques ?
2. Chaque personne organise sa critique d'une manière personnelle. Par exemple, la première personne a) donne son évaluation ; b) donne une liste des points forts du film ; c) parle des acteurs. Comment est-ce que les autres critiques sont organisées ?
3. Dans les trois premières critiques, trouvez une phrase ou une expression qui résume l'opinion de la personne qui l'a écrite.

D. Après avoir lu. Discutez des questions suivantes avec vos camarades de classe.

1. Est-ce que vous pouvez résumer l'opinion de chaque critique ? Quelle critique vous semble la plus convaincante et pourquoi ?
2. D'après ce que vous avez lu, quelle impression est-ce que vous avez de ce film ? Est-ce que vous voudriez le voir ? Pourquoi ? Est-ce que vous avez déjà vu un film semblable ? Si oui, décrivez-le.

Écrivons

11-40 La critique d'un film

Stratégie

To write a review of a film or a book, be sure to include the expected factual information as well as your personal assessment.

A. Avant d'écrire. Choisissez un film que vous avez vu récemment et écrivez une petite critique. D'abord, pensez aux éléments importants d'une bonne critique en répondant aux questions suivantes :

1. Notez le nom du réalisateur et des acteurs principaux. Quels rôles est-ce qu'ils jouent ?
2. Faites un résumé assez bref de l'intrigue. Pour vous guider, pensez aux critiques de films que vous avez déjà lues.
3. Enfin, quelle est votre opinion de ce film ?

Implementation: Avant d'écrire You might want to arrange to show a Francophone movie or have students rent one for the purposes of this assignment. This helps curb the need, or desire, for unnecessary translation from English to French.

B. En écrivant. Écrivez votre critique avec les détails que vous avez notés dans l'exercice A, et n'oubliez pas de donner votre opinion du film. Utilisez le vocabulaire que vous connaissez.

C. En révisant. Réfléchissez aux questions suivantes et puis faites tous les changements nécessaires.

1. Relisez votre critique pour analyser le contenu : est-ce que vous avez inclus tous les éléments nécessaires : le titre du film, le nom du réalisateur et des acteurs principaux, un résumé de l'intrigue avec quelques précisions sur l'histoire et votre opinion ?
2. Relisez de nouveau votre critique pour analyser le style et la forme : est-ce que vous avez utilisé les expressions appropriées pour donner votre opinion du film ? Est-ce que votre résumé du film est bref mais suffisamment clair ? Est-ce que le lecteur aura une bonne idée s'il faut aller voir ce film ou pas après avoir lu votre critique ?

D. Après avoir écrit. Échangez votre critique avec un/e camarade de classe ou lisez votre critique pour vos camarades de classe. Ne donnez pas le titre du film. Les autres vont essayer de deviner de quel film il s'agit (*it's about*).

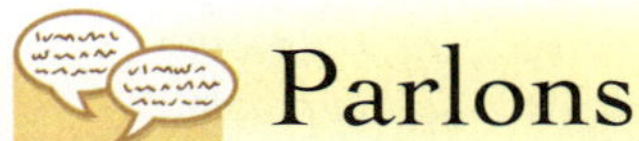

Parlons

11-41 Un questionnaire sur le cinéma

Implementation: Avant de parler Divide students into groups of four or five to prepare the survey questions or have students prepare the questions together as a whole-class activity. Then have students ask each other the survey questions and tabulate the results.

A. Avant de parler. Tout le monde aime le cinéma, n'est-ce pas ? Peut-être pas. En groupes de quatre ou cinq, préparez un questionnaire et puis faites un sondage dans votre classe pour savoir les opinions de vos camarades de classe à propos du cinéma. D'abord, il faut préparer trois ou quatre questions et les réponses possibles. Vous pouvez poser des questions, par exemple, sur le genre de films que les gens préfèrent voir (les films d'action, les comédies romantiques, ...), sur la fréquence avec laquelle ils voient des films (régulièrement, de temps en temps, rarement, jamais...), sur l'endroit où ils ont l'habitude de voir des films (à la maison en DVD, au cinéma, sur ordinateur...). Voici une question modèle et ses réponses pour vous aider :

MODÈLE Parmi les choses suivantes, qu'est-ce qui vous donne le plus envie d'aller voir un film ?

- ☐ les acteurs
- ☐ le réalisateur
- ☐ le sujet
- ☐ les critiques
- ☐ les opinions de mes amis qui ont déjà vu le film
- ☐ les publicités à la télé ou les bandes-annonces dans les salles de cinéma

B. En parlant. Maintenant, faites votre sondage en posant les questions que vous avez préparées à vos camarades de classe. Notez leurs réponses.

C. Après avoir parlé. Avec votre groupe, analysez vos réponses et présentez-les à vos camarades de classe. Comparez les résultats du sondage de chaque groupe. Est-ce que les différents groupes ont beaucoup de similarités ou beaucoup de différences ?

Now that you have completed *Chapitre 11*, can you do the following in French?

- ☐ talk about television, films, and the print media?
- ☐ talk about the use of electronic media and equipment?
- ☐ talk about hypothetical situations using the conditional?
- ☐ express concurrent and consecutive events in the past, present, and future?
- ☐ discuss the use of the Internet in France?
- ☐ discuss cinema in the French-speaking world?

Leçon 1

des genres d'émissions	***kinds of programs***
un dessin animé	*cartoon, animated film*
un divertissement	*variety show*
un documentaire	*documentary*
une émission de musique	*music program*
une émission sportive	*sports event*
une émission de téléachat	*infomercial*
une émission de téléréalité	*reality show*
un feuilleton	*soap opera*
un jeu télévisé	*game show*
le journal télévisé (le JT)	*news broadcast*
les informations (les infos)	*news*
un magazine	*news magazine*
un reportage	*special report*
une série	*series*
un téléfilm	*made-for-TV movie*

pour regarder la télévision	***to watch TV***
allumer	*to turn on (an appliance)*
une chaîne	*TV station*
un écran	*screen*
un épisode	*episode*
un magazine télé	*listing of TV programs*
une télécommande	*remote control*

des genres de films	***types of films***
une comédie	*comedy*
une comédie dramatique	*dark comedy*
une comédie musicale	*musical*
une comédie romantique	*romantic comedy*
un drame (psychologique)	*(psychological) drama*
un film d'action	*action film*
un film d'animation	*animated film*
un film d'aventures	*adventure film*
un film d'espionnage	*spy film*
un film historique	*historical movie*
un film d'horreur	*horror movie*
un film policier	*detective/police movie*
un film de science-fiction	*science fiction movie*
un western	*western*

pour parler des films	***to talk about films***
célèbre	*famous*
doublé/e	*dubbed*
le personnage (principal)	*(main) character*
plein de	*full of*
raconter (une histoire)	*to tell (a story)*
un réalisateur/une réalisatrice	*film director*
des sous-titres (m.)	*subtitles*
tourner (un film)	*to shoot (a film)*
une vedette	*a movie star*
en version originale (en V.O.)/en version originale avec des sous-titres en français (en V.O.S.T.F.)	*in the original language / in the original language with French subtitles*

quelques conjonctions	***some conjunctions***
aussitôt que	*as soon as*
dès que	*as soon as*
lorsque	*when*
pendant	*during, for*
pendant que	*while*

pour exprimer une opinion	***to express an opinion***
Je pense / Je crois / Je trouve que...	*I think / I believe / I find that . . .*
À mon avis, ...	*In my opinion, . . .*
Pour moi, ...	*For me, . . .*

pour réagir à une opinion	***to react to an opinion***
Je suis (tout à fait) d'accord...	*I agree (completely)*
Je ne suis pas (tout à fait) d'accord...	*I do not (completely) agree*
Au contraire, ...	*On the contrary, . . .*
D'un autre côté, ...	*On the other hand, . . .*

Vocabulaire

Leçon 2

un ordinateur (un ordi)	***computer***
un baladeur MP3	*MP3 player*
un clavier	*keyboard*
une clé USB	*USB key-drive, thumb drive*
un graveur CD/DVD	*CD/DVD burner*
un disque dur	*hard drive*
une imprimante (multifonction)	*(multifunction) printer*
un lecteur CD/DVD	*CD drive, DVD drive*
un lien	*(Web) link*
la messagerie instantanée	*instant messaging*
un moniteur (avec un écran plat)	*(flat screen) monitor*
un ordinateur portable	*laptop*
un PDA	*PDA*
un scanner	*scanner*
une souris (sans fil)	*(wireless) mouse*
une webcam	*webcam*

pour travailler à l'ordinateur	***to work at the computer***
un clip (vidéo)	*(video) clip*
une connexion sans fil	*wireless connection/card*
un e-mail	*e-mail message*
le courrier électronique	*e-mail*
en ligne	*online*
envoyer	*to send*
un fichier	*computer file*
imprimer	*to print*
un logiciel	*software program*
multimédia	*multimedia*
une pièce jointe	*attachment*
recevoir	*to receive*
la recherche	*research*
un réseau (sans fil), Wi-Fi	*(wireless) network*
retoucher	*to edit a picture, to touch up*
sauvegarder (un fichier)	*to save (a file)*
surfer sur Internet	*to surf the Internet*
un site Web	*Web site*
télécharger	*to download*

autres mots utiles	***other useful words***
C'est génial !	*It's great!*
échanger	*to exchange*
se servir de (quelque chose)	*to use (something)*
tout le monde	*everyone*

pour situer l'action dans le temps	***to order events in time***
avant de + inf. ...	*before . . .*
après avoir/être + participe passé ...	*after having . . .*

Leçon 3

à lire	***to read***
un atlas	*atlas*
une bande dessinée (une BD)	*comics, comic book*
une biographie	*biography*
une encyclopédie	*encyclopedia*
un hebdomadaire	*weekly (publication)*
un journal (des journaux)	*newspaper(s)*
un livre d'art	*art book*
un livre de cuisine	*cookbook*
un livre d'histoire	*history book*
un livre de loisirs	*book on leisure time or hobbies*
un magazine	*magazine*
un mensuel	*monthly (publication)*
un ouvrage de référence	*reference book*
la poésie	*poetry*
la presse	*the press*
une publicité (une pub)	*advertisement, commercial*
un quotidien	*daily (publication)*
un roman	*novel*

pour choisir un livre	***to choose a book***
un auteur	*author*
un critique	*(movie, literary) critic*
une critique	*(critical) review*
une recommandation	*recommendation*

pour exprimer la durée	***to express duration***
depuis combien de temps ?	*for how long?*
depuis quand ?	*since when?*
il y a... que	*it's been . . ., for . . .*

quelques mots utiles	***some useful words***
se distraire	*to amuse oneself*
s'informer	*to get information*
s'instruire	*to educate oneself, to improve one's mind*

12 Les beaux-arts

Cette représentation de l'opéra d'*Aïda* a lieu dans un théâtre romain en Provence. Est-ce que vous pouvez trouver l'orchestre ? les acteurs principaux ? le chœur ?

After completing this chapter, you should be able to:

- Talk about the arts
- Narrate events in the past, present, and future
- Use pronouns appropriately to avoid redundancy
- Discuss the arts in the French speaking world

Leçon  Fêtons la musique !

POINTS DE DÉPART

Tu es musicien ?

Presentation: Begin the lesson by reviewing music vocabulary from Ch. 2, L. 2, reminding students to use *jouer de* with a musical instrument. Have them listen to the dialogue as they look at the text. Ask simple questions to test comprehension: *De quel instrument est-ce que Claire joue ? Et Ben ?*, etc. Point out useful conversational expressions such as *Bof, C'est entendu, Tu plaisantes !* The children's book *Sophie la vache musicienne*, written by Geoffroy de Pennart (Kaléidoscope, 1999), can be used as a complement to this lesson. Written mostly in the present tense, the text is quite accessible. You may wish to play the video clip *J'aime beaucoup le jazz*, in which the speaker discusses her music preferences and a concert she attended. Have students pick out the details she uses to describe the singer's style.

Claire arrive au café avec son violon.

BEN : Tiens, je ne savais pas que tu étais musicienne !
CLAIRE : Bof, pas vraiment. Je joue pour le plaisir.
BEN : Tu fais partie d'un orchestre ?
CLAIRE : Non, je joue quelquefois avec des copains, c'est tout.
BEN : De la musique classique ?
CLAIRE : Non, c'est surtout de la musique traditionnelle ou folklorique.
BEN : Ah, c'est intéressant ! Tu me diras quand tu feras un concert ?
CLAIRE : C'est entendu. Mais est-ce que ça t'intéresserait de jouer avec nous ? On a une répétition demain soir chez moi.
BEN : Tu plaisantes ! Avec mon saxophone ?
CLAIRE : Et pourquoi pas ?

Presentation: Display the musicians and their instruments (MFL, Ch. 12) and describe each group. Test comprehension by having students point to the instrument you name; find out if students in the class, or anyone in their family, play any of the instruments pictured. Depending on your class, you may wish to introduce additional musical instruments, such as *des instruments à cordes – la contrebasse, la viole, la harpe ; des instruments à vent – les bois : le basson, le hautbois ; les cuivres : le cor* (French horn), *le tuba ; des instruments à percussion : le tambour, le triangle, les cymbales (f.), le xylophone.* Note that in France, *une flûte* is a recorder; the expression used for a flute is *une flûte traversière.*

Quelques instruments

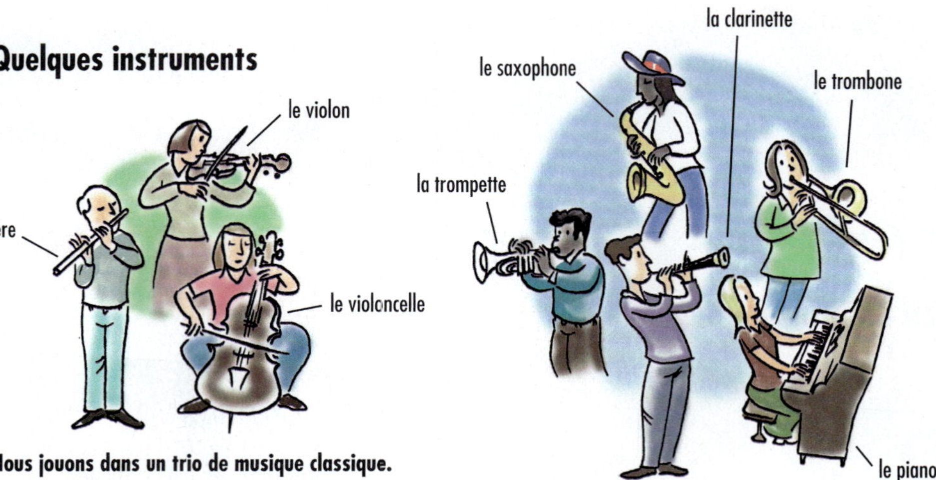

Nous jouons dans un trio de musique classique.

Ils font partie d'un groupe de jazz.

la batterie

le clavier

la guitare électrique

la guitare basse

Eux, ils ont formé un groupe de rock.

À vous la parole

Expansion: Have students listen to snippets of music to identify the instruments they hear.

12-1 Ils jouent de quel instrument ? De quel instrument est-ce que ces personnes jouent ?

MODÈLE Marie-Hélène joue de la clarinette.

Marie-Hélène

1. Claire et moi

2. Thomas

3. Sylvie et toi

4. Adrien

5. Fred

6. Vanessa et David

Note: *La Fête de la Musique* always occurs on the summer solstice, the longest day of the year. Since its inception in 1982, it has gained in popularity and has spread to countries far beyond France. North American cities, from Montreal and New York City to Kalamazoo, Michigan, have instituted their own versions of this annual event. It has also spread to Yemen, Katmandu (in Nepal), and in 2008 to Iraq. Ask students if they have ever participated in a *Fête de la Musique* event. Consult the *Chez nous* Companion Website for links to sites with more information.

Vie et culture

La Fête de la Musique

Regardez cette affiche pour la Fête de la Musique en France. Où est-ce que cette fête se déroule[1] ? Quelle est la date de la fête ? Pourquoi, à votre avis, est-ce que l'on a choisi cette date ?

En 1982, Maurice Fleuret, ancien Directeur de la musique et de la danse au Ministère de la Culture, a remarqué que cinq millions de Français, y compris un jeune sur deux[2], jouaient d'un instrument. Son rêve[3], c'était de créer un jour où tous les Français pourraient fêter la musique ensemble — non seulement dans les salles de spectacle, mais aussi chez eux, dans les cafés et dans la rue. Alors en 1982, la première Fête de la Musique a eu lieu en France. Pendant toute la journée et toute la soirée, vous pouvez entendre des musiciens amateurs et professionnels qui jouent de la musique dans les parcs et les cafés, dans la rue ou chez des gens. Maintenant la Fête de la Musique est devenue internationale, présente dans plus de 100 pays sur les cinq continents, de Katmandou à Kalamazoo. Est-ce que cela existe chez vous ? Aimeriez-vous participer à la Fête de la Musique ?

[1] *take place* [2] *one out of two young people* [3] *dream*

Implementation: 12-2 Before completing this exercise, ask students to look up the musicians they do not know; alternatively, complete this as a group activity. 1) Placido Domingo is a Spanish opera singer 2) Eric Clapton is a British singer and guitarist 3) Yo Yo Ma is a Chinese-American cello player 4) Elton John is a British singer and pianist 5) Stevie Wonder is an American singer and pianist 6) Céline Dion is a French-Canadian singer 7) Kenny G is an American saxophone player 8) Louis Armstrong was an American jazz musician who played the cornet and the trumpet 9) Sting is a British singer who also plays the guitar, the piano, the harmonica, and the saxophone.

Implementation: 12-3 Follow up by having each group tell which concert they would most like to attend.

 **12-2 Des musiciens célèbres.** Avec un/e partenaire, identifiez ces musiciens célèbres.

MODÈLE Ella Fitzgerald

É1 C'était une chanteuse américaine.

É2 Oui, elle chantait du jazz.

1. Placido Domingo
2. Eric Clapton
3. Yo Yo Ma
4. Elton John
5. Stevie Wonder
6. Céline Dion
7. Kenny G
8. Louis Armstrong
9. Sting

 **12-3 Choisir un concert.** Regardez cet extrait de journal pour choisir un concert avec votre partenaire, selon la situation décrite.

MUSIQUE

L'heure musicale au Marais À 15 h : Gérôme Simon, violon, Juliana Laska, violoncelle, Yumiko Yamaji, piano. Œuvres de Ravel. À 17 h : Choko Gamo, piano. Œuvres de Schumann, Chopin. Cathédrale Sainte-Croix des Arméniens. Entrée libre.

Orchestre National de France Dir : Kurt Masur. Katia Skanavi, piano. Cycle Beethoven. 20 h. Théâtre des Champs-Élysées. Pl : 8 à 65 €.

Chœur et orchestre Paul Kuentz Dir : Paul Kunetz. Kristina Vahrenkamp, Joëlle Fleury, soprano, Yété Queiroz, alto, Henner Leyhe, ténor, Philip Langshaw, basse. Mozart : Messe du Couronnement et la Grande messe en ut mineur. 20 h 30. Église Saint-Germain-des-Prés. Pl : 20 à 40 €.

Festival « À fleur de note » Raquele Maghales, flûte, Romain Garioud, violoncelle, Pieter-Jelle de Boer, piano. Œuvres de Duruflé, Weber, Haydn. 18 h. Eglise réformée du Saint-Ésprit. Pl : 15 et 25 €.

MODÈLE Vous voulez écouter de la musique pendant l'après-midi.

É1 Est-ce que nous pouvons assister à un concert pendant l'après-midi ?

É2 Oui, à la Cathédrale Sainte-Croix il y a un concert à 15 heures et aussi à 17 heures.

1. Vous voudriez assister à un concert avec plusieurs styles de musique.
2. Vous aimez entendre un grand orchestre.
3. Vous aimez les concerts de piano et surtout la musique classique.
4. Vous adorez écouter des gens qui chantent.
5. Vous préférez la flûte.
6. Vous aimez la musique, mais vous n'avez pas beaucoup d'argent.

FORMES ET FONCTIONS

Vue d'ensemble : les verbes suivis de l'infinitif

Many verbs in French can be followed by an infinitive. Some are followed directly by an infinitive, and some require a preposition before the infinitive.

- As you have learned, the **futur proche** is one case where the verb **aller** is directly followed by an infinitive.

Elle **va chanter** avec sa chorale mercredi prochain.	*She is going to sing with her chorus next Wednesday.*

- Verbs expressing likes and dislikes, including **adorer**, **aimer**, **désirer**, **détester**, and **préférer**, are also directly followed by the infinitive.

J'**aime** bien **écouter** de la musique classique, mais mon copain **préfère écouter** du jazz.	*I like listening to classical music, but my boyfriend prefers listening to jazz.*

- The verbs **devoir**, **pouvoir**, and **vouloir** are directly followed by an infinitive.

—Tu **veux venir** avec nous à un concert ce soir ?	*—Do you want to come with us to a concert tonight?*
—Malheureusement, je ne **peux** pas **venir**. Je **dois travailler** ce soir.	*—Unfortunately, I can't come. I have to work tonight.*

- Other verbs directly followed by the infinitive are: **espérer**, **falloir** (**il faut**), and **savoir**.

—Vous **savez jouer** du violon ?	*—Do you know how to play the violin?*
—Non, mais **j'espère apprendre** bientôt.	*—No, but I hope to learn soon.*

- Many other verbs require a preposition, either **à** or **de**, before the infinitive. The particular preposition required for each verb must be memorized. Here are some of the most frequently used verbs.

These verbs, among others, require **à** before an infinitive:

aider à	*to help*	Il m'**aide à chanter** mieux.
apprendre à	*to learn*	J'**apprends à jouer** du piano.
commencer à	*to begin*	Elle **a commencé à jouer** de la flûte traversière quand elle avait neuf ans.
continuer à	*to continue*	Nous **continuons à apprécier** le jazz.
inviter à	*to invite*	Je t'**invite à aller** à un concert avec moi.
réussir à	*to succeed*	Vous **avez réussi à jouer** du piano.

Note: Ch. 12 has only one **Formes et fonctions** per lesson: these synthesize major topics and introduce more sophisticated structures. Three additional topics are treated in the Appendices: *le plus-que-parfait, le futur antérieur,* and *le passé du conditionnel.* You may wish to introduce these if you are using *Chez nous* over three semesters or have a more advanced class. Explanations and exercises integrate thematically with Ch. 12. We suggest using *le futur antérieur* (Appendix 3) as a second grammar topic in L. 1; *le plus-que-parfait* (Appendix 2) as the second grammar topic in L. 2; and *le passé du conditionnel* (Appendix 4) as the first grammar topic in L. 3.

Note: This material combines review (of modal verbs, verbs of preference followed by an infinitive, and the *futur proche*) with new information about prepositions following certain verbs when used with an infinitive.

Note: Additional verbs that take *à* before an infinitive include: *s'amuser à, avoir du mal à, chercher à.* Note that *continuer* can be followed by either *à* or *de* : *continuer à parler, continuer de parler.*

Note: Additional verbs that take *de* before an infinitive include: *avoir besoin de, avoir envie de, avoir peur de, conseiller de, demander de, se dépêcher de.*

These verbs, among others, require **de** before an infinitive:

accepter de	*to agree*	Il **a accepté de jouer** avec nous.
arrêter de	*to stop*	J'**ai arrêté de jouer** du piano il y a longtemps.
décider de	*to decide*	Ils **ont décidé de former** un orchestre ensemble.
essayer de	*to try*	Je vais **essayer de chanter** plus.
finir de	*to finish*	Elle **finit de suivre** des cours lundi.
oublier de	*to forget*	J'**ai oublié d'apporter** ma clarinette à la répétition.
refuser de	*to refuse*	La diva **refuse de chanter** cette aria.
rêver de	*to dream of*	Elle **rêve d'être** musicienne professionnelle.

Note that **venir** can also be followed by **de** but that this expression has a special meaning: *to have just done something.*

Je **viens d'apprendre** cette chanson.	*I've just learned that song.*

À vous la parole

Implementation: 12-4 To simplify, provide verbs as cues:
1) faire, réviser
2) suivre, aimer
3) venir, aller, assister
4) danser, faire
5) écouter, faire, jouer
6) jouer, apprendre
7) chanter, jouer
8) écouter, jouer

12-4 Des détails. Pour chaque phrase, ajoutez un verbe logique pour donner plus de détails.

MODÈLE Adrien apprend la flûte à l'école.
→ Adrien apprend à jouer de la flûte à l'école.

1. Elle finit ses devoirs pour le prof de piano.
2. Je continue mes leçons de chant.
3. Tu as oublié le concert hier soir ?
4. Delphine arrête la danse.
5. Nous adorons le jazz.
6. J'essaie le saxophone.
7. Vous commencez avec ce groupe folklorique ?
8. Tu préfères quel type de musique ?

Implementation: 12-5 This type of exercise is familiar, but the qualities students are looking for are more complex. Encourage students to engage in longer conversations with fewer students to discover the hidden musical talents and desires among class members.

12-5 Les talents et les projets musicaux. Identifiez qui dans votre classe a des talents et des projets musicaux. Posez des questions à vos camarades de classe pour découvrir qui fait quoi. N'oubliez pas d'inclure le professeur !

MODÈLE savoir jouer d'un instrument

É1 Est-ce que tu sais jouer d'un instrument ?
É2 Non, je ne sais pas jouer d'un instrument.
OU Oui, je sais jouer un peu de piano, mais j'aimerais apprendre à jouer du saxophone.

1. savoir jouer d'un instrument
2. aimer chanter
3. commencer récemment à jouer d'un instrument
4. vouloir faire partie d'un groupe musical
5. rêver d'être chanteur/euse de rock (de rap, de jazz, d'opéra)
6. refuser d'écouter du rap
7. réussir à chanter de l'opéra
8. essayer de jouer d'un instrument

12-6 Pendant les vacances. C'est bientôt les vacances. Avec un/e partenaire, discutez de vos projets.

Implementation: 12-6 Compare answers and decide who has the most ambitious vacation plans, the most realistic, the funniest, the most original.

MODÈLE Pendant les vacances, je refuse...
É1 Pendant les vacances, je refuse de me lever tôt. Et toi ?
É2 Et moi, je refuse de travailler. Je voudrais me reposer à la plage.

1. Pendant les vacances, j'ai accepté...
2. Je vais certainement ...
3. Mais, j'ai aussi décidé ...
4. J'aimerais apprendre ...
5. Si j'avais le temps, je voudrais ...
6. Je pourrais toujours ...
7. En fait, je rêve ...
8. Finalement, je sais que je vais réussir ...

Note: American students are most likely to be familiar with French traditional songs such as *Frère Jacques* and *Alouette*. See the *Chez nous* Companion Website for links to sites with the words and music to many traditional French songs. You might have students listen to some of these in class or research the topic further outside of class.

Écoutons

TEXT AUDIO
CD 6 TRACK 24

12-7 À la claire fontaine

Daniel Le Mée qui chante « À la claire fontaine »

A. Avant d'écouter. Est-ce que vous connaissez des chansons traditionnelles en anglais — *Auld lang syne*, ou *Greensleeves*, par exemple ? Est-ce que vous connaissez aussi des chansons traditionnelles françaises ? Si oui, quelles chansons ? Quels sont souvent les sujets ou les thèmes des chansons traditionnelles ?

Dans cette chanson, *À la claire fontaine*, il s'agit d'une personne — Pierre ; d'une fleur — la rose ; et d'un oiseau — le rossignol (*nightingale*). Souvent, dans les chansons traditionnelles, il y a beaucoup de répétitions, et c'est le cas pour cette chanson. Il y a un refrain, mais d'autres vers (*lines*) dans chaque strophe (*verse*) se répètent aussi. Ces répétitions vont vous aider à comprendre la chanson.

Key: En écoutant 1) la guitare, le piano, le xylophone (Note that in this recording, all three of these instruments were digitally produced. Students who are involved in music might notice this.) 2) b 3) a, c 4) Il y a longtemps que je t'aime / Jamais je ne t'oublierai 5) Le refrain est répété après chaque strophe. De plus, les deux derniers vers de chaque strophe sont répétés comme les deux premiers vers de la strophe suivante. Cela établit un certain rythme et fonctionne comme un aide-mémoire.

Script: Écoutons
À la claire fontaine / M'en allant promener / J'ai trouvé l'eau si claire / Que je m'y suis baignée
Il y a longtemps que je t'aime / Jamais je ne t'oublierai
J'ai trouvé l'eau si claire / Que je m'y suis baignée / À la feuille d'un chêne / Je me suis essuyée
Il y a longtemps que je t'aime / Jamais je ne t'oublierai
À la feuille d'un chêne / Je me suis essuyée / Sur la plus haute branche / Le rossignol chantait
Il y a longtemps que je t'aime / Jamais je ne t'oublierai
Sur la plus haute branche / Le rossignol chantait / Chante, rossignol, chante / Toi qui as le cœur gai
Il y a longtemps que je t'aime / Jamais je ne t'oublierai
Chante, rossignol, chante / Toi qui as le cœur gai / Tu as le cœur à rire / Moi je l'ai à pleurer
Il y a longtemps que je t'aime / Jamais je ne t'oublierai
Tu as le cœur à rire / Moi je l'ai à pleurer / C'est de mon ami Pierre / Qui ne veut plus m'aimer
Il y a longtemps que je t'aime / Jamais je ne t'oublierai
C'est de mon ami Pierre / Qui ne veut plus m'aimer / Pour un bouton de rose / Que tantôt j'ai donné
Il y a longtemps que je t'aime / Jamais je ne t'oublierai
Pour un bouton de rose / Que tantôt j'ai donné / Je voudrais que la rose / Fût encore au rosier
Il y a longtemps que je t'aime / Jamais je ne t'oublierai
Je voudrais que la rose / Fût encore au rosier / Et que mon ami Pierre / Fût encore à m'aimer
Il y a longtemps que je t'aime / Jamais je ne t'oublierai

B. En écoutant. Trouvez les réponses aux questions suivantes.

1. Identifiez les instruments que vous entendez.
2. Identifiez la voix que vous entendez : est-ce que c'est une voix...
   a. de baryton ? **b.** de ténor ? **c.** de basse ?
3. Quels sont les thèmes de la chanson ?
   a. l'amour **b.** la nature **c.** le regret
4. Dans cette chanson, il y a plusieurs couplets et un refrain ; quel est le refrain ?
5. Dans cette chanson, il y a beaucoup de répétitions. Quels sont les vers (*lines*) répétés ? Pourquoi, à votre avis ?

Une fontaine dans le village de Nérac dans le sud-ouest de la France.

C. Après avoir écouté. Discutez de ces questions avec vos camarades de classe.

1. Quelle est votre réaction à cette chanson ? Est-ce que elle vous a plu ? Pourquoi ?
2. Les chansons traditionnelles sont très populaires parmi les Français. On les chante pendant les fêtes et surtout aux mariages. À quels moments est-ce qu'on chante des chansons traditionnelles (ou d'autres chansons) chez vous ?

Leçon 2 L'art et ses formes d'expression

POINTS DE DÉPART

Les artistes et leurs œuvres d'art

Presentation: Begin by presenting artists using the line art (MFL, Ch. 12) and asking questions such as *Qui peint ? Qui sculpte ? Qui fait/prend une photo ?* The noun *peintre* is only used in the masculine form, *photographe* can be both masculine and feminine, and *sculpteur* has a distinct feminine form: *une sculptrice* or *une femme sculpteur*. You may wish to present the corresponding verbs: *peindre, sculpter, dessiner, photographier* or *faire/prendre une photo*. Present artistic styles using the images in the textbook or other reproductions you may have. Discuss students' preferences and their knowledge of works of art and artists.

Les artistes au travail

un sculpteur
une sculpture

un tableau
un peintre

un portrait
une photographie (une photo)
une photographe

un dessin
une dessinatrice
un pastel
un dessinateur

Jean-Baptiste Siméon Chardin a peint cette nature morte. Cette composition représente des objets de cuisine. C'est un tableau réaliste avec des couleurs assez sombres.

Jean-Baptiste Siméon Chardin (1699–1779), *Menu de gras et ustensiles de cuisine*, Louvre. Paris, France. Bridgeman Art Library.

Henri Rousseau a peint ce tableau dans le style primitif. Le sujet de ce tableau est une femme qui se promène dans une forêt exotique avec des fleurs et des arbres immenses. Les couleurs sont très vives.

Henri J.F. Rousseau (1844–1910), *Femme se promenant dans une forêt fantastique*, 1905. Oil on canvas/The Barnes Foundation, Merion, Pennsylvania, USA/The Bridgeman Art Library.

Ce tableau abstrait et cubiste de Fernand Léger s'intitule *Éléments mécaniques*. C'est un bon exemple d'art moderne avec ses formes géométriques qui se répètent.

Éléments mécaniques, 1918–1923 (Oil on canvas) by Fernand Léger (1881–1955). Kunstmuseum, Basle, Switzerland/ Peter Willi/Bridgeman Art Library.

Claude Monet (1840–1926) a peint ce paysage d'hiver. Regardez l'utilisation de la lumière et surtout ses reflets sur la neige. Monet a été le grand maître des impressionnistes.

Claude Monet (1840–1926), *La pie, Effet de neige*, Musée d'Orsay. Paris.

Fiche pratique

To learn visually oriented vocabulary, try associating each term with an example you can picture clearly. For instance, you might identify **le style abstrait et cubiste** with a painting by Fernand Léger.

Note that the verb **peindre** is irregular:

—Qu'est-ce que vous **peignez** en ce moment?

—Je **peins** une nature morte avec des belles fleurs.

PEINDRE *to paint*			
je	peins	nous	peign**ons**
tu	peins	vous	peign**ez**
il / elle / on	peint	ils / elles	peign**ent**

PASSÉ COMPOSÉ : Renoir **a peint** beaucoup de portraits.

Initial practice: Begin with a discrimination drill: *une personne ou plus ? Elle peint un tableau. Elles peignent un portrait. Ils peignent souvent le week-end. Il peint beaucoup. Elle peint bien. Elles peignent comme des vraies artistes.* Follow up with a substitution drill: *Pablo peint un tableau ; toi ? — Tu peins un tableau*, etc.

Vie et culture

Presentation: Students can complete a virtual visit of many of these museums. Visit the *Chez nous* Companion Website for links. For cross-cultural comparison, ask students to list museums in their city and/or region, or to make a list of museums they have visited and have enjoyed. Have students compare answers.

Les musées à Paris

Testez votre connaissance des musées à Paris : Quel est le plus grand musée du monde qui s'y trouve ? Quel musée d'art parisien était autrefois[1] une gare ? Dans quel musée est-ce que vous pouvez voir des sculptures dans un beau jardin ? Dans quel musée est-ce que vous pouvez admirer les tableaux *les Nymphéas* de Monet ? Des musées, il y en a pour tous les goûts à Paris. Par exemple :

Le musée du Louvre et sa pyramide.

Le Centre Pompidou	l'art moderne et l'art contemporain
Le musée de Cluny	l'art médiéval et les tapisseries de *la Dame à la Licorne*[2]
Le musée d'Orsay	les impressionnistes et les post-impressionnistes
Le musée des Arts décoratifs	les meubles, les céramiques, les tapisseries, les textiles
L'Orangerie	les impressionnistes et surtout *les Nymphéas* de Monet
Le musée Picasso	des œuvres des maîtres modernes, surtout Picasso
Le musée Rodin	une collection de sculptures de l'artiste, exposées dans le jardin et la maison

Trouvez des renseignements sur un des musées mentionnés sur Internet et parlez-en avec vos camarades de classe. Pourquoi est-ce que vous aimeriez visiter ce musée ?

[1]*formerly* [2]*unicorn*

À vous la parole

Implementation: 12-8 As a follow-up, ask students what type of art they prefer and which works of art they would like to have in their room or apartment. You could also have students discuss these questions in pairs.

12-8 Qu'est-ce que c'est ? Identifiez ces œuvres d'art.

MODÈLE C'est une nature morte.

1. 
2. 
3. 
4. 
5. 
6. 
7. 
8. 

12-9 Artistes célèbres. Avec un/e partenaire, choisissez un/e artiste qui vous intéresse dans la liste suivante. Faites quelques recherches et présentez-le devant la classe. Parlez du style de l'artiste et de ses œuvres d'art. Si possible, montrez une photo d'une de ses œuvres à vos camarades de classe.

Vincent Van Gogh, *Autoportrait*, 1889, Musée d'Orsay, Paris.

MODÈLE É1 Nous avons choisi Vincent Van Gogh.

É2 Van Gogh était un peintre néerlandais de style post-impressionniste. Il a peint surtout des paysages et des portraits.

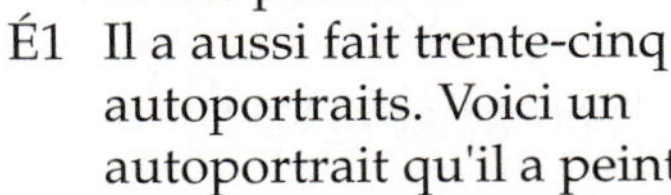

É1 Il a aussi fait trente-cinq autoportraits. Voici un autoportrait qu'il a peint vers la fin de sa vie.

1. Marc Chagall
2. Eugène Delacroix
3. Mary Cassatt
4. Pablo Picasso
5. Berthe Morisot
6. Camille Claudel
7. Auguste Rodin
8. Georges Braque
9. Robert Doisneau
10. Henri Matisse
11. Auguste Renoir
12. Claude Lorrain

Implementation: 12-9 You may wish to assign pairs of students to certain artists, or to allow students to choose their artists based on their own tastes. Ask them to find a picture or two to illustrate the work of each artist they describe. After the brief presentations, follow up by asking students which artists they are most familiar with and which works of art they prefer. Marc Chagall was a Russian painter who spent much of his life in France; Eugène Delacroix was a French Romantic painter; Mary Cassatt was an American Impressionist painter, the only woman to exhibit with the original Impressionists; Pablo Picasso was a Spanish painter and sculptor known for cubism; Berthe Morisot was one of the few women Impressionist painters in France; Camille Claudel was a French sculptress; Auguste Rodin was a French sculptor; Georges Braque was a French cubist painter; Robert Doisneau was a French photographer known for interesting pictures of people in Paris streets and cafés; Henri Matisse was a French painter, sculptor, and collage artist; Auguste Renoir was a French Impressionist who painted many portraits; Claude Lorrain was a seventeenth-century French artist known for his landscapes.

12-10 Une œuvre d'art que vous aimez. Apportez en classe une œuvre d'art ou une reproduction d'œuvre d'art. Présentez-la à vos camarades de classe. N'oubliez pas de parler de l'artiste, du type d'art et de dire pourquoi vous l'aimez.

MODÈLE Voici une œuvre d'Henri Matisse. C'est un collage qui s'appelle *Les bêtes de la mer*. C'est assez abstrait et très coloré. J'aime la technique de Matisse et le sujet de ce collage. Les couleurs sont très vives et très intenses. Il y a beaucoup d'énergie exprimée dans ce collage.

Implementation: 12-10 To help students describe color in the piece of art they have chosen, review color adjectives such as *pâle* and introduce terms such as *clair/e* and *foncé/e*. To encourage more active listening as students present their art, collect all the pieces of art or photos and put them in a central spot in the classroom. Have each student read his or her description as the class determines which piece of art is being described.

FORMES ET FONCTIONS

Vue d'ensemble : l'emploi des temps verbaux

Presentation: For each example, have students identify the time reference: present, present progressive, past, or future.

- The present indicative is the most versatile tense in French. As you know, it is used to express habitual actions or states and ongoing actions or events. When used with an appropriate time expression, the present can also be used to recount past events and describe future ones:

Il **parle** français couramment.	*He speaks French fluently.*
Elle **peint** une nature morte pour l'anniversaire de sa mère.	*She is painting a still life for her mother's birthday.*
En 1874, Monet, Degas, Renoir et d'autres artistes **exposent** leurs tableaux. C'**est** le début de l'impressionnisme.	*In 1874, Monet, Degas, Renoir and other artists exhibited their paintings. It was the beginning of Impressionism.*
Nous **allons** au musée **demain**.	*We're going to the museum tomorrow.*

Note: You may wish to mention that there is also a literary past tense, *le passé simple*, which students have seen in several reading passages in the textbook and the SAM/MFL. If you would like to include a discussion of *le passé simple* with your class, you could use one of these passages: **Lisons** in Ch. 7, VCN or Ch. 9, L. 2 in the textbook, or the **Lisons** in Ch. 5, 7, 10 and 12 of the SAM/MFL. At this stage, students should simply be expected to recognize the forms of the verbs and to understand that the tense functions in a similar way to *le passé composé*.

Presentation: Ask students to explain the particular use of the *passé composé* or *l'imparfait* for each excerpt. You may also provide other examples or ask them to provide other examples, even from samples of their own writing for the course. Other **Lisons** selections that include past tenses include: *La pluralité culturelle* in Ch. 6, VCN and *Critiques d'un film* in Ch. 11, VCN. Selections that feature *le passé simple* include: *L'enfant noir* in Ch. 7, VCN; *Martinique guide pratique* in Ch. 8, VCN; *le Tour du Monde en quatre-vingts jours* in Ch. 9, L. 2; and *Un détective à Paris* in Ch. 9, VCN. The following selections illustrate the use of the present to refer to a variety of time frames : *Familiale* in Ch. 4, L. 1; *Frère Jacques, dormez-vous ?* in Ch. 4, VCN; *Je suis cadien* in Ch. 7, L. 3; *Le Malade Imaginaire* in Ch. 10, L. 1; and *La découverte de l'art africain* in Ch. 12, VCN.

- You have learned two of the tenses that can be used in French to express the past: **le passé composé** and **l'imparfait**. As you know, **l'imparfait** is used to express repeated or continuous actions; mental states and emotions; and descriptions of people, places, or the weather in the past. In a narrative, it provides background information, while **le passé composé** expresses completed actions that advance the storyline. Consider these examples from texts you may have read in *Chez nous*.

En 1815, M. Charles-Francois-Bienvenu Myriel était évêque de Digne. C'était un vieillard d'environ soixante-quinze ans. (Hugo, *Les Misérables*, Chapitre 2)

Il s'est levé
Il a mis
Son chapeau sur sa tête
Il a mis
Son manteau de pluie
Parce qu'il pleuvait
Et il est parti. ...
(Prévert, « Déjeuner du Matin », *Paroles*, Chapitre 5)

Zinna commençait toujours ainsi. Elle s'asseyait sur la plage, et Tomi se mettait à côté d'elle. C'était généralement le matin ... (Le Clézio, *Printemps et autres saisons*, Chapitre 6)

Il y avait la famine au village. Oncle Hyène et Oncle Lièvre ont décidé d'aller chercher de la nourriture pour leurs familles. Oncle Hyène est parti mais n'a rien trouvé. Oncle Lièvre s'est mis aussi en route. (*L'arbre nourricier*, Chapitre 10)

Initial practice: Begin with an exercise including multiple tenses and ask students to identify the time frame: *On y va la semaine prochaine : présent employé pour parler du futur immédiat. Je joue au tennis avec Jean-Claude : présent. En 2004, le Président Reagan meurt à l'âge de 93 ans : présent employé pour parler du passé. Elle sort ce soir : présent employé pour parler du futur immédiat. Demain, ils partent en vacances : présent employé pour parler du futur immédiat. Quand elle était petite, elle jouait de la clarinette : passé. Ils viennent d'arriver : présent pour parler du passé. J'allais éteindre la télé quand j'ai vu ton émission : passé.* Alternatively, you could produce only the first part of the sentence and ask students to complete it in an appropriate manner.

À vous la parole

12-11 Bien dit. Déterminez si chaque phrase évoque le présent, le futur ou le passé et suggérez d'autres façons de dire la même chose si c'est possible.

MODÈLE On va au musée ce week-end pour voir la nouvelle exposition.
On pourrait dire : On va aller au musée pour voir la nouvelle exposition.

1. Elle vient nous voir la semaine prochaine.
2. Il apprend le français à la fac.
3. Le jeune artiste s'installe à Paris à l'âge de 23 ans pour y faire fortune.
4. Ce week-end, je travaille samedi et dimanche.
5. On part cet après-midi.
6. Elle termine sa sculpture.
7. En ce moment, il peint un tableau abstrait.
8. Ils arrivent en France le 18 mai.

Implementation: 12-11 Encourage students to provide as many different ways of saying each sentence as they can. In some cases, the time frame of the sentence may be ambiguous. For example, *ils arrivent le 18 mai* could refer to either a past or a future event.

Key: 12-11 1) Elle va venir nous voir. 2) Il a appris le français à la fac. 3) Le jeune artiste s'est installé/s'installait à Paris ... 4) Ce week-end, je vais travailler samedi et dimanche. 5) On va partir. 6) Elle a terminé sa sculpture. 7) Il peint un tableau abstrait. 8) Ils vont arriver en France le 18 mai. / Ils sont arrivés en France ...

12-12 Toujours le sport. Racontez cette histoire au passé ; employez le passé composé ou l'imparfait, selon le cas.

MODÈLE C'est un samedi après-midi au début du mois de juin.
C'était un samedi après-midi au début du mois de juin.

(1) Il y a un match de football à deux heures de l'après-midi. (2) Il fait très chaud et lourd. (3) Le ciel est gris. (4) Les parents sont anxieux. (5) Ils pensent qu'il va pleuvoir. (6) On fait nos derniers préparatifs quand il commence à pleuvoir très fort. (7) L'arbitre (*referee*) nous dit qu'on doit jouer sous la pluie. (8) Les spectateurs ne sont pas contents. (9) Nous allons commencer le match quand on voit un éclair à l'horizon. (10) Juste après, on entend du tonnerre. (11) L'arbitre siffle (*whistles*). (12) Tout le monde doit quitter le terrain. (13) On attend une demi-heure dans les voitures des spectateurs mais la pluie ne s'arrête pas. (14) Finalement, le match est annulé et on rentre à la maison. (15) Je ne suis pas heureux. Quelle mauvaise journée !

Key: 12-12 1) avait 2) faisait 3) était 4) étaient 5) pensaient, allait 6) faisait, a commencé 7) a dit, devait 8) n'étaient pas 9) allions, a vu 10) a entendu 11) a sifflé 12) a dû 13) a attendu, ne s'est pas arrêté 14) a été, est rentrés 15) étais

12-13 Histoire à suivre. En groupes de cinq ou six, choisissez un début et puis imaginez la suite de l'histoire. Chaque membre du groupe va ajouter une phrase à tour de rôle.

MODÈLE Il faisait sombre.
É1 Il pleuvait depuis trois jours et ...
É2 ... les petits chats n'étaient pas contents parce que ...
É3 ... ils avaient faim.
É4 Ils cherchaient à manger quand soudainement ...
É5 ... un gros chien est arrivé.
É1 Les petits chats ...

1. Il faisait sombre ...
2. C'était une journée ordinaire ...
3. Il faisait beau et le soleil brillait ...
4. C'était la première fois que ...
5. Ils ont toujours voulu ...

Implementation: 12-13 Divide students into groups of five or six for this activity and assign a secretary for each group to record the story they create so it can be shared with the rest of the class. Decide which story is the most creative, the most plausible, the most far-fetched, the funniest.

Variation: 12-13 If you have a computer lab, conduct this activity as a group writing project. Have each student (or pair of students, depending on the size of the lab) sit in front of a computer and complete the first sentence of the story. At regular intervals, have students get up and move to the next computer, where they will read the sentence written by the previous student and add the next sentence. After each student (or pair of students) has had a chance to write six or seven sentences, call time and ask several students to read out loud the story on the computer screen in front of them. You could also have students save and print out or e-mail the various stories.

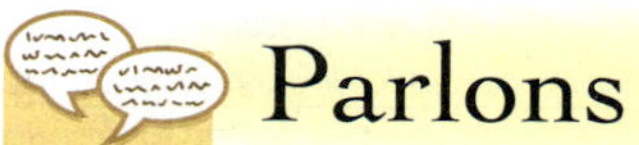

Parlons

Implementation: 12-14 This oral presentation is most effective if accompanied by visuals, perhaps using a poster or presentational software. Encourage students to think about how they can best organize the information verbally and visually to make it appealing. If you decide to grade this activity, give points for the visual as well as the oral aspects of the presentation: visual appeal, organization, clarity, completeness, and comprehensibility (i.e., were classmates able to follow the presentation?). Encourage listeners to ask questions and provide feedback. See the *Chez nous* Companion Website for links to additional Francophone art museums.

12-14 Visites de musées

Avec un/e partenaire, présentez un musée d'un pays francophone à vos camarades de classe. Choisissez un musée de la liste ci-dessous, ou trouvez un autre musée qui vous intéresse particulièrement :

en Afrique :

le musée Manéga [au Burkina Faso]
le musée national du Mali
le musée d'art africain de Dakar [au Sénégal]

au Canada :

le musée d'art contemporain de Montréal
le musée des beaux-arts de Montréal
le musée national des beaux-arts du Québec

en Europe :

le musée d'art moderne et d'art contemporain de Liège [en Belgique]
le musée de l'art wallon [en Belgique]
le musée d'art et d'histoire de Genève [en Suisse]
le musée d'art et d'histoire de Neuchâtel [en Suisse]
le musée d'art moderne Lille Métropole [en France]
le musée Marc Chagall à Nice [en France]
la Fondation Maeght [en France]

Une visite guidée de l'exposition **¡ Cuba ! Art et histoire de 1868 à nos jours** au musée des beaux-arts de Montréal. Avec plus de 400 œuvres, c'était la plus grande exposition de l'art cubain jamais réalisée.

A. Avant de parler. Cherchez des renseignements dans les catégories suivantes :

- Description générale :

MODÈLE Le musée national des beaux-arts de Montréal contient plus de 35 000 objets de l'Antiquité jusqu'à l'époque moderne.

- Informations pratiques : l'adresse du musée, les jours et les heures d'ouverture, les tarifs

MODÈLE Le musée se trouve dans la rue Sherbrooke dans la ville de Montréal. Il est ouvert de 11 h à 17 h le mardi, de 11 h à 21 h le mercredi, le jeudi et le vendredi et de 10 h à 17 h le samedi et le dimanche. Le musée est fermé le lundi. L'entrée à la collection du musée est gratuite ; il faut seulement payer pour les expositions temporaires. C'est 15 $ pour les adultes et 7,50 $ pour les étudiants de moins de 30 ans avec une carte d'étudiant.

- Les collections et les expositions

MODÈLE Il y a des collections de cultures anciennes, d'art canadien et européen, d'arts décoratifs et d'art contemporain.

- Une ou deux œuvres d'art (ou une exposition) que vous allez présenter avec plus de précision.

MODÈLE Nous avons choisi une sculpture et un paysage. Le tableau s'appelle *Arbre déraciné* et Marc-Aurèle Fortin l'a peint vers 1928. C'est un tableau d'un gros arbre qui ...

- Votre commentaire personnel

MODÈLE Nous pensons que ce musée serait intéressant à visiter. On peut y voir des œuvres d'artistes connus comme Cézanne, Matisse et Renoir et aussi des artistes canadiens qui ne sont pas très connus en dehors (*outside of*) du Canada.

B. En parlant. Avec votre partenaire, faites votre exposé à vos camarades de classe. Pensez à rendre votre exposé plus intéressant avec quelques images du musée et des œuvres d'art qu'on y trouve.

C. Après avoir parlé. Considérez les questions suivantes avec vos camarades.

1. Quels étaient les musées les plus intéressants ?
2. Quels musées est-ce que vous aimeriez visiter ? Pourquoi ?

Leçon 3 Allons voir un spectacle !

POINTS DE DÉPART

TEXT AUDIO
CD 6 TRACK 26

Le spectacle

Pour voir un ballet ou un opéra, vous pouvez aller au palais Garnier à Paris. Le palais Garnier est un chef-d'œuvre de l'architecture théâtrale du XIXe siècle. Dans la salle de spectacle, le plafond (*ceiling*) a été peint par Marc Chagall en 1964.

Presentation: In conjunction with this **Points de départ**, you may wish to show the video segment *Le théâtre et l'opéra*, in which Christian, pictured here, describes visits to the theater and the opera in Nice. Point out that the verb *s'abonner* is equivalent to having "season tickets" to the theater.

Christian et sa femme vont souvent au Théâtre National de Nice pour voir des spectacles. Ils y sont abonnés. Ce théâtre est assez moderne ; il a été construit en 1989.

Presentation: Have students listen to the dialogue as they look at the text. Have students list activities Rémi and Sophie are considering: which would they like to do, and which have they decided not to do? Ask students to pick out expressions used to express the idea that one is not interested in doing something or is hesitating: *pas si vite, je ne suis pas un fanatique de danse, ça (ne) me dit rien, ça risque d'être assez cher* ; and expressions used to indicate this might be a possibility: *un spectacle plutôt, pourquoi pas, j'aimerais bien voir ça, ça ne fait rien, ça vaut le coup, après tout, on va se faire un petit plaisir.* Point out the structure *Ça fait longtemps que* and mention that it is a version of *il y a... que*, which students learned in Ch. 11, L. 3.

Rémi et Sophie planifient leur week-end.

SOPHIE : Alors, qu'est-ce qu'on fait samedi soir ?
RÉMI : Je ne sais pas. Tu as acheté *Pariscope* ?
SOPHIE : Bien sûr, mais ... il y a beaucoup de choix. Qu'est-ce que tu veux faire ? voir un film ? aller à un concert ? aller au musée ?
RÉMI : Un spectacle plutôt, pourquoi pas une pièce de théâtre ?
SOPHIE : Ou un opéra ... ou même un ballet ! Ça fait longtemps qu'on n'est pas allé voir un spectacle de danse.
RÉMI : Eh, pas si vite ! Tu sais bien que je ne suis pas un fanatique de danse. Regarde les pièces qui passent en ce moment.
SOPHIE : Eh bien, il y a les classiques à la Comédie-Française : *Le Misanthrope* de Molière et *Cyrano de Bergerac* d'Edmond Rostand.
RÉMI : Bof. Ça me dit rien.

SOPHIE : Tiens, à l'Opéra Bastille, il y a *La flûte enchantée* de Mozart ; j'aimerais bien voir ça !

RÉMI : Ah oui, moi aussi. Tu crois qu'il y aura encore des places ?

SOPHIE : Je vais téléphoner pour voir s'il en reste. Mais ça risque d'être assez cher.

RÉMI : Ça ne fait rien. Pour un bon opéra, ça vaut le coup. Après tout, c'est bientôt ton anniversaire. On va se faire un petit plaisir.

Vie et culture

Pariscope

Pariscope, c'est un périodique indispensable pour planifier une visite à Paris. Il sort tous les mercredis. Son nom est un mot-valise qui combine « Paris » et « périscope ». Regardez le sommaire pour découvrir ce que vous pourriez faire à Paris.

ET VOUS ?

1. Quels renseignements est-ce que vous y trouvez ? Qu'est-ce que vous choisiriez de faire ?
2. Est-ce qu'il y a un magazine semblable pour votre ville ou votre région ? Qu'est-ce que vous faites pour trouver des idées et des renseignements, quand vous avez envie de sortir ?

Presentation: You may wish to treat the *sommaire* from *Pariscope* as a reading before addressing the questions in the **Vie et Culture**. Have students identify the time period and list the various types of activities covered in this publication: theater, music, cinema, etc. If you have a copy of an old *Pariscope*, bring it to class to show students. You may wish to replay the video clip *Je lis la presse* from Ch. 11, especially the last section where the speaker shows and describes *Pariscope*.

sommaire

du mercredi 25 juin au mardi 1er juillet 2008

Implementation: 12-15 Students may complete this activity in pairs. Give them time to scan the listings and decide on a few possibilities for each category.

Note: *La Villette* is a large urban park and redevelopment project on the outskirts of the 19e *arrondissement,* located on the site of a former meat market and slaughterhouse. The first structure, a concert hall named *le Zénith,* opened in 1984. The complex was completed in 2000 and features *la Cité des sciences et de l'industrie, la Cité de la musique, le Conservatoire national supérieur de musique et de danse de Paris,* several concert venues, an IMAX theater, a large park, and much more. For more information, see the *Chez nous* Companion Website.

À vous la parole

12-15 Sorties à la Villette. Regardez les pages *la Villette* de *Pariscope* qui proposent une gamme d'activités pour toute la famille au Parc de la Villette, un énorme complexe dans le 19e arrondissement de Paris. Suggérez une ou deux possibilités de sorties dans les catégories suivantes :

MODÈLE cinéma
On pourrait voir *Sauvegardons notre planète* au cinéma Louis-Lumière.

1. cinéma
2. théâtre
3. concerts
4. spectacles de danse
5. expositions

Presentation: Students should notice that there are a variety of discount ticket prices for most events. The abbreviation TR stands for *tarif réduit ; une Carte Villette* refers to a discount card which is purchased for a year and allows the bearer to reductions on most events. Note also that there are a variety of reductions for youth of various ages.

Musique, danse...

La Villette vit au rythme de l'Afrique !

« Afrique[s] »

Concerts, danse, colloque

du 24 juin au 12 juillet - Grande Halle de la Villette
Une invitation au voyage au cœur des cultures africaines.
Un rendez-vous unique !
Programme détaillé sur www.villette.com

À ne pas manquer

cette semaine :

jusqu'au 28 juin 20 h *« 2147, l'Afrique »*
Moïse Touré, Jean-Claude Gallotta, Rokia Traoré.
Une mise en récit par la danse, le théâtre et la musique de l'Afrique à l'horizon 2147.
15 €/TR 10 € Carte Villette 9 € - 16 ans 8 €

27 juin 10 h-18 h *Colloque*
« La création artistique en Afrique et ses liens avec l'Europe »
Accès libre.

Afrique[s]

continue avec :

3 juillet 21 h 30 *Salif Keita*
25 €/TR et Carte Villette 20 €

8 et 9 juillet 21 h 30 *Les lauréats 2008 des Rencontres « Danse l'Afrique danse »*
12 €/TR et Carte Villette 9 €

du 8 au 12 juillet 20 h *« Le Sacre du Printemps »*
Une reprise contemporaine du chef-d'œuvre classique de Stravinsky, 14 danseurs livrent une danse brute, colorée et efficace. Chorégraphie de Heddy Maalem
15 €/TR 10 €/Carte Villette 9 €/-16 ans 8 €

la villette

Pour petits et grands, expos, animations, spectacles...

Cité des sciences

Les expositions de la Cité sont une invitation à découvrir l'univers des sciences et des techniques : jouez avec la lumière, décodez votre carte génétique, faites parler la Joconde, plongez au cœur de mises en scène sonores, montez à bord d'un vrai sous-marin... Autant d'expériences qui vous font explorer les secrets de la science.

Nouvelles expositions

Le grand récit de l'Univers
Une vaste enquête interactive sur l'origine de la matière, la lumière et l'énergie, un voyage de 13,7 millards d'années, de la Terre jusqu'au vide extragalactique. Permanent.

Expo 2CV
Plein feux sur la grande histoire d'une petite voiture populaire.
Jusqu'au 30 novembre.

Les expositions : 8 €
Les expositions + le planétarium : 11 €
Sous-marin Argonaute : 3 € (gratuit - de 7 ans)

Spectacles

– **Au planétarium : À l'aube de la conquête spatiale** ou la rétrospective, en images, de cinquante années d'exploration.
– **Au cinéma Louis-Lumière : Paroles d'insecte et Sauvegardons notre planète,** deux films en relief.
– **À la Géode :** avec un écran hémisphérique de 1000 m2, plongez dans l'image ! Programme (voir pages cinéma). *Géode : 9 €*

12-16 Qu'est-ce qu'on fait ? Avec un/e partenaire, proposez quelques sorties pour ce week-end.

MODÈLE É1 Qu'est-ce qu'on fait ce week-end ?
É2 Pourquoi pas aller au cinéma ? Il y a un nouveau film avec Nicole Kidman que j'aimerais voir.
É1 Non, ça me dit rien. Je n'aime pas cette actrice. Un concert plutôt ?
É2 Peut-être, mais ...

Implementation: 12-16 Have several groups perform their dialogue in front of the class. To vary the activity, specify the number of activities that students must suggest before agreeing on one. You might also have students work with one partner for a specified length of time and then switch partners to determine with whom they have more compatible interests.

12-17 Les sorties. Avec un/e partenaire, discutez de vos préférences culturelles.

MODÈLE Est-ce que vous préférez le théâtre, le cinéma, la danse ou l'opéra ?
É1 J'adore l'opéra. Je sais que c'est un peu curieux parce que beaucoup d'étudiants n'aiment pas l'opéra. Mais moi, j'adore ça.
É2 Pas moi. J'aime plutôt la danse. Je fais de la danse classique depuis 12 ans et j'aime bien aller à des spectacles de danse.
É1 Tu y vas beaucoup ? Moi, je ne vais pas très souvent à l'opéra parce que c'est cher.
É2 Je vais assez souvent à des spectacles de danse sur le campus. Tu sais, ce n'est pas très cher et ça vaut vraiment le coup ...

Implementation: 12-17 You could have students work in small groups to complete this activity as well. Follow up with a brief whole-class discussion.

1. Est-ce que vous préférez le théâtre, le cinéma, la danse ou l'opéra ?
2. Est-ce que vous assistez régulièrement à des spectacles ? Combien de fois par semaine, par mois ou par an ? Avec qui est-ce que vous y allez ?
3. Combien d'argent est-ce que vous consacrez (*devote*) aux sorties culturelles par semaine ou par mois ?
4. Est-ce qu'il y a des spectacles sur votre campus qui ne sont pas très chers pour les étudiants ? Est-ce que vous y allez ? Pourquoi ?
5. Est-ce que vos habitudes culturelles sont différentes des habitudes de vos parents ? Est-ce qu'ils sont abonnés à un théâtre ou à un opéra par exemple ? Et vous ?
6. Est-ce que vous avez les mêmes préférences pour les spectacles de musique et de danse, les pièces de théâtre et les films que vos parents ou que vos amis ?

Au Théâtre des Bouffes du Nord à Paris, Carole Bouquet et Lambert Wilson répètent une scène de la pièce *Bérénice*, écrite par Racine.

FORMES ET FONCTIONS

Vue d'ensemble : les combinaisons de pronoms compléments d'objet

Presentation: This feature is presented mainly for recognition with limited productive control of the most frequent combinations, based on the extensive corpus of conversational French presented in O'Connor Di Vito's 1997 book *Patterns Across Spoken and Written French: Empirical Research on the Interaction Among Forms, Functions, and Genres.* Provide a general review of pronoun forms and placement before introducing the new material.

You have learned about direct- and indirect-object pronouns **le**, **la**, **les**, **lui**, **leur**, **me**, **te**, **nous**, **vous**, the reflexive pronoun **se**, the partitive pronoun **en**, and the locative pronoun **y**. As you know, these pronouns are used to avoid repetition and are generally placed before the conjugated verb. There are some special rules to learn when you use two pronouns in the same sentence.

- Certain pronoun combinations are quite common in French:
  - The expression **il y en a**:

—Il y a des places qui restent à 25 euros ?	—*Are there any seats left for 25 euros?*
—Oui, **il y en a** quelques-unes, mais il faut vous dépêcher.	—*There are a few (of them) left, but you must hurry.*

  - Combinations involving a person and a thing (or things):

Tu **me le** prêtes ?	*Will you lend it to me?*
Je **te l'**offre.	*I'm giving it to you.*
Il **me l'**a déjà dit.	*He already told me.*
Tu pourrais **me l'**apporter ?	*Could you bring it to me?*
Ne **leur en** donne pas !	*Don't give them any!*

- When two object pronouns (direct, indirect, reflexive) occur together, their order is as follows:

subject	me te se nous vous	le/l' la les	lui leur	y	en	**verb**

Presentation: Make it clear to students that statements such as *Voilà mon billet ; apporte-le-moi !* and *Donnez-nous-en !* would be considered impolite in many contexts. It is better for students to avoid these constructions and use the modal verbs they have learned: *Tu pourrais me l'apporter ?* Point out the use of the hyphen to connect pronouns to the verb in written affirmative commands and the elision of *moi* and *toi* before *en*. For the second-person singular imperative, native speakers will use both *Donne-le-moi !* and *Donne-moi-le !*

- In affirmative commands, the order is somewhat different:

Voilà mon billet ; apporte-**le-moi** !	*There's my ticket; bring it to me!*
Donnez-**nous-en** !	*Give us some!*

verb	le la les	moi/m' toi/t' lui nous vous leur	y	en

À vous la parole

12-18 À un concert. Vous écoutez des gens qui parlent pendant l'entracte (*intermission*) d'un concert de musique classique. Avec un/e partenaire, imaginez de quoi ils parlent probablement.

MODÈLE Il y en a beaucoup.
É1 Il y a beaucoup de musiciens.
É2 Il y a beaucoup de violons.

1. Tenez, je vous le donne.
2. Non, il n'y en a pas.
3. Vous m'en donnez deux, s'il vous plaît ?
4. Est-ce que vous le lui avez donné ?
5. Passez-les-moi, s'il vous plaît.
6. Pas de problème ; il y en a pour tout le monde.

Implementation: 12-18 This comprehension-based exercise asks students to focus on the potential meanings of pronoun combinations. Before completing, brainstorm with students about what people do during intermission of a show and what they might talk about.

12-19 Il y en a combien ? Avec un/e partenaire, trouvez la bonne réponse.

MODÈLES musiciens dans un trio
É1 Il y a combien de musiciens dans un trio ?
É2 Il y en a trois.

francophones au Québec
É1 Il y a combien de francophones au Québec ?
É2 Il y en a environ six-millions.

1. musiciens dans un quartette
2. flûtes traversières dans un orchestre
3. semaines dans un semestre/trimestre
4. examens pour le cours de français
5. étudiants dans le cours de français
6. ordinateurs dans le labo de langues
7. étudiants à l'université
8. personnes dans votre ville

Variation: 12-19 Vary by reversing question and response: for example, a student might say: *il y en a vingt* and a classmate might guess *ordinateurs au labo* or *étudiants dans la classe.* As another variation, have students tell how many numbers are found in: telephone numbers, social security numbers, dates, etc.; tell how many of certain items there are in their rooms—windows, electronic devices, magazines, etc.

12-20 Qui en prend ? Après le concert, il y a une réception pour les musiciens et leurs invités. On arrose (*toast*) l'évènement avec du champagne. À qui est-ce qu'on en sert ?

MODÈLE au chef d'orchestre ?
Oui, on lui en sert.

1. à sa mère ?
2. à son fils de sept ans ?
3. au pianiste ?
4. à ses amis ?
5. à sa femme ?
6. à sa petite fille ?
7. aux membres de l'orchestre ?

 **12-21 Donnant donnant.** Est-ce que vous faites les choses suivantes pour votre colocataire ou votre meilleur/e ami/e et est-ce qu'il ou elle les fait pour vous ?

MODÈLES prêter l'iPod

É1 Tu lui prêtes ton iPod ?
É2 Non, je ne le lui prête jamais.
É1 Et il te prête son iPod ?
É2 Non, il ne me le prête jamais.

1. prêter l'iPod
2. prêter le dictionnaire de français
3. prêter des vêtements
4. prêter des livres
5. emprunter des CD
6. envoyer une carte d'anniversaire
7. s'offrir des cadeaux
8. demander des conseils

Lisons

TEXT AUDIO
CD 6 TRACK 27

Stratégie

When reading dialogue from a play, be alert to changes in pace and tone that signal development in the characters and the plot. When such changes occur, ask yourself what they mean and how they reinforce the buildup of dramatic tension.

Presentation: Avant de lire Have students examine the photo of the interior of the theater in order to visualize the context for the play.

12-22 La Leçon

A. Avant de lire. Depuis plus de cinquante ans, dans une petite rue du Quartier latin à Paris, le **Théâtre de la Huchette** présente les deux pièces les plus connues d'Eugène Ionesco (1909–1994) : ***La cantatrice chauve*** (*The Bald Soprano*) et ***La Leçon*** (tous deux publiés en 1953). Dans ce petit théâtre de quatre-vingt-dix places, des millions de spectateurs ont vu ces deux œuvres modèles du théâtre de l'absurde, un genre littéraire qui a fleuri après la Seconde Guerre mondiale. Le théâtre de l'absurde rejette la structure, les personnages (*characters*) et la logique du théâtre conventionnel dans l'objectif d'exposer un monde à l'envers (*upside down*).

L'intérieur du Théâtre de la Huchette. Est-ce que vous aimeriez voir une pièce dans cette salle ?

Vous allez lire un extrait de ***La Leçon***. Cet échange entre un professeur et son élève semble bizarre, mais il y a une progression dans le ton et le style qui prédit l'évènement violent, un meurtre, qui sera la fin dramatique de la pièce. Pour bien saisir la tension qui monte, remarquez le changement dans les répliques du professeur et de son élève du début à la fin de cette scène.

Key: En lisant 1) le professeur pense que l'élève est brillante parce qu'elle sait combien font un et un ; il dit qu'elle est très avancée et qu'elle va obtenir facilement son doctorat ; la nature rapide des questions et des réponses est drôle ; il y a aussi le commentaire du professeur que l'élève est magnifique (simplement à cause de l'addition simple) 2) Au début, l'élève a beaucoup de confiance et elle est très sûre d'elle. Elle devient de moins en moins sûre d'elle. Quand le professeur continue à poser des questions « difficiles », elle ne sait pas comment répondre. Elle commence à paniquer et elle donne des réponses sans réfléchir. 3) Au début, le professeur est poli, il a beaucoup de patience et il encourage l'élève. Ensuite, il devient de plus en plus agressif. Il devient impatient et on a l'impression qu'il veut dominer l'élève. Il essaie de montrer que c'est lui le maître et le plus intelligent. 4) À la fin, le professeur a complètement dominé l'élève. Elle se questionne et elle hésite avant chaque réponse. Il y a un rapport de maître-élève.

B. En lisant. Lisez le texte et ensuite répondez aux questions suivantes.

1. Identifiez quelques aspects comiques de cet extrait.

MODÈLE Le professeur est très surpris parce que l'élève sait combien font un et un ; …

2. Quelle est l'attitude de l'élève au début : est-ce qu'elle est timide ou est-ce qu'elle est sûre d'elle ? Comment est-ce que ses réponses évoluent pendant la leçon ? Pourquoi ?
3. Comment est le professeur au début : est-ce qu'il est poli et patient, par exemple ? Comment est-ce qu'il change d'attitude au cours de la leçon ? Pourquoi ?
4. Comment est-ce que la relation entre le professeur et son élève a changé à la fin ?

LE PROFESSEUR : Bon. Arithmétisons donc un peu.
L'ÉLÈVE : Oui, très volontiers, Monsieur.
LE PROFESSEUR : Cela ne vous ennuierait pas de me dire …
L'ÉLÈVE : Du tout[1], Monsieur, allez-y.
LE PROFESSEUR : Combien font un et un ?
L'ÉLÈVE : Un et un font deux.
LE PROFESSEUR : *émerveillé[2] par le savoir de l'Élève :* Oh, mais c'est très bien. Vous me paraissez[3] très avancée dans vos études. Vous aurez facilement votre doctorat total, Mademoiselle.
L'ÉLÈVE : Je suis bien contente. D'autant plus que[4] c'est vous qui le dites.
LE PROFESSEUR : Poussons plus loin : combien font deux et un ?
L'ÉLÈVE : Trois.
LE PROFESSEUR : Trois et un ?
L'ÉLÈVE : Quatre.
LE PROFESSEUR : Quatre et un ?
L'ÉLÈVE : Cinq.
LE PROFESSEUR : Cinq et un ?
L'ÉLÈVE : Six.
LE PROFESSEUR : Six et un ?
L'ÉLÈVE : Sept.
LE PROFESSEUR : Sept et un ?
L'ÉLÈVE : Huit.
LE PROFESSEUR : Sept et un ?
L'ÉLÈVE : Huit … *bis.*
LE PROFESSEUR : Très bonne réponse. Sept et un ?
L'ÉLÈVE : Huit *ter.*
LE PROFESSEUR : Parfait. Excellent. Sept et un ?
L'ÉLÈVE : Huit *quater.* Et parfois neuf.

[1]*Not at all* [2]*amazed* [3]*seem, appear* [4]*All the more so because*

LE PROFESSEUR : Magnifique. Vous êtes magnifique. Vous êtes exquise. Je vous félicite chaleureusement[5], Mademoiselle. Ce n'est pas la peine[6] de continuer. Pour l'addition, vous êtes magistrale. Voyons la soustraction. Dites-moi, seulement, si vous n'êtes pas épuisée[7], combien font quatre moins trois ?

L'ÉLÈVE : Quatre moins trois ? ... Quatre moins trois ?

LE PROFESSEUR : Oui. Je veux dire : retirez[8] trois de quatre.

L'ÉLÈVE : Ça fait ... sept ?

LE PROFESSEUR : Je m'excuse[9] d'être obligé de vous contredire[10]. Quatre moins trois ne font pas sept. Vous confondez[11] : quatre plus trois font sept, quatre moins trois ne font pas sept... Il ne s'agit plus[12] d'additionner, il faut soustraire maintenant.

L'ÉLÈVE : *s'efforce de comprendre :* Oui ... oui...

LE PROFESSEUR : Quatre moins trois font ... Combien ? ... Combien ?

L'ÉLÈVE : Quatre ?

LE PROFESSEUR : Non, Mademoiselle, ce n'est pas ça.

L'ÉLÈVE : Trois, alors.

LE PROFESSEUR : Non plus, Mademoiselle ... Pardon, je dois le dire ... Ça ne fait pas ça ... mes excuses.

L'ÉLÈVE : Quatre moins trois ... Quatre moins trois ... Quatre moins trois ? ... Ça ne fait tout de même pas dix ?

LE PROFESSEUR : Oh, certainement pas, Mademoiselle. Mais il ne s'agit pas de deviner[13], il faut raisonner. Tâchons[14] de le déduire ensemble. Voulez-vous compter ?

L'ÉLÈVE : Oui, Monsieur. Un ... , deux ... , euh ...

LE PROFESSEUR : Vous savez bien compter ? Jusqu'à combien savez-vous compter ?

L'ÉLÈVE : Je puis[15] compter ... à l'infini.

LE PROFESSEUR : Cela n'est pas possible, Mademoiselle.

L'ÉLÈVE : Alors, mettons[16] jusqu'à seize.

LE PROFESSEUR : Cela suffit[17]. Il faut savoir se limiter[18]. Comptez donc, s'il vous plaît, je vous en prie.

L'ÉLÈVE : Un ... , deux ... , et puis après deux, il y a trois ... quatre ...

LE PROFESSEUR : Arrêtez-vous, Mademoiselle. Quel nombre est plus grand ? Trois ou quatre ?

L'ÉLÈVE : Euh ... trois ou quatre ? Quel est le plus grand ? Le plus grand de trois ou quatre ? Dans quel sens le plus grand ?

LE PROFESSEUR : Il y a des nombres plus petits et d'autres plus grands. Dans les nombres plus grands il y a plus d'unités que dans les petits ...

L'ÉLÈVE : ... Que dans les petits nombres ?

LE PROFESSEUR : À moins que[19] les petits aient des unités plus petites. Si elles sont toutes petites, il se peut qu[20]'il y ait plus d'unités dans les petits nombres que dans les grands ... s'il s'agit d'autres unités ...

L'ÉLÈVE : Dans ce cas, les petits nombres peuvent être plus grands que les grands nombres ?

LE PROFESSEUR : Laissons cela[21]. Ça nous mènerait beaucoup trop loin ...

[5] *warmly* [6] *There's no point* [7] *exhausted* [8] *take away* [9] *I am sorry* [10] *to contradict* [11] *confuse* [12] *It's no longer a question* [13] *to guess* [14] Essayons [15] peux [16] Disons [17] *That's enough* [18] *We have to know our limits* [19] *Unless* [20] *it may be that* [21] *Let's drop it*

C. En regardant de plus près. Maintenant examinez quelques caractéristiques du texte.

1. Observez la rapidité du dialogue : à quel moment est-ce que les questions et les réponses se suivent très rapidement ? À quel moment est-ce que les réponses ralentissent (*slow down*) ? Qu'est-ce que cela signale ?
2. Examinez les répliques (*lines*) du professeur et de l'élève séparément : qu'est-ce que cela révèle sur le développement de chaque personnage ?

Key: En regardant de plus près 1) Le dialogue est le plus rapide avec les problèmes d'addition. Il ralentit avec la soustraction. Cela signifie un changement dans les attitudes des personnages. C'est peut-être aussi un commentaire sur la nature du système éducatif et l'importance de la mémorisation par cœur. 2) Pour l'élève, on voit qu'elle devient de plus en plus confuse et de moins en moins sûre d'elle et qu'elle pose plus de questions. Pour le professeur, on voit qu'il devient de plus en plus impatient et qu'il commence à donner des explications plus complexes (même si elles ne sont pas toujours logiques).

D. Après avoir lu. Discutez des questions suivantes avec vos camarades de classe.

1. Dans cet extrait, il s'agit d'un dialogue absurde entre le professeur et l'élève. Est-ce que c'est, à votre avis, une critique du système éducatif ? Dans quel sens ?
2. Comment sont les relations entre les professeurs et les élèves, d'après Ionesco ?
3. À la fin de la pièce, il y a un meurtre ; qui va tuer qui, à votre avis ? Expliquez votre réponse.

Key: Après avoir lu 1) Une interprétation possible, c'est que le système éducatif encourage la mémorisation par cœur à un tel point que les élèves ne peuvent pas raisonner et ne sont pas créatifs. 2) Ionesco essaie de démontrer que les professeurs ont trop de pouvoir par rapport aux élèves, même le pouvoir de la vie et la mort. 3) Dans cette pièce, c'est le professeur qui tue l'élève comme il l'a fait avec les quarante élèves précédents. À la fin de la pièce, la sonnette annonce l'arrivée d'un autre élève...

Le Théâtre de la Huchette à Paris. À quelle date est-ce que la première représentation de *La Leçon* a eu lieu ?

Le Théâtre de la Huchette se trouve dans le Quatier Latin près de la place St. Michel. Qu'est-ce qu'on peut visiter aussi dans ce quartier ?

Presentation: To preview this lesson, show the opening montage for *Modes d'expression artistique*. Have students identify the various types of art and music they see expressed in the montage. Help students understand the meaning of the words *artisan* and *artisanat* through the **Observons** activity and the discussion of *artisanat* that follows.

Venez chez nous ! Modes d'expression artistique

Un artiste dessine devant une sculpture au Louvre.

Partout dans le monde, les gens s'expriment à travers l'art. Dans le monde francophone, on trouve une grande variété de modes d'expression artistique : des grands maîtres de l'impressionnisme français aux masques et sculptures africains en passant par l'art de style primitif haïtien. Côté musique, on trouve le zydeco en Louisiane, l'Afropop à Madagascar ou en Guinée ainsi que des grands compositeurs comme Bizet, Debussy et Ravel et les rappeurs de nos jours. Il y a également des nombreux artisans. Ce sont des personnes qui travaillent pour eux-mêmes et qui produisent des choses qui, sans être des œuvres d'art, ont une valeur artistique.

Observons

12-23 L'art et l'artisanat

A. Avant de regarder. Est-ce que vous connaissez des artistes ou des artisans ? De quelles sortes ? Où est-ce qu'ils vendent leurs créations ? Écoutez Sylviane, une artiste sérigraphe à Seillans, qui nous montre son art, son atelier et son magasin à côté.

B. En regardant. Entourez toutes les réponses possibles.

1. Sylviane dit qu'elle est ...
   - **a.** une sérigraphe parmi (*among*) beaucoup d'autres en France.
   - **b.** une des dernières sérigraphes manuelles en France.
   - **c.** la meilleure artiste sérigraphe en France.
2. La sérigraphie moderne se fait ...
   - **a.** à la main.
   - **b.** dans les usines.
   - **c.** avec des machines sophistiquées.
3. Sylviane travaille comme ...
   - **a.** les Chinois il y a 3000 ans.
   - **b.** les artisans du Moyen Âge.
   - **c.** ses parents il y a 30 ans.
4. Elle réalise ses créations ...
   - **a.** chez elle dans une petite pièce.
   - **b.** chez des amis qui ont un bon atelier.
   - **c.** dans un atelier à côté de son magasin.
5. Elle peut faire des choses ...
   - **a.** personnalisées.
   - **b.** dans le style demandé par ses clients.
   - **c.** très sophistiquées.

Key: En regardant 1) b 2) c 3) a 4) c 5) a, b 6) b, c, e

Script: Observons
Note that the elements in brackets reflect standard usage and have been added to the written transcripts. They were not pronounced by the speaker in question.
Bonjour, je m'appelle Sylviane Leibovitz. Je suis euh artisan ou artiste sérigraphe. Je suis une des dernières sérigraphes manuelles qui existent en France. Euh la sérigraphie se fait maintenant avec des appareils très sophistiqués. Euh moi, je travaille encore presque comme travaillaient les Chinois il y a trois-mille ans avec des produits un peu plus modernes mais le principe est le même. Euh, tout ce que vous voyez dans ce magasin euh a été produit à l'atelier, là, à côté. Je travaille euh aussi en fonction des des de ce qu'on me demande les les clients c'est-à-dire [que] je peux faire des choses tout à fait personnalisées euh dans le style de de ce qu'on me demande avec des motifs, des motifs tirés du folklore, ou de la nature ou des animaux ou bien enfin, tu sais, il y a des inspirations très très diverses... mais toujours en adaptant euh au goût de de la clientèle.

6. Pour ses motifs, elle s'inspire ...
   a. des fruits et légumes.
   b. du folklore.
   c. de la nature.
   d. des enfants.
   e. des animaux.

Note: The definition of an artisan, according to the *Petit Robert*, is *Personne qui exerce un métier manuel pour son propre compte, aidée souvent de sa famille, de compagnons, apprentis*, etc. In France, the term is also used to describe the production of food in expressions such as *du pain artisanal*, *du chocolat artisanal*, and so forth. Question 2 leads into the discussion of art and *artisanat* below. Ask students their opinion as to whether a jewelry maker or a watch repair person, for example, is an artisan or an artist and why they think so.

C. Après avoir regardé. Maintenant discutez des questions suivantes avec vos camarades de classe.

1. Est-ce que vous connaissiez la sérigraphie ? Qu'est-ce que vous pensez des objets que vous avez vus dans la vidéo ? Est-ce que vous aimeriez avoir un tee-shirt ou un foulard décoré selon la technique de la sérigraphie?
2. Sylviane dit qu'elle est « **artisan ou artiste sérigraphe** ». Quelle est la différence à votre avis ? Est-ce que vous pensez qu'elle est artiste ou plutôt artisan ? Pourquoi ?

L'artisanat

Les artisans peuvent avoir un métier très créatif. En France, comme dans d'autres pays francophones, les artisans travaillent à leur compte[1] et gagnent leur vie avec la vente des œuvres qu'ils ont créées. Dans certains cas, il peut être assez difficile de déterminer s'il s'agit[2] d'art ou d'artisanat, parce qu'après tout, le mot « artisan » contient bien le mot « art ». Par exemple, est-ce que les masques africains sont considérés comme de l'artisanat ou comme des œuvres d'art, ou comme les deux à la fois[3] ? Il est certain que ces masques ont inspiré des artistes modernes comme Pablo Picasso et Henri Matisse. Ils font partie aussi des grandes collections d'art dans certains musées du monde et dans des collections privées.

[1]*are self-employed* [2]*if it's about* [3]*at the same time*

Au Bénin, on peut trouver des belles tapisseries comme ce « Lion dans la forêt ».

Cet artisan haïtien vend ses tableaux aux amateurs (*aficionados*) d'art folklorique.

Presentation: Looking at the pictures, continue the discussion about the differences between *l'art* and *l'artisanat*. Is one more valued than the other? Is one more practical? Is there a cultural dimension to what is termed art? Use this as a springboard to discuss African art in particular and as an introduction to the **Lisons** that follows.

Stratégie

Use what you know about the famous people, historical events, and general subject matter of an expository text to better understand the content. If you are not familiar with some of the people or events mentioned, consider doing some preliminary research before you tackle the text.

Presentation: 12-24 You might have students look at the pictures and discuss similarities between the African masks and Picasso's paintings. Alternatively, have students read the text first, then look at and discuss the pictures.

Note: The text mentions the fifteenth and twentieth centuries. When Africa was first discovered by the West, its art was considered mainly a curiosity or the crude expression of an "inferior" people. In the twentieth century, modern artists such as Matisse and Picasso appreciated African art on its own terms and found inspiration in it to break with the canons of traditional art. The artists mentioned are Matisse, Picasso, Gauguin, and Vlaminck (an artist of Flemish origins born in Paris in 1876, contemporary with Matisse and Picasso). These artists can all be classified as representative of *l'art moderne. Cubisme* is the artistic movement mentioned in the text. The first cubist work is *Les demoiselles d'Avignon* by Picasso, shown in the textbook. The connection to African art is quite explicit in this painting.

Key: En lisant 1) les navigateurs portugais au xve siècle 2) la puissance, l'abstraction, la richesse, la variété, la vitalité, les valeurs humanistes 3) pendant « les années folles » (1919–1929) 4) dans des musées et des galeries d'art

Lisons

12-24 La découverte de l'art africain

Des masques africains.

En 1907, Pablo Picasso lance un nouveau style, le cubisme, avec ce tableau, *Les demoiselles d'Avignon*. Regardez le visage de ces femmes. Quelle est la ressemblance avec les masques africains ?

Pablo Picasso, *Les demoiselles d'Avignon*. 1907. Art Resource. NY.

A. Avant de lire. Ce passage décrit des artistes connus, des mouvements artistiques et des époques historiques. Avant de le lire, examinez rapidement le texte pour identifier les deux siècles (*centuries*) indiqués par des chiffres romains. D'après le texte, comment est-ce que la connaissance du continent africain par les Européens a changé à travers les siècles ? Ensuite, trouvez le nom de quatre artistes dans le texte. Est-ce que vous les connaissez ? Finalement, trouvez le mouvement artistique qui est cité dans ce texte. Quels artistes faisaient partie de ce mouvement ? Maintenant, lisez le texte en vous servant de ces connaissances qui vont vous aider à bien comprendre.

B. En lisant. Répondez aux questions suivantes.

1. D'après le texte, qui a découvert l'art africain et quand ?
2. Au vingtième siècle, plusieurs artistes ont reconnu les qualités de l'art africain. D'après le texte, quelles sont ces qualités ?
3. D'après le texte, quand est-ce que les grandes collections privées ont commencé ?
4. Où est-ce qu'on peut voir de l'art africain de nos jours ?

La découverte de l'art africain

À partir du XVe siècle les navigateurs portugais explorent l'Afrique et l'Europe et découvrent peu à peu l'art africain ...

La véritable rencontre de l'art africain et de l'Europe se fait au XXe siècle.

Il y est décelé[1] une nouvelle écriture qui va répondre pour certains artistes comme Matisse, Picasso, Gauguin, Vlaminck, à leur préoccupation[2] et marquer le point de départ de la rupture avec les normes académiques. Ces artistes occidentaux sont les premiers à reconnaître autant de valeurs humanistes chez les artistes africains. Ils admirent la puissante abstraction de cette expression, la richesse, la variété, la vitalité qui rayonnent[3] dans cet art. Ils y trouvent une nouvelle source d'inspiration et même un style nouveau, le Cubisme, art abstrait qui casse le carcan[4] des lois imposées aux artistes depuis la Renaissance.

Enfin, les objets d'art africain vont être regardés comme des œuvres d'art. Il n'était plus[5] question de beauté, de laideur, mais bien d'une émotion directe, d'une manifestation spontanée.

L'engouement[6] pour l'art africain caractérise « les années folles ». C'est aussi bien sûr le temps des grandes collections privées.

De nos jours, des centaines d'expositions d'art africain sont organisées chaque année dans le monde. Des musées, des galeries d'art et des collectionneurs privés s'arrachent[7] ces œuvres dans les grandes ventes aux enchères[8] internationales et atteignent[9] des prix records.

[1] *revealed* [2] *concerns* [3] *shine forth* [4] *yoke* [5] *no longer* [6] l'enthousiasme [7] *grab up* [8] *auctions* [9] *reach*

Source : Babette Gazeau, http://www.danse-africaine.net

C. En regardant de plus près. Maintenant, examinez les aspects suivants du texte.

1. Regardez l'expression **une nouvelle écriture** à la ligne 4. Vous savez que le mot **écriture** a un rapport avec le verbe **écrire.** Normalement, ce mot veut dire « les signes graphiques qu'on utilise pour écrire ». Mais ici ce mot a une autre signification. Quelle est la signification du mot **écriture** dans ce texte ?
2. Regardez le verbe **reconnaître** à la ligne 7. Vous remarquez sans doute le verbe **connaître** dans ce verbe. Si vous considérez en plus le contexte, qu'est-ce que ce verbe veut dire en anglais ?
3. À la ligne 14, on parle de **beauté** et de **laideur**. Ces deux noms sont dérivés d'adjectifs qui décrivent l'apparence physique. Quel est l'adjectif qui correspond à **beauté** ? Si vous savez que **laid** est un synonyme de l'adjectif **moche**, quelle est la signification de **laideur** ?
4. Regardez le mot **centaines** à la ligne 18. Quel chiffre est-ce que vous remarquez dans ce mot ? D'après cela, que veut dire la phrase : **des centaines d'expositions** ?

Key: En regardant de plus près 1) Cette expression a un sens plus abstrait ici. Elle fait référence au système que les artistes utilisent pour créer leur art. 2) *to recognize* 3) beau, belle ; laid/e : ce qui n'est pas beau 4) cent ; deux-cents ou trois-cents (ou plus !) d'expositions.

Key: Après avoir lu Certains styles de musique aux États-Unis sont très influencés par la culture africaine : par exemple, la musique gospel, le jazz, le zydeco. La danse aussi : par exemple le « *step-dancing* ». L'artisanat aux États-Unis connaît également des influences africaines. Certains artistes Afro-américains qui utilisent un style naïf font partie du mouvement artistique qui s'appelle « *outsider art* » (l'art brut).

D. Après avoir lu. Discutez des questions suivantes avec vos camarades de classe.

1. Est-ce que vous avez déjà vu des expositions d'art africain dans un musée ou dans une galerie ? Qu'est-ce que vous pensez des œuvres d'art que vous avez vues ?
2. À votre avis, est-ce que les civilisations africaines ont eu une influence sur d'autres mouvements artistiques en Occident ? Dans quels domaines ? Est-ce que cette influence est toujours reconnue ? Pourquoi, à votre avis ?

Écrivons

Stratégie

To write an interesting, coherent essay, decide how you can articulate your topic clearly in an introductory paragraph, then determine how you will develop it on a paragraph-by-paragraph basis. This process will give you a clear plan for presenting your ideas effectively.

12-25 L'art chez moi

A. Avant d'écrire. Pensez aux œuvres d'art et à leurs reproductions qu'il y a dans votre chambre, dans votre appartement ou chez vos parents et faites-en une petite liste. Est-ce que vous pouvez identifier un style ou des préférences pour un certain type d'art ou pour un certain artiste ? Quel est l'œuvre d'art que vous préférez ?

B. En écrivant. Rédigez un texte de trois ou quatre paragraphes qui décrivent le(s) type(s) d'art que vous préférez et une œuvre chez vous que vous aimez en particulier.

1. Pour commencer, complétez ce tableau qui va vous aider à organiser votre texte.

Introduction Pour écrire une bonne introduction : ◆ Identifiez les œuvres d'art qu'il y a chez vous. ◆ Donnez-en quelques exemples précis. ◆ Indiquez vos préférences (pour le style, les matières, les artistes, les œuvres). ◆ Indiquez votre œuvre préférée.	**MODÈLE** ◆ l'art africain chez mes parents ◆ des masques, des sculptures, des batiks, des tableaux ◆ j'adore les petites sculptures et les batiks ◆ je préfère le grand batik au-dessus (*above*) de la cheminée	VOUS :
Paragraphe 2 Décrivez votre œuvre d'art préférée.	**MODÈLE** ◆ le grand batik a beaucoup de couleurs très vives ... ◆ c'est une scène de village	VOUS :

Paragraphe 3 Dites pourquoi vous aimez cette œuvre et expliquez son importance pour vous.	**MODÈLE** ◆ c'est un souvenir du village de ma grand-mère au Ghana	VOUS :
Conclusion Écrivez deux ou trois phrases pour terminer votre essai.	**MODÈLE** L'art africain est très important pour mon père et aussi pour moi. Quand j'étais petite, je ne l'aimais pas beaucoup parce que c'était différent de l'art chez mes amis. Mais maintenant, je l'apprécie.	VOUS :

2. Maintenant, utilisez vos notes pour rédiger votre texte. Si vous voulez, vous pouvez accompagner votre texte d'une image ou d'une photo.

MODÈLE J'aime bien l'art africain. Mon père vient du Ghana et donc nous avons chez nous beaucoup d'œuvres d'art qui viennent de son pays. Il y a des masques, des sculptures, des batiks et des tableaux. J'aime surtout un grand batik que nous avons au-dessus de la cheminée.

Mon batik préféré montre une scène de village avec des petites maisons, des baobabs, des femmes qui préparent à manger, des enfants qui jouent, des hommes qui travaillent dans les champs. Il y a beaucoup de couleurs très vives surtout dans des tons jaunes et orange. Je peux contempler ce batik pendant des heures ...

Ce batik me rappelle le village de ma grand-mère au Ghana et quand je le regarde, je pense à elle ...

L'art africain est très important pour mon père et aussi pour moi. Quand j'étais petite je ne l'aimais pas beaucoup parce que c'était différent de l'art chez mes amis. Mais maintenant, j'apprécie beaucoup.

C. En révisant. Réfléchissez aux questions suivantes et puis faites tous les changements nécessaires.

1. Relisez votre texte pour en analyser le contenu : est-ce que vous avez utilisé les notes que vous avez prises pour décrire l'art chez vous ?
2. Relisez de nouveau votre texte pour analyser le style et la forme : est-ce que vous avez bien organisé votre information en paragraphes logiques qui se suivent, y compris une bonne introduction ? Est-ce que vous avez utilisé une variété de mots ou d'expressions pour décrire les œuvres d'art que vous mentionnez ?
3. Donnez un titre à votre texte et si vous avez une photo ou un dessin, écrivez une légende (*caption*).

D. Après avoir écrit. Échangez votre texte avec vos camarades de classe. Est-ce que vous avez les mêmes goûts artistiques ou est-ce que vos goûts sont différents ?

Implementation: 12-25 Have students exchange drafts and encourage them to revise based on peer feedback. You might collect the final version and create an "art catalogue" for the class. Alternatively, you might post the best compositions, accompanied by illustrations, on a class or school Web site.

Les musiques cadienne et zydeco en Louisiane

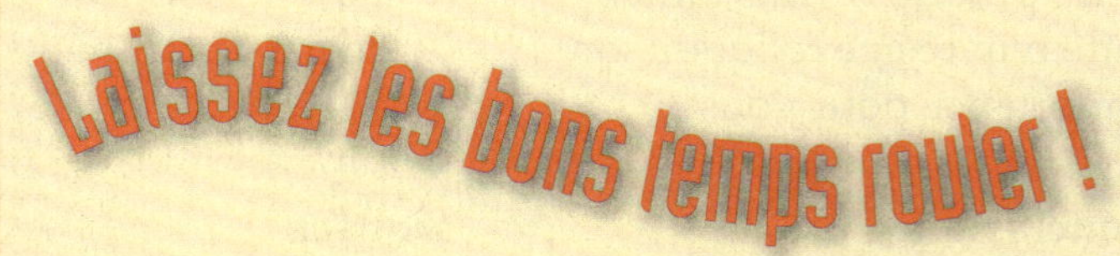

Les musiques cadienne et zydeco sont très populaires aux États-Unis comme en Europe pour danser et faire la fête. Mais il faut être en Louisiane pour aller à une soirée « fais dodo » où l'on peut manger les spécialités locales, écouter de la bonne musique, danser et s'amuser. Quelle est la différence entre ces deux musiques louisianaises ?

La musique cadienne est la musique des descendants d'Acadiens. Les Acadiens ont quitté le Canada et sont arrivés en Louisiane au dix-huitième siècle. Ils ont été chassés de leur région, l'Acadie (aujourd'hui le Nouveau-Brunswick et la Nouvelle-Écosse), parce qu'ils refusaient de se soumettre totalement à l'autorité du gouvernement britannique. Cette musique a été influencée par la valse, la mazurka et la polka qui venaient d'Europe, et par la musique folklorique, country et swing d'Amérique du Nord. Les deux instruments essentiels sont le violon et l'accordéon. On y entend aussi souvent le triangle ou ti-fer (petit fer).

BeauSoleil, un groupe de musiciens cadiens, en concert en Louisiane. Michael Doucet joue du violon, Jimmy Breaux joue de l'accordéon et David Doucet joue de la guitare.

La musique zydeco, au rythme syncopé, a été créée par des Louisianais d'origine africaine. Ses influences sont plutôt le blues, le jazz et le rock. Au lieu du violon, c'est la guitare qui est l'instrument de base du zydeco à côté de l'accordéon. On y trouve aussi des guitares et des contrebasses électriques et même de la batterie.

Presentation: Play samples of Cajun and Zydeco music and have students identify the instruments they hear. To illustrate Cajun music, play songs performed by the late, great Cajun fiddler Dewey Balfa and various groups made up of his family members—the *Balfa Brothers* and *Balfa Toujours*. Zydeco musicians include the late "king of Zydeco" Clifton Chénier, Beau Jocque (now deceased), John Delafose, or Buckwheat Zydeco. The popular group *BeauSoleil* plays Cajun and Zydeco music. See the *Chez nous* Companion Website for links to Web sites devoted to both types of music.

Implementation: 12-26 As a model, show the video clip *J'aime beaucoup le jazz*. Have students note expressions used by the speaker to describe this music and a particular musician, and have them note how she incorporates a musical selection into her description. See the IRM for suggestions on assessing an oral presentation. Encourage students to practice before making their presentation. Bring a CD player to class to allow them to share their musical sample. For a particularly large class, you may have students complete this assignment in pairs.

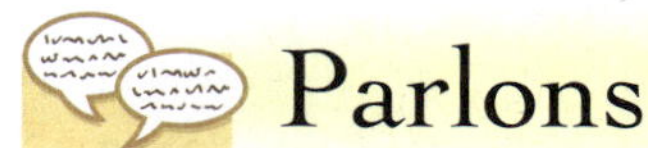

Parlons

12-26 La musique que je préfère

Quel type de musique est-ce que vous préférez ? le jazz ? la musique pop ? le rock ? le rap ? la musique punk ? Qui est votre musicien/ne préféré/e ? Préparez un exposé sur la musique que vous aimez et présentez-le à votre classe.

A. Avant de parler. Pour faire un bon exposé oral, il faut se préparer à l'avance :

1. D'abord, pensez à la musique et au musicien ou à la musicienne que vous voudriez présenter.
2. Ensuite, pensez aux choses que vous aimeriez dire : par exemple, vous pourriez décrire le style de musique, parler un peu de son histoire et donner ses caractéristiques. Si vous présentez un/e musicien/ne ou un groupe, vous pourriez mentionner quelques aspects de sa biographie, parler de sa musique et dire pourquoi vous l'appréciez.
3. Il est important que vos camarades de classe puissent comprendre votre exposé, donc ne cherchez pas de mots compliqués dans le dictionnaire. Essayez plutôt d'utiliser des mots que vous connaissez et d'accompagner votre exposé de supports visuels.
4. Pour rendre votre présentation plus intéressante, pensez aussi à apporter quelques extraits que vous pouvez faire écouter aux autres.

B. En parlant. Présentez votre exposé à vos camarades.

MODÈLE D'habitude, je préfère le rock, mais la semaine dernière, je suis allée à un concert de *BeauSoleil* avec mes parents et j'ai décidé de faire mon exposé sur ce groupe cadien. Le musicien principal du groupe s'appelle Michael Doucet, il joue du violon et chante. Son frère, David Doucet, fait partie du groupe aussi. Lui, il joue de la guitare. Bien sûr, il y a un accordéon dans ce groupe ; c'est Jimmy Breaux, le petit-fils d'un célèbre joueur d'accordéon cadien, qui joue de l'accordéon pour *BeauSoleil*. Les autres musiciens du groupe jouent de la batterie, de la guitare électrique et aussi du violon.

Les musiciens de *BeauSoleil* jouent ensemble depuis plus de 30 ans. Ils font de la musique traditionnelle et composent aussi des nouvelles chansons ...

Le concert était super. Il y avait beaucoup d'énergie et d'enthousiasme. En fait, Michael Doucet a encouragé tout le monde à danser ...

Voici un extrait d'une de leurs dernières chansons ...

C. Après avoir parlé. Quelles présentations ont été particulièrement intéressantes ? Pourquoi ? Est-ce que vous aimeriez en savoir plus sur un style de musique ou sur un/e musicien/ne en particulier ?

Now that you have completed *Chapitre 12*, can you do the following in French?

- ☐ talk about the performing and visual arts?
- ☐ tell stories and recount events using the past, present, and future as appropriate?
- ☐ describe various artistic movements, artists, and practices in the Francophone world?

Vocabulaire

Leçon 1

la musique	***music***
... classique	*classical music*
folklorique	*folk music*
traditionnelle	*traditional music*
un chœur	*chorus*
un opéra	*opera*
un orchestre	*orchestra*
une répétition	*rehearsal*
une représentation	*production*
un trio	*trio*

quelques instruments (m.)	***some instruments***
la clarinette	*clarinet*
le clavier	*keyboards*
la flûte traversière	*flute*
la guitare basse	*bass guitar*
la guitare électrique	*electric guitar*
le trombone	*trombone*
la trompette	*trumpet*
le violon	*violin*
le violoncelle	*cello*

quelques verbes suivis de *à* ou *de* devant l'infinitif	***verbs followed by* à *or* de *before an infinitive***
accepter de	*to accept*
aider à	*to help*
apprendre à	*to learn*
arrêter de	*to stop*
commencer à	*to begin*
continuer à	*to continue*
décider de	*to decide*
essayer de	*to try*
finir de	*to finish*
inviter à	*to invite*
oublier de	*to forget*
refuser de	*to refuse*
réussir à	*to succeed*
rêver de	*to dream of*
venir de + inf.	*to have just (done something)*

d'autres mots utiles	***other useful words***
C'est entendu	*It's understood; OK*
espérer	*to hope*
pourquoi pas ?	*why not?*

Leçon 2

les artistes et leur art	***artists and their art***
un dessin	*sketch/drawing*
un dessinateur/une dessinatrice	*draftsman/woman*
un maître	*master*
une nature morte	*still life*
une œuvre d'art	*work of art*
un pastel	*pastel*
un paysage	*landscape*
peindre	*to paint*
un/e peintre	*painter*
un/e photographe	*photographer*
une photo(graphie)	*photo(graph)*
un portrait	*portrait*
un sculpteur	*sculptor*
un tableau	*painting*
une tapisserie	*tapestry*

pour parler d'art	***to talk about art***
la composition	*composition*
une couleur	*color*
sombre	*somber, dark*
vive	*bright, vivid*
l'utilisation de la lumière	*use of light*
s'intituler	*to be titled*
un reflet	*reflection*
le style	*style*
abstrait	*abstract*
cubiste	*cubist*
impressionniste	*Impressionist*
primitif	*primitive*
le sujet	*subject*

quelques expressions pour se décider	***expressions used in deciding***
après tout	*after all*
ça (ne) me dit rien	*I'm not interested in that*
ça (ne) fait rien	*that doesn't matter*
ça vaut le coup	*it's worth it (fam.)*
un choix	*choice*
être fanatique de	*to be a fan of*
pas si vite	*not so fast*
planifier	*to plan*
plutôt	*rather*
risquer de ...	*to run the risk of . . .*
se faire un petit plaisir	*to treat oneself*

d'autres mots utiles	***other useful words***
s'abonner, être abonné/e	*to subscribe. to buy season tickets/to be subscribed, to have season tickets*
un chef-d'œuvre, des chefs-d'œuvre	*masterpiece(s)*
un spectacle	*show*

Appendices

Appendice 1

L'ALPHABET PHONÉTIQUE INTERNATIONAL

a	**à**, l**a**	b	le **b**ureau
e	**é**cout**ez**	k	le **c**ahier, **qu**i, **k**ilo
ɛ	**e**lle	ʃ	la **ch**aise
i	**i**l, le st**y**lo	d	**d**ans
o	le styl**o**, bient**ô**t, le tabl**eau**	f	la **f**emme
ɔ	la g**o**mme	g	le **g**arçon
u	n**ou**s	ɲ	espa**gn**ol
y	d**u**	ʒ	le **j**our, **g**entil
ø	d**eu**x	l	**l**a, vi**ll**age
œ	l**eu**r, la s**œu**r	m	**m**ada**m**e
ɑ̃	l'**en**fan**t**	n	**n**euf
ɛ̃	le cous**in**	ŋ	le campi**ng**
ɔ̃	b**on**jour	p	le **p**ère
œ̃	**un**	r	la **r**ègle
j	la n**i**èce, la f**ill**e, le cra**y**on	s	**s**alut, **c**inq, fran**ç**ais, la bro**ss**e
ɥ	l**u**i	t	la **t**an**t**e
w	m**oi**, j**ou**er, le **w**eek-end	v	**v**oici
		z	**z**éro, la cou**s**ine

Appendice 2

LE PLUS-QUE-PARFAIT

You have learned that the **passé composé** and the **imparfait** are used to narrate events in the past. Another past tense, the **plus-que-parfait**, is used as indicated below.

- Use the **plus-que-parfait** to order events in the past or to describe an event in the past that occurred before another past event (even an implied event).

J'ai appris que l'exposition sur Renoir **avait** déjà **finie**.	*I learned that the Renoir exhibit had already finished.*
Quand on est arrivé, le spectacle **avait** déjà **commencé**.	*When we arrived, the show had already begun.*
Elles ne **s'étaient** jamais **rencontrées**.	*They had never met.*

- To form the **plus-que-parfait**, use the imperfect of **avoir** or **être** and the past participle.

j'**avais** joué	nous **avions** joué
tu **avais** joué	vous **aviez** joué
il / elle / on } **avait** joué	ils / elles } **avaient** joué
j'**étais** parti/e	nous **étions** parti/e/s
tu **étais** parti/e	vous **étiez** parti/e/s
il **était** parti	ils **étaient** partis
elle **était** partie	elles **étaient** parties
on **était** partis	

Note: Point out to students that the final *s* on *partis* in the form *on était partis* reflects the fact that *on* is used here as the equivalent of *nous*. In actual fact, this usage is variable. Grammatical agreement can be made with *on* as either a singular or plural subject, even though the subject is semantically plural when used as the equivalent of *nous*.

- The **plus-que-parfait**, as in the second example below, is also used to report what someone said she *had done* in the past. Note that in the first example, the imperfect is used to report what someone said she *was doing* in the past.

Elle dit : « Je lis le programme. »	Elle a dit qu'elle lisait le programme.
Elle dit : « J'ai lu le programme. »	Elle a dit qu'elle **avait lu** le programme.

À vous la parole

A2-1 Histoire d'amour. Voici quelques moments dans la vie de Camille Claudel et d'Auguste Rodin, deux sculpteurs français qui étaient ensemble pendant dix ans. Ils se sont séparés définitivement en 1898. Est-ce que les actions suivantes se sont passées avant ou après cette rupture ?

MODÈLE Camille Claudel était allée à Paris pour sculpter.
avant la rupture

1. Ils s'étaient souvent disputés.
2. Ils s'étaient rencontrés à Paris.
3. Elle a sculpté *La Vague*.
4. Elle avait commencé à travailler dans l'atelier (*studio*) de Rodin.
5. Ils étaient tombés amoureux.
6. Camille Claudel avait beaucoup influencé l'œuvre de Rodin.
7. Auguste Rodin est retourné à sa maîtresse Rose Beuret.
8. Camille Claudel est morte à l'âge de 79 ans.

A2-2 Une sortie. Un après-midi, Pierre et Nathalie sont sortis ensemble. Pour chaque phrase, indiquez l'ordre des évènements.

MODÈLE Ils étaient arrivés au café quand Nathalie a suggéré d'aller voir une exposition.
1. Ils sont arrivés au café. 2. Nathalie a suggéré d'aller voir une exposition.

1. Ils avaient fini de boire leur café quand ils ont décidé d'aller au musée.
2. Avant de choisir une exposition, ils avaient acheté *Pariscope*.
3. Quand ils sont entrés dans le musée, la visite guidée avait déjà commencé.
4. Pierre avait déjà vu l'exposition, mais il n'a rien dit.
5. Après avoir vu l'exposition, ils sont allés chez Nathalie.
6. Ils avaient parlé de l'exposition avant de manger.
7. Pierre avait rangé la cuisine un peu avant de partir.

A2-3 Explications. Complétez ces phrases avec un verbe au **plus-que-parfait** choisi de la liste suivante pour mieux expliquer la situation.

acheter	commencer	étudier	jouer
lire	manger	répéter	terminer

MODÈLE Le groupe s'est arrêté de chanter plus tôt que prévu parce qu'il … à pleuvoir.
avait déjà commencé

1. Nous sommes arrivés tellement en retard que le concert…
2. Quand le nouveau réalisateur est finalement arrivé, les acteurs … pendant trois semaines.
3. C'est dommage mais quand il a téléphoné pour m'inviter au restaurant, j'…
4. J'ai perdu le *Pariscope* que mon copain…
5. Quand nous avons vu cet opéra, nous … le livret (*libretto*).
6. Quand elle est allée au Louvre, elle … l'histoire de l'art.
7. Il ne savait pas que ce groupe … ta chanson préférée.

Implementation: A2-1, A2-2 These exercises test students' comprehension of the *plus-que-parfait*. To begin productive practice, use substitution drills: *J'avais déjà téléphoné ; lui — Il avait déjà téléphoné*, etc. *J'étais déjà partie ; nous — Nous étions déjà partis*, etc. Continue with meaningful practice — for example, having students describe things they had done before a particular time: *À huit heures... — je m'étais déjà levé*, etc. or *Quand mon colocataire est rentré... — j'avais déjà mangé ; j'avais terminé mes devoirs ; j'avais déjà fait la cuisine*, etc.

Implementation: A2-1 This simple discrimination drill is designed to help students learn to recognize the *plus-que-parfait* and its functional usage. To follow up, have students construct a narrative about the lives of these two sculptors and reorder the sentences logically. *Camille Claudel était allée à Paris. Ils s'étaient rencontrés...* For further productive practice, put students in small groups and have them present the tragic, romantic histories of famous couples (e.g., Romeo and Juliet, Princess Di and Prince Charles, Mark Anthony and Cleopatra) or of friends or family members.

Additional activity: For further practice with the *plus-que-parfait*, show students the following cues and have them transform these direct statements into indirect statements. *Laure a dit : « J'ai rencontré mes amis au concert hier soir. » — Laure a dit qu'elle avait rencontré ses amis au concert hier soir. Kevin nous a dit : « Je n'ai pas pu inviter mes parents au spectacle. » Manon a dit : « Romain et moi n'avons pas aimé le concert. » Pauline a dit : « J'ai adoré ce concert de jazz. » Hugo a écrit : « La mise en scène de l'opéra a été magnifique. » Gregory nous a dit : « Mes parents sont venus pour l'exposition. » Aurore a écrit : « J'ai obtenu le rôle principal dans la pièce de théâtre qu'on présente ce semestre. »*

Appendice 3

LE FUTUR ANTÉRIEUR

Presentation: This point was introduced in Ch. 11, L. 1. It is important to remind students that these types of sentences contain two future tenses in French; either the *futur simple* when the events are simultaneous, or the *futur antérieur* and the *futur simple* when one action in the future precedes the other. This usage is quite different from English and bears stressing.

- You have learned that when two future events are simultaneous, the future tense is used in both clauses.

Dès que j'**aurai** vingt-et-un ans, j'**irai** au nouveau club.	*As soon as I'm twenty-one, I'll go to the new club.*

- When one future event will have been completed before a second future event occurs, use the **futur antérieur** to convey the order of these events. Use the **futur antérieur** in a clause introduced by an expression such as **aussitôt que**, **dès que**, **quand**, or **lorsque** to express the earlier event.

Quand Rachid **aura terminé** cette sculpture, il la montrera à sa femme.	*When Rachid has finished this sculpture, he'll show it to his wife.*
Nous irons voir l'exposition **aussitôt qu'**il **aura terminé** ses devoirs.	*We will go to see the exhibit as soon as he has finished his homework.*
Dès que nous **aurons dîné**, nous sortirons.	*As soon as we have eaten, we will go out.*

- The **futur antérieur** can also be used with a temporal expression to indicate that an action will have been finished at that moment.

En l'an 2050 on **aura** tout **vu**.	*In the year 2050, we will have seen it all.*
J'espère que la pièce **aura fini avant dix heures et demie.**	*I hope that the play will have ended by 10:30.*

- To form the **futur antérieur**, use the future tense of **avoir** or **être** plus the past participle.

j'**aurai** joué	nous **aurons** joué
tu **auras** joué	vous **aurez** joué
il / elle / on **aura** joué	ils / elles **auront** joué
je **serai** parti/e	nous **serons** parti/e/s
tu **seras** parti/e	vous **serez** parti/e/s
il **sera** parti	ils **seront** partis
elle **sera** partie	elles **seront** parties
on **sera** partis	

Note: Point out to students that the final *s* on *partis* in the form *on sera partis* reflects the fact that *on* is used here as the equivalent of *nous*. In actual fact, this usage is variable. Grammatical agreement can be made with *on* as either a singular or plural subject, even though the subject is semantically plural when used as the equivalent of *nous*.

 À vous la parole 

Initial practice: Begin with a simple substitution drill. Have students change short sentences from the *futur simple* to the *futur antérieur*. *Il rentrera.* — *Il sera rentré ; On viendra.* — *On sera venus* ; etc.

 **A3-1 Des projets.** Qu'est-ce que vous ferez dans les situations suivantes ? Avec un/e partenaire, parlez de vos projets.

MODÈLE Dès que j'aurai terminé mes devoirs ce soir, …

É1 Dès que j'aurai terminé mes devoirs ce soir, je regarderai un peu la télé.

É2 Pas moi. Je préfère dormir. Dès que j'aurai terminé mes devoirs, je me coucherai.

1. Aussitôt que je me serai réveillé/e demain matin, je…
2. Dès que le week-end sera arrivé, je…
3. Lorsque j'aurai fini avec les examens finals, je…
4. Quand les grandes vacances seront arrivées, je…
5. Lorsque j'aurai terminé mes études, je…
6. Quand j'aurai trouvé un bon travail, je…
7. Quand j'aurai rencontré le/la partenaire idéal/e, je…
8. Quand j'aurai eu des enfants, je…

A3-2 Allons au musée. Complétez chaque phrase logiquement en employant le **futur antérieur**.

Key: A3-2 1) h 2) d 3) i 4) f 5) c 6) e 7) b 8) a 9) g

MODÈLE Il y aura des critiques dans le journal dès que l'exposition…

Il y aura des critiques dans le journal dès que l'exposition aura commencé.

1. Il y aura des critiques dans le journal dès que l'exposition…
2. J'obtiendrai mon billet avec une réduction aussitôt que je…
3. Nous achèterons le programme quand nous…
4. Vous pourrez entrer dans le musée lorsque vous…
5. Vous pourrez visiter librement les salles quand la visite guidée…
6. Nous sortirons dans le jardin dès qu'on…
7. On prendra un café dès qu'on…
8. On achètera des cartes postales lorsqu'on…
9. Je mettrai ma nouvelle affiche au mur dès que…

a. arriver dans la boutique du musée
b. arriver devant la caféteria
c. terminer
d. montrer ma carte d'étudiant
e. visiter toutes les salles
f. acheter des billets à l'entrée
g. rentrer à la maison
h. commencer
i. arriver à la caisse

Expansion: When each pair has finished, compare answers among the whole class. Who has the most interesting plans for the future? the most realistic? the most ambitious?

A3-3 En l'an 2030. Qu'est-ce que vous aurez fait en l'an 2030 ? Parlez de votre avenir avec un/e partenaire.

MODÈLE É1 En l'an 2030, j'aurai terminé mes études et je serai médecin. Je me serai marié et j'habiterai à New York avec ma femme.

É2 Et moi, en l'an 2030, j'aurai gagné un million de dollars avec ma propre société et je serai très riche. J'aurai acheté un appartement à Paris, une grande maison à Long Island et une maison en Floride pour les vacances.

Appendice 4

LE PASSÉ DU CONDITIONNEL

- Use the past conditional to express a hypothetical action or event in the past. In this case, the past conditional is often used with such expressions as **à ta place**, **à votre place**, or with the stressed pronouns **moi**, **nous**.

À ta place, je n'**aurais** pas **dépensé** 60 euros pour une place à l'opéra.	*If I were you, I wouldn't have spent 60 euros for an opera ticket.*
Moi, je **serais sortie** quand même.	*I still would have gone out.*

- To express what should have or could have been done in the past, use the past conditional of **devoir** or **pouvoir**.

Il s'est trompé pendant le concert. Il **aurait dû** répéter plus.	*He made a mistake during the concert. He should have practiced more.*
Je ne suis pas allée au théâtre parce que j'avais du retard, mais j'**aurais pu**.	*I didn't go to the theater because I was late, but I could have.*

Note: Although standard English employs the same sequence of tenses, there are regional variants in American colloquial usage which differ, for example: "If I would have known, I would have come." Students should be aware of this and be careful to use the appropriate tenses in French.

- You have learned that the conjunction **si** is used in a clause expressing a condition that is followed by another clause expressing the result. To express a past hypothetical situation, use **si** plus the **plus-que-parfait** followed by the result in the past conditional.

Si j'**avais su**, je ne **serais** pas **venu**.	*If I had known, I would not have come.*
Si on **avait eu** de l'argent, on **aurait acheté** des places pour l'opéra.	*If we had had money, we would have bought tickets for the opera.*

- To form the past conditional, use the conditional of **avoir** or **être** plus the past participle. The forms of the past conditional are illustrated with the verbs **devoir** and **partir**.

j'**aurais** dû	nous **aurions** dû
tu **aurais** dû	vous **auriez** dû
il / elle / on } **aurait** dû	ils / elles } **auraient** dû
je **serais** parti/e	nous **serions** parti/e/s
tu **serais** parti/e	vous **seriez** parti/e/s
il **serait** parti	ils **seraient** partis
elle **serait** partie	elles **seraient** parties
on **serait** partis	

Note: Point out to students that the final *s* on *partis* in the form *on serait partis* reflects the fact that *on* is used here as the equivalent of *nous*. In actual fact, this usage is variable. Grammatical agreement can be made with *on* as either a singular or plural subject, even though the subject is semantically plural when used as the equivalent of *nous*.

À vous la parole

Initial practice: Begin practice by having students transform the conditional to the past conditional in short sentences: *À ta place, je prendrais le bus. —À ta place, j'aurais pris le bus*, etc.

Implementation: A4-1, A4-2 These exercises offer initial practice with the conditional past by limiting students to the commonly used verbs *pouvoir* and *devoir*. Ex. A4-3 offers more varied, open-ended practice.

A4-1 Pour être un grand artiste. Dites ce que ces gens auraient dû faire ou auraient pu faire pour être un grand artiste.

MODÈLE Sophie n'a pas pris de leçons de chant.
→ Elle aurait dû prendre des leçons de chant.
OU Elle aurait pu prendre des leçons de chant.

1. Hélène n'a pas beaucoup joué de violon quand elle était petite.
2. Ces peintres n'ont pas utilisé beaucoup de couleurs.
3. Je ne suis pas allée à toutes les répétitions.
4. Les garçons n'ont pas bien appris leurs rôles.
5. Suzanne n'a pas considéré l'opinion des critiques.
6. Elle n'a pas eu le temps de se concentrer.
7. Nous n'avons pas trouvé d'inspiration.

A4-2 Des conseils tardifs. Vos amis n'ont pas de chance. Ils ont raté un bon spectacle pour des raisons diverses. Dites ce qu'ils auraient pu faire pour pouvoir y aller.

MODÈLE J'avais perdu les billets pour le spectacle.
→ Tu aurais pu les garder dans un endroit sûr.

1. Elle ne savait pas à quelle heure le spectacle commençait.
2. Nous n'avions pas assez d'argent.
3. Janique avait trop de devoirs à faire.
4. Mes amis ne savaient pas où se trouvait le théâtre.
5. Mon père ne voulait pas que j'y aille un mardi soir.
6. Nous sommes arrivés en retard pour le premier acte.
7. Elles ne savaient pas le prix des billets.

A4-3 Des regrets. Ce week-end ne s'est pas bien passé. Avec un partenaire, dites ce que ces personnes auraient pu faire selon les cas suivants.

Implementation: A4-3 All of these hypothetical situations in the past could have more than one answer. Begin by brainstorming as a class possible answers to a few of the situations. Then put students in pairs or small groups to compare their reactions to each situation. You could vary the activity by providing the result clause and having students suggest plausible reasons. For example:... *j'aurais dansé jusqu'à trois heures du matin. —Si je n'avais pas eu mal aux pieds... ; Si je n'avais pas porté des nouvelles chaussures... ; Si le club n'était pas fermé à deux heures du matin...*, etc.

MODÈLE S'il avait fait beau ce week-end...

É1 ... j'aurais joué au tennis avec ma copine.
É2 ... et moi, j'aurais fait de la planche à voile.

1. Si j'avais eu de l'argent...
2. Si j'avais eu plus de temps libre...
3. Si je n'avais pas eu cet examen de philosophie à préparer...
4. Si mes parents étaient venus ce week-end...
5. Si mes copains avaient voulu aller à ce concert avec moi...
6. Si mon prof de français avait été plus raisonnable...
7. Si l'examen n'avait pas duré si longtemps...

Appendice 5 VERBES RÉGULIERS

VERBE INFINITIF	PRÉSENT DE L'INDICATIF	PRÉSENT DU SUBJONCTIF	IMPARFAIT	PASSÉ COMPOSÉ	FUTUR	CONDITIONNEL	IMPÉRATIF
verbes **-er**							
regarder *to look at*	*je regarde* *tu regardes* *il regarde* *nous regardons* *vous regardez* *ils regardent*	*que je regarde* *que tu regardes* *qu'il regarde* *que nous regardions* *que vous regardiez* *qu'ils regardent*	*je regardais* *tu regardais* *il regardait* *nous regardions* *vous regardiez* *ils regardaient*	*j'ai regardé* *tu as regardé* *il a regardé* *nous avons regardé* *vous avez regardé* *ils ont regardé*	*je regarderai* *tu regarderas* *il regardera* *nous regarderons* *vous regarderez* *ils regarderont*	*je regarderais* *tu regarderais* *il regarderait* *nous regarderions* *vous regarderiez* *ils regarderaient*	*regarde* *regardons* *regardez*
verbes **-ir**							
dormir *to sleep*	*je dors* *tu dors* *il dort* *nous dormons* *vous dormez* *ils dorment*	*que je dorme* *que tu dormes* *qu'il dorme* *que nous dormions* *que vous dormiez* *qu'ils dorment*	*je dormais* *tu dormais* *il dormait* *nous dormions* *vous dormiez* *ils dormaient*	*j'ai dormi* *tu as dormi* *il a dormi* *nous avons dormi* *vous avez dormi* *ils ont dormi*	*je dormirai* *tu dormiras* *il dormira* *nous dormirons* *vous dormirez* *ils dormiront*	*je dormirais* *tu dormirais* *il dormirait* *nous dormirions* *vous dormiriez* *ils dormiraient*	*dors* *dormons* *dormez*
verbes **-ir/-iss**							
choisir *to choose*	*je choisis* *tu choisis* *il choisit* *nous choisissons* *vous choisissez* *ils choisissent*	*que je choisisse* *que tu choisisses* *qu'il choisisse* *que nous choisissions* *que vous choisissiez* *qu'ils choisissent*	*je choisissais* *tu choisissais* *il choisissait* *nous choisissions* *vous choisissiez* *ils choisissaient*	*j'ai choisi* *tu as choisi* *il a choisi* *nous avons choisi* *vous avez choisi* *ils ont choisi*	*je choisirai* *tu choisiras* *il choisira* *nous choisirons* *vous choisirez* *ils choisiront*	*je choisirais* *tu choisirais* *il choisirait* *nous choisirions* *vous choisiriez* *ils choisiraient*	*choisis* *choisissons* *choisissez*
verbes **-re**							
attendre *to wait for*	*j'attends* *tu attends* *il attend* *nous attendons* *vous attendez* *ils attendent*	*que j'attende* *que tu attendes* *qu'il attende* *que nous attendions* *que vous attendiez* *qu'ils attendent*	*j'attendais* *tu attendais* *il attendait* *nous attendions* *vous attendiez* *ils attendaient*	*j'ai attendu* *tu as attendu* *il a attendu* *nous avons attendu* *vous avez attendu* *ils ont attendu*	*j'attendrai* *tu attendras* *il attendra* *nous attendrons* *vous attendrez* *ils attendront*	*j'attendrais* *tu attendrais* *il attendrait* *nous attendrions* *vous attendriez* *ils attendraient*	*attends* *attendons* *attendez*
verbes pronominaux							
se laver *to wash oneself*	*je me lave* *tu te laves* *il se lave/on se lave* *nous nous lavons* *vous vous lavez* *ils se lavent*	*que je me lave* *que tu te laves* *qu'il se lave/qu'on se lave* *que nous nous lavions* *que vous vous laviez* *qu'ils se lavent*	*je me lavais* *tu te lavais* *il se lavait* *nous nous lavions* *vous vous laviez* *ils se lavaient*	*je me suis lavé/e** *tu t'es lavé/e* *il s'est lavé/elle s'est lavée* *nous nous sommes lavé/e/s* *vous vous êtes lavé/e/s* *ils/elles se sont lavés/lavées*	*je me laverai* *tu te laveras* *il se lavera* *nous nous laverons* *vous vous laverez* *ils se laveront*	*je me laverais* *tu te laverais* *il se laverait* *nous nous laverions* *vous vous laveriez* *ils se laveraient*	*lave-toi* *lavons-nous* *lavez-vous*

Comme **dormir :** *s'endormir, mentir, partir, ressentir, servir, sortir.* *Comme* **choisir :** *désobéir (à), finir, grandir, grossir, maigrir, obéir (à), pâlir, punir, réfléchir (à), réussir (à), rougir.*
Comme **attendre :** *descendre, se détendre, (s')entendre, perdre, rendre (à), rendre visite (à), répondre (à), vendre.*

*Although agreement of the past participle is shown with reflexive verbs like *se laver*, recall that when a noun follows the verb, no past participle agreement is made. For example, *Elle s'est lavé les cheveux.*

VERBES IRRÉGULIERS EN -ER

VERBE INFINITIF	PRÉSENT DE L'INDICATIF	PRÉSENT DU SUBJONCTIF	IMPARFAIT	PASSÉ COMPOSÉ	FUTUR	CONDITIONNEL	IMPÉRATIF
verbes **-er**							
acheter *to buy*	*j'achète* *tu achètes* *il achète* *nous achetons* *vous achetez* *ils achètent*	*que j'achète* *que tu achètes* *qu'il achète* *que nous achetions* *que vous achetiez* *qu'ils achètent*	*j'achetais*	*j'ai acheté*	*j'achèterai*	*j'achèterais*	*achète* *achetons* *achetez*
appeler *to call*	*j'appelle* *tu appelles* *il appelle* *nous appelons* *vous appelez* *ils appellent*	*que j'appelle* *que tu appelles* *qu'il appelle* *que nous appelions* *que vous appeliez* *qu'ils appellent*	*j'appelais*	*j'ai appelé*	*j'appellerai*	*j'appellerais*	*appelle* *appelons* *appelez*
commencer *to call*	*je commence* *tu commences* *il commence* *nous commençons* *vous commencez* *ils commencent*	*que je commence* *que tu commences* *qu'il commence* *que nous commencions* *que vous commenciez* *qu'ils commencent*	*je commençais* *nous commencions*	*j'ai commencé*	*je commencerai*	*je commencerais*	*commence* *commençons* *commencez*
s'essuyer *to wipe, to dry oneself*	*je m'essuie* *tu t'essuies* *il s'essuie* *nous nous essuyons* *vous vous essuyez* *ils s'essuient*	*que je m'essuie* *que tu t'essuies* *qu'il s'essuie* *que nous nous essuyions* *que vous vous essuyiez* *qu'ils essuient*	*je m'essuyais*	*je me suis essuyé/e**	*je m'essuierai*	*je m'essuierais*	*essuie-toi* *essuyons-nous* *essuyez-vous*
manger *to eat*	*je mange* *tu manges* *il mange* *nous mangeons* *vous mangez* *ils mangent*	*que je mange* *que tu manges* *qu'il mange* *que nous mangions* *que vous mangiez* *qu'ils mangent*	*je mangeais* *nous mangions*	*j'ai mangé*	*je mangerai*	*je mangerais*	*mange* *mangeons* *mangez*
préférer *to prefer*	*je préfère* *tu préfères* *il préfère* *nous préférons* *vous préférez* *ils préfèrent*	*que je préfère* *que tu préfères* *qu'il préfère* *que nous préférions* *que vous préfériez* *qu'ils préfèrent*	*je préférais*	*j'ai préféré*	*je préfèrerai***	*je préfèrerais***	

Comme **acheter :** *amener, geler, (se) lever, (se) promener.* *Comme* **appeler :** *(s')appeler, épeler, jeter, (se) rappeler.* *Comme* **commencer :** *recommencer.* *Comme* **s'essuyer :** *(s')ennuyer, essayer, essuyer, nettoyer, payer.* *Comme* **manger :** *(s')arranger, exiger, loger, nager, partager, protéger, ranger, voyager.* *Comme* **préférer :** *compléter, espérer, s'inquiéter, posséder, protéger, répéter, suggérer.*

*Although agreement of the past participle is shown with reflexive verbs like *s'essuyer*, recall that when a noun follows the verb, no past participle agreement is made. For example, *Elle s'est essuyé les cheveux.*

**Note that the future and conditional forms of the *préférer*-type verbs (*préférer, espérer, répéter, suggérer*) are spelled here with an accent grave, based on the 1990 Orthographic reform (*règle 3A*): « *On accentue sur le modèle de semer les futurs et conditionnels des verbes du type céder : je cèderai, je cèderais...* ». The accent grave clearly indicates the pronunciation of [ɛ].

D'AUTRES VERBES IRRÉGULIERS

VERBE INFINITIF	PRÉSENT DE L'INDICATIF		PRÉSENT DU SUBJONCTIF		IMPARFAIT	PASSÉ COMPOSÉ	FUTUR	CONDITIONNEL	IMPÉRATIF
aller *to go*	*je vais tu vas il va*	*nous allons vous allez ils vont*	*que j'aille que tu ailles qu'il aille*	*que nous allions que vous alliez qu'ils aillent*	*j'allais*	*je suis allé/e*	*j'irai*	*j'irais*	*va ; vas-y allons ; allons-y allez ; allez-y*
avoir *to have*	*j'ai tu as il a*	*nous avons vous avez ils ont*	*que j'aie que tu aies qu'il ait*	*que nous ayons que vous ayez qu'ils aient*	*j'avais*	*j'ai eu*	*j'aurai*	*j'aurais*	*aie ayons ayez*
boire *to drink*	*je bois tu bois il boit*	*nous buvons vous buvez ils boivent*	*que je boive que tu boives qu'il boive*	*que nous buvions que vous buviez qu'ils boivent*	*je buvais*	*j'ai bu*	*je boirai*	*je boirais*	*bois buvons buvez*
connaître *to know, be acquainted with*	*je connais tu connais il connaît*	*nous connaissons vous connaissez ils connaissent*	*que je connaisse que tu connaisses qu'il connaisse*	*que nous connaissions que vous connaissiez qu'ils connaissent*	*je connaissais*	*j'ai connu*	*je connaîtrai*	*je connaîtrais*	
courir *to run*	*je cours tu cours il court*	*nous courons vous courez ils courent*	*que je coure que tu coures qu'il coure*	*que nous courions que vous couriez qu'ils courent*	*je courais*	*j'ai couru*	*je courrai*	*je courrais*	*cours courons courez*
croire *to believe*	*je crois tu crois il croit*	*nous croyons vous croyez ils croient*	*que je croie que tu croies qu'il croic*	*que nous croyions que vous croyiez qu'ils croient*	*je croyais*	*j'ai cru*	*je croirai*	*je croirais*	*crois croyons croyez*
devoir *must, to have to; to owe*	*je dois tu dois il doit*	*nous devons vous devez ils doivent*	*que je doive que tu doives qu'il doive*	*que nous devions que vous deviez qu'ils doivent*	*je devais*	*j'ai dû*	*je devrai*	*je devrais*	
dire *to say*	*je dis tu dis il dit*	*nous disons vous dites ils disent*	*que je dise que tu dises qu'il dise*	*que nous disions que vous disiez qu'ils disent*	*je disais*	*j'ai dit*	*je dirai*	*je dirais*	*dis disons dites*
se distraire *to amuse oneself*	*je me distrais tu te distrais il se distrait*	*nous nous distrayons vous vous distrayez ils se distraient*	*que je me distraie que tu te distraies qu'il se distraie*	*que nous nous distrayions que vous vous distrayiez qu'ils se distraient*	*je me distrayais*	*je me suis distrait/e*	*je me distrairai*	*je me distrairais*	*distrais-toi distrayons-nous distrayez-vous*
écrire *to write*	*j'écris tu écris il écrit*	*nous écrivons vous écrivez ils écrivent*	*que j'écrive que tu écrives qu'il écrive*	*que nous écrivions que vous écriviez qu'ils écrivent*	*j'écrivais*	*j'ai écrit*	*j'écrirai*	*j'écrirais*	*écris écrivons écrivez*
envoyer *to send*	*j'envoie tu envoies il envoie*	*nous envoyons vous envoyez ils envoient*	*que j'envoie que tu envoies qu'il envoie*	*que nous envoyions que vous envoyiez qu'ils envoient*	*j'envoyais*	*j'ai envoyé*	*j'enverrai*	*j'enverrais*	*envoie envoyons envoyez*

Comme **devoir :** *recevoir* (passé composé : *j'ai reçu*). *Comme* **écrire :** *décrire.*

VERBE INFINITIF	PRÉSENT DE L'INDICATIF		PRÉSENT DU SUBJONCTIF		IMPARFAIT	PASSÉ COMPOSÉ	FUTUR	CONDITIONNEL	IMPÉRATIF
être *to be*	*je suis tu es il est*	*nous sommes vous êtes ils sont*	*que je sois que tu sois qu'il soit*	*que nous soyons que vous soyez qu'ils soient*	*j'étais*	*j'ai été*	*je serai*	*je serais*	*sois soyons soyez*
faire *to do, make*	*je fais tu fais il fait*	*nous faisons vous faites ils font*	*que je fasse que tu fasses qu'il fasse*	*que nous fassions que vous fassiez qu'ils fassent*	*je faisais*	*j'ai fait*	*je ferai*	*je ferais*	*fais faisons faites*
falloir *to be necessary*	*il faut*		*qu'il faille*		*il fallait*	*il a fallu*	*il faudra*	*il faudrait*	
s'instruire *to educate oneself*	*je m'instruis tu t'instruis il s'instruit*	*nous nous instruisons vous vous instruisez ils s'instruisent*	*que je m'instruise que tu t'instruises qu'il s'instruise*	*que nous nous instruisions que vous vous instruisiez qu'ils s'instruisent*	*je m'instruisais*	*je me suis instruit/e*	*je m'instruirai*	*je m'instruirais*	*instruis-toi instruisons-nous instruisez-vous*
lire *to read*	*je lis tu lis il lit*	*nous lisons vous lisez ils lisent*	*que je lise que tu lises qu'il lise*	*que nous lisions que vous lisiez qu'ils lisent*	*je lisais*	*j'ai lu*	*je lirai*	*je lirais*	*lis lisons lisez*
mettre *to put, put on*	*je mets tu mets il met*	*nous mettons vous mettez ils mettent*	*que je mette que tu mettes qu'il mette*	*que nous mettions que vous mettiez qu'ils mettent*	*je mettais*	*j'ai mis*	*je mettrai*	*je mettrais*	*mets mettons mettez*
mourir *to die*	*je meurs tu meurs il meurt*	*nous mourons vous mourez ils meurent*	*que je meure que tu meures qu'il meure*	*que nous mourions que vous mouriez qu'ils meurent*	*je mourais*	*je suis mort/e*	*je mourrai*	*je mourrais*	
naître *to be born*	*je nais tu nais il naît*	*nous naissons vous naissez ils naissent*	*que je naisse que tu naisses qu'il naisse*	*que nous naissions que vous naissiez qu'ils naissent*	*je naissais*	*je suis né/e*	*je naîtrai*	*je naîtrais*	
ouvrir *to open*	*j'ouvre tu ouvres il ouvre*	*nous ouvrons vous ouvrez ils ouvrent*	*que j'ouvre que tu ouvres qu'il ouvre*	*que nous ouvrions que vous ouvriez qu'ils ouvrent*	*j'ouvrais*	*j'ai ouvert*	*j'ouvrirai*	*j'ouvrirais*	*ouvre ouvrons ouvrez*
peindre *to paint*	*je peins tu peins il peint*	*nous peignons vous peignez ils peignent*	*que je peigne que tu peignes qu'il peigne*	*que nous peignions que vous peigniez qu'ils peignent*	*je peignais*	*j'ai peint*	*je peindrai*	*je peindrais*	*peins peignons peignez*
pleuvoir *to rain*	*il pleut*		*qu'il pleuve*		*il pleuvait*	*il a plu*	*il pleuvra*	*il pleuvrait*	
pouvoir *to be able to*	*je peux tu peux il peut*	*nous pouvons vous pouvez ils peuvent*	*que je puisse que tu puisses qu'il puisse*	*que nous puissions que vous puissiez qu'ils puissent*	*je pouvais*	*j'ai pu*	*je pourrai*	*je pourrais*	
prendre *to take*	*je prends tu prends il prend*	*nous prenons vous prenez ils prennent*	*que je prenne que tu prennes qu'il prenne*	*que nous prenions que vous preniez qu'ils prennent*	*je prenais*	*j'ai pris*	*je prendrai*	*je prendrais*	*prends prenons prenez*

Comme **lire :** *élire, relire.* *Comme* **mettre :** *permettre, promettre, remettre, soumettre.* *Comme* **ouvrir :** *couvrir, découvrir, offrir soumettre.* *Comme* **peindre :** *éteindre.* *Comme* **prendre :** *apprendre, comprendre, surpren-*

VERBE INFINITIF	PRÉSENT DE L'INDICATIF		PRÉSENT DU SUBJONCTIF		IMPARFAIT	PASSÉ COMPOSÉ	FUTUR	CONDITIONNEL	IMPÉRATIF
réduire *to reduce*	*je réduis tu réduis il réduit*	*nous réduisons vous réduisez ils réduisent*	*que je réduise que tu réduises qu'il réduise*	*que nous réduisions que vous réduisiez qu'ils réduisent*	*je réduisais*	*j'ai réduit*	*je réduirai*	*je réduirais*	*réduis réduisons réduisez*
savoir *to know*	*je sais tu sais il sait*	*nous savons vous savez ils savent*	*que je sache que tu saches qu'il sache*	*que nous sachions que vous sachiez qu'ils sachent*	*je savais*	*j'ai su*	*je saurai*	*je saurais*	*sache sachons sachez*
suivre *to follow*	*je suis tu suis il suit*	*nous suivons vous suivez ils suivent*	*que je suive que tu suives qu'il suive*	*que nous suivions que vous suiviez qu'ils suivent*	*je suivais*	*j'ai suivi*	*je suivrai*	*je suivrais*	*suis suivons suivez*
valoir *to be worth*	*il vaut*		*qu'il vaille*		*il valait*	*il a valu*	*il vaudra*	*il vaudrait*	
venir *to come*	*je viens tu viens il vient*	*nous venons vous venez ils viennent*	*que je vienne que tu viennes qu'il vienne*	*que nous venions que vous veniez qu'ils viennent*	*je venais*	*je suis venu/e*	*je viendrai*	*je viendrais*	*viens venons venez*
vivre *to live*	*je vis tu vis il vit*	*nous vivons vous vivez ils vivent*	*que je vive que tu vives qu'il vive*	*que nous vivions que vous viviez qu'ils vivent*	*je vivais*	*j'ai vécu*	*je vivrai*	*je vivrais*	*vis vivons vivez*
voir *to see*	*je vois tu vois il voit*	*nous voyons vous voyez ils voient*	*que je voie que tu voies qu'il voie*	*que nous voyions que vous voyiez qu'ils voient*	*je voyais*	*j'ai vu*	*je verrai*	*je verrais*	*voyons voyez*
vouloir *to want*	*je veux tu veux il veut*	*nous voulons vous voulez ils veulent*	*que je veuille que tu veuilles qu'il veuille*	*que nous voulions que vous vouliez qu'ils veuillent*	*je voulais*	*j'ai voulu*	*je voudrai*	*je voudrais*	*veuillez*

Comme **réduire :** *construire, produire.* *Comme* **venir :** *devenir, maintenir, obtenir, retenir, revenir, soutenir, (se) souvenir, tenir.* *Comme* **voir :** *revoir.*

Appendice 6

LEXIQUE FRANÇAIS-ANGLAIS

This glossary lists most French words found in the text. The vocabulary can be divided into two types: productive vocabulary and receptive vocabulary. Productive vocabulary words appear in the **Points de départ** and **Formes et fonctions** sections and occasionally in the **Vie et culture** sections; these words reappear periodically. You are expected to recognize these words when you read and hear them and to use them yourself in exercises and conversational activities. All other words, including those presented in readings and realia, are receptive vocabulary; you are expected only to recognize them and to know their meanings when you see them in written form or hear them in context.

- For all productive vocabulary items, the numbers following an entry indicate the chapter and lesson in which that vocabulary item is first introduced. Since verbs in their infinitive form are occasionally introduced as vocabulary items before their conjugation is presented, refer to the Index to locate where the conjugation is introduced. You will also find the complete conjugation information for each verb (or type of verb) in Appendix 5.
- To find the meaning of an expression, try to locate the main word in the expression and look that up. For example, the expression **Cela vous convient** is found with the entry for the verb **convenir**; the expression **faire du sport** is found under the entry for the noun **sport**.
- The gender of nouns is indicated by the abbreviations *m.* for masculine and *f.* for feminine. Feminine and masculine nouns that are closely related in meaning and identical or similar in pronunciation are listed under a single entry: **architecte** *m./f.*; **étudiant** *m.*, **étudiante** *f.* Nouns that occur only in the plural form are followed by the gender indication and *pl.*: **beaux-arts** *m. pl.*, **vacances** *f. pl.* Nouns and adjectives that show no agreement and do not change in the plural or feminine are indicated by the abbreviation *inv.*: **CD** *m. inv.*
- Adjectives with differing masculine and feminine written forms are shown in the masculine form followed by the feminine ending: **allemand/e**, **ambitieux/-euse**, **canadien/ne**. For adjectives whose masculine and feminine forms vary considerably, both forms are listed: **cher/chère**. Special prenominal forms of adjectives are given in parentheses: **beau** (**bel**), **belle**. When necessary for clarity, adjectives and adverbs are indicated by *adj.* and *adv.*, respectively.
- The object pronouns **le, la, les, lui, leur, me, te, nous**, etc., have been indicated by the abbreviation *pron.*
- An asterisk (*) before a word indicates that the initial **h** is aspirate.

- The hashmark (†) appears after productive verbs showing some irregularity in conjugation; these verbs appear in their full conjugation in the verb charts, Appendix 5. Verbs showing irregularities in conjugation that are considered part of receptive vocabulary are not always included in Appendix 5, since you are only expected to recognize and not produce these verbs. However, the conjugations of many of these verbs are similar to conjugations you will find in Appendix 5. For example, the verb **admettre** is conjugated just like the verb **mettre**. For verbs that require a preposition under certain conditions, the latter appears in parentheses: **commencer (à)**, (**il commence son travail, il commence à travailler**); for verbs that always require a preposition, the preposition is indicated without parentheses: **s'occuper de** (**il s'occupe de moi**).

A

à to, at, in, on, P-1
abbaye *f.* abbey, 9-3
abîmé/e worn, worn out, 6-2
abominable abominable
abondant/e abundant
  pluies *f.* **abondantes** heavy rains
abonnement *m.* subscription
s'abonner (à) to subscribe (to), to buy season tickets, 12-3
  être abonné/e to be subscribed (to), to have season tickets, 12-3
d'abord first (of all), 5-3
absence absence
absent/e absent, missing, 7-1
absolument absolutely
abstrait/e abstract, 12-2
accent accent
accepter (de) to accept, 12-1
accès *m.* access
accessoire *m.* accessory
accident *m.* accident
accompagner to accompany, 8-3
  Tu veux/Vous voulez m'accompagner ? Do you want to come with me?, 8-3
d'accord OK, all right, 5-3
  être (tout a fait) d'accord to agree completely, 11-1
  Je suis d'accord... I agree . . . , 11-1
  Je ne suis pas d'accord... I disagree . . . , 11-1
accordéon *m.* accordion
accueillir to welcome
achat *m.* purchase
  émission *f.* **de téléachat** infomercial, 11-1
  faire † des achats to shop, 8-2
acheter † to buy, 5-2
acteur *m.*, **actrice** *f.* actor/actress, 3-3
actif/-ive active
action *f.* action
  film *m.* **d'action** action film, 11-1
activité *f.* activity, 1-3
actuel/le current
addition *f.* bill, 5-1
additionner to add
adjectif *m.* adjective
admettre † to admit
administratif/-ive administrative, 3-1
administration *f.* administration
admirer to admire
adolescent/e (ado) adolescent
adorable adorable
adorer to adore, love, 2-1
adresse *f.* address
adulte *m.; adj.* adult
adverbe *m.* adverb
aéroport *m.* airport, 9-1
aérosol *m.* aerosol
affaires *f. pl.* belongings, things, 6-2; business
  faire des affaires to be in business
  femme *f.* **d'affaires** businesswoman, 3-3
  homme *m.* **d'affaires** businessman, 3-3
affectueux/-euse affectionate, warm-hearted
affiche *f.* poster, P-2
afficher to post
affilée : d'affilée in a row
affirmatif/-ive affirmative
afin de + *inf.* in order to + *verb*
africain/e African
Afrique *f.* Africa, 9-2
âge *m.* age, 1-2
  Quel est ton/votre âge ? What is your age?, 1-2
  Quel âge as-tu/avez-vous ? How old are you?, 1-2
  d'un certain âge middle-aged, 2-1
âgé/e aged, elderly, old, 2-1
agence *f.* agency
  agence de voyage travel agency
  agence immobilière real estate agency
agenda *m.* datebook
agent/e de police *m./f.* police officer, 3-3
agent immobilier *m.* real estate agent
s'agir de to be about
  il s'agit de... it's about . . .
agneau *m.* lamb, 5-3
  côtelette *f.* **d'agneau** lamb chop, 5-3
agréable pleasant, 6-2
agricole agricultural
agriculteur *m.*, **agricultrice** *f.* farmer
aide *f.* help, assistance
aider (à) to help, 12-1
  aider les gens to help people, 3-3
ail *m.* garlic
aimable lovable
aimer to like, to love, 1-3
  aimer beaucoup to like or love a lot, 3-2
  aimer bien to like fairly well, 3-2
  aimer mieux to prefer, 10-2
aîné/e older (brother/sister)
ainsi (que) thus, in such a way
air *m.* air, 10-2
  air frais fresh air
  avoir l'air (d'être) + *adj.* to seem/to appear (to be) + *adj.*, 7-3
  en plein air outdoors, 3-3
aisance *f.* ease
aisé/e easy, well off
ajouter to add
alarme *f.* alarm
album *m.* album
alcool *m.* alcohol, 10-1
  alcoolisé/e *adj.* containing alcohol, 5-1
alerte *adj.* alert
Algérie *f.* Algeria, 9-2
algérien/ne Algerian, 9-2
alimentaire *adj.* relating to food
  banque *f.* **alimentaire** food bank, 10-3
aliments *m. pl.* food, 5-2
allant (de) going (from)
Allemagne *f.* Germany, 9-2
allemand/e *adj.* German, 9-2
allemand *m.* German (language), 3-2
aller † to go, 2-3
  aller sur Internet to go online, 9-3
  Ça ne va pas. Things aren't going well., P-1
  Ça va, et toi ? Fine, and you?, P-1

Comment allez-vous ? How are you?, P-1
Comment ça va ? How are you?, P-1
On y va ? Shall we go?, 8-3
allô hello (telephone only)
allumer to turn on (an appliance), 11-1
alors so, 2-3; then
alphabet *m.* alphabet
alpinisme *m.* mountain climbing, 8-2
faire † de l'alpinisme to go mountain climbing, 8-2
ambassadeur *m.*, **ambassadrice** *f.* ambassador
ambitieux/-euse ambitious, 2-1
améliorer to improve
amener † to bring (along) a person
américain/e American, 9-2
Amérique *f.* **centrale** Central America
Amérique *f.* **du Nord** North America, 9-2
Amérique *f.* **du Sud** South America, 9-2
Amérique *f.* **latine** Latin America
ami *m.*, **amie** *f.* friend, P-1
amoureux/-euse in love, 7-3
tomber amoureux/-euse (de) to fall in love (with), 7-3
amphithéâtre *m.* amphitheater, lecture hall, 3-1
ampoule *f.* **(électrique)** (light)bulb, 10-2
ampoule basse consommation energy-saving lightbulb, 10-2
amputé/e amputated
amusant/e funny, 2-1
s'amuser to have fun, 7-3
an *m.* year, 1-2
J'ai 19 ans. I am 19 years old., 1-2
analyse *f.* analysis
analytique analytical
anchois *m.* anchovy
ancien/ne old, antique, 6-2; former, 7-1
anglais/e *adj.* English, 9-2
anglais *m.* English (language), P-2
Angleterre *f.* England, 9-2
angoisse *f.* anguish
angoissé/e anguished
animal *m.* animal, 1-1
animal familier pet, 1-1
animateur *m.*, **animatrice** *f.* organizer
animation *f.* animation, excitement
film *m.* **d'animation** animated film, 11-1
animé/e animated, excited
année *f.* year, 2-3
l'année dernière last year, 5-2
l'année prochaine next year, 2-3
anniversaire *m.* birthday, 1-2
Joyeux anniversaire ! Happy birthday!, 7-2
annonce *f.* advertisement
annoncer to announce
annuaire *m.* phone book
anorak *m.* ski jacket, parka, 4-3
Antarctique *f.* Antarctica
anthropologie *f.* anthropology, 3-2
antibiotique *m.* antibiotic
anxiété *f.* anxiety
anxieux/-euse anxious, 7-3
août August, 1-2
apéritif *m.* **(un apéro)** before-meal drink
appareil *m.* **électrique,** electrical appliance, 10-2
appareil *m.* **(photo)** camera, 9-1
appareil *m.* **(photo) numérique** digital camera, 9-1
appartement *m.* apartment, 4-1
appartement sous les toits attic apartment, 6-2
appartenir † to belong to
appel *m.* call
appeler † to call, 5-2
s'appeler to be called, 7-3
Je m'appelle... My name is . . . , P-1
appliquer to apply (sthg)
apporter to bring (an object), 6-2
apprécier to appreciate
apprendre † to learn, 5-1
apprendre à † to teach, to learn, 7-1
apprentissage *m.* learning, apprenticeship
approprié/e appropriate
après after, after that, 3-1
après avoir/être... after having . . . , 11-2
après-midi *m.* afternoon, 1-3
après tout after all, 12-3
d'après vous according to you
de l'après-midi in the afternoon, P.M., 4-2
aquarelle *f.* watercolor
aquarium *m.* aquarium
arabe *m.* Arabic
arbre *m.* tree, 6-3
arbre fruitier fruit tree, 6-3
archéologie *m.* archaeology
archipel *m.* archipelago
architecte *m./f.* architect, 3-3
architecture *f.* architecture
argent *m.* money, 3-3
argentin/e Argentinian, 9-2
Argentine *f.* Argentina, 9-2
argot *m.* slang
argument *m.* argument
armoire *f.* armoire, 6-2
s'arranger † to be all right, to work out, 7-3
arrêt *m.* stop
arrêter (de) to stop, 12-1
Arrête ! Stop it!, 2-1
s'arrêter to stop oneself
arrière back, rear
arrière-grand-parent *m.* great-grandparent
arrivée *f.* arrival
arriver to arrive, 1-3
arrondissement *m.* Parisian city district
arroser to water; to celebrate with wine or champagne
art *m.* art, 11-3
arts *pl.* **décoratifs** decorative arts, interior design
arts *pl.* **du spectacle** performing arts, 3-2
article *m.* article
articles *pl.* **de toilette** toiletries, 4-1
articulatoire *adj.* articulatory
artifice *f.* artifice
feu *m.* **d'artifice** fireworks, 7-2
artificiel/le artificial
artisan *m.* craftsman
artisanal/e handcrafted
artisanat *m.* arts and crafts
artiste *m./f.* artist, 3-3
artistique artistic
asiatique Asiatic
ascenseur *m.* elevator, 6-1
Asie *f.* Asia, 9-2
aspect *m.* aspect, side
asperge *f.* asparagus, 5-2
aspiré/e aspirated
aspirine *f.* aspirin
s'asseoir to sit down
Asseyez-vous ! Sit down!, P-2
assez rather, 1-1; enough, 4-1
assiette *f.* plate, 5-3
assistant *m.* **social, assistante** *f.* **sociale** social worker, 3-3
assister à to attend, 2-3
association *f.* association
association étudiante student association, 3-1
association humanitaire humanitarian association, 10-3
associé/e associate(d)
astrologie *f.* astrology
astrologue *m./f.* astrologer
astronomie *f.* astronomy, 3-2
atelier *m.* studio (artist); workshop
athlète *m./f.* athlete
atlas *m.* atlas, 11-3
atmosphérique atmospheric
pollution *f.* **atmosphérique** air pollution, 10-2
attendre to wait (for), to expect, 3-1
attention *f.* attention
faire † attention (à) to pay attention (to); to be careful
attentivement attentively
attraper to catch
au (à + le) 2-2
au revoir good-bye, P-1
auberge *f.* inn, 9-3
auberge de jeunesse youth hostel, 9-3
au-dessous *adv.* below
au-dessus *adv.* above
augmenter to increase, 10-2

aujourd'hui today, 1-3
auprès de next to, close to
aussi also, P-1
aussi ... que as . . . as, 4-2
aussi bien que as well as, 9-2
moi aussi me too
aussitôt que as soon as, 11-1
Australie *f.* Australia, 9-2
australien/ne Australian, 9-2
autant (de) ... que as many/much . . . as, 4-2
auteur *m.* author, 11-3
(auto)bus *m.* city bus
automatique automatic
auto(mobile) *f.* car
automne *m.* fall, 8-1
autonome independent, 3-3
autonomie *f.* autonomy
autoritaire authoritarian, 7-1
autorité *f.* authority
autoroute *f.* highway
autour de around
autre other, another, 2-1
d'autres *adj.* other
autrefois in the past
autrement otherwise
Autriche *f.* Austria, 9-2
autrichien/ne Austrian, 9-2
aux (à + les) 2-2
avance : (être) en avance (to be) early, 4-2
avant de + *inf.* before . . . , 11-2
avant-hier the day before yesterday, 5-2
avantage *m.* advantage
avec with, 1-3
avenir *m.* future
aventure *f.* adventure
film *m.* **d'aventures** adventure film, 11-1
aventurier *m.*, **aventurière** *f.* adventurer
avenue *f.* avenue, 9-3
aveugle *adj.* blind
avion *m.* plane, 9-1
avis *m.* opinion, 11-1
à mon avis, ... in my opinion, . . . , 11-1
à votre avis, ... in your opinion, . . .
avocat *m.*, **avocate** *f.* lawyer, 3-3
avoir † to have, 1-2
avoir † le droit to have the right
avril April, 1-2
ayant having

B

bac(calauréat) *m.* high school exit exam (*France*), 3-2
bacc(alauréat) *m.* **(en)** B.A. or B.S. degree (in) (*Can.*), 3-2
bacon *m.* bacon, 5-2
bagage *m.* luggage
baguette *f.* French bread (long, thin loaf), 5-3
baignoire *f.* bathtub
bain *m.* bath
maillot *m.* **de bain** bathing suit, 4-3
prendre un bain to take a bath
salle *f.* **de bains** bathroom, 6-1
baisser to lower
bal *m.* ball, dance
bal populaire *m.* street dance, 7-2
balade *f.* walk, stroll
baladeur *m.* **MP3** MP3 player, 11-2
balcon *m.* balcony, 6-1
ballet *m.* ballet, 2-3
banaliser to make commonplace
banane *f.* banana, 5-2
bande-annonce *f.* (movie) trailer
bande dessinée *f.* **(une BD)** comic, comic strip, 11-2
banlieue *f.* suburbs
banque *f.* bank
banque alimentaire food bank, 10-3; food pantry
banque de données data bank
banquier *m.*, **banquière** *f.* banker
baptême *m.* baptism, 7-2
bar *m.* bar
barbe *f.* beard
bas/se low
en bas downstairs
base de données *f.* database
basilic *m.* basil
baskets *m. pl.* sports shoes, 4-3
basket(-ball) *m.* basketball, 2-2
basket-fauteuil *m.* wheelchair basketball, 10-1
bateau *m.* boat, 6-3
bateau à voile sailboat, 6-3
bâtiment *m.* building, 6-1
batterie *f.* percussion, drum set, 2-2
battre to beat, to break (record)
se battre to fight
battu/e beaten
beau (bel), belle beautiful, handsome, 2-1
Il fait beau. It's beautiful weather., 8-1
beaucoup a lot, 1-1
beau-frère *m.* brother-in-law, 7-1
beau-père *m.* stepfather, father-in-law, 1-1
beaux-arts *m. pl.* fine arts, 3-2
beige beige, 4-3
belge Belgian, 9-2
Belgique *f.* Belgium, 9-2
belle-mère *f.* stepmother, mother-in-law, 1-1
belle-sœur *f.* sister-in-law, 7-1
bénévolat *m.* volunteering, 10-3
bénévole *m./f.* volunteer, 10-3
besoin *m.* need, 5-3
avoir besoin de to need, 5-3
bête stupid, 2-1
beurre *m.* butter, 5-2
bibliothèque *f.* library, 2-3
bibli *f.* (Can.) library, 3-1
bibliothèque municipale municipal library, 2-3
bibliothèque universitaire (la B.U.) university library, 3-1
bien well, fine, P-1
être bien dans sa peau to have confidence in oneself, 7-1
faire † du bien to do (someone) good
bien sûr of course, 2-1
bien-être *m.* well-being, 10-1
bientôt soon, 2-3
à bientôt see you soon, P-1
bienvenu/e *adj.* welcome
bienvenue *f.* welcome; you're welcome (Can.)
bière *f.* beer, 5-1
bifteck *m.* steak, 5-3
bifteck haché ground beef, 5-3
bijou *m.* piece of jewelry
bilingue bilingual
billet *m.* ticket, 9-1
billet aller-retour round-trip ticket
billet d'avion airplane ticket, 9-2
billet d'entrée entrance ticket
bimensuel *m.* semi-monthly publication
bio = biologique
biodégradable biodegradable, 10-2
biographie *f.* biography, 11-3
biologie *f.* biology, 3-2
biologique organic, 5-3
biscuit *m.* cookie, 5-2
bise *f.* kiss
faire † une/la bise to kiss hello/good-bye on the cheeks
blanc/blanche white, 4-3
bleu/e blue, 4-3
blond/e blond, 2-1
bloquer to block
blouson *m.* heavy jacket, 4-3
boire † to drink, 5-1
bois *m.* woods, 6-3; wood
boisson *f.* drink, 5-1
boisson alcoolisée alcoholic beverage, 5-1
boisson chaude hot drink, 5-1
boisson rafraîchissante cold drink, 5-1
boîte *f.* can 5-3
boîte de conserve can of food
boîte postale post office box
bol *m.* bowl, 5-2
bonbon *m.* piece of candy
bon/ne good, 3-1
Bon anniversaire ! Happy birthday!, 7-2
bonjour hello, P-1
bon marché *adj. inv.* inexpensive, 4-3

Bonne année ! Happy New Year!, 7-2
Bonnes vacances ! Have a good vacation!, 7-2
bonsoir good evening, P-1
Bon voyage ! Have a good trip!, 7-2
Il fait bon. It's nice weather., 8-1
bonheur *m.* happiness
bonnet *m.* **de laine** knit/wool cap, 4-3
bord *m.* edge, shore
au bord (du lac) at the shore (of the lake), 6-3
au bord de la mer at the seashore, 6-3
bordé/e par bordered by, limited by, flanked by
border to border, to line up with, to limit
botanique *f.* botany, 3-2
botte *f.* boot, 4-3
boubou *m.* African robe, dress
bouche *f.* mouth, 10-1
boucher *m.*, **bouchère** *f.* butcher
boucherie *f.* butcher shop; 5-3
bougie *f.* candle, 7-2
bouillabaisse *f.* seafood stew
bouillir to boil
bouillon *m.* broth, stock
boulanger *m.*, **boulangère** *f.* baker
boulangerie *f.* bakery, 5-3
boulevard *m.* boulevard, 9-3
boulot *m.* work (*colloq.*), 4-1
bout *m.* tip, end
au bout at the end
bourgeois/e *adj.* bourgeois, middle-class
bouteille *f.* bottle, 5-1
boutique *f.* boutique, shop
branché/e plugged in, connected with
bras *m.* arm, 10-1
bravo ! great! well done!, 8-2
bref/brève brief
Brésil *m.* Brazil, 9-2
brésilien/ne Brazilian, 9-2
Bretagne *f.* Brittany
breton/ne Breton
bricolage *m.* do-it-yourself, 2-2
faire † du bricolage to do do-it-yourself projects, 2-2
bricoler to do odd jobs, to tinker 2-2
bricoleur *m.*, **bricoleuse** *f.* do-it-yourselfer
brise *f.* breeze
brocante *f.* flea market
brochure *f.* brochure, pamphlet
brodé/e embroidered
bronzé/e (sun)tanned
se bronzer to get a suntan, 8-2
brosse *f.* chalkboard eraser, P-2; brush, 4-1
brosse à cheveux hairbrush, 4-1
brosse à dents toothbrush, 4-1
se brosser to brush one's . . . , 4-1
se brosser les cheveux to brush one's hair, 4-1
se brosser les dents to brush one's teeth, 4-1
brouillard *m.* fog, 8-1
Il y a du brouillard. It's foggy., 8-1
brouillon *m.* rough draft
bruit *m.* sound, noise, 10-2
brûlé/e burned
brûler to burn, 10-2
brun/e brunette, 2-1
bruyant/e noisy
budget *m.* budget
bulletin *m.* **de vote** ballot, 10-3
bureau *m.* desk, office, P-2; office, 3-3
bureau de vote polling station, 10-3
bureau des inscriptions registrar's office, 3-1
bureaux administratifs administrative offices 3-1
bus *m.* (city) bus, 9-1
but *m.* goal, aim, purpose

C

ça that
Ça depend. That depends.
Ça (ne) fait rien. That doesn't matter. 12-3
Ça (ne) me dit rien. I'm not interested in that. 12-3
Ça ne va pas. Things aren't going well., P-1
Ça va ? How are things?, P-1
Ça va. It's going fine., P-1
Ça vaut le coup. It's worth it. (*fam.*), 12-3
C'est ça. That's right.
Comment ça va ? How's it going?, P-1
câble *m.* cable (television)
caché/e hidden
cacher to hide, 7-2
cadeau *m.* present, gift, 7-2
cadre *m.* business executive; frame (for a picture)
café *m.* café, 2-3; coffee, 5-1
café au lait with milk, 5-2
café crème with cream, 5-1
café déca(féiné) decaffeinated coffee
café serré strong cup of expresso coffee
pause-café *f.* coffee break
caféine *f.* caffeine
cafétéria *f.* cafeteria, 3-1
cahier *m.* notebook, P-2
caisse *f.* cash register, 5-3
caissier *m.*, **caissière** *f.* cashier
calcul *m.* calculus, 3-2
calculatrice *f.* calculator, P-2
calendrier *m.* calendar
calme calm, 1-1
se calmer to calm down, 7-3
camarade *m./f.* friend, buddy
camarade de classe classmate, P-1
Cameroun *m.* Cameroon, 9-2
camerounais/e Cameroonian, 9-2
campagne *f.* countryside, 8-2; campaign
à la campagne in the country, 6-2
campagne électorale electoral campaign
pain *m.* **de campagne** round loaf of bread, 5-3
camping *m.* campground, 9-3
faire † du camping to camp, to go camping, 8-2
camping-car *m.* RV, 9-3
campus *m.* campus
Canada *m.* Canada, 9-2
canadien/ne Canadian, 9-2
canapé *m.* couch, 6-2
candidat/e *m./f.* candidate, 10-3
canne *f.* cane, walking stick
cannette *f.* (soda) can, 5-1
canoë *m.* canoe
capacité *f.* ability
car *m.* excursion bus, intercity bus, 9-1
caractère *m.* nature, disposition, 1-1
carafe *f.* **(d'eau)** carafe (of water), 5-2
caravane *f.* camper (vehicle), 9-3
cardinal/e cardinal
carnet *m.* small notebook
carnet d'adresses address book, 9-1
carotte *f.* carrot, 5-3
carrière *f.* career, 3-3
carte *f.* map, P-2; playing card, 2-2
à la carte from the menu; cafeteria-style
carte bancaire debit card, 9-1
carte de crédit credit card, 9-1
carte mémoire memory card
carte météorologique weather map
carte postale postcard, 8-2
jouer aux cartes to play cards, 2-2
carton *m.* cardboard
cas *m.* case
casquette *f.* baseball cap, 4-3
casse-croûte *m. inv.* snack, 5-1
casser to break, to crack
cassette *f.* cassette tape
catégorie *f.* category
cathédrale *f.* cathedral, 9-3
catholicisme *m.* Catholicism
catholique Catholic
cause *f.* cause
à cause de due to, because of, 8-3
causer to cause; to chat
cave *f.* wine cellar, 9-3
CD *m. inv.* CD, compact disk, P-2
ce (c') it, that
c'est... this/it is . . . , P-1
c'est-à-dire that is to say
ce sont... these/they are. . ., P-1
ce (cet), cette this, that, 4-3
ces these, those, 4-3
céder to relinquish

ceinture *f.* belt
cela that
Cela vous convient ? Does this suit you?, 9-3
célèbre famous, 11-1
célébrer to celebrate
célébrité *f.* celebrity
céleste celestial
célibataire single, 1-1
mère *f.*/**père** *m.* **célibataire** single mother/father, 7-1
cendre *f.* ash
cendrier *m.* ashtray
cent hundred, 1-2
centre *m.* center
centre étudiant student center, 3-1
centre informatique computer center, 3-1
centre sportif sports complex, 3-1
centre urbain urban center, downtown area
centre-ville *m.* downtown, 6-2
cèpe *m.* type of mushroom
cependant however
céramique ceramic
céréales *f. pl.* cereal, 5-2
cérémonie *f.* ceremony, 7-2
cérémonie civile civil (wedding) ceremony, 7-2
cérémonie religieuse religious ceremony
cerise *f.* cherry, 5-3
certain/e certain
certainement certainly
ces *see* **ce**
chacun/e each one
chaîne *f.* chain; TV (or radio) station, 11-1
chaise *f.* chair, P-2
chambre *f.* bedroom, 4-1
champ *m.* field, 6-3
champignon *m.* mushroom, 5-3
champion *m.*, **championne** *f.* champion
championnat *m.* championship
chance *f.* luck
avoir de la chance to be lucky
changement *m.* change
changer to change
chanson *f.* song
chant *m.* singing
chanter to sing, 4-2
chanteur *m.*, **chanteuse** *f.* singer, 3-3
chapeau *m.* hat, 2-1
chapelle *f.* chapel
chaque each, 6-1
char *m.* (carnival) float
charcuterie *f.* pork butcher shop; cooked pork meats, 5-3
charmant/e charming
charges *f. pl.* utilities, 6-1
charges comprises utilities included, 6-1
chariot *m.* shopping cart
charte *f.* charter
chasse *f.* hunting
chat/te *m./f.* cat, 1-1
châtain *adj. inv.* chestnut-colored, auburn, 2-1
château *m.* castle, 9-3
château fort fortress, 9-3
chaud hot, 5-1
chocolat *m.* **chaud** hot chocolate, hot cocoa, 5-1
Il fait chaud. It's hot (weather)., 8-1
J'ai chaud. I'm hot. 8-1
chauffeur *m.* driver
chausser to put shoes on
chaussette *f.* sock, 4-3
chausson *m.* slipper
chausson de danse ballet slipper
chaussure *f.* shoe, 4-3
chaussure à talon high-heeled shoe, 4-3
chef *m.* boss; chef
chef d'entreprise corporate manager
chef d'œuvre *m.* **(chefs-d'œuvre** *pl.*) masterpiece, 12-3
chemin *m.* way, 9-3; path
indiquer le chemin to give directions, 9-3
chemin de fer railroad
cheminée *f.* chimney
chemise *f.* man's shirt, 4-3
chemisier *m.* blouse, 4-3
chêne *m.* oak; oak tree
cher/chère expensive, 4-3
chercher to look for, 2-3
chéri/e *m./f.* love, darling
cheval *m.* horse, 8-2
faire † du cheval to go horseback riding, 8-2
cheveux *m. pl.* hair, 4-1
avoir † les cheveux courts/longs/bouclés to have short/long/curly hair
cheville *f.* ankle, 10-1
chez at the home of, at the place of, 1-1
chez (les jeunes) among (the young)
chez nous at our place, 1-1
chic *adj. inv.* chic, stylish, 4-3
chien/ne *m./f.* dog, 1-1
chien d'assistance service dog
chien guide guide dog
chiffre *m.* numeral, digit
chimie *f.* chemistry, 3-2
Chine *f.* China, 9-2
chinois/e *adj.* Chinese, 9-2
chinois *m.* Chinese (language)
chocolat *m.* **chaud** hot chocolate, 5-1
chœur *m.* chorus, 12-1
choisir to choose, 6-1
choix *m.* choice, 12-3
cholestérol *m.* cholesterol
chômage *m.* unemployment
choquant/e shocking
chorale *f.* choir
chose *f.* thing, 10-1
quelque chose something, 8-3
ne pas faire † grand-chose to not do much, 2-2
chou *m.* cabbage
choucroute *f.* sauerkraut
chouette ! neat!, 8-2
Chunnel *m.* undersea rail tunnel linking France with England
chute *f.* fall
ci-dessous below
ci-dessus above
cidre *m.* cider
ciel *m.* sky, 8-1
Le ciel est couvert. The sky is overcast., 8-1
cigarette *f.* cigarette
cimetière *m.* cemetery
ciné = **cinéma**
cinéaste *m.* filmmaker
cinéma *m.* cinema, the movies, 2-3
cinématographe *m.* cinematographer
cinq five, 1-2
cinq-pièces *m.* three-bedroom apartment/house, 6-1
cinquante fifty, 1-2
cinquième fifth, 6-1
circulation *f.* traffic
citer to cite
citoyen *m.*, **citoyenne** *f.* citizen, 10-3
citron *m.* lemon, 5-1
citron pressé lemonade, 5-1
civil/e civil
civique civic
clair/e clear; light (for colors)
clarinette *f.* clarinet, 12-1
classe *f.* class of students, school year, grade; school classroom
classes *pl.* **préparatoires (classes prépas)** prepatory classes for entrance to **les Grandes Écoles**
classique classic
musique *f.* **classique** classical music, 1-3
clavier *m.* computer keyboard, 11-2; musical keyboard, 12-1
clé/clef *f.* key, 9-1
clé USB USB key, flash drive, 11-2
climat *m.* climate
clinique *f.* private hospital, 3-3
clip (vidéo) *m.* video clip, 11-2
CO_2 *m.* **(dioxyde de carbone)** carbon dioxide, 10-2
coca(-cola) *m.* cola, 5-1
cocher to check off
code *m.* code
code postal postal code
cœur *m.* heart, 10-1
avoir mal au cœur to be nauseated, 10-1
se coiffer to fix one's hair, 4-1
coin *m.* corner
au coin de at the corner (of)

avec coin cuisine with a kitchenette, 6-2
colère *f.* anger, 7-3
en colère angry, 7-3
collant *m.* pantyhose, 4-3, tights
collège *m.* middle school, 1-3
collier *m.* necklace
colline *f.* hill, 6-3
coloc(ataire) *m./f.* roommate, housemate, 2-1
colocation *f.* renting a house or an apartment together
Colombie *f.* Colombia, 9-2
colombien/ne Colombian, 9-2
colonie *f.* colony
colonie de vacances summer camp
colonisation *f.* colonization
colonne *f.* column
combattre to fight, to combat
combien how much, 2-1
combien de how many, 2-1
combinaison *f.* combination
combiner to combine
comédie *f.* comedy; drama 11-1
comédie dramatique dark comedy, 11-1
comédie musicale musical, 11-1
comédie romantique romantic comedy, 11-1
commander to order, 5-1
comme like, as
Comme ci, comme ça. So-so., P-1
commencer (à) † to begin, to start, 4-2
comment how, 2-1
Comment ça va ? How's it going?, P-1
Comment dit-on... ? How do you say. . . ?, P-2
Comment tu t'appelles ? What is your name?, P-1
Comment vous appelez-vous ? What is your name?, P-1
commentaire *m.* comment
commenter to comment on, to give a commentary on
commerçant *m.*, **commerçante** *f.* merchant, 5-3
communauté *f.* community
communément communally, in common
communication *f.* communication
communiquer to communicate
compagnie *f.* company
comparaison *f.* comparison
comparatif/-ive comparative
comparer to compare, 4-2
compliment *m.* compliment
compliqué/e complicated
comportement *m.* behavior
se comporter to behave, to act
composé/e composite
composition *f.* composition, 12-2
compréhension *f.* comprehension
comprendre † to understand, 5-1
Je ne comprends pas. I don't understand., P-2
compris/e *adj.* included, 6-1
y compris including, 10-3
comptabilité *f.* accounting, 3-2
comptable *m./f.* accountant, 3-3
compte *m.* account
compter to count
comptine *f.* nursery rhyme
concentration *f.* (*Can.*) concentration in area of studies
concept *m.* concept
concerner to concern
en ce qui concerne as to, in relation to
concert *m.* concert, 2-2
concierge *m./f.* caretaker, manager
concombre *m.* cucumber, 5-3
condamner to condemn
condiment *m.* condiment, 5-3
conditionnel *m.* conditional tense
conduire to drive
confiserie *f.* confectionery, candy store
confiture *f.* jam, 5-2
conflit *m.* conflict
conformiste conformist, 1-1
confort *m.* comfort
confortable comfortable (material objects), 6-2
congé *m.* leave
congé de maternité maternity leave
prendre congé to take leave, say good-bye
congélateur *m.* freezer
congrès *m.* conference
conjonction *f.* conjunction
conjugaison *f.* conjugation
conjugué/e conjugated
connaissance *f.* knowledge, understanding, 7-1; acquaintance
connaître † to know, be familiar with, 8-2
connecté/e connected
connexion *f.* **sans fil** wireless connection/card, 11-2
connu/e known
conquête *f.* conquest
consacrer to devote
conseil *m.* piece of advice; council
conseil de classe meeting of teachers, administration, and elected parent and student representatives
conseil universitaire elected university governing body
demander un conseil to ask for advice
conseiller to advise
conseiller *m.*, **conseillière** *f.* advisor
conséquence *f.* consequence
conservateur/-trice conservative
conservation *f.* conservation
conserver to store
consister to consist
consommateur *m.*, **consommatrice** *f.* consumer
consommation *f.* drink
consommer to consume, 10-2
consonne *f.* consonant
constituer to be, to constitute, to form
construire † to construct, build
consultation *f.* visit with a health professional
consulter to consult
consulter le médecin to see a doctor, 10-1
contaminer to contaminate
contempler to contemplate
contemporain/e contemporary
contenir † to contain
content/e happy, 7-3
conteur *m.* storyteller
continent *m.* continent, 9-2
continuer to go on/keep going, 9-3
continuer (à) to continue, 12-1
continuer tout droit keep going straight ahead, 9-3
contraire *m.* opposite
au contraire, ... to the contrary, . . . , 11-1
contraste *m.* contrast
contribuer to contribute
contrôle *m.* inspection, control, test
convaincre to convince
convenir † to suit
Cela vous convient ? Does this suit you?, 9-3
copain *m.*, **copine** *f.* friend, 2-1
copieux/-euse copious, hearty, 5-2
corail *m.* coral
Corée *f.* Korea, 9-2
coréen/ne Korean, 9-2
corps *m.* body, 10-1
corps humain human body, 10-1
correspondance *f.* correspondance
correspondant/e *m./f.* pen pal
correspondre to correspond
corriger to correct
corso *m.* procession (of floats)
costume *m.* man's suit, 4-3
costume-cravate *m.* suit and a tie
côte *f.* coast
côté *m.* side
à côté de next to, beside 3-1
d'un autre côté, ... on the other hand, . . . , 11-1
Côte-d'Ivoire *f.* Ivory Coast, 9-2
côtelette *f.* **(d'agneau)** (lamb) chop, 5-3
coton *m.* cotton, 4-3
côtoyer to rub shoulders with
cou *m.* neck, 10-1
se coucher to go to bed, 4-1
coude *m.* elbow, 10-1
couleur *f.* color, 4-3
de quelle couleur est... ? what color is . . . ?, 4-3

couloir *m.* hallway, 6-1
coup *m.* blow, strike, punch
ça vaut le coup it's worth it, 12-3
coup de soleil sunburn
coup de téléphone phone call
couper to cut, to chop
couper l'eau du robinet to turn off the running water (from the faucet), 10-2
couple *m.* couple
couplet *m.* verse of a poem
cour *f.* courtyard, 6-1
courant/e current
au courant up-to-date (for a person)
courant *m.* **d'air** draft, breeze
courir † to run, 4-2
couronne *f.* crown
courriel *m. (Can.)* e-mail message
courrier électronique *m.* e-mail, 11-2
cours *m.* course, class, 3-1
au cours de during
course *f.* errand, 2-2
faire † des courses to run errands, including grocery shopping, 2-2
faire † les courses to do the weekly grocery shopping, 5-3
court/e short, 4-3
cousin *m.*, **cousine** *f.* cousin, 1-1
coussin *m.* cushion
coussinet *m.* small cushion
coûter to cost, 6-2
coutume *f.* custom
couture *f.* sewing, dressmaking
haute couture designer fashion
couturier *m.* fashion designer
couturière *f.* dressmaker, seamstress
couvert : Le ciel est couvert The sky is overcast., 8-1
couvrir † to cover
covoiturage *m.* carpooling, 10-2
craie *f.* stick of chalk, P-2
cravate *f.* tie, 4-3
crayon *m.* pencil, P-2
créer to create
crème *f.* cream, 5-1
crème glacée (*Can.*) ice-cream
crèmerie *f.* dairy store
créole *adj.* Creole
créole *m.* Creole (language)
crevette *f.* shrimp, 5-3
crier to yell, 7-3
crime *m.* crime
crise *f.* crisis
cristal *m.* crystal
critère *m.* criterion
critique *f.* critique, criticism, (critical) review, 11-3
critique *m.* (movie, literary) critic (person), 11-3
croire † **(à, en)** to believe, 7-3
Je crois/Je crois que oui. I think so., 7-3
Je crois que... I believe that . . . , 7-3
Je ne crois pas/Je crois que non. I don't think so., 7-3
croisière *f.* cruise
croissant *m.* croissant, 5-2
croque-madame *m. inv.* grilled ham and cheese sandwich topped with a fried egg
croque-monsieur *m. inv.* grilled ham and cheese sandwich, 5-1
croustillant/e crusty
crudités *f. pl.* cut-up raw vegetables, 5-1
cubiste cubist, 12-2
cuiller, cuillère *f.* spoon, 5-1
cuir *m.* leather, 4-3
cuisine *f.* kitchen, 6-1
avec coin cuisine with a kitchenette, 6-2
faire † la cuisine to cook, 2-2
cuisinière *f.* stove, 6-2
culturel/le cultural
cupidité *f.* greed

D

d'abord first, 5-3
d'accord OK, agreed, 5-3
dame *f.* lady, P-2
danger *m.* danger
dans in, into, inside, P-2
danse *f.* dance, 3-2
faire † de la danse to dance, to study dance, 2-2
danser to dance
d'après... according to . . .
date *f.* date, 1-2
Quelle est la date ? What is the date?, 1-2
d'autres *adj.* other
davantage more
de (d') from, of, about, P-1
De rien. Not at all., You're welcome., P-2
déambulateur *m.* walker
débarquer to disembark
débat *m.* debate
debout standing, on one's feet
être debout to be up, 4-1
début *m.* beginning
décédé/e deceased, 1-1
décembre December, 1-2
déception *f.* disappointment
déchet *m.* waste, refuse, 10-2
déchets *pl.* **domestiques** household garbage, 10-2
déchets *pl.* **industriels** industrial waste, 10-2
déchèterie *f.* waste collection center, 10-2
décider (de) to decide, 12-1
se décider to make up one's mind, 12-3
déclaration *f.* declaration
décontracté/e relaxed
décorer to decorate
découverte *f.* discovery
découvrir † to discover; to uncover
décrire † to describe, 7-1
déçu/e disappointed, 10-3
être déçu/e que to be disappointed that, 10-3
déduire to deduce
défaire † to undo
défaite *f.* defeat, loss
défi *m.* challenge
défilé *m.* parade, 7-2
défilé de mode fashion show
définir to define
définition *f.* definition
déforestation *f.* deforestation, 10-2
degré *m.* degree; step
Il fait vingt degrés. It's 20 degrees (Celsius)., 8-1
se déguiser to disguise oneself, to dress up in costume
dehors outside
en dehors de outside of
déjà already, 4-1
déjeuner *m.* lunch, 5-2
déjeuner to have lunch, 1-3
délégué/e *m./f.* delegate
délégué/e de classe elected class representative
délicieux/-euse delicious, 5-3
demain tomorrow, 2-3
à demain see you tomorrow, P-1
demander to ask, request, 6-2
démarrer to begin, to start
demi/e half
demi-frère *m.* half-brother, stepbrother, 7-1
demi-kilo *m.* half-kilo
demi-sœur *f.* half-sister, stepsister, 7-1
demi-tour *m.* U-turn
et demi/e and a half, 4-2
faire † demi-tour to make a U-turn
démocratie *f.* democracy
démocratique *adj.* democratic
démodé/e old-fashioned, out-of-date, 4-3
demoiselle *f.* young lady, single woman
démonstratif/-ive demonstrative
dent *f.* tooth, 4-1
se brosser les dents to brush one's teeth, 4-1
se laver les dents to brush one's teeth
dentifrice *m.* toothpaste, 4-1
dentiste *m./f.* dentist, 3-3
départ *m.* departure
au départ de leaving from, originally
département *m.* department, regional administrative unit in France

dépasser to exceed
se dépêcher to hurry up, 4-1
dépendant/e *adj.* dependent
dépendre de to depend on
  Ça depend. That depends.
dépense *f.* expenditure
dépenser to spend
déposer to drop off, to place
depuis since, 11-3
depuis combien de temps... ? for how long . . . ?, 11-3
depuis quand... ? since when . . . ?, 11-3
dernier/-ière last, 3-1
derrière behind, 3-1
des *pl.* some, P-2
dès que as soon as, 11-1
désagréable disagreeable, 1-1
désastre *m.* disaster
descendant (de) *m.* descendant (of)
descendre to go down, 3-1
  descendre de to get off, 3-1
  descendre en ville to go downtown, 3-1
descente *f.* descent
désert *m.* desert
se déshabiller to undress, 4-1
désignation *f.* name, designation
désirer to desire, to want, 10-2
désobéir à to disobey, 6-1
désolé/e sorry, 8-3
  Je suis désolé/e... I am sorry..., 8-3
dessert *m.* dessert, 5-2
desservir to serve, to stop at
dessin *m.* drawing, 3-2
  dessin animé cartoon, animated film, 11-1
dessinateur/-trice *m./f.* draftsman/woman, 12-2
dessiner to draw
dessous : en dessous underneath
destination *f.* destination, 8-2
se détendre to relax, 6-3
détente *f.* relaxation; release (of a consonant)
déterminer to determine, to work out
détester to detest, 3-2
deux two, 1-2
  deux fois par jour twice a day, 4-1
deuxième *m.* second, 1-1
devant in front of, 3-1
développement *m.* development
  développement durable sustainable development
développer to develop
devenir † to become, 5-3
deviner to guess
devoir † must, to have to, should, 3-3
devoir *m.* essay, assignment 3-2
devoirs *m. pl.* homework, P-2
  faire † des devoirs to do homework
d'habitude usually, 6-3
diagnostic *m.* diagnosis
dialecte *m.* dialect
dialogue *m.* dialogue
dictionnaire *m.* **(un dico)** dictionary, 3-2
différence : à la différence de unlike
différent/e different
différer † to differ
difficile difficult, 3-2
diffusion *f.* (commercial) distribution
dimanche Sunday, 1-3
diminuer to decrease, to lower
dîner *m.* dinner, 5-2; lunch (*Can.*)
dîner to have dinner, 1-3; to have lunch (*Can.*)
dioxyde *m.* **de carbone (CO_2)** carbon dioxide
diplomate *m./f.* diplomat
diplôme *m.* degree, 3-2
  avoir un diplôme to have a degree
dire † to say, 7-1
  Ça (ne) me dit rien. I'm not interested in that., 12-3
direct : en direct *adv.* live
  émission *f.* **en direct** live broadcast
directeur *m.* **directrice** *f.* manager
discipliné/e disciplined, 1-1
discuter de to have a discussion, to talk
disjoint/e disjointed, stressed (pronouns)
disparaître to disappear
disparition *f.* disappearance
disponible available
se disputer to argue, 7-3
disque *m.* **dur** hard drive, 11-2
disquette *f.* diskette
distractions *f. pl.* amusements, diversions, 8-3
se distraire to amuse oneself, 11-3
divers/e various
diversité *f.* diversity
divertissement *m.* variety show, 11-1
divisé/e divided, split
diviser to divide, to split
divorcé/e divorced, 1-1
divorcer to divorce, 7-1
dix ten, 1-2
dixième tenth, 6-1
dix-huit eighteen, 1-2
dix-huitième eighteenth, 6-1
dix-neuf nineteen, 1-2
dix-neuvième nineteenth, 6-1
dix-sept seventeen, 1-2
dix-septième seventeenth, 6-1
doctorat *m.* doctorate, Ph.D.
documentaire *m.* documentary, 11-1
dodo (*colloq.*) sleep, 4-1
  faire † dodo (*colloq.***)** go to sleep, 4-1
doigt *m.* finger, 10-1
domaine *m.* area, field
domicile *m.* place of residence
dommage *m.* damage
  C'est dommage. It's too bad. It's a pity., 8-3
  Il est/C'est dommage que... It's too bad that . . . , It's a shame that . . . , 10-3
  Quel dommage. What a pity.
donc then, therefore, 2-1
donnée *f.* data
  base *m.* **de données** database
donner to give, P-2
  donner sur to look onto or lead out to, 6-1
doré/e golden brown, glazed
dormir to sleep, 4-2
dos *m.* back, 10-1
dossier *m.* file, case, folder
double double
doublé/e dubbed, 11-1
doubler to dub
doucement gently, softly
douche *f.* shower
  prendre une douche to take a shower, 4-1
se doucher to shower, 4-1
doué/e to be talented, 3-3
douleur *f.* pain
doute *m.* doubt
  sans aucun doute without a doubt
  sans doute probably
douter to doubt, 10-3
doux/douce gentle, soft, sweet
douzaine *f.* dozen, 5-3
douze twelve, 1-2
douzième twelfth, 6-1
drame *m.* **(psychologique)** (psychological) drama, 11-1
drapeau *m.* flag
dresser (une liste) to make (a list)
se droguer to take drugs, to be on drugs
drogue *f. sg.* (illegal) drugs
droit *adv.* straight, 9-3
  tout droit straight ahead, 9-3
droit *m.* law, 3-2
droite *f.* right, 3-1
  à droite (de) to the right (of), 3-1
drôle amusing, funny, strange, 2-1
du (= de + le) 2-2
durable sustainable
dur/e hard, difficult, stiff
durée *f.* length of time, duration
durer to endure, last
duvet : manteau *m.* **en duvet** down coat
DVD *m. inv.* DVD, P-2
dynamique dynamic, 1-1

E

eau *f.* water, 5-1
  eau minérale mineral water, 5-1
  eau minérale gazeuse carbonated mineral water
  eau minérale plate still mineral water
  eau potable drinkable water, 10-3

échange *m.* exchange
échanger to exchange, 11-2
échappement *m.* exhaust; escape
  gaz *m. pl.* **d'échappement** exhaust fumes, 10-2
échapper to escape
écharpe *f.* scarf, 4-3
échecs *m. pl.* chess, 2-2
échelle *f.* ladder
éclair *m.* lightning, 8-1
  Il y a des éclairs. There is lightning., 8-1
éco-geste *m.* ecological act, gesture, 10-2
école *f.* school, 1-3
  école de commerce business school
  école maternelle preschool, nursery school
  école primaire elementary school
  école secondaire secondary school
écologie *f.* ecology
écologique ecological, 10-2
économie *f.* economy; economics, 3-2
  faire † des économies *pl.* to save money
économique economical
  sciences *f. pl.* **économiques** economics, 3-2
économiser to save, economize, 10-2
écosystème *m.* ecosystem
écotourisme *m.* ecotourism
écoute *f.* listening
écouter to listen, P-2
  écouter de la musique to listen to music, 1-3
écran *m.* screen, 11-1
  écran (plat) (flat-screen) monitor, 11-2
écraser to crush
écrire † to write, 7-1
écrivain *m.* writer, 3-3
écureuil *m.* squirrel
éducatif/-ive educational
effacer to erase, P-2
effet *m.* effect
  en effet yes, indeed, 6-3
efficace efficient, effective
effort *m.* effort
égal/e equal
église *f.* Catholic church, 2-3
égoïste selfish, 2-1
élaborer to elaborate
électricité *f.* electricity
électrique electric
électronique electronic
élégance *f.* elegance
élégant/e elegant, 2-1
éléphant *m.* elephant
élève *m./f.* pupil, student (elementary age)
éliminer to eliminate
élire to elect, 10-3
elle *f.* she, her, it, P-1
  elle-même *f.* herself
elles *f. pl.* they, them, P-1
  elles-mêmes *f. pl.* themselves
élu/e elected
e-mail *m.* e-mail message, 11-2
emballage *m.* packaging, 10-2
embarras *m.* trouble
embarrassé/e embarrassed, 7-3
s'embrasser to kiss, 7-3
émission *f.* program, 11-1
  émission de musique music program, 11-1
  émission de téléachat infomercial, 11-1
  émission de téléréalité reality show, 11-1
  émission sportive televised sports event, 11-1
emmener † to bring someone along
émotion *f.* emotion
empêcher to prevent
emploi *m.* use; job
employé/e *m./f.* employee, white-collar worker
employer † to use
emporter to bring something, to take with
empreinte *f.* **écologique** ecological footprint
emprunter to borrow, 6-2
en *prep.* to, at, P-1; *pron.* some, any, 5-3
  en ligne online, 11-2
enchaînement *m.* linking
enchanté/e delighted (to meet you), P-1
encore still, yet, again, another, 4-2
  encore un quart d'heure another fifteen minutes, 4-2
encyclopédie *f.* encyclopedia, 11-3
s'endormir to fall asleep, 4-1
endroit *m.* place, 6-3
énergie *f.* energy
  énergie renouvelable renewable energy, 10-2
  énergie solaire solar energy, 10-2
énergique energetic, 2-1
énervé/e irritable
s'énerver to become irritated/worked up
enfance *f.* childhood
enfant *m./f.* child, 1-1
enfin finally, 5-3
enfourner to put in the oven
engagement *m.* involvement, commitment
s'engager to get involved, 10-3
s'ennuyer † to become bored, 7-3
ennuyeux/-euse boring, tedious, 3-2
enquête *f.* poll, survey
enrichir to enrich
enseignant/e *m./f.* teacher, instructor
enseignement *m.* teaching
enseigner to teach
ensemble together, 1-3
ensuite next, then, 5-3
entendre to hear, 3-1
  s'entendre (avec) to get along (with), 7-3
  entendu : C'est entendu. It's understood. OK. 12-1
enthousiaste enthusiastic
entourer to surround; to circle
entraînement *m.* practice (sport)
s'entraîner to practice (sport)
entraîneur *m.* trainer, coach
entre between, 4-2
entrée *f.* appetizer or starter, 5-2; entrance, foyer, 6-1
entreprise *f.* firm, place of business
entrer to go/come in, 5-3
entretien *m.* interview
énumérer to enumerate, to list
envie *f.* urge, craving
  avoir envie de (+ *nom*, + *inf.*)... to want, desire (sthg, to do sthg) . . . , 4-3
environ about, approximately
environnement *m.* environment, 10-2
environs *m. pl.* surroundings
envoyer † to send, 11-2
épaule *f.* shoulder, 10-1
épeler † to spell, 5-2
épice *f.* spice, 5-2
épicerie *f.* grocer's shop, 5-3
épicier *m.*, **épicière** *f.*, grocer
épinards *m. pl.* spinach, 5-3
épisode *m.* episode, 11-1
époque *f.* era, time
époux *m.*, **épouse** *f.* spouse
épreuve *f.* test, 7-1
éprouver to feel, to experience
équilibré/e balanced, 10-1
équipe *f.* team
équipé/e equipped, 6-2
équivalent *m.* equivalent
érosion *f.* erosion
erreur *f.* mistake, error
escalier *m.* staircase, stairs, 6-1
espace *m.* place, space
  espace vert green, grassy area
Espagne *f.* Spain, 9-2
espagnol/e *adj.* Spanish, 9-2
espagnol *m.* Spanish (language), 3-2
espion *m.* spy
espionnage *m.* spying, 11-1
  film *m.* **d'espionnage** spy film, 11-1
en espèces in cash
espérer † to hope, 12-1
essai *m.* essay, 3-2
essayer (de) † to try, 10-1
essence *f.* gas
essuyer † to dry
  s'essuyer † to dry oneself off, wipe off, 4-1
est *m.* east
estimer to consider, to believe, to judge, 10-3
estomac *m.* stomach, 10-1
et and, P-1

établir to establish
établissement *m.* establishment
étage *m.* floor, 6-1
premier étage second floor, 6-1
étagère *f.* bookcase, (book)shelf, 6-2
étape *f.* stage, step (in a process)
état *m.* state
état civil marital status, 1-1
États-Unis *m. pl.* the United States, 9-2
été *m.* summer, 2-3
l'été prochain next summer, 2-3
éteindre † to turn off, 10-3
éteindre les lumières to turn off the lights, 10-2
étendu/e extended, 7-1
étoile *f.* star, 9-3
étonnant/e surprising, 10-3
étonné/e surprised, 10-3
étranger/-ère foreign, 3-2
étranger/-ère *m./f.* stranger, foreigner
être † to be, P-1
être (tout à fait) d'accord to agree (completely), 11-1
être en train de + *inf.* to be busy doing something, 4-1
Ne sois pas... Don't be . . . , 7-3
sois, soyez... ! be . . . ! , 7-3
Soyez calme ! Be calm!, 7-3
être *m.* **humain** human being
études *f. pl.* studies, 3-2
faire † des études (de) to study (sthg)
étudiant *m.*, **étudiante** *f.* student, P-2
étudier to study
Europe *f.* Europe, 9-2
européen/ne European
eux *m. pl.* they, them, P-1
eux-mêmes *m. pl.* themselves
évènement *m.* event, 7-2
éventuel/le probable
éventuellement probably, perhaps
évident obvious
évier *m.* (kitchen) sink, 6-2
éviter to avoid, 10-1
exacte exact
exactement exactly
exagérer to exaggerate
examen *m.* exam, 3-2
passer un examen to take an exam
préparer un examen to study for an exam, 3-2
réussir un examen to pass an exam
excès *m.* excess
exercer to exercise, exert
exercice *m.* exercise
faire † de l'exercice to exercise, 10-1
exigeant/e demanding, 7-1
exiger † to require, to demand, 10-2
exotique exotic
expérience *f.* experience; experiment
explication *f.* explanation
expliquer to explain, 6-2
exposé *m.* oral presentation, report, 3-2
exposer to state, to explain; to exhibit
exposition *f.* exhibition, 2-3
expression *f.* expression
expression fixe set expression, idiom
expresso *m.* small cup of strong coffee
exprimer to express
s'exprimer to express oneself
externe external
extrait *m.* exerpt, extract
extrême extreme
extrêmement extremely

F

fabriquer to make, to produce
fac = faculté
face *f.* face, side
en face (de) facing, across from, 3-1
fâché/e angry, upset, 7-3
se fâcher (contre) to get angry (at, with), 7-3
facile easy, 3-2
facilement easily
faciliter to facilitate, to make easier
façon *f.* way
de toute façon in any case
facteur *m.*, **factrice** *f.* mail carrier, 3-3
facture *f.* bill
faculté *f.* college, university, 2-1
faible weak
faim *m.* hunger, 5-1
avoir faim to be hungry, 5-1
faire † to do, to make, 2-2
Ça (ne) fait rien. That doesn't matter., 12-3
deux et deux font quatre 2 + 2 = (equals) 4
faire partie de to belong to, 7-1
faire penser à to remind one of
Il fait beau. It's beautiful weather., 8-1
Ne t'en fais pas !/Ne vous en faites pas ! Don't worry!, 7-3
se faire du souci to worry, 7-3
se faire un petit plaisir to treat oneself, 12-3
faire-part *m. inv.* (birth, wedding) announcement
fait *m.* fact
en fait in fact
falloir † to be necessary, 8-1
Il faut... to need, 5-3; you have to/must, 8-1
Il ne faut pas... you must not, 8-1
Il faut que... It is necessary that/You must . . . , 10-1
Il ne faut pas que... You must not . . . , 10-1
fameux/-euse famous
familial/e familial, related to family
familier/-ière familiar
famille *f.* family, 1-1
famille étendue extended family, 7-1
famille monoparentale single-parent family, 7-1
famille nombreuse big family, 1-1
famille recomposée blended family, 7-1
fanatique *m.* fan, fanatic
être fanatique de to be a fan of, 12-3
fantaisiste fantastic (not based in reality)
fantastique fantastic (great, wonderful); fantasy
film *m.* **fantastique** fantasy film
fantôme *m.* phantom, ghost
farine *f.* flour
fariné/e floured
fasciné/e fascinated
fatigué/e tired, P-1
faune *f.* wildlife, fauna
faut *see* **falloir**
faute *f.* mistake
faire † une faute to make a mistake
fauteuil *m.* armchair, 6-2
basket-fauteuil *m.* wheelchair basketball, 10-1
fauteuil roulant wheelchair, 10-1
faux/-sse false
favoriser to favor
Félicitations ! Congratulations!, 7-2
féliciter to congratulate
féminin/e feminine
féminisation *f.* feminization (esp. names of professions)
femme *f.* wife, woman, 1-1
femme au foyer stay-at-home mother, 7-1
femme d'affaires businesswoman, 3-3
fenêtre *f.* window, P-2
férié : jour *m.* **férié** legal holiday, 7-2
ferme *f.* farm, 6-3
fermer to close, P-2
festival *m.* festival
fête *f.* party, 2-2; holiday, 7-2
fête religieuse *f.* religious holiday, 7-2
fêter to celebrate, 7-2
feu *m.* fire
feu d'artifice fireworks, 7-2
feu rouge stoplight
feuille *f.* sheet of paper; leaf
feuilleton *m.* series, soap opera, 11-1
feutre *m.* felt-tip pen, marker, P-2
fève *f.* broad bean, favor baked in **la Galette des rois**
février February, 1-2
fiançailles *f. pl.* engagement
fiancé/e engaged, 1-1
se fiancer to get engaged, 7-3
fichier *m.* computer file, 11-2
fidèle faithful
fièvre *f.* fever
avoir de la fièvre to have a temperature, to run a fever

figure *f.* face, 4-1; figure, shape
figure géométrique geometric shape
fil *m.* thread, wire
fille *f.* daughter, girl, 1-1
film *m.* film, 1-3
fils *m.* son, 1-1
fin *f.* end
fin de semaine (*Can.*) weekend
fin/e thin, elegant, delicate, 4-3
final/e final, 3-2
finalement finally, 11-2
finir to finish, 6-1
fitness *m.* cardio workout
fixer to set (an appointment)
flamand *m.* Flemish (language)
fleur *f.* flower, 7-2
fleurir to flourish
fleuve *m.* river, 6-3
flore *f.* flora, plant life
flûte *f.* recorder
flûte traversière flute, 12-1
foie *m.* liver
foire *f.* fair
fois *f.* time
deux fois par jour twice a day, 4-1
x fois par semaine x times a week
une fois once, one time
folklorique folkloric
musique *f.* **folklorique** folk music, 12-1
foncé/e dark (color)
fonction *m.* function
fonctionnaire *m./f.* government worker, 3-3
fonctionner to function
fond *m.* bottom, end
à fond deeply; loudly
fondre to melt, 10-2
fondu/e melted
fontaine *f.* fountain
football *m.* **(le foot)** soccer, 1-3
football *m.* **américain** American football, 2-2
foraine : fête foraine *f.* fair
forcément inevitably, necessarily
forêt *f.* forest, 6-3
formation *f.* formation; training
avoir une formation to have training
forme *f.* shape; form
être en forme to be fine, P-1
être en pleine forme to be in good shape
former to form, to train
formidable great, 6-3
fort *adv.* loudly, 7-3
fort/e *adj.* strong, stout, 2-1
forum *m.* forum
forum de discussion discussion forum, newsgroup
foulard *m.* silk scarf, 4-3
foule *f.* crowd
four *m.* oven, 6-2
fourchette *f.* fork
fourrure *f.* coat, fur
foyer *f.* home, household, 7-1
femme *f.* **au foyer** stay-at-home mother, 7-1
homme *m.* **au foyer** stay-at-home father, 7-1
frais/fraîche fresh
Il fait frais. It's cool (weather)., 8-1
fraise *f.* strawberry, 5-3
français/e *adj.* French, 9-2
français *m.* French (language), P-2
faire † du français to study French, 2-2
France *f.* France, 9-2
francophone French-speaking
francophonie *f.* French-speaking world
fréquence *f.* frequency
frère *m.* brother, 1-1
frigo *m.* (*colloq.*) fridge
frite *f.* French fry, 5-1
froid cold, 8-1
Il fait froid. It's cold (weather)., 8-1
J'ai froid. I'm cold., 8-1
fromage *m.* cheese, 5-2
fromager *m.* cheese maker, cheese seller
frontière *f.* border, 9-2
fruit *m.* fruit, 5-2
fruits *pl.* **de mer** seafood
fruitier/fruitière *adj.* fruit, 6-3
arbre *m.* **fruitier** fruit tree, 6-3
fumé/e *adj.* smoked
fumée *f.* smoke
fumer to smoke, 10-2
fumet *m.* aroma
furieux/-euse furious, 7-3
futur *m.* future tense
futur proche immediate future

G

gadget *m.* gadget
gagner to win
gagner de l'argent to earn money, 3-3
galérie *f.* (art) gallery
galette *f.* cake for the Epiphany, 7-2; savory dinner crepe made with buckwheat flour
gant *m.* glove, 4-3
gant de toilette wash mitt, 4-1
garage *m.* garage, 3-1
garantir to guarantee
garçon *m.* boy, 1-1
gare *f.* train station, 2-3
garer to park, 6-1
gaspiller to waste, 10-2
gâteau *m.* cake, 7-2
gauche *f.* left, 3-1
à gauche (de) to the left (of), 3-1
gaz *m.* gas, 10-2
gaz à effet de serre greenhouse gas, 10-2
gaz carbonique carbon gas, 10-2
gaz *pl.* **d'échappement** exhaust fumes, 10-2
gazeux/-euse carbonated
geler † to freeze, 8-1
Il gèle. It's freezing (weather)., 8-1
gêné/e bothered, embarrassed, 7-3
général/e general
généralement generally
généreux/-euse generous, warm-hearted, 2-1
générique *m. sg.* screen credits
génial : C'est génial. It's great/awesome. 11-2
genou *m.* knee, 10-1
genre *m.* (grammatical) gender; kind, type
genre littéraire literary genre
gens *m. pl.* people, 3-3
gentil/le kind, nice, 2-1
C'est gentil à toi/vous. That's kind (of you)., 8-3
géographie *f.* geography
géologie *f.* geology
gérant *m.*, **gérante** *f.* manager
gestion *f.* management, 3-2
gilet *m.* cardigan sweater, 4-3
gîte (rural) *m.* (rural) bed and breakfast, 9-3
glace *f.* ice cream, 5-1
glace au chocolat chocolate ice cream, 5-1
glacé/e ice-cold, frozen, iced
crème *f.* **glacée** (*Can.*) ice cream
thé *m.* **glacé** iced tea
glacier *m.* glacier, 10-2
glaçon *m.* ice cube, 5-1
golf *m.* golf, 1-3
gomme *f.* eraser, P-2
gorge *f.* throat, 10-1
avoir mal à la gorge to have a sore throat
goulu/e gluttonous
goût *m.* taste, liking
avoir le goût du travail to have a strong work ethic, 7-1
goûter *m.* afternoon snack, 5-2
goûter to have a snack, to taste
goutte *f.* drop
gouvernement *m.* government, 10-3
grâce à thanks to
graisse *f.* fat, grease
graissé/e greased
gramme *m.* (*abbr.* gr) gram
grand-chose *m. inv.* : **pas grand-chose** not very much, not a great deal, 2-2
ne pas faire † grand-chose to not do much, 2-2
grand/e tall, 2-1
grand magasin *m.* department store, 4-3

grande surface *f.* superstore, 5-3
grandes vacances *f. pl.* summer vacation, 7-2
grandir to grow taller, to grow up (for children), 6-1
grand-mère *f.* grandmother, 1-1
grand-père *m.* grandfather, 1-1
grand-parent *m.*, (grands-parents *pl.*) grandparent, 1-1
grasse *adj.* fatty, oily, greasy
gratuit/e free
gratuitement for free
grave serious, 7-3
Ce n'est pas grave. It's not serious., 7-3
graveur *m.* **CD/DVD** CD/DVD burner, 11-2
gravité *f.* gravity, seriousness
grève *f.* strike, 10-3
grignoter to snack, 10-2
grillé/e grilled, toasted, 5-2
grimper to climb up
grippe *f.* flu
gris/e gray, 4-3
Groenland *m.* Greenland
gros/se fat, 2-1
grossir to gain weight, 6-1
grotte *f.* **(préhistorique)** (prehistoric) cave, 9-3
groupe *m.* group
groupe de consonnes *m.* consonant cluster
guerre *f.* war
guerre de Sécession (American) Civil War
Première Guerre mondiale First World War
Seconde Guerre mondiale Second World War
guide *m.* guide (tour guide or guidebook), 9-3
guidé/e guided
guitare *f.* guitar, 1-3
guitare basse bass guitar, 12-1
guitare électrique electric guitar, 12-1
gymnase *m.* gym, 2-3
gymnastique *f.* exercises; gymnastics
faire de la gym to do exercises, to work out

H

s'habiller to get dressed, 4-1
habitation *f.* dwelling, housing
habiter to live (in a physical sense), 1-1
habitude *f.* habit
d'habitude usually, 6-3
habituel/le habitual
habituellement usually
s'habituer à to get used to
***haché/e** chopped, ground, 5-3
***hamburger** *m.* hamburger, 5-1
***handicap** *m.* handicap, disability, 10-1
***handicapé/e** handicapped, 10-1
être *handicapé/e to be handicapped/disabled, 10-1
***haricot** *m.* bean, 5-3
***haricot vert** green bean, 5-2
harmonica *m.* harmonica, 2-2
harmonie *f.* harmony
***haut** high
hebdomadaire *adj.* weekly, 11-3
***hein !** huh!, understood?
heure *f.* hour, 4-2
être à l'heure to be on time, 4-2
Il est une heure. It's one o'clock., 4-2
Quelle heure est-il ? What time is it?, 4-2
Vous avez l'heure ? Do you have the time?, 4-2
heureusement luckily, 7-1
heureux/-euse happy, 7-3
***heurter** to strike
hexagone *m.* hexagon
L'Hexagone (*colloq.*) France
hier yesterday, 5-2
histoire *f.* history, 3-2; story
histoire drôle joke, 2-1
historique historical
film *m.* **historique** historical movie, 11-1
hiver *m.* winter, 5-1
***hockey** *m.* hockey, 2-2
***hollandais/e** Dutch, hollandaise (sauce)
***Hollande** *f.* Holland
***homard** *m.* lobster
homme *m.* man, 1-1
homme au foyer stay-at-home father, 7-1
homme d'affaires businessman, 3-3
honte *f.* shame
hôpital *m.* public hospital, 3-3
horaire *m.* schedule
horaires *pl.* **d'ouverture** opening hours, business hours
horloge *f.* clock, 4-2
horreur *f.* horror
film *m.* **d'horreur** horror movie, 11-1
Quelle horreur ! How awful!, 5-1
***hors** except; outside
hôte *m.* guest or host
hôtel *m.* hotel, 2-3
huile *f.* oil, 5-3
huile d'olive olive oil
huile usagée waste (used) oil, 10-2
***huit** eight, 1-2
***huitième** eighth, 6-1
huître *f.* oyster
humain/e human
corps *m.* **humain** human body, 10-1
sciences *f. pl.* **humaines** social sciences, 3-2
***hyène** *f.* hyena
hygiéniste *m./f.* **dentaire** dental hygienist
hypermarché *m.* superstore

I

ici here, 3-1
idéal/e ideal
idéaliste idealistic, 1-1
idée *f.* idea
identifier to identify
identité *f.* identity
idiomatique idiomatic
il *m.* he, it, P-1
île *f.* island
ils *m. pl.* they, P-1
il y a there is/are, P-2; ago, 5-2
il n'y a pas de... there isn't/aren't . . . , P-2
il y a deux jours two days ago, 5-2
il y a longtemps a long time ago, 5-2
il y a ... que it's been . . . , for . . . , 11-3
illogique illogical
illustre illustrious
imaginaire imaginary
imaginer to imagine
imam *m.* imam, leader of prayers in a Muslim mosque
imbécile *m./f.* idiot
immense huge, immense
immeuble *m.* building, 6-1
immigré/e immigrant
immobilier *m.* real estate business
immunodéficitaire immunodeficient
imparfait *m.* imperfect tense
impatience *f.* impatience
impératif *m.* imperative
imper(méable) *m.* raincoat, 4-3
impliquer to involve, to implicate
importance *f.* importance
important important, 8-1
impression *f.* impression
impressionnisme *m.* Impressionism
impressionniste Impressionist, 12-2
imprimante *f.* **(multifonction)** (multifunction) printer, 11-2
imprimer to print, 11-2
inclure to include
inclus/e included
inconvénient *m.* disadvantage, inconvenience
incorporer to blend
Inde *f.* India, 9-2
indéfini/e indefinite
indication *f.* sign, indication
indien/ne Indian, 9-2
indifférence *f.* indifference
indigestion *f.* indigestion
indiquer to indicate, 9-3
indiscipliné/e undisciplined, 1-1
indiscret/-ète indiscreet

indispensable necessary
individualiste individualistic, 1-1
individu *m.* individual
individuel/le individual
indulgent/e indulgent, lenient, 7-1
industriel/le industrial, 10-2
industriel/le *m./f.* manufacturer, industrialist
infection *f.* infection
infinitif *m.* infinitive
infirmerie *f.* health center/clinic, 3-1
infirmier *m.*, **infirmière** *f.* nurse, 3-3
informaticien *m.*, **informaticienne** *f.* programmer, 3-3
information *f.* information
informations *f. pl.* **(les infos)** news, 11-1
informatique *f.* computer science, 3-2
s'informer to get information, 11-3
ingénieur *m.* engineer, 3-3
innovateur/-trice innovative
innovation *f.* innovation
inondation *f.* flood, 10-2
inquiet/-ète worried, uneasy, anxious, 7-3
s'inquiéter † to worry, 7-3
inquiétude *f.* worry
insatisfait/e unsatisfied
inscription *f.* registration, enrollment
  bureau *m.* **des inscriptions** registrar's office, 3-1
s'inscrire to register, to enroll
  s'inscrire sur la liste électorale to register to vote, 10-3
insensible insensitive
instable unstable
installer to put in, to install
instant *m.* moment, instant
s'instruire † to educate oneself, to improve one's mind, 11-3
instrument *m.* instrument, 12-1
  instrument de musique musical instrument
insulter to insult
insupportable unbearable
intégrer † to incorporate, integrate
  s'intégrer to integrate, to fit in
intelligent/e intelligent, smart, 2-1
intensité *f.* intensity
interactif/-ive interactive
interdiction *f.* ban
interdire † to ban, to forbid
intéressant/e interesting, 3-2
s'intéresser (à) to be interested (in), 3-3
intérieur *m.* inside, interior
interlocuteur *m.* partner in dialogue, interlocutor
internaute *m.* Internet user
Internet *m.* Internet
  aller sur Internet to go on the Internet
  surfer sur Internet to surf the Internet
interpréter † to interpret; to perform
interrogatif/-ive interrogative
interrogation *f.* quiz
interviewer to interview
intime intimate
s'intituler to be titled, 12-2
intrigue *f.* plot, scheme
invariable invariable
inventer to invent
invitation *f.* invitation, 8-3
invité/e *m./f.* guest
inviter to invite, 1-3
Irak *m.* Iraq
Iran *m.* Iran
irrégularité *f.* irregularity
irrégulier/-ière irregular
Italie *f.* Italy, 9-2
italien/ne *adj.* Italian, 9-2
italien *m.* Italian (language)
item *m.* item
ivoirien/ne Ivorian, 9-2

J

jalousie *f.* jealousy
jaloux/-ouse jealous, 7-3
jamais ever
  ne ... jamais never, 4-1
jambe *f.* leg, 10-1
jambon *m.* ham, 5-1
janvier January, 1-2
Japon *m.* Japan, 9-2
japonais/e *adj.* Japanese, 9-2
japonais *m.* Japanese (language)
jardin *m.* garden, yard, 1-3
jardinage *m.* gardening, 2-2
  faire † du jardinage to garden, to do some gardening, 2-2
jaser (*Can.*) to chatter, prattle
jaune yellow, 4-3
jazz *m.* jazz, 2-2
je (j') I, P-1
jean *m. sg.* jeans, 4-3
jet *m.* spurt, spray; jet
jeter † to throw/throw out, 5-2
jeu *m.* game, 2-2
  jeu de mot pun
  jeu de société board game, 2-2
  jeu électronique computer game
  jeu télévisé game show, 11-1
  jeu vidéo video game
  Jeux *pl.* **Olympiques** Olympic games
jeudi Thursday, 1-3
jeune *adj.* young, 2-1
jeune *m./f.* young person
jeûne *m.* fast
jeûner to fast
jeunesse *f.* youth, young people
jogging *m.* jogging, 2-2
  faire † du jogging to go jogging, to jog, 2-2
joie *f.* joy
joli/e pretty, 2-1
jouer to play, 1-3
  jouer une pièce to perform a play, 8-3
  jouer à to play (a sport), 1-3
  jouer de to play (an instrument), 1-3
jour *m.* day, 1-3
  ce jour-là that day, 5-2
  jour férié legal holiday, 7-2
journal *m.* newspaper, 11-3
  journal télévisé (le JT) news broadcast, 11-1
journalisme *m.* journalism, 3-2
journaliste *m./f.* journalist, 3-3
journée *f.* day, 4-1
joyeux/-euse *adj.* merry, cheerful
  Joyeux Anniversaire ! Happy Birthday!, 7-2
  Joyeux Noël ! Merry Christmas!, 7-2
juger to judge
juif *m.*, **juive** *f.* Jewish, 7-1
juillet July, 1-2
juin June, 1-2
jumeau *m.*, **jumelle** *f.* twin
jupe *f.* skirt, 4-3
jus d'orange *m.* orange juice, 5-1
jusqu'à until, 4-2
justifier to justify
juteux/-euse juicy

K

kayak *m.* kayak
kilo *m.* kilo, 5-3
kiosque *m.* newsstand

L

la (l') *f.* the, P-1; *pron.* her, it, 6-1
là there, 6-3
là-bas there, over there, 6-3
labo(ratoire) *m.* laboratory, 3-1
  labo(ratoire) de chimie chemistry lab, 3-1
  labo(ratoire) de langues language lab, 3-1
lac *m.* lake, 6-3
laid/e ugly
laine *f.* wool, 4-3
laïque secular
laisser to leave (alone)
  laisser les lumières allumées to leave the lights on, 10-2
lait *m.* milk, 5-2
lampe *f.* lamp, 6-2
lancer to throw
  lancer un pari to make a wager
langage *m.* language
langagier/-ière linguistic, of language
langue *f.* language, 3-2; tongue, 10-1
  langue étrangère foreign language, 3-2
  langue maternelle native language, 9-2
laquelle *f.* which one, 8-1
lapin *m.* rabbit

large big, large, loose-fitting, roomy, 4-3
lavabo *m.* bathroom sink, 4-1
laver to wash
se laver to wash oneself, 4-1
se laver les cheveux to wash one's hair, 4-1
se laver les dents to brush one's teeth
se laver la figure to wash one's face, 4-1
se laver les mains to wash one's hands, 4-1
le (l') *m.* the, P-1; *pron.* him, it, 6-1
leçon *f.* lesson, 1-3
leçon de chant singing lesson, 1-3
lecteur *m.*, **lectrice** *f.* reader
lecteur CD *m.* CD player, P-2
lecteur CD/DVD *m.* CD/ DVD drive, 11-2
lecteur DVD *m.* DVD player, P-2
lecture *f.* reading
légende *f.* caption; legend; key
leger/-ère light
légume *m.* vegetable, 5-2
lémur *m.* lemur
lequel *m.* which one, 8-1
les *pl.* the, P-2 ; *pron.* them, 6-1
lesquels *m. pl.*, **lesquelles** *f. pl.* which ones, 8-1
lettre *f.* letter
lettres *f. pl.* humanities, 3-2
leur *adj.* their, 1-2; *pron.* to them, 6-2
leurs *adj. pl.* their, 1-2
lever † to raise, 5-2
lever le doigt to raise one's hand
se lever † to get up, 4-1
Levez-vous ! Get up/Stand up!, P-2
lèvre *f.* lip, 10-1
liaison *f.* link, liaison
libraire *m./f.* bookseller
librairie *f.* bookstore, 2-3
libre free (a person), available, 8-3
Je ne suis pas libre. I'm not free., 8-3
Tu es/vous êtes libre(s) ? Are you free?, 8-3
libre-service *m.* self-service
licence *f.* Bachelor's degree (in French university system)
licorne *f.* unicorn
lien *m.* (Web) link, 11-2; connection, tie
lieu *m.* place
au lieu de instead of
avoir lieu to take place, 7-2
lieu de travail workplace
lièvre *m.* hare
ligne *f.* line
en ligne online, 11-2
limite *f.* border, limit
limité/e limited
limité/e à limited to
limité/e par bordered by, limited by
limiter to limit, to restrict
limonade *f.* lemon-lime soft drink, 5-1
linguistique *f. sg.* linguistics
lire † to read, 7-1
Je lis un roman. I'm reading a novel, 3-2
Lisez les mots... ! Read the words . . . !, P-2
liste *f.* list
lit *m.* bed, 6-2
litre *m.* liter, 5-3
littérature *f.* literature, 3-2
livre *m.* book, P-2
locataire *m./f.* tenant, renter, 6-1
location *f.* renting
logement *m.* lodgings, accommodation, 9-3
loger † to stay temporarily, 9-3
logiciel *m.* software program, 11-2
logique logical
loin *adv.* far away, a long way
C'est loin. It's far.
au loin in the distance
loin (de) far from, 3-1
lointain/e *adj.* distant, faraway
loisir *m.* leisure time, 2-2
long/longue long, 4-3
longtemps a long time, 5-2
il y a longtemps a long time ago, 5-2
lors de during, at the time of
lorsque when, 11-1
loto *m.* lottery, 2-2
louer to rent, 6-1
louisianais/e *adj.* from Louisiana
lourd/e heavy, 8-1
Il fait lourd. It's humid., 8-1
loyer *m.* rent, 6-1
lui *m.* him, P-1; *pron.* to him, to her, 6-2
lui-même *m.* himself
luisant/e gleaming, shining
lumière *f.* light, 9-3
éteindre les lumières to turn off the lights, 10-2
spectacle *m.* **son et lumière** sound and light historical production, 9-3
lunaire lunar, pertaining to the moon
lundi Monday, 1-3
le lundi every Monday, on Mondays, 6-3
lune (Lune) *f.* moon (the Moon)
être dans la lune to have one's head in the clouds
lune de miel honeymoon
lunettes *f. pl.* eyeglasses, 4-3
lunettes de soleil pair of sunglasses, 4-3
lutte *f.* struggle; wrestling
lutter to struggle, fight
luxe *m.* luxury
luxueux/-euse luxurious
lycée *m.* high school, 1-3

M

ma *f.* my, 1-1
McDo *m.* McDonald's restaurant
machine *f.* machine
macroéconomique *adj.* macroeconomic
madame (Mme) Mrs., Ms., P-1
mademoiselle (Mlle) Miss, P-1
magasin *m.* store, 4-3
grand magasin department store, 4-3
magasiner (*Can.*) to shop
magazine *m.* news show, 11-1; magazine, 11-3
magazine télé listing of TV programs, 11-1
maghrébin/e North African, 7-1
magistral/e *adj.* brillant
magnétophone *m.* tape player
magnétoscope *m.* videocassette player/recorder
magnifique magnificent, 4-3
mai May, 1-2
maigre skinny, thin, 2-1
maigrir to lose weight, 6-1
maillot *m.* **(de bain)** swimsuit, 4-3
main *f.* hand, 4-1
maintenant now, 1-3
maintenir † to affirm, to uphold, 9-2
maire *m.* mayor
mairie *f.* city hall, 2-3
mais but, P-2
maison *f.* house, home, 1-3
rester à la maison to stay home, 1-3
maître *m.* master, 12-2
maîtrise *f.* mastery; M.A. or M.S. degree in former French academic system
majeur/e *adj.* principal, major
majeure (en) *f.* (*Can.*) academic major (in), 3-2
majoritairement predominantly
mal *adv.* badly, P-1
pas mal not bad, P-1
mal *m.* **(maux** *pl.***)** pain, ache, 10-1
avoir du mal à respirer to have difficulty breathing
avoir mal to hurt, 10-1
avoir mal à la tête to have a headache, 10-1
avoir mal au cœur to be nauseated, 10-1
avoir mal partout to hurt all over, 10-1
malade *adj.* sick, P-1
malade *m./f.* sick person
malade imaginaire hypochondriac
maladie *f.* sickness, disease
malentendant/e *m./f.* hearing-impaired
malgache *adj.* from Madagascar
malgré in spite of
malheureux/-euse unhappy, unfortunate, 7-3
mandat *m.* term (of office), 10-3
manière *f.* **de vivre** way of life

manifestation *f.* protest, demonstration, 10-3
manger † to eat, 2-3
manque *m.* lack
manquer to miss, to be lacking
manteau *m.* overcoat, 4-3
manuel *m.* manual, handbook
maquillage *m.* makeup, 4-1
se maquiller to put on makeup, 4-1
marche *f.* walking, pace; step
faire de la marche to walk for exercise, 2-2
marché *m.* market, 2-3
bon marché *adj.* inexpensive, 4-3
marché en plein air open-air market
marcher to walk
mardi Tuesday, 1-3
mari *m.* husband, 1-1
mariage *m.* wedding, 7-2; marriage
marié *m.*, **mariée** *f.* bridegroom/bride, 7-2
marié/e married, 1-1
se marier to get married, 7-3
marier to marry
marier les expressions to match the expressions
marin/e related to the sea
maritime coastal, seaside, maritime
marmotte *f.* groundhog; sleepy head (*colloq.*)
Maroc *m.* Morocco, 9-2
marocain/e Moroccan, 9-2
marraine *f.* godmother, 7-2
marron *adj. inv.* brown, 4-3
marquant/e *adj.* outstanding
mars March, 1-2
masque *m.* mask
masse *f.* group, mass
master : diplôme *m.* **de master** M.A. or M.S. degree in current French academic system
match *m.* (**matchs** *pl.*) game (sports), 2-2
mathématiques *f. pl.* (**les maths**) mathematics, 3-2
matière *f.* matter, material, subject
matin *m.* morning, 1-3
dix heures du matin ten o'clock in the morning, 4-2
du matin in the morning; A.M., 4-2
mauvais/e bad, 3-1
Il fait mauvais. The weather's bad., 8-1
maux *see* **mal**
mazurka *f.* mazurka, Polish folk dance
me (m') *pron.* me, to me, 7-2
mécanicien *m.*, **mécanicienne** *f.* mechanic
méchant/e mean, naughty, 2-1
médecin *m.* doctor (M.D.), 3-3
médecine *f.* medicine, 3-2
médias *m. pl.* media, 11-1
médical/e medical
médicament *m.* medicine, drug
médiocre mediocre, 3-2
se méfier to be suspicious
meilleur/e *adj.* better, best, 4-3
meilleur/e ami/e *m./f.* best friend
Meilleurs vœux ! Best wishes!, 7-2
mél *m.* e-mail address (*France*)
mélange *m.* mixture, blend, combination
mélanger to mix
melon *m.* cantaloupe, 5-3
membre *m.* member, limb
même same; even, 6-1
en même temps at the same time
mémoire *f.* memory
mémoire *m.* long essay, M.A. thesis
ménacé/e threatened, 10-2
ménacer to threaten
ménage *m.* household
mener † to lead, to carry out
mener à sa fin to lead to one's end
mensuel/le monthly, 11-3
mental/e mental
menthe *m.* mint
thé *m.* **à la menthe** mint tea
tisane *f.* **à la menthe** herbal mint tea
mentionner to mention
mentir to lie, 4-2
mer *f.* sea, 6-3
au bord de la mer at the seashore, 6-3
merci thank you, P-2
mercredi Wednesday, 1-3
mère *f.* mother, 1-1
mériter to earn, merit
merveilleux/-euse marvelous, wonderful
mes *pl.* my, 1-1
mésaventure *f.* misfortune
message *m.* message
messagerie instantanée *f.* instant messaging, 11-2
messe *f.* Catholic mass
mesure *f.* measurement
mesurer to measure
métaphore *f.* metaphor
météo(rologie) *f.* weather forecast, 8-1
métier *m.* occupation, job, 3-3
métro *m.* subway, 9-1
metteur en scène *m.* film or stage director
mettre † to put on, 4-3
mettre à jour to update
mettre la musique à fond to turn the music up loud
mettre la table to set the table
mettre une heure to take an hour
meublé/e furnished, 6-2
meuble *m.* piece of furniture, 6-2
meurtre *m.* murder
mexicain/e Mexican, 9-2
Mexique *m.* Mexico, 9-2
micro(phone) *m.* microphone
micro-trottoir *m.* sidewalk interview
midi noon, 4-2
mieux better, 4-2
mieux ... que better . . . than, 4-2
militaire military
militant/e *m./f.* political activist
militer to be a political activist
mille thousand, 6-2
milliard billion, 6-2
million million, 6-2
mince *adj.* thin, slender, 2-1
Mince ! Shoot!, 4-2
mincir to lose weight
mineure *f.* **(en)** (*Can.*) minor, 3-2
mini-jupe *f.* miniskirt, 4-3
ministère *m.* ministry, department
ministre *m.* minister, secretary
minorité *f.* minority
minuit midnight, 4-2
minute *f.* minute, 4-1
mitaine *f.* (*Can.*) mitten
se mobiliser (contre) organize (against), 10-3
mobylette *f.* moped, motor scooter, 9-1
mocassin *m.* loafer, 4-3
moche ugly, 2-1
modalité *f.* form, modality
mode *f.* fashion, 4-3
à la mode stylish, fashionable, 4-3
mode *m.* form, mode
mode articulatoire articulatory mode
mode d'emploi directions
modèle *m.* model
moderne modern, 6-2
modeste modest
modifier to modify
moelle *f.* marrow
moelleux/-euse moist
moi me, P-1
moi-même myself
moins less, 4-2
moins (de) ... que less . . . than, 4-2
moins le quart a quarter to, 4-2
moins vingt twenty to, 4-2
mois *m.* month, 1-2
le mois prochain next month, 2-3
moitié *f.* half
moment *m.* moment, 5-2
à ce moment-là at that moment, 5-2
mon *m.* my, 1-1
monde *m.* world
avoir une vision du monde to have a worldview, 7-1
tout le monde everyone, everybody, 11-2
mondial/e worldwide
moniteur *m.* monitor, 11-2
moniteur avec un écran plat flat-screen monitor, 11-2
moniteur *m.*, **monitrice** *f.* (sports) instructor, (camp) counselor

monnaie *f.* currency; change
mononucléose *f.* mononucleosis
monoparental/e single-parent, 7-1
monotone monotonous
monsieur (M.) Mr., P-1
monsieur *m.* man, P-2
monstre *m.* monster
montagne *f.* mountain, 6-3
montée *f.* climb
monter to go up, 5-3
montre *f.* watch, 4-2
montrer to show, P-2
monument *m.* monument, 2-3
  monument aux morts veterans' memorial, 2-3
se moquer de to tease, mock
morceau *m.* piece, 5-3
mort *f.* death
mort *m.* deceased person, cadaver
mortel/le mortal
mosquée *f.* mosque
mot *m.* word
  mot à mot word for word
  mot apparenté cognate
  mot-clé *m.* keyword
  mot juste right word
  mot-valise *m.* portmanteau word
moteur *m.* engine, 10-2
  moteur de recherche search engine
moto *f.* motorcycle, 8-2
  faire † de la moto to ride a motorcycle, 8-2
motoneige *f.* snowmobile
  faire † de la motoneige to go snowmobiling, 8-2
mouche *f.* fly (insect)
  bateau-mouche *m.* Paris river boat
mouiller to moisten
mourir † to die, 5-3
moutarde *f.* mustard, 5-3
moyen *m.* way, means
  moyen de transport means of transportation, 9-1
moyen/ne *adj.* medium, average
  le Français moyen the average French person
moyenne *f.* average
muet/te silent, mute
muguet *m.* lily of the valley, 7-2
multiculturel/le multicultural, 7-1
multiethnique multiethnic
multifonction multifunction, 11-2
multimédia multimedia, 11-2
multiple multiple
municipal/e municipal, 2-3
mur *m.* wall, 6-2
musculation *f.* bodybuilding, 10-1
  faire † de la musculation to do strength/resistance training; to lift weights, 10-1
musée *m.* museum, 2-3
musical/e *adj.* musical
  comédie *f.* **musicale** musical, 11-1
musicien *m.*, **musicienne** *f.* musician, 3-3
musique *f.* music, 1-3
  faire † de la musique to play (make) music, 2-2
musulman/e Muslim
mystérieux/-euse mysterious
mythe *m.* myth

N

nager † to swim, 2-3
naissance *f.* birth
naître † to be born, 5-3
narratif/-ive narrative
narration *f.* narrative, account
nasal/e nasal
natation *f.* swimming, 2-2
  faire † de la natation to swim, 2-2
nationalité *f.* nationality, 9-2
nature *f.* nature, 6-3
  nature morte still life, 12-2
navet *m.* turnip
navette *f.* shuttle, bus, 3-1
ne ... jamais never, 4-1
ne ... pas not, 1-3
ne ... personne no one, 8-3
ne ... rien nothing, 8-3
nécessaire necessary, 8-1
nécessairement necessarily
nécessité *f.* need, necessity
néerlandais/e Dutch, 9-2
néerlandais *m.* Dutch (language)
négatif/-ive negative
neiger to snow, 8-1
  Il neige. It's snowing., 8-1
nettoyer † to clean, 10-2
neuf nine, 1-2
neuf/ve *adj.* brand-new, 6-2
neuvième ninth, 6-1
neveu *m.* nephew, 1-1
  neveux *pl.* nieces and nephews, 1-1
nez *m.* nose, 10-1
nièce *f.* niece, 1-1
Noël *m.* Christmas, 7-2
noir/e black, 4-3
nom *m.* last name, P-2
  nom de plume pen name
nombre *m.* number, 1-2
nombreux/-euse numerous, 1-1
nommer to name
non no, P-1
  non plus neither
  moi non plus me neither
non biodégradable nonbiodegradable, 10-2
non-voyant/e *m./f.* visually handicapped person
nord *m.* north, 9-2
normalement normally, 1-3
nos *pl.* our, 1-2
note *f.* grade, 3-2
  avoir une (bonne/mauvaise) note to have/receive a (good/bad) grade, 3-2
notre *m./f.* our, 1-2
nourricier/-ière nourishing
nourrir to nourish
  se nourrir to feed, to eat
nourriture *f.* food, nourishment
nous we, P-1; *pron.* us, to us, 7-2
  nous-mêmes ourselves
nouveau (nouvel), nouvelle new, 3-1
  de nouveau again, 4-1
nouveauté *f.* novelty, new release, new publication, new model
nouvelle *f.* piece of news, 7-3
nouvelles *f. pl.* news
novembre November, 1-2
nuage *m.* cloud, 8-1
  Il y a des nuages. It's cloudy., 8-1
nucléaire *adj.* nuclear
  centrale *f.* **nucléaire** nuclear power plant
  énergie *f.* **nucléaire** nuclear power
nuisance *f.* something harmful, environmental problem; nuisance
nuit *f.* night, 4-1
numéro *m.* number
numéroter to number
nymphéa *m.* water lily

O

obéir à to obey, 6-1
obésité *f.* obesity
obligatoire required, 3-2
observer to observe
obtenir † to obtain, 9-2
occasion *f.* chance, opportunity, occasion
  avoir l'occasion de to have the opportunity to
Occident *m.* the West
occupé/e busy, P-1
s'occuper de to take care of, 6-3
océan *m.* ocean, 8-2
Océanie *f.* Pacific, 9-2
octobre October, 1-2
odeur *f.* odor
œil *m.* (**yeux** *pl.*) eye, 10-1
œuf *m.* egg, 5-2
  œuf en chocolat chocolate egg, 7-2
  œufs sur le plat/au plat fried eggs, 5-2
œuvre *f.* work (esp. literary or artistic)
  œuvre d'art work of art, 12-2
office *m.* **de tourisme** tourism office, 9-3
officiel/le official
offrir † to give (a gift), 6-2
oignon *m.* onion, 5-3
oiseau *m.* bird, 1-1
olive *f.* olive
omelette *f.* omelet
omniprésent/e omnipresent
on one, people in general, 1-3
  On y va ensemble ? Shall we go (there) together?, 8-3

oncle *m.* uncle, 1-1
onze eleven, 1-2
onzième eleventh, 6-1
opéra *m.* opera, 12-1
opinion *f.* opinion
optimiste optimistic, 1-1
orage *m.* (thunder)storm, 8-1
  Il y a un orage. There is a (thunder)storm., 8-1
oral/e oral
orange *adj. inv.* orange (color), 4-3
orange *f.* orange (fruit), 5-1
Orangina *m.* Orangina orange soda, 5-1
orchestre *m.* orchestra, 12-1
ordinaire ordinary
ordi(nateur) *m.* computer, P-2
  ordinateur portable laptop computer, 11-2
ordonnance *f.* prescription
ordre *m.* order
ordures *f. pl.* trash, waste, 10-2
oreille *f.* ear, 10-1
organiser to plan, to organize, 2-2
originaire (de) originally (from), native (of)
origine *f.* origin
orphelin/e orphaned
orteil *m.* toe
ou or, P-1
où where, 2-1
ouest *m.* west
oublier (de) to forget, 2-3
Ouf ! Whew!, 4-2
oui yes, P-1
ouragan *m.* hurricane, 10-2
ours *m.* bear
  ours blanc polar bear, 10-2
ouvrage *m.* **de référence** reference book, 11-3
ouvert/e open
ouverture *f.* opening
ouvrier *m.*, **ouvrière** *f.* worker, laborer
ouvrir † to open, P-2

P

PACS *m.*, **pacte** *m.* **civil de solidarité** legal document recognizing a civil union in France
se pacser to sign a PACS agreement
pagne *m.* wrap, piece of (African) cloth
pain *m.* bread, 5-2
  du pain avec du chocolat bread with chocolate, 5-2
  pain au chocolat chocolate croissant, 5-2
  pain de campagne round loaf of bread, 5-3
  pain de mie loaf of sliced bread, 5-3
  pain grillé toast, 5-2
  petit pain roll, 5-3
paire *f.* pair
paix *f.* peace
pâle pale, 6-1
pâlir to become pale, 6-1
panier *m.* basket, 10-2
pantalon *m. sg.* slacks, 4-3
pantouflard/e homebody, stay-at-home, 2-1
paquet *m.* package, 5-3
par by, through
  par exemple for example
  (deux fois) par jour/semaine (twice) a day/week, 4-1
  par terre on the floor, 6-2
paradoxalement paradoxically
parapluie *m.* umbrella, 4-3
parc *m.* park, 2-3
  parc de loisirs theme park
parce que because, 2-1
pardon excuse me, P-2
parent *m.* parent; relative, 1-1
paresseux/-euse lazy, 2-1
parfaitement perfectly, completely
parfois sometimes
pari *m.* bet, wager
parité *f.* **(politique)** political parity
parler to speak, P-2
  parler au telephone to talk on the phone, 1-3
  Parlez plus fort ! Speak louder!, P-2
parmi among
paroisse *f.* parish; county in Louisiana
parrain *m.* godfather, 7-2
part *f.* slice, share, proportion
partager † to share, 5-1
partenaire *m./f.* partner
participer à to participate in
particulier/-ière particular, specific, exceptional, special
  en particulier particularly, in particular
particularité *f.* special feature
partie *f.* part
  faire † partie de to belong to, 7-1
partir to leave, 4-2
  à partir de from
  partir en vacances to go on vacation, 8-2
partitif/-ive partitive
partout everywhere, all over, 10-1
pas not, P-1
  ne … pas not, 1-3
  pas du tout not at all
  pas mal not bad, P-1
  pas si vite not so fast, 12-3
  pas tout à fait not quite, 8-2
passage *m.* passage
passager *m.*, **passagère** *f.* passenger
passant *m.*, **passante** *f.* passerby
passé *m.* past
  passé composé compound past tense
passeport *m.* passport, 9-1
passer to go/come by, 5-3
  passer (du temps) to spend time, 8-3
  passer une soirée tranquille to spend a quiet evening, 8-3
  se passer to happen, 7-3
passion *f.* passion
passionné/e passionate
pastel *m.* pastel, 12-2
pasteur *m.* pastor, Protestant minister
pâte *f.* pasta, dough, 5-2
pâté *m.* pâté, 5-3
patience *f.* patience
patin *m.* **à glace** ice skate; ice-skating
patin *m.* **à roulettes** roller skate; roller-skating
patinage *m.* skating
pâtisserie *f.* pastry shop, 5-3
pâtissier *m.*, **pâtissière** *f.* pastry chef
patron *m.*, **patronne** *f.* boss
pauvre poor
pavillon *m.* building, 3-1
  pavillon principal main building, 3-1
payer † to pay
pays *m.* country, 9-2
paysage *m.* landscape, 12-2
Pays-Bas *m. pl.* The Netherlands, 9-2
PDA *m.* PDA, 11-2
peau *f.* skin
  être bien dans sa peau to have confidence in oneself, 7-1
pêche *f.* peach, 5-3; fishing, 6-3
  aller à la pêche to go fishing, 6-3
peigne *m.* comb, 4-1
se peigner to comb one's hair
peindre † to paint, 12-2
peintre *m.* painter, 12-2
peinture *f.* painting, 3-2
pellicule *f.* roll of film
pendant during, for, 4-2
  pendant que while, 11-1
pénicilline *f.* penicillin
pensée *f.* thought
penser to think, 4-3
  penser (à) to think of
  penser (de) to think about
  Je pense que non. I don't think so.
  Je pense que oui. I think so.
  Je pense que ... I think that . . . , 7-3
perdre to lose, to waste, 3-1
  perdre son sang-froid to lose one's composure, 7-3
père *m.* father, 1-1
  père célibataire single father, 7-1
période *f.* period
périodique *m.* periodical
perle *f.* pearl
permettre † (à, de) to permit, 7-1
permis *m.* permit, 3-1
  permis de conduire driver's license, 9-1
persan/e *adj.* Persian
persil *m.* parsley
personnage *m.* character, 11-1

personnage principal main character, 11-1
personnalisé/e personalized
personne *f.* person, P-1
personne âgée elderly person
personne du troisième âge senior citizen
personne en difficulté person in difficult situation, disadvantaged
ne ... personne no one, nobody, 8-3
personnel/le personal
perspective *f.* perspective
persuader to persuade
perte *f.* loss
pessimiste pessimistic, 1-1
petit-déjeuner *m.* breakfast, 5-2
petit/e short, small, little, 2-1
petite annonce *f.* classified ad
petit commerçant *m.* owner of a small retail shop
petit-enfant *m.* grandchild, 1-1
petite-fille *f.* granddaughter, 1-1
petit-fils *m.* grandson, 1-1
petit pois *m.* pea, 5-3
peu *m.* a little, 1-1
un petit peu a little bit
peur *f.* fear
avoir † peur to be afraid, 10-3
faire † peur to frighten, scare
peut-être maybe, 2-1
phare *m.* lighthouse, beacon
pharmacie *f.* pharmacy
pharmacien *m.*, **pharmacienne** *f.* pharmacist, 3-3
phénomène *m.* phenomenon
philosophie *f.* philosophy, 3-2
photographe *m./f.* photographer, 12-2
photo(graphie) *f.* photograph, photography, 2-1
phrase *f.* sentence
physiologie *f.* physiology, 3-2
physique *adj.* physical
physique *f.* physics, 3-2
physique *m. sg.* physical traits, 2-1
piano *m.* piano, 1-3
pièce *f.* play, 2-3; room 6-1
un cinq-pièces *m.* three-bedroom apartment, 6-1
pièce de monnaie coin
pièce jointe (e-mail) attachment, 11-2
pied *m.* foot, 10-1
à pied on foot, 9-1
pierre *f.* stone
piétonnier/-ière for pedestrians
pincée *f.* pinch (in cooking)
pingouin *m.* penguin
piquant/e spicy, hot
pique-nique *m.* picnic, 6-3
faire † un pique-nique to have a picnic, 6-3
piquer to sting
pire worse
piscine *f.* swimming pool, 2-3
pizza *f.* pizza, 5-1
placard *m.* cupboard, kitchen cabinet, 6-2
place *f.* (city) square, 2-3; seat, place, 8-3
plage *f.* beach, 6-3
se plaindre to complain
plaisanter to joke
Tu plaisantes ! You're joking!
plaisir *m.* pleasure, 8-3
avec plaisir with pleasure, 8-3
se faire un petit plaisir to treat oneself, 12-3
plan *m.* map, blueprint
plan de ville city map, 9-1
plan du campus map of campus, 3-1
planche *f.* board
planche à voile windsurfing, windsurfing board, 8-2
faire † de la planche à voile to windsurf, 8-2
planète *f.* planet, 10-2
planifier to plan, 12-3
plantain *m.* plantain
plante *f.* plant
plastique *m.* plastic, 10-2
plat *m.* dish or course, 5-2
plat préparé prepared dish, 5-3
plat principal main dish, 5-2
plein/e (de) full (of), 11-1
en plein air *adj./adv.* in the open air, outdoors
faire † le plein to fill up the gas tank of a car
pleurer to cry, 7-3
pleuvoir † to rain, 8-1
Il pleut. It's raining., 8-1
pluie *f.* rain, 8-1
plupart *f.* majority, most
plus *adv.* more; plus
de plus en plus more and more
en plus additionally, besides
non plus neither
moi non plus me neither
plus (de) ... que more . . . than, 4-2
plusieurs several
plutôt more, rather, 12-3
pneumonie *f.* pneumonia
poche *f.* pocket
poêle *f.* pan
poème *m.* poem
poésie *f.* poetry, 11-3
poète *m./f.* poet
poignet *m.* wrist, 10-1
point *m.* point, period, spot
pointe : de pointe high-tech, state-of-the-art
poire *f.* pear, 5-2
poirier *m.* pear tree
poison *m.* poison
poisson *m.* fish, 5-2
poissonnerie *f.* seafood shop, 5-3
poitrine *f.* chest, 10-1
poivre *m.* pepper, 5-2
poivron *m.* (bell) pepper
poivron rouge red pepper
poivron vert green pepper
policier : film *m.* **policier** detective/police film, 11-1
polluer to pollute, 10-2
pollution *f.* pollution, 10-2
pollution atmosphérique air pollution, 10-2
pollution sonore noise pollution, 10-2
polo *m.* polo shirt, 4-3
pommade *f.* ointment, salve
pomme *f.* apple, 5-2
pomme *f.* **de terre** potato, 5-2
populaire popular
popularité *f.* popularity
porc *m.* pork, 5-3
portable *m.* laptop computer 11-2; cell phone
porte *f.* door, P-2
portée *f.* reach
portefeuille *m.* wallet, 9-1
porte-monnaie *m. inv.* change purse, 9-1
porter to wear, 4-3; to carry
portrait *m.* portrait, 12-2
portugais/e *adj.* Portuguese, 9-2
Portugal *m.* Portugal, 9-2
poser to place, put
poser une question to ask a question, 2-1
posséder † to possess, 6-3
posséssif/-ive possessive
possibilité *f.* possibility
possible possible
postal/e postal
poste *m.* job, position
poste *f.* post office
poster *m.* poster
pot *m.* jar, 5-3
potable *adj.* drinkable
eau *f.* **potable** drinking water, 10-2
potager *m.* vegetable garden, 6-3
poubelle *f.* trash can, 10-2
poudre *f.* powder
poudre à pâte baking powder (Louisiana)
poule *f.* hen
poulet *m.* chicken, 5-2
pouls *m.* pulse
poumon *m.* lung, 10-1
pour for, 2-1
pour + *inf.* in order to
pour moi for me, 11-1
pourboire *m.* tip
pourcentage *m.* percentage
pourquoi why, 2-1
pourquoi pas ? why not?, 12-1
pousser to push, encourage
pouvoir *m.* power
pouvoir † to be able to, 3-3
poux *m. pl.* lice

pratiquant/e practicing
être pratiquant/e to practice a faith, 7-1
pratique *adj.* practical, 6-2
pratique *f.* practice
pratiquer to do, to engage in
pré *m.* meadow
précedent/e previous
précis/e precise
prédécesseur *m.* predecessor
prédiction *f.* prediction
préfecture *f.* **(de police)** prefecture (police headquarters)
préféré/e favorite, 8-1
préférence *f.* preference, 3-2
préférer † to prefer, 3-2
préhistorique prehistoric, 9-3
premier/-ière first, 1-1
C'est le premier mai. It's May first., 1-2
prendre † to take; to have a meal, 5-1
prendre congé to take leave, say good-bye
prendre le petit-déjeuner to have breakfast, 5-2
prendre un bain to take a bath
prendre une douche to take a shower, 4-1
Prenez un stylo ! Take a pen!, P-2
prénom *m.* first name, P-2
prénominal/e prenominal, before the noun
préparer to prepare, 1-3
préparer le dîner to fix dinner, 1-3
préparer un diplôme (en) to do a degree (in), 3-2
préparer un examen to study for an exam, 3-2
préparer une leçon to prepare for a lesson/class, 1-3
préposition *f.* preposition
près (de) close (to), near, 3-1
tout près very near
présent *m.* present, present tense
présentateur *m.*, **présentatrice** *f.* presenter; newscaster
présenter to introduce, present, P-1
Je te/vous présente Loïc. Let me introduce Loïc to you., P-1
se présenter to introduce oneself
se présenter candidat/e to stand for election
préservation *f.* conservation, preservation
préserver to preserve
président/e *m./f.* president
presque almost
presse *f.* press, 11-3
pressé/e squeezed; in a hurry
citron *m.* **pressé** lemonade, 5-1
prestige *m.* prestige, 3-3
prêt/e ready
prêter to lend, 6-2
prétexte *m.* excuse
prêtre *m.* Catholic priest
prévenir † to prevent, to avoid; to warn someone
prévu/e predicted, foreseen, anticipated
prier to beg, to pray
Je vous/t'en prie. You're welcome., 9-3
prière *f.* prayer
primaire primary
primitif/-ive primitive, 12-2
principal/e main, principal, 3-1
printemps *m.* spring, 8-1
au printemps in the spring, 8-1
priorité *f.* priority
pris/e : Je suis pris/e. I'm busy. I have a previous engagement., 8-3
privé/e private
privilégier to favor
prix *m.* price, 4-3; prize
probable probable
probablement probably
problème *m.* problem
sans problème no problem, 5-1
prochain/e next, 2-3
proche close
producteur *m.*, **productrice** *f.* producer
produire † to produce, to bring in
se produire to occur, to happen
produit *m.* product
produit chimique chemical product
prof *m.* = **professeur**
professeur *m.* professor, P-2; teacher, 3-2
professeure *f.* *(Can.)* professor, teacher
profession *f.* profession, 3-3
profond/e deep
programme *m.* **d'études** course of study
projet *m.* (future) plan
projets *pl.* **de vacances** vacation plans, 8-2
promenade *f.* walk, stroll, 2-2
faire † une promenade to take a walk, 2-2
se promener † to take a walk, 6-3
promettre † **(à, de)** to promise
pronom *m.* pronoun
pronom complément d'objet direct direct-object pronoun
pronom complément d'objet indirect indirect-object pronoun
pronom disjoint stressed pronoun
pronom réfléchi reflexive pronoun
pronom relatif relative pronoun
pronom sujet subject pronoun
pronominal/e pronominal
prononcer to pronounce
prononciation *f.* pronunciation
propos *m.* remark
à propos de on the subject of, about
proposer to propose, to suggest
propre one's own, 6-1; clean
propriétaire *m./f.* landlord/landlady; homeowner, 6-1
protéger † to protect, 10-2
protester to protest, 10-3
prothèse *f.* artificial limb, prosthesis
proverbe *m.* proverb
province *f.* province
provisions *f. pl.* food supplies
provoquer to provoke
proximité *f.* nearness, closeness, proximity
à proximité de near
prune *f.* plum
psychologie *f.* psychology, 3-2
psychologique psychological
psychologue *m./f.* psychologist
public *m.* public, 3-3
avoir un contact avec le public to have contact with the public, 3-3
public/publique *adj.* public
publicitaire *adj.* promotional, advertising
publicité *f.* (**une pub**) advertisement, 11-3
travailler dans la publicité to work in advertising
puce *f.* flea
marché *m.* **aux puces** flea market
puis then, 5-3
pull(-over) *m.* pullover sweater, 4-3
punir to punish, 6-1

Q

qualification *f.* label, description, qualification
quand when, 2-1
quand même anyway, just the same
quantité *f.* quantity, 5-3
quarante forty, 1-2
quart *m.* quarter, 4-2
et quart a quarter after, 4-2
moins le quart a quarter to, 4-2
quart d'heure *m.* quarter of an hour, 4-2
quartier *m.* neighborhood, 6-1
quatorze fourteen, 1-2
quatorzième fourteenth, 6-1
quatre four, 1-2
quatrième fourth, 6-1
quatre-vingts eighty, 1-2
quatre-vingt-dix ninety, 1-2
quatre-vingt-onze ninety-one, 1-2
que (qu') what, whom, which, that, 8-2
qu'est-ce que/qui ... ? what . . . ?, 8-2
Qu'est-ce que tu as ? What's wrong?, 7-3
quel/le which, 8-1
Quel âge as-tu/avez-vous ? How old are you?, 1-2

Quel est ton/votre âge ? What's your age?, 1-2
Quelle est la date ? What's the date?, 1-2
Quelle heure est-il ? What time is it?, 4-2
Quel temps fait-il ? What's the weather like?, 8-1
quelque some
quelque chose something, 5-1
quelquefois sometimes, 4-1
quelque part somewhere, 8-3
quelqu'un someone, 8-3
question *f.* question, 2-1
poser une question to ask a question, 2-1
questionnaire *m.* questionnaire, survey of questions
queue *f.* line (of people)
qui who, which, whom, 2-1
quinze fifteen, 1-2
quinze jours two weeks
quinzième fifteenth, 6-1
quitter to leave, 4-2
quoi what, 8-2
n'importe quoi anything, no matter what
Quoi de neuf ? What's new?
quotidien *m.* daily publication, 11-3
quotidien/ne daily

R

rabbin *m.* rabbi
racine *f.* root, origin, 7-1
avoir des racines to have roots/origins, 7-1
raconter to tell a story, 11-1
radio *f.* radio, 1-3
écouter la radio to listen to the radio, 1-3
radio-revéil *m.* clock radio, 4-2
rafraîchissant/e refreshing, 5-1
raisin *m.* grape, 5-3
raison *f.* reason
avoir raison to be right
raisonnable reasonable, 1-1
rajouter to add (some) more
randonnée *f.* hike, 8-2
faire † une randonnée to take a hike, 8-2
ranger † to arrange, to tidy up, 6-2
rap *m.* rap music
rapide quick, rapid
rapidement quickly, rapidly
rappel *m.* reminder
se rappeler † to remember, 7-3
rapport *m.* relationship, 7-1; report
avoir des bons rapports avec qqn to get along well with sb, 7-1
rare rare
rarement rarely, 4-1
se raser to shave, 4-1
rasoir *m.* razor, 4-1
rater to miss, 7-1
ravi/e delighted, 7-3
rayon *m.* supermarket section, aisle, 5-3
rayon boucherie meat counter, 5-3
rayon boulangerie-pâtisserie bakery/pastry aisle, 5-3
rayon charcuterie deli counter, 5-3
rayon crèmerie dairy aisle
rayon fruits et légumes produce aisle, 5-3
rayon poissonnerie fish counter, 5-3
rayon surgelés frozen foods, 5-3
rayonnement *m.* influence
réagir to react
réalisateur *m.*, **réalisatrice** *f.* film director, 11-1
réaliste realistic, 1-1
rebelle rebellious, 7-1
récemment recently
recensement *m.* census
récent/e recent
réception *f.* welcome; reception (room)
réceptionniste *m./f.* receptionist
recette *f.* recipe
recevoir † to receive, 11-2
réchauffement *m.* **climatique** global warming, 10-2
réchauffer to reheat
recherche *f.* research, 11-2
à la recherche de in search of
faire † de la recherche to do research
récipient *m.* container
réciprocité *f.* reciprocity
récit *m.* narrative, 5-3
réciter to recite
recommandation *f.* recommendation, 11-3
recommander to recommend
recommencer (à) † to begin again
récompense *f.* reward, award
recomposé/e blended, put together again
famille *f.* **recomposée** blended family, 7-1
reconnaître † to recognize
reconstitué/e reconstituted
recyclage *m.* recycling, 10-2
recycler to recycle, 10-2
rédacteur *m.*, **rédactrice** editor
rédaction *f.* composition, short essay
rédiger to compose, write
réduction *f.* reduction, cut
réduire † to reduce, 10-1
réduit/e reduced, lower
réfléchi/e reflexive; thoughtful
pronom *m.* **réfléchi** reflexive pronoun
réfléchir à to think of/about, 6-1
reflet *m.* reflection, 12-2
refléter to reflect
réflexion *f.* reflection
réforme *f.* reform
refrain *m.* chorus, refrain
réfrigérateur *m.* (**un frigo**, *colloq.*) refrigerator, 6-2
refroidir to cool down
refuser (de) to refuse, 8-3
regarder to watch, 1-3
regarder la télé to watch TV, 1-3
Regardez le tableau ! Look at the board!, P-2
regarder un film to watch a film on TV, 1-3
régime *m.* diet, 10-1
être au régime to be on a diet
faire † / suivre † un régime to diet, 10-1
région *f.* area, region
régional/e regional
règle *f.* ruler, P-2
régler to adjust, to regulate
regret *m.* regret
regretter to be sorry, to regret, 8-3
régulier/-ière regular
régulièrement regularly
reine *f.* queen
relation *f.* relation, relationship
relation familiale family relation, 1-1
relier to join, link together
religieux/-euse religious
religion *f.* religion
relire † to reread
remarié/e remarried, 1-1
remarquer to notice, to observe; to point out
rembourser to reimburse
remède *m.* remedy
remercier to thank, P-2
Je te/vous remercie. Thank you.
Je te/vous remercie d'être venu/e. Thank you for coming.
remettre † to hand in/over, 6-2; to put off
remplacer to replace
remue-méninges *m. inv.* brainstorming
rencontre *f.* meeting, encounter
rencontrer to meet
se rencontrer to meet (each other), 7-3
rendez-vous *m.* meeting, date, appointment, 8-3
rendre (à) to hand in, P-2; to give back, 3-1
rendre visite à to visit someone, 3-1
se rendre to go
rénové/e renovated, 6-2
renseignement *m.* information, 9-3
renseigner to inform
se renseigner to get information, 9-3
rentrée *f.* back-to-school
rentrer to return home, 4-1; to go/come back, 5-3
répandu/e widespread
réparer to repair

repartir to leave again
repas *m.* meal, 5-2
  repas équilibré well-balanced meal, 10-1
répéter † to repeat, P-2; to rehearse
répétition *f.* rehearsal, 12-1; repetition
replanter to replant
réplique *f.* line in a play; retort
répondre (à) to answer, 3-1
  Répondez en français ! Answer in French!, P-2
répondeur *m.* **(automatique)** answering machine
reportage *m.* report (esp. news), 11-1
repos *m.* rest, 8-2
se reposer to rest, 7-3
reprendre † to take back
représentant *m.*, **représentante** *f.* **de commerce** sales representative, 3-3
représentation *f.* (theatrical) production, 12-1; representation
réputation *f.* reputation
réseau *m.* network, 11-2
  réseau sans fil wireless network, 11-2
réservation *f.* reservation
réserve *f.* **naturelle** nature reserve
réservé/e reserved, 1-1
réserver to reserve
résidence *f.* dormitory, 3-1
résidentiel/le residential, 6-1
résolu/e *adj.* resolved
résoudre to resolve, to solve, 10-3
respirer to breathe
responsabilité *f.* responsibility, 3-3
ressembler à to look like, to resemble
  se ressembler to look alike, to be alike
ressentir to feel, be affected by, 7-1
ressource *f.* resource
  ressource naturelle natural resource, 10-2
restaurant *m.* restaurant, 2-3
  restaurant universitaire (resto U) dining hall, 3-1
restauration *f.* restaurant business, catering
  restauration à la chaîne chain restaurant business
rester to stay, 1-3
  rester à la maison to stay home, 1-3
  rester à la résidence to stay in the dorm, 2-2
  rester en forme to stay in shape, 10-1
résultat *m.* result
résumé *m.* summary
résumer to summarize
résurrection *f.* resurrection
retard : être en retard to be late, 4-2
retenir † to retain, 9-2
retomber to fall again
retoucher to edit pictures, to touch up, 11-2
retour *m.* return
retourner to go back, 5-3
retraite *f.* retirement
  prendre † sa retraite to retire
retransmettre † to broadcast, to retransmit
retrouver (qqn) to meet up with (sb), 3-1
  se retrouver to meet, 7-3
réunion *f.* meeting, 9-2
se réunir to get together
réussir (à) to succeed/pass, 6-1
  réussir un examen to pass an exam, 3-2
réutiliser to reuse
rêve *m.* dream
  faire † un rêve to have a dream
réveil *m.* alarm clock, 4-2
se réveiller to wake up, 4-1
réveillon *m.* Christmas or New Year's Eve
revenir † to return, 5-3
rêver (de) to dream, 12-1
réviser to review, 1-3
revoir † to see again
  au revoir good-bye, P-1
révolution *f.* revolution
revue *f.* review, journal
rez-de-chaussée *m.* **(RdeCh)** ground floor, 6-1
rhume *m.* cold
rideau *m.* curtain, 6-2
rien *m.* nothing
  De rien. Not at all. You're welcome., P-2
  ne … rien nothing, 8-3
rire *m.* laugh
rire to laugh
ris *m. pl.* **de veau** veal sweetbreads
risque *m.* risk
risquer (de) to risk, run the risk of, 12-3
rite *m.* rite, ritual
rituel *m.* ritual
rivière *f.* large stream or river (tributary), 6-3
riz *m.* rice, 5-2
robe *f.* dress, 4-3
robot *m.* robot
rock *m.* rock music, 2-2
roi *m.* king
rôle *m.* role, part
roman *m.* novel, 11-3
romanche *m.* Romansch (language spoken in Switzerland)
rond/e round
rosbif *m.* roast beef, 5-3
rose pink, 4-3
rose *f.* rose (flower)
rosé *m.* rosé wine, 5-1
rôti *m.* roast, 5-3
  poulet *m.* **rôti** rotisserie chicken
  rôti de porc pork roast, 5-3
rôtie *f.* (*Can.*) piece of toast, 5-2
rouge red, 4-3
rougir to blush, 6-1
routine *f.* routine, 4-1
roux/-sse redhead, redhaired, 2-1
rue *f.* street, 6-1
rugby *m.* rugby, 2-2
rupture *f.* break, rupture
rural/e rural, 9-3
rythme *m.* rhythm

S

sa *f.* his, her, 1-1
sac *m.* purse, 4-3; sack
  sac à dos backpack, 9-1
  sac à main ladies' handbag
  sac en plastique plastic bag, 10-2
sage wise; well-behaved (for children)
saison *f.* season, 8-1
salade *f.* salad, lettuce, 5-1
  salade de fruits fruit salad
  salade verte green salad, 5-1
salaire *m.* salary, 3-3
salle *f.* room, P-2
  salle à manger dining room, 6-1
  salle de bains bathroom, 6-1
  salle de classe classroom, P-2
  salle de séjour living room, 6-1
  salle de spectacle auditorium
salon *m.* lounge, living room
  salon de coiffure hairdressing salon
saluer to greet, P-1
salut hi, bye, P-1
samedi Saturday, 1-3
  samedi dernier last Saturday, 5-2
sandale *f.* sandal, 4-3
sandwich *m.* (**sandwichs** *pl.*) sandwich, 5-1
  sandwich au jambon ham sandwich, 5-1
  sandwich au fromage cheese sandwich, 5-1
sang *m.* blood
sang-froid *m.* composure, 7-3
sanglot *m.* sob
sans without, P-2
  sans doute undoubtedly
  sans problème no problem, 5-1
sapin *m.* pine tree, 6-3; Christmas tree, 7-2
satellite *f.* satellite
satisfait/e satisfied, happy
sauce *f.* sauce
saumon *m.* salmon, 5-3
sauter to jump, to skip
  sauter un repas to skip a meal, 10-1
sauvage wild, savage
sauvegarder (un fichier) to save (a file), 11-2; to protect, 10-2
sauver to protect, 10-2
savane *f.* savannah

savoir † to know (how), 8-2
savon *m.* soap, 4-1
saxophone *m.* saxophone, 2-2
scanner *m.* scanner, 11-2
scénario *m.* screenplay, script, scenario
science *f.* science, 3-2
  sciences *pl.* **de l'éducation** education, 3-2
  sciences *pl.* **économiques** economics, 3-2
  sciences *pl.* **humaines** social sciences, 3-2
  sciences *pl.* **naturelles** natural sciences, 3-2
  sciences *pl.* **physiques** physical sciences, 3-2
  sciences *pl.* **politiques** political science, 3-2
science-fiction *f.* science fiction, 11-1
  film *m.* **de science-fiction** science fiction film, 11-1
scientifique *adj.* scientific
scientifique *m.* scientist
scolarité *f.* schooling
sculpteur *m.* sculptor, 12-2
sculpture *f.* sculpture, 3-2
séance *f.* showing at a movie theater
sec/sèche dry
secondaire secondary
secrétaire *m./f.* secretary, 3-3
secteur *m.* sector
  secteur privé private sector
  secteur public public sector
sécurisant/e reassuring, 7-1
sécurité *f.* security
sédentaire unmoving, sedentary
seize sixteen, 1-2
seizième sixteenth, 6-1
séjour *m.* living room, 6-1; stay (abroad)
sel *m.* salt, 5-2
selon according to
semaine *f.* week, 1-3
  la semaine prochaine next week, 2-3
  par semaine per week
semblable *adj.* similar
sembler to appear
  il me semble it seems to me, 6-3
semestre *m.* semester, 3-2
semi-voyelle *f.* semivowel, glide
semoule *f.* semolina
Sénégal *m.* Senegal, 9-2
sénégalais/e Senegalese, 9-2
sens *m.* meaning; direction, way
sensible sensitive, 7-3
sentiment *m.* feeling, 7-3
sentimental/e sentimental
sentir to smell
se sentir to feel
séparer to divide, to pull apart, to separate
  se séparer to separate (couple), 7-3
sept seven, 1-2
septembre September, 1-2
septième seventh, 6-1
série *f.* TV serial, 11-1; series
sérieux/-euse serious, 2-1
sérigraphie *f.* silkscreen printing
se serrer la main to shake hands
serveur *m.*, **serveuse** *f.* server (in restaurant), 3-3
service *m.* service, tip
  Le service est compris ? Is the tip included?
  service compris gratuity included
services *m. pl.* service sector, 3-3
serviette *f.* **(de toilette)** towel, 4-1
servir to serve, 4-2
  se servir de (qqch) to use (sthg), 11-2
ses *pl.* his, her, 1-1
seul/e *adj.* alone, only
seulement only, 5-1
Seychelles *f. pl.* Seychelle Islands
shampooing *m.* shampoo, 4-1
short *m. sg.* shorts, 4-3
si yes, 1-3; if, whether, 7-3
SIDA *m.* AIDS
siècle *m.* century
sieste *f.* nap
  faire † la sieste to take a nap
sigle *m.* initials, acronym
signaler to indicate, to be a sign of
signe *m.* sign
silence *m.* silence
s'il te/vous plaît please, P-2
similaire alike, similar
similarité *f.* likeness, similarity
simplifier to simplify
singulier/-ière singular
sinon *adv.* otherwise, or else
sirène *f.* siren, foghorn; mermaid
sirop *m.* syrup
site *m.* site, 9-3
  site culturel cultural site, 9-3
  site historique historical site, 9-3
  site Web Web site, 11-2
situé/e located, situated, 6-1
situer to situate
six six, 1-2
sixième sixth, 6-1
ski *m.* skiing, 8-2
  faire † du ski to ski, 8-2
  faire † du ski nautique to water ski, 8-2
  ski de fond cross-country skiing
  ski de piste downhill skiing
slogan *m.* slogan
SNCF *f.* (**Société** *f.* **nationale des chemins de fer français**) French national railway company
snack-bar *m.* snack bar
soccer *m.* (*Can.*) soccer
sociable outgoing, 1-1
socialisme *m.* socialism
sociologie *f.* sociology, 3-2
sœur *f.* sister, 1-1
  belle-sœur sister-in-law, 7-1
  demi-sœur stepsister
se soigner to take care of oneself
soie *f.* silk, 4-3
soif *f.* thirst, 5-1
  avoir † soif to be thirsty, 5-1
soin *m.* care
  soins *pl.* **dentaires** dental care
  soins *pl.* **médicaux** medical care, treatment
soir *m.* evening, 1-3
  ce soir tonight, 2-3
  du soir in the evening, P.M., 4-2
soirée *f.* evening, 8-3
  Bonne soirée ! Have a good evening!
soixante sixty, 1-2
soixante-et-un sixty-one, 1-2
soixante-dix seventy, 1-2
soixante-et-onze seventy-one, 1-2
sol *m.* ground, earth
  sous-sol *m.* basement, under ground 6-1
solde *f.* sale, 4-3
  en solde on sale
soldé/e *adj.* on sale
soleil *m.* sun, 8-1
  Il y a du soleil. It's sunny., 8-1
solidarité *f.* solidarity
solution *f.* solution
sombre somber, dark, 12-2
sommaire *m.* brief table of contents
somme *f.* amount, sum
sommeil *m.* sleep
  avoir sommeil to be tired
sommet *m.* top, summit
son *m. adj.* his, her, 1-1
son *m.* sound, volume
  baisser le son to turn down the volume
sondage *m.* survey, poll
sonner to ring, 4-2
sonore resonant, sonorous
  pollution *f.* **sonore** noise pollution, 10-2
sophistiqué/e sophisticated
sortie *f.* outing, trip
sortir to go out, 4-2
souci *m.* worry, concern
  se faire † du souci to worry, 7-3
souhaiter to hope, to wish, 10-2
soulier *m.* (*Can.*) shoe
soumettre † to submit
soupe *f.* soup, 5-2
souper *m.* (*Can.*) dinner, 5-2
souper to have supper/dinner
source *f.* source, credit
sourd/e *adj.* deaf
souris *f.* mouse, 11-2
  souris sans fil wireless mouse, 11-2
sous under, below, 6-2
  sous les toits in the attic, 6-2
sous-sol *m.* basement, 6-1

sous-titre *m.* subtitle, 11-1
sous-titré/e subtitled
soutenir † to support, 9-2
soutien *m.* support; aid
souvenir *m.* memory, recollection; souvenir, memento
se souvenir † de to remember
souvent often, 4-1
soyez *see* **être**
spécial/e peculiar, special
spécialisation *f.* **(en)** major (in), 3-2
spécialité *f.* speciality
spectacle *m.* show, 12-3
  spectacle son et lumière sound and light historical production, 9-3
sport *m.* sport, 2-2
  faire † du sport to do/play sports, 2-2
  sports d'hiver winter sports, 8-2
sportif/-ive athletic, 2-1
stade *m.* stadium, 2-3
stage *m.* internship, professional training
standardiste *m./f.* telephone operator, receptionist
station *f.* **de métro** subway stop, 3-1
statistique *f.* statistic
stéréotype *m.* stereotype
stress *m.* stress
stressé/e stressed, P-1
strophe *f.* stanza
studio *m.* studio apartment, 6-1
style *m.* style, 12-2
stylo *m.* pen, P-2
subjonctif *m.* subjunctive mood
subventionné/e subsidized
succès *m.* success
succession *f.* sequence, succession
sucre *m.* sugar, 5-1
sucré/e sweet (for food)
sud *m.* south
suggérer † to suggest, 3-2
suisse *adj.* Swiss, 9-2
Suisse *f.* Switzerland, 9-2
suivant/e *adj.* following, next
suivi/e *adj.* consistent, continuous; followed by
suivre † to follow, 3-2
  suivre un cours to take a course, 3-2
  suivre un régime to be on a diet, 10-1
sujet *m.* subject, 12-2
super super, 4-2
superbe superb
superlatif *m.* superlative
supermarché *m.* supermarket
superstition *f.* superstition
supplément *m.* extra or additional part
  en supplément extra charge
supplémentaire extra or additional
sur over, on, 6-2
surconsommation *f.* overconsumption
sûr/e sure
  bien sûr of course, 2-1
surf *m.* surfing, 8-2
  faire † du surf to surf, 8-2
  faire † du surf des neiges to snowboard, 8-2
surface *f.* surface area
  grande surface superstore, 5-3
surfer (sur Internet) to surf (the Internet), 10-3
surgelé/e *adj.* frozen, 5-3
surgelés *m. pl.* frozen foods, 5-3
surpopulation *f.* overpopulation
surprenant/e surprising
surprendre † to surprise
surpris/e surprised, 7-3
surtout above all, 6-2
surveiller to oversee
survol *m.* overview, survey
sympa(thique) nice, 1-1
symptôme *m.* symptom
synagogue *f.* synagogue
syncopé/e syncopated, irregular (rhythm)
syndicat *m.* (trade) union
  Syndicat d'initiative tourist office
système *m.* system

T

ta *f.* your, 1-1
tabac *m.* specialty shop for tobacco products, newspapers, magazines
table *f.* table
  table basse coffee table, 6-2
tableau *m.* board, P-2; painting 12-2; chart, table
tâche *f.* chore, task
taille *f.* waist, 10-1; size
  de taille moyenne average height, 2-1
tailleur *m.* women's suit, 4-3
talon *m.* heel
  chaussure *f.* **à talons** high-heeled shoe, 4-3
  talons *pl.* **hauts** high heels
  talons *pl.* **plats** flat heels
tant *adv.* (so) much
  tant d'autres so many others
tante *f.* aunt, 1-1
taper to type
tapis *m.* rug, 6-2
tapisserie *f.* tapestry, 12-2
tard late, 4-1
tarte *f.* pie, 5-3
  tarte aux pommes apple pie, 5-2
tartelette *f.* small pie or tart
tartine *f.* slice of bread, 5-2
tasse *f.* cup, 5-1
taux *m.* rate, level
  taux de cholestérol cholesterol level
taxi *m.* taxi, 9-1
te (t') *pron.* you, to you, 7-2
technicien *m.* **(de labo), technicienne** *f.* **(de labo)** lab technician, 3-3
technologie *f.* technology
technologique technological
technophile *m.* technology-lover
technophobe *m.* technology-hater
tee-shirt *m.* T-shirt, 4-3
télé *f.* = **télévision**
téléachat *m.* infomercial, 11-1
télécharger to download, 11-2
télécommande *f.* TV remote control, 11-1
téléfilm *m.* made-for-TV film, 11-1
téléphoner (à qqn) to phone (sb), 1-3
  se téléphoner to phone one another, 7-3
téléréalité *f.* reality TV, 11-1
téléspectateur *m.*, **téléspectatrice** *f.* TV viewer
télévisé/e televised
télévision *f.* TV, television, P-2
  télévision numérique digital TV
  télévision satellite satellite TV
tempérament *m.* disposition, temperament
température *f.* temperature, 8-1
tempéré/e temperate
temple *m.* (Protestant) church
temps *m.* weather, 8-1; time; tense
  depuis combien de temps...? for how long . . . ?, 11-3
  de temps en temps from time to time
  Quel temps fait-il ? What's the weather like?, 8-1
  temps libre free time
tendance *f.* tendency
tendre tender, affectionate
tendresse *f.* tenderness
tenir † to hold, 9-2
tennis *m.* tennis, 1-3; *m. pl.* tennis shoes
tension *f.* tension; blood pressure
tente *f.* tent
terminer to end, to finish, 7-1
terrain *m.* **de sport** playing field, court, 3-1
terrasse *f.* terrace, 6-1
terre (Terre) *f.* earth (the Earth), 10-2
  par terre on the floor, 6-2
terrine *f.* loaf made of ground meats, fish, and/or vegetables
territoire *m.* territory
tes *pl.* your, 1-1
tête *f.* head, 10-1
têtu/e stubborn, 1-1
TGV *m.* (**train** *m.* **à grande vitesse**) TGV, high-speed train
thé *m.* tea, 5-1
  thé au citron with lemon
  thé au lait with milk, 5-1

théâtre *m.* theater, 2-3
théâtre romain Roman theater, 9-3
thème *m.* theme
thèse *f.* thesis
thon *m.* tuna, 5-3
ticket *m.* (subway) ticket, 9-1
tigre *m.* tiger
timide shy, 1-1
tirage *m.* printing, circulation in print
tirer to pull, to draw, to fire
tirer une conclusion to draw a conclusion
tirer un feu d'artifice to shoot fireworks
tisane *f.* herbal tea
tisane à la menthe mint herbal tea
tissu *m.* fabric, 4-3
titre *m.* title
toilette : faire † sa toilette to wash oneself
toilettes *f. pl.* toilets, restroom, 6-1
articles *m. pl.* **de toilette** toiletries, 4-1
toi you, P-1
toi-même yourself
toit *m.* roof, 6-2
sous les toits in the attic, 6-2
tomate *f.* tomato, 5-3
tomate bio(logique) organic tomato, 5-3
tombe *f.* grave, gravestone
tombée : à la tombée de la nuit at nightfall
tomber to fall, 5-2
tomber amoureux/-euse (de) to fall in love (with), 7-3
ton *adj.* your, 1-1
ton *m.* shade, tone
tonnerre *m.* thunder, 8-1
Il y a du tonnerre. There is thunder., 8-1
tornade *f.* tornado, 10-2
tôt early, 4-1
toujours always, 4-1
tour *f.* tower
tour *m.* trip, outing, visit; round
faire † un tour take a walk
premier tour first round of voting
second tour second round of voting
tour de scrutin voting round
tourisme *m.* tourism
faire † du tourisme *m.* to go sightseeing, 8-2
tourner to turn, 9-3
tourner un film to shoot a film, 11-1
tous *m. pl.* all
tout *m.* everything
tout, tous, toute, toutes all, 4-1
tous/toutes les... every . . . , 4-1
tous les jours every day, 4-1
tout à fait completely, 11-1
tout de suite right away, immediately
tout droit straight ahead, 9-3
tout le monde everyone, everybody, 11-2
tousser to cough
toux *f.* cough
toxique toxic
trace *f.* trace
tradition *f.* tradition
traditionnel/le traditional, 7-1
musique *f.* **traditionnelle** traditional music, 12-1
traduction *f.* translation
traduire translate
tragédie *f.* tragedy
train *m.* train, 9-1
être en train de + *inf.* to be busy doing sthg, 4-1
traitement de texte *m.* word processing, editing
tramway *m.* tram, 9-1
tranche *f.* slice, 5-2
tranquil/le calm, tranquil, 6-1
transfert *m.* transfer
transport *m.* **en commun** public transportation, 10-2
travail *m.* work, 3-3
avoir le goût du travail to have a strong work ethic, 7-1
travailler to work, to study, 1-3
travailler dans le jardin to work in the garden/yard, 1-3
travailleur/-euse hardworking, 7-1
travers : à travers across, through
traverser to cross, 9-3
treize thirteen, 1-2
treizième thirteenth, 6-1
trente thirty, 1-2
trente-et-un thirty-one, 1-2
très very, P-1
Très bien, merci. Very well, thank you., P-1
triangle *m.* triangle
trier to sort, 10-2
trimestre *m.* trimester, quarter, 3-2
trio *m.* trio, 12-1
triste sad, 7-3
trois three, 1-2
troisième third, 6-1
trombone *m.* trombone, 12-1
trompette *f.* trumpet, 12-1
trop too much, 1-1
troupe *f.* troop
trouver to find, 4-2
Je trouve que... I find that . . . , 11-1
se trouver to be located, 3-1
truite *f.* trout
tu you, P-1
tuer to kill
tulipe *f.* tulip
tuque *f.* (*Can.*) ski cap
typique typical, 1-3

U

un one, 1-2
un/e a, an, one, P-2
-unième : vingt-et-unième twenty-first, 6-1
uni/e united
uniforme *adj.* regular, uniform
uniforme *m.* uniform
union *f.* **libre** cohabitation, 7-1
universel/le universal
universitaire related to the university
université *f.* university, 3-1
urbain/e related to the city, urban
urgence *f.* emergency
urgent urgent, 10-1
usage *m.* use, custom, (language) usage
usé/e waste, used
usine *f.* factory, 10-2
utile useful, 8-1
utilisation *f.* use
utilisation de la lumière use of light, 12-2
utiliser to use, 10-3

V

vacances *f. pl.* vacation, 6-3
grandes vacances summer vacation, 7-2
vague *f.* (ocean) wave, 10-2
vaisselle *f.* dishes
faire † la vaisselle to do the dishes, 5-2
valise *f.* suitcase, 9-1
vallée *f.* valley, 6-3
valoir † to be worth
ça vaut le coup it's worth it, 12-3
Il vaut/vaudrait mieux que... It is/would be better (best) that . . . , 10-1
valse *f.* waltz
vaste vast
vaut *see* **valoir**
vedette *f.* movie star, 11-1
veille : en veille on stand-by (an appliance)
vélo *m.* bicycle, 2-2
faire † du vélo to ride a bicycle, to go bike riding, 2-2
vendeur *m.*, **vendeuse** *f.* sales clerk, 3-3
vendre to sell, 3-1
vendredi Friday, 1-3
venir † to come, 5-3
venir de + *inf.* to have just (done sthg), 9-2
vent *m.* wind, 8-1
Il y a du vent. It's windy., 8-1
vente *f.* sales
ventre *m.* belly, abdomen, 10-1
avoir † mal au ventre to have a stomachache, 10-1

verbal/e verbal
verbe *m.* verb
  verbe pronominal reflexive verb
verglas *m.* sleet, ice on the ground, 8-1
  Il y a du verglas. It's icy, slippery., 8-1
vérifier to check, verify
vérité *f.* truth, 7-1
verre *m.* glass, 5-1
vers toward, around, 4-2
vers *m.* line of verse
verser to pour
version *f.* version
  version française (V.F.) dubbed in French
  version multilingue (V.M.) available dubbed in several languages using digital TV
  version originale (V.O.) in the original language, 11-1
  en version originale avec des sous-titres en français (en V.O.S.T.F.) in the original language with French subtitles, 11-1
vert/e green, 4-3 ; unripe
veste *f.* jacket, suit coat, 4-3
vestimentaire *adj.* pertaining to clothes
vêtement *m.* clothing, 4-3
viande *f.* meat, 5-2
vidéocassette *f.* videotape
vie *f.* life, 6-3
vieux (vieil), vieille old, 3-1
Vietnam *m.* Vietnam, 9-2
vietnamien/ne *adj.* Vietnamese, 9-2
vif/vive *adj.* bright, vivid, 12-2
villa *f.* house in a residential area, villa, 6-3
village *m.* village, 9-3
  village médiéval medieval village, 9-3
  village perché village perched on a hillside, 9-3
ville *f.* city, 2-1
vin *m.* wine, 5-1
  vin blanc white wine, 5-1
  vin rosé rosé wine, 5-1
  vin rouge red wine, 5-1
vinaigre *m.* vinegar, 5-3
vingt twenty, 1-2
vingt-et-un twenty-one, 1-2
vingt-deux twenty-two, 1-2
vingtième twentieth, 6-1
violon *m.* violin, 12-1
violoncelle *m.* cello, 12-1
virtuel *m.* virtual reality
virus *m.* virus
visage *m.* face, 10-1
vision *f.* vision
  avoir une vision du monde to have a worldview, 7-1
visite *f.* visit, 3-1
  rendre visite à to visit a person, 3-1
visiter to visit a place, 8-2
vitesse *f.* speed
vitrine *f.* display window, 4-3
vive... (les vacances) ! hurray for . . . (vacation)!, 5-2
vivre † to live, 7-1
vœu *m.* wish, 7-2
  Meilleurs vœux ! Best wishes!, 7-2
voici ... here is/are . . . , P-1
voilà ... here/there is/are . . . , P-2
voile *f.* sail, sailing
  faire † de la voile to go sailing, 8-2
voile *m.* veil
voilé/e veiled
voir † to see, 2-3
  voir une exposition to see an exhibit, 2-3
  voir un film to see a film (in a cinema), 2-3
  voir une pièce to see a play, 2-3
  Voyons ! See here!, 7-3
  Voyons ... Let's see . . . , 9-1
voisin *m.*, **voisine** *f.* neighbor, 6-1
voiture *f.* automobile, car, 3-1
  voiture hybride hybrid car
voix *f.* voice
  à haute voix out loud
vol *m.* flight, 9-1
voler to fly; to steal
volley(-ball) *m.* volleyball, 2-2
volonté *f.* wish, will
  de bonne volonté *adv.* willingly
Volontiers. With pleasure, gladly., 8-3
vomir to vomit
vos *pl.* your, 1-2
voter to vote, 10-3
votre *m./f.* your, 1-2
vouloir † to want, to wish, 3-3
  je voudrais I would like, 5-1
vous you, P-1; *pron.* to you, 7-2
  vous-même yourself
  vous-mêmes yourselves
voyage *m.* trip, voyage, 9-1
voyager † to travel, 3-3
voyant/e *m./f.* fortune-teller
voyelle *f.* vowel
voyons *see* **voir**
vrai/e true
  C'est vrai. That's true.
  C'est pas vrai ! It can't be!, 8-2
vraiment really, 1-1
vue *f.* view
  vue d'ensemble overview
vulnérable vulnerable

W

W.-C. *m. pl.* toilets, restroom (*lit.* water closet), 6-1
webcam *f.* webcam, 11-2
week-end *m.* weekend, 1-3
  ce week-end this weekend, 2-3
  le week-end on weekends, every weekend, 6-3
western *m.* western (film), 11-1
Wi-Fi *m.* wireless network, 11-2
wolof *m.* Wolof (language spoken in Senegal)

Y

y *pron.* there, 9-1
  y compris including, 10-3
yaourt *m.* yogurt, 5-2
yeux *m. pl. see* œil

Z

zèbre *m.* zebra
zéro *m.* zero, 1-2
zoologie *f.* zoology, 3-2
Zut (alors) ! Darn!, 4-2

Appendice 7

LEXIQUE ANGLAIS-FRANÇAIS

A

a, an un/e
abdomen ventre *m.*
able: to be able to pouvoir †
about de, environ
  it is about . . . il s'agit de...
abroad à l'étranger
absent, missing absent/e
accident accident *m.*
according to d'après
accountant comptable *m./f.*
accounting comptabilité *f.*
ache mal (des maux) *m.*
acquaintance connaissance *f.*
across from en face de
action film film *m.* d'action
active actif/-ive
activity activité *f.*
actor/actress acteur *m.*, actrice *f.*
address adresse *f.*
  address book carnet *m.* d'adresses
to adore adorer
adventure movie film d'aventures *m.*
advertisement annonce *f.*, publicité *f.* (pub)
to be affected by ressentir
affectionate affectueux/-euse
afraid: to be afraid avoir peur
Africa Afrique *f.*
African africain/e
after, afterward après
  after having . . . après avoir/être + part. passé...
afternoon après-midi *m.*
  in the afternoon, P.M. de l'après-midi
again encore
age âge *m.*
  What is your age? Quel est ton/votre âge ?, Quel âge as-tu/avez-vous ?
aged, old âgé/e
ago il y a...
  two days ago il y a deux jours
to (not) agree (ne pas) être † d'accord
air air *m.*
  air conditioning climatisation *f.*
  air pollution pollution *f.* atmosphérique
airplane avion *m.*
airport aéroport *m.*
aisle (in a store) rayon *m.*
alarm clock réveil *m.*
alcohol alcool *m.*
Algeria Algérie *f.*
Algerian algérien/ne
alive vivant/e
all tout, tous, toute, toutes
  all alone tout/e seul/e
  all of a sudden tout d'un coup
  all right d'accord
  all the same quand même
  all the time tout le temps, toujours
to allow permettre † de
almost presque, à peu près
alone seul
along: to get along (with) s'entendre (avec)
Alps Alpes *f. pl.*
already déjà
also aussi
always toujours
ambitious ambitieux/-euse
America Amérique *f.*
  Central America Amérique centrale
  Latin America Amérique latine
  North America Amérique du nord
  South America Amérique du sud
American américain/e
amphitheater amphithéâtre *m.*
amputated amputé/e
to amuse oneself se distraire, s'amuser
amusements distractions *f. pl.*
amusing drôle, amusant/e
and et
anger colère *f.*
angry fâché/e, en colère
  to become angry se fâcher
animal animal *m.*
animated film film *m.* d'animation
ankle cheville *f.*
to announce annoncer
announcement (public) annonce *f.*
  birth announcement faire-part *m. inv.* de naissance
  civil union announcement faire-part *m. inv.* de PACS
  wedding announcement faire-part *m. inv.* de mariage
to answer répondre (à)
  to answer the phone répondre au téléphone
  to answer a question répondre à une question
answer réponse *f.*
  answering machine répondeur *m.*
anthropology anthropologie *f.*
antique ancien/ne
antibiotic antibiotique *m.*
anxious anxieux/-euse ; inquiet/-ète
anyway quand même
apartment appartement *m.*
to appear (good) avoir l'air (bon)
appetizer entrée *f.*
apple pomme *f.*
April avril
Arabic arabe *m.*
architect architecte *m./f.*
Argentina Argentine *f.*
Argentinian argentin/e
to argue se disputer
arm bras *m.*
armchair fauteuil *m.*
armoire armoire *f.*
around vers, autour de
to arrange ranger †
to arrive arriver
arrival arrivée *f.*
art art *m.*
  art book livre *m.* d'art
article article *m.*
as comme
  as . . . as aussi... que
  as many/much . . . as autant (de)... que
  as soon as dès que, aussitôt que
Asia Asie *f.*
Asian asiatique
to ask demander
  to ask a question poser une question
  to ask for directions demander le chemin
asleep endormi/e
asparagus asperge *f.*
aspirin aspirine *f.*
assignment devoir *m.*
association association *f.*
  humanitarian association association humanitaire
  student association association étudiante
astronomy astronomie *f.*
at à
  at last enfin
  at once tout de suite
  at X's house chez X
  at the same time en même temps
  at the side of au bord de
athletic sportif/-ive
Atlantic Ocean océan *m.* Atlantique
atlas atlas *m.*
to attend assister à
attention attention *f.*
  to pay attention faire † attention
attorney avocat/e *m./f.*
August août
aunt tante *f.*
Australia Australie *f.*
Australian australien/ne
Austria Autriche *f.*
Austrian autrichien/ne
author auteur *m.*
authoritarian autoritaire
autumn automne *m.*

avenue avenue *f.*
awake réveillé/e
away: right away tout de suite
automobile voiture *f.*

B

baby bébé *m.*
  to babysit faire † du baby-sitting
back dos *m.*
  to come back revenir †
  backpack sac *m.* à dos
bacon bacon *m.*
bad mauvais/e
  Not bad. Pas mal.
  It's too bad. C'est dommage.
badly mal
bag sac *m.*
bakery/pastry aisle rayon *m.* boulangerie-pâtisserie
balcony balcon *m.*
ballot bulletin *m.* de vote
banana banane *f.*
baptism baptême *m.*
bare nu/e
basement sous-sol *m.*
basket panier *m.*
basketball basket(-ball) *m.*
bathing suit maillot *m.* (de bain)
bathroom salle *f.* de bains
to be être †
beach plage *f.*
bean *haricot *m.*
  green bean *haricot vert
bear ours *m.*
  polar bear ours blanc
to bear supporter
beautiful beau (bel), belle
  It's beautiful weather. Il fait beau.
because parce que
  because of à cause de
to become devenir †
bed lit *m.*
  to get out of bed se lever †
  to go to bed se coucher
  (rural) bed and breakfast gîte (rural) *m.*
bedroom chambre *f.*
beef bœuf *m.*
  ground beef bifteck *m.* haché
beer bière *f.*
before avant
  before (doing something) . . . avant de + *inf.*
to beg prier
to begin commencer †
beginning début *m.*
behind derrière
beige beige
Belgian belge
Belgium Belgique *f.*
to believe croire † (à, en)
  I believe that . . . Je crois que...
  I don't believe so. Je ne crois pas.
belly ventre *m.*
to belong to faire † partie de, appartenir † à
belongings affaires *f. pl.*
beside à côté de
best le/la meilleur/e
  Best wishes! Meilleurs vœux !
better meilleur/e *adj.*, mieux *adv.*
  better . . . than meilleur/e... que, mieux... que
  it is better (to) il vaut mieux
  it would be better (to) il vaudrait mieux
between entre
beverage boisson *f.*
  alcoholic beverage boisson alcoolisée
bicycle vélo *m.*
  to go for a bike ride faire † du vélo
big grand/e, gros/se, large
bill (restaurant) addition *f.*
  utility bill facture *f.*
billion milliard *m.*
biography biographie *f.*
biology biologie *f.*
bird oiseau *m.*
birthday anniversaire *m.*
  Happy birthday! Joyeux anniversaire ! Bon anniversaire !
black noir/e
blackboard tableau *m.*
blind *adj.* aveugle
blond blond/e
blouse chemisier *m.*
blue bleu/e
to blush rougir
board planche *f.*
board game jeu *m.* de société
boat bateau *m.*
  sailboat bateau à voile
body corps *m.*
book livre *m.*
bookcase étagère *f.*
bookstore librairie *f.*
boot botte *f.*
border frontière *f.*
bored ennuyé/e
  to become bored s'ennuyer †
boring ennuyeux/-euse
born: to be born naître †
to borrow emprunter
boss patron/ne *m./f.*, chef *m.*
botany botanique *f.*
both tous/toutes les deux
to bother gêner
bothered gêné/e
bottle bouteille *f.*
bowl bol *m.*
box carton *m.*, boîte *f.*
  box of cereal paquet *m.* de céréales
boy garçon *m.*
  boyfriend petit ami *m.*, copain *m.*
brand-new neuf/neuve
Brazilian brésilien/ne
Brazil Brésil *m.*
bread pain *m.*
  round loaf of bread pain de campagne
  sliced bread pain de mie
  slice of bread tranche *f.* de pain
to break casser
  to break up se séparer
breakfast petit-déjeuner *m.*
  to have breakfast prendre † le petit-déjeuner
to breathe respirer
bride mariée *f.*
bridegroom marié *m.*
to bring (along) a person amener †
to bring (something) apporter, emporter
British anglais/e
brochure brochure *f.*
bronchitis bronchite *f.*
brother frère *m.*
  brother-in-law beau-frère *m.*
  half-brother demi-frère *m.*
  step-brother demi-frère *m.*
brown marron *adj. inv.*
brunette brun/e, châtain *inv.*
to brush se brosser
  to brush one's teeth se brosser les dents, se laver les dents
  to brush one's hair se brosser les cheveux, se coiffer
building bâtiment *m.*, immeuble *m.*, pavillon *m.*
to burn brûler
bus (city) bus *m.*
  bus (between cities) car *m.*
business les affaires *f. pl.*, entreprise *f.*
  businessman homme *m.* d'affaires
  businesswoman femme *f.* d'affaires
to be busy doing something être en train de...
  I'm busy. Je suis pris/e. Je suis occupé/e.
but mais
butcher shop boucherie *f.*
butter beurre *m.*
to buy acheter †
by par
bye salut

C

cable cable *m.*
cafeteria cafétéria *f.*, restaurant *m.* universitaire
cake gâteau *m.*
calculator calculatrice *f.*
calendar calendrier *m.*
  day planner agenda *m.*
call appel *m.*
to call appeler †
  to be called/named s'appeler †
calm calme
  to calm down se calmer
camera appareil *m.* photo
  camcorder, video camera caméscope *m.*
  digital camera appareil *m.* (photo) numérique
Cameroon Cameroun *m.*
Cameroonian camerounais/e
campground camping *m.*
to camp/go camping faire † du camping
camper (vehicle) caravane *f.*
campus campus *m.*
can boîte *f.*, **(soda)** cannette *f.*
can (to be able to do something) pouvoir †
Canada Canada *m.*
Canadian canadien/ne
candidate candidat/e
candle bougie *f.*
candy bonbon *m.*
cantaloupe melon *m.*
cap casquette *f.*
  knit/wool cap bonnet *m.* de laine

caption légende *f.*
car voiture *f.*
carpooling covoiturage *m.*
carafe carafe *f.*
card carte *f.*
  to play cards jouer aux cartes
care: to take care of s'occuper de
  to take care of oneself se soigner
career carrière *f.*
careful prudent/e
carrot carotte *f.*
to carry apporter
  to carry out (food) emporter
cartoon dessin *m.* animé
cash argent *m.*
  cash register caisse *f.*
cashier caissier *m.*, caissière *f.*
castle château *m.*
cat chat/te *m./f.*
cathedral cathédrale *f.*
CD, compact disk CD *m. inv.*
  CD burner graveur *m.* CD
  CD player lecteur *m.* CD
to celebrate fêter
celebrity célébrité *f.*, vedette *f.*
cello violoncelle *m.*
cell phone portable *m.*
center centre *m.*
century siècle *m.*
cereal céréales *f. pl.*
chair chaise *f.*
  armchair fauteuil *m.*
  wheelchair fauteuil *m.* roulant
chalk (stick of) craie *f.*
change purse porte-monnaie *m.*
channel chaîne *f.*
character personnage *m.*
  main character personnage principal
to chat bavarder, jaser (*Can.*)
  to chat online t'chatter (*Can.*)
cheese fromage *m.*
chemical product produit chimique *m.*
chemistry chimie *f.*
chemistry lab labo(ratoire) *m.* de chimie
chess échecs *m. pl.*
chest poitrine *f.*
chicken poulet *m.*
child enfant *m./f.*
  grandchild petit-enfant *m.*
China Chine *f.*
Chinese chinois/e
chocolate chocolat *m.*
  dark chocolate chocolat noir
  hot chocolate chocolat chaud
  milk chocolate chocolat au lait
  white chocolate chocolat blanc
choir chorale *f.*
chorus chœur *m.*
to choose choisir
church (Catholic) église *f.*, **(Protestant)** temple *m.*
citizen citoyen/ne *m., f.*
city ville *f.*
  in the city en ville
  city bus bus *m.*
  city hall mairie *f.*
  city map plan *m.* de ville
civil wedding cérémonie *f.* civile
clarinet clarinette *f.*
class (subject) cours *m.*
  chemistry class cours de chimie
  elective class cours facultatif
  required class cours obligatoire
class (group of people) classe *f.*
  French class classe de français
classical classique
  classical music musique *f.* classique
classified ad petite annonce *f.*
classmate camarade *m./f.* de classe
classroom classe *f.*, salle *f.* de classe
clean *adj.* propre
to clean nettoyer †
clear clair/e
climate climat *m.*
  climate change changement *m.* climatique
clock horloge *f.*
  clock radio radio-réveil *m.*
to close fermer
  closed fermé/e
closet placard *m.*
clothing vêtement *m.*
cloud nuage *m.*
  It's cloudy. Il y a des nuages. Le ciel est couvert.
coast côte *f.*
  East Coast côte est
  West Coast côte ouest
coat manteau *m.*
  down coat anorak *m.*
  raincoat imperméable *m.*
  suit coat veste *f.*
coffee café *m.*
  coffee break pause-café *f.*
  coffee with cream café crème
  coffee with milk café au lait
  decaffeinated coffee café déca(féiné)
  strong cup of expresso coffee café serré
coffee table table *f.* basse
cohabitation union *f.* libre
coin pièce *f.* (de monnaie)
cola coca(-cola) *m.*
cold froid/e ; rhume *m.*
  I have a cold. J'ai un rhume. Je suis enrhumé/e.
  I'm cold. J'ai froid.
  It's cold (weather). Il fait froid.
cold cuts charcuterie *f.*
college fac(ulté) *f.*
Colombia Colombie *f.*
Colombian colombien/ne
color couleur *f.*
comb peigne *m.*
to comb se peigner
to come venir †
  to come back revenir †
  to come by passer
  to come home rentrer
  to come in entrer
comedy comédie *f.*
comfortable (material objects) confortable
  (person) à l'aise
comic strip bande *f.* dessinée (BD)
communication communication *f.*
completely tout à fait
composition rédaction *f.*, composition *f.*
computer ordinateur *m.*
  computer center centre *m.* informatique
  computer file fichier *m.*
  computer science informatique *f.*
  laptop computer ordinateur portable, portable *m.*
concert concert *m.*
condiments condiments *m. pl.*
conformist conformiste
Congratulations! Félicitations !
connection (wireless) connexion *f.* (sans fil)
to consume consommer
to contaminate contaminer
continent continent *m.*
to cook faire † la cuisine
cookie biscuit *m.*
cooking cuisine *f.*
  to do the cooking faire † la cuisine *f.*
cool: It's cool weather. Il fait frais.
contrary: To the contrary, . . . au contraire, ...
copious copieux/-euse
corner coin *m.*
  at the corner (of) au coin de
  corner café café *m.* du coin
co-renter colocataire *m./f.*
corridor couloir *m.*
to cost coûter
cotton coton *m.*
couch canapé *m.*
cough toux *f.*
to cough tousser
country pays *m.*
  foreign country pays étranger
  in this country dans ce pays
country(side) campagne *f.*
  in the country à la campagne
course cours *m.*
  to take a course suivre † un cours
of course bien sûr
courtyard cour *f.*
cousin cousin *m.*, cousine *f.*
credit card carte *f.* de crédit
critic (person) critique *m.*
criticism critique *f.*
critique critique *f.*
croissant croissant *m.*
  chocolate croissant pain *m.* au chocolat
to cross traverser
cruise croisière *f.*
to cry pleurer
cucumber concombre *m.*
cuisine cuisine *f.*
culture culture *f.*
cup tasse *f.*
cupboard placard *m.*
curtain rideau *m.*
customer client/e *m./f.*
to cut couper
cute mignon/ne

D

dairy: dairy aisle rayon *m.* crèmerie
  dairy products produits *m. pl.* laitiers
dance danse *f.*
to dance faire † de la danse, danser
dangerous dangereux/-euse

dark-haired brun/e
Darn! Zut (alors) !
database base *m.* de données
date date *f.*, **(meeting)** rendez-vous *m.*
  birth date date de naissance
to date sortir avec
datebook agenda *m.*
daughter fille *f.*
day jour *m.*, journée *f.*
  day before yesterday avant-hier
  Have a good day! Bonne journée !
  that day ce jour-là
dead mort/e
dear cher/chère
death mort *f.*
debate débat *m.*
debit card carte *f.* bancaire
deceased décédé/e
December décembre
to decide décider
deep profond/e
deeply profondément
degree (in) diplôme *m.* (en)
  to do a degree (in) préparer un diplôme (en)
  to have a degree avoir un diplôme, une formation
deli: deli counter rayon *m.* charcuterie
  deli meats charcuterie *f.*
delicious délicieux/-euse
delighted enchanté/e, ravi/e
dentist dentiste *m./f.*
department store grand magasin *m.*
departure départ *m.*
to descend descendre
to describe décrire †
desert désert *m.*
to desire désirer, vouloir †
desk bureau *m.*
dessert dessert *m.*
detective movie film *m.* policier
to detest détester
dictionary dictionnaire *m.*
to die mourir †
diet régime *m.*
  to be on a diet suivre † un régime, faire † un régime
different différent/e
difficult difficile
difficulty: to have difficulty avoir † du mal à + *inf.*
dining hall restaurant *m.* universitaire (resto U), cafétéria *f.*
dining room salle *f.* à manger
dinner dîner *m.*, souper *m.* *(Can.)*
  to have dinner dîner, souper (*Can.*)
  to fix dinner préparer le dîner
  Dinner's ready! À table !
director directeur *m.*, directrice *f.* ; administrateur *m.*, administratice *f.*
  film director réalisateur *m.*, réalisatrice *f.*
  stage director metteur *m.* en scène
disability handicap *m.*
  to have a disability être handicapé/e
disagreeable désagréable
disappointed déçu/e
disciplined discipliné/e
to discuss discuter
dish assiette *f.*, plat *m.*
  to do the dishes faire † la vaisselle
to disobey désobéir à
disposition caractère *m.*
display window vitrine *f.*
to divorce divorcer
divorced divorcé/e
to do faire †
  to do do-it-yourself projects bricoler, faire du bricolage
  to not do much ne pas faire grand-chose
do-it-yourselfer bricoleur *m.*, bricoleuse *f.*
do-it-yourself projects bricolage *m.*
doctor (M.D.) médecin *m.*, docteur *m.*
documentary documentaire *m.*
dog chien/ne *m./f.*
  guide dog chien *m.* guide
  service dog chien *m.* d'assistance
door porte *f.*
dormitory résidence *f.*
to doubt (that) douter (que)
  without a doubt sans doute
downtown centre-ville *m.*
  to go downtown descendre en ville
dozen douzaine *f.*
draftsman/woman dessinateur *m.*, dessinatrice *f.*
drama drame *m.*, comédie *f.*
to draw dessiner
drawing dessin *m.*
dream rêve *m.*
to dream rêver
dress robe *f.*
  to get dressed s'habiller
  to get undressed se déshabiller
dressing (oil and vinegar) vinaigrette *f.*
drink boisson *f.*
  cold drink boisson rafraîchissante
  hot drink boisson chaude
to drink boire †
to drive aller † en voiture, conduire †
  to go for a drive faire † un tour en voiture
driver's license permis *m.* de conduire
drug (medicine) médicament *m.*
  (illegal) drogue *f. sg.*
drum set batterie *f.*
to dry essuyer †
  to dry oneself off s'essuyer †
to dub doubler
dubbed doublé/e
due to à cause de
dumb bête
during pendant
dynamic dynamique

E

each chaque
  each one chacun/e
ear oreille *f.*
  to have an earache avoir † mal aux oreilles
early tôt
  to be early être † en avance
to earn money gagner de l'argent
earth (the Earth) terre (la Terre) *f.*
east est
  East Coast côte *f.* est
easy facile
to eat manger †
  to eat between meals grignoter
  to eat breakfast prendre † le petit-déjeuner
  to eat dinner dîner, souper (*Can.*)
  to eat lunch déjeuner, dîner (*Can.*)
  to eat a snack goûter
ecological écologique
  ecological footprint empreinte *f.* écologique
ecology écologie *f.*
economics sciences *f. pl.* économiques, économie *f.*
economy économie *f.*
edge bord *m.*
to edit pictures retoucher
to educate oneself s'instruire †
education (academic discipline) sciences *f. pl.* de l'éducation
egg œuf *m.*
  fried egg œuf sur le plat, œuf au plat
eight huit
eighteen dix-huit
eighty quatre-vingts
elbow coude *m.*
elderly âgé/e
electronic game jeu *m.* éléctronique
elegant élégant/e
elementary school école *f.* primaire
elevator ascenseur *m.*
eleven onze
e-mail e-mail *m.*, courrier *m.* électronique, courriel *m.* (*Can.*)
  e-mail message e-mail *m.*, message *m.* électronique, courriel *m.* (*Can.*)
embarrassed embarrassé/e, gêné/e
employee employé/e
empty vide
to encourage encourager
encyclopedia encyclopédie *f.*
end fin *f.*
energetic énergique
engaged fiancé/e
  to get engaged se fiancer
engagement fiançailles *f. pl.*
engine moteur *m.*
engineer ingénieur *m.*
England Angleterre *f.*
English *adj.* anglais/e
English (language) anglais *m.*
enough assez
  enough of assez de
to enter entrer
entertainment (TV show) divertissement *m.*
enthusiastic enthousiaste
entrance (foyer) entrée *f.*
environment environnement *m.*
equipped équipé/e
errand course *f.*
  to run errands faire † des courses
eraser (pencil) gomme *f.*
eraser (board) brosse *f.*
especially surtout
essay essai *m.*, rédaction *f.*
Europe Europe *f.*
European européen/ne
even (same) même
even (number) (nombre) pair
evening soir *m.*, soirée *f.*

event évènement *m.*
eventually finalement
every chaque ; tout, tous, toute, toutes
every day tous les jours
every evening tous les soirs
everyone tout le monde
everything tout
everywhere partout
exam examen *m.*
final exam examen final
midterm exam examen partiel
oral exam examen oral
to pass an exam réussir un examen
to study for an exam préparer un examen
to take an exam passer un examen
example exemple *m.*
for example par exemple
except sauf
except for à part
excited enthousiaste, agité/e, impatient/e
excursion bus car *m.*
excuse excuse *f.*
Excuse me. Pardon, Excusez-moi.
exercise exercice *m.*
to exercise faire † de l'exercice
exhaust fumes gaz *m. pl.* d'échappement
exhibit exposition *f.*
expensive cher/chère
to explain expliquer
eye (eyes) œil *m.* (yeux)

F

face figure *f.*, visage *m.*
to face donner sur
facing face à, en face de
factory usine *f.*
to fail rater
to fail an exam échouer à un examen
fair juste
It's not fair! Ce n'est pas juste !
fairly assez
faithful fidèle
fall automne *m.*
to fall tomber
to fall asleep s'endormir
to fall in love (with) tomber amoureux/-euse (de)
false faux/fausse
family famille *f.*
big family famille nombreuse
blended family famille recomposée
extended family famille étendue
single-parent family famille monoparentale
family relations relations *f. pl.* familiales
family room séjour *m.*
famous célèbre, connu/e
fan fanatique *m.*
to be a fan of être fanatique de
far (from) loin (de)
farm ferme *f.*
farmer fermier *m.*, fermière *f.*, agriculteur *m.*, agricultrice *f.*
fashion mode *f.*
to be in fashion être à la mode
fashion designer couturier *m.*
high fashion haute couture *f.*
out of fashion démodé/e
fashionable à la mode
fast rapide *adj.*, vite *adv.*
to fast jeûner
to break a fast déjeûner
fat *adj.* gros/se
fat graisse *f.*
father père *m.*
father-in-law beau-père *m.*
single father père célibataire
stepfather beau-père *m.*
favorite préféré/e
fear peur *f.*
to fear avoir † peur de
February février
to feel se sentir, toucher ; ressentir
to feel bad aller † mal
to feel better aller † mieux
to feel good aller † bien
to feel great être † en forme
to feel like doing something avoir † envie de + *inf.*
feminine féminin/e
fever fièvre *f.*
few peu, un peu de, quelques
fiancé/e fiancé *m.*, fiancée *f.*
field champ *m.*
playing field terrain *m.* de sport
fifteen quinze
fifty cinquante
to fill remplir
film film *m.*
filmmaker cinéaste *m./f.*
film director réalisateur *m.*, réalisatrice *f.*
final final/e
finally finalement, enfin
to find trouver
I find that . . . Je trouve que…
fine bien
to be fine être en forme
Fine, also. Bien aussi.
Fine, and you? Ça va, et toi ?
fine arts beaux-arts *m. pl.*
finger doigt *m.*
to finish finir, terminer
first premier/-ière
first (of all) d'abord
first course entrée *f.*
first floor rez-de-chaussée *m.*
fish poisson *m.*
fish counter rayon *m.* poissonnerie
to fish pêcher
fishing pêche *f.*
to go fishing aller † à la pêche
five cinq
to fix réparer
to fix one's hair se coiffer
fixed-price meal menu *m.*, prix *m.* fixe
flight vol *m.*
flood inondation *f.*
floor étage *m.*
first (ground) floor rez-de-chaussée *m.*
second floor premier étage *m.*
on the floor par terre
flour farine *f.*
to flow couler
flower fleur *f.*
flu grippe *f.*
flute flûte *f.* traversière
to fly aller † en avion, voler
fog brouillard *m.*
It's foggy. Il y a du brouillard.
follow suivre †
food aliment *m.*, nourriture *f.*
food bank banque *f.* alimentaire
foot pied *m.*
on foot à pied
football football *m.* américain
football game match *m.* de football américain
football stadium stade *m.*
for pour ; depuis (+ time expression) ; pendant (+ time expression)
foreign *adj.* étranger/-ère
foreigner étranger *m.*, étrangère *f.*
forest forêt *f.*
to forget oublier
former ancien/ne
fortunately heureusement
forty quarante
four quatre
fourteen quatorze
France France *f.*
free (a person) libre ; **(a thing)** gratuit/e
I'm not free. Je ne suis pas libre.
to freeze geler †
It's freezing. Il gèle.
French *adj.* français/e
French bread (long, thin loaf) baguette *f.*
French toast pain *m.* perdu
French fries frites *f. pl.*
French (language) français *m.*
fresh frais/fraîche
Friday vendredi
friend ami/e, camarade *m./f.*, copain *m.*, copine *f.*
best friend meilleur/e ami/e *m./f.*
(my) boyfriend (mon) petit ami *m.*, (mon) copain *m.*, (mon) ami *m.*
(my) girlfriend (ma) petite amie *f.*, (ma) copine *f.*, (mon) amie *f.*
Your friend, Amitiés
friendly sociable
friendship amitié *f.*
from de (d')
front: in front of devant
frozen foods surgelés *m. pl.*
fruit fruit *m.*
fruit juice jus *m.* de fruit
fun: to have fun s'amuser
to be fun être † agréable, être † amusant/e
for fun pour s'amuser
It's fun. C'est amusant.
to make fun of se moquer de
funny amusant/e, drôle
furious furieux/-euse
furnished meublé/e
furniture meuble *m.*
future avenir *m.*
future tense futur *m.*

G

to gain weight grossir
game jeu *m.* ; **(sports)** match *m.*
game show jeu *m.* télévisé
garage garage *m.*
garden jardin *m.*

to garden faire † du jardinage, travailler dans le jardin
garlic ail *m.*
gas gaz *m.*
gas (for a car) essence *f.*
carbon gas gaz carbonique
greenhouse gas gaz *m.* à effet de serre
generous généreux/-euse
gentle doux/douce
geography géographie *f.*
geology géologie *f.*
German *adj.* allemand/e
German (language) allemand *m.*
Germany Allemagne *f.*
to get obtenir †
to get a (good) grade avoir † une (bonne) note
to get along (with someone) s'entendre avec (quelqu'un)
to get angry (with) se fâcher (contre)
to get a degree obtenir † un diplôme
to get divorced divorcer
to get dressed s'habiller
to get engaged se fiancer
to get information s'informer, se renseigner
to get involved s'engager
to get married se marier
to get off descendre
to get ready se préparer
to get a tan se bronzer
to get together se retrouver, se réunir
to get undressed se déshabiller
to get up se lever †
Get up/stand up! Levez-vous !
to get used to s'habituer à
gift cadeau *m.*
girl fille *f.*, jeune fille *f.*
girlfriend petite amie *f.*, copine *f.*
to give donner, offrir †
to give advice conseiller
to give back rendre
to give a present offrir † (un cadeau)
glacier glacier *m.*
glad content/e
glass verre *f.*
glasses lunettes *f. pl.*
sunglasses lunettes de soleil
global warming réchauffement *m.* climatique, changement *m.* climatique
glove gant *m.*
to go aller †
to go around faire † un tour
to go around the world faire † le tour du monde
to go back retourner
to go by passer
to go down descendre
to go downtown descendre en ville
to go home rentrer
to go in entrer
to go on/keep going continuer
to go online aller † sur Internet
to go on vacation partir en vacances
to go out sortir
to go to bed se coucher
to go to the doctor aller † chez le médecin
to go up monter
God Dieu
godfather parrain *m.*
godmother marraine *f.*
golf golf *m.*
good bon/ne *adj.*, bien *adv.*
good-bye au revoir, salut
Good evening. Bonsoir.
Good morning. Bonjour.
Good night. Bonne nuit.
Have a good day. Bonne journée.
Have a good evening. Bonne soirée.
grade note *f.*
to have/get a (bad) grade avoir † une (mauvaise) note
grandchild petit-enfant *m.*
granddaughter petite-fille *f.*
grandfather grand-père *m.*
grandmother grand-mère *f.*
grandparents grands-parents *m. pl.*
grandson petit-fils *m.*
grape raisin *m.*
bunch of grapes grappe *f.* de raisins
gray gris/e
grease graisse *f.*
Great! Génial !
green vert/e
green bean *haricot *m.* vert
green salad salade *f.* (verte)
grilled grillé/e
grilled ham-and-cheese sandwich croque-monsieur *m.*
grocery store épicerie *f.*, supermarché *m.*
ground sol *m.*, terre *f.*
ground floor rez-de-chaussée *m.*
on the ground par terre
to grow pousser
to grow larger, fatter grossir
to grow old vieillir
to grow taller grandir
to grow up (for children) grandir
guest invité *m.*, invitée *f.*
guide (tour guide or guidebook) guide *m.*
guinea pig cochon *m.* d'Inde
guitar guitare *f.*
bass guitare guitare basse
electric guitar guitare électrique
gym gymnase *m.*

H

hair cheveux *m. pl.*
to do one's hair se coiffer
to have short/long/curly hair avoir † les cheveux courts/longs/bouclés
to wash one's hair se laver les cheveux
half demi/e
half-brother demi-frère *m.*
half-kilo demi-kilo *m.*
half-past et demi/e
half-sister demi-sœur *f.*
hallway couloir *m.*
ham jambon *m.*
ham sandwich sandwich *m.* au jambon
hamburger *hamburger *m.*
hand main *f.*
to hand in/over remettre †
on the other hand, . . . d'autre part, en revanche
to raise your hand lever † le doigt, lever † la main
handicap handicap *m.*
to be handicapped être handicapé/e
handsome beau (bel), belle
to happen se passer, avoir † lieu
What happened? Qu'est-ce qui s'est passé ?
happy heureux/-euse, content/e
Happy birthday! Joyeux anniversaire ! , Bon anniversaire !
Happy New Year! Bonne année !
hard (difficult) difficile ; dur/e
hardworking sérieux/-euse, travailleur/-euse
harmonica harmonica *m.*
hat chapeau *m.*
to hate détester
to have avoir †
to have a drink prendre † une boisson
to have a good time s'amuser
Have a nice weekend! Bon week-end !
to have just (done something) venir † de + *inf.*
to have to (do something) devoir †
he *(pron.)* il
head tête *f.*
headline gros titre *m.*
health santé *f.*
health center/clinic infirmerie *f.*
healthy bon/ne pour la santé
to be healthy (person) être † en bonne santé
hear entendre
heart cœur *m.*
heart attack crise *f.* cardiaque
hearty copieux/-euse
heavy lourd/e
heavy jacket blouson *m.*
height taille *f.*
of average height de taille moyenne
Hello. Bonjour.
Hello (telephone only). Allô.
to help aider (à)
her elle ; la ; son, sa, ses
to her lui
herself elle-même
herbal tea tisane *f.*
here ici
Here is/are . . . Voici...
Here/there is/are . . . Voilà...
Hi! Salut !
high *haut/e
high school lycée *m.*
hike randonnée *f.*
to go on a hike faire † une randonnée
hill colline *f.*
him le ; lui
to him lui
himself lui-même
his son, sa, ses
history histoire *f.*
hockey *hockey *m.*
to hold tenir †
holiday fête *f.*
legal holiday jour *m.* férié
religious holiday fête religieuse

home maison *f.*
at my/our home chez moi/nous
stay-at-home mother/father femme *f.* au foyer, homme *m.* au foyer
homeowner propriétaire *m./f.*
homebody pantouflard/e
homework devoirs *m.*
to do homework faire † des devoirs *m.*
to hope espérer †, souhaiter
horror movie film *m.* d'horreur
horse cheval *m.*
to go horseback riding faire † du cheval
hospital (public) hôpital *m.*
private hospital clinique *f.*
hostel (youth) auberge *f.* de jeunesse
hot chaud
hot (food) épicé/e
hot chocolate chocolat *m.* chaud
I am hot. J'ai chaud.
It's hot (weather). Il fait chaud.
hotel hôtel *m.*
hour heure *f.*
for an hour pendant une heure, pour une heure, depuis une heure
in an hour dans une heure, en une heure
house maison *f.*
at the home of chez
housemate colocataire *m./f.*
how comment
How are you? Comment allez-vous ?
how many combien de
how much combien
How's it going? Comment ça va ?
human being être *m.* humain
human body corps *m.* humain
humanities lettres *f.*
humid lourd/e
It's humid. Il fait lourd.
hundred cent
hunger faim *m.*
to be hungry avoir † faim
Hurray for . . . ! Vive...!
hurricane ouragan *m.*
to hurry up se dépêcher
in a hurry pressé/e
hurt blessé/e
to hurt (somewhere) avoir † mal à
to hurt (someone) faire † mal à
husband mari *m.*

I

I je (j')
ice glace *f.*
ice cream glace *f.* ; crème *f.* glacée (*Can.*)
ice cube glaçon *m.*
ice on the ground verglas *m.*
icy: It's icy. Il y a du verglas.
idealistic idéaliste
if si
If I were you À ta/votre place
important important/e
in à, dans, en
in-laws beaux-parents *m. pl.*
including y compris
independent autonome
India Inde *f.*
Indian indien/ne
individualistic individualiste
indulgent indulgent/e
industrial industriel/le
industrial waste déchets *m. pl.* industriels
inexpensive bon marché
infection infection *f.*
information renseignement *m.*
to get information se renseigner, s'informer
injured blessé/e
inn auberge *f.*
inside dans, à l'intérieur de, dedans
instant messaging messagerie *f.* instantanée
instead of au lieu de
intelligent intelligent/e
intensity intensité *f.*
interesting intéressant/e
to be interested (in) s'intéresser (à)
Internet Internet *m.*
connect to the Internet se connecter sur Internet
to go on the Internet aller † sur Internet
Internet access accès *m.* à Internet
Internet browser browser *m.*
on the Internet sur Internet
interview interview *f.*, entretien *m.*
to interview interviewer
into dans
to introduce présenter
Je vous/te présente X. This is X.
invitation invitation *f.*
to invite inviter
irritable énervé/e
irritated: to become irritated s'énerver
island île *f.*
Israel Israël *m.*
Israeli israélien/ne
it ce (c') ; il ; elle ; le ; la
it is . . . c'est...
Italian (*adj.*) italien/ne
Italian (language) italien *m.*
Italy Italie *f.*
Ivorian ivoirien/ne
Ivory Coast Côte *f.* d'Ivoire

J

jacket blouson *m.*
(suit coat) jacket veste *f.*
jam confiture *f.*
January janvier
Japan Japon *m.*
Japanese (*adj.*) japonais/e
Japanese (language) japonais *m.*
jar pot *m.*
jazz jazz *m.*
jealous jaloux/-ouse
jeans jean *m. sg.*
job poste *m.*, travail *m.*, métier *m.*
full-time job travail à plein temps
part-time job travail à mi-temps
to jog faire † du jogging
joke histoire drôle *f.*, blague *f.*, plaisanterie *f.*
to joke plaisanter, blaguer, raconter des histoires drôles
journalism journalisme *m.*
journalist journaliste *m./f.*
July juillet
June juin

K

kayak kayak *m.*
kangaroo kangourou *m.*
keyboard clavier *m.*
key clé *f.*, clef *f.*
key word mot *m.* clé
kilo(gram) kilo(gramme) *m.*
kilometer kilomètre *m.*
kind gentil/le
That's kind (of you). C'est gentil à toi/vous.
king roi *m.*
to kiss s'embrasser
kitchen cuisine *f.*
kitchen cabinet placard *m.*
(with) kitchenette (avec) coin *m.* cuisine
knee genou *m.*
to kneel se mettre † à genoux
to know (how to) savoir †
to know or be familiar with connaître †
knowledge connaissance *f.*
koala (bear) koala *m.*
Korea Corée *f.*
Korean *adj.* coréen/ne
Korean (language) coréen *m.*

L

lab(oratory) laboratoire *m.* (labo)
lab technician technicien *m.*, technicienne *f.* de laboratoire
lacrosse crosse *f.*
to play lacrosse jouer à la crosse
lady dame *f.*
lake lac *m.*
lamb agneau *m.*
lamb chop côtelette *f.* d'agneau
leg of lamb gigot *m.* d'agneau
lamp lampe *f.*
landlord/landlady propriétaire *m./f.*
language langue *f.*
in the original language en version *f.* originale (en V.O.)
foreign language langue *f.* étrangère
language lab labo(ratoire) *m.* de langues
native language langue *f.* maternelle
laptop (ordinateur) portable *m.*
last dernier/dernière
last month le mois dernier
last Saturday samedi dernier
last week la semaine dernière
last year l'année dernière, l'an dernier
to last durer
late tard
to be late être † en retard
to laugh rire †
law loi *f.*
law school faculté *f.* de droit
study of law droit *m.*
lawyer avocat *m.*, avocate *f.*
lazy paresseux/-euse
to learn apprendre (à) †

leather cuir *m.*
to leave partir ; **(someone, something)** quitter
to leave the lights on laisser les lumières allumées
lecture conférence *f.*
lecture hall amphithéâtre *m.*
left gauche *f.*
leftovers restes *m. pl.*
to the left à gauche
leg jambe *f.*
leisure activities loisirs *m. pl.*
leisure time temps *m.* libre
lemon citron *m.*
lemonade citron *m.* pressé
lemon-lime soft drink limonade *f.*
to lend prêter
lenient indulgent/e
less moins
less . . . than moins (de)... que
letter lettre *f.*
lettuce salade *f.*
library bibliothèque *f.* ; bibli (*Can.*)
public (city) library bibliothèque *f.* municipale
university library bibliothèque *f.* universitaire (B.U.)
license permis *m.*
driver's license permis de conduire
to lie mentir
life vie *f.*
to lift lever †
light (color) clair/e ; **(weight)** léger, légère
light lumière *f.*
to turn on the lights allumer les lumières
to turn out the lights éteindre les lumières
to leave the lights on laisser les lumières allumées
lightbulb ampoule *f.* (électrique)
energy-saving lightbulb ampoule basse consommation
lightning éclair *m.*
There's lightning. Il y a des éclairs.
likable sympa(thique)
like comme
to like aimer
to like fairly well aimer bien
to like or love a lot aimer beaucoup
line ligne *f.*
online en ligne
to stand in line faire † la queue
linguistics linguistique *f.*
lip lèvre *f.*
lipstick rouge *m.* à lèvres
to listen to écouter
to listen to music écouter de la musique
list liste *f.*
listing of TV programs magazine *m.* télé
to make a list faire † une liste
liter litre *m.*
literature littérature *f.*
little petit/e
little bit peu *m.*
a little bit un petit peu
to live habiter ; vivre †
to live together without being married cohabiter ; vivre † en union *f.* libre
liver foie *m.*
chicken liver foie de volaille
goose liver paté foie gras
living room séjour *m.*, salle *f.* de séjour
loaf of sliced bread pain *m.* de mie
to locate trouver
located situé/e
to be located se trouver
long long/ue
a long time longtemps
a long time ago il y a longtemps
for how long . . . ? depuis combien de temps...?
to look (seem) avoir † l'air (+ *adj.*)
to look after soigner
to look at regarder
to look for chercher
to look like ressembler à
to look onto donner sur
to lose perdre
to lose one's composure perdre son sang-froid
to lose weight maigrir, mincir
a lot beaucoup (de)
lottery loto *m.*
to play the lottery jouer au loto
loudly fort
lovable aimable
love amour *m.*
to love aimer
to be in love (with) être † amoureux/-euse (de)
to fall in love (with) tomber amoureux/-euse (de)
luck chance *f.*
good luck bonne chance *f.*
luckily heureusement
to be lucky avoir † de la chance
luggage bagages *m. pl.*
to carry up luggage monter les bagages
lunch déjeuner *m.*
to eat lunch déjeuner, dîner (*Can.*)
lung poumon *m.*

M

Madam, ma'am madame *f.* (Mme)
mad fâché/e, en colère
to get mad se fâcher
magazine magazine *m.*
monthly magazine mensuel *m.*
weekly magazine hebdomadaire *m.*
mail courrier *m.*
e-mail e-mail *m.*, courriel *m.* (*Can.*)
mail carrier facteur *m.*, factrice *f.*
main character personnage *m.* principal
main dish plat *m.* principal
major (in) spécialisation *f.* (en), majeure *f.* (en) (*Can.*)
majority plupart *f.*
to make faire †
to make a mistake faire † une faute
makeup maquillage *m.*
to put on makeup se maquiller
man homme *m.*, monsieur *m.*
manager directeur *m.*, directrice *f.*
map carte *f.*
city map plan *m.* de ville
March mars
market marché *m.*
flea market marché aux puces
open-air market marché en plein air
supermarket supermarché *m.*
marital status état *m.* civil
marriage mariage *m.*
married marié/e
to get married se marier
masculine masculin
mathematics mathématiques *f.* (les maths)
May mai
maybe peut-être
mayonnaise mayonnaise *f.*
mayor maire *m.*
me moi
me neither moi non plus
me too moi aussi
not me pas moi
meal repas *m.*
before-meal drink apéritif *m.*
balanced meal repas *m.* équilibré
mean méchant/e
to mean (to say) vouloir † dire
means of transportation moyen *m.* de transport
meat viande *f.*
meat counter rayon *m.* boucherie
mechanic mécanicien *m.*, mécanicienne *f.*
media médias *m. pl.*
medicine (field of study) médecine *f.*
medicine (drug) médicament *m.*
mediocre médiocre
to meet se rencontrer, se retrouver, se connaître, faire la connaissance de qqn
to meet up with (se) retrouver, se réunir
meeting rendez-vous *m.*, réunion *f.*, rencontre *m.*
melon (cantaloupe) melon *m.*
to melt fondre
Merry Christmas! Joyeux Noël !
meter mètre *m.*
Mexican mexicain/e
Mexico Mexique *m.*
microwave (oven) (four à) micro-ondes *m.*
middle milieu *m.*
to be in the middle of doing sthg être † en train de faire qqch
in the middle au milieu de
in the middle of May à la mi-mai
middle-aged d'un certain âge
middle school collège *m.*
midnight minuit
milk lait *m.*
milk chocolate chocolat *m.* au lait
million million *m.*
mineral water eau *f.* minérale
minor (in) mineure *f.* (en) (*Can.*)
mint menthe *f.*
mint tea thé *m.* à la menthe
herbal mint tea tisane *f.* à la menthe
minute minute *f.*
mirror miroir *m.*, glace *f.*
Miss Mademoiselle *f.* (Mlle)
to miss manquer, rater
I miss him/her. Il/Elle me manque.
I miss them. Ils/Elles me manquent.

I miss you. Tu me manques. Vous me manquez.
missing absent/e
mistake faute *f.*, erreur *f.*
to make a mistake faire † une faute, se tromper
Mister Monsieur *m.* (M.)
modern moderne
moment moment *m.*
at that moment à ce moment-là
Monday lundi
money argent *m.*
monitor moniteur *m.*, écran *m.*
flat-screen monitor moniteur avec un écran plat, écran plat
month mois *m.*
last month le mois dernier
next month le mois prochain
moon (the Moon) lune (la Lune) *f.*
moped mobylette *f.*
more . . . than plus (de)... que
morning matin *m.*
Good morning. Bonjour.
(X o'clock) in the morning (X heures) du matin
Moroccan *adj.* marocain/e
Morocco Maroc *m.*
most plupart *f.*
mother mère *f.*
mother-in-law belle-mère *f.*
single mother mère célibataire
stepmother belle-mère *f.*
motorcycle moto *f.*
motorscooter mobylette *f.*
mountain montagne *f.*
to go mountain climbing faire † de l'alpinisme *m.*
mouse souris *f.*
wireless mouse souris sans fil
mouth bouche *f.*
to move (an object) bouger
to move (one's home) déménager
movie film *m.*
movie star vedette *f.*, star *f.*
movie theater cinéma *m.*
MP3 player baladeur *m.* MP3
Mr. Monsieur *m.* (M.)
Mrs. Madame *f.* (Mme)
Ms. Madame *f.* (Mme)
multimedia multimédia
museum musée *m.*
mushroom champignon *m.*
music musique *f.*
musical comédie *f.* musicale
musician musicien *m.*, musicienne *f.*
must devoir †
You (One) must . . . Il faut...
You (One) must not . . . Il ne faut pas...
mustard moutarde *f.*
my mon, ma, mes
My name is . . . Je m'appelle...
myself moi-même

N

name (last) nom *m.*
first name prénom *m.*
nickname surnom *m.*
My name is . . . Je m'appelle...
What is your name? Comment vous appelez-vous/tu t'appelles ?
to name nommer
nationality nationalité *f.*
natural sciences sciences *f.* naturelles
nature nature *f.*, caractère *m.*
nausea mal *m.* au cœur
to be nauseated avoir † mal au cœur
near (to) près (de)
very near tout près (de)
nearly à peu près, presque
Neat! Chouette !
necessary nécessaire, indispensable
to be necessary falloir † : il faut, être † nécessaire, être † indispensable
neck cou *m.*
necklace collier *m.*
to need avoir † besoin de, il faut
need besoin *m.*
neighbor voisin/e *m./f.*
neighborhood quartier *m.*
neighboring voisin/e
neither non plus, ne... ni... ni
nephew neveu *m.*
nieces and nephews neveux *pl.*
nervous agité/e, nerveux/-euse
Netherlands Pays-Bas *m. pl.*
network réseau *m.*
wireless network réseau *m.* sans fil
never ne... jamais
new nouveau (nouvel), nouvelle
brand-new neuf, neuve
news informations *f. pl.*, (infos) nouvelles *f. pl.*
news broadcast journal *m.* télévisé
newsgroup forum *m.* de discussion
newspaper journal *m.*
newsstand kiosque *m.* à journaux
next prochain/e, ensuite
next to à côté de
nice sympa(thique), gentil/le, agréable
niece nièce *f.*
nieces and nephews neveux *m. pl.*
night nuit *f.*
at night la nuit, le soir
nine neuf
nineteen dix-neuf
ninety quatre-vingt-dix
no non
no longer ne... plus
no matter what n'importe quoi
no more ne... plus
no one ne... personne
noise bruit *m.*
to make noise faire † du bruit
noise pollution pollution *f.* sonore
nonbiodegradable non-biodégradable
noon midi
normally normalement
north nord *m.*
North America Amérique *f.* du nord
nose nez *m.*
to have a runny nose avoir † le nez qui coule
not pas, ne... pas
not at all pas du tout
not bad pas mal
not me pas moi
not yet pas encore
notebook cahier *m.*
nothing ne... rien
novel roman *m.*
November novembre
now maintenant
number chiffre *m.*, numéro *m.*
nurse infirmier *m.*, infirmière *f.*

O

to obey obéir à
to obtain obtenir †
obvious évident/e
occupation métier *m.*, profession *f.*
October octobre
odd bizarre
odd jobs: to do odd jobs around the house bricoler, faire † du bricolage
of de (d')
of course bien sûr
offer offre *f.*
job offer offre d'emploi
to offer offrir †
office bureau *m.*
administrative offices bureaux *pl.* administratifs
registrar's office bureau des inscriptions
often souvent
oil huile *f.*
olive oil huile d'olive
waste (used) oil huile usagée
ointment pommade *f.*
OK d'accord
old vieux (vieil), vieille ; ancien/ne
to be X years old avoir † X ans
How old are you? Quel âge avez-vous/as-tu ?
old-fashioned démodé/e
older person personne *f.* âgée
olive olive *f.*
omelet omelette *f.*
on à, sur
on foot à pied
on purpose exprès
on sale en solde
on TV à la télé
on the contrary si, au contraire
once une fois
once upon a time il était une fois
one un/e
onion oignon *m.*
online en ligne
to go online aller † sur Internet
only seulement, ne... que, uniquement
open ouvert/e
to open ouvrir †
opinion opinion *f.*, avis *m.*
in my opinion à mon avis, d'après moi
opposite contraire *m.* ; *prep.* en face (de)
optimistic optimiste
optional facultatif/-ive
or ou
orange (color) orange *adj. inv.*
orange (fruit) orange *f.*
orange juice jus *m.* d'orange
Orangina orange soda Orangina *m.*
order (in restaurant) commande *f.* ; **(general)** ordre *m.*
to be out of order être † en panne
to give orders donner des ordres
in order to pour + *inf.*, afin de + *inf.*
to order (food) commander

organic biologique, bio
to organize organiser
to organize (against) se mobiliser (contre)
other autre
our notre, nos
ourselves nous-mêmes
outdated démodé/e
outdoors en plein air, dehors
outgoing sociable
outside dehors, à l'extérieur
oven four *m.*
microwave oven four à micro-ondes, micro-ondes *m.*
over sur
over there là-bas
overcast: It's overcast. Le ciel est couvert.
overcoat manteau *m.*
to overlook donner sur
to owe devoir †
to own posséder †, avoir †
owner propriétaire *m./f.*

P

Pacific Océanie *f.*
Pacific Ocean océan *m.* Pacifique
to pack faire † ses valises *f. pl.*
package paquet *m.*, colis *m.*
packaging emballage *m.*
page page *f.*
on page X à la page X
pain mal (des maux) *m.*, douleur *f.*
to paint peindre †
painter peintre *m.*
painting peinture *f.*, tableau *m.*
pair paire *f.*
in pairs en groupes *m. pl.* de deux
pale pâle
to become pale pâlir
pants pantalon *m. sg.*
pantyhose collant *m.*
paper papier *m.*
paper (written for a course) dissertation *f.*, un essai *m.*, un devoir *m.* écrit
parent parent *m.*
park parc *m.*
to park garer
parking garage garage *m.*, parking *m.*
to participate in participer à
partner partenaire *m./f.*
part-time à mi-temps
party fête *f.*, soirée *f.*
to pass by passer
to pass (an exam/a course) réussir (à)
passerby passant *m.*, passante *f.*
passport passeport *m.*
pasta pâtes *f. pl.*
pastime passe-temps *m.*
pastry pâtisserie *f.*
pastry chef pâtissier *m.*, pâtissière *f.*
pâté pâté *m.*
path chemin *m.*
to pay payer †
to pay attention (be careful) faire † attention
peach pêche *f.*
pear poire *f.*
peas petits pois *m. pl.*
pedestrian piéton *m.*
pedestrian street rue *f.* piétonne
pen stylo *m.*
pencil crayon *m.*
penicillin pénicilline *f.*
people gens *m. pl.*
pepper poivre *m.*
chili pepper piment *m.* rouge
green pepper poivron *m.* vert
hot pepper piment *m.*
red pepper poivron *m.* rouge
percussion batterie *f.*
perfect parfait/e, idéal/e
perfectly parfaitement
performing arts arts *m. pl.* du spectacle
perhaps peut-être
permit permis *m.*
to permit permettre †
person personne *f.*
personality personnalité *f.*, caractère *m.*
pessimistic pessimiste
pet animal *m.* familier
pharmacist pharmacien *m.*, pharmacienne *f.*
pharmacy pharmacie *f.*
philosophy philosophie *f.*
to phone téléphoner à, appeler †
to phone one another se téléphoner
photo(graph) photo(graphie) *f.*
photographer photographe *m./f.*
physical sciences sciences *f. pl.* physiques
physics physique *f.*
physiology physiologie *f.*
piano piano *m.*
to play the piano jouer du piano
picnic pique-nique *m.*
to have a picnic faire † un pique-nique
to picnic pique-niquer
picture photo(graphie) *f.*, tableau *m.*, peinture *f.*, image *f.*, dessin *m.*, illustration *f.*
pie tarte *f.*
apple pie tarte aux pommes
piece morceau *m.*
piece of advice conseil *m.*
piece of furniture meuble *m*
piece of information renseignement *m.*
piece of news nouvelle *f.*
piece of toast tartine *f.*, rôtie *f.* (*Can.*), toast *m.*
pig cochon *m.*
pineapple ananas *m.*
pink rose
pizza pizza *f.*
place endroit *m.*, lieu *m.*
at my/our place chez moi/nous
at X's place chez X
at your place chez toi/vous
to take place avoir † lieu
in your place à ta/votre place
to plan organiser, planifier
plan projet *m.*
to have plans être pris/e, avoir † des projets
to make plans faire † des projets
plane avion *m.*
planet planète *f.*
plastic plastique *m.*
plastic bag sac *m.* en plastique
plate assiette *f.*
play (theater) pièce *f.* (de théâtre)
to play jouer
to play an instrument jouer (de)
to play a sport jouer (à)
to play sports faire † du sport
playing field terrain *m.* de sport
player joueur *m.*, joueuse *f.*
pleasant agréable
please s'il te plaît, s'il vous plaît
poem poème *m.*
poet poète *m.*
poetry poésie *f.*
police officer agent *m.* de police
political science sciences *f. pl.* politiques
poll (opinion) sondage *m.*, enquête *f.*
polling station bureau *m.* de vote
to pollute polluer
pollution pollution *f.*
air pollution pollution atmosphérique
noise pollution pollution sonore
pork porc *m.*
Portugal Portugal *m.*
Portuguese *adj.* portugais/e
Portuguese (language) portugais *m.*
possible possible
It's possible. C'est possible.
possibly éventuellement
to post afficher, annoncer
postcard carte *f.* postale
poster affiche *f.*, poster *m.*
post office poste *f.*
potato pomme *f.* de terre, patate *f.* (*fam.*)
position (job) poste *m.* ; position *f.*
to pour verser
practical pratique
practice répétition *f.* (musique, théâtre), entraînement *m.* (sport)
to practice répéter † (musique, théâtre), s'entraîner (sport)
to prefer préférer †, aimer mieux
to prepare préparer
prepared dish plat *m.* préparé
prescription ordonnance *f.*
present cadeau *m.*
to present présenter, offrir †, donner, remettre †
to press appuyer † sur; insister
to press the button appuyer † sur le bouton
press presse *f.*
prestige prestige *m.*
pretty joli/e
pretty good pas mal du tout
to prevent empêcher
price prix *m.*
printer imprimante *f.*
multifunction printer imprimante multifonction
probably probablement
problem problème *m.*
no problem sans problème
produce aisle rayon *m.* fruits et légumes
profession profession *f.*
professor professeur *m.*, professeure *f.* (*Can.*)
program (TV) émission *f.*
programmer informaticien *m.*, informaticienne *f.*

project projet *m.*
to promise promettre †
to protect protéger †, sauver, sauvegarder
protest manifestation *f.*
to protest manifester (contre), protester
psychological drama drame *m.* psychologique
psychology psychologie *f.*
public public *m.* ; *adj.* public/publique
public transportation transport *m.* en commun
pullover sweater pull(-over) *m.*
to punish punir
purple violet/-te
purse sac *m.* à main
to push pousser
to push (a button) appuyer † sur (un bouton)
to put mettre †, placer †
to put away ranger †
to put in installer
to put makeup on se maquiller
to put on (clothes) mettre †
to put on shoes chausser

Q

quantity quantité *f.*
quarter quart *m.* ; trimestre *m.*
quarter past et quart
quarter to moins le quart
Quebec Québec *m.*
Quebecois québécois/e
queen reine *f.*
question question *f.*
to answer a question répondre à une question
to ask a question poser une question
quiet *adj.* réservé/e, silencieux/-ieuse
quiet silence *m.*, tranquillité *f.*
quietly en silence, doucement, sans bruit, silencieusement
quite assez
quiz interrogation *f.*

R

rabbit lapin *m.*
radio radio *f.*
rain pluie *f.*
to rain pleuvoir †
It's raining. Il pleut.
raincoat imper(méable) *m.*
to raise lever †
to raise one's hand lever † le doigt, lever † la main
to raise a child élever † un enfant
rapid rapide
rapidly vite, rapidement
rarely rarement
rather assez, plutôt
raw vegetables crudités *f. pl.*
razor rasoir *m.*
to read lire †
to read out loud lire † à haute voix
ready prêt/e
real vrai/e, réel/le, véritable, authentique
realistic réaliste
reality show émission *f.* de téléréalité
really vraiment
Really? Ah bon ?
reason raison *f.*
the reason why la raison pour laquelle
reasonable raisonnable
reassuring sécurisant/e
rebellious rebelle
to receive recevoir †
receptionist réceptionniste *m./f.*
recipe recette *f.*
recommendation recommandation *f.*
recorder flûte *f.*
to recycle recycler, faire † du recyclage
recycling recyclage *m.*
red rouge
redhead, redhaired roux/-sse
reference book ouvrage *m.* de référence
to reflect (on) réfléchir (à)
refrigerator réfrigérateur *m.*, frigo *m.*
region région *f.*
to register s'inscrire
to register to vote s'inscrire sur la liste électorale
rehearsal répétition *f.*
to rehearse répéter †
relative parent *m.*
relax se détendre, se décontracter, se relaxer
remarried remarié/e
remedy remède *m.*
to remember se rappeler †, se souvenir † de
remote control télécommande *f.*
renovated renové/e
rent loyer *m.*
to rent louer
renter locataire
co-renter colocataire *m./f.*
to repeat répéter †
report exposé *m.*, rapport *m.*, reportage *m.*
to request demander (à, de)
to require exiger
required obligatoire
reservation réservation *f.*
to reserve réserver, faire † une réservation
reserved réservé/e
residential résidentiel/le
residential neighborhood quartier *m.* résidentiel
resource ressource *f.*
natural resource ressource naturelle
responsibility responsabilité *f.*
responsible responsable
rest repos *m.*
to rest se reposer
restaurant restaurant *m.*
restroom toilettes *f. pl.*, W.-C. *m. pl.*
to return revenir †
to return home rentrer
to return (object) rendre
rice riz *m.*
to ride a bicycle faire † du vélo *m.*
right droite *f.*
to the right à droite
to be right avoir † raison
It will be all right. Ça va s'arranger.
ring bague *f.*, anneau *m.*
diamond ring bague en diamants
engagement ring bague de fiançailles
wedding ring alliance *f.*
to ring sonner
ripe mûr/e
river (to the sea) fleuve *m.*
river (tributary) rivière *f.*
roast rôti *m.*
pork roast rôti de porc
roast beef rosbif *m.*
rock music rock *m.*
role (film or theater) rôle *m.*
role play jeu *m.* de rôle
roll of film pellicule *f.*
roll (bread) petit pain *m.*
roof toit *m.*
room pièce *f.*, salle *f.*
bedroom chambre *f.*
classroom salle (de classe)
roommate colocataire *m./f.*, camarade de chambre *m./f.*
routine routine *f.*
rug tapis *m.*
rugby rugby *m.*
ruler règle *f.*
to run courir †
to run errands faire † des courses *f.*
RV camping-car *m.*

S

sad triste
sailboat bateau *m.* à voile
to go sailing faire † de la voile
salad salade *f.*
salary salaire *m.*
sale solde *f.*, promotion *f.*
to be on sale être † en solde
sales clerk vendeur *m.*, vendeuse *f.*
sales representative représentant *m.*, représentante *f.* de commerce
salmon saumon *m.*
smoked salmon saumon fumé
salt sel *m.*
salty salé/e
same même
just the same quand même
the same thing la même chose *f.*
sandal sandale *f.*
sandwich (ham, cheese) sandwich *m.* (au jambon, au fromage)
Santa Claus Père *m.* Noël
Saturday samedi
to save (money) économiser, faire † des économies
to save a file sauvegarder un fichier
saxophone saxophone *m.*
to say dire †
to scan scanner, passer au scanner
scanner scanner *m.*
to scare faire † peur à
to be scared avoir † peur
scarf écharpe *f.*
silk scarf foulard *m.*
schedule emploi *m.* du temps
school école *f.*
business school école de commerce
elementary school école primaire
middle school collège *m.*
high school lycée *m.*
nursery school école maternelle
school within a university faculté *f.*
secondary school école secondaire

science science *f.*
science-fiction science-fiction *f.*
screen écran *m.*
flat screen écran *m.* plat
sculpture sculpture *f.*
sea mer *f.*
seafood fruits *m. pl.* de mer
search engine moteur *m.* de recherche
seashore bord *m.* de la mer
season saison *f.*
to have season tickets être † abonné/e, avoir † un abonnement
seat place *f.*, siège *m.*
second (unit of time) second *m.*
second (order) deuxième ; second/e (when there are only two items in a series)
second floor premier étage *m.*
secretary secrétaire *m./f.*
to see voir †
Let's see . . . Voyons...
See you soon! À bientôt !
See you tomorrow! À demain !
to seem (good) avoir † l'air (bon)
selfish égoïste
to sell vendre
to send envoyer †
semester semestre *m.*
Senegal Sénégal *m.*
Senegalese sénégalais/e
sensitive sensible
to separate se séparer
separated séparé/e
September septembre
series feuilleton *m.*, série *f.*
serious sérieux/-euse, grave
to serve servir
service sector services *m. pl.*
to set mettre †
to set the table mettre † la table
seven sept
seventeen dix-sept
seventy soixante-dix
several plusieurs
shampoo shampooing *m.*
shape forme *f.*
to be in shape être † en forme
to get back in shape retrouver la forme, se remettre † en forme
to get in shape se mettre † en forme
square shape forme carrée
to take shape prendre forme
to share partager †
to shave se raser
she elle
sheet of paper feuille *f.* de papier
shelf étagère *f.*
shirt (man's) chemise *f.*
shirt (woman's) chemisier *m.*
shoe chaussure *f.*
to shop faire † du shopping
to shop for groceries faire † les courses *f. pl.*
shopkeeper commerçant *m.*, commerçante *f.*
shore plage *f.*, bord *m.* de la mer
short petit/e, court/e
shorts short *m. sg.*
shoulder épaule *f.*
to shout crier
show spectacle *m.*, représentation *f.*, émission *f.* (TV)
to show montrer
to shower se doucher, prendre † une douche
shrimp crevette *f.*
shuttle (bus) navette *f.*
shy timide, réservé/e
sick malade
side côté *m.*
sightseeing tourisme *m.*
to go sightseeing faire † du tourisme *m.*
silk soie *f.*
since (because) puisque
since (time) depuis
since when . . . ? depuis quand...?
to sing chanter
singer chanteur *m.*, chanteuse *f.*
singing lesson leçon *f.* de chant
single célibataire
sink (bathroom) lavabo *m.*
sink (kitchen) évier *m.*
Sir Monsieur *m.*
sister sœur *f.*
half-sister demi-sœur *f.*
sister-in-law belle-sœur *f.*
stepsister demi-sœur *f.*
to sit down s'asseoir †
Sit down! Asseyez-vous !
site site *m.*
Web site site *m.* (Web)
to situate situer
to be situated at être † situé/e à
six six
sixteen seize
sixty soixante
size taille *f.*
middle-sized de taille *f.* moyenne
to ski faire † du ski *m.*, skier
skin peau *f.*
skinny maigre
to skip (a meal) sauter (un repas)
to skip (a class) sécher † (un cours)
skirt jupe *f.*
miniskirt mini-jupe *f.*
sky ciel *m.*
slacks pantalon *m. sg.*
to sleep dormir
to be asleep être endormi/e
to fall asleep s'endormir
to go back to sleep se rendormir
sleet verglas *m.*
slice tranche *f.*, part *f.*
slim mince
slow lent/e
to slow down ralentir
slowly lentement
small petit/e
smart intelligent/e
smoke fumée *f.*
to smoke fumer
smoked fumé/e
to snack grignoter, goûter
snack casse-croûte *m. inv.*, en-cas *m.*, collation *f.*
afternoon snack goûter *m.*
snack bar snack-bar *m.*
snake serpent *m.*
sneakers baskets *m. pl.*, tennis *m. pl.*
snow neige *f.*
snowman bonhomme *m.* de neige
snowmobile motoneige *f.*
to go snowmobiling faire † de la motoneige
to snow neiger
It's snowing. Il neige.
snowboard planche *f.* à neige
to snowboard faire † du surf des neiges
so alors
so do I moi aussi
soap savon *m.*
laundry soap lessive *f.*
soap opera feuilleton *m.*
soccer football (foot) *m.*, soccer *m. (Can.)*
soccer game match *m.* de football
sociable sociable
social sciences sciences *f. pl.* humaines
social worker assistant *m.*, assistante *f.* social/e
sociology sociologie *f.*
sock chaussette *f.*
software (program) logiciel *m.*
some des ; en ; quelques
someone quelqu'un
something quelque chose
sometimes quelquefois
somewhere quelque part
son fils *m.*
grandson petit-fils *m.*
son-in-law gendre *m.*, beau-fils *m.*
stepson beau-fils *m.*
song chanson *f.*
soon bientôt
sorry désolé/e
to be sorry être † désolé/e, regretter
to sort trier
so-so comme ci, comme ça
sound bruit *m.*
soup soupe *f.*
soup kitchen soupe *f.* populaire
south sud *m.*
South America Amérique *f.* du sud
souvenir souvenir *m.*
Spain Espagne *f.*
Spanish *adj.* espagnol/e
Spanish (language) espagnol *m.*
to speak parler
Speak louder! Parlez plus fort !
speciality spécialité *f.*
to spell épeler †
to spend (money) dépenser
to spend (time) passer
spice épice *f.*
spicy épicé/e
spinach épinards *m. pl.*
spoon cuillière *f.*
soupspoon grande cuillière
spoonful (of) cuillerée (de)
tablespoon grande cuillière
teaspoon petite cuillière
sport sport *m.*
sport coat veste *f.*
sports show émission *f.* sportive
to do/play sports faire † du sport
spring printemps *m.*
in the spring au printemps
spouse époux *m.*, épouse *f.*
spy movie film *m.* d'espionnage

square carré *m.*
square (in a city) place *f.*
to squeeze presser
stadium stade *m.*
staircase escalier *m.*
stairs escalier *m.*
star étoile *f.*
movie star vedette *f.*, star *f.*
to start commencer †
to start exercising again se remettre † à faire de l'exercice
to stay rester
to stay home rester à la maison
to stay in a hotel loger † à l'hôtel
to stay overnight passer la nuit
to stay with a friend loger † chez un/e ami/e
steak biftek *m.*, steak, *m.*
stepbrother demi-frère *m.*
stepdaughter belle-fille *f.*
stepfather beau-père *m.*
stepmother belle-mère *f.*
stepsister demi-sœur *f.*
stepson beau-fils *m.*
still encore
stomach estomac *m.*, ventre *m.*
to have a stomachache avoir † mal au ventre
stop arrêt *m.*
bus stop arrêt *m.* de bus
stoplight feu *m.* rouge
stop sign stop *m.*, arrêt *m.* (*Can.*)
to stop (s')arrêter
Stop it! Arrête !
store magasin *m.*, boutique *f.*
story (of a building, house) étage *m.*
first story rez-de-chaussée *m.*
second story premier étage
story histoire *f.*
stout fort/e
stove cuisinière *f.*
straight ahead tout droit
strange bizarre, drôle
stranger étranger *m.*, étrangère *f.*
strawberry fraise *f.*
stream (large) rivière *f.*
street rue *f.*
streetcar tramway *m.*
strength training musculation *f.*
to do strength training faire † de la musculation
strep throat angine *f.*
stressed stressé/e
strike grève *f.*
to strike faire † (la) grève
to be on strike être † en grève
strong fort/e
stubborn têtu/e
student étudiant *m.*, étudiante *f.*
studies études *f. pl.*
studio atelier *m.*
studio apartment studio *m.*
to study étudier, travailler
to study for an exam préparer un examen
to study (French) faire † du (français)
to study tonight, this weekend travailler ce soir, ce week-end
stuff affaires *f. pl.*
stupid bête, idiot/e, stupide
to do something stupid faire † une bêtise
stylish chic, à la mode
to subscribe (to) s'abonner (à)
suburb banlieue *f.*
subtitle sous-titre *m.*
to subtitle doubler
subway métro *m.*
to succeed réussir (à)
sugar sucre *m.*
brown sugar sucre roux
powdered sugar sucre glace
to suggest suggérer †, proposer
suit (man's) costume *m.*
suit (woman's) tailleur *m.*
suitcase valise *f.*
summer été *m.*
summer camp colonie *f.* de vacances
summer vacation grandes vacances *f. pl.*
sun soleil *m.*
It's sunny. Il y a du soleil.
sunburn coup *m.* de soleil
Sunday dimanche
sunglasses lunettes *f. pl.* de soleil
super super
supermarket aisles rayons *m. pl.* du supermarché
supper souper *m.*
to have supper souper
to support soutenir †
sure sûr/e
surfing surf *m.*
to surf faire † du surf
to surf the Web surfer sur Internet
surprised étonné/e, surpris/e
sweater (cardigan) gilet *m.*
to swim nager †, faire † de la natation
swimming la natation *f.*
swimming pool piscine *f.*
swimsuit maillot *m.* (de bain)
Swiss suisse
Switzerland Suisse *f.*
symptom symptôme *m.*

T

T-shirt tee-shirt *m.*
table table *f.*
to set the table mettre † la table
to take prendre †
to take a nap faire † la sieste
to take a test passer un examen
to take a trip faire † un voyage
to take care of s'occuper de
to take care of oneself se soigner
to take courses suivre † des cours
to take someone somewhere emmener †
to take something somewhere emporter
talented doué/e
to talk parler
tall grand/e
to tan se bronzer
taste goût *m.*
to taste goûter
taxi taxi *m.*
tea thé *m.*
teacher professeur *m.*, enseignant/e *m./f.*
team équipe *f.*
to tease someone plaisanter avec quelqu'un, taquiner
tedious ennuyeux/-euse
teenager adolescent *m.*, adolescente *f.*
telephone téléphone *m.*
cell phone portable *m.*
phone number numéro *m.* de téléphone
phone book annuaire *m.*
to telephone (someone) téléphoner à
television télévision *f.* (télé)
to tell dire †
to tell a joke raconter une histoire drôle
to tell a lie mentir
to tell a story raconter (une histoire)
ten dix
tenant locataire *m./f.*
tender tendre
tennis tennis *m.*
tennis shoes tennis *m. pl.*
tent tente *f.*
terrace terrasse *f.*
term (of office) mandat *m.*
test examen *m.*, épreuve *f.*
to thank remercier
Thank you! Merci !
Thank you for coming. Je te/vous remercie d'être venu/e.
that cela, ça
That's all. C'est tout.
That's it. Ça y est.
That's too bad. C'est dommage.
that (*rel. pron.*) qui, que
theater théâtre *m.*
their leur/s
them eux, elles, les
to them leur
themselves eux-mêmes, elles-mêmes
then alors, ensuite, puis
there là ; y
there is/are . . . voilà, il y a…, voici
therefore donc
these ces
they ils, elles, on
thin fin/e, mince
thing chose *f.*
something quelque chose
something interessing quelque chose d'intéressant
the same thing la même chose
think penser, réfléchir à
I don't think so. Je pense que non. Je (ne) pense pas.
I think so. Je pense que oui.
I think that . . . Je pense que…
thirst soif *f.*
to be thirsty avoir † soif
thirteen treize
thirty trente
this ce (cet), cette
this is . . . c'est/ce sont…, voici
thousand mille
three trois
throat gorge *f.*
to have a sore throat avoir † mal à la gorge
through par, à travers
to throw (out) jeter †

thunderstorm orage *m.*
thunder tonnerre *m.*
  There is thunder. Il y a du tonnerre.
Thursday jeudi
ticket billet *m.*
  museum ticket entrée *f.*
  subway ticket ticket
  theater/concert ticket place *f.*
to tidy up ranger †
tie (clothing) cravate *f.*
  tie (game) match *m.* nul
  tie (link) attache *f.*, lien *m.*
to tie attacher, lier ; nouer (une cravate, un foulard) ; faire † match nul
tights collant *m.*
time l'heure *f.* ; temps *m.*
  for a long time depuis longtemps
  full-time à plein temps
  long time longtemps
  part-time à mi-temps
  What time is it? Quelle heure est-il ?
tip (money) pourboire *m.*
  tip (advice) conseil *m.*, tuyau *m.* (*fam.*)
tired fatigué/e
title titre *m.*
to à, en
today aujourd'hui
toe orteil *m.*
together ensemble
toilet toilettes *f. pl.*
toiletries articles *m. pl.* de toilette
tomato tomate *f.*
tomorrow demain
  day after tomorrow après-demain *m.*, lendemain *m.*
tonight ce soir
too aussi
  me too moi aussi
  too much trop
tooth dent *f.*
  toothbrush brosse *f.* à dents
  toothpaste dentifrice *m.*
tornado tornade *f.*
tourism office office *m.* de tourisme, Syndicat *m.* d'initiative
tourist touriste *m./f.*
toward vers
towel serviette *f.* (de toilette)
to towel off s'essuyer †
town ville *f.*
  town hall mairie *f.*
toxic toxique
traffic circulation *f.*
  traffic circle rond-point *m.*
  traffic jam embouteillage *m.*
train train *m.*
  train station gare *f.*
tramway tramway *m.*
transportation (means of) moyen *m.* de transport
  mass transportation transports *m. pl.* en commun
trash ordures *f. pl.*
  trash can poubelle *f.*
to travel voyager †
tree arbre *m.*
  Christmas tree sapin *m.* de Noël
  pine tree sapin *m.*
  fruit tree arbre fruitier
tremendous formidable
trimester trimestre *m.*
trip voyage *m.*
  to go on a trip faire † un voyage, voyager †, partir
  Have a good trip! Bon voyage !
trombone trombone *m.*
trousers pantalon *m. sg.*
true vrai/e
  That's true. C'est vrai.
trumpet trompette *f.*
truth vérité *f.*
to try essayer † (de)
Tuesday mardi
tuna thon *m.*
turkey dinde *f.*
to turn tourner
  to turn off (the lights) éteindre † (les lumières)
  to turn off the running water (from the faucet) couper l'eau du robinet
  to turn on (an appliance) allumer
TV télévision *f.* (télé)
  TV (or radio) station chaîne *f.*
  TV remote control télécommande *f.*
  TV series série *f.*
twenty vingt
twin jumeau *m.*, jumelle *f.*
two deux
typical typique

U

ugly moche, laid/e
umbrella parapluie *m.*
uncle oncle *m.*
under sous
underground au sous-sol
to understand comprendre †
undisciplined indiscipliné/e
to undress se déshabiller
uneasy inquiet/e
unfortunately malheureusement
unhappy malheureux/-euse
unhealthy mauvais/e pour la santé
United States États-Unis *m. pl.*
university université *f.*, faculté *f.* (fac)
  university dining hall restaurant *m.* universitaire (resto U)
  university library bibliothèque *f.* universitaire (B.U., bibli, *Can.*)
unmarried célibataire
until jusqu'à
up: to be up être † debout
  to get up se lever †
  to go up monter
  Time's up! C'est l'heure !
to update mettre † à jour
to be upset être † fâché/e, en colère
upstairs en *haut
urgent urgent
us nous
to use (something) se servir de (quelque chose) employer †, utiliser
useful utile
usually d'habitude, habituellement
utilities charges *f. pl.*

V

vacation vacances *f. pl.*
  vacation plans projets *m. pl.* de vacances
  to go on vacation partir en vacances
valley vallée *f.*
vanilla vanille *f.*
  vanilla ice cream glace *f.* à la vanille
variety show divertissement *m.*
VCR magnétoscope *m.*
vegan végétalien/ne
vegetable légume *m.*
  vegetable garden potager *m.*
  cut-up raw vegetables crudités *f. pl.*
vegetarian végétarien/ne
very très
  very good très bon/ne
  very much beaucoup
  very well très bien
video vidéo *f.*
  video games jeux *m. pl.* vidéos, jeux *m. pl.* électroniques
  videotape vidéocassette *f.*
Vietnam Vietnam *m.*
Vietnamese vietnamien/ne
village village *m.*
vinaigrette vinaigrette *f.*
vinegar vinaigre *m.*
  balsamic vinegar vinaigre balsamique
  cider vinegar vinaigre de cidre
viola violon *m.* alto
violin violon *m.*
to visit (someone) rendre visite à
to visit (someplace, something) visiter
volleyball volley(-ball) *m.*
volunteer bénévole *m./f.*, volontaire *m.*, *f.*
volunteering bénévolat *m.*
to vote voter

W

waist taille *f.*
to wait (for) attendre
waiter/waitress serveur *m.*, serveuse *f.*
to wake up se réveiller
walk promenade *f.*
to walk marcher, aller † à pied
  to take a walk se promener †, faire † une promenade
  to walk for exercise faire † de la marche
  to walk the dog promener † le chien, sortir le chien
wall mur *m.*
wallet portefeuille *m.*
to want vouloir †, avoir † envie de, désirer
war guerre *f.*
  World War I la Première Guerre mondiale
  World War II la Seconde Guerre mondiale
wardrobe (furniture) armoire *f.*, (clothing) garde-robe *f.*
warm chaud/e
  It's warm weather. Il fait chaud. Il fait bon.
  I'm warm. J'ai chaud.
  warm-hearted affectueux/-euse
to wash se laver
  to wash one's face se laver la figure
  to wash one's hands se laver les mains
  to wash oneself faire † sa toilette
wash mitt gant *m.* de toilette
waste gaspillage *m.*, déchet *m.* ; perte *f.*

industrial waste déchets *pl.* industriels
household waste déchets *pl.* domestiques
to waste (resources) gaspiller
to waste time perdre du temps
wasted *adj.* usé/e
watch montre *f.*
to watch regarder, voir †
to watch a game voir † un match
to watch a game on TV regarder un match (à la télé)
to watch a movie voir † un film
to watch a movie on TV regarder un film (à la télé)
to watch a play voir † une pièce (de théâtre)
to watch TV regarder la télé
water eau *f.*
mineral water eau minérale
sparkling water eau gazeuse/pétillante
tap water eau du robinet
water skiing ski *m.* nautique
to go water skiing faire † du ski nautique
wave (ocean) vague *f.*
way of life manière *f.* de vivre
we nous, on
to wear porter, mettre †
weather temps *m.*
weather forecast météo(rologie) *f.*
What's the weather like? Quel temps fait-il ?
The weather's bad. Il fait mauvais.
It's nice weather. Il fait bon.
Web Web *m.*, toile *f.*
Web address adresse *f.* Web
webcam webcam *f.*
Web page page *f.* Web
Web site site *m.* Web
wedding mariage *m.*
Wednesday mercredi
week semaine *f.*
weekend week-end *m.*, fin *f.* de semaine (*Can.*)
to weigh peser †
weight poids *m.*
weight lifting musculation *f.*
to do weight lifting faire † de la musculation
welcome *(adj.)* bienvenu/e ; bienvenue *f.*
You're welcome. Je t'en prie/Je vous en prie. Bienvenue. *(Can.)*
Welcome to . . . Soyez la bienvenue !
well bien
Well done! Bravo !
well-done (cooked) bien cuit/e
west ouest *m.*
western western *m.*
What . . . ? Qu'est-ce que/qui...?, Quel/le...?
What? Quoi ?
What about you? Et toi ?/Et vous ?
What color is . . . ? De quelle couleur est...?
What did you say? Comment ?
What happened? Qu'est-ce qui s'est passé ?
What is that? Qu'est-ce que c'est ?
What's the matter? Qu'est-ce que tu as/vous avez ?
What's your name? Comment tu t'appelles/vous appelez-vous ?
wheelchair fauteuil *m.* roulant
wheelchair basketball basket-fauteuil *m.*
when quand, lorsque, où
where où
whether si
which quel/le ; que (qu'), qui
which one/s lequel, laquelle, lesquels, lesquelles
while pendant que
white blanc/blanche
who qui
why pourquoi
wife femme *f.*
willingly volontiers
to win gagner
the winner le/la gagnant/e ; le vainqueur ; le/la champion/ne
wind vent *m.*
It's windy. Il y a du vent.
window fenêtre *f.*
shop window vitrine *f.*
to window-shop faire du lèche-vitrine
to windsurf faire † de la planche à voile
wine vin *m.*
red wine vin *m.* rouge
white wine vin *m.* blanc
winter hiver *m.*
winter sports sports *m. pl.* d'hiver
to wipe (off) essuyer †
to wish vouloir †, souhaiter
wish(es) vœu(x) *m.*
Best wishes! Meilleurs vœux !
with avec
within dans
without sans
woman femme *f.*
to wonder se demander
wonderful génial/e, merveilleux/-euse
wood bois *m.*
woods bois *m.*, forêt *f.*
wool laine *f.*
word mot *m.*
in other words en d'autres termes
word-for-word mot à mot
words (song) paroles *f. pl.*
work travail *m.*
to work travailler
hardworking travailleur/-euse
It'll work out. Ça va s'arranger.
to work at the computer travailler à l'ordinateur
to work out faire † du sport, s'entraîner
worker (manual labor) ouvrier *m.*, ouvrière *f.*
worker (white-collar) employé/e *m./f.*
workplace lieu de travail *m.*
workshop atelier *m.*
world monde *m.*
around the world tour *m.* du monde
worn, worn out (objects) abîmé/e
worried inquiet/-ète, anxieux/-euse
to worry s'en faire † (du souci), s'inquiéter †
wounded blessé/e
wrist poignet *m.*
to write écrire †, rédiger
writer écrivain *m.*

Y

yard jardin *m.*
year an *m.*, année *f.*
I am 19 years old. J'ai 19 ans.
Happy New Year! Bonne année !
to yell crier
yellow jaune
yes oui ; si (*after negative question*)
yesterday hier
yet encore
not yet pas encore
yogurt yaourt *m.*
young jeune
you tu, vous, toi
to you te (t'), vous
your ton, ta, tes ; votre, vos
yourself toi-même, vous-même
yourselves vous-mêmes

Z

zero zéro *m.*
zoology zoologie *f.*

Source

TEXT CREDITS

Page 25 (top left and middle left): « Le vaccin antigrippal serait utile » and « Un dinosaure rare découvert à Lisbonne » Le Soir en Ligne, 12 octobre 2007 sur le site: *Headline reproduced by permission of the publisher's permisssion, all rights reserved*; **page 25 (top right):** Courtesy of Haïti en marche. www.haitienmarche.com; **page 25 (bottom right):** L'Express (Neuchâtel) www.lexpress.ch; **page 90:** © edesade.com; **page 136:** Courtesy of Moving to Magazines Ltd., Toronto, Canada, www.movingto.com; **page 215:** Saveurs du Monde – http://www.saveursdumonde.net; **page 216:** Courtesy of Jean Perrin; **page 250:** Courtesy of Bordas; **page 254:** Office du Tourisme et des Congrès; **page 286–287:** Editions Perce-Neige, *Je suis Cadien* (suite poétique); **page 300:** Michel Barelli, *Nice-Matin*, 9 avril 2003. Tous droits réservés; **pages 314–315:** Courtesy of éditions Quo Vadis; **page 322:** J. Cardonna, C. Lacroix, /Mini chiffres clés 2008/, Paris, Ministère de la Culture et de la Communication-Deps / La Documentation française; **page 323:** Used by permission of Centre Pompidou. www.centrepompidou.com; **page 332:** « Guide du Voyageur - Textes Comité Martiniquais du Tourisme »; **page 341:** Courtesy of la SNCF; **page 419 (middle left and middle right):** Used by permission of France TV; **page 419 (right):** M6 logo used by permission; **page 421 (middle bottom):** M6 logo used by permission; **page 421:** © 2008 TeleObs.com. Used by permission; **page 432:** INSEE; **page 441:** AEPM survey. Used by permission of Audipresse; **page 475–476:** Pariscope. Used by permission; **page 487:** Babette Gazeau, Danseuse Chorégraphe de danse africaine, http://www.danse-africaine.net.

PHOTO CREDITS

Page 2: Simon Harris/Robert Harding World Imagery; **page 5 (left):** Romilly Lockyer/Getty Images Inc - Image Bank - Rights Ready; **page 5 (right):** Yellow Dog Productions/Getty Images Inc - Image Bank - Rights Ready; **page 14:** GoldPitt LLC; **page 22 (top left):** Eric Ryan/Contributor/Getty Images, Inc.; **page 22 (bottom left):** Francois Durand/ Stringer/Getty Images, Inc. - Getty News; **page 22 (middle):** Jean Bapiste Lacroix/Contributor/Getty Images - WireImage.com; **page 22 (right):** Sophie Bassouls/Corbis/Sygma; **page 23 (right):** G Roli/Robert Harding World Imagery; **page 23 (left):** Dallas and John Heaton/Stock Connection; **page 24 (top and top middle):** Owen Franken/Stock Boston; **page 24 (bottom middle):** Pierre Desrosiers/Getty Images; **page 24 (bottom):** Gavin Hellier/Getty Images - Robert Harding World Imagery; **page 26 (all):** GoldPitt LLC; **page 30:** Nacivet/Taxi/Getty Images; **page 33 (left):** GoldPitt LLC; **page 33 (right):** Annette Brieger/Goldpitt; **page 34:** Bazille,Frédéric (1841-1870) Family Reunion, 1867. Oil on canvas, 152 x 230 cm. Inv. RF2749. Photo: Hervé Lewandowski. Réunion des Musées Nationaux/Art Resource, NY; **page 35 (all):** Mary Ellen Scullen; **page 55:** Mary Ellen Scullen; **page 59:** Taxi/Getty Images; **page 60 (bottom right):** Cathy Pons; **page 60 (left):** Susan Kuklin/Photo Researchers, Inc.; **page 60 (top right):** Dannielle Hayes/Omni-Photo Communications, Inc.; **page 63:** GoldPitt LLC; **page 64:** John Eastcott/Yva Momatiuk/The Image Works; **page 68:** Alexandra & Pierre Boulat/Alexandra Boulat; **page 69:** Mary Ellen Scullen; **page 71:** Owen Franken/Stock Boston; **page 77:** Erin Patrice O'Brien/Taxi/Getty Images; **page 78 (all):** Courtesy of the Library of Congress; **page 87:** GoldPitt LLC; **page 88 (left):** Andrew D. Bernstein/Allsport Concepts/Getty Images; **page 88 (middle):** Ian Walton/Allsport Concepts/Getty Images; **page 88 (right):** Phillip MacCallum/Allsport Concepts/Getty Images; **page 91:** Annette Brieger/Goldpitt; **page 98:** François Guillot/Getty Images, Inc. AFP; **page 99:** Chung Sung-Jun/Stringer/Allsport Concepts/Getty Images; **page 101 (top):** Samuel Kubani/Getty Images, Inc. AFP; **page 101 (bottom left):** Getty Images, Inc. AFP; **page 101 (bottom right):** Dean Mouhtaropoulos/Allsport Concepts/Getty Images; **page 106:** Ulrike Welsch/PhotoEdit Inc.; **page 109 (top):** Guy Schiele/Publiphoto, Inc.; **page 109 (bottom):** GoldPitt LLC; **page 115 (left):** Michael Krasowitz/Getty Images, Inc. - Taxi; **page 115 (right):** Chip Henderson/Photolibrary.com; **page 117:** Annette Brieger/GoldPitt; **page 121:** Will & Deni McIntyre/Getty Images Inc. - Stone Allstock; **page 126:** Masterfile Royalty Free Division; **page 132:** Robert Fried/Robert Fried Photography; **page 133 (top):** Wim Van Cappellen/Peter Arnold, Inc.; **page 133 (bottom):** Annette Brieger/Goldpitt; **page 134:** Creative Eye/mira.com; **page 138:** Tatiana Markow/Corbis/Sygma; **page 142:** Eric Feferberg/Getty Images, Inc. AFP; **page 155 (all):** Cathy Pons; **page 164 (left):** Eric Ryan/Getty Images, Inc.; **page 164 (right):** Seyllou/AFP/Agence France Presse/Getty Images; **page 170:** Getty Images, Inc. AFP; **page 171 (left):** Mary Ellen Scullen; **page 171 (middle and right):** GoldPitt LLC; **page 172:** Chad Ehlers/Stock Connection; **page173 (left):** Chad Ehlers/Stock Connection; **page 173 (middle):** Abdelhak Senna/Getty Images, Inc. AFP; **page 173 (right):** Corbis/© Vince Streano; **page 175 (top left):** Yves Foestier/Corbis/Sygma; **page 175 (top right):** © Dacid Brabyn/Corbis. All Rights Reserved; **page 175 (bottom left):** GoldPitt LLC; **page 175 (bottom right):** Werner Otto/AGE Fotostock America, Inc.; **page 176:** Image Bank/Getty Images; **page 180:** © Catherine Karnow/Corbis. All Rights Reserved; **page 181:** © Owen Franklin/Corbis. All Rights Reserved; **page 184 (left):** Cathy Pons; **page 184 (right):** Mary Ellen Scullen; **page 193 (top):** Mary Ellen Scullen; **page 193 (bottom):** R. Lucas/The Image Works; **page 194:** Mary Ellen Scullen; **page 201:** Corbis Royalty Free; **page 204 (left):** IPA/The Image Works; **page 204 (right):** AP Wide World Photos; **page 205 (left):** GoldPitt LLC; **page 205 (top right):** SGM/Stock Connection; **page 205 (bottom right):** Mary Ellen Scullen; **page 210:** Mary Ellen Scullen; **page 211:** © Walter Rawlings/Robert Harding World Imagery/Corbis. All Rights Reserved; **page 212 (top and middle):** Envision Stock Photography, Inc.; **page 212 (bottom):** © P. Hussenot/Corbis. All Rights Reserved; **page 213 (top left and right):** Beryl Goldbergh; **page 213 (top middle):** © F. Subiros/Corbis. All Rights Reserved; **page 213 (bottom left and right):** GoldPitt LLC; **page 216 (top):** Dorling Kindersley © Paul Wilkinson; **page 220:** Michael Busselle/Getty Images Inc. - Stone Allstock; **page 221:** Mary Ellen Scullen; **page 223:** Beryl Goldberg; **page 231 (all):** Mary Ellen Scullen; **page 232:** Mary Ellen Scullen; **page 233:** GoldPitt LLC; **page 241:** Bill Bachmann/mira.com; **page 246:** Peter Cade/Getty Images - Iconica;

page 247: Bruno Morandi/Image Bank/Getty Images; **page 250 (top):** EschCollection/Photographer's Choice/Getty Images; **page 250 (middle):** Angelo Cavalli/Image Bank/Getty Images; **page 250 (bottom):** Rubberball/Getty Images Inc - Rubberball Royalty Free; **page 252 (top left):** Mary Ellen Scullen; **page 252 (bottom):** GoldPitt LLC; **page 255 (all):** Simeone Huber/Getty Images Inc. - Stone Allstock; **page 258:** GoldPittLLC; **page 259 (top):** Yolanda Perez/Omni-Photo Communications, Inc.; **page 259 (middle):** Scott Cunningham/Getty Images Inc. - Stone Allstock; **page 259 (bottom):** David R. Frazier Photolibrary, Inc.; **page 260:** David Simson/Stock Boston; **page 261 (bottom):** GoldPitt LLC; **page 261 (top left and right):** Robert Fried/robertfriedphotography.com; **page 261 (middle):** Robert Frerck/Getty Images Inc. - Stone Allstock; **page 268 (all):** Michèle Delefortrie; **page 269 (top):** © Beryl Goldberg; **page 269 (bottom left):** Mary Ellen Scullen; **page 269 (bottom right):** Cathy Pons; **page 277:** Owen Franken/Stock Boston; **page 285:** Philip Gould Photography; **page 288:** Corbis. All Rights Reserved; **page 290 (top):** Daninielle Hayes/Omni-Photo Communications, Inc.; **page 290 (bottom right):** Dr. Henri Bastien; **page 290 (bottom left):** Chris Brown/Stock Boston; **page 291:** Mary Ellen Scullen; **page 294 (top):** Fayez Nureldine/Getty Images; **page 294 (bottom):** Barry Ancelet; **page 298:** Mary Ellen Scullen; **page 302 (top left):** Esbin-Anderson/The Image Works; **page 302 (bottom left):** Lawrence Migdale/Stock Boston; **page 302 (bottom right):** Mark Junak/Getty Images Inc. - Stone Allstock; **page 302 (top right):** Kim Sayer © Dorling Kindersley; **page 303 (all):** Mary Ellen Scullen; **page 309:** Corbis/Bettmann; **page 320:** David Sanger/Creative Eye/mira.com; **page 330:** Patrick Aventurier/Zuma Press - Gamma; **page 331:** Robert Fried/robertfriedphotography.com; **page 333 (top):** Édouard Fleuriau-Château; **page 333 (bottom):** GoldPitt LLC; **page 334 (middle):** Robert Harding/Robert Harding World Imagery; **page 334 (right):** Jess Stock/Getty Images Inc. - Stone Allstock; **page 338:** Chad Ehlers/Stock Connection; **page 341:** © G. Bowater/Corbis. All Rights Reserved; **page 348 (all):** GoldPitt LLC; **page 349 (all):** GoldPitt LLC; **page 350 (top):** Owen Franken/Stock Boston; **page 350 (middle):** John Rowley/Getty Images/Digital Vision; **page 350 (bottom):** Jean Claude Francolon; **page 352 (top right):** Courtesy of Médecins Sans Frontières **page 352 (left):** Courtesy of the International Committee of the Red Cross; **page 352 (bottom right):** Pharmaciens Sans Frontières; **page 357:** The Granger Collection, New York; **page 360:** Kim Sayer © Dorling Kindersley; **page 362 (left):** David Simson/Stock Boston; **page 362 (top right):** Ray Stott/The Image Works; **page 362 (bottom right):** John Elk Photography; **page 369:** Mary Ellen Scullen; **page 370 (left):** Chad Ehlers/AGE Fotostock America, Inc.; **page 370 (right):** GoldPitt LLC; **page 371:** A. Autenzio/Explorer/Photo Researchers, Inc.; **page 372:** Mary Ellen Scullen; **page 373:** Keystone/Everett Collection; **page 374:** Mary Ellen Scullen; **page 376 (left):** Hulton Getty/MPI/Getty Images, Inc - Liaison; **page 376 (right):** Walery/Getty Images Inc. - Hulton Archive Photos; **page 380:** Teo Lannie/Getty Images - PhotoAlto Royalty Free; **page 383:** GoldPitt LLC; **page 391:** National Library of Medicine; **page 392:** Pierre Verdy/Agence France Presse/Getty Images; **page 393 (left):** © Franck Guiziou/Corbis. All Rights Reserved; **page 393 (middle):** François Guillot/Agence France Presse/Getty Images; **page 393 (right):** Mary Ellen Scullen; **page 399:** Mary Ellen Scullen; **page 401 (top):** Franck Perry/Agence France Presse/Getty Images; **page 401 (bottom left):** Pierre Verdy/Agence France Presse/Getty Images; **page 401 (bottom right):** Mychele Daniau/Agence France Presse/Getty Images; **page 402:** Mary Ellen Scullen; **page 409:** Peter McCabe/Agence France Presse/Getty Images; **page 411 (left):** Frans Lanting/Minden Pictures; **page 411 (right):** Cyril Ruoso/Getty Images, Inc.; **page 418:** Marc Susset- Lacroix/Getty Images - WireImage.com; **page 422:** Agence France Presse/Getty Images; **page 423:** Philippe Huguen/Agence France Presse/Getty Images; **page 431:** © Glenn McLaughlin; **page 432:** Mary Ellen Scullen; **page 433:** Mary Ellen Scullen; **page 436:** Mary Ellen Scullen; **page 440:** Stephen Simpson/Getty Images, Inc. - Taxi; **page 446:** Mary Ellen Scullen; **page 447 (left):** Picture Desk, Inc./Kobal Collection; **page 449 (top):** MJ Kim/Getty Images, Inc.; **page 449 (bottom):** Issouf Sanogo/Agence France Presse/Getty Images; **page 450:** Christal Films/Everett Collection; **page 456:** © Gail Mooney/Corbis; **page 457:** George Haling/AGE Fotostock America, Inc.; **page 459 (left):** Crédits affiche de la Fête de la Musique 2008; Fanette Mellier; **page 459 (right):** Thomas Coex/Agence France Presse/Getty Images; **page 463:** Cathy Pons; **page 464:** Debi Trelaor/Stone/Getty Images; **page 466 (bottom right):** Herve Lewandowski/Art Resource/Réunion des Musées Nationaux; **page 467:** DEA/C. Sappa/Getty Images/De Agostini Editore Picture Library; **page 469 (top):** Corbis/Bettmann; **page 469 (bottom):** Matisse, Henri. Beasts of the Sea. National Gallery of Art, Washington, D.C. Image © Board of Trustees, National Gallery of Art, Washington.; **page 472 (all):** Agence France Presse/Getty Images; **page 474 (left):** Thomas Coex/Agence France Presse/Getty Images; **page 474 (right):** GoldPitt LLC; **page 477:** Jacques Demarthon/Agence France Presse/Getty Images; **page 480:** De Malglaive Etienne/Zuma Press - Gamma; **page 483 (all):** Mary Ellen Scullen; **page 484:** Erica Lansner/Getty Images Inc. - Stone Allstock; **page 485 (left):** John Elk Photography; **page 485 (right):** Connie Coleman/Getty Images Inc. - Stone Allstock; **page 486 (left):** Ken Gillham/Robert Harding World Imagery; **page 490:** © Philip Gould/Corbis. All Rights Reserved;

Index

This index is divided into two parts: Part I (Structures) covers topics related to grammar and pronunciation; here you will find references for information on spelling, pronunciation, grammatical form, and language functions. Part II (Topics) includes vocabulary and cultural topics, as well as information on how to find people, places, and strategies for learning French.

Part I: Structures

Part II: Topics

Famous Francophones

Francophony

French life and culture

Learning strategies (Fiches pratiques)

Reading strategies (Stratégies)

Vocabulary

Writing strategies (Stratégies)

La France
L'ANGLETERRE
Londres
La Mer
Du Nord
LES PAYS-BAS
N
L'ALLEMAGNE
Bruxelles
Bonn
LA BELGIQUE
Calais
Lille
NORD-PAS
DE CALAIS
LE LUXEMBOURG
Luxembourg
La Manche
Cherbourg
Le Havre
HAUTE-
NORMANDIE
Rouen
Amiens
PICARDIE
Reims
Verdun
Metz
Caen
BASSE-
NORMANDIE
la Seine
Paris
ÎLE-DE-FRANCE
la Marne
CHAMPAGNE-
ARDENNE
la Meuse
LORRAINE
Nancy
Strasbourg
Brest
BRETAGNE
Rennes
Le Mans
PAYS DE
LA LOIRE
Troyes
Chaumont
la Moselle
LES VOSGES
le Rhin
ALSACE
Mulhouse
Orléans
Angers
Tours
la Loire
Dijon
Besançon
Nantes
CENTRE
BOURGOGNE
FRANCHE-
COMTÉ
Berne
LA SUISSE
le Lac
Léman
Poitiers
Genève
la Saône
La Rochelle
POITOU-
CHARENTES
Vichy
Annecy
Chamonix
Mont
Blanc
Limoges
LIMOUSIN
Clermont-
Ferrand
Lyon
RHÔNE-ALPES
L'OCÉAN
ATLANTIQUE
AUVERGNE
St.-Étienne
Grenoble
L'ITALIE
Bordeaux
la Dordogne
LE MASSIF
CENTRAL
le Rhône
AQUITAINE
la Garonne
Avignon
PROVENCE-ALPES-
CÔTE-D'AZUR
MIDI-PYRÉNÉES
Nîmes
Nice
Cannes
Bayonne
Toulouse
Montpellier
Aix-en-Provence
Marseille
Toulon
LANGUEDOC-
ROUSSILLON
Perpignan
L'ANDORRE
Bastia
CORSE
Ajaccio
L'ESPAGNE
La Mer
Méditerranée
200 kilomètres
200 milles

Le Canad
LA RUSSIE
L'OCÉAN ARCTIQUE
l'île de Ellesmere
GROENLAND (Dan.)
Les îles de la Reine-Élisabeth
l'île Victoria
l'île de Baffin
L'ALASKA
TERRITOIRE DU YUKON
Whitehorse
Mackenzie
le Grand lac de l'Ours
LES TERRITOIRES DU NORD-OUEST
Yellowknife
le Grand lac des Esclaves
L'OCÉAN ATLANTIQUE
la Baie d'Hudson
L'OCÉAN PACIFIQUE
LES MONTAGNES ROCHEUSES
LA CHAÎNE CÔTIÈRE
le lac Athabasca
L'ALBERTA
Athabasca
LE SASKATCHEWAN
LE MANITOBA
Nelson
LE QUÉBEC
TERRE-NEUVE
St-Jean
L'ÎLE DU PRINCE-ÉDOUARD
St-Pierre-et-Miquelon (Fr.)
LA COLOMBIE BRITANNIQUE
Saskatchewan
Edmonton
l'île de Vancouver
Vancouver
Calgary
Saskatoon
le lac Winnipeg
L'ONTARIO
LE NOUVEAU-BRUNSWICK
Charlottetown
Moncton
Victoria
Regina
Winnipeg
Québec
Fredericton
Halifax
Seattle
le lac Supérieur
Montréal
LA NOUVELLE-ÉCOSSE
1,000 kilomètres
1,000 milles
le lac Huron
Ottawa
St-Laurent
LES ÉTATS-UNIS
Toronto
le lac Ontario
Boston
le lac Michigan
Hamilton
le lac Érié
Chicago
Détroit
Le Québec
LA PÉNINSULE D'UNGAVA
La Baie d'Ungava
Arnaud
George
L'OCÉAN ATLANTIQUE
Rivière aux Feuilles
Rivière à la Baleine
Koksoak
Caniapiscau
La Baie d'Hudson
TERRE-NEUVE
LABRADOR
le lac Bienville
le lac à l'Eau Claire
les îles Belcher
Rivière du Petit-Mécatina
Grande Rivière de la Baleine
La Grande Rivière
Réservoir de Caniapiscau
Natashquan
LES MONTS OTISH
Eastmain
l'île d'Anticosti
Sept-Îles
QUÉBEC
Le Golfe du St-laurent
Gaspé
le lac Mistassini
Baie-Comeau
Matane
St-Pierre-et-Miquelon (Fr.)
Chibougamau
L'ÎLE DU PRINCE-EDOUARD
Rimouski
Harricana
LES LAURENTIDES
le lac St-Jean
Saguenay
L'ONTARIO
Roberval
Chicoutimi
LE NOUVEAU-BRUNSWICK
Québec
Montmagny
La Tuque
Lévis
LA NOUVELLE-ÉCOSSE
Rouyn-Noranda
Val-d'Or
Shawinigan
St-Laurent
Thetford Mines
MAINE
Sorel
St-Hyacinthe
St-Jérôme
Sherbrooke
Hull
Montréal
Granby
Ottawa
VERMONT
le lac Huron
NEW HAMPSHIRE
NEW
500 kilomètres
500 milles